GILBERT ODD

THE ENCYCLOPEDIA OF
BOXING

CHARTWELL
BOOKS, INC.

Pictures on preliminary pages:
Endpapers: A Boxing Match by George Cruikshank
Half-title page: Dick Curtis (1802–43)
Title spread: Mike Tyson v. James 'Bonecrusher' Smith

Published by Chartwell Books, Inc.
A Division of Book Sales, Inc.
110 Enterprise Avenue
Secaucus, New Jersey 07094

© 1983, 1989 The Hamlyn Publishing Group Limited, London

ISBN 1-55521-395-2

Printed in Portugal

Contents

Introduction

Compiling an Encyclopedia of Boxing from the historic days of the prize ring until the modern version has been a fascinating task; the objective being to provide ardent followers of the sport with the fullest possible book of reference. It has taken considerable time to collect all the essential facts, and while every endeavour has been made to ensure accuracy, anything that might seem essential, but has not been included, has only been omitted because of insufficient space.

The prize ring details have been taken from such volumes as *Boxiana* and *Pugilistica*; those of the early days of boxing under Marquess of Queensbury Rules, from newspapers of the times; the era from the start of this century to World War I, from the wealth of magazines and periodicals produced during that time; while from 1920 to the present time, from my own extensive library and collection of individual records and lists of championship contests throughout the world.

Unfortunately, the recording of boxing contests was not carried out in 100% detail until the late 1930s when I first came to be associated with *Boxing*, a weekly publication. Ringside reporters at that time were, in the main, concerned only with the major bouts on a programme, the rest going unrecorded. This I considered to be unfair to the minor boxers setting out on a ring career. When, after World War II, the name of the paper was changed to *Boxing News* and I became its editor, the policy of printing every result was adopted and has been maintained until the present day. This means that prior to that time, the result of many a bout has been lost, except perhaps in the memory of the contestants.

The present edition of the Encyclopedia of Boxing has had to be enlarged considerably not only because of the passage of time, but also because of the activities of the World Boxing Association (W.B.A.), the World Boxing Commission (W.B.C.) and the International Boxing Federation (I.B.F.) all of whom have their own versions of the World Titles, which also now number 17, instead of the original eight. It now means that aspiring boxers have no fewer than 51 World Championship titles (or 54 if the newly arrived 'Strawweights' are included) at which to aim, thus widening the field for the ardent records keeper. However, no account has been taken of the 'Champions' set up by either the United States Boxing Association or the North American Boxing Federation, nor of the Junior or International titles created by the W.B.C. (i.e. those competed for by boxers not rated in the official Top Ten).

Birth dates of ring battlers are always of interest, but not alas always reliable. Today, when a boxer applies for a professional licence, he must give proof of his age, whereas in the past he could deduct a few years in order to preserve his youth for publicity purposes, the true facts coming to light in after years. An outstanding case was that of Archie Moore, former light-heavyweight champion of the world. For years he claimed his birth date to be Dec. 13, 1916, whereas his mother always declared that he first saw the light of day three years earlier. It was not until 1983 that Ancient Archie admitted that she was right. I know of only one instance where a boxer, either by design or accident, advanced his age. This was Bob Fitzsimmons, who told everyone that he 'guessed' he was born on June 4, 1862, whereas his birth certificate disclosed the fact that the true date was May 26, 1863.

To any boxer who does not find his name and exploits recorded in this work, I offer apology and regret. It is not because of unawareness of his existence or his record, but solely because there had to be space boundaries in a work of this kind and this has necessitated the exclusion of some who might justifiably think themselves worthy of being represented.

Gilbert Odd 1989

Boxer's Score Guide

Score 171: *w*124 (53) *d*24 *l*19 *ND*. 2 *Dnc*. 2

At the end of each boxer's biography is a summary of his professional fighting career. It shows: his total number of bouts, how many he won, how many he won inside the distance, how many he drew, how many he lost, in how many there was 'no decision' and how many were 'declared no contest.'

For example, above is the career summary of Abe Attell. It shows that he had 171 fights and won 124 of them (including 53 inside the distance), he drew 24 bouts and lost 19. There was 'no decision' in 2 bouts and 2 bouts were 'declared no contest.'

A-Z Guide to the Great Boxers

Accavallo, Horacio

World Flyweight Champion (W.B.A.) 1966–67

(b. Parque Patricios, Argentina, Oct. 14, 1934). Began pro boxing: Sept. 21, 1956.

He made his start just before his 22nd birthday and was unbeaten in his first 30 bouts. He then went to Rome where he was outpointed by Salvatore Burruni, the Italian flyweight champion. It was the only decision he ever lost in 83 bouts, of which he won 75 and drew 6. He suffered one setback inside the distance, losing to Kiyoshi Tanabe at Tokyo when, after a clash of heads, Accavallo sustained a severe cut on the brow that caused the referee to call a halt. In 1961 he won the Argentine flyweight title by beating Carlos Rodriguez at Buenos Aires and three months later took the South American title by winning over Jupiter Mansilla. He held both these championships for the next four years, then secured a W.B.A.-recognized world title contest against Katsuyoshi Takayama, a Japanese southpaw, at Tokyo. Recovering from a severe battering in the first three rounds, Accavallo went on to win handsomely on points. Accavallo twice defended his title claim, against Hiroyuki Ebihara (former Japanese champion) in Buenos Aires, and Efren Torres of Mexico, also in the Argentine capital. He retired on Oct. 1, 1968 at the age of 34.
Score 83: *w*75 (34) *d*6 *l*2.

Adigue, Pedro

World Junior-Welterweight Champion (W.B.C.) 1968–70

(b. Palanas, Masbate, Philippines, Dec. 22, 1943). Began pro boxing: Feb. 18, 1962.

He fought for the Filipino flyweight title in 1963, winning it two years later. In 1967 he won the Oriental lightweight title and successfully defended it four times. He gained the world junior-welterweight title, declared vacant by the W.B.C., by outpointing Adolph Pruitt at Manila on Dec. 14, 1968. He lost his crown to Bruno Arcari (Italy) in 1970. Adigue regained the Oriental world junior-welterweight title but lost it in 1973. He won the Filipino welterweight championship in 1975 and kept it before retiring the following year.
Score 61: *w*35 (13) *l*20.

Akins, Virgil

World Welterweight Champion 1958

(b. St. Louis, Missouri, March 10, 1928). Began pro boxing: March 11, 1948.

A classy box-fighter, he won 14 of his 15 amateur bouts before turning professional in 1948. In his second fight he was stopped by Charlie Baxter in three rounds, but secured revenge 16 days later with a fine points victory. For nine years he was just a good travelling club warrior, but at the end of 1957, following two startling kayo wins over Tony DeMarco, he found himself matched with Isaac Logart in an eliminating bout for the world welter crown. He knocked out Logart in six rounds and three months later won the vacant title by halting Vince Martinez in four rounds before his home-town fans. He had slipped into the championship almost without anyone noticing it and he went out just as quietly, suffering a points defeat at the hands of Don Jordan. Akins had made sure there was a return title fight clause in the contract, but Jordan was again too good for him and he lost another 15 rounds verdict. He continued to box in the hope of fighting his way back to the top, but early in 1962 he was forced to retire from active boxing because of an eye injury.
Score 93: *w*60 (34) *d*2 *l*31.

Albarado, Oscar

World Junior-Middleweight Champion 1974–7

(b. Pecos, Texas, Sept. 15, 1948). Began pro boxing: April 12, 1966.

This tough Texan started at the age of 18, but although he piled up a respectable record, he did not get a real break until he had been warring for over eight years, when he secured a fight in Tokyo with Koichi Wajima who had held the junior-middleweight title for upwards of three years. Albarado gained a dramatic 15 rounds knockout victory and returned to the Japanese capital to retain his title with a seventh round stoppage. However, on a third trip, in another fight with Wajima, he was beaten on points and lost the crown he had held for only six months. He retired, was inactive for nearly four years, and then made a return that proved disastrous.
Score 71: *w*57 (43) *d*1 *l*13.

Ali, Muhammad

World Heavyweight Champion 1964–80

(b. Louisville, Kentucky, Jan. 17, 1942). Began pro boxing: Oct. 29, 1960.

Cassius Marcellus Clay (later Muhammad Ali) began boxing as an 11-year-old in a boys' club. In a distinguished amateur career he won the Kentucky Golden Gloves tourney, two National Golden Gloves championships, and two National Amateur Athletic Union titles. These earned him the light-heavyweight position in the U.S. Olympic Games team of 1960, and he was far too speedy for the opposition at his weight, knocking out a Belgian and outpointing a Russian, an Australian and a Pole to win the gold medal.

When Ali returned home he found 11 white men – most of them millionaires – eager to sponsor him as a professional boxer. This syndicate hired Angelo Dundee, a trainer of high reputation and the promoter of a boxing arena in Miami, to convert the ex-amateur into a professional. His task was simple, for Ali had natural talent and a unique style which Dundee did not attempt to change. All he did was teach Ali how to put more power behind his punches and how to deal with the tougher professionals he would now meet.

After eight wins Ali confidently began nominating the round in which he would finish off an opponent. He proved an amazing prophet; only Doug Jones spoilt his record by staying the full ten rounds with him in New York. Against Henry Cooper at Wembley, London, in June, 1963 Ali predicted that he would win in five rounds. In round four the British champion put him down with a left hook. Until the bell he stayed down. But in the next round he set about Cooper with gusto, opening a cut over the left eye that caused the referee to stop the fight. Prophecy was fulfilled. Ali had boasted that he would win the world heavyweight championship before he was 21, which would have been a record. But he had to wait for a return bout between Sonny Liston and Floyd Patterson before his big chance came. By then he was just 39 days past his 22nd birthday.

Few thought that Ali, in spite of his nimbleness, would be able to stand up to the immensely strong, savage-punching Liston, who had twice annihilated Patterson in a single round. But Ali boxed him to a

Above: *Cassius Clay (Muhammad Ali), then an under-rated challenger, hurls insults at Sonny Liston at the official weigh-in for their title bout.*

Right: *Ali ducks under a left jab from Floyd Patterson (left) during their title fight on Nov. 23, 1965 which Ali won in 12 rounds.*

stand-still with cool, long-range punching and amazing ringcraft. After round six, Liston sat in his corner and refused to come out, complaining of an injured shoulder. Ali had won the world heavyweight championship after only 20 professional fights.

In a return match 15 months later, Ali again astounded the world. He produced a right-hand punch that nobody thought he possessed (and few saw) to knock out Liston in the first minute of round one. After that Ali successfully defended his title against Patterson (w.rsf.12), George Chuvalo (w.pts.15), Cooper (w.rsf.6), Brian London (w.ko.3), Karl Mildenberger (w.rsf.12) and Cleveland Williams (w.rsf.13). He then took on the giant Ernie Terrell, who had been declared heavyweight champion by the W.B.A. Ali gave Terrell an unmerciful beating, taunting him in every round,

jeeringly demanding to know which of them was the true champion. He won the unanimous decision of the referee and two judges after 15 gory rounds. Ali made another successful defence of his title, against Zora Folley (w.ko.7), but on April 28, 1967, he was stripped of his title by both the W.B.A. and the New York State Athletic Commission for his refusal to be conscripted into the U.S. army, because of his religious convictions (he had become a Muslim and had changed his name from Clay to Ali).

Despite this, he was still 'the Greatest' in the eyes of many. In the ring he gave full value for money and his boxing skill improved with every appearance. Ali's superb defence, the way he made full use of his long reach, his uncanny timing and anticipation, his clever footwork and his use of every square inch of the ring more than compensated for any deficiency he had in punching power. He was also always supremely fit and thus able to shake off the effects of any hard blow he might have to take – as in the first

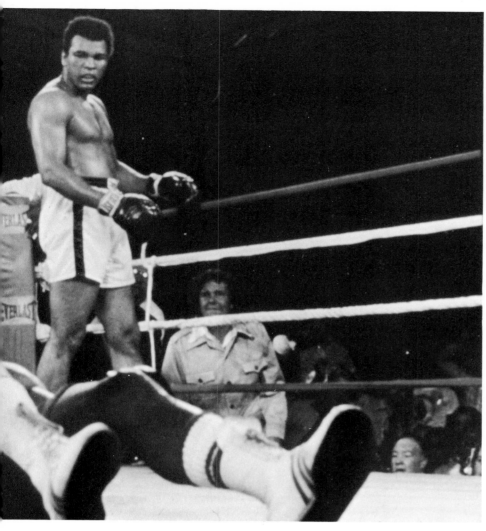

Above: *In 1966 Ali's anti-Vietnam War views made him so unpopular he was forced to fight abroad. Englishman Brian London (left) was badly outclassed and lasted only three rounds.*

Left: *On Oct. 29, 1974 Ali became the second man to win the world heavyweight title twice when he knocked out George Foreman in Kinshasa, Zaïre.*

Below: *Ali glances a right off Joe Frazier's head in their third fight–in Manila, the Philippines on Oct. 1, 1975. Ali won a gruelling contest in 14 rounds.*

contest with Henry Cooper. In late 1970, and in his 29th year, he announced his return to boxing. The come-back seemed doomed to disaster when he was beaten on points by the world champion, Joe Frazier, but Ali was undaunted. Slowly but surely he destroyed one contender after another until Frazier (now an ex-champion) was forced to meet him again. This time Ali won convincingly and then became world champion once more when he knocked out the formidable George Foreman in eight rounds in Zaïre.

Ali made ten successful defences of his title but on 15 Feb. 1978, he was, surprisingly, outpointed by Leon Spinks, a 24-year-old Olympic Gold Medallist who had had only seven professional bouts. However, Ali easily outpointed Spinks in the return bout to take the world heavyweight title for a record-breaking third time.

Almost immediately he again announced his retirement, but two years later (he was now 38) challenged Larry Holmes, holder of the W.B.C. version of the title. His showing was pathetic and it was a relief for all when he was forced to retire in the 11th round. He had kept the boxing world enthralled for 20 years and it was sad to see him go. Yet there

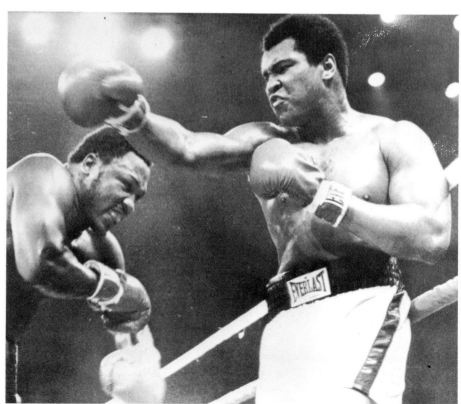

was a final appearance 14 months later, when he met Trevor Berbick, the Commonwealth Heavyweight Champion, over ten rounds at Nassau in the Bahamas, and was beaten on points.
Score 61: *w*56 (37) *d*0 *l*5.

Allen, Terry

World, European and British Flyweight Champion 1950–54

(b. Islington, London, June 18, 1924) – d. London, April 8, 1987. Began pro boxing: Sept. 3, 1942.

A fast-moving, sharp-punching boxer of orthodox style, Albert Edward Govier adopted the name of Terry Allen after a friend who had been killed in World War II, and vowed to make it famous. As an amateur he won 102 of his 107 bouts and became a professional on Sept. 3, 1942, at the age of 18 years and three months. Rapidly he rose into title class and showed his enthusiasm and determination by overcoming a disheartening one-round knockout defeat by Rinty Monaghan. He had to wait until 1949 before getting a title chance, fighting Monaghan in Belfast for the World, European and British titles, but was held to a draw. When the Irishman retired from boxing, Allen fought Honore Pratesi for the World and European titles and won on points. He did not hold his world crown for very long, losing it in Hawaii to Dado Marino at Honolulu on 1 Aug., 1950. He had been world champion for 98 days. The same year he lost his European title to Jean Sneyers of Belgium. Twice he was given the opportunity to win back the world crown, but lost each time – to Marino, again in

Terry Allen who was a world champion for just 98 days.

Dennis Andries being chaired by his cornermen after the W.B.C. light-heavyweight championship.

Honolulu, and to Yoshio Shirai in Tokyo. Allen did achieve fame, however, by winning, losing and regaining the British flyweight championship. He retired in 1954.
Score 77: *w*62 (18) *d*1 *l*14.

Ambers, Lou

World Lightweight Champion 1936–37 1939–40

(b. Herkimer, New York, Nov. 8, 1913). Began pro boxing: June 16, 1932.

A bustling, two-fisted box-fighter whose hustling methods earned him the nickname of the Herkimer Hurricane, Ambers (real name Louis D'Ambrosio) was a great box-office draw, his two exciting title fights with Henry Armstrong being the stand-outs of his career. He began pro boxing at 18½ and in three years had become contender for the world lightweight championship, but lost on points to Tony Canzoneri on May 10, 1935. In a return match the following year he defeated Canzoneri to become title-holder two months before his 23rd birthday. He made two successful title defences before losing a points decision to Armstrong, winning back the title a year later. Surprisingly he lost the lightweight championship to Lew Jenkins in three rounds in 1940, after which he joined the U.S. Coast Guard, his war service seeing his retirement from active boxing.
Score 100: *w*86 (27) *d*6 *l*8.

Anaya, Romeo

World Bantamweight Champion 1973

(b. Cahuare, Mexico, April 5, 1946). Began pro boxing: Aug. 14, 1968.

He became Mexican bantam champion in

1971, taking the world title from Enrique Pinder on Jan. 20, 1973, at Panama City. He defended the title successfully before losing it to Arnold Taylor (South Africa) at the end of the same year. Failing on two occasions to regain the crown, he retired in 1980.
Score 65: *w*45 (37) *d*1 *l*19.

Andries, Dennis

World Light-Heavyweight Champion (W.B.C.) 1986, British Light-Heavyweight Champion 1984–86

(b. Georgetown, Guyana, Nov. 5, 1953). Began pro boxing: May 16, 1973.

In his 14th pro bout he challenged Bunny Johnson for his British light-heavyweight title, but was outpointed over 15 rounds. He had to wait over two years for another chance and was then beaten on points by Tom Collins over the same course. Another ten months lapsed before he could get his third attempt, but he made the most of it by outpointing Collins on Jan. 26, 1984. Four months later he gave his old enemy a chance to win it back, but again was a points victor over 12 rounds. In his first defence seven months later he stopped Devon Bailey by a kayo in round 12 and really rose to the heights on April 30, 1986 when in London he outpointed J. B. WIlliamson in a contest for the vacant W.B.C. light-heavyweight crown. On Sept. 10 the same year, he halted Tony Sibson in nine rounds in London and he kept his title until March 7, 1987 when he succumbed in ten rounds to the great Thomas Hearns at Detroit.
Score 37: *w*28 (19) *d*2 *l*7.

Vito Antuofermo takes a left hook from Alan Minter in their title bout on June 28, 1980 which Minter won on points.

Angelmann, Valentin

World Flyweight Champion (I.B.U.) 1936

(b. Colmar, France, March 7, 1910). Began pro boxing Jan. 6, 1927.

A strong and resolute flyweight, this Frenchman, who stood only 5 ft. 1 in., started pro boxing at the age of 16 and in his fourth year became both fly and bantam champion of his own country, and lost on points over 15 rounds when challenging Frankie Genaro of America for the world crown. Two years later, in 1933, he was outpointed by Jackie Brown for the world title, lost to him again, then held him to a draw. This induced the I.B.U. to press for another chance against Brown and when this was not forthcoming the I.B.U. recognized a fight between Angelmann and Kid David for the 'vacant' championship. Angelmann won in five rounds and the same year successfully defended the title against Ernst Weiss of Austria. This fight covered the European flyweight crown which Angelmann retained against Baltazar Sangchilli of Spain. He then became a bantam and continued to box regularly from 1940 to 1944 throughout the German occupation of France. His last bout, at the age of 36, saw him draw with Camille Dormont at Limoges over ten rounds.
Score 176: w121 (40) d16 l39.

Angott, Sammy

World Lightweight Champion 1940–44

(b. Washington, Pennsylvania, Jan. 17, 1915 – d. Cleveland, Ohio, Oct. 22, 1980). Began pro boxing: March 1935.

Angott (real name Samuel Engotti) had 63 contests before being given a title chance when matched by the N.B.A. with Davey Day in 1940. Angott won on points over 15 rounds and defended his title against Lew Jenkins and Allie Stolz. In Nov. 1942 he startled the boxing world by retiring from the ring, leaving the championship vacant,

but a year later he changed his mind and won back the N.B.A. lightweight title by outpointing Luther (Slugger) White. In 1944, however, he was outpointed by Juan Zurita for his crown and soon afterwards again decided to hang up his gloves. This time his retirement lasted nine months and on his return he continued to box for six years, but without finding an opportunity to regain his title or win another. Angott was a clever masterful boxer and a stiff puncher but not a knockout specialist.
Score 132: w97 (23) d8 l27.

Antuofermo, Vito

World Middleweight Champion 1979–80, European Light-Middleweight Champion 1976

(b. Bari, Italy, Feb. 9, 1953). Began pro boxing: Nov. 30, 1971.

A strong, courageous battler, he started boxing at 18 in America and was soon making a name for himself in New York rings. In 1976 he created a big impression when winning the European light-middleweight crown from Eckhard Dagge in Berlin, but after one successful defence he dropped the title to Maurice Hope. Undaunted, he returned to America and after seven winning bouts was matched with Hugo Corro, the Argentine holder of the world middleweight crown. Antuofermo won a surprising points victory to become champion and five months later did well to hold Marvin Hagler to a draw in a title defence. At Las Vegas, however, in 1980, he was outpointed by Alan Minter, and in a return match in London was forced to retire in eight rounds. Later in the year Hagler took the title from Minter and at once Antuofermo made a brave attempt to win back his championship, but was forced to give up in five rounds. In Dec. 1981 he announced his retirement.
Score 59: w50 (21) d2 l7.

Apostoli, Fred

World Middleweight Champion 1937–39

(b. San Francisco, California, Feb. 2, 1913 – d. San Francisco, Nov. 29, 1973). Began pro boxing: Oct. 8, 1934.

Known as the 'Boxing Bell-Hop' because he was a hotel page boy before becoming a pro fighter, Apostoli was an upstanding, straightforward boxer with good punching power. He won his world crown in unusual circumstances. In 1937 the promoter, Mike Jacobs, staged a Carnival of Champions at the Polo Grounds in New York, with four world title bouts. In one of these Apostoli was matched with Marcel Thil of France for the latter's world middleweight crown but, because it had already recognized Freddie Steele as champion, the New York State Boxing Commission refused title status to

the Apostoli v. Thil bout, which the American won on the retirement of the Frenchman in round ten. Ignoring the New York body, Apostoli successfully defended his crown twice before losing it to Ceferino Garcia of the Philippines on Oct. 2, 1939. He was never given a chance to regain his laurels and retired from the ring in 1948.
Score 72: w61 (31) d1 l10.

Arcari, Bruno

World Junior-Welterweight Champion (W.B.C.) 1970–74

(b. Latina, Italy, Jan. 1, 1942). Began pro boxing: Dec. 11, 1964.

The remarkable thing about this Italian southpaw is the fact that in 73 contests, he was only twice stopped (both in his first two years as a pro), was held to a draw only once – and was never defeated on points. Of his 70 wins, 38 were scored inside the scheduled course, proving what a devastating puncher he was. He began fighting professionally 21 days before his 23rd birthday and lost in five rounds to Franco Colella. He took the European junior-welterweight title by defeating Johan Orsolics of Austria at Vienna on May 7, 1964. He made four successful defences of this championship, beating British, German, Spanish and Italian challengers, all inside the distance. In 1970 a Rome promoter induced Pedro Adigue, Philippines holder of the world title, to defend his championship against Arcari, who won on points over 15 rounds. He never lost his title, in the next five years retaining it against all comers. In 1975 he began to lose interest in boxing and had his last bout at the age of 36.
Score 73: w70 (38) d1 l2.

Archibald, Joey

World Featherweight Champion 1938–41

(b. Providence, Rhode Island, Dec. 6, 1915). Began pro boxing: 1932

This sprightly feather holds several distinctions – he had to beat two champions before being recognized as undisputed title-holder, he twice became world champion and could win only four of his last 31 contests. Not until he had been beaten 12 times in succession did his manager decide it was time to retire him. Archibald had all the moves, plenty of pluck but not a lot in punch power, although he is credited with 28 stoppages, most of which, however, came in the early years of his career. In 1938, in his 23rd year, he startled New Yorkers by outpointing their own world champion, Mike Belloise. However, the N.B.A. had its own featherweight champion in Leo Rodak, but six months later, Archibald outpointed him to become universally recognized as world titleholder. He defended this successfully against Harry Jeffra in Washington, but in a return title fight eight months later

Jeffra out-pointed Archibald in Baltimore. Joey then lost his next four contests and was stopped in four rounds by Larry Bolvin. He revenged himself in a return battle and then astonished everyone by regaining the championship from Jeffra on July 1, 1941. Alas, his second reign was short-lived, since two months afterwards he was knocked out by Chalky Wright, a Mexican-born Negro, and lost his crown. When Archibald finally retired in 1943 he joined the U.S. Navy.
Score 108: *w*61 (30) *d*5 *l*42.

Arguello, Alexis

World Feather (W.B.A.), Junior- Light (W.B.C.) and Lightweight Champion (W.B.C.) 1974–82

(b. Managua, Nicaragua, April 19, 1952). Began pro boxing: Nov. 18, 1968.

One of the later surge of great box-fighters from South America, he created a new record by holding world titles at three different weights. Tall, with destructive punching power, he began pro fighting in his home town at the tender age of 16 and in his first five years had engaged in 37 bouts, winning all but two, 29 of these inside the distance. Success brought him a shot at the W.B.A. featherweight title on Feb. 16, 1974, but he was outpointed by Ernesto Marcel. Undaunted, on Nov. 23, 1974, Alexis knocked out Ruben Olivares in 13 rounds to become champion and he kept the title with four successful defences, the last taking place in June 1976. Later the same year he relinquished the crown and went in among the junior-lightweights. At first try he won the W.B.C. world junior-lightweight championship, which he retained against eight challengers before giving up his second crown to go after the lightweights. In London he took the W.B.C. title from Jim Watt and stopped Ray Mancini in his first defence. At Miami, on July 31, 1982, he tried to establish a record by winning a fourth world title, the world light-welterweight crown, but was stopped in 14 rounds by Aaron Pryor.
Score 86: *w*80 (65) *d*0 *l*6.

Arizmendi, Alberto (Baby)

World Featherweight Champion 1934–36

(b. Torreon, Coahila, Mexico, March 17, 1914 – d. Los Angeles, California, Dec. 31, 1963). Began pro boxing: before 1927.

Nicknamed 'Baby' because of his broad smiling face, he was, according to record, pro boxing in 1927, which gives him an incredibly early start. At first his activities were confined to Mexico City and he won the Mexican bantam title there by beating Kid Pancho when in his 18th year. He had a rushing, two-fisted, bruising style and seemed completely impervious to punishment: they all came alike to him, bantams,

Henry Armstrong, the only boxer to hold three titles simultaneously.

feathers, lightweights and welters. In 1933 he challenged Freddie Miller for the N.B.A. featherweight title, but lost on points over ten rounds. His next attempt to win the championship came 18 months later and this time he was successful, outscoring Mike Belloise over 15 rounds in New York to win recognition there. In Jan. 1935 he was credited with winning the Mexican version of the world featherweight crown, by outscoring the fabulous Henry Armstrong in a 12-rounder. In all they met five times and each was head-on battle. Arizmendi lost his Mexican crown to Armstrong and when the latter became world welter king, he challenged him for it, but lost over ten tempestuous rounds. Arizmendi was a great crowd-pleaser and was active for 15 years.
Score 109: *w*70 (12) *d*13 *l*26.

Armstrong, Henry

World Feather, Light and Welterweight Champion 1937–41

(b. Columbus, Mississippi, Dec. 12, 1912 – d. Los Angeles, California, Oct. 1988). Began pro boxing: Dec. 27, 1931.

Armstrong was one of the most spectacular fighters of all time – the personification of perpetual motion: his fighting was of the non-stop variety that earned him the nickname 'Homicide Hank'. He had an abnormal heart-beat that enabled him to fight at a ferocious pace for 15 rounds, finishing scarcely out of breath. He is the only man in the history of boxing to hold three world titles simultaneously, and nearly won a fourth, being held to a draw by the reigning middleweight champion. He gained his trio of titles within ten months: feather, welter and light in that order.

Brought up in St. Louis, he came of poor parents and a large family, boxing as an 'amateur' in his early 'teens and selling his prizes to swell the meagre family budget. At 19 he left home and hitch-hiked to Los Angeles where he fought professionally in the clubs, winning, losing or boxing to a 'draw', according to instructions. He was fortunate to attract the attention of Al Jolson, the crooner, who found him a new manager in Eddie Mead. Henry changed his name from Jackson to Armstrong to cover up his early record and in 1937 burst upon the New York boxing scene with a knockout win over Mike Belloise, one of the claimants to the world featherweight title. Seven months later Armstrong gained universal recognition as champion by knocking out Petey Sarron in six rounds. In that year he had 27 bouts without defeat, only one contest going the full distance.

In May 1938 Armstrong added the welterweight title to his featherweight crown by outpointing another great warrior, Barney Ross, over 15 rounds, so battering the champion that he never fought again. Three months later he went on to gain his third title, outpointing Lou Ambers for his lightweight crown after another tremendous contest. He never defended his featherweight title because of difficulty in making the weight and lost his lightweight crown to Ambers when they had a return bout a year after their first meeting.

Armstrong now concentrated on his welterweight crown which he defended successfully on 19 occasions, beating all but four of his challengers inside the distance. However, by 1940 the all-action machine began to slow down and he lost his last title to Fritzie Zivic, who out-savaged him over 15 rounds to take the welterweight crown. In a return with Zivic, three months later, Armstrong was saved from a humiliating knockout defeat by the referee who stopped the contest in the 12th round.

After this Armstrong slipped out of the fight game for 18 months, then returned to engage in 49 fights in the next three years, winning most of them. But he had lost his former brilliance and, after being beaten by a comparative unknown, he retired permanently in 1945. Although he earned an immense fortune with his flailing fists, Armstrong had little to show for it and went swiftly downhill. However, he pulled himself together and became an ordained minister.
Score 181: *w*152 (100) *d*8 *l*21.

Arrendondo, Ricardo

World Junior-Lightweight Champion (W.B.C.) 1971–74

(b. Apatzingan, Mexico, May 26, 1949). Began pro boxing: 1966.

Arrendondo started battling around Mexico City by the time he was 17 and soon proved that he possessed a knockout punch, scoring 36 inside-the-distance wins in his first five years. Qualifying for a fight for the world junior lightweight title, he went to Tokyo in 1971 but was outpointed by Hiroshi Kobayashi. To show his disappointment he won seven bouts in a total of 29 rounds, including a ten-rounds victory over Yoshiaki Numata, who had been installed as champion by the W.B.C. Arrendondo made four successful defences of his world crown, finally dropping it to Kuniaki Shibata in Tokyo on a points verdict. He fought on for a while, but his form deteriorated and after a run of disastrous defeats he retired in 1979.
Score 99: w76 (57) d1 l22.

Arthur, Johnny

South African Heavyweight Champion 1953–57

(b. Springs, Transvaal, South Africa, Aug. 29, 1929). Began pro boxing: 1949.

Big and bulky, if somewhat clumsy, Arthur made so much progress as an amateur that he was selected to represent his country in the 1948 Olympic Games in London. He came away with a bronze medal and the following year turned professional. He tried unsuccessfully to wrest the Commonwealth heavyweight championship from Johnny Williams, but did win his native title by stopping Lou Strydom in nine, and made three successful defences. He spent 1954–55 in North America, winning four of eight bouts. Back in Johannesburg he tried again to gain the Commonwealth crown, but found Don Cockell too experienced for him and lost on points. He twice more defended his native title and retired in 1957.
Score 38: w30 (24) d0 l8.

Attell, Abe

World Featherweight Champion 1904–12

(b. San Francisco, California, Feb. 22, 1884 – d. New Paltz, New York, Feb. 7, 1970).

A smart, teasing boxer with clever ringcraft, he reigned for seven years as world 9 stone (126 pounds) champion, first claiming the title in 1904 when he knocked out Harry Forbes in five rounds. The following year he was knocked out in five rounds by Tommy Sullivan, but Attell claimed that his challenger was overweight and therefore his title had not been at stake. He fought off all contenders for the next two years, then had the first of two famous fights with Owen

Moran from Birmingham. The first was declared a 'draw' after 25 rounds, but the Englishman was dissatisfied with the decision, so the promoter rematched them. This time Attell wanted the distance reduced to 20 rounds, but Moran insisted on 25. The promoter therefore made it for 23 rounds, thus creating a world record. Again the verdict was a 'draw'. The following year, in New York, Attell lost every one of ten rounds fought against Jim Driscoll, the British champion, but it was a no-decision contest and again his title was saved. He went on reigning as featherweight king until, at the age of 28, he lost on points to Johnny Kilbane. In 1917, after a lay-off of three years, he made a single return to the ring but was stopped by Phil Virgets in the fourth.
Score 171: w124 (53) d24 l19 ND.2 Dnc.2.

Avelar, Antonio

World Flyweight Champion (W.B.C.) 1981–82

(b. Guadalajara, Mexico, Aug. 25, 1958). Began pro boxing: June 30, 1975.

Avelar scored a two-rounds knockout win on his professional debut, two months before his 17th birthday. His subsequent career was chequered, though in his fourth year he was matched with his fellow-countryman, Miguel Canto, for the latter's world flyweight crown, but lost on points. He went on to win the N.A.B.F.'s flyweight title by stopping Alberto Morales in ten rounds. This success he followed by going to Mito City, Japan, to stop Shoji Oguma in seven rounds and become holder of the W.B.C. (112 pounds) crown. At Seoul in South Korea Avela shook off a challenge from Tae-Shik Kim with a two-rounds win, but March 20, 1982, saw the end of his reign, when he was knocked out in a single round by the Colombian flyweight, Prudencio Cardona. He was still fighting, mainly in Mexican rings, up to May 31, 1986 when he stopped Wilfredo Vasquez in eight rounds at Miami. Vasquez subsequently became W.B.A. world bantamweight champion.
Score 48: w35 (28) d1 l8.

Backus, Billy

World Welterweight Champion 1970–71

(b. Canastota, New York, March 5, 1943). Began pro boxing: March 9, 1962.

A strong two-fisted southpaw, Backus had a bad start, losing as many fights as he won, but later showed considerable improvement and prowess. On Dec. 3, 1970, he managed to secure a title fight with Jose Napoles for the world welterweight title and caused a sensation by stopping this outstanding Cuban in four rounds. Backus had gone into the ring an underdog at odds of 9 to 1. These odds were justified when six months later, in

a return title bout, Backus was badly battered and stopped in round four. In 1972 he made two attempts to win the New York State version of the championship, but was beaten on points each time by Hedgemon Lewis. He continued to box until 1978 when, fighting for the W.B.A. welterweight crown, he was halted in a single round by Pipino Cuevas, a disastrous defeat that brought his immediate retirement.
Score 73: w48 (22) d5 l20.

Baer, Buddy

World Heavyweight Contender 1941–42

(b. Denver, Colorado, June 11, 1915 – d. Martinez, California, July 18, 1986). Began pro boxing: Sept. 23, 1934.

Buddy was the bigger Baer, standing 6 ft 6½ in. and weighing 245 pounds. Carrying great power in his gloves, he won most of his contests inside the distance and, after beating Tony Galento in seven rounds in 1941, was matched with Joe Louis for the heavyweight title. He had the satisfaction of knocking the champion out of the ring, but the 'Brown Bomber' came back to win on a disqualification. Louis struck Baer and put him down after the bell had sounded to end round six. He was helped to his corner and Louis was declared the winner when Baer's manager, Ancil Hoffman, claimed a foul and refused to let his fighter come out for the seventh round. In a return title match eight months later Baer was knocked out in 2 min. 56 sec. of the opening round. Soon afterwards he joined the army and did not resume his boxing career.
Score 55: w48 (43) d0 l7.

Baer, Max

World Heavyweight Champion 1934–35

(b. Omaha, Nebraska, Feb. 11, 1909 – d. Hollywood, California, Nov. 21, 1959). Began pro boxing: May 16, 1929.

Son of a Californian cattle butcher, Baer (nicknamed 'The Livermore Larruper' and 'The Merry Madcap') had all the physical assets to make a heavyweight champion, but not the necessary dedication. With a mighty right hand he enjoyed knocking his opponents off their feet, delighting the fans with his big hitting and comic ring antics. By stopping Max Schmeling in ten rounds he gained a fight for the world crown against Primo Carnera. Baer put the giant Italian down 11 times in 11 rounds to win the title, clowning and joking throughout the contest. But when he behaved in the same way against James J. Braddock, a year later, he was well beaten on points. Endeavouring to fight his way back to the top, he was knocked out in four rounds by Joe Louis, a humiliating defeat from which he never recovered. Baer continued until beaten by Lou Nova in April 1941.
Score 83: w70 (52) d0 l13.

Baldock, Teddy

*World and British Bantamweight Champion
1927–28*

(b. Poplar, London, May 20, 1907 – d. Romford, Essex, March 15, 1971). Began pro boxing: March 14, 1921.

When this tall, auburn-haired youngster made his first appearance in a pro ring at the age of 13 years, 10 months, he astonished everyone by his rapid punching and fast footwork. By 1927 he had advanced so rapidly that a consortium of boxing enthusiasts invited Archie Bell of America to London to fight Baldock for the world bantam crown. To the joy of his compatriots, Baldock won a brilliant points victory at the Albert Hall, London, and was acclaimed world champion. Five months later, however, when Willie Smith of South Africa was brought to London to challenge Baldock, the Poplar lad could not produce the same form and lost on points. He compensated by winning the British title from Johnny Brown on a two rounds kayo and then had a terrific battle with Alf 'Kid' Pattenden when defending it for the only time. Damaged hands caused his eventual downfall and he retired early in 1933. He died in poverty.
Score 80: w72 (37) d3 l5.

Ballas, Gustavo

*World Super-Flyweight Champion
(W.B.A.) 1981*

(b. Villa Maria, Argentina, Feb. 10, 1958). Began pro boxing: Dec. 3, 1976

Ballas was unbeaten in his first 54 bouts, with one drawn result. On Sept. 12, 1981, in Buenos Aires, he stopped Suk Chui-Bae

(Korea) to win the W.B.A. version of the super-fly or junior-bantam world title. However, he was champion for less than three months, being outpointed by Rafael Pedroza (Panama) and losing his crown.

An attempt to regain his crown was frustrated by Jiro Watanabe (Japan) who stopped him in nine rounds at Osaka. Ballas continued to box until the end of 1986 by which time he had become South American junior bantamweight champion.
Score 93: w84 (26) d4 l5.

Alexis Arguello (left) was one of the great champions. On June 20, 1981 he met Jim Watt and took his world lightweight crown on points.

Max Baer (wearing the Star of David) attacks James J. Braddock in his first world title defence.

Ballerino, Mike

World Junior-Lightweight Champion 1925

(b. Ashbury Park, New Jersey, April 10, 1901). Began pro boxing: 1920.

He spent his early fighting days in the Philippines where he had more than 40 bouts, most of them of four or six rounds. He came to New York in 1923 and gradually worked his way into a fight with Steve 'Kid' Sullivan for the world junior-lightweight title.

Ballerino was knocked out in five rounds, but six months later he outpointed Sullivan to become champion. He defended his position in a hard battle with Vincent 'Pepper' Martin but, when challenged by Ted Morgan, he lost his crown by a knockout in the tenth round. Ballerino continued to box for two more years, but a series of losses caused him to retire in 1928.
Score 100: w47 (8) d18 l30 ND.5.

Barnes, George

Australian and Commonwealth Welterweight Champion 1954–60

(b. Temora, N.S.W., Australia, Feb. 20, 1927). Began pro boxing: Nov. 15, 1948.

A hard-hitting and skilled boxer, Barnes built himself into a national hero in Australia, winning first the light- then the welterweight titles. He won the Commonwealth title by knocking out Barry Brown (New

Zealand) in 11 rounds in Sydney and held on to his titles for six years, never refusing a challenger. He was 33 when he went to Swansea, Wales, to defend his crown against Brian Curvis, ten years his junior. Even so Barnes put up a great battle and was defeated only on points. He retired in 1960.

In the 1920s his father (boxing as Frankie Burns) campaigned in England for some considerable time. He boxed as a middleweight and endeavoured to win the Commonwealth title in a fight with Ted 'Kid' Lewis, but was knocked out in 11 rounds.

Score 65: w42 (22) d4 l19.

Barrientos, Rene

World Junior-Lightweight Champion (W.B.C.) 1969–70

(b. Balite, Philippine, Feb. 1942). Began pro boxing: 1964.

He won his native junior-lightweight title in his first year and became Oriental lightweight champion the following year, but lost this title in 1967. An effort to win the world title in Tokyo failed when the best he could get against the Japanese holder, Hiroshi Kobayashi, was a draw. In 1969 he outpointed Ruben Navarro to win the W.B.C. version of the title, which he lost a year later to Yoshiaki Numata in Tokyo on points. An attempt to regain his crown failed, when he was again outpointed by Numata in Japan. He retired in 1971 and a come-back six years later did not continue after two winning bouts.

Score 46: w37 (14) d2 l7.

Barry, Jimmy

World Bantamweight Champion 1894–98

(b. Chicago, Illinois, March 7, 1870 – d. Chicago, April 3, 1943). Began pro boxing: 1891

One of the few professional boxers who retired undefeated, Barry came into prominence on Dec. 5, 1893, when he knocked out Jack Levy in 17 rounds in a bout advertised as being for the world 100 pounds championship. The men wore skin-tight gloves. Barry went on to beat all-comers and in 1897 travelled to London to fight Walter Croot for the title at the National Sporting Club, where he knocked out the Englishman in the 20th round. A few days later Croot died of a brain injury and Barry was charged with manslaughter, but was exonerated by the magistrate. The tragedy appeared to affect the 27-year-old American. He kept his title twice against Casper Leon, who held him to a 20 rounds 'draw' each time, although previously he had knocked Leon out in 28 rounds. Following his last title defence, Barry had only one more bout, with Harry Harris in Chicago, which ended in a 'draw' after six rounds.

Score 69: w58 (40) d11 l0.

Bartolo, Sal

World Featherweight Champion (N.B.A.) 1944–46

(b. Boston, Massachusetts, Nov. 5, 1917). Began pro boxing: April 3, 1937.

A good upstanding boxer of considerable skill, he fought mainly in and around Boston during his early days and worked his way steadily into the top bracket of the 126-pounds class. After six years of honest endeavour, he fought with the famous Willie Pep for the world title before his own supporters in Boston, but he was outpointed over 15 rounds after a classic contest. Bartolo could never get past Pep who beat him the three times they met. In March 1944 the N.B.A. matched Bartolo with Phil Terranova in a featherweight title bout and Sal came away with a fine points victory. He successfully defended his crown against Terranova, Willie Roache and Spider Armstrong but, meeting Pep in a clearing-up championship battle in New York on June 7, 1946, Bartolo was knocked out in the 12th round. He continued to box, but after two fights in 1949, decided to hang up his gloves for good.

Score 97: w74 (16) d5 l18.

Basham, Johnny

European, British and Commonwealth Welter and Middleweight Champion 1914–21

(b. Newport, Wales, Sept. 13, 1890 – d. Newport, June 7, 1947). Began pro boxing: Jan. 1, 1910.

A soldier in the early years of his career, he was billed as Private, Corporal and finally Sergeant Johnny Basham. A skilful boxer of the highest degree, Basham was a joy to watch: his leading was superb and his footwork delightful. He made a bad start, being knocked out in his first two fights, but the confidence and zeal was there and soon he

Carmen Basilio (right) swaps punches with Sugar Ray Robinson in their first world middleweight title contest. Basilio won a split decision.

was up among the top-liners at his weight. From 1914 to 1921 he was involved in ten championship fights of one sort or another. He won a Lonsdale Belt outright at welterweight and remained champion for five years, adding the Commonwealth crown, but was knocked out by Albert Badoud (Switzerland) when he attempted to win the European title. His arch enemy was Ted 'Kid' Lewis. They met three times in championship matches and the smashing, dashing London East Ender won on each occasion, depriving the Welshman of all his titles. Basham's last contest, at the age of 39, was also against Lewis who stopped him in three rounds.

Score 91: w68 (21) d6 l17.

Basilio, Carmen

World Middle and Welterweight Champion 1953–57

(b. Canastota, New York, April 2, 1927). Began pro boxing: Nov. 24, 1948.

One of the toughest of his time, this Syracuse onion-picker did not make a paid start until he was past 21 and then proved a fierce, two-fisted warrior, who always gave a colourful showing. He had been boxing for five years before he won the New York version of the world welter title by outpointing Billy Graham over 12 rounds. In a return match seven weeks later the result was a draw. Basilio's reign was restricted to 55 days when he lost to Kid Gavilan, but two years later he regained his crown by stopping Tony De Marco in 12 rounds on June 10, 1955. A return match ended in precisely the same manner; then Basilio lost his laurels to Johnny Saxton, on points. He regained the welter title with a nine-rounds victory and then stopped Saxton in two rounds in a rubber match. Relinquishing his crown because of weight difficulties, he challenged Sugar Ray Robinson for the world middleweight title and gained an astounding points win after a tempestuous battle. Another toe-to-toe slugfest six months later saw Robinson regain the title, but when the N.B.A. declared the championship to be vacant, Basilio was in there for another try, only to be stopped by big-hitting Gene Fullmer in 14 rounds of vicious mauling. Basilio tried twice more to become middleweight champion again, but was stopped, first by Fullmer and then by Paul Pender who had come into the title. Basilio retired in April 1961 after a hard and memorable career.

Score 79: w56 (27) d7 l16.

Bass, Benny

World Feather and Junior-Lightweight Champion 1927–31

(b. Kiev, Russia, Dec. 4, 1904 – d. Philadelphia, Pennsylvania, June 25, 1975) Began pro boxing: 1923.

Hogan 'Kid' Bassey aims a straight left at London feather Sammy McCarthy. Bassey was Nigeria's first world boxing champion.

This very active box-fighter, who fought out of Philadelphia, Pennsylvania, carried plenty of power in his punches. In 1927 he won the vacant world featherweight title by outpointing Red Chapman over ten rounds in Philadelphia, but at his first defence, five months later, he lost it to the irrepressible Tony Canzoneri in New York on a 15-rounds points verdict. Bass continued to fight with great frequency and at the end of 1929 took the world junior-lightweight crown from Tod Morgan in two rounds. He kept this title for 19 months, but was then knocked out by the famed Kid Chocolate in seven rounds. Although he never again fought for a championship, Bass continued as a top-liner for the next eight years, retiring in 1940 at the age of 36.
Score 227: w176 (63) d10 l38 ND.1 Dnc 1.

Bassey, Hogan

World and Commonwealth Featherweight Champion 1955–59

(b. Calibar, Nigeria, June 3, 1932). Began pro boxing: 1949.
A stocky, well-built man, Hogan 'Kid' Bassey was an uncommon combination of boxer-fighter. He carried tremendous power in both hands, which he tempered with a scientific know-how. Bassey, whose African name was Okon Bassey Asuguo, went to England at the beginning of 1952, by which time he was already bantamweight champion of Nigeria and West Africa. In England he worked his way through the professional ranks to win the Commonwealth featherweight title in 1955 by knocking out Billy Kelly, who had previously beaten him in the eighth round in Belfast.

In 1957 Bassey won an eliminator for the vacant world featherweight title on points against Miguel Berrios in Washington. Later the same year, on June 24, in Paris, he battered the European champion, Cherif Hamia of France, into submission after ten rounds to become featherweight champion of the world. This feat also brought him an M.B.E. – the first awarded to a Nigerian boxer.

After voluntarily relinquishing his Commonwealth title, Bassey went to America again in 1958 to successfully defend his world title with a third-round knock-out win over the Mexican, Ricardo Moreno.

In March 1959 Bassey defended his world crown for the third time but was forced to retire with eye injuries in round 13 against Davey Moore of Springfield, Ohio. He tried to regain his title in August 1959, but was again stopped by Moore, this time in 11 rounds. Bassey retired from boxing soon afterwards.
Score 74: w59 (21) d2 l13.

Battalino, Battling

World Featherweight Champion 1929–32

(b. Hartford, Connecticut, Feb. 18, 1908 – d. Hartford, July 25, 1977). Began pro boxing: June 6, 1927.
This most competent box-fighter was U.S. amateur champion before fighting for cash. 'Battling' Battalino (real name Christopher Battaglia) was a relentless, worrying scrapper and in only his third year he proved too strong for André Routis of France, and won the world featherweight crown with a 15-rounds points verdict. In the next two years he defended this title four times against the best opposition in the world: Kid Chocolate, Fidel LaBarba, Freddie Miller and Earl Mastro, all of whom were outpointed. In 1929 he tried to pass his title to his stable-mate Freddie Miller, but their 'championship' fight was such a fake that it was declared 'no contest'. Three months later Battalino was forced to relinquish his title, which Miller won in due course. Battalino continued to fight until 1935 and, after a brief comeback four years later, retired early in 1940.
Score 87: w57 (23) d3 l26 Dnc 1.

Batten, Jimmy

British Light-Middleweight Champion 1977–78

(b. Millwall, London, Nov. 7, 1955). Began pro boxing: June 4, 1974.
A pleasing box-fighter with a knockdown punch, he became the third holder of the British light-middle title by stopping Albert Hillman in seven rounds. He retained the championship by halting the former champion Larry Paul in four rounds and Tony Poole in 13 to win the Lonsdale Belt outright in 19 months. Attempting to win the European crown, he was knocked out in three rounds by Gilbert Cohen (France) at Wembley Arena. In 1979 he lost his British title to Pat Thomas who stopped him with a cut eye in nine rounds.
Score 43: w36 (16) d0 l7.

Becerra, José

World Bantamweight Champion 1959–60

(b. Guadalajara, Mexico, April 15, 1936). Began pro boxing: Aug. 30, 1953.
A tough little ko king, he spent his first six years fighting in Mexican rings and building up a big reputation. In 1959 in Los Angeles Alphonse Halimi, French holder of the bantam crown, defended his title against Becerra but was knocked out in eight rounds. Halimi had a return fight clause in his contract and he fought hard to get back his crown, but the Mexican proved too powerful a hitter and this time Halimi was stopped in nine. Becerra made one more successful defence in 1960, outpointing Kenji Yonekura in Tokyo. Then, in a catchweights contest in Juarez, he was sensationally stopped in eight rounds by Eloy Sanchez. Becerra immediately retired from the ring as unbeaten world bantam king. He returned to the ring in 1962 for one contest in which he outpointed Alberto Martinez over six rounds.
Score 79: w72 (43) d2 l5.

Beckett, Joe

British and Commonwealth Heavyweight Champion 1919–23

(b. Wickham, Hampshire, April 4, 1892 – d. Southampton, March 12, 1965). Began pro boxing: 1912.
He learned the profession in the family

fairground travelling booth with his elder brother, George. On the short side, but burly, Beckett knew how to use a left hook. His first appearance was at the National Sporting Club in London where he entered a novice middleweight competition and was beaten in the final. Growing into a light-heavy, he was outpointed over 20 rounds by Dick Smith, but won two heavyweight competitions in 1918 while serving in the Royal Flying Corps. Beaten in the final of an all-services competition by Bombardier Billy Wells, he later gained revenge by knocking out Wells in five rounds to become British and Commonwealth heavyweight champion, two titles he never lost. Trying to win the European crown as a stepping-stone to a world title fight with Jack Dempsey, Beckett suffered a humiliating defeat, being knocked out in a matter of seconds by Georges Carpentier of France. In a return match he suffered an equally early fate, after which he retired. His greatest fight was with Frank Moran of America. When they first met the 'Pittsburgh Dentist' won easily in two rounds, but their return fight two years later was unforgettable, with Beckett getting off the floor to stop his rival in seven rounds.
Score 60: w48 (34) d1 l11.

Belanger, Albert 'Frenchy'

Flyweight Champion (N.B.A.) 1927–28

(b. Toronto, Canada, May 17, 1906 – d. Toronto, May 27, 1969). Began pro boxing: 1924.

In 1927 this popular performer outpointed Newsboy Brown in Toronto to win N.B.A. recognition as world champion. He defended his title successfully against Ernie Jarvis of England, but lost it to Frankie Genaro on an adverse points decision on Feb. 6, 1928. Belanger won, lost and regained the Canadian flyweight title and was then invited to New York to meet Izzy Schwartz for the New York State version of the world crown. He lost on points over 12 rounds. In 1930, in Toronto, he tried to regain his N.B.A. crown from Genaro, but was again outpointed. Belanger retired in 1932.
Score 65: w38 (12) d9 l18.

Benitez, Wilfred

World Junior-Welter, Welter and Light-Middleweight Champion 1976–82

(b. Bronx, New York, Sept. 12, 1958). Began pro boxing: Nov. 22, 1973.

A rapid, two-fisted fighter of great skill, on March 6, 1976 he gained the junior-welterweight title by outpointing Antonio Cervantes at San Juan in his native Puerto Rico, and thus became the youngest-ever boxer to win a world championship. He twice defended the title successfully but was then stripped of it by the W.B.A. for failing to grant Cervantes a return title contest.

After a fourth defence Benitez challenged Carlos Palomino for the world welterweight crown and won a fine points victory. He retained his second world title against Harold Weston, but lost it to Sugar Ray Leonard in the 15th and last round of a terrific contest. In 1981 he won his third world championship by stopping Maurice Hope in 12 rounds at Las Vegas to gain the light-middleweight crown.

Benitez outpointed Carlos Santos and Roberto Duran in title defences, but was himself outpointed by Thomas Hearns for the light-middleweight title at Houston, Texas on Dec. 3, 1982.
Score 58: w51 (30) d1 l6.

Benn, Nigel

British Commonwealth Middleweight Champion 1988–

(b. Ilford, London, Jan. 26, 1964). Began pro boxing: Jan. 28, 1987.

Benn came up from the amateurs where he was A.B.A. middleweight champion in 1986. A dynamic punching machine, his first 18 contests ended inside the distance, few going beyond the second round. He became Commonwealth titleholder on April 20, 1988 by stopping Abdul Umaru Sanda, from Ghana, in two rounds in London and proved one of late 1980s' big box-office attractions.
Score 18: w18 (18) d0 l0.

Benvenuti, Giovanni (Nino)

World Junior-Middle and Middleweight Champion 1966–70

(b. Trieste, Italy, April 26, 1938). Began pro boxing: Jan. 20, 1961.

A brilliant amateur, he won the welterweight gold medal at the 1960 Rome Olympic Games, took the vacant Italian middleweight title in 1963 and retained it

Nino Benvenuti, Olympic gold medallist and world junior-middleweight and middleweight champion.

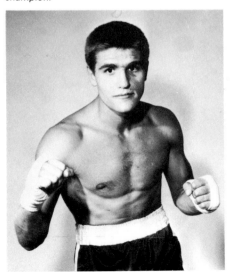

three times. After winning the world junior-middleweight title from his fellow countryman, Sandro Mazzinghi, in 1965, Benvenuti defended it successfully and also gained the European middleweight title the same year. This he retained, but in Korea he lost his junior crown to Ki-Soo Kim. In 1967, in New York, he took the world middleweight crown from the formidable Emile Griffith. They fought twice more for the championship, with Benvenuti winning the rubber. He retained his title against Don Fullmer and others, ultimately losing to the sensational Carlos Monzon, who stopped him in 12 rounds in Rome in 1970. In a return title fight Monzon again won, this time in three rounds, where upon Benvenuti announced his retirement.
Score 90: w82 (35) d1 l7.

Berbick, Trevor

World Heavyweight Champion (W.B.C.) 1986, British Commonwealth Heavyweight Champion 1981–85

(b. Port Anthony, Jamaica, Aug. 1, 1952). Began pro boxing in Canada: Nov. 20, 1976.

In his fourth year Berbick won the Canadian heavyweight title by stopping Earl McCready in seven rounds at Glace Bay. He defended his crown with a kayo win over Ron Rousselle. When attempting to win the W.B.C. world heavyweight title from Larry Holmes on April 11, 1981 at Las Vegas he was outpointed over 15 rounds after a gallant try. He won the Commonwealth crown when knocking out Conroy Nelson in two rounds at Halifax, N.S. and kept it until 1985 when he relinquished it to go after the world title again. On January 17, 1987, he secured W.B.C. recognition when he outpointed Pinklon Thomas over 12 rounds at Las Vegas on March 22, 1986. Taking on the daunting Mike Tyson eight months later, he suffered the fate of all others and was stopped in two rounds.
Score 37: w31 (23) d1 l5.

Berg, Jack 'Kid'

World Junior-Welterweight Champion 1930–31, British Lightweight Champion 1934–36

(b. London, June 28, 1909). Began pro boxing: June 8, 1924.

Berg (real name Judah Bergman) started just before his 15th birthday, most of his early bouts taking place in London's East End. An all-action, non-stop puncher, he was nicknamed 'the Whitechapel Whirlwind'. In May 1928 he went to America, where he remained for two years, coming home to fight Mushy Callahan of New York for the much-maligned junior-welterweight championship, Lord Lonsdale protesting at the Albert Hall ringside that there was no such title. Berg stopped his rival in ten

Jack 'Kid' Berg scored more wins inside the distance than any other world junior-welterweight champion.

rounds and immediately returned to America to cash in on his crown. Nine times he put it successfully at stake, but when fighting for the world lightweight title against Tony Canzoneri in 1931, Berg was stopped in three rounds. The winner claimed both titles which Berg disputed, so they met again five months later and this time Canzoneri won a hard-earned points verdict. Berg's best wins in America were over Kid Chocolate, Billy Petrolle and Tony Canzoneri the first time they met (1930). In 1934 Berg was back in London to take the British lightweight title from Harry Mizler who was stopped in ten rounds. Berg then went to South Africa but failed to win the Commonwealth lightweight crown, being outpointed by Laurie Stevens over 12 rounds. The same year he lost his British championship to Jimmy Walsh, being halted in nine rounds at Liverpool Stadium. This amazing man continued ring battling for another nine years, finally hanging up his gloves in May 1945.
Score 192: *w*157 (57) *d*9 *l*26.

Berlenbach, Paul

World Light-Heavyweight Champion 1925–26

(b. New York City, Feb. 18, 1901 – d. Port Jefferson, New York, Sep. 30, 1985). Began pro boxing: Oct. 4, 1923.

Starting as a wrestler and becoming a National Amateur Champion before changing to boxing, Berlenbach (nicknamed 'The Astoria Assassin') was a tremendous hitter but not a great boxer. He won the world light-heavyweight title by outpointing Mike McTigue over 15 rounds in his 28th contest, having won 23 inside the distance. He defended the title successfully three times, including a great slugfest with Jack Delaney. When they had a return battle in 1926 the

Canadian turned the tables and took the title after another terrific fight. Berlenbach went back to wrestling, tried to make a comeback as a boxer, but finally retired in 1933.
Score 52: *w*40 (33) *d*3 *l*8 *Dnc* 1.

Bernstein, Jack

World Junior-Lightweight Champion 1923

(b. New York City, Nov. 5, 1899 – d. Yonkers, New York, Dec. 26, 1945). Began pro boxing: 1914.

A good consistent fighting force with plenty of fan appeal, Bernstein (real name John Dodick) fought sparingly in his first seven years, then rose into top company with great success. By outpointing Johnny Dundee over 15 rounds in New York in 1923, he became the second holder of the somewhat unpopular junior-lightweight title. His tenure of the title was restricted to seven months, Dundee regaining his crown on another points verdict. Bernstein continued to be a top-liner for the next five years and went on until 1931 before giving up.
Score 89: *w*60 (14) *d*8 *l*21.

Bettina, Melio

World Light-Heavyweight Champion (N.Y.S. and N.B.A.) 1939–41

(b. Bridgeport, Connecticut, Nov. 18, 1916). Began pro boxing: Oct. 6, 1934.

A stocky light-heavy with a good punch, durability and boxing skill, he was stopped only three times in 99 bouts. In his fifth year

Wilfred Benitez (left) was one of the few boxers to become a world champion at three different weights.

as a pro he stopped Jack (Tiger) Fox in nine rounds to win the vacant New York State version of the world title. Bettina reigned for five months, but was outpointed by Billy Conn, who defeated him again when he tried to regain his crown ten weeks afterwards. In Jan. 1941 he was recognized as the world champion by the N.B.A. after he had outpointed Anton Christoforidis. Although he continued boxing for the next eight years, he never defended his title and retired in 1949.
Score 100: *w*84 (37) *d*3 *l*13.

Beynon, Bill

British Bantamweight Champion 1913

(b. Talback, Wales, April 8, 1891 – d. Bryn, Wales, July 20, 1932). Began pro boxing: June 3, 1911.

Many great fighters came out of the Welsh mining pits and one of the most rugged and durable of them was Beynon. He just loved fighting, and when he had made a name for himself in his own locality, he set off to find contests all over England in the many boxing halls that were flourishing in his day. He became British bantam champion in his third year, causing an upset by outpointing the renowned Digger Stanley on points over 20 rounds. His success was short-lived, however, as the Digger took the verdict in a return title bout. In all the years that followed Beynon did not get another title shot and when he retired at the age of 39 he expected to be able to live on his fight memories for a long time. Alas, he was killed in a colliery disaster soon after.
Score 154: *w*53 (13) *d*23 *l*77 *ND*.1.

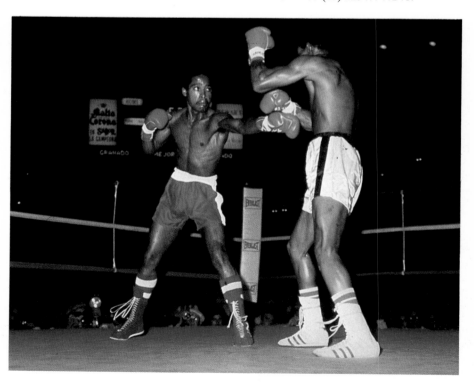

Bodell, Jack

*European, Commonwealth and British
Heavyweight Champion 1969–71*

(b. Swadlincote, Derbyshire, Aug. 11,
1940). Began pro boxing: Feb. 13, 1962.

A southpaw, in his sixth year he challenged Henry Cooper for the British and
Commonwealth titles at Wolverhampton but
was stopped in two rounds. He made his way
back by beating Brian London and Carl
Gizzi in eliminators, and when the British
title became vacant, he outpointed Gizzi at
Nottingham on Oct. 13, 1969, to become
champion. Five months later he lost his
crown to Cooper on a points verdict and
then caused a first-class sensation by defeating Joe Bugner on points for the European,
Commonwealth and British titles. Bodell
lost the E.B.U. title to José Urtain (Spain)
by a stoppage in two rounds, and his other
two titles to Danny McAlinden, who knocked him out in two rounds at Birmingham in
1972. Bodell never fought again.
Score 71: *w*58 (33) *d*0 *l*13.

Boon, Eric

British Lightweight Champion 1938–44

(b. Chatteris, Cambridgeshire, Dec. 28,
1914 – d. Jan. 19, 1981). Began pro boxing:
Jan. 17, 1935.

A blacksmith's apprentice, he had the big
biceps and heavy muscles that enabled him
to punch with full power. He swept through
the lightweight ranks, leaving a trail of
battered victims until he was matched with
Dave Crowley, holder of the 135-pounds
British crown. Boon won by a kayo in round
13, and in his first defence of his title came a
memorable battle with Arthur Danahar. On
the verge of defeat more than once, Boon
fought back with such ferocity that the
referee had to halt the contest in the 14th
round. A knockout win in a return with
Crowley gave Boon full ownership of the
Lonsdale Belt. He had to find fights where
he could during the war years and after, and
it was not until the end of 1947 that he finally
stepped into the ring as challenger to Ernie
Roderick for the British welterweight title.
After a tremendous contest, the champion
kept his title. Not many matches followed
and Boon eventually retired.
Score 118: *w*95 (64) *d*5 *l*17 *Dnc.* 1.

Borkorsor, Venice

World Flyweight Champion 1973

(b. Thailand, 1950). Began pro boxing:
March 4, 1970.

In his 13th contest Borkorsor (real name
Pravas Polchiangkwang) won the W.B.C.
version of the world flyweight title from
Betulio Gonzalez of Venezuela, who was
knocked out in the tenth round. Then

followed a successful defence against Erbito
Salavarria of the Philippines. Borkosor
gave up the crown eight months later to challenge
Rafael Herrera for the W.B.C. bantam
crown, but was beaten on points. A second
challenge three years later against Rodolfo
Martinez had the same result. As a bantam
he won the Oriental title and the championship of his own country, for which he
was unbeaten when he stopped boxing in
1980.
Score 57: *w*49 (35) *d*0 *l*8.

Bossi, Carmelo

*World Junior-Middleweight Champion
1970–71*

(b. Milan, Italy, Oct. 15, 1939). Began pro
boxing: March 4, 1961.

This smart Italian box-fighter gained a
silver medal at the 1960 Rome Olympics in
the light-middleweight class. He won the
Italian welterweight title in his fourth year
and the European crown two years later.
This he retained against Johnny Cooke
(U.K.) and Jean Josselin (France) but lost it
to Edwin 'Fighting' Mack (Netherlands) by a
stoppage in round ten. Bossi spent a year in
the wilderness, then came back as a welter to
try and take the European title from Johann
Orsolics of Austria. He was outpointed, but
three months later defeated Freddie Little to
win the world junior-middleweight crown.
This he kept for 15 months, but lost it when
he was outpointed by Koichi Wajima in
Tokyo. Bossi retired in 1971.
Score 51: *w*40 (10) *d*3 *l*8.

Bowker, Joe

*World and British Bantamweight Champion,
British Featherweight Champion, 1902–06*

(b. Salford, Manchester, July 20, 1883 – d.
London, Oct. 1955). Began pro boxing:
1900.

This stalwart Lancashire Lad, whose real
name was Tommy Mahon, came into prominence in 1901 when he won a 115 pounds
novices' competition at the National Sporting Club in London. The following year he
beat Harry Ware for the British bantam title
which he defended against Andrew Tokell,
Bill King, Alf Fellows and Owen Moran. In
1904 Bowker won a great 20-rounds points
victory over Frankie Neil of America for the
world bantam crown. He never defended
this title, almost immediately going into the
featherweight division where he knocked out
Pedlar Palmer for the British title in the 12th
round of a furious battle. He kept this crown
by outpointing Spike Robson over 20
rounds, but dropped it to Peerless Jim
Driscoll over 15 rounds. Bowker boxed
infrequently for the next ten years, finally
retiring in 1919.
Score 51: *w*40 (8) *d*1 *l*8 *ND.*2.

*Above: A triumphant Boza-Edwards. On March
8, 1981 he outpointed Rafael Limon to become
the world junior-lightweight title-holder.*

Boza-Edwards, Cornelius

World Super-Featherweight Champion 1981

(b. Kampala, Uganda, May 27, 1956). Began pro boxing: Dec. 12, 1976.

A sterling fighter with a powerful punch,
he had 17 fights in London arenas, winning
all but four inside the distance. After several
fights in America in 1979, he was matched to
fight Rafael Limón of Mexico for the
W.B.C. junior-lightweight title. Boza scored
an impressive points win to become champion and, defending his crown against Bobby
Chacon at Las Vegas, stopped his challenger
in the 13th round. Three months later he
was, surprisingly, knocked out in five rounds
by Rolando Navarrete of the Philippines. On
June 26, 1982, Boza made a good start to
regaining his world crown by outpointing
world-ranked Robert Elizondo over ten
rounds at Las Vegas, and notched up five
other wins during the year. He regained
some of his lost prestige in winning the
European super-featherweight title by stopping Carlos Hernandez (Spain) in four
rounds in London, but surrendered this title
to concentrate on regaining the world crown.
In 1983, however, he was outpointed by
Bobby Chacon over 12 rounds at Las Vegas,
but fought his way to another title bid by
Sept. 26, 1986 when he lost a disputed
verdict to Hector Camacho at Miami in a
W.B.C. lightweight title bout. The following
year his championship aspirations seemingly
came to an end when on Oct. 8, 1987 he was
knocked out by Jose Luis Ramirez (Mexico)
in Paris, France.
Score 52: *w*44 (34) *d*1 *l*7.

Braddock, James

World Heavyweight Champion 1935–57

(b. New York City, June 7, 1906 – d. North Bergen, New Jersey, Nov. 29, 1974). Began pro boxing: April 14, 1926.

Fame came very late for Braddock, who started as a welter and grew into a heavy. His first seven years were very uneven and included a failure to win the light-heavyweight title from Tommy Loughran who outpointed him in 1929. Braddock, with a family to support, was reduced to the breadline in the depression of the early 1930s, but in 1934 was given a contest at Madison Square Garden against a rising young heavy named Corn Griffin. Braddock was expected to be a stepping-stone, but created a sensation by winning in three rounds. Two more good wins and he was challenging Max Baer for the world heavyweight title, and he astounded everyone by winning comfortably on points. He did not defend his title for two years, then dropped it to Joe Louis by a knockout in eight rounds. He had one more fight, outpointing Tommy Farr over ten rounds in New York at the age of 31.
Score 86: w46 (27) d4 l23 ND.11 Dnc.2.

Jack Britton, welterweight champion 1915–22.

Britt, Jimmy

World Lightweight Title Claimant 1904

(b. San Francisco, California, Oct. 5, 1879 – d. San Francisco, Jan. 29, 1940). Began pro boxing: Feb. 18, 1902.

In the early days of the great lightweights, Britt shone as a skilful boxer and right from the start mingled with the best. Fighting Joe Gans for the world lightweight title in 1904, he lost on an alleged foul in round five, but two months later created a stir by outpointing the renowned Battling Nelson over 20 rounds at San Francisco, where he had most of his bouts. He defeated Jabez White and Kid Sullivan over 20 rounds, but in a return with Nelson was knocked out in the 18th. In a third match with the Battler he again beat him on points, but in 1907, when fighting a return with Gans, he broke his wrist in the fourth round and was stopped in the sixth. In 1909 he came to London for three fights with Johnny Summers. He won the first on points over ten rounds, was outpointed over 20 and in the third match, before an enormous outdoor crowd, he was knocked out in the ninth. Britt went on the stage after that and when the Australian Hugh D. McIntosh came to London to promote in 1911, Britt was with him as adviser and manager.
Score 23: w13 (3) d1 l7 ND.2.

Britton, Jack

World Welterweight Champion 1915–22

(b. Clinton, New York, Oct. 14, 1885). Began pro boxing: 1905

A brilliant stand-up boxer of the classical school who took little out of himself during a bout, most of his many bouts going the scheduled distance, Britton (real name William J. Breslin) fought frequently and continuously for 22 years. He claimed the vacant world welterweight title after outpointing Mike Glover over 12 rounds in 1915. Two months later he lost it to Ted (Kid) Lewis of England, and these two then tossed the world crown back and forth until 1921, when Britton finally proved himself the master. In all, Briton fought Lewis 20 times (w4 l3 d1 ND.12). Dave Shade held Britton to a draw over 15 rounds in a title fight, and when the welter king met Benny Leonard, the reigning lightweight champion, the contest had a dramatic ending. Well outpointed from the start, Leonard put in a borderline left to the body in round 13 and Britton went to one knee. Immediately Leonard cracked a left hook on the fallen man's jaw to earn instant disqualification. In 1921, at the age of 36, Britton lost his crown to Mickey Walker, who was 16 years his junior, but Britton was only beaten on a points verdict. He continued to fight until Nov. 14, 1927, when he was outpointed by Jimmy Jones at Canton, Ohio.
Score 299: w83 (21) d19 l20 ND.177.

Brouillard, Lou

World Middle and Welterweight Champion 1931–33

(b. St. Eugene, Quebec, Canada, May 23, 1911). Began pro boxing: 1928.

When Mickey Walker relinquished the middleweight title in 1931, among the many claimants to the title was Brouillard, a French Canadian southpaw who was a rugged, hard puncher with plenty of stamina. Brouillard had started as a welter and won the world crown by outpointing Young Jack Thompson on Oct. 31, 1931, but lost it three months later to Jackie Fields. He grew into a middle and, having outpointed Walker over ten rounds, was matched to fight Ben Jeby who held the New York version of the world middleweight crown.

The fight took place on Aug. 9, 1933, and Brouillard won by a stoppage in round seven, but again his tenure of the title was shortlived, as he lost his crown to Vince Dundee less than three months later. He continued to box in top company and in 1935 went to Paris where he met Marcel Thil, the real world middleweight champion. They met over ten rounds and Lou put up such a good show that they were rematched twice more – Brouillard being disqualified on both occasions. He retired from the ring in 1940.
Score 141: w110 (66) d3 l28.

Brown, Al

World Bantamweight Champion 1929–35

(b. Panama, July 5, 1902 – d. New York, April 11, 1951). Began pro boxing: 1919.

This elongated bantam stood 5 ft. 11 in. and used his correspondingly long reach to perfection. In his own country he won the flyweight title and in 1923 moved to New York, where he at once attracted great attention although he had to wait until 1929 before being given a title chance. The world crown was vacant and Brown outpointed Vidal Gregorio to be acclaimed champion. Once it was in his grasp, he took it round the world, defending it successfully during the next six years in Denmark, France, Canada, Great Britain and Italy. In Spain, however, he dropped a decision to Baltazar Sangchilli that cost him his long-kept crown and signalled the beginning of the end. But he kept going for another seven years before retiring at the end of 1942.

Score 152: *w*120 (58) *d*11 *l*19 *ND*.2.

Brown, Jackie

World, European and British Flyweight Champion 1929–35

(b. Ancoats, Manchester, Nov. 29, 1909 – d. Manchester, March 15, 1971). Began pro boxing: March 23, 1926.

Fleet-footed, fast punching, durable – this lad had champion written all over him from the start. He won the British flyweight title on a Sunday morning in West Bromwich, the first and only time a championship has been decided on the Sabbath. The bout, on Oct. 13, 1929, ended in a third-round knockout of Bert Kirby who took his revenge and the title in a return match in London when Brown suffered an identical fate. In a rubber match Brown regained his crown by out-

Jackie Brown.

Joe Brown (left) ducks to avoid a left from Dave Charnley. Brown went on to retain his world welterweight title on points.

pointing Kirby over 15 rounds in Manchester in 1931.

Later the same year he took the European crown from Lucien Popescu and he hung on to these two prizes for five years, meanwhile winning the world title by knocking out Victor Perez of France in three rounds. He made four successful defences of his world championship, but against the redoubtable Benny Lynch of Scotland he was deprived of all his holdings by a knock-out in the second round. Brown became a bantam but failed to win the British title, being knocked out by his fellow-Mancunian, Johnny King, in 13 rounds. He continued to box in the top class until the outbreak of the war when he immediately enlisted.

Score 132: *w*100 (38) *d*7 *l*25.

Brown, Joe

World Lightweight Champion 1956–62

(b. New Orleans, Louisiana, May 18, 1926). Began pro boxing: Jan. 13, 1946.

An all-services lightweight champion before turning professional, Brown was, at 5 ft. 7½ in., tall for his weight and had a long reach, of which he made skilful use, while he could finish off a beaten opponent with some keen right-hand punches. It took him nearly ten years to get his first title chance and he made the most of it by cleverly outpointing Wallace (Bud) Smith. In the next five years he defended his crown against all-comers – 12 times in all, losing it on the last occasion to Carlos Ortiz on a points verdict in April 1962, his conqueror being his junior by ten years. Brown went on

boxing for the next eight years, performing in many countries. He retired in 1970 at the age of 44.

Score 160: *w*104 (48) *d*12 *l*42 *Dnc*.2.

Brown, Johnny

European and British Bantamweight Champion 1923–28

(b. St. Georges, London, July 18, 1902 – d. South Africa, June 1976). Began pro boxing: March 13, 1919.

Although reared in London's East End, Brown (real name: Philip Hickman) started his paid career on the south side of the River Thames, at the famous Ring at Blackfriars. Brown soon proved himself a harder puncher than the average bantam, and in his fourth year decided to further his fistic education in American rings. After staying there for nearly two years and getting in 26 bouts, some of the no-decision variety, he returned to England as a more formidable boxer and hustled Harry Lake out of his European and British titles. Bantams and feathers fell before him, with an occasional points setback, but he demolished Harry Corbett in 16 rounds in a title defence and then made the Lonsdale Belt his own property by disposing of Mick Hill in 12 rounds. Back he went to America, but this time the trip was most disappointing as he failed to win one of six bouts, and going on to South Africa, he dropped a decision to Willie Smith. There were ten fights to follow with mixed fortunes for Brown and in his last appearance he was forced to retire in two rounds to Teddy Baldock, losing his titles, and bringing about his retirement. He went to live in South Africa and remained there until his death in June 1976.

Score 97: *w*53 (32) *d*6 *l*25 *ND*.13.

Frank Bruno, facing camera, unsuccessfully challenges Tim Witherspoon for the W.B.A. title.

Brown, Newsboy

World Flyweight Champion (Californian State A.C.) 1928

(b. Russia, 1904 – d. 1977). Began pro boxing: Feb. 27, 1922.

Fast on his feet and speedy with his punches, Brown (real name David Montrose) boxed principally in California and, after he had been outpointed by Izzy Schwartz for the New York version of the world flyweight title in Dec. 1927, he was immediately offered a championship contest with Johnny McCoy at Los Angeles that carried the Californian state's official blessing. He took the title but not for long, being tempted to London where he was well outpointed by Johnny Hill, the British and European flyweight king. He kept in the limelight for more than ten years, hanging up his gloves early in 1933.
Score 81: *w*51 (10) *d*5 *l*13 *ND*.12.

Bruno, Frank

European Heavyweight Champion 1985,
World Heavyweight Title Contender 1986

(b. Hammersmith, London, Nov. 16, 1961). Began pro boxing: March 17, 1982.

After winning the A.B.A. heavyweight title in 1980, Frank turned pro two years later. A magnificently built heavyweight, he surged through his early bouts, winning 21 inside the scheduled distance. He appeared a world-beater until he came up against James (Bonecrusher) Smith, whom he outboxed easily until caught by a swiping punch in the tenth round that put him down for the full count. Bruno came back from that disaster to win the European heavyweight title by knocking out Anders Eklund in four rounds. Disposing of Gerrie Coetzee in the opening round gained Bruno a shot at the W.B.A. heavyweight title held by Tim Witherspoon. They fought at Wembley before a huge crowd and Bruno was winning on points until the 11th round when he was submerged under a fearsome two-fisted assault by the American and was being badly battered when the referee called a halt. In the autumn of 1988 Bruno was matched against Mike Tyson in London, but the contest did not materialise.
Score 32: *w*30 (29) *d*0 *l*2.

Buchanan, Ken

World Lightweight Champion 1970–72,
European Lightweight Champion 1974–79,
British Lightweight Champion 1968–73

(b. Edinburgh, Jan. 28, 1945). Began pro boxing: Nov. 20, 1965.

Tall and stylish, he confined his early contests to clubs, but in his 17th start he won his national title and a year later became British titleholder when he knocked out Maurice Cullen in 11 rounds. Buchanan failed to win the European crown from Miguel Velásquez in Madrid, but gained a second notch on his Lonsdale Belt by disposing of Brian Hudson in five rounds and then went off to San Juan where he created an upset by taking the world lightweight title from Ismael Laguna on points. He made two successful defences: against Ruben Navarro in Los Angeles and Laguna in New York. On June 26, 1972, against rough and tough Roberto Duran, he was stopped in the 13th round. Coming home, Buchanan outpointed his fellow-countryman, Jim Watt, to win the Lonsdale trophy outright, then knocked out Antonio Puddu of Italy in six rounds at Cagliari to become European lightweight king. He kept this title for several years before losing to Charlie Nash on a 12-rounds points verdict. He continued to box in England for several years, but the old skill and guile had gone.
Score 69: *w*62 (28) *d*0 *l*7.

Buff, Johnny

World Bantamweight Champion, 1921–22

(b. Perth Amboy, New Jersey, June 12, 1888 – d. East Grange, New Jersey, Jan. 14, 1955). Began pro boxing: 1918.

This very competent and stylish boxer (real name John Leskey) began while serving in the U.S. navy and soon showed the makings of a champion. In his fourth professional year he became American flyweight champion by knocking out Abe Goldstein in two rounds. Six months later he defeated Pete Herman to become world bantam champion. The year 1922 was a disastrous one for Buff. In July Joe Lynch took his bantam crown by a knock-out in round 14 and two months later, in an attempt to win the world flyweight crown, he was stopped in 11 rounds by the renowned Pancho Villa. Johnny boxed on for four more years, but after being put away in two rounds by the unknown Johnny Hamm, he announced his retirement and re-enlisted in the U.S. navy.
Score 94: *w*28 (13) *d*4 *l*16 *ND*.45 *Dnc*.1.

Bugner, Joe

European, Commonwealth and British Heavyweight Champion 1971–76

(b. Hungary, March 13, 1950). Began pro boxing: Dec. 20, 1967.

Bugner, who grew up in England, possessed all the physical requisites and boxing know-how to become heavyweight champion of the world, but lacked the aggression and 'killer' instinct to make the most of it. He made a bad start, being knocked out in his first paid bout, but became a popular performer in the big London halls, although many thought him lucky to take a trio of championship titles from Henry Cooper at Wembley in 1971. He lost all his title holdings to southpaw Jack Bodell six months later, but regained the European crown the following year and kept it against five challengers. He put up a good show against Muhammad Ali at Las Vegas in a 12 rounds non-title fight, but lost on points. He was beaten in similar fashion after putting up terrific resistance to Joe Frazier, the former heavyweight king. Bugner fought Ali for the world crown at Kuala Lumpur and should have beaten him, but could not stir himself to go all out for victory and was outpointed over 15 rounds. He announced his retirement, but came back to regain his former three titles by knocking out Richard Dunn in a single round in 1976. Bugner made further comebacks in 1982 and 1987.
Score 67: *w*58 (39) *d*1 *l*8.

Ken Buchanan, in the tartan shorts, is jolted by a fierce punch from Roberto Duran.

Joe Bugner (right) covers up against Frank Bruno during Bugner's 1987–8 comeback.

Burge, Dick

British Lightweight Champion 1891–97

(b. Cheltenham, Gloucestershire, 1865 – d. London, March 15, 1918). Began pro boxing: 1887.

There is no doubt that this very strong and competent fighter had many bouts that evaded the record books, both with and without the gloves. He started his career in the Newcastle area, but his fame reached London and in 1891 in the Borough Hop Exchange, he won on a disqualification over Jim Carney in the 11th round and claimed the lightweight championship of England. All his fights were wars, if not between him and his opponent, then between the supporters of both sides. He made two superb defences of his crown, then was surprisingly knocked out in two rounds by Ted Pritchard, and then was saved by the referee against Jem Smith in the ninth round of a brawling battle. In 1896 the National Sporting Club in London invited George Lavigne of America to dispute the world lightweight title with Burge. Despite putting up a great fight, Dick found himself outsmarted by the visitor and in the 17th round the referee halted the contest in Lavigne's favour. Burge had seven fights after that, including two riotous affairs with Tom Causer, and he retired in 1900. In

Tommy Burns – Canadian world heavyweight king.

1910 Burge became a prominent promoter of boxing at the celebrated Ring at Blackfriars, in South London.
Score (incomplete) 19: *w*10 (8) *d*2 *l*7.

Burns, Tommy

World Heavyweight Champion 1906–08

(b. Chesley, Ontario, Canada, June 17, 1881 – d. Vancouver, May 10, 1955). Began pro boxing: 1900.

Tommy Burns (real name Noah Brusso) was the smallest of the heavyweight kings (5 ft. 7 in.) and also the most business-like, practically managing himself. When Jim Jeffries retired, he paired Jack Root with Martin Hart to fight for the vacant title. Hart won, but lost to Burns over 20 rounds on Feb. 23, 1906. Burns' claim to be heavyweight champion did not get serious consideration, so he set out to prove his right to the title. He made four defences in America, and went abroad to beat the British champion and several others. He fought in France, then went to Australia, where he made two further successful defences in his crown. He had met all-comers bar one, the giant Jack Johnson, who followed him to Sydney where Burns was forced to put his title at stake on Boxing Day, 1908. Tommy was topped by 6¼ inches and outweighed by 20 pounds, yet he fought gamely against a superb boxer until the police intervened in round 14. After that Burns became a manager and promoter and in 1920 made an amazing comeback to fight Joe Beckett for the British and Commonwealth titles in London, putting up a good show until age told and he was forced to retire in the seventh round.
Score 60: *w*46 (37) *d*9 *l*5.

Burruni, Salvatore

World and European Flyweight Champion, 1961–66

(b. Sardinia, Italy, April 11, 1933). Began pro boxing: April 3, 1957.

This 5ft 2½-in flyweight, strong, tough and bustling in his action, won the Italian title in his second year and never lost it. In 1961 he became European champion and he defended this championship successfully on five occasions in the next three years. In 1965, in Rome, he outpointed Pone Kingpetch of Thailand to gain the world crown, a title he later defended in Sydney against Rocky Gattellari, who was stopped in the 13th round. At his next defence, however, he was outpointed by Walter McGowan of Scotland at Wembley Arena. As he had already defeated the Scot when defending his European crown in Rome, this seemed to call for a rubber match, but Burruni never got it. Two years later he won the European bantamweight title, of which he was still the holder when he retired in 1969.
Score 109: *w*99 (31) *d*1 *l*9.

Buxton, Alex

British Light-Heavyweight Champion 1953–55

(b. Watford, Hertfordshire, May 10, 1925). Began pro boxing: March 10, 1942.

Of four fighting brothers, he was the only one to reach championship status. After his nine minor bouts, he became a merchant seaman and when his ship reached Australia, he found there were plenty of opportunities for fighters and remained there for over three years, during which he met the best, including the phenomenal Dave Sands. Back home he won a British middleweight title eliminator, but then decided he was best at light-heavyweight and challenged the holder, Dennis Powell, winning on the referee's intervention in round ten. He defended his

crown against Albert Finch, who was knocked out in eight rounds. Buxton's arch-enemy was Randolph Turpin. He had lost in seven rounds before becoming champion, and when defending his title against the Leamington Larruper, was put away in two rounds. Fifteen months later they again met for the British light-heavyweight title which had fallen vacant, and once more Turpin proved his master, this time in five rounds. Giving up the idea of being given another title chance, Alex packed his boxing kit into a bag and went round the world, taking fights wherever he could get them. He fought in every European boxing city, and even went to Lima in Peru. He lost more often than he won, but he had a yen for travelling and loved boxing. His last fight was in 1963.
Score 125: *w*79 (55) *d*4 *l*42.

Bygraves, Joe

British Commonwealth Heavyweight Champion 1956–57

(b. Kingston, Jamaica, May 26, 1931). Began pro boxing: Feb. 12, 1953.

A strong, hard-punching heavyweight, he had his pro debut in Liverpool, England, and made steady progress until in 1955 he began venturing abroad for his fights. He won bouts in Dortmund (West Germany), Milan (Italy), Bologna (Italy) and then, going to Gothenburg, did well to stay ten rounds with Ingemar Johansson and lost a points verdict. At Wembley Arena, on Harry Levene's opening show there, he outpointed Kitione Lave (Tonga) to win the British Commonwealth title, which he defended against Henry Cooper (k.o.9) and Dick Richardson (draw 15). He lost his crown eventually to Joe Erskine, who outpointed him. After that this pleasing West Indian boxed on for six more years, but fairly infrequently. In his last 19 bouts, 13 were fought out of England and a decisive defeat in Berlin by Gerhard Zeck in 1963 brought about his retirement.
Score 67: *w*41 (21) *d*2 *l*24.

Caldwell, John

World Bantamweight Champion 1961–62

(b. Belfast, Northern Ireland, May 7, 1938). Began pro boxing: Feb. 6, 1958.

He won a bronze medal in the flyweight class at the 1956 Melbourne Olympic Games and had a brief but exciting career as a pro. Caldwell won his first 21 bouts as a paid fighter, 12 inside the distance, including the British flyweight crown which he took from Frankie Jones in three rounds. There was some dispute as to the ownership of the world title, so promoter Jack Solomons matched the Irishman with Alphonse Halimi of France, and secured agreement that the fight should be for the vacant championship.

Caldwell won a close contest on points and in a return with Halimi repeated his victory. However, in a title bout with Eder Jofre, Caldwell was stopped in ten rounds.

In an all-Irish battle in Belfast in 1962 he was beaten by Freddie Gilroy in ten rounds for the British and Commonwealth bantam titles, but then came back two years later to knock out George Bowes in seven rounds and regain both crowns. He kept these for exactly a year, then passed them on to Alan Rudkin, who stopped him in ten rounds. He retired in 1965.

Score 35: *w*29 (15) *d*1 *l*5.

Callahan, Mushy

World Junior-Welterweight Champion 1926–30

(b. New York City, Nov. 3, 1905 – d. Los Angeles, California, June 16, 1986). Began pro boxing: 1924.

Callahan (real name Vincent Morris Scheer) was a talented boxer but lacking colour. He won his title by outpointing the holder, Pinkey Mitchell, over ten rounds and held on to it for four years, making three winning defences. In 1930, however, the promoter Jeff Dickson brought him to London where he defended his crown against Jack (Kid) Berg and had to retire in the tenth round.

Score 65: *w*47 (20) *d*4 *l*14.

Callura, Jackie

World Featherweight Champion (N.B.A.) 1943

(b. Hamilton, Ontario, Canada, Sept. 24, 1917). Began pro boxing: 1936.

This hard-working, dedicated boxer had to wait seven years and engage in 79 contests before a title chance came his way in 1943. Then he took the N.B.A. featherweight title on a points decision from Jackie Wilson and beat him again the same way in a return fight two months later. The same year he dropped his crown to Phil Terranova by a stoppage in eight rounds and in a return match suffered a similar fate, being halted in six rounds. No more opportunities came his way and after three disastrous defeats he retired in 1947.

Score 102: *w*57 (14) *d*10 *l*35.

Camel, Marvin

World Cruiserweight Champion (W.B.C.) 1979–80

(b. Missoula, Montana, Dec. 24, 1951). Began pro boxing: Sept. 20, 1973.

He became the first holder of the newly created world cruiserweight championship when it was introduced in 1979 by the World Boxing Council, the new weight limit being 190 pounds (later raised to 195 pounds.) He had to go to Yugoslavia for his chance, but

could only get a 'draw' with the local hero, Mate Parlov. In a return match at Las Vegas on March 31, 1980, Camel secured a points decision and the new title. On Nov. 26, 1980, however, he dropped the championship to Carlos De Leon of Puerto Rico on a points verdict, and was stopped in seven rounds in a re-match on Feb. 24, 1982. A year later he secured the I.B.F. crown by stopping Rick Sekorski in nine rounds, a title he lost to Lee Roy Murphy, who stopped him in 14 rounds on October 6, 1984. He retired in 1986.

Score 52: *w*43 (21) *d*2 *l*7.

Campi, Eddie

World Bantamweight Champion 1913

(b. San Francisco, California, July 4, 1989 – d. June 10, 1918). Began pro boxing: 1908.

His full name was Eddie de Campus, and his willingness to do battle made him a box-office attraction. In 1913 an enterprising promoter matched him with Charles Ledoux in a contest which was advertised as for the world bantam title, to which the Frenchman laid claim. Campi gained a hard-fought points win over 20 rounds and styled himself 'King of the Bantams'. His reign was restricted to seven months and then, in the same ring, he was stopped in 12 rounds by Kid Williams. Campi continued as a top-line fighter for the next four years, then he was fatally injured in a hunting accident.

Score 98: *w*76 (11) *d*8 *l*12 *ND.1 Dnc.*1.

Canto, Miguel

World Flyweight Champion (W.B.C.) 1973–79

(b. Merida, Mexico, Jan. 30 1949). Began pro boxing: Feb. 5, 1969.

An all-action flyweight, Canto fought mainly in his own country and in South America. He won the W.B.C. version of the vacant flyweight title by outpointing Shoji Oguma in Japan, and made 14 successful title defences in the next five years, eventually dropping his championship to Chan-Hee Park in Korea. In a return match he failed to regain the title, although he held the Korean to a draw. Canto retired in 1981.

Score 74: *w*61 (15) *d*4 *l*9.

Canzoneri, Tony

World Feather, Light and Junior-Lightweight Champion 1928–36

(b. Slidell, Louisiana, Nov. 6, 1908 – d. New York, Dec. 9, 1959). Began pro boxing: June 17, 1925.

Epitomizing the 'poor-boy-makes-good' legend, ex-shoeshine boy Tony Canzoneri contested boxing championship at four weights, was world's champion at three of them, and became the first man in the history of the ring to win the world light-

weight title twice. This tough little Italian-American moved to New York when he was a schoolboy and there found plenty of scope for his desire to box. He turned professional after winning the New York State Amateur Athletic Union bantam title in 1924.

Canzoneri's aggressive style and busy fists made him a favourite of the fans wherever he fought. He made two unsuccessful attempts to win the vacant world bantam title in 1927, but gained the featherweight crown the following year, losing it seven months later. He then turned his attention to the lightweights and in 1930 created a sensation by winning the championship from Al Singer in 66 seconds, a world record for the weight division.

He lost the title in 1933 but regained it in 1935. In the interim he had three great battles with Jack (Kid) Berg, losing the first on points over ten rounds, but knocking out the Englishman in three rounds to defend his lightweight title and win Berg's junior-welterweight crown. In a return contest for the lightweight championship, Canzoneri beat Berg on points. Canzoneri lost the world lightweight title to Lou Ambers in 1936 but still fought at championship status until 1937, when he was again outpointed by Lou Ambers in an attempt to win back the lightweight title, and retired two years later after sustaining the only inside-the-distance defeat of his long career, when he was stopped by Al Davis in three rounds.

Score 175: *w*141 (44) *d*10 *l*24.

Cardona, Ricardo

World Super-Bantamweight Champion 1978–80

(b. Bolivar, Colombia, Nov. 9, 1952). Began pro boxing: Sept. 15, 1973.

One of the first to win world title honours for his country, Cardona gained his native junior-featherweight title in 1976 and the W.B.A. version of the world super-bantam crown two years later by going to Korea and stopping Soo-Hwan Hong in 12 rounds. After five successful title defences, he was finally stopped in the 15th and last round by Leo Randolph at Seattle. He had a chance to win back his crown a year later but was again stopped, this time by Sergio Palma in 12 rounds in Buenos Aires. A few unimportant contests followed in the next three years and he retired in 1984.

Score 37: *w*26 (13) *d*1 *l*10.

Carmona, Erubey

World Lightweight Champion (W.B.C.) 1972

(b. Mexico City, Sept. 29, 1944). Began pro boxing: Jan. 18, 1964.

This hard-punching, aggressive fighter (real name Eidibiel Chapin) won his native lightweight title in his fourth year as a pro by outscoring Arturo Lomeli over 12 rounds.

Seven weeks later, however, he was outpointed by Alfredo Urbina. His punching power carried him through the next four years, in which he stopped 19 opponents, but was himself halted on three occasions. Undaunted, he scored five more inside-the-distance wins, including one of eight rounds over Mando Ramos to win the W.B.C. version of the world lightweight title in 1972. He kept this for less than two months before being stopped in 13 rounds by Rodolfo Gonzalez, a fellow countryman. Losing his title took a lot of the enthusiasm out of Carmona, and after a knockout defeat by Shinichi Kadota in Honolulu he faded out of the fight game.

Score 66: *w*51 (42) *d*2 *l*13.

Carnera, Primo

World Heavyweight Champion 1933–34

(b. Sequals, Italy, Oct, 26, 1906 – d. June 29, 1967). Began pro boxing: Sept. 12, 1928.

Primo Carnera, 'the Ambling Alp', was the heaviest boxing champion in history. He scaled 19 stone (266 pounds) when he was 21 and gazed down at his challengers from a height of 6 ft. 5¾ in. Although he could box

Primo Carnera's massive physique made up for his lack of skill. He won the championship by stopping Jack Sharkey but lost it to Max Baer.

quite well, Carnera did not punch with his full weight. Even so, he won 69 of his 103 fights inside the distance.

He worked as a labourer, wrestler and strongman in a travelling circus until Leon See, a French manager of boxers, took him over and taught him how to use his fists. In London and Paris he became a great box-office draw, losing only one contest in his first 18 bouts – all crammed into 15 months.

When Carnera went to the United States, he was exploited by his American managers who took him on a tour of the country. There he won 23 contests inside the scheduled distance in nine months. For the next two years he boxed in Europe and America, running up a great many victories. Then in 1933 he was matched with Jack Sharkey for the world heavyweight championship and won by a knock-out in round six. He made two successful defences of his title, winning on points, but was deprived of the championship by the swashbuckling Max Baer, who put him down 11 times before the referee stopped the contest in the 11th round.

A year later Carnera was badly beaten by the up-and-coming Joe Louis, who stopped him in six rounds. After losing twice to Leroy Haynes in 1936 his boxing career was virtually at an end. He went back to wrestling and made enough money to open a liquor store in California, where he lived for many years before going home to Sequals.

Score 103: *w*88 (69) *d*0 *l*14 *ND*.1.

Carney, Jem

British Lightweight Champion 1884–90

(b. Birmingham, Nov. 5, 1856 – d. London, Sept. 8, 1941).

One of the last of the bare knuckle fighters, this tough and durable Midlander

Georges Carpentier walks away after downing British champion Joe Beckett in just 74 seconds – one of the shortest European title fights.

fought many marathon contests, in and around his home town where he was the local hero. He beat Paddy Lee in two hours and drew with Punch Callon over 74 rounds. He faced Jimmy Highland in a fight that was called a draw after 43 rounds, but Carney was arrested the day after and imprisoned for six months because his opponent died after the contest.

Carney won the championship of England by beating Jake Hyams in London after 45 rounds, for which feat his friends presented him with a handsome belt that completely covered his midsection. Moreover, they found the money to send him to Boston to meet the American champion, Jack McAuliffe, for the world title. They fought in a barn for 74 rounds that lasted five hours; then McAuliffe's backers broke into the ring and the fight ended as a 'draw'. No record has been kept of all Carney's fights but in 11 recorded contests he was never beaten.

Carpentier, Georges

World Light-Heavyweight Champion 1920–22, European Heavyweight Champion 1913–23

(b. Lens, France, Jan. 12, 1894 – d. Paris, Oct. 28, 1975). Began pro boxing: Nov. 1, 1908.

Georges Carpentier, the 'Pride of Paris', reigned supreme among light-heavyweight boxers in the years immediately before and after World War I. Handsome, debonair, and the idol of the ladies, he won the French lightweight title at the age of 15, and went on to become light-heavyweight champion of the world. He was a master of long-range boxing, measuring his man with an unerring straight left before smashing a devastating right to the chin that usually brought his fights to a swift and dramatic close.

The son of a miner, Carpentier was, at the age of 12, an amateur flyweight, and had his first professional contest a year later. As he grew up, he passed through all the weight divisions, winning French and European championships until he came into the heavyweight picture by knocking out Bombardier Billy Wells, the British champion, in four rounds in 1913. He repeated the victory six months later by knocking out Wells in 73 seconds. On the eve of World War I he fought the American Ed 'Gunboat' Smith at Olympia, London. Smith was disqualified in the sixth round, and with this victory Carpentier won the unofficial white heavyweight championship of the world (Jack Johnson, the true champion, was a black).

On the outbreak of war, Carpentier joined the French Air Force, became a lieutenant, and was awarded the Croix de Guerre and the Médaille Militaire. He did not box again until 1919, losing five precious years at the most important stage of his career. On returning to the ring after the war Carpentier defended his European title against the former British light-heavyweight champion, Dick Smith, in Paris, winning by a knockout in eight rounds. In 1919 he went back to London and caused a sensation by knocking out the British champion, Joe Beckett, in 74 seconds. This win earned Carpentier the right to challenge Jack Dempsey for the heavyweight championship of the world.

This fight, the first of the 'million-dollar gates' promoted by Tex Rickard, took place in July 1921. A special outdoor arena had been built at Jersey city to accommodate the 80,183 fans who paid $1,729,238 for the privilege of watching the contest. Carpentier, who was conceding some 24 pounds, put up a plucky show. He broke his thumb on the champion's iron jaw, and was eventually punched into submission by the 'Manassa Mauler' in the fourth round.

In 1922 he defended his world light-heavyweight title against Ted (Kid) Lewis in London, winning by a controversial one-round knockout. But four months later he was dramatically beaten in Paris by the Senegalese fighter, Battling Siki. Caught by a wild punch from his opponent in round six, Carpentier went down and his manager threw in the towel. This was disregarded by the referee, who proceeded to disqualify Siki for allegedly tripping his opponent. Shortly afterwards, amid a storm of booing, the judges reversed the decision.

In 1923 Carpentier had a return fight with Beckett, again defeating him inside a round – the fight lasting a mere 15 seconds. Then a year later the Frenchman embarked on another American tour, but was stopped in 15 rounds by Gene Tunney. He retired in 1927.

Score 109: *w*88 *d*6 *l*14 *ND*.1.

Carrasco, Pedro

World (W.B.C.) 1971–72 and European Lightweight Champion 1967–69

(b. Huelva, Spain, July 11, 1943). Began pro boxing: Oct. 24, 1962.

This fine Spanish fighter with the magnificent knockout record fought the majority of his contests in his own country where his hard, crisp punching made him a national idol. He won the European lightweight title by stopping Borge Krogh, a tough Dane, in eight rounds and for the next two years beat off all his five challengers. He then relinquished the title because of weight worries and won the European junior-welterweight crown by outpointing René Roque (France). When the opportunity came for him to contest the W.B.C. world lightweight title, in Madrid, he reduced to make the weight and won the fight when his opponent, Mando Ramos (U.S.A.), was ruled out in the 11th round for allegedly hitting below the belt. Pedro had been down four times before the end came and it seemed that weight-reducing had weakened him. This was made clearer when he fought a return with Ramos in Los Angeles three months later and was beaten on points. In a third match between them, in Madrid, Carrasco was again a points loser and soon after he retired.

Score 110: *w*105 (66) *d*2 *l*3.

Carruthers, Jimmy

World Bantamweight Champion 1952–54

(b. Paddington, N.S.W., Australia, July 5, 1929). Began pro boxing: Aug. 15, 1950.

Jimmy Carruthers, a southpaw bantamweight, was the first Australian to win an undisputed world boxing championship. He secured the world bantamweight title by knocking out South Africa's Vic Toweel in the first round, and retired undefeated in 1954 after 19 professional bouts. Carruthers, who stood 5 ft. 6½ in. high, with spindly legs and powerful shoulders, moved very fast and used every inch of the ring.

He first represented his country as an amateur at the 1948 Olympic Games in London. When he returned to Sydney he had no intention of turning professional until he heard that Vic Toweel, whom he had watched in London, had become world bantam champion.

He immediately resolved to fight for pay, and in his ninth bout won the Australian title by defeating the highly regarded aboriginal champion, Elley Bennett. Five winning fights later Carruthers went to Johannesburg to challenge Toweel, and scored his sensational victory. In a return contest four months later, Carruthers knocked out Toweel in the tenth round. After defending his crown against Henry Gault of America in 1953 Carruthers successfully made one more

Jimmy Carruthers forces his opponent into a corner.

title defence and then retired. Unwisely, he returned in 1961, after an absence of seven years, and after several disappointing displays hung up his gloves for good.
Score 25: *w*21 (13) *d*0 *l*4.

Carter, James

World Lightweight Champion 1951–55

(b. Aiken, South Carolina, Dec. 15, 1923). Began pro boxing: March 14, 1946.

This modest, likeable box-fighter was one of the most dedicated boxers ever to win the world lightweight crown. In his first four years he went into action 58 times: his big chance came in 1951 when he met the long-reigning Ike Williams in New York and won the world lightweight title when the referee stopped the contest in the 14th round to save the champion from unnecesary punishment. There followed three contests with Lauro Salas: win, lose, win. Art Aragon, Tommy Collins, George Araugo and Armand Savoie were all losing challengers, then Carter dropped the title to Paddy DeMarco, only to win it back in a return contest. He had thus won the world crown three times, which was something of a record. When Wallace (Bud) Smith gained the championship on a points win, Carter thought he could get it back again. But his luck had run out and Smith won the return fight, also on points. Carter continued to box for several more years and finally retired at the age of 38.
Score 120: *w*81 (31) *d*9 *l*30.

Castellini, Miguel

*World Junior-Middleweight Champion
(W.B.A.) 1976–77*

(b. Santa Rosa, Argentina, Jan. 26, 1947).
Began pro boxing: May 28, 1973.

After suffering some setbacks in his early
years, he ran up a sequence of knockout
wins, during which he won and retained his
native junior-middleweight crown. This success decided him to tour Europe and in
Madrid he outpointed José Durán to become
world titleholder. He kept the crown for
only five months, losing it at the first defence
to Eddie Gazo at Managua, Nicaragua, on a
points decision. He did not get a chance to
regain his title and after three more years of
battling, with fair success, he retired in 1980.
Score 93: w73 (49) d12 l8.

Castillo, Freddie

*World Junior-Flyweight Champion 1978,
Flyweight Champion (W.B.C.) 1982*

(b. Mérida, Mexico, June 15, 1955). Began
pro boxing: Sept. 22, 1971.

This tiny Mexican carried a powerful
punch, as witnessed by the fact that he won
so many of his contests inside the scheduled
distance. His career as a world-beater was
not, however, a long one. He won the
W.B.C. light-flyweight title by stopping Luis
Estaba in 14 rounds at Caracas, Venezuela,
on Feb. 19, 1978, but lost it three months
later to Netrnoi Sor Vorasingh in Bangkok.
He continued boxing and on Feb. 26, 1982
captured the N.A.B.F. flyweight title by
stopping Gabriel Bernal in eight rounds and
followed this by outpointing Prudencio Cardona to become W.B.C. flyweight champion. He lost his crown four months later to
Eleoncio Mercedes on a points verdict, and
when he tried to regain it he was outpointed
by Sot Chitalada on Feb. 22, 1986. He then
retired.
Score 69: w46 (29) d5 l18.

Castillo, Jesus

World Bantamweight Champion 1970–71

(b. Nuevo Vaile de Moreno, Mexico, June
17, 1944). Began pro boxing: April 26, 1962.

A hard, free-punching fighter, Castillo
won his native title by outpointing Joe Medel
over 12 rounds at Mexico City. He kept this
against two challengers, then fought Lionel
Rose (Australia) for his world crown at
Inglewood, California. The champion won
on points and, back home, Castillo made
two more winning defences of his Mexican
title. He then tried once again to win the
world crown, but lost on points to his
fellow-countryman, Ruben Olivares. In a
return fight six months later, Castillo caused
a surprise by halting Olivares in the 14th
round, the referee stopping the contest

because a badly cut eye, sustained by the
champion in round one, had become an ugly
wound. Ruben got his own back when he
outpointed Castillo in a third title fight. The
latter had reigned for less than a year and,
after fighting spasmodically and without
much success in four years, decided to retire.
Score 65: w65 (20) d2 l18.

Cerdan, Marcel

*World and European Middleweight
Champion 1948–49*

(b. Sidi Bel-Abbes, Algeria, 1917 – d.
Azores, Oct. 27, 1949). Began pro boxing:
Nov. 4, 1934.

Marcel Cerdan, the French-Algerian
middleweight boxing champion of the world,
had everything that it takes to reach the top:
true fighting spirit, strength, stamina, courage, and the punch that pays. Cerdan's elder
brothers boxed for a living, and at 17 he
decided to follow their example and turned
professional. He built up such a reputation
that the fans in Paris clamoured to see him.
In 1938, at the age of 22, he became French
welterweight champion. The following year
he went to Milan where he relieved the
Italian champion, Salverio Turiello, of his
European title.

On the outbreak of World War II Cerdan
joined up and remained in the French army
until the fall of France. He then defended his
European title against Omar Kouidri in
Oran, in 1941, and against the Spaniard,
José Ferrer, in Paris a year later. In 1945 he
gained the French middleweight title in
Paris.

During a brief trip to the United States in
1946 he scored a notable win over Georgie
Abrams and then returned to take the
European championship with a sensational

*Marcel Cerdan, French middleweight champion
of the world 1948–49.*

one-round win over Léon Fouquet of Belgium. In 1948 his unblemished record was
slightly marred when he lost his championship to Cyrille Delannoit of Belgium, by
the narrowest of margins – the only time he
was ever beaten on points. In a return match
he regained the title by easily outpointing
the Belgian.

In Sept. 1948 Cerdan challenged the
American, Tony Zale, for the world title at
Jersey City, and punched Zale into subjection in the 12th round. In June 1949 Cerdan
defended his world title in Detroit against
Jake LaMotta – a bruiser whose main asset
was his sheer toughness. The Frenchman
suffered a damaged shoulder during the first
round, survived for nine rounds and then
retired. There was a return fight clause in the
contract, and on Oct. 27, 1949, Cerdan and
his manager took off in an airliner for New
York. The plane crashed in the Azores and
the boxing world was stunned to learn that
Marcel Cerdan had been killed at the age of
33.
Score 123: w119 (74) d0 l4.

Cervantes, Antonio

*World Junior-Welterweight Champion
(W.B.A.) 1971–80*

(b. Bolívar, Colombia, Dec. 23, 1945).
Began pro boxing: Jan. 31, 1964.

A strong, heavy puncher, he came into
world prominence when he was matched
with Nicolino Loche (Argentina) for the
world junior-welterweight title at Buenos
Aires in 1971. He lost on points but, when
given a second chance a year later, stopped
Alfonso Franser (Panama) in ten rounds to
become world champion. He put this at
stake almost every time he fought thereafter,
making no fewer than ten successful defences against all comers. Eventually he lost
his crown to Wilfred Benitez (U.S.A.), who
outpointed him at San Juan. When the
W.B.A. declared the title vacant in 1977,
Cervantes was there to stop Carlos Giminez
in six rounds and became champion again.
Once more he proved himself a fighting
champion, beating off six challengers in the
next three years. But at 35 he lost his world
crown to Aaron Pryor (U.S.A.) in four
rounds at Cincinnati. Cervantes had three
bouts in the next three years and retired in
1983.
Score 79: w66 (37) d1 l12.

Chacon, Bobby

*World Junior-Light and Featherweight
Champion 1974–83*

(b. Los Angeles, California, Nov. 28, 1951).
Began pro boxing: April 17, 1972.

A dashing fighter with hard punch, he
romped through his first 25 bouts with only
one defeat and 23 wins inside-the-distance.
His sole defeat was at the hands of Ruben
Olivares when they fought for the North

American Boxing Federation featherweight title, and Chacon lost in nine rounds. A year later, however, he took the W.B.C. championship by stopping Alfredo Marcano in nine rounds. He held this against a challenge from Jesus Estrada but, in 1975, meeting Ruben Olivares again, he was stopped in two rounds and lost his crown. He became a junior-lightweight, but two attempts to win this championship, from Alexis Arguello and Cornelias Boza-Edwards, ended in defeats inside the distance. Eventually he won the title by outpointing Rafael Limon at Sacramento on Dec. 11, 1982 after being on the canvas twice. He successfully defended this title by outpointing Boza-Edwards over 12 rounds, but lost it in three rounds to Ray Mancini the following year. He retired in 1985.
Score 65: w57 (46) d1 l7.

Chambers, Arthur

World Lightweight Champion 1872–73

(b. Salford, Lancashire, Dec. 3, 1847 – d. Philadelphia, Pennsylvania, May 25, 1925). Began pro boxing: 1864.

Chambers fought in the days of the long-distance fights: with Fred Finch in London (64 rounds), Arthur Webber (20), Ned Evans (44), Jem Brady (28), Jem Brady (63), Tom Scatterwood (40), Bob Mullins (D.43), George Fletcher (56) and George Siddons (39). When he defeated the American champion, Billy Edwards, on a foul in the 26th round of their title battle on Squirrel Island in Canada, Chambers had every reason to claim the world lightweight title. He fought a draw with Dick Goodwin at Acton, London, that went 105 rounds and lasted 3 hrs. 4 mins., but his greatest performance, when he was 32, was to go 136 rounds with Johnny Clark, at Chippewa Falls, Canada, to win by a knockout.
Score 14: w11 d2 l1.

Chandler, Jeff

World Bantamweight Champion (W.B.A.) 1980–84

(b. Philadelphia, Pennsylvania, Sept. 3, 1956). Began pro boxing: Feb. 25, 1976.

A complete boxer with a sizeable punch, he won an American title in his 19th bout and gained the W.B.A. version of the world title by scoring a 14th round win over Julian Solis at Miami at the end of his fifth year as a pro. He retained the title against Jorge Lugan (points), Eijiro Murata (draw), Julian Solis (7th round), Eijiro Murata (13th round), Johnny Carter (6th round), and Miguel Iriate (9th round). He became U.S.B.A. bantam champion in 1979 and N.A.B.F. titleholder the following year, winning also the world title at the end of 1980. He kept this crown against nine challengers in the next three years, finally

losing it to Richard Sandoval on April 7, 1984, being stopped in the 15th and last round at Atlantic City.
Score 37: w33 (18) d2 l2.

Chaney, George

World Featherweight Contender 1916

(b. Baltimore, Maryland, 1893 – d. 1958). Began pro boxing: Jan. 2, 1910.

Although never a world champion, this hard-punching, durable fighter fought for 15 years against all comers, scoring such a high rate of knockout wins that they called him KO Chaney. He was ready to fight at the drop of a hat and, although only a featherweight, was always ready to fight men bigger and heavier than himself. He got the sole chance in his long career to win a world title when he had already been fighting for seven years, obtaining a match with Johnny Kilbane for his world featherweight title. But the champion was too good for him and ended the fight dramatically in round two with a clean-cut kayo. Chaney was 32 when he gave up fighting for pay.
Score 178: w109 (86) d0 l14 ND.55

Charles, Ezzard

World Heavyweight Champion 1949–51

(b. Lawrenceville, Georgia, July 7, 1921 – d. Chicago, May 27, 1970). Began pro boxing: March 15, 1940.

A skilful, upstanding boxer with a sizeable punch, he started as an amateur and in 1939

Ezzard Charles sends Jersey Joe Walcott to the canvas in the first of their four title fights. Charles won this encounter on points.

became Golden Gloves Champion at middleweight. He made a good start as a paid fighter, but it took him through the light-heavies and into 1949 before he got a real break. Joe Louis had threatened retirement, so the National Boxing Association declared his title vacant and nominated Charles to meet Jersey Joe Walcott to fight for it. Charles won on points, defended it successfully on three occasions and then got himself recognized as heavyweight champion of the world by outpointing Louis, who had resolved on a comeback. Four more times he put his championship at stake, and then came up against Walcott, who caused a sensation by scoring a kayo in round seven. In a return bout Jersey Joe outpointed him, but Charles went on trying to regain his lost laurels, even taking on the redoubtable Rocky Marciano when he was 33. He stayed the course against the Rock and deserved a return contest. This took place three months later and, although Charles was stopped in eight rounds, he put up such a fight and damaged Marciano's features so badly that it was one of the causes of the latter's retirement.
Score 122: w96 (58) d1 l25.

Charnley, Dave

European, Commonwealth and British Lightweight Champion 1957–65

(b. Dartford, Kent, Oct. 10, 1935). Began pro boxing: Oct. 19, 1954.

Charnley's strong punching won him the A.B.A. featherweight championship of 1954, and he turned professional the same year. He became British lightweight champion at 21 by outpointing Joe Lucy, another

29

southpaw in 1957, but in his first attempt to win the Commonwealth title later that year he was beaten on points by the brilliant South African champion, Willie Toweel. In a return match Charnley punched with such authority that the championship changed hands in the tenth round.

Charnley challenged for the world title at Houston, Texas, in 1959, against Joe Brown, but was forced to retire in the fifth round with a badly damaged eye. He fought Brown again – this time in London – and just lost a bitterly contested duel that many fans thought he had won. By way of consolation he knocked out Brown in six rounds in a third meeting – but after the American had already lost his world title. Before his second bout against Brown, Charnley added the European to his British and Commonwealth titles.

In 1961 Charnley met challenger David (Darkie) Hughes of Wales for his three titles and stopped the Welshman in 40 seconds including the count – a record win for the British lightweight class. In 1962 he went to Jamaica, losing his Commonwealth title on a close points verdict to Bunny Grant, but won his Lonsdale Belt outright by defeating Maurice Cullen in 1963. That year he forfeited his European title.

Moving into the welterweight division, Charnley was game enough to challenge world champion Emile Griffith. But he took a bad beating before the fight was stopped in round eight. Charnley retired from the ring in 1965, unbeaten British lightweight champion.

Score 61: *w*48 (30) *d*1 *l*12.

Chartvanchai, Berkrerk

World Flyweight Champion (W.B.A.) 1970

(b. Bangkok, Thailand, 1946). Began pro boxing: Jan. 5, 1966.

An exciting little fighter, he went through his first 28 bouts without defeat, which included the winning of the W.B.A. flyweight crown with a points victory over Bernabe Villacampo. Chartvanchai remained champion for six months and was then stopped in 13 rounds by Masao Ohba of Japan. He did not get a chance to win back his crown and, after three more unsatisfactory years, decided to retire.

Score 40: *w*29 (7) *d*3 *l*8.

Chavez, Julio Cesar

World Super-Featherweight Champion (W.B.C.) 1984–87, World Lightweight Champion (W.B.A.) 1987–

(b. Sonora, Mexico, July 12, 1962). Began pro boxing: Feb. 5, 1980.

One of four boxing brothers, he learned his boxing the hard way with eight bouts in his first year, 14 in the second, all of which he won by knockouts. He won the W.B.C. super-featherweight title on Sept. 13, 1984

by stopping Mario Martinez in eight rounds at Los Angeles, subsequently defending it successfully nine times, beating such strong contenders as Roger Mayweather, Refugio Rojas, Rocky Lockridge, Juan LaPorte, Francisco Tomas and Daniel Cabrera, the majority of his wins being inside the distance. He relinquished his crown in 1987 and completed as a lightweight, winning the W.B.A. title on Nov. 21 from Edwin Rosario of Puerto Rico in 11 rounds at Las Vegas. His first defence of his second world crown was against Rodolfo Aguilar, from Panama, who could last only into the sixth round. He is a consistently good box-fighter.

Score 57: *w*57 (48) *d*0 *l*0.

Chionoi, Chartchai

World Flyweight Champion 1966–74

(b. Bangkok, Thailand, Oct. 10, 1942). Began pro boxing: Oct. 12, 1957.

A truly remarkable box-fighter, Chionoi went on winning and losing the world fly-

weight title until past 32. He first won the Orient title and then, when he had been boxing for ten years, had a stroke of luck. A Thailand promoter brought Walter McGowan, the British champion, to Bangkok in defence of his world crown and Chionoi caused a sensation by stopping the Scot in nine rounds with a damaged nose. Chionoi defended his crown against Puntip Keosuriya in three rounds, then went to London to give McGowan a chance to recover his title. This time the champion stopped his challenger in seven rounds. Two more successful defences followed. Chionoi subsequently lost his crown to Efren Torres, regained it in a return fight, then lost it once more, to Erbito Salavarria. Making an attempt to win the W.B.A. version of the flyweight title, Chionoi was stopped in 12 rounds by Masao Ohba but five months later regained the crown with a five-rounds win over Fritz Chervet. He retained the title against Susu-

Julio Cesar Chavez, one of the outstanding boxers of the 1980s.

mu Hanagata on a points verdict five months later, and defended it against Chervet with a fine points win. In a return match with Hanagata, however, he was halted in six rounds on Oct. 18, 1974. A year later, after one more inside-the-distance defeat, he gave up.
Score 85: *w*63 (39) *d*3 *l*19.

Chip, George

World Middleweight Champion 1913–14

(b. Scranton, Pennsylvania, Aug. 25, 1888 – d. Nov. 8, 1960). Began pro boxing: 1909.

Chip (real name Chipulonia), a strong, two fisted fighter of the old school, did most of his battling in no-decision contests. But in 1913 he came up against an even more durable opponent in Frank Klaus and caused a big surprise by winning on a knockout in six rounds. A return fight two months later saw Chip again successful, this time in five rounds. At 25 he seemed destined to keep his crown as middleweight king for some time, but going to Brooklyn to defend his title against a notoriously light hitter, Al McCoy, he made the mistake of not finding out beforehand that his challenger was a southpaw, a little-known complication in those days. At the start Chip rushed his rival into the ropes, McCoy leant back into them and, rebounding with a wild left swing to the chin, put Chip down and out in 45 seconds. Chip went on boxing for the next seven years, but never got a chance to become champion again.
Score 160: *w*72 (36) *d*14 *l*46 *ND*.27 *Dnc*.1.

Chocolate, Kid

World Feather and Junior-Lightweight Champion 1931–33

(b. Cerro, Cuba, Jan. 6, 1910 – d. Cuba, Aug. 8, 1988). Began pro boxing: 1927.

Kid Chocolate (real name Eligio Sardinias) started in his own country and is credited with over 100 wins as an amateur. Becoming a professional, he scored 21 wins inside the distance and it was then decided he should make his fortune in American rings. A superlative boxer, with knockdown power, in four years he had his first title chance. He muffed this by losing on points to the more experienced Bat Battalino, but in Philadelphia he won the junior-lightweight title from Benny Bass in a single round. An attempt to take the lightweight crown from Tony Canzoneri ended in a points defeat, so Chocolate went back to fighting men of his own weight. In 1932 he took the New York State version of the featherweight championship from Lew Feldman. He defended this successfully against Fidel LaBarba (U.S.A.) on a points verdict, and Seaman Tom Watson (England), also on points. He found himself growing out of the class, but lost his junior-lightweight crown to Frankie Klick, being stopped in seven rounds. Kid Chocolate went on boxing in both Cuba and America for more than four years and then retired.
Score 148: *w*132 (50) *d*6 *l*10.

Christoforidis, Anton

World Light-Heavyweight Champion (N.B.A.) 1941

(b. Messina, Greece, May 26, 1917 – d. Athens, Nov. 1986). Began pro boxing: 1934.

After a few bouts in Athens, this good-looking Greek made his fistic headquarters in Paris, where he was managed by Pierre Grandon, one-time French middleweight champion. Christoforidis won the European middleweight crown by defeating Bep Van Klaveren (Netherlands) but quickly lost it to Edouard Tenet (France). He then made tracks for America and with a series of wins found himself matched with Melio Bettina for the N.B.A. version of the world light-heavyweight title, Jan. 13, 1941. He won on points, but lost his crown to Gus Lesnevich four months later. He had one more busy year in America, then faded out and finally retired in 1947.
Score 74: *w*52 (13) *d*7 *l*15.

Clabby, Jimmy

Welterweight Contender

(b. Norwich, Connecticut, July 14, 1890 – d. Calumet City, Indiana, Jan. 18, 1934). Began pro boxing: Aug. 1906.

Although he was never a champion, he fought the very best at his weight in his day – and they *were* good at that time. Throughout a long career, he averaged 12 fights a year and was stopped only four times, twice in his early days and twice towards the close. In 1908 he did feature in a contest at New Orleans that was billed as for the world welter crown, but lost on points to Jimmy Gardner. In 1915 Clabby took off for Australia where he remained for five years, twice meeting the legendary Les Darcy, but being outpointed on both occasions. Jimmy kept going until 1923, when he was 33, a two rounds defeat by Morrie Schaiffer deciding him to call it a day.
Score 155: *w*79 (40) *d*20 *l*21 *ND*.34 *Dnc*.1.

Clarke, Elky

European, British Empire and British Flyweight Champion 1924–27

(b. Bridgeton, Glasgow, Jan. 4, 1898 – d. Glasgow, Sep. 22, 1956). Began pro boxing: Nov. 14, 1921.

A stalwart, dour Scot, Clarke seemed to be able to go on for ever. He was not very impressive in his early years and failed in his first attempt to win his native title. When he did become Scottish flyweight king, he soon added the bantam championship and then set out to win the British crown. He won his way through a series of eliminators and then stopped Kid Kelly of Plymouth in the 20th and final round. He took the British Empire title by beating Jim Hanna, then the European crown at the expense of Michel Montreuil (Belgium), also over 20 rounds. He kept all three titles against George (Kid) Socks, who was stopped in the 20th round and successfully defended his European title against Francois Morrachini (France). He went to New York in Jan. 1927 to fight Fidel La Barba for the world's flyweight title, but lost over 12 rounds. Had it been over the marathon course to which the little Scot was used, there might have been a different ending. As it was he sustained a damaged eye and on reaching home announced that his fistic career was at an end. One of the greatest of British flyweights, he became the boxing correspondent of a Scottish paper.
Score 44: *w*29 (20) *d*4 *l*11.

Clayton, Ronnie

British, European and British Empire Featherweight Champion 1947–54

(b. Blackpool, Lancashire, Feb. 9, 1923). Began pro boxing: Jan. 3, 1941.

Formerly a schoolboy champion, he yearned to be a pro boxer and each week would pack his meagre fighting gear into a cardboard attache case and go along to the Tower Circus in his home town where regular shows were staged. At last the promoter gave him a chance in a four-round bout that ended in a draw – and Clayton was on his way. He had no luck as a bantam, twice being beaten in eliminators, but as a feather-weight he was a greater force and fought his way through to a fight with Al Phillips that carried three titles: British, European and British Empire. He won on points, but in a few months dropped his European crown to that talented Frenchman, Ray Famechon. But no one could take away his British title and he fought off five challengers to win two Lonsdale Belts outright. Eventually he lost his Commonwealth title to Roy Ankrah and failed to regain his E.B.U. title from Famechon. For over 12 years he was a popular performer, a capable boxer and a sportsman through and through. When he finally lost his British title to Sammy Mc-Carthy, eight years his junior, Ronnie decided to retire.
Score 110: *w*77 (47) *d*8 *l*25.

Cochrane, Freddie

World Welterweight Champion 1941–46

(b. Elizabeth, New Jersey, May 6, 1915). Began pro boxing: June 4, 1933.

Because of the colour of his hair, he was known as Red Cochrane and he must be considered one of the unluckiest of all the world champions. It took Freddie eight years of very active fighting to get himself into

range for a title fight, but as soon as he had taken the title from Fritzie Zivic on a points verdict, America entered World War II and Cochrane went into the U.S. navy, his world title being frozen in the meantime. When he resumed his career in 1945, he was twice stopped in ten rounds by the renowned Rocky Graziano, and was then stopped in four rounds when making the first defence of his championship against Marty Servo. This final setback brought about Cochrane's retirement.
Score 117: *w*73 (27) *d*9 *l*35.

Cockell, Don

European and British Light-Heavyweight Champion, British and Commonwealth Heavyweight Champion 1953-56

(b. Battersea, London, Sept. 22, 1928 – d. 1983). Began pro boxing: June 26, 1946.

Cockell took to boxing when he attended fair booths on a Saturday night to earn enough money to get married. He did so well that he left his work as a blacksmith to start a career in the ring. A fine boxer and a solid puncher, in his fifth year he won the vacant British light-heavyweight title, added the European crown and kept these for 2½ years before, weakened by weight-making, he lost his titles to Randolph Turpin. Beating the aged Tommy Farr in an eliminator, he took the British and Commonwealth heavyweight crowns from Johnny Williams. He went to South Africa to defend successfully the Commonwealth title and then started his onslaught on the contenders for the world heavyweight title. Cockell was too short to have any chance of winning the world crown, but he defeated such American heavies as Harry Matthews and Roland La Starza to earn himself a title bout with the unbeaten Rocky Marciano. The champion's non-stop bulldozing tactics proved too much and Cockell had to retire after nine rounds. He

Don Cockell (right) is jolted by a straight left from Rocky Marciano in the opening round of their championship bout.

then lost his form completely and was stopped by the giant Cuban, Nino Valdes, in three rounds and by Kitione Lave, from Tonga, in two. These setbacks prompted him to relinquish all his holdings and retire.
Score 79: *w*64 (37) *d*1 *l*14.

Cohen, Robert

World, French and European Bantamweight Champion 1954–56

(b. Bône, Algeria, Nov. 15, 1930). Began pro boxing: Sept. 12, 1951.

A hard-hitting, resolute fighter, Cohen had the majority of his early bouts in Paris, where he became a most popular performer because of his punching power. He won the French bantam title by outpointing Maurice Sandeyron and the European title from John Kelly in Belfast, knocking out the Irishman in three rounds. In Thailand he won the vacant world crown by outpointing Chamrern Songkitrat over 15 rounds at Bangkok. In South Africa Cohen successfully defended his title against Willie Toweel at Johannesburg, but was held to a draw. The following year, in Rome, he lost his crown to Mario D'Agata, who battered him to defeat, forcing him to retire at the end of the eighth round. Cohen hung up his gloves after that.
Score 43: *w*36 (14) *d*3 *l*4.

Cokes, Curtis

World Welterweight Champion (W.B.A.) 1966–69

(b. Dallas, Texas, June 15, 1937). Began pro boxing: March 24, 1958.

This extremely good boxer and powerful puncher had to battle his way through for five years before getting near a title fight. He won the Texas State welter title in 1965 and a bout billed as for the Southern title the same year. In 1966 he stopped Luis Rodriguez in the final round of a W.B.A. eliminating contest and this paved the way for the championship itself, which he won by outscoring Manuel Gonzalez. Three months later he defeated the European champion, Jean Josselin (France), to strengthen his claim to the world crown. He successfully defended this four times in the next two years, but in 1969 dropped the title to Jose Napoles (Cuba), being stopped in 13 rounds. A return title match had the same result, except that Napoles cut it down to ten rounds this time. Cokes retired in 1972.
Score 80: *w*62 (30) *d*4 *l*14.

Collins, Tom

British and European Light-Heavyweight Champion 1982–

(b. Curacao, Dutch West Indies, July 1, 1955).

An ambitious boxer with a good punch, but not too strong in defence, Collins be-

came Central Area champion by knocking out Greg Evans in one round, and outpointed Karl Canvell (who held a kayo win over him) in an eliminator for the British light-heavyweight championship. He won this on March 15, 1982 by outpointing Dennis Andries (his other inside-the-distance conqueror) over 15 rounds at Bradford. Two months later he gained a second notch on his Lonsdale Belt by knocking out Trevor Cattouse (Balham) in six rounds at Leeds. He made the Lonsdale Belt his own property on March 9, 1983, in the short time of 359 days by stopping Antonio Harris in six rounds. He lost his crown to his arch-enemy Dennis Andries on a points verdict in London on Jan. 26, 1984, but when the title became vacant, regained it in a terrific battle with John Moody, of Wales, the referee stopping the contest in the tenth round. Tom captured the European crown on Nov. 11, 1987 with a stunning two-round kayo of Alex Blanchard, the Dutch holder. He defended both his titles against Mark Kaylor on May 20, 1988 and stopped him in nine rounds but was unlucky when defending his E.B.U. crown against Pedro van Raamsdamk from the Netherlands – the bout being halted in the seventh round because of an eye wound sustained in the opening round.
Score 40: *w*24 (17) *d*1 *l*15.

Conn, Billy

World Light-Heavyweight Champion 1939–41

(b. Pittsburgh, Pennsylvania, Oct. 8, 1917). Began pro boxing: 1935.

Colourful and clever, but not a heavy puncher, Conn started as a welter at the age of 18 and advanced as he grew until, in 1939, when the world light-heavyweight title fell vacant, he was matched with Melio Bettina by the New York State Athletic Commission and won a points verdict. The fact that Len Harvey had climbed on to the vacant throne three days earlier did not bother the Americans. Conn kept his half of the championship for two years, beating off two challengers in such style that the promoter Mike Jacobs thought him good enough to put up against Joe Louis for the heavyweight crown. His faith was justified, because for the first 12 rounds Conn outboxed the vaunted Brown Bomber. Then he got overconfident and endeavoured to go for a knockout. He played right into Joe's hands, and was promptly stopped in the 13th. Both men joined the U.S. Army for the duration of World War II. Afterwards Jacobs did not hesitate to rematch them in a title bout. Louis had grown old and fat, but Conn had lost his zeal for fighting. He made a very poor showing and the end came in the eighth, with Louis scoring a clean-cut knockout win. Conn was inactive for a year, made some sort of a comeback, but it fizzled out and he retired.
Score 76: *w*63 (14) *d*1 *l*12.

John Conteh was the first British light-heavyweight champion of the world since Freddie Mills in 1950.

Conteh, John

British, Commonwealth, European and World Light-Heavyweight Champion (W.B.C.) 1973–78

(b. Liverpool, May 27, 1951). Began pro boxing: Oct. 18, 1971.

When this keen-punching ex-amateur champion began to fight for pay the majority of his early bouts took place in London where he built up a huge following. In his first 26 fights he lost only one (a ten-rounds points decision) and all but five of his wins ended inside the distance. Conteh's first title win was the European one which he took from Rudiger Schmidtke (West Germany). He took the British and Commonwealth titles from Chris Finnegan. He got his big break in 1974 when Jorge Ahumada (Argentina) was brought to London to fight him for the world light-heavyweight title, declared vacant by the W.B.A. Conteh won a popular victory, retained his crown on three occasions and then remained idle while his business affairs were sorted out. In consequence he lost W.B.C. recognition as champion, and then had to challenge Mate Parlov for the title. He went to Belgrade and returned a points loser. He was given two more chances to become world champion again, but each time he was beaten by Matthew Saad Muhammad, the first time on points and then on a stoppage in the fourth round. He retired in 1980.
Score 39: w34 (24) d1 l4.

Cook, George

Heavyweight Contender 1916–38

(b. Cobraha, N.S.W., Australia, Jan. 23, 1898 – d. Thames Ditton, Surrey, Oct. 8, 1943). Began pro boxing: 1916.

Cook made a name for himself in England where he went in 1921, claiming to be the heavyweight champion of Australia. Only 5 ft. 9 ins. in height and weighing 190 pounds, he had to fight at close range against his taller opponents. He was matched with the best in England and in Europe. He then went to America, where he campaigned in the major fight cities, returning to England via Australia and South Africa, keeping busy all the way. In 1932 he met Primo Carnera for the second time but, beyond showing the utmost bravery, could not cope with the giant Italian. Cook fought for the British Empire crown without success against Joe Beckett, Phil Scott, Larry Gains and Jack Petersen. He kept going until he was 40, making his home in London for the last few years of his career.
Score 108: w50 (19) d8 l48 ND.2.

A blood-spattered Henry Cooper on the attack against Cassius Clay (Muhammad Ali) on 18 June, 1963.

Cooper, Henry

European, British and Commonwealth Heavyweight Champion 1959–70

(b. Bellingham, Kent, May 3, 1934). Began pro boxing: Sept. 14, 1954.

Henry Cooper held the British and Commonwealth heavyweight boxing titles for a record ten years, and twice won the European crown. Only a modicum of bad luck and a tendency to cut easily deprived Cooper, indisputably Britain's best post-war heavyweight, of the very highest ring honours.

One of boxing twins, Cooper soon showed more ability than his brother George (who later fought professionally as Jim Cooper), and in 1952 and 1953 won the A.B.A. light-heavyweight title.

He turned professional in 1954 under the management of Jim Wicks, and made his debut at Harringay. In an eliminator for the British title – his 13th bout – he was beaten by Joe Erskine and subsequent title attempts were equally disastrous. In 1957 he was knocked out in nine rounds by Joe Bygraves when trying to win the Commonwealth Championship, and by Ingemar Johansson in five while endeavouring to take the European title in Stockholm. In September of that year his efforts to capture the British title from Erskine ended in a points defeat.

Cooper made a quiet comeback during the following year, beating Britain's Dick Richardson and the American Zora Folley, and on Jan. 12, 1959, defeated Brian London for the British and Commonwealth titles. During the next ten years he defeated all his challengers and created a record by winning three Lonsdale Belts outright.

Cooper was always a popular boxer be-

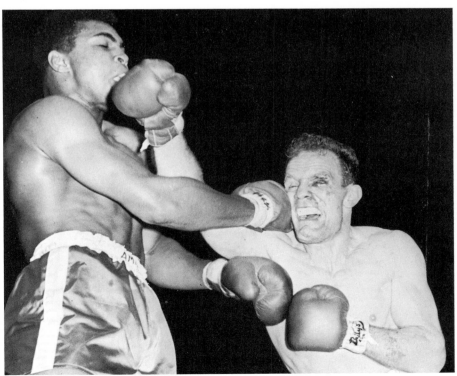

cause of his gentlemanly behaviour and sheer grit, and his greatest moment came on the night he first fought Muhammad Ali at Wembley Stadium in 1963. He put the future champion down with his formidable left hook in round four and was robbed of an almost certain knock-out victory by the bell. A badly cut eye in the following round lost him the fight. Three years later he challenged Ali for the world heavyweight title and, after putting up a most determined assault, was forced to surrender with another severe eye injury in round six.

In 1969 Cooper was awarded the OBE, and later that year was voted Boxer of the Year by the Italian press, after he had defeated their champion, Piero Tomasoni, in defence of his European title in March. He was matched to fight Jimmy Ellis of America for the heavyweight championship of the world, as recognized by the World Boxing Association, but the contest was refused official recognition by the British Boxing Board of Control, whereupon Cooper relinquished his British title.

In 1970 he made a successful comeback by outscoring Jack Bodell for the British heavyweight crown, following this by defeating Jose Urtain, the former Spanish holder of the E.B.U. title. However, defending his British crown against Joe Bugner, he was declared a points loser. It was a hotly disputed verdict and Cooper expressed his feelings by announcing his retirement from the ring.
Score 55: *w*40 (27) *d*1 *l*14.

Corbett, Dick

British and British Empire Bantamweight Champion 1929–34

(b. Bethnal Green, London, Sept. 28, 1908 – d. London, March 3, 1943). Began pro boxing: May 20, 1926.

His real name was Richard Truman Ford Coleman but, like his boxing brother, Harry, he changed it to Corbett. If the elder brother was an artist, the younger was a superlative boxer and there were high hopes that he would develop into world class. Dick did not carry a weighty punch, but he boxed his opponents dizzy. After three years of progress and six contests without defeat in Australia he secured a fight with Willie Smith of South Africa for the vacant British Empire bantamweight title. Corbett was the winner and the following year he got a bout with Johnny King for the British crown. Again he was successful, but it was so close that a return was demanded and this time it was King who was the winner. In a third meeting Corbett regained two titles; then they fought 15 rounds to a draw so that he remained champion. One more meeting was called for, but Corbett could not make the weight and had to forfeit the two championships. He fought as a feather for the next six years without getting a title shot and

finally gave up in 1940. On March 3, 1943, during an air raid on London, Corbett was trampled to death while protecting a baby whose mother had fallen on some steps.
Score 175: *w*129 (39) *d*15 *l*31.

Corbett, Harry

British Featherweight Champion 1928–29

(b. Bethnal Green, London, Feb. 14, 1904 – d. Bow, London, May 1957). Began pro boxing: Sept. 25, 1921.

An artist with the gloves and carrying the power to put away an opponent given the opportunity, Henry William Coleman boxed mainly in London's East End and, not wanting his relatives to know, changed his name to Young Corbett in honour of his boyhood hero, Gentleman Jim Corbett. When he got older he altered it to Harry Corbett. He fought his way upwards for four years and then was given a shot at the British bantam title, but had to retire after 16 rounds against the more experienced Johnny Brown. A year later he received another title chance, but could not get past the educated fists of Johnny Cuthbert, who outpointed him. After two more years he was given a return with Cuthbert and boxed splendidly to win a 20-rounds points verdict. His first defence was against the Yorkshireman and this time the result was a draw. Accordingly they had yet another meeting, when Cuthbert took back the championship on points. There were no more title fights for Corbett. He went on boxing for another four years, but failing eyesight caused his retirement. He was then 32.
Score 208: *w*137 (54) *d*23 *l*46 *Dnc.*2.

Corbett, James J.

World Heavyweight Champion 1892–97

(b. San Francisco, California, Sept. 1, 1866 – d. Bayside, New York, Feb. 18, 1933). Began pro boxing: 1884.

'Gentleman Jim' Corbett was the first man to win the world heavyweight boxing title under the Marquess of Queensbury Rules, which demanded the use of gloves. He is also regarded as one of the first scientific boxers, as opposed to the bare-fisted, toe-to-toe fighters who preceded him. After building an outstanding reputation as an amateur, Corbett turned professional. His keenest local rival at first was Joe Choynski, with whom he had four bitterly fought contests, one of which took place in June 1889 on a barge, and ended with a knock-out victory for Corbett in the 27th round.

His next important contest was in 1891 with Peter Jackson, the talented West Indian Negro whom John L. Sullivan had refused to fight because of his colour. Jackson and Corbett fought until they and the referee were exhausted, and at the end of 61 rounds a draw was declared. The following year

James J. Corbett, world heavyweight champion 1892–97.

Corbett met Sullivan at the Olympic Club in New Orleans, both men wearing 5-oz gloves. Sullivan outweighed Corbett by more than 40 pounds and was favoured to win at 4 to 1 on. But the challenger, at 26 the younger by eight years, was too fast for the heavily muscled 'Boston Strong Boy' and knocked him out in the 21st round.

Corbett's greatest rival was now Bob Fitzsimmons, the Cornish blacksmith. Although Fitzsimmons was only a middleweight, he bowled over heavyweights with such regularity that he was regarded as the leading contender for the title. It took nearly three years to get Corbett and Fitzsimmons together and when they eventually met it was at Carson City, Nevada, in March 1897, in a specially constructed outdoor arena.

Corbett had the best of the early rounds, putting his challenger down and cutting his face to ribbons, but he had slowed down by the 14th. Perceiving this, Mrs Fitzsimmons, who was seated in a private box at the ringside, urged her husband to go for the body. Fitzsimmons smashed a tremendous left swing to the champion's body, catching him in the solar plexus, Corbett went down gasping and, although fully conscious, was unable to get to his feet in time to beat the count.

Two years later Corbett set out to win back the championship, which had by that time fallen into the hands of James J. Jeffries, who had knocked out Fitzsimmons. Corbett trained for a year before making his challenge and then put up a superb performance, so as to be far ahead on points by the end of the 22nd round. But in the 23rd round he was trapped on the ropes and went down for the full count. Three years later, at the age of 37, he made another gallant attempt to retrieve his lost laurels, but Jeffries knocked him out in ten rounds. Corbett never fought again.

Corbett was the first man to bring science into boxing. He used the orthodox stance and, although not renowned for his hitting power, had a good straight left, a clipping right, and knew how to use his feet. His manners were polished (earning him the name of 'Gentleman Jim') and he spoke and wrote well, in contrast to the other members of his rough, tough fraternity. That is probably why he was something of an oddity, and never received the whole-hearted adulation of the boxing fans.
Score 19: w11 (7) d2 l4 Dnc.2.

Corbett II, Young

World Featherweight Champion 1901–04

(b. Denver, Colorado, Oct. 4, 1880 – d. Denver, April 10, 1927). Began pro boxing 1897.

This fierce-punching, tough featherweight (whose real name was William H. Rothwell) got his chance when a promoter thought he would be able to stay a few rounds with the reigning featherweight champion, Terry McGovern. However, Corbett was so confident of success that he rapped on McGovern's door on the way to the ring and shouted: "Come on out, you Irish rat, and take a licking." He was as true as his word. McGovern was so furious that he fought recklessly and took the full count from a right to the chin in the second round. Corbett gave him a chance to win back his title 16 months later, but again he proved the bigger hitter of the two and won by a knockout in the 11th. Corbett then gave up his world crown and went after the lightweights, but he could not get past the top-notchers in the higher class and eventually retired at the age of 30.
Score 101: w62 (41) d17 l21 ND.1.

Corbett III, Young

World Welterweight Champion 1933

(b. Campania, Italy, May 27, 1905). Began pro boxing: Oct. 3, 1919.

This useful and durable southpaw started his career in America and had to wait many years before he got a world title chance. This came in 1933 when he was two days past his 28th birthday, but he won a ten rounds verdict at San Francisco over Jackie Fields, and the reigning champion was considered to have lost his title. Corbett held the welter crown for a little more than three months and then lost it quickly to Jimmy McLarnin, who put him away in 2 min. 37 secs. of the

opening round. Corbett became a middleweight after that and worked his way into a title fight with Fred Apostoli in New York. He was now 33 and did well to stay eight rounds before being stopped. There were four more minor matches, then he retired.
Score 151: w123 (33) d17 l11.

Corro, Hugo

World Middleweight Champion 1978–79

(b. Mendoza, Argentina, Nov. 5, 1953). Began pro boxing: Aug. 30, 1973.

An exciting fighter, carrying plenty of knockdown power, he won both his native title and the South American championship at middleweight. These honours gained him a chance at the world crown against Rodrigo Valdez (Colombia) at San Remo and Corro came out a points winner after a great contest. He retained his title against Ronnie Harris and in a return with Valdez, but in Monte Carlo was outpointed by Vito Antuofermo (Italy) over 15 terrific rounds. He made a comeback in 1981, but after two defeats, hung up his gloves for good.
Score 53: w48 (25) d1 l4.

Coulon, Johnny

World Bantamweight Champion 1910–14

(b. Toronto, Canada, Feb. 12, 1889 – d. Chicago, Illinois, Oct. 29, 1973). Began pro boxing: 1905.

A two-fisted little scrapper, he started before his 16th birthday, being managed by his father. He won the American title from Kid Murphy over ten rounds in 1908 and was never beaten for it in spite of numerous challengers. In 1910 Jim Kendrick came from England as a contender and lost a close decision over ten rounds. This encouraged a New Orleans promoter to match them in a title fight and Coulon outstayed the Londoner to win in the 19th round. He made five winning defences of his title, but eventually lost it to Kid Williams on a knockout in three rounds. He was never given the opportunity to regain his lost laurels and joined the U.S. Army during World War I. Fighting in Paris after the Armistice, he was knocked out by Charles Ledoux and retired to become an instructor.
Score 97: w56 (24) d4 l4 ND.32 Dnc.1.

Cowdell, Pat

European and British Featherweight Champion 1979–82, European and British Super-Featherweight Champion 1984–88

(b. Smethwick, Aug. 18, 1953). Began pro boxing: July 5, 1977.

A.B.A. featherweight champion in 1976–77 and an Olympic Games bronze medallist, Cowdell did not look a world-beater when

he made his pro debut at Wolverhampton, but fought on to win an eliminator for the British title and then had the first of three contests with the reigning featherweight king, Dave Needham. Cowdell was outpointed in the first, took the decision in the second and in the rubber match Needham was stopped in the 12th. In between he made a successful defence against Jimmy Flint who retired after 11 rounds. He thus won a Lonsdale Belt outright in the record time of 6 months and 5 days. Five more impressive wins and he was off to Houston, Texas, to challenge Salvador Sanchez for the W.B.C. version of the world crown. Cowdell put up the fight of his life but the Mexican titleholder was just that much stronger and was returned a points winner. Cowdell won the E.B.U. featherweight title on March 30, 1982, by stopping Salvatore Melluzzo (Italy) in ten rounds at Marsala, and on Oct. 30, 1982, at Zurich, he successfully defended it against Sepp Iten (Switzerland). He retired on Jan. 1, 1983, but returned to action the following year and won the European super-featherweight title by outpointing Jean Marc Renard at Birmingham on July 7. He defended this crown, beating Roberto Castanon (5 rounds) and Carlos Hernandez (12), but was stripped of his title by the E.B.U. for failure to defend it. On October 12, 1985, in an attempt to win the W.B.C. featherweight title, he lost sensationally in 2 min 24 sec to Azumah Nelson, from Ghana. In spite of this disaster, he won the British super-featherweight title by stopping John Doherty in six rounds on April 17, 1986, but lost it in 38 days to Najib Daho (Morocco) in another single-round defeat. He gained full revenge by stopping Daho in eight rounds the following year. His triumph was short-lived, however, as he lost his championship to Floyd Havard, from Swansea, on May 18, 1988, being saved by the referee in round eight, following which he again announced his retirement.
Score 39: w34 (15) l5.

Criqui, Eugène

World and European Featherweight Champion 1922–23

(b. Belleville, France, Aug. 15, 1893 – d. Villepinte, March 7, 1977). Began pro boxing: 1910.

Criqui proved a scourge for European fighters from flyweight to feather in the years he was active. He won his native flyweight title in 1912, but when he challenged Percy Jones (Great Britain) for the world crown in 1914, he was a points loser over 20 rounds. Called up for military service in World War I, he was struck in the jaw by a German bullet and had to have a silver plate screwed to the shattered bone. Finding this gave him increased resistance to a punch, he resumed fighting in 1917 and built up an impressive record, in spite of two setbacks at the hands of Tommy Noble

(Great Britain) who stopped him in 19 rounds, and Pal Moore, who did the trick in 14. Criqui went to Australia where he proved a sensation, scoring eight decisive wins and one points victory. Back home he won the French featherweight title from Auguste Grassi, defended it against Ledoux with a sensational one-round win, and then upset British hopes by knocking out Joe Fox in 14 rounds. He won the European title, defended it three times, then went to America and knocked out the veteran Johnny Kilbane to gain the world crown. His retention of the title was limited to 54 days, Johnny Dundee taking the referee's nod at the end of 15 rounds. Back in France, Criqui, now in his 31st year, lost his European title to his fellow-countryman, Edouard Mascart, and after he had been stopped by Britain's Danny Frush in eight rounds, he virtually gave up boxing.
Score 117: *w*95 (56) *d*8 *l*14.

Crowley, Dave

British Lightweight Champion 1938

(b. Clerkenwell, London, May 4, 1910 – d. London, Dec. 11, 1974).

A hotel page boy before he joined a local boxing club, he soon showed that he had all the makings of a future champion. Fast on his feet, quick with his fists, he was both confident and game. He barred no one and before he became champion, he was mingling with the best, including Al Brown, bantamweight champion of the world, and Freddie Miller, world featherweight titleholder. When he was 23 he gave Nel Tarleton one of the hardest fights of his life and was only just beaten on points. Going to New York he was counted out following a dubious body blow in the ninth round against Mike Belloise, and the following year he beat another world champion, Petey Sarron, who was ruled out in round nine in London. He was 27 when he became British lightweight king by outpointing Jimmy Walsh, but six months later hard-punching Eric Boon took away his title by a knockout in the 13th round. Trying to regain his title he was again knocked out by Boon, this time in seven rounds. World War II interfered with Crowley's career, but he got in some bouts, remaining a star fighter until 1946 when an eye injury forced his retirement.
Score (incomplete) 100: *w*67 (46) *d*5 *l*28½.

Cruz, Carlos Teo

World Lightweight Champion 1968–69

(b. Santiago, Dominican Republic, Nov. 4, 1937 – d. Dominican Republic, Feb. 15, 1970). Began pro boxing: Oct. 23, 1959.

A fast performer, he boxed his way through the lightweight ranks for eight years before a promoter in Santo Domingo could tempt Carlos Ortiz to put his world title at

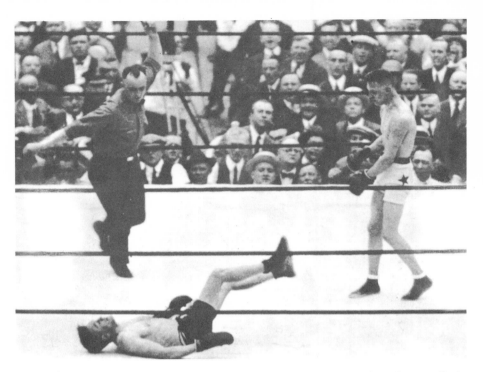

The moment Eugene Criqui won the world featherweight championship: Johnny Kilbane is knocked out in the sixth round.

risk against Cruz, who won on points over 15 rounds. Three months later he successfully defended the crown against Mando Ramos (U.S.A.), but in a return bout Cruz was stopped in 11 rounds. There was no opportunity to have a rubber fight as a year later, almost to the day, Carlos, his wife and two children, were killed in an air crash.
Score 57: *w*41 (13) *d*2 *l*14.

Cuello, Miguel Angel

World Light-Heavyweight Champion (W.B.C.) 1977–78

(b. Santa Fé, Argentina, Feb. 27, 1946). Began pro boxing: July 25, 1973.

Cuello established himself as a kayo king from the start, winning his native title in 1975 by stopping Raul Loyola in four rounds at Córdoba. When the world light-heavyweight title became vacant according to the W.B.A., he was matched with Jesse Burnett (Los Angeles). The bout took place at Monte Carlo and resulted in the Californian being stopped in nine rounds. Eight months later, however, in Milan, Cuello suffered an identical fate and lost his crown to Mate Parlov. He retired soon after.
Score 22: *w*21 (20) *d*0 *l*1.

Cuevas, Pipino

World Welterweight Champion (W.B.A.) 1976–80

(b. Mexico City, Dec. 27, 1957). Began pro boxing: Jan. 1, 1972.

A real kayo king, Cuevas could put them away with either hand or batter all the resistance out of his opponents. Occasionally out-pointed, he took the full count only once, when he lost his world title to Hearns. He first won the Mexican welter championship in 1975 and the following year took the world crown from Angel Espada in two rounds at Mexicali. He was only 18 years 6 months old at the time, one of the youngest to win a world crown. He defended this successfully on 11 occasions, against all comers, in the next four years; finally losing it to Thomas Hearns at Detroit on August 2, 1980. He boxed on for six more years, but never got another title chance.
Score 45: *w*33 (29) *l*12.

Curley, Johnny

British Featherweight Champion 1925–27

(b. Lambeth, London, Nov. 9, 1898). Began pro boxing: Nov. 18, 1915.

Auburn-haired Johnny Curley did not have to go far for his fights when he decided, at 17, to fight for money, most of his early bouts, and a lot of others afterwards, taking place at the celebrated Ring at Blackfriars or at Premierland on the other side of the River Thames. Gradually he rose from a six-rounder to a top-liner taking 15 and 20 rounds bouts in his stride. It took him ten years to get a title chance because the competition was so fierce at that time. Then he defeated George McKenzie (Scotland) to win the title and gain a first notch on a Lonsdale Belt. Outpointing Harry Corbett gained him a second, but when he defeated his third challenger, Billy Hindley, the fight at Manchester was outside the jurisdiction of the National Sporting Club, and in their eyes did not count. Called upon to put his title at stake against Johnny Cuthbert, Curley was

adjudged a points loser and had to hand back his treasured trophy. He went off to Australia for a few fights and came back to stay highly rated in the featherweight ranks until, at the age of 33, he called it quits.
Score 143: w99 (41) d14 l29 Dnc.1.

Curvis, Brian

British and Commonwealth Welterweight Champion 1960–65

(b. Swansea, Wales, Aug. 14, 1937). Began pro boxing: June 2, 1959.

The youngest of this Welsh fighting family (there were three of them), he won the A.B.A. title under his true name, Nancurvis, in 1958. A harder puncher than his brothers, he gained the Commonwealth title in his 14th paid fight, added the British crown six months later, and reigned as dual champion until he retired undefeated at the age of 28. Curvis had the distinction of making two Lonsdale Belts his own property, having beaten all challengers as they came up. His big chance came in 1964 when the world champion, Emile Griffith (U.S.A.), was brought to London in a title defence. Against a superlative fighter, the Welshman put up the fight of his life and was still on his feet at the finish, only to lose on points. On April 25, 1966 he went to Paris to fight Jean Josselin for the vacant European title, but was forced to retire in the 13th round, afterwards announcing his retirement.
Score 41: w37 (18) l4.

Curvis, Cliff

British and Commonwealth Welterweight Champion 1952–53

(b. Swansea, Wales, Nov. 20, 1927). Began pro boxing: Aug. 26, 1945.

One of a family of fighting brothers, this southpaw could both box and punch. A featherweight to start with, he grew into a welter and in his sixth year challenged his fellow-countryman, Eddie Thomas, for the British title. Outpointed, he fought on until he got a second chance to become a champion and in a terrific battle of the southpaws at Liverpool Stadium, finally knocked out Wally Thom in nine rounds. In South Africa he dropped the Commonwealth crown on a points decision to Gerald Dreyer and, in a fight for the European title against Gilbert Lavoine in Paris, he was ruled out for alleged holding. Earlier in the fight he had put down the Frenchman in the second round. There were no more bouts after that. Ordered to defend his British title against Peter Fallon, Cliff decided that the purse offered was insufficient and relinquished the championship.
Score 55: w42 (12) d1 l12.

Cuthbert, Johnny

British Feather and Lightweight Champion 1927–34

(b. Sheffield, July 23, 1904 – d. Boston, Aug. 29, 1987). Began pro boxing: July 23, 1921.

Short of stature, but strong and resolute, Cuthbert was taught to box by his father in a shed at the bottom of their garden. On his 17th birthday he took the plunge into pro fighting and very soon he was an established top-of-the-bill performer, most of his bouts being over 15 rounds. He was in great demand and fought all over Britain and in Europe, especially Paris where he was a great favourite because of his fighting spirit. Cuthbert became British champion in 1927 by outpointing Johnny Curley, then had a long series of defences until he was finally beaten by Nel Tarleton. Going into the lightweight class, he held hard-punching Al Foreman to a draw and then took over the British title by knocking out Jim Hunter in ten rounds. This was a considerable feat as Johnny was a light hitter, even guilty at times of using the inside of the glove. He was in his 30th year when he finally dropped his lightweight crown to Harry Mizler on a points verdict. Two more defeats and he announced his retirement.
Score 152: w109 (40) d14 l29.

Dade, Harold

World Bantamweight Champion 1947

(b. Chicago, Illinois, Oct. 9, 1924 – d. Los Angeles, California, July 17, 1962). Began pro boxing: Dec. 18, 1942.

A smart, light-punching boxer, he surprised everyone when, at the age of 22, he took a 15-rounds decision off Manuel Ortiz and captured the world bantam crown. The champion had held the title for more than three years, had beaten many challengers, and seemed invincible. Dade's reign was short, however. Obliged to give Ortiz a return fight, he met him two months later, when the decision was reversed. His famous victory put Dade in demand and for the next six years he enjoyed plenty of work, although he could never get back to the top, the best at his weight being too good for him. He retired in 1952.
Score 77: w41 (9) d6 l30.

D'Agata, Mario

World and European Bantamweight Champion 1955–58

(b. Arezzo, Italy, May 29, 1926). Began pro boxing: Oct. 14, 1950.

The astonishing thing about this tough, hard-hitting Italian was the fact that he was a deaf mute. This handicap did not deter him nor did it cause him any embarrassment, since he was never disqualified and was stopped only once, towards the end of his career. He became bantam champion of Italy in his fourth year. In 1955 he captured the vacant European crown and eight months later became world champion by knocking out Robert Cohen (France) in six rounds. He reigned for only ten months, losing on a points verdict to Alphonse Halimi (France). But he regained the E.B.U. title and held this until Piero Rollo took it from him on a points verdict on Oct. 12, 1958. He fought on until 1962 when he failed to win the Italian bantamweight title and then retired.
Score 67: w54 (23) d3 l10.

Dagge, Eckhard

World Light-Middleweight Champion (W.B.C.) 1976–77

(b. Berlin, Feb. 27, 1948). Began pro boxing: March 2, 1973.

This 5 ft. 11½ in. East German carried plenty of knockout power and in his 14th paid fight won his native title with a five-rounds kayo over Klaus-Peter Tombers. The following year he disposed of José Durán (Spain) in 11 rounds to win the European crown, a title he defended successfully and then lost to Vito Antuofermo. Going for the world championship, he knocked out Elisha Obed in ten rounds, beat off a challenge from the once-eminent Emile Griffith (U.S.A.), and was held to a drawn decision by Maurice Hope (England). However, six months later he dropped his world title to Rocky Mattioli, who stopped him in five rounds. Dagge won six bouts after that but a two-rounds stoppage by Brian Anderson at Kiel caused him to retire.
Score 32: w26 (16) d1 l5.

Damiani, Francesco

European Heavyweight Champion 1988–

(b. Bagnocavallo, Italy, Oct. 4, 1958). Began pro boxing: Jan. 5, 1985.

Following an excellent amateur career, in which he won a silver medal at the 1984 Olympics and other trophies, this 6 ft. 4 in. Italian giant started off by winning all his bouts in his first year, all but one inside the distance. He was equally successful the following year with eight more victories, only one opponent hearing the final bell. He became E.B.U. champion on Oct. 9, 1987 by stopping Anders Ekland at Copenhagen in six rounds. On April 22, 1988 he successfully defended his crown against John Emmen, of the Netherlands, stopping his challenger in the third round.
Score 22: w22 (18) d0 l0.

Darcy, Les

World Middleweight Champion 1915–16

(b. Maitland, N.S.W., Australia, 1895 – d. Memphis, Tennessee, May 27, 1917). Began pro boxing: 1910.

On leaving school Darcy became a blacksmith's apprentice, where his strong build stood him in good stead. He also took up boxing. At 15 he was winning every tournament he entered and so his professional debut a year later seemed a logical move. At that time he weighed 140 pounds but, with training, he developed into a formidable middleweight. This together with his inborn fighting spirit, instinctive talent, and powerful punching quickly made him the favourite of the Sydney Stadium fans.

Very soon he was fighting 20-round contests and, by the end of 1915, had disposed of all home-grown opposition, winning the welter, middle, and even the heavyweight championships of Australia. After he had beaten the American, Jeff Smith, a man with a strong claim to the world title, Darcy was matched with Eddie McGoorty, another high-ranking American. The bout was advertised as being for the world middleweight title, although this was actually held by the unpopular Al McCoy. Darcy beat McGoorty in 15 rounds and later repeated the performance in eight. He also stopped the renowned Buck Crouse, and strengthened his claim to the title by twice outpointing the world-ranking Jimmy Clabby, a man of wide experience.

When in 1916 he knocked out the Lithuanian-American, George Chip, in nine rounds, Darcy reached the pinnacle of his success. He received an offer to go to the United States and take part in contests that would lead to a championship fight. Unfortunately, Australia was at war with Germany and all men between 18 and 40 were forbidden to leave the country.

Darcy could see that several years of army service would ruin his boxing career, so one night he slipped away on a cargo boat and eventually arrived in the United States, only to find that the Americans too, had just entered the war. The young Australian was branded a slacker and money-grabber. No promoter dared make use of his services, and, after embarking on a disappointing theatrical tour, he died of a fever aged 21.
Score 50: w46 (30) d0 l4.

De Jesus, Esteban

World Lightweight Champion (W.B.C.) 1976–78

(b. Carolina, Puerto Rico, Aug. 2, 1951). Began pro boxing: Feb. 10, 1969.

Hard punching, two-fisted and aggressive, de Jesus made an excellent start in his first five years, winning the NABF lightweight title by outpointing Ray Lampkin in a 12-rounder. However, his attempt to take the world lightweight crown from Roberto Duran ended in an 11th-round stoppage and when, a year later, he tried to collect the world junior-lightweight crown from Antonio Cervantes, he was outpointed. Things came right in 1976 when he won the W.B.C. version of the lightweight crown by outpoint-

ing Ishimatsu Suzuki, a title he retained three times. Then he came up against his former conqueror, Duran, and with the same result, Esteban being stopped in 12 rounds this time. An attempt to win the world junior-welterweight title in 1980 failed and he retired forthwith.
Score 62: w57 (32) d0 l5.

Delaney, Jack

World Light-Heavyweight Champion 1925–26

(b. St. Francis, Quebec, Canada, March 18, 1900 – d. Katonah, New York, Nov. 27, 1948). Began pro boxing: 1919.

This heavy-punching French-Canadian (real name Ovila Chapdelaine) soon developed the reputation for possessing a killer punch in his right glove. When he disposed of tough Tiger Flowers in two rounds, the loser could not believe it, so they were rematched and this time Delaney did it in four. He won the world title from Paul Berlanbach, another renowned kayo specialist, but beat him handsomely on points, repeating the dose when they fought again seven months later. Delaney then decided to cast his lot among the big boys, but a knock-out defeat in a single round by Jack Sharkey convinced him he could not give weight away. There were only a few more bouts after that and he retired in 1932.
Score 93: w79 (45) d1 l11 Dnc.2.

De Leon, Carlos

World Cruiserweight Champion (W.B.C.) 1980–88

(b. Rio Piedras, Puerto Rico, May 3, 1959). Began pro boxing: Aug. 3, 1974.

He became the second holder of the newly created cruiserweight title by outscoring Marvin Camel on 26 Nov. 1980. In a return title fight he beat camel in seven rounds, the referee stopping the contest. DeLeon kept the title for only four months, being halted in two rounds by S. T. Gordon at Highland Heights, Ohio, on June 27, 1982. He regained the title on July 17, 1983 in a return match with Gordon and this time kept it until April 9, 1988 when he lost on a kayo to Evander Holyfield.
Score 47: w42 (28) d1 l4.

DeMarco, Paddy

World Lightweight Champion 1954–55

(b. Brooklyn, New York, Feb. 10, 1928). Began pro boxing: March 20, 1945.

Starting as a featherweight, De Marco had a remarkable run of success in his first five years as a pro until he ventured out of his class and was stopped by that fistic master, Sandy Saddler, in nine rounds. Going into the lightweight ranks, De Marco found the

opposition heavier, but eventually secured a match with Jimmy Carter for the world title. He jumped for joy when he was adjudged a points winner, but it must have been an off-night for Carter. Eight months later, in a return battle, DeMarco was halted in the 15th and last round. He continued to fight but his form declined and he retired in 1959.
Score 104: w75 (8) d3 l26.

DeMarco, Tony

World Welterweight Champion 1955

(b. Boston, Massachusetts, Jan. 14, 1932). Began pro boxing: Oct. 21, 1948.

DeMarco (real name Leonard Liotta) fought the majority of his early fights around his home town and built up a reputation as a knockout specialist, in 1953 scoring six inside-the-distance wins in a row. He came into world class in his seventh year of scrapping and took the title from the talented Johnny Saxton, who was stopped in 14 rounds. In a little more than two months DeMarco was back in the ring to defend his newly-won crown against Carmen Basilio, who stopped him in 12 rounds. When DeMarco was given the chance to win back his title, Basilio accomplished an identical performance. DeMarco retired in 1962.
Score 71: w58 (33) d1 l12.

Dempsey, Jack

World Middleweight Champion 1884–91

(b. County Kildare, Ireland, Dec. 15, 1862 – d. Portland, Oregon, Nov. 2, 1895). Began pro boxing: April 7, 1883.

Dempsey won his first recorded bout with Ed McDonald, in 21 rounds, by a knockout. They called him the 'Nonpareil' because no one could be found to beat him. He won the world middleweight title by beating George Fulljames in 22 rounds and defended it successfully on three occasions. Against George LaBlanche, however, he was knocked out, but since the challenger had done the trick with the illegal back-handed punch, Dempsey kept his crown. He beat off a challenger from Australia, Billy Murphy, with a 28th round kayo, but came unstuck when British-born Bob Fitzsimmons caused a world upset by winning on a knockout in 15 rounds. Dempsey more or less retired after that disaster, in which his backers lost a fortune.
Score 68: w48 (25) d7 l3 ND.17 Dnc.3.

Dempsey, Jack

World Heavyweight Champion 1919–26

(b. Manassa, Colorado, June 24, 1895 – d. New York, May 31, 1983). Began pro boxing: 1914.

Born William Harrison Dempsey, he was the ninth child of poorish parents. His elder brother, Bernie, had made boxing his career, taking the name of 'Jack' Dempsey from the former middleweight champion, and William followed suit as soon as he was old enough, boxing as 'Young' Dempsey until his brother gave up the profession. Then he, too, became 'Jack' Dempsey.

Most of his early fights were in the nearby states of Utah and Nevada, and all the time he was working in mining and timber camps. Fights among the workers were frequent in these camps and Dempsey gained vast experience and developed his fighting in the betting matches that formed part of the rough and ready means of entertainment. The turning point in his career came when he teamed up with Jack Kearns, and together they became one of the greatest partnerships the fight game has ever known. Kearns carefully chose his boxer's opponents, whittling down the contenders until no one stood between Dempsey and the champion – the giant cowboy, Jess Willard.

The Dempsey – Willard fight took place at Toledo, Ohio, and as he sat in his corner awaiting the starting bell, Dempsey was surprised to hear Kearns say: "You'd better get busy, because I've bet our purse ($27,500) at ten to one that you'll win in the first round." Dempsey tore into Willard, dropped him seven times, and then left the ring thinking he had won by a knock-out. But he was recalled, the timekeeper having informed the referee that the bell had saved the champion from being counted out. In the excitement and noise no one had heard it. Dempsey returned to maul Willard still further until he retired in his corner at the end of the third round. Dempsey had won

Jack Dempsey (in white shorts) savages Jess Willard in the first round of their title fight. Willard was floored seven times in this round yet lasted until the third before retiring.

the title, but he received nothing for doing it. The following year Dempsey made two successful title defences in knock-out style. Then promoter Tex Rickard thought up the first 'Battle of the Century', a meeting between Dempsey and the Frenchman, Georges Carpentier, war hero and champion of Europe. For this fight he built a huge outdoor stadium at Jersey City and was rewarded by the first million-dollar gate in ring history. The fight attracted over 80,000 people, who paid $1,789,238 to see Dempsey slaughter his lighter opponent in four rounds after Carpentier had broken his right thumb on Dempsey's chin. Two years later Kearns arranged for Dempsey to defend his title against Tom Gibbons, and he won easily. Rickard imported Dempsey's next challenger, Luis Firpo, a giant from Argentina, who had nothing except size and gameness. Dempsey floored him seven times in the first round and was himself knocked out of the ring by a mighty right to the chin before he stopped Firpo in the second. It was another million-dollar gate, but it was also Dempsey's last title defence for three years.

Much to Kearns' disgust, Dempsey married Estelle Taylor, a film star, and the marriage eventually resulted in the break-up of the partnership. There were long-drawn out lawsuits, and when Dempsey did finally defend his title against Gene Tunney over ten rounds at Philadelphia, he was so ring rusty that he lost on points. Preparing for the return match against Tunney, Dempsey enjoyed another million-dollar gate from his fight against Jack Sharkey, whom he knocked out in the seventh round. And then, in Sept. 1927 at Chicago, Dempsey almost regained the heavyweight crown when he dropped Tunney with a combination of vicious hooks from each hand. But he failed to go to a neutral corner when ordered by the referee, and the count did not start until he had done so. It was estimated that

Tunney was down for a total of 14 seconds and the extra respite allowed him to get up with wits restored. He defied all Dempsey's efforts to score another knock-down and by outboxing the challenger Tunney gained his second points verdict over him.

Dempsey announced his retirement after the second Tunney fight, but four years later made a comeback that lasted only six months. He was certainly one of the greatest heavyweights of all time: game and tough with a ruthless fighting spirit, he was a box office magnet because of his colourful style of battling and he carried a punch in both hands capable of settling a fight both conclusively and dramatically.
Score 80: *w*60 (49) *d*7 *l*7 ND.5 Dnc.1.

De Oliveira, Miguel

World Light-Middleweight Champion 1973

(b. São Paulo, Brazil, Sep. 30, 1947). Began pro boxing: June 16, 1968.

Possessed of a 'killer' punch, De Oliveira became the idol of home-town fans as he stopped 18 of his first 29 opponents and was undefeated when he tried to take the world light-middleweight title from the Japanese holder, Koichi Wajima. The best he could get was a draw and, when given a return bout a year later, he was beaten on points. His third chance came at Monte Carlo on May 10, 1975, where he became champion by outpointing Jose Duran. Success was short-lived, however. In Paris, against Elisha Obed, he was stopped for the first time in his career and lost his crown. Going back to Brazil, he tried to win his native middleweight title but lost on points to Luis Fabre. After two years of inactivity he attempted a comeback, but retired in 1980.
Score 52: *w*45 (28) *d*1 *l*6.

Dillon, Jack

World Light-Heavyweight Champion 1911–16

(b. Frankfort, Indiana, Feb. 2, 1891 – d. Chattahoochee, Florida, Aug. 7, 1942). Began pro boxing: April 18, 1908.

This tough individual (real name Ernest Cutler) seemed to be able to go on for ever. He started as a middleweight and travelled all over the United States, fighting as frequently as he could and never refusing a contest. Moving into the light-heavyweight class, in 1911 he engaged in 27 contests, mostly ten rounds, and the following year he enjoyed 29 contests. They called him 'The Giant Killer' because he beat so many bigger than himself. Going up into the light-heavyweight class, he claimed the vacant title, but it was three years before he was recognized as champion. He kept his crown until 1916 when he lost over 12 rounds to Battling Levinsky. Dillon remained active for another five years until finally his friends persuaded him to stop.
Score 245: *w*162 (64) *d*36 *l*28 ND.22 Dnc.1.

Dixie Kid, The

World Welterweight Champion 1904

(b. Fulton, Missouri, Dec. 23, 1883 – d. Los Angeles, California, April 6, 1934). Began pro boxing: 1899.

A sound boxer and fine puncher, Dixie (real name Aaron Brown) would box anyone, anywhere, regardless of size and reputation. On April 30, 1904, he took on the great Joe Walcott who was ruled out for a foul in the 20th round, leaving Dixie to claim the world crown. Twelve days later they fought again when the decision was a draw. Soon afterwards Dixie outgrew the welter division, packed his fighting kit and went anywhere he could find employment. He made several visits to France and England, being based there for his last four years in the ring. Win or lose, it was all the same to Dixie, and he proved he had a stopping punch right up to the last.
Score 126: w78 (63) d6 l18 ND.23 Dnc.1.

Dixon, George

World Featherweight Champion 1892–1900

(b. Halifax, Nova Scotia, Canada, July 29, 1870 – d. New York, Jan. 6, 1909). Began pro boxing: Nov. 1, 1886.

Called 'Little Chocolate' because of his colour and his height of 5 ft. 3½ in. he was an immaculate boxer, a joy to watch, and commanded respect wherever he went. Before he was 20 he fought Cal McCarthy to a draw over 70 rounds at Boston on Feb. 7, 1890 for the American featherweight title and three months later went to London and won the world championship by knocking out Nunc Wallace in 18 rounds at the

National Sporting Club. He defended his title against all comers no fewer than eight times in the next seven years, ultimately losing it on a points verdict to Solly Smith at San Francisco on Oct. 4, 1897. He again assumed the role of world featherweight champion by outpointing Eddie Santry over 20 rounds and 25 days later put it at stake against the British champion, Ben Jordan, from Bermondsey, London, who outpointed him over 25 rounds in New York on July 1, 1898. Dixon was again recognized as world featherweight champion when he won over Dave Sullivan (dis. ten), a title he successfully defended eight times in the next 12 months. Finally he was knocked out by 'Terrible' Terry McGovern on Jan. 9, 1900 and that saw the end of his world title ventures. In 1902 he went to England and remained there until 1905, meeting all comers. He retired at the end of 1906.
Score 131: w51 (27) d46 l28 ND.3 Dnc.3.

Michael Dokes, looking battered but happy after a victory.

George Dixon, a skilful Canadian boxer, was one of the earliest of the undisputed world featherweight champions.

Dokes, Michael

World Heavyweight Champion (W.B.A.) 1982–83

(b. Akron, Ohio, Aug. 10, 1958). Began pro boxing: Oct. 15, 1976.

A former National Golden Gloves champion, weighing 215 lb and standing 6 ft. 2 in. Dokes was named 'Dynamite' because of his aggression and punching power, but he was a very able boxer. He beat Lucien Rodriguez, the European champion, on points and the British champion, John L. Gardner, in three rounds. Held to a draw by Ossie Occasio, he stopped him in one round in a return bout. At Las Vegas on Dec. 12, 1982 he stopped Mike Weaver for the W.B.A. world heavyweight title in 65 seconds, establishing a world record. He drew a return with Weaver, but lost his title to a tenth-round knockout by Gerrie Coetzee in Richfield on September 23, 1983. After a quiet period, he began a comeback.
Score 37: w34 (21) d2 l1.

Dower, Dai

*European, British and Commonwealth
Flyweight Champion 1954–56*

(b. Abercynon, Wales, June 20, 1933).
Began pro boxing: Feb. 16, 1953.

This black-haired Welsh boy became
A.B.A. champion in 1952 and went to
Helsinki the same year as a member of the
British Olympic team. As a pro he showed a
brilliance that could only take him to the top
and, after being unbeaten in his first 20
bouts, outpointed Jake Tuli of South Africa
on Oct. 19, 1954, to win the Commonwealth
crown. He followed this by winning the
British title by outpointing Eric Marsden in
Feb. 1955 and, a month later, gained a
decision over Nazzareno Gianelli to become
European champion. Up to now he seemed
a likely candidate for world honours, but
Young Martin, a tough Spaniard, relieved
him of the E.B.U. crown with a knockout in
12 rounds. Some prestige was restored when
Dower again outpointed Tuli in defence of
his Commonwealth title. After completing
National Service, Dower went to Buenos
Aires to challenge Pascual Perez for the
world title, but the Argentine champion
knocked him out in 2 min. 48 sec. of the first
round. Dower relinquished his titles after
that, had two more minor bouts and then
announced his retirement.
Score 37: *w*34 (14) *d*0 *l*3.

Downes, Terry

*World and British Middleweight Champion
1958–62*

(b. Paddington, London, May 9, 1936).
Began pro boxing: April 9, 1957.

Downes began his boxing career as a
junior in Paddington, London. At the age of
15, he went to America with his parents and
joined the U.S. Marines, resuming his
amateur boxing career. He adopted the
aggressive, two-fisted American style of
boxing and won the U.S. All-Services title.
Returning to England in 1957, Downes set
his sights on winning an A.B.A. title, but
subsequently turned professional, making
his debut against Peter Longo, whom he
knocked out in round one.

Immediately he was the brightest star in
British boxing. He won the vacant British
middleweight title in his 19th bout, lost it on
a disqualification to John McCormack the
next year, but regained it seven weeks later,
after a memorably punishing fight by stopping the Scot in round eight. He made the
Lonsdale Belt his own property when he
forced Phil Edwards to retire in 12 rounds.

Then came his three contests with Paul
Pender involving the world title. In the first,
held in Boston in Jan. 1961, Downes was
stopped in round seven with a damaged
nose. Six months later he took the title from
Pender at Wembley. In their third meeting
Downes was outpointed.

When the British Boxing Board of Control
insisted that he should defend his British title
at the end of 1962, Downes reluctantly gave
up the championship because he had pros-
pects of more lucrative matches. Two years
later he made a tremendous effort to gain a
second world title by challenging the American, Willie Pastrano, for the light-
heavyweight crown at Manchester. He was
winning right up until round 11 when, tired
from his own exertions, he was put down.
Although Downes beat the count, the referee decided he was in no condition to
continue and the fight was stopped.

Downes retired in 1965, and became the
successful owner of a chain of betting shops.
His whirlwind, non-stop punching style had
made him a tremendous draw. The fans
loved every minute he was in the ring from
the moment he did his flashy, limbering-up
'war-dance' in the corner to the time he left
the ring, usually an inside-the-distance
winner.
Score 44: *w*35 (28) *d*0 *l*9.

Downey, William Bryan

World Middleweight Champion 1921–22

(b. Columbus, Ohio, Sept. 7, 1896 – d.
Wadsworth, California, March 28, 1970).
Began pro boxing: Feb. 2, 1914.

After more than eight years of hard
fighting, Downey at last succeeded in coax-
ing Johnny Wilson into a championship
defence at Cleveland, Ohio. Wilson was a
southpaw and difficult to catch with a decisive punch, but Downey got one in during
the seventh that put the champion down and
then had the mortification of being disqualified for a low blow. Both the Cleveland and
the Ohio State Boxing Commissions disputed the referee's decision and Downey
was recognized by them as world champion.
He did get a second fight with Wilson but
only in a no-decision affair, in which he
failed to score a knockout that would have
gained him the title. He retained his Ohio
title until 1923, when he secured a ten-
rounds fight with Harry Greb, who had
taken the crown from Wilson. Downey lost
on points and that virtually brought his long
career to an end.
Score 121: *w*36 (18) *d*14 *l*10 ND.60 Dnc.1.

Driscoll, Jim

*European, British Empire and British
Featherweight Champion 1906–14*

(b. Cardiff, Dec. 15, 1881 – d. Cardiff, Jan.
31, 1925). Began pro boxing: 1899.

As a boy employed in a newspaper office
Driscoll learnt to box using wastepaper
wrapped round his hands. He won the
British featherweight title in 1906 and
accounted for all his challengers. After
gaining the British Empire and European
titles, he went to America in an attempt to

*'Peerless Jim' Driscoll was one of the first men
to win a Lonsdale Belt: it was awarded after he
beat Seaman Arthur Hayes on Feb. 14, 1910.*

force a fight with Abe Attell who claimed
the world title. The champion would meet
Driscoll only in a no-decision bout; Driscoll
won every round by wide margins and was
regarded as the uncrowned titleholder thereafter. Coming home, he beat three more
challengers to make a Lonsdale Belt his own
property in the quick time of 11 months and
16 days. Persuaded against his will, he met
his fellow-countryman, Freddie Welsh, in a
bout that turned into a dirty fight, Driscoll
being finally ruled out for 'butting'. He
retired in 1913, but six years later made one
more appearance. His opponent was a two-
fisted, solid puncher named Charles Ledoux,
younger by 11 years. Driscoll boxed him
dizzy for the best part of 16 rounds, but a
punch to his ulcerated body forced him to
retire.
Score 69: *w*59 (36) *d*7 *l*3.

Duane, Carl

*World Super-Bantamweight Champion
1923–26*

(b. New York City, June 25, 1902). Began
pro boxing: 1920.

Duane never boxed out of New York in a
career lasting ten years, a rare occurrence.
In his fourth year he was matched with Jack
(Kid) Wolfe, the first holder of the junior-
featherweight title, as it was called then.
Duane won on points over 12 rounds, but

Terry Downes had an all-action style which made him immensely popular.

never defended his crown. Instead, three years later, he tried to take the world junior-lightweight title from Tod Morgan, but was a points loser over 15 rounds. He boxed on for two more years and retired in 1929.
Score 63: *w*43 (14) *d*5 *l*12 *ND*.3.

Dundee, Joe

World Welterweight Champion 1927–29

(b. Rome, Aug. 16, 1903, – d. Baltimore, Maryland, March 31, 1982). Began pro boxing: March 14, 1919.

Dundee (real name Samuel Lazzaro) was an older brother of Vince Dundee, and lighter because he fought at welterweight. When his family reached America they established themselves in Baltimore and it was there that Joe had the majority of his early bouts. He was not a big hitter, but an honest slugger and tough with it. He had ten years of hard battling before he got a title chance, when he took a points decision off Pete Latzo to gain the world welterweight title. He kept the crown for over two years, then lost it to Jackie Fields, being ruled out for an alleged foul blow to the body.
Score 122: *w*85 (23) *d*11 *l*20 *ND*.4 *Dnc*.2.

Dundee, Johnny

World Feather and Junior-Lightweight Champion 1921–24

(b. Shaikai, Italy, Nov. 22, 1893 – d. East Orange, New Jersey, April 22, 1965). Began pro boxing: 1910.

His real name was Joseph Corrara, so one of his managers called him 'The Scotch Wop' and the name stuck. He was a fast-moving, rapid-hitting boxer, who carried little stopping power in his gloves, but had such a wealth of stamina that he seemed to be able to go on for ever. He had a habit of reeling

back into the ropes and then bouncing off the hemp to land surprise punches. He did this once too often in 1917 when Willie Jackson caught him on the rebound with a right to the chin and knocked him cold in round one. Dundee became junior-lightweight champion in 1921, winning on a fifth-round foul from George Chaney. He showed that this was no fluke victory by holding the title for three years, losing and regaining it from Jack Bernstein meanwhile. His greatest feat was to take a 15-rounds points verdict off Eugene Criqui (France) and so become world featherweight champion. He never defended this title and went on fighting until 1932.
Score 337 *w*230 (22) *d*33 *l*69 *ND*.4 *Dnc*.1.

Dundee, Vince

World Middleweight Champion 1933–34

(b. Baltimore, Maryland, Oct. 22, 1907 – d. Glendale, California, July 27, 1949). Began pro boxing: Sept. 19, 1923.

A strong and resolute fighter, Dundee (real name Vincent Lazzaro) boxed for ten years before getting any real recognition. Twice he was adjudged a winner over Len Harvey, the British champion, and this enabled him to obtain a match with Ben Jeby, which the New York Commission recognized as being for the world title. It ended in a draw, but seven months later he outpointed Lou Brouillard to gain title recognition. He beat off two challengers, but was outscored by Teddy Yarosz, having reigned for 18 months.
Score 152: *w*117 (28) *d*13 *l*21 *Dnc*.1.

Dunn, Richard

European, British and Commonwealth Heavyweight Champion 1975–76

(b. Bradford, Yorkshire, Jan. 19, 1945). Began pro boxing: July 7, 1969.

This southpaw heavy did not promise to be very great until in his seventh year as a paid fighter he outpointed Bunny Johnson to win the British and Commonwealth titles. He then scored an impressive two rounds victory over Danny McAlinden to keep his crowns and gained a third by stopping Bernd August (Germany) for the European title. This prompted his advisers to accept a match for the world crown against Muhammad Ali, which took place in Munich. Dunn put up determined resistance until the referee called a halt in round five. Five months later he defended his three titles against Joe Bugner and lost the lot in 2 min. 14 sec. of round one. Dunn later tried his luck in South Africa but was stopped in five rounds by Kallie Knoetze, after which he retired.
Score 45: *w*33 (17) *d*0 *l*12.

Dupas, Ralph

World Light-Middleweight Champion 1963

(b. New Orleans, Louisiana, Oct. 14, 1935). Began pro boxing: Aug. 7, 1950.

A sound fighter, Dupas relied on his strength and durability to see him through the many bouts he undertook during his 16 years of ring activity. He was in his ninth year when he received his first shot at a title. Challenging Joe Brown for the lightweight crown, he was stopped in eight rounds. Five more years elapsed before he secured his second championship chance, against Emile Griffith for the welter title, but was outpointed over 15 rounds. At last success came his way. Denny Moyer, first holder of the light-middleweight title, was brought to New Orleans and Dupas clinched a points verdict, as he did when they met in a return fight two months later. Going to Milan, however, he was stopped in nine rounds by Allesandro Mazzinghi. He got a chance to win back his crown but was again stopped by the Italian, this time in 13 rounds. He had been world champion for only five months. He retired in 1966.
Score 134: *w*105 (19) *d*6 *l*23.

Duran, José

World Light-Middleweight Champion 1976

(b. Madrid, Oct. 9, 1945). Began pro boxing: Nov. 30, 1968.

This very talented Spaniard became champion of his own country in his fourth year as a pro by beating José Mario Madrazo over 12 rounds. Two years later he took the E.B.U. title from Jacques Kechichian (France) on a points verdict. He made three successful defences, but in trying to pick up the world title was outpointed by Miguel DeOliveira (Brazil). In his next title defence he was stopped by Eckhard Dagge (Germany) in nine rounds, and lost his E.B.U. crown. Undeterred, he had a final shot at the world crown, going to Tokyo where he stopped the Japanese champion, Koichi Wajima, in 14 rounds on May 18, 1976. At home he put his world honours at stake against Miguel Castellini in Madrid and lost on points. Inactive for two years, he made a last effort to be a world-beater again, but was stopped by Rocky Mattioli in five rounds and promptly retired.
Score 78: *w*63 (23) *d*9 *l*6.

Duran, Roberto

World Light, Welter and Light-Middleweight Champion 1972–83

(b. Guarare, Panama, June 16, 1951). Began pro boxing: March 8, 1967.

Right from the start Duran showed plainly that he was to be a great champion. Winning 23 of his first 27 contests, this two-fisted

Roberto Duran (left) and Sugar Ray Leonard (right) fought for the world welterweight title twice in 1980. Duran won the first; Leonard won the second.

warrior proved invincible for over 13 years, a remarkable record. To gain the world light-weight championship he stopped Ken Buchanan (Scotland) in 13 rounds, then defended his crown twice a year thereafter, eventually relinquishing it in 1979 to try and win the welterweight title. Here he was up against the phenomenal Sugar Ray Leonard, but fought true to form to win a points verdict in a brilliant contest. The inevitable return bout five months later was eagerly anticipated, but this time Duran was forced to retire in eight rounds. This did not mean the end. Two wins in 1981 and he was challenging Wilfred Benitez for the W.B.C. light-middleweight title on Jan. 20, 1982, only to lose on points over 15 rounds. Three more wins and he won the W.B.A. version of the title from Davey Moore, stopping him in eight rounds. He relinquished this and challenged 'Marvelous' Marvin Hagler for the middleweight title and took him the full distance before losing on points. He was inactive until June 15, 1984, when, at Las Vegas, he was stopped in two rounds by Thomas Hearns in a contest labelled as for the vacant world junior middleweight title. After another rest, he made a return to the ring in 1986.
Score 86: w79 (59) l7.

Durelle, Yvon

Commonwealth and Canadian Light-Heavyweight Champion 1953–58

(b. Baie Ste. Anne, New Brunswick, Canada, Oct. 14, 1929). Began pro boxing: Aug. 1948.
A big-swinging, hard-punching lumber-jack, he gave every sign of becoming a world-beater. He could knock them out with left or right, but against a sharp-shooter who could move, he very often came off second best. He won his Canadian title in 1953 and the Commonwealth crown in 1957 – he was never beaten for either. His big moment came when he challenged Archie Moore for this world title in 1958. Just 28 seconds after the start, a solid left hook to the chin put the champion down. Somehow he scrambled up to beat the count, but two more knockdowns followed as Durelle did his utmost to knock him out. He tried so hard that by the 11th round he had exhausted himself and it was Moore who won by a kayo. Eight months later Durelle tried again, but Moore had his measure by now and checked his challenge with a knockout in the third. An attempt to win the Canadian heavyweight title from George Chuvallo ended in a 12th-round defeat and Durelle announced his retirement.
Score 109: w83 (44) d2 l23 Dnc.1.

Ebihara, Hiroyuki

World Flyweight Champion (W.B.A.) 1963–69

(b. Tokyo, March 26, 1940). Began pro boxing: Sept. 20, 1959).
This fast-moving, vicious-punching Japanese lost only one bout (on points) on his way to the top, taking part in 38 contests, with 20 wins inside the distance. To gain the world title, he knocked out the holder, Pone Kingpetch (Thailand), in 2 min 7 sec. of the opening round on Sept. 18, 1963. Kingpetch got revenge in a return bout, winning on points. In 1966 Ebihara had another title chance and then he was outpointed by Horacio Accavallo, who repeated this performance a year later. Ever resolute and determined, Ebihara secured another opportunity when the W.B.A. declared the title vacant. This time he scored a points win over Jose Severino, but seven months later dropped a decision to Bernabe Villacampo, after which he retired, never having been stopped or knocked out.
Score 69: w63 (34) d1 l5.

Edwards, Llew

British and British Empire Featherweight Champion, Australian Lightweight Champion 1915–20

(b. Porth, Wales, 1894 – d. 1965). Began pro boxing: Jan. 25, 1913.
The small Welsh town of Porth was a breeding place for boxers at that time and Edwards did so well in bouts around there, Tonypandy and Cardiff that the celebrated Jim Driscoll took him under his wing and obtained fights for him outside his native country. However, title fights did not come quickly and Edwards had to fight his way through stout opposition in the feather-weight class before he secured a fight with Owen Moran for the British championship. It was a desperate struggle that ended in the tenth round when Moran was ruled out for a low punch. Seven months later Edwards went to Australia and stopped Jimmy Hill for the British Empire crown. He liked it there, and settled in Sydney. He grew into a lightweight and won the Australian title by outpointing Herb McCoy over 20 rounds. He made a number of successful defences in the following years until Harry Stone out-pointed him to take the crown. Edwards retired soon afterwards to become a trainer.
Score 99: w79 (42) d6 l12 ND.2.

Ellis, Jimmy

World Heavyweight Champion (W.B.A.) 1967–70

(b. Louisville, Kentucky, Feb. 24, 1940). Began pro boxing: April 19, 1961.
Up to the time when Muhammad Ali was deprived of his title in 1967, Ellis had been his chief sparring-partner. When the title became vacant, he asserted himself and won a heavyweight tournament sponsored by the W.B.A., beating Leotis Martin, Oscar Bonavena and Jerry Quarry. He defended successfully against Floyd Patterson and then in 1970 met Joe Frazier, who had been installed as champion by New York, and was beaten in five rounds. The following year, when Ali had made a comeback, Ellis met his old master and was stopped in 12 rounds. That was his last real fling as a heavyweight contender and he retired in 1975.
Score 53: w40 (24) d1 l12.

Elorde, Gabriel (Flash)

World Junior-Lightweight Champion 1960–66

(b. Bogo, Philippines, March 22, 1935 – d. Manila, Philippines, Jan. 2, 1985). Began pro boxing: June 16, 1951.

This colourful character kept going for 20 years and always in good company. Apart from being champion of the Orient from bantam to lightweight, he fought Sandy Saddler for the world featherweight title, Carlos Oritz for the lightweight crown and won the world junior-lightweight crown from Harold Gomez. He was involved in a title fight of some sort in every year from 1952 to 1967 when he retired. He made a comeback two years later, but this fizzled out after nine bouts.
Score 115: *w*88 (34) *d*2 *l*25.

Erne, Frank

World Lightweight Champion 1899–1902

(b. Zurich, Switzerland, Jan. 8, 1875 – d. New York, Sept. 17, 1954). Began pro boxing: Jan. 7, 1894.

A fine upstanding boxer, he started his career in New York State as a featherweight. Going up a class in 1898, he challenged George Lavigne over 20 rounds but was held to a draw. At a second attempt ten months later he outpointed Lavigne over the long distance and retained the title in a 25-rounder with Jack O'Brien. In a title bout with Joe Gans he won unexpectedly in 12 rounds when the coloured boy asked the referee to stop the fight. Trying to wrest the world welter crown from Rube Ferns, he was stopped in nine rounds and then, in a return with Gans, he was knocked out in 1 min. 40 secs. There was little fighting after that and he retired.
Score 40: *w*22 (10) *d*12 *l*6.

Erskine, Joe

British and Commonwealth Heavyweight Champion 1956–58

(b. Cardiff, Jan. 26, 1934). Began pro boxing: March 9, 1954.

A.B.A. champion in 1953, he did not carry a great punch, but was an expert boxer and relied on his ringcraft to bring him success. At the end of 1955 he outpointed Henry Cooper in an eliminator and the following year took the British title from Johnny Williams on a well-merited decision. He held off a challenge from Cooper over 15 rounds and two months later added the Commonwealth championship by outpointing Joe Bygraves (Jamaica). Unfortunately that ended Erskine's run of title successes. He was forced to retire to Ingemar Johansson in 13 rounds, in an attempt on the E.B.U. crown, and was then knocked out in eight by Brian London to lose his two titles. Erskine kept winning ordinary fights, but in three more matches with Cooper, all for the British and Commonwealth titles, he was stopped in 12, 5 and 9 rounds respectively. He continued to box until 1964.
Score 54: *w*45 (15) *d*1 *l*8.

Escalera, Alfredo

World Junior-Lightweight Champion (W.B.C.) 1975–78

(b. Carolina, Puerto Rico, March 21, 1952). Began pro boxing: Sept. 24, 1970.

An energetic, capable fighter with plenty of power in his punches, he dominated the world junior-lightweight division for three years. He went to Tokyo to gain his title and scored a knockout win over Kuniaki Shibata. He beat off no fewer than ten challengers, but coming up against that superlative box-fighter, Alexis Arguello, he was stopped in 13 rounds. A year later he tried hard to regain the crown from his conqueror, but lost by the identical number of rounds, again being stopped. He made a comeback in 1982.
Score 69: *w*52 (30) *d*3 *l*14.

Escobar, Sixto

World Bantamweight Champion 1934–39

(b. Barcelona, Puerto Rico, March 23, 1913, – d. Puerto Rico, Nov. 17, 1979). Began pro boxing: 1931.

Busy and hard punching, Sixto fought his way through the bantam ranks until he secured a match with Baby Casanova (Mexico) for the N.B.A. version of the world title. He defended this against Eugène Huat (France), but lost it to Lou Salica (U.S.A.). Regaining it from Salica, he then met Tony Marino in a universally recognized contest for the championship. Marino was stopped in 13 rounds and Escobar then scored an amazing victory over challenger Indian Quintana, knocking him out in 1 min. 49 sec. He next beat Salica again, lost the title to Harry Jeffra and regained it within five months. He made one more defence – against Kayo Morgan – but increasing weight problems caused him to give up his crown in Oct. 1939. He retired soon after, never having been knocked out or stopped.
Score 72: *w*45 (22) *d*4 *l*23.

Espada, Angel

World Welterweight Champion (W.B.A.) 1975–76

(b. Salinas, Puerto Rico, Feb. 2, 1948). Began pro boxing: March 11, 1967.

Like most of his fellow-countrymen Espada was a hard slugger. He had to wait nine years before he got a title chance and then outpointed Clyde Gray (Canada) for the W.B.A. version of the welter championship which was vacant at the time. Successful defences against Johnny Gant and Alfonso Hayman followed, but against Pipino Cuevas he was stopped in two rounds. A return match with the fierce-punching Mexican saw Espada stopped in 11, while a third match between them ended in ten rounds in

Cuevas' favour. When at his next appearance he was defeated by Thomas Hearns, he called it a day.
Score 57: *w*43 (27) *d*3 *l*11.

Espadas, Gustavo

World Flyweight Champion (W.B.A.) 1976–78

(b. Mérida, Mexico, Dec. 20, 1954). Began pro boxing: April 4, 1971.

This bustling Mexican did the first five years of his pro fighting in and around his home town. He picked up the W.B.A. version of the flyweight title by stopping Alfonso López in 13 rounds and made successful defences in Tokyo, Mérida, Los Angeles and again in Japan. He ran into trouble with Betulio González, who outpointed him to win the championship, and a year later, in trying to retrieve his crown, was knocked out in two rounds by Chan-Hee Park of Korea.
Score 48: *w*37 (27) *d*5 *l*6.

Espana, Ernesto

World Lightweight Champion (W.B.A.) 1979–80

(b. La Flor, Venezuela, Nov. 7, 1954). Began pro boxing: March 17, 1975.

This kayo specialist got away to a good start by winning 21 of his first 25 bouts inside the distance. This made his supporters think he was ready for a title shot and he did not disappoint them, knocking out Claude Noel (Trinidad) in 13 rounds. He scored another knockout win when he beat challenger Johnny Lira in the tenth, but those were the total of his successes as a champion. Challenged by Hilmer Kenty seven months later, he was stopped in nine rounds and when Espana tried to regain his crown he was halted again, this time in four. In 1981 he set out to fight his way back and scored seven wins, but was stopped in six rounds by Ray 'Boom-Boom' Mancini at Warren, Ohio, on July 24, 1982.
Score 48: *w*37 (27) *d*5 *l*6.

Estaba, Luis Alberto

World Junior-Flyweight Champion (W.B.C.) 1975–78

(b. Puerto La Cruz, Venezuela, Aug. 13, 1941). Began pro boxing: Feb. 28, 1967.

A hurricane little hitter, he ran up 29 wins, mostly inside the distance, in his first eight years of scrapping, then got a chance to challenge for the W.B.C. version of the world light-flyweight crown and won it by knocking out Rafael Lovera in four rounds. He defended this successfully 11 times in the next two years, finally losing it to Freddie Castillo, who stopped him in the 14th round. Estaba tried to win back his title five months later, but was forced to retire in five rounds to Netrnoi Sor Vorasingh.
Score 52: *w*41 (27) *d*2 *l*9.

Famechon, Johnny

World Featherweight Champion 1969–70

(b. Paris, March 28, 1945). Began pro boxing: June 7, 1961.

Johnny Famechon came from a family of French boxers but when the frail-looking boy wanted to become a professional boxer at 16, his father – who had emigrated to Australia in 1950 – was not keen on the idea. Famechon never boxed as an amateur and he won the Australian featherweight championship at the age of 19½. With a record of only four losses in 47 bouts, he earned his first international contest when Scotland's John O'Brien went to Melbourne to defend his British Commonwealth featherweight title. Famechon produced a surprise inside-the-distance victory in 11 rounds and so won his second title.

He successfully defended his Commonwealth crown against Billy McGrandle of Canada, and was then matched with Cuban José Legra for the world title at the Albert Hall in London. For round after round Famechon danced about the ring, scoring with his neat left jab. his clever evasive tactics frustrating all Legra's efforts to gain a knock-out. Famechon, the underdog at 5-1 against, brought off one of the biggest boxing upsets in years, outpointing Legra by 74½ to 73¼.

Although not recognized as world champion by the W.B.A. who had installed Sho Saijyo of Japan as titleholder, Famechon had the full support of the British Boxing Board of Control, the New York State Boxing Commission, and all those countries affiliated to the World Boxing Council.

After an easy points win over Jimmy Anderson, the British junior-lightweight champion, Famechon returned to Australia to defend his world title against Fighting Harada of Japan. He was given the fight of his life, being put down three times and having to use his defensive wits as never before in order to survive.

After two more successes in London against foreign opposition, Famechon went to Tokyo to give Harada the inevitable return contest. Most experts expected the title to change hands this time, but Famechon got off the floor to score a sensational knockout in 69 seconds of the 14th round. Famechon remained champion until May 1970 when he went to Rome and dropped a 15 rounds points decision to Vicente Saldivar, a former champion who was making a comeback. It was a disappointing trip and Famechon did not fight again. *Score* 67: *w*56 (20) *d*6 *l*5.

Famechon, Ray

French and European Featherweight Champion 1947–55

(b. Souis-le-Bois, Maubeurge, France, Nov. 8, 1924). Began pro boxing: Nov. 12, 1944.

The youngest and most accomplished of three fighting brothers, Ray was an expert boxer, relying on his skill more than his hitting power, although he stopped a fair number of his opponents. He became French featherweight champion in 1947 and took the E.B.U. crown from Ronnie Clayton (U.K.) the following year. He defended this title twice and then went to New York to challenge Willie Pep for his world title. After a brilliant battle between stylists, Famechon lost on points. He returned home to defend his European title three times. He was then outpointed by Jean Sneyers (Belgium), but retrieved the title in a return bout a year later. He made two more defences, but at the end of 1955 he was stopped in seven rounds by Fred Galiana (Spain). The following year he announced his retirement. *Score* 113: *w*98 (35) *d*3 *l*12.

Farr, Tommy

British and Commonwealth Heavyweight Champion 1937–38

(b. Tonypandy, Wales, March 12, 1913 – d. Brighton, East Sussex, March 1, 1986). Began pro boxing: Dec. 18, 1926.

Farr's long ring career began at the age of

Tommy Farr leads with his left in Joe Louis's first defence of his title.

13 when he fought in the travelling boxing booths on a Saturday night. He quickly learnt the finer points of boxing and never took a punch that could be avoided. Not a powerful hitter, he developed a puzzling crouching and weaving style, knew how to whittle away a rival's stamina, and was a good finisher at the right moment. Farr became Welsh light-heavyweight champion four months after his 19th birthday, but when he attempted to win the British title at this weight he was outpointed by Eddie Phillips. The following year he moved into the heavyweight ranks and won his second Welsh title by knocking out Jim Wilde in seven rounds.

This contest was recognized as an eliminator for the British crown, and six months later Farr became champion by outpointing Ben Foord. It was a victory that brought the Welshman right into the limelight, and he added to his fame by outpointing the former world heavyweight champion, Max Baer, and knocking out Walter Neusel of Germany, who had long been the scourge of British heavies.

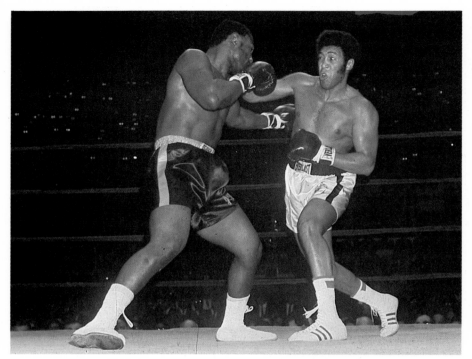

Jimmy Ellis (right) was beaten by Joe Frazier in five rounds in their title bout on Feb. 16, 1970.

Then came Farr's big chance. Joe Louis had just become world champion and Farr was appointed his first challenger. No Briton had fought for the world heavyweight crown (which Americans regarded as a national heirloom) for nearly 30 years, and boxing fans throughout the United Kingdom got up in the early morning to listen to the radio commentary of the title bout, staged in New York on Aug. 30, 1937. Farr fought fiercely and skilfully, and for most of the fight he forced the pace and made the formidable 'Brown Bomber' back off. But Louis came back strongly and clinched a narrow points verdict. The Welshman's fine performance earned him more American contests and he relinquished his British title to attend to them. He had a further four fights in the States but lost points decisions to Max Baer, Lou Nova, Red Burman and James J. Braddock. He then went home determined to win back his British title before the war put a stop to his career.

In Sept. 1950, at the age of 36 and after ten years absence from the ring, Farr made an astonishing comeback. In three years he won his way into a final eliminator for the British title, but was stopped by Don Cockell in seven rounds at Nottingham. It was his last appearance in the ring.
Score 107: *w*71 (22) *d*11 *l*25.

Feeney, George

British Lightweight Champion, 1982

(b. County Durham, Feb. 9, 1957). Began pro boxing: Aug. 22, 1977.

The brother of John, the British featherweight champion, Feeney was outpointed by Rickey Beaumont in an eliminator for the British lightweight championship in his 16th pro bout. The following year he was more successful, stopping Winston Spencer in nine rounds in another eliminator. At the start of 1982 he outpointed Ken Buchanan, the former world lightweight champion. On Oct. 12 the same year he stopped Ray Cattouse in 14 rounds of a thrilling battle to win the British lightweight title at London's Albert Hall. He won a Lonsdale Belt outright when defeating the challenger, Paul Chance, in his third title defence. He retired on Jan. 16, 1985 due to eye trouble.
Score 29: *w*19 (8) *d*0 *l*10.

Feeney, John

British Bantamweight Champion 1981–85

(b. Hartlepool, County Durham, May 15, 1958). Began pro boxing: July 10, 1977.

Feeney got away to a good start by winning his first 18 bouts spread over three years. Attempting to wrest the British and Commonwealth titles from the ill-fated Johnny Owen, he lost on points. He then showed courage in going to Italy to challenge for the European crown, but was outpointed by Valerio Nati. Three months later he became British champion by stopping Dave Smith, the holder, in eight rounds.

In 1982 he challenged for the Commonwealth title but was stopped in Sydney, Australia, by Paul Ferreri in 13 rounds. Two months later he was outpointed by Guiseppe Fossati in Italy for the European title. He lost his British title when disqualified in the 13th against Hugh Russell, in Belfast in Jan. 1983, but won it back in Nov. by stopping Davy Larmont, also in Belfast. Two other attempts on the European title failed in 1983 and 1984 when he was outpointed by Walter Giorgetti in Campobasso, Italy, and by Ciro de Leva, in Salerno, Italy. He then lost his British title when outpointed by Ray Gilbody in Hartlepool on June 15, 1985, and he failed in a challenge for the vacant British featherweight title when outpointed by Robert Dickie in Kensington on April 9, 1986.
Score 45: *w*34 (13) *d*0 *l*11.

Fenech, Jeff

World Bantam (I.B.F.) 1985–87, Super-Bantam (W.B.C.) 1987–88 and Featherweight Champion (W.B.C.) 1988–

(b. Sydney, N.S.W., Australia, May 28, 1964). Began pro boxing: Nov. 5, 1984.

A smart and strong boxer, a worthy hero to Australian fans, he won his native super-flyweight title in his third contest and the State title in his fifth. His rapid progress towards the highest honours continued when he won the I.B.F. bantamweight crown by stopping Satoshi Shingaki in nine rounds. He defended this three times, against Shingski (stopped 3), Jerome Coffee (points 15), and Steve McGrory (stopped 14). He then relinquished his title to challenge for the W.B.C. super-bantam crown, which he won by knocking out Samart Payakaroon in the fourth. Two defences of this crown followed in the next five months; Greg Richardson (stopped 5) and Carlos Zarate (stopped 4). Again he surrendered his title to box as a full featherweight, winning the W.B.C. title by stopping Victor Callejas, of Puerto Rico, in ten rounds on March 7, 1988. Apart from going to Bangkok to fight Payakaroon, the remainder of his contests have taken place in Australia.
Score 20: *w*20 (16) *d*0 *l*0.

Johnny Famechon in training before his clash with Fighting Harada.

Fernández, Périco

World Junior-Welterweight Champion (W.B.C.) 1974–75

(b. Zaragoza, Spain, Nov. 19, 1952). Began pro boxing: May 20, 1972.

This tough Spaniard with a dynamite-laden punch, was a very busy performer. He won his native title in his second year by outpointing Kid Tano and in the following year picked up the European title by disposing of Tony Ortiz in 12 rounds (July 26, 1974). Two months later he was matched with Lion Furuyama of Japan to fight for the vacant W.B.C. title in Rome and came out a points winner. He retained this against Joâo Henrique (Brazil). Venturing outside Spain, he went to Bangkok where he lost his crown to Saensak Muangsurin in eight rounds. The Thailander was lured to Madrid to give Fernandez a chance to win back his title and was outpointed. Seven months later Jim Watt (Scotland) relieved Fernández of his E.B.U. crown and then he lost his Spanish title to Fernando Ságnchez at Bilbao. He was still only 26 and went on battling, but without success.
Score 122: w82 (47) d14 l24 Dnc.2.

Ferns, Jim 'Rube'

World Welterweight Champion 1900

(b. Pittsburg, Kansas, Jan. 20 1874 – d. Pittsburg, June 11, 1952). Began pro boxing: 1896.

Jeff Fenech of Australia won world titles at three weights without being beaten in his first 20 contests.

He proved a strong fighter with a knock-out punch and in his fifth year he fought Mysterious Billy Smith for the welter title, being awarded the decision on a foul in the 21st round. Ten months later he was out-decisioned by Matty Matthews in a title defence, but won back his crown by a ten rounds knockout in a return bout. A challenger, Frank Erne, was stopped in nine rounds, but up against Joe Walcott, the Barbados Demon, Ferns found himself out-punched and took the full count in the fifth. He continued fighting for a while and retired in 1906.
Score 65: w43 (32) d8 l14.

Fields, Jackie

World Welterweight Champion 1929–32

(b. Chicago, Illinois, Feb. 9, 1908). Began pro boxing: Sept. 18, 1924.

An Olympic Gold Medallist at the 1924 Olympic Games, Fields (real name Jacob Finkelstein) came into the championship reckoning at a time when the welter crown was being tossed about like a shuttlecock between a clique of managers who had some class welters between them. A good boxer with a solid punch and unlimited stamina,

Fields was in his fifth year as a pro when he outpointed Young Jack Thompson over ten rounds in a bout the N.B.A. recognized as being for the world title. He defended this against Joe Dundee, then passed it back to Thompson on a 15-rounds points decision. Two years later he was back on the throne, having outpointed Lou Brouillard in a ten-rounder, and a year later lost over the same distance to Young Corbett III, who claimed the crown. Fields retired in 1933.
Score 87: w74 (30) d3 l9 Dnc.1.

Finch, Albert

British Middleweight Champion 1949–54

(b. Croydon, Surrey, May 16, 1916). Began pro boxing: Aug. 14, 1945.

He loved fighting and was taught the rudiments when a baby by his father. A believer in the straight left to pave the way to victory, he was not a dynamic puncher with the right. He challenged for the British middleweight title in his fourth year, but was outpointed by wily Dick Turpin. He succeeded the following year with a points win over Dick, but lost the crown after six months to Turpin's younger brother, the mighty Randy. He turned his attention to the light-heavies, but was thwarted by Don Cockell who stopped him in seven rounds. Resolutely fighting on, Finch, had to wait three years for another title chance, when despite a great effort he was beaten by Alex Buxton in eight rounds and two years later he was beaten by Ron Barton, also in eight. Albert kept on until he was 32 and enjoyed every moment of it.
Score 102: w71 (21) d9 l21 Dnc.1.

Finnegan, Chris

European, British and Commonwealth Light-Heavyweight Champion 1971–76

(b. Iver, Buckinghamshire, June 4, 1944). Began pro boxing: Dec. 9, 1968.

Finnegan was the only member of the British team in the 1968 Olympic Games to return with a gold medal. As a pro he was a popular success and fought for the E.B.U. crown before successfully challenging Eddi Avoth for the British and Commonwealth titles. He earned a draw against Connie Velensek for the European title, then out-pointed him in a return match. He was now holder of three crowns and fit to fight for the world title. Against the talented Bob Foster, he put up a courageous performance, the referee ending the contest in round 14 when Finnegan was exhausted. Two months later he dropped his E.B.U. honours to Rudiger Schmidtke (Germany). John Conteh took away his remaining crowns, but Finnegan got them back two years later by outpointing Johnny Frankham. He retired with eye trouble in 1976.
Score 37: w29 (16) d1 l7.

Chris Finnegan (left) is made an honorary deputy by Bob Foster, deputy-sheriff of Albuquerque and also world light-heavyweight king.

Finnegan, Kevin

European and British Middleweight Champion 1974–80

(b. Iver, Buckinghamshire, April 18, 1948). Began pro-boxing: Nov. 23, 1970.

The younger brother of Chris Finnegan, but not so big, he was a tough and courageous middleweight with plenty of action. He achieved the double in his fourth year as a pro, winning the British title from Bunny Sterling and the European crown from Jean-Claude Bouttier (France). He lost the latter a year later to Gratien Tonna in Monte Carlo and had already relinquished the British title, so when it became vacant, he and Alan Minter fought for it, Finnegan losing on points. When the British crown was once more without a wearer, he successfully fought Frankie Lucas for it. Again he was thwarted by Minter, so he went to Boston and had two fights with the great Marvin Hagler. Finnegan lost both bouts, each time retiring with cuts. Then at the age of 31 he made a remarkable comeback to outpoint Tony Sibson and make the Lonsdale Belt his own property. He continued his triumphs in 1980, winning the vacant European title from Tonna on a points verdict in Paris, but losing the crown to Matteo Salvemini (Italy) at San Remo. He then retired. *Score* 47: *w*35 (12) *d*1 *l*11.

Fitzsimmons, Bob

World Middle, Light-Heavy and Heavyweight Champion 1891–99

(b. Helston, Cornwall, May 26, 1863 – d. Chicago, Illinois, Oct. 22, 1917). Began pro boxing: 1883.

Bob Fitzsimmons was the first man ever to win three world titles and the only world heavyweight champion produced by Eng-

land. An undoubted fistic phenomenon, he never weighed much more than 170 pounds, was 28 years old when he won his first world championship and 41 when he took his third.

Taken to New Zealand as a child and brought up in Timaru, he became an apprentice blacksmith. In 1880 Jem Mace, the acknowledged founder of modern boxing, visited New Zealand. Fitzsimmons won a competition organized by Mace and started on a professional career. He moved to Australia, fought there intermittently for the next ten years, then left for America where he won instant success as a middleweight. In 1891 he gained the world title in his third American fight by knocking out Jack Dempsey, the 'Nonpareil', in 13 rounds.

After twice defending his title successfully, Fitzsimmons had to fight his way through the heavyweight ranks for another three years and take out American citizenship before he could get James J. Corbett to recognize him as a challenger. They finally

Bob Fitzsimmons.

met in a specially constructed arena in Carson City, Nevada, the only state that would permit the match. 'Gentleman Jim' Corbett outboxed Fitzsimmons for 13 rounds, cutting him severely with precision punches while warding off the challenger's attempts to land a knockout blow to the head. But in the 14th round, when victory for Corbett seemed certain, Mrs Fitzsimmons called to her husband from the ringside: 'Go for the body, Bob. Hit him in the slats (ribs).' The challenger swung a heavy left to the solar plexus, Corbett sank to his knees and was counted out.

In 1899 Fitzsimmons lost the title when the burly James J. Jeffries, 13 years younger and over 50 pounds heavier, knocked him out in the 11th round. In their return match in 1902 Fitzsimmons was beaten in eight rounds after breaking his right hand attempting to knock out Jeffries. Next year he won the newly created light-heavyweight title from George Gardner, but after losing it to Jack O'Brien in 1905 gradually drifted out of boxing, finally retiring in 1914 at the age of 52.
Score 62: *w*40 (32) *d*0 *l*9 *ND*.10 *Dnc*.1.

Flowers, Tiger

World Middleweight Champion 1926

(b. Camile, Georgia, Aug. 5, 1895 – d. New York, Nov. 16, 1927). Began pro boxing: 1918.

Flowers was the first Black middleweight champion and his southpaw style made him an awkward opponent. Immensely popular, he had 36 bouts in 1924 and 25 the following year. The only man to cause him trouble was Jack Delaney, but he was light-heavy and a big puncher. He knocked the Tiger cold in two rounds. Flowers could not believe it and demanded a return bout. This time Delaney did it in the fourth. For his first fight in 1926 Flowers challenged Harry Greb, a tearaway like himself, and they had a rough fight until the final bell when the Tiger got the verdict to become world middleweight champion.

He had a return match with Greb and again came out successful. Then he was lured to Chicago to meet Mickey Walker in what was intended to be a ten rounds no-decision affair. But at the end the referee raised Walker's arm aloft and he was announced as the new champion. Flowers had been tricked out of his title, but he did not get the chance for revenge. In less than a year, after 18 more bouts, he died in hospital during an operation on one of his eyes.
Score 156: *w*133 (52) *d*8 *l*15 *Dnc*.1.

Foord, Ben

British and British Empire Heavyweight Champion 1936–37

(b. Vrede, Orange Free State, South Africa, Jan. 21, 1913 – d. Sept. 29, 1942). Began pro boxing: June 4, 1932.

A full-scale heavyweight, Foord had all the physical requirements to make a world-beater, but no one had taught him how to box or punch. Many of his wins came from sheer strength and stamina. He won the South African title in 1934 by knocking out Willie Storm in four rounds at Cape Town. It was a title he retained until 1940, as he spent most of the intervening years in England, where he was popular both in and out of the ring. In his 23rd bout in Britain he stopped a fading Jack Petersen in three rounds to win the British and Empire titles. Then he was outpointed by both Walter Neussel and Tommy Farr, the last-named depriving him of his twin titles. There followed a run of heavy defeats and his career virtually came to an end when Eddie Phillips knocked him out in nine rounds in a final eliminator for the British crown. In 1939 Foord returned to South Africa where he had four more fights and lost his native title. The boxing world was shocked when he ended his own life.
Score 59: w40 (13) d4 l15.

Forbes, Harry

World Bantamweight Champion 1901–03

(b. Rockford, Illinois, May 13, 1879 – d. Chicago, Illinois, Dec. 19, 1946). Began pro boxing: Jan. 16, 1897.

A smart little boxer, Forbes had three years of hard, busy fighting, at the end of which he had earned a shot at the bantam title held by Terry McGovern. The bout was short-lived, Terrible Terry scoring a kayo in round two. Less than a year later, however, when the title became vacant, Forbes had another try, but was held to a draw by Casper Leon. This called for a return which Forbes won on points, and he remained as champion for more than two years. Then he lost to Frankie Neil in two rounds. Undaunted, he challenged Abe Attell for the featherweight crown, but was stopped in five rounds and, when trying to regain his 118 pounds title from Neil, suffered another kayo defeat, this time in three. That was in 1904, but Forbes kept on fighting until his career faded out in 1913.
Score 136: w90 (43) d25 l17 Dnc.1.

Foreman, Al

British and British Empire Lightweight Champion 1930–32

(b. Bow, London, Nov. 3, 1904 – d. Montreal, Canada, Dec. 23, 1954). Began pro boxing: 1920.

During the years he fought in London rings at the start of his career, he used the name of Bert Harris. Then the family moved to Canada, where his brothers set up a gymnasium, and Al developed a big right-hand punch and boxed as Foreman. Soon he acquired fame as a kayo king, especially when he disposed of Ruby Levine in 1½

seconds at Montreal. Becoming Canadian lightweight champion, he returned to England with his brother, Maurice. Between them they obtained a title fight with the reigning British champion, Fred Webster. That ended in the first round and Foreman met all comers until the British Boxing Board of Control stripped him of his titles because he refused to accept an inadequate purse offer. A most likeable man, he was a great box-office draw and kept his punching power up to his retirement at the age of 30.
Score 154: w125 (78) d9 l20.

Foreman, George

World Heavyweight Champion 1973–74

(b. Marshall, Texas, Jan. 22, 1948) Began pro boxing: June 23, 1969.

An Olympic Games heavyweight gold medallist in 1968, he turned pro the following year and from the start looked a championship prospect. At 6 ft. 3 in. and weighing 220 pounds, he was big enough and he soon showed that he possessed a lethal right hand punch. He was unbeaten in his first 37 bouts, all but three of which ended inside the scheduled course. Even so, it was not thought that he could beat Joe Frazier when he challenged for the title, yet he did so, knocking the champion all over the ring and out for the count in two rounds. Foreman made two easy defences and then faced Muhammad Ali who was making his second comeback. Ali was 32 and he was not expected to stand up to the champion's thundering punches. But, cleverly, he let Foreman wear himself out on the empty air and then proceeded to box him dizzy and knock him out in eight rounds. Foreman did little serious boxing after that debacle and retired in 1977. Ten years later Foreman made a comeback and was successful in a number of contests.
Score 57: w55 (52) d0 l2.

Foster, Bob

World Light-Heavyweight Champion 1968–74

(b. Albuquerque, New Mexico, Dec. 15, 1938). Began pro boxing: March 27, 1968.

A supreme boxer, he could beat anyone at his weight and the two setbacks he suffered before winning the world crown were both against heavies, Doug Jones and Ernie Terrell. To win the title he achieved the feat of knocking out Dick Tiger in four rounds and he made no fewer than 14 successful defences against the cream of the world light-heavies. Taking on Joe Frazier was a mistake and ended in the second round, similarly his bout with Muhammad Ali was halted in the eighth. One of his hardest challengers was Chris Finnegan, the British champion, who took him 14 rounds, while Pierre Fourie, the South African titleholder, twice went the full distance to a points

verdict. The last time Foster put his title on the line, he only kept it by a drawn verdict with Jorge Ahumada. Three months later he announced his retirement.
Score 65: w56 (46) d1 l8.

Fox, Joe

British Bantam and Featherweight Champion 1915–22

(b. Leeds, Yorkshire, Feb. 8, 1894 – d. 1965). Began pro boxing: Nov. 21, 1910.

A smart, precise boxer, he was fighting 20-rounders in his second year as a pro. True fight fans liked his intelligent boxing and ringcraft and he was always in demand. In 1914, at the age of 20, he went to America to gain extra experience. On his return he outpointed Alex Lafferty in a bantam eliminator and won the title by stopping Jimmy Berry in 16 rounds. Tommy Harrison was outpointed and Joe Symonds stopped in 18, thus giving Fox the outright ownership of a Lonsdale Belt. He gave up his crown soon after and fought among the featherweights, eventually winning the British title from Mike Honeyman on a points verdict. When he fought Eugène Criqui for the European title, Fox won every round up to the 12th, then caught a jaw-crunching punch from the Frenchman and was put down and out. He spent a lot of time in Australia and America, his career coming to an end when he was 30.
Score 130: w70 (29) d12 l22 ND.24 Dnc.2.

Frazer, Alfonso

World Junior-Welterweight Champion 1972–73

(b. Panama City, Panama, Jan. 17, 1948). Began pro boxing: April 10, 1965.

Like many specialist knockout kings, he could also be put away, and while he stopped almost half his opponents, he was 11 times prevented from going the distance. He won the world title in his home town by outpointing the accomplished Nicolino Loche (Argentina), but his tenure of the championship only lasted four months. He made one successful defence by knocking out Al Ford, but Antonio Cervantes (Colombia) stopped him in ten and in a return title fight cut the time down by half. Frazer continued to box for another eight years before retiring.
Score 63: w44 (29) d2 l17.

Frazier, Joe

World Heavyweight Champion 1968–73

(b. Beaufort, South Carolina, Jan. 12, 1944). Began pro boxing: Aug. 16, 1965

The Olympic medallist, Joe Frazier, had his first professional contest at Philadelphia in August 1965. During the next few years he made steady progress, entering the ratings

George Foreman in training.

with impressive wins over Oscar Bonavena, Eddie Machen, Doug Jones, and George Chuvalo. In August 1967 the World Boxing Association (W.B.A.) launched an open competition to find a successor to Muhammad Ali, but Frazier refused to enter it. While the W.B.A. eliminations were in progress the rival World Boxing Council (W.B.C.) matched Frazier with Buster Mathis in a 'world title' fight. Frazier won in 11 rounds and then defeated four challengers. After Jimmy Ellis won the W.B.A. tourney in April 1968 and defended his title successfully against Floyd Patterson, the boxing world waited for Frazier and Ellis to settle the question of heavyweight supremacy, but it took 17 months to get them into the Madison Square Garden ring. The result, however, was conclusive. Frazier proved the undoubted master, forcing Ellis to retire when the bell signalled the start to round five.

At 205 pounds and standing 5 ft. 11½ in. with a reach of 73½ in. Frazier was shortish for a heavyweight but he was solidly built and hustled an opponent for the full three minutes of every round, never taking a backward step and hooking viciously with his left.

He looked a worthy champion until Muhammad Ali appeared on the scene, having made a comeback to take him into championship class again. However, Frazier beat Ali decisively, even putting him down for a count. He went on defending his crown against mediocre opposition until George Foreman gave him the first set-back of his career, putting him down and out in two rounds with ponderous right-hand punches. That was virtually the end. He beat Joe Bugner, Jerry Quarry and Jimmy Ellis, but lost a ten-rounder to Ali and, at their third meeting (this time with the title at stake), he was stopped in 14 rounds. When, in a return with Foreman, he was stopped in five rounds that was the finish.
Score 37: *w*32 (27) *d*1 *l*4.

Freeman, Tommy

World Welterweight Champion 1930–31

(b. Hot Springs, Arkansas, Jan. 22, 1904 – d. Little Rock, Arkansas, Feb. 25, 1986). Began pro boxing: 1921.

A strong, workmanlike fighter, he was not only an accomplished boxer but very much a kayo king as well. Yet it took him ten years to get within reach of a title chance, when he took a decision off Young Jack Thompson. Then he had five lucrative defences in the space of two months before losing to Thompson by a stoppage in 12 rounds. Although Freeman went on campaigning for a further seven years, he never got another shot at the welter title. In 1938 he joined the U.S. Navy.
Score 196: *w*162 (77) *d*14 *l*20.

Frias, Arturo

World Lightweight Champion (W.B.A.) 1981–82

(b. Montebello, California, Oct. 27, 1956). Began pro boxing: Feb. 7, 1975.

In the first six years of his career, he went into the ring only 18 times and showed no signs of being a world-beater. In 1981 he made another start and in his sixth bout was fortunate to be given a chance at the W.B.A. version of the lightweight title, being matched with the holder, Claude Noel (Trinidad). Frias won by a knockout in eight rounds at Las Vegas. On Jan. 30, 1982 he kept his crown against Ernesto Espana (Venezuela) in a controversial decision in round nine at Los Angeles. Returning to Las Vegas, on May 8, in another title defence, he was destroyed in 2 min. 34 secs. of the first round by Ray 'Boom-Boom' Mancini.
Score 33: *w*28 (8) *d*0 *l*5.

Joe Frazier (left) defeats Jimmy Ellis to become the undisputed world heavyweight champion.

Fujii, Paul Takeshi

World Junior-Welterweight Champion 1967–68

(b. Honolulu, Hawaii, July 6, 1940). Began pro boxing: April 14, 1964.

Getting off to a good start in his homeland, with a string of kayo wins, he moved to Japan where he won the junior-welterweight championship of the Orient in his 21st bout. Seven months later he acquired the world title by knocking out the holder, Sandro Lopopolo (Italy), in two rounds. In Tokyo he retained his crown against Willi Qhatour (Germany) with a win in four rounds, but 13 months later he had to bow the knee to Nicolino Loche of Argentina, being stopped in the tenth round. He retired in 1970.
Score 36: *w*32 (27) *d*1 *l*3.

Fullmer, Gene

World Middleweight Champion 1957–63

(b. West Jordan, Utah, July 21, 1931). Began pro boxing: June 9, 1931.

One of the toughest middles ever to win the title and a solid puncher. Fullmer made a memorable start in which he won all his 17 bouts, only three going the distance. He then took two years off before resuming with another good run of successes. Fullmer astounded critics by outpointing the great Sugar Ray Robinson to win the world crown, but had to hand it back four months later. Another year went by and then he took the N.B.A. version of the title by stopping rock-hard Carmen Basilio in 14 rounds. Seven defences against the best in the world proved successful, but he had to give way to Dick Tiger, who not only outpointed him but proved a future stumbling block. In a return Fullmer was held to a draw and when they met for the third time, Tiger made sure by knocking out Fullmer in seven rounds.
Score 64: *w*55 (24) *d*3 *l*6.

Gains, Larry

*British Empire Heavyweight Champion
1931–34*

(b. Toronto, Canada, Dec. 12, 1901 – d. Cologne, West Germany, July 26, 1983). Began pro boxing: June 23, 1923.

Gains boxed as an amateur in his own country, going to England to start a pro career at the age of 21, where he had one bout which he lost. He spent the best part of the next three years fighting in European rings, basing himself in West Germany. Returning to England, he made his home in Leicester and at once proved he was a heavyweight threat. Tall and beautifully built, he carried a big punch and gained the British Empire title by knocking out Phil Scott in two rounds. He defended this in two hectic fights with Don McCorkindale (South Africa) and George Cook (Australia), losing it finally to Len Harvey, who outpointed him. He failed to regain the title in bouts with Jack Petersen and Harvey, but continued as a star boxer, liked by everyone for his gentlemanly behaviour both in and out of the ring. Gains had his last fight when he had turned 40.
Score 146: *w*116 (63) *d*5 *l*23 *Dnc*.2.

Gallindez, Victor

*World Light-Heavyweight Champion
(W.B.A.) 1974–79*

(b. Buenos Aires, Argentina, Nov. 2, 1948 – d. De Mayo, Argentina, Oct. 26, 1980). Began pro boxing: May 10, 1969.

A good boxer with a strong punch, Galindez won his native title in his 25th pro bout and the South American title three fights later. He came into the world championship (W.B.A. version) by stopping Len Hutchins in 13 rounds. After making ten successful

Ceferino Garcia (right) attacks Barney Ross in Mike Jacob's 'Festival of Champions'. Garcia lost on points.

title defences in the next four years in places all round the world, he succumbed at New Orleans to Mike Rossman, who stopped him in 13 rounds. He got back the championship in a return bout, but seven months later was halted by Marvin Johnson in 11 rounds. That brought his career to an end.
Score 70: *w*55 (34) *d*4 *l*9 *Dnc*.2.

Gans, Joe

World Lightweight Champion 1902–08

(b. Baltimore, Maryland, Nov. 25, 1874 – d. Baltimore, Aug. 10, 1910). Began pro boxing: 1891.

Gans was a highly-talented boxer, but because of the hostile attitude towards coloured fighters in his day, very often had to box 'to orders'. There is no record of his very early fights and it was not until he was 26 that he got a title chance against Frank Erne. For some unknown reason Gans quit in the 12th, asking the referee to stop the fight. Yet, on May 12, 1902, when he again challenged Erne, he knocked out the champion in 1 min. 40 secs. of the first round. Two years later he attempted to take the welter crown from Joe Walcott, but was held to a draw after 20 rounds. His fifth challenger for lightweight honours was Battling Nelson, who was ruled out in the 42nd round for low hitting. In a second meeting Gans weakened himself by severe weight reduction and was stopped in 17 rounds. Trying to win back his cherished crown, but only a shadow of his former greatness, Gans was knocked out in the 21st round. He retired in 1909 and died of tuberculosis a year later.
Score 156: *w*120 (55) *d*10 *l*8 *ND*.18.

Joe Gans, world lightweight champion 1902–08.

Garcia, Ceferino

World Middleweight Champion 1939–40

(b. Manila, Philippines, Aug. 26, 1910 – d. San Diego, California, Jan. 1, 1981). Began pro boxing: 1927

After five years battling in his own country, this strong and durable Filipino grew into a welterweight while campaigning in American rings and won the California state title by knocking out Johnny Romero in eight rounds. He had to wait four years and another 67 hard fights before he got his chance. Then he found Barney Ross too smart for him and, a year later, Henry Armstrong outpunched him to win the decision. Suddenly he became world middleweight champion by halting Fred Apostoli in seven rounds in New York. He made a successful defence against Glen Lee (ko. 13) and then again met Armstrong, holding him to a ten-rounds draw. Soon afterwards, however, he lost his world crown to Ken Overlin, after which his career petered out.
Score 130: *w*95 (65) *d*9 *l*26.

Gardner, George

World Light-Heavyweight Champion 1903

(b. Lisdoonvarna, County Clare, Ireland, March 17, 1877 – d. Chicago, Illinois, July 8, 1954). Began pro boxing: 1897.

A workmanlike fighter with no special talent, Gardner became the second boxer to become holder of the world light-heavyweight title, which had been created in 1903. He knocked out the first champion, Jack Root, in 12 rounds, but four months later was out-smarted by the 40-year old Bob Fitzsimmons. Gardner mingled with the heavies in the next five years, but without much success and brought a mixed career to an end by retiring in 1908.
Score 65: *w*41 (19) *d*10 *l*11 *ND*.2 *Dnc*.1.

Gardner, Jack

European, British and Commonwealth Heavyweight Champion 1950–52

(b. Market Harborough, Leicestershire, Nov. 6, 1926 – d. Market Harborough, Nov. 11, 1978). Began pro boxing: Dec. 6, 1948.

An ex-guardsman, Gardner carried a good knockdown punch in his right, but was weak on defence. He won many Army titles and the A.B.A. heavyweight championship in 1948 before making his pro debut by winning a heavyweight novices competition at Haringay Arena in London. He became British and Commonwealth champion by stopping Bruce Woodcock in 11 rounds, then took the European title from Jo Weiden (Austria) on a points verdict. In Germany he lost this to Hein Ten Hoff, being outpointed over 15 rounds, and then lost similarly to Johnny Williams, who took his two remaining titles. He died five days after his 52nd birthday.
Score 34: *w*28 (24) *d*0 *l*6.

Gavilan, Kid

World Welterweight Champion 1950–54

(b. Camaguey, Cuba, Jan. 6, 1926). Began pro boxing: June 5, 1943.

Gavilan (real name Gerado Gonzalez) fought in and around Havana for his first few years, then headed for America, where his blustering, aggressive style and seemingly unlimited stamina made him a great crowd-pleaser. He grew into a welter and in 1949 went 15 rounds with Sugar Ray Robinson for the world crown. This was a good perform-ance, but Gavilan did not get another chance until two years later when the title had fallen vacant. He then outpointed Johnny Bratton to become champion and at his first defence was somewhat lucky to take a decision over Billy Graham. He followed with six more successful title defences, was outpointed in an attempt to take the middleweight title from Bobo Olson and finally lost his welter crown to Johnny Saxton on a points verdict. He kept on fighting for four more years and then retired in 1958 after a busy and success-ful career.
Score 143: *w*106 (27) *d*61 *l*30 *Dnc*.1.

Gazo, Eddie

World Junior-Middleweight Champion 1977–78

(b. San Lorenzo, Nicaragua, Sept. 12, 1950). Began pro boxing: Oct. 6, 1971.

One of the few fighters to emerge from this part of Central America, Gazo hardly boxed out of his own territory in the ten years he was active. He became Central American champion by knocking out Rodri-go Delgardo in ten rounds in 1976 and the following year became world king by out-scoring Miguel Castellini over 15 rounds. He made three successful defences the same year but, risking his title in Japan for the second time, dropped his crown to Madashi Kudo on a points defeat. Gazo fought on for a few years but after he had been stopped a number of times he gave up in 1981.
Score 57: *w*44 (24) *d*2 *l*11.

Genaro, Frankie

World Flyweight Champion 1928–31

(b. New York, Aug. 26, 1901 – d. New York, Dec. 27, 1966). Began pro boxing: 1920.

Very fast on his feet and with his leading? Genaro surprised New York fans when he outpointed Pancho Villa in 1923 to win the American flyweight title. He retained this for three years, but was then outpointed by Fidel LaBarba. In Canada two years later he took the N.B.A. version of the 112-pound crown from Frenchy Belanger at the second attempt and then went to Paris where he was outed in 58 seconds by Emile Pladner. A month later he got his title back when the Frenchman was ruled out in the fifth round. Making successful defences in London, Paris and Toronto, Genaro was then held to a draw by Midget Wolgast in New York. Taking his half share of the flyweight crown back to Europe, he defeated two more challengers, but was finally stopped by Vic-tor Perez in two rounds to lose his crown. He had one more year of activity and retired in 1934.
Score 131: *w*98 (20) *d*8 *l*22 *ND*.3.

Giardello, Joey

World Middleweight Champion 1963–65

(b. Brooklyn, New York, July 16, 1930). Began pro boxing: Oct. 1948.

A strong and vigorous warrior, Giardello (real name Carmine Titelli) enjoyed every moment in the ring and piled up an impres-sive record in his 20 years of activity. He had to wait until he was almost 30 before a title chance came his way and then he could secure only a draw against Gene Fullmer. His next attempt came on Dec. 7, 1963, when he got the better of Dick Tiger over 15 rounds, and he retained the title against

Rubin Carter on a points decision. A year later in a return with Tiger, he had to give back the crown and retired in 1967.
Score 133: *w*100 (32) *d*7 *l*25 *ND*.1.

Gilroy, Freddie

European, British and Commonwealth Bantamweight Champion 1959–63

(b. Belfast, Northern Ireland, March 7, 1936). Began pro boxing: Feb. 9, 1957.

A breezy bantam with great crowd appeal, he scattered opponents right, left and centre until he became British and Commonwealth champion in 1959 by stopping Peter Keenan in 11 rounds. Gilroy added the E.B.U. crown the same year by outpointing Piero Rollo (Italy), keeping the Commonwealth title against a challenge by Bernie Taylor (South Africa) in five rounds and all three titles against Billy Rafferty (Scotland), who was halted in 13. In a match advertised as for the world title and involving the European title, he was outpointed by Alphonse Halimi (France). Making an attempt to win back the E.B.U. crown, he lost in nine rounds to Pierre Cossemyns (Belgium). Unperturbed, he beat Rafferty again, this time by a kayo in 12 rounds. He had one final fling, stopping fellow-countryman John Caldwell in defence of his two remaining titles and then announced his retirement.
Score 31: *w*28 (18) *d*0 *l*3.

Glover, Mike

World Welterweight Champion 1915

(b. Lawrence, Massachusetts, Dec. 18, 1890 – d. Middlesboro, Mass, July 11, 1917). Began pro boxing: 1908.

Active in the busy 'no-decision' era that swamped America, Glover was a vigorous journeyman fighter who could always find plenty of work, especially around New York. Eventually he went back to the Boston area and there he outpointed Matt Wells of England over 12 rounds, promptly styling himself welterweight champion of the world. His claim lasted exactly three weeks, for in his next fight he lost a decision to Jack Britton. He fought on for a while, but retired in 1916.
Score 95: *w*31 (18) *d*4 *l*4 *ND*.56.

Godwin, Bob

World Light-Heavyweight Champion (N.B.A.) 1933

(b. Moultrie, Georgia, May 5, 1911). Began pro boxing: 1927.

A good, upstanding fighter with a sound defence and good striking power, Godwin fought very frequently in his early days. In one year he had 28 bouts, winning all of them except three that were drawn. In 1933 the N.B.A. decided it could not recognize Maxie Rosenbloom as light-heavyweight

champion and matched Godwin to fight Joe Knight for the title thus declared vacant. Godwin won a ten-rounds points verdict and was then enticed to New York to meet Rosenbloom, who put the upstart in his place by handing out a four-rounds kayo. In all Godwin fought Rosenbloom seven times and could outpoint him only once and that was in a non-title bout. His career finished in 1938.
Score 168: *w*120 (51) *d*21 *l*25 *ND*.1 *Dnc*.1.

Goldstein, Abe

World Bantamweight Champion 1923–24

(b. New York, 1900 – d. St. Petersburg, Florida, Feb. 12, 1977). Began pro boxing: 1916.

Lively as well as busy, he thought nothing of fighting once every two weeks if given the chance. On Oct. 15, 1923, he scored a two-rounds win over Johnny Naselle and four days later he presented himself as a substitute for the bantam champion, Joe Lynch, who was supposed to defend his title against Joe Burman, but failed to turn up. At the weigh-in, the New York Boxing Commission solemnly hailed Burman as world champion, declaring Lynch to have forfeited his crown. That evening Burman's reign as bantam king came to an end, for Goldstein outpointed him over 12 rounds. To show he was no cardboard champion, Goldstein next proceeded to outpoint Lynch and then twice defended his title successfully. However, at the end of a great year he was adjudged a points loser to Eddie 'Cannonball' Martin and was never given the chance to win the title back. He retired in 1927.
Score 130: *w*85 (30) *d*5 *l*14 *ND*.26.

Gomes, Harold

World Junior-Lightweight Champion (N.B.A.) 1959

(b. Providence, Rhode Island, Aug. 22, 1933). Began pro boxing: Sept. 17, 1951.

Useful box-fighter in his early days, Gomes was in his eighth year when the N.B.A. installed him as world champion after he had beaten Paul Jorgensen on points over 15 rounds before his hometown fans. He kept the title five months, went to Manila and came home without it, having been stopped in seven rounds by the phenomenal Flash Elorde. Trying to win it back in San Francisco, Gomes was halted in the opening round. He retired in 1961.
Score 60: *w*50 (24) *d*0 *l*10.

Gomez, Antonio

World Featherweight Champion (W.B.A.) 1971–73

(b. Cumana, Venezuela, Sept. 30, 1945). Began pro boxing: Feb. 28, 1967.

A stout-hearted, busy warrior, he spent most of his time fighting in his own country, venturing out when opportunity offered. In 1971 he went to Tokyo and won the W.B.A. version of the featherweight title by stopping Shozo Saijyo in five rounds. He retained his title against Ernesto Marcel the following year (ko.7), but lost it on a points decision in a return match six months later. The following year he made another attempt to regain his lost laurels, but Marcel was again too good for him and won in 12 rounds. Gomez retired in 1975.
Score 50: *w*40 (18) *d*2 *l*7 *Dnc*.1.

Gomez, Wilfredo

World Super-Bantam, Feather and Junior-Lightweight Champion 1977–86

(b. Puerto Rico, Oct. 29, 1956). Began pro boxing: Nov. 16, 1974.

This astonishing Puerto Rican, carrying a big punch, came into the championship picture in his 17th pro bout, winning the W.B.C. version of the super-bantamweight title by knocking out Dong-Kyun Yum in 12 rounds. Following that he made 15 successful defences and suffered only one defeat, when he tried to give weight to Salvador Sánchez in an attempt to win the featherweight crown, being stopped in eight rounds after a heroic try. He successfully defended his title by stopping Lupe Pintor (world bantamweight champion) at Houston, Texas, on Dec. 3, 1982. He relinquished his title to go after the W.B.C. world featherweight crown which he won on March 31, 1984 by outpointing Juan LaPorte, but later in the year lost it to Azuma Nelson on a kayo in round 11. Notwithstanding, he went after the junior-lightweight title and won it by outpointing Rocky Lockridge at San Juan after 15 rounds. But a year later he lost his third world crown when Alfredo Layne stopped him in nine rounds at Hato Rey.
Score 46: *w*42 (40) *d*1 *l*3.

González, Betulio

World Flyweight Champion (W.B.C. and W.B.A.) 1972–79

(b. Maracaibo, Venezuela, Oct. 24, 1949). Began pro boxing: 1968.

This busy little man fought so many times with the world flyweight title at stake that it is difficult to keep track of his progress. He began his assault on the championship in 1971 and during the next ten years engaged in 16 title bouts, first those recognized by the W.B.C., and then switched to the W.B.A. He was champion four times and made five successful defences, but in his last attempt to get back to the top was outpointed by Santos Laciar. He retired in 1982, but returned to the ring two years later with disastrous results.
Score 88: *w*75 (50) *d*3 *l*11.

González, Rodolfo

World Junior-Lightweight Champion (W.B.C.) 1972–74

(b. Jalisco, Mexico, Dec. 16, 1945). Began pro boxing: Nov. 17, 1959.

González proved himself as a kayo king when he won 29 of his first 31 bouts inside the distance. Then he dropped a decision and remained inactive for the best part of three years. He resumed boxing to add to his big total of kayo wins, but was twice stopped. In 1972 he took the world crown from Chango Carmona in 13 rounds, successfully defended it twice the following year, and then went to Tokyo, where Ishimatsu Suzuki relieved him of his crown with a stoppage in round eight. Returning to Japan to try and regain his lost title, González managed to stay 13 rounds. He had one more bout then retired.
Score 70: *w*62 (50) *d*1 *l*7.

Goodrich, Johnny

World Lightweight Champion 1925

(b. Scranton, Pennsylvania, July 30, 1900 – d. Fort Myers, Florida, Sept. 25, 1982). Began pro boxing: 1921.

Goodrich (real name James Edward Moran), a clean-hitting, stylish boxer, was a real professional, ready to go anywhere to earn his fight pay. He had been fighting for five years when the great Benny Leonard retired, leaving the lightweight title vacant. The New York Commission then selected Goodrich to take part in an eliminating competition, in the final of which he disposed of Stanislaus Lloauza in two rounds to be acclaimed as the new lightweight champion. Six months later, when defending his title against Rocky Kansas, he was outpointed and never again figured in a championship contest. Nevertheless, he went on fighting for five more years, retiring in 1930.
Score 182: *w*109 (10) *d*22 *l*49 *ND*.2.

Graham, Bushy

World Bantamweight Champion 1928

(b. Italy, June 18, 1903 – d. Utica, New York, Aug. 5, 1982). Began pro boxing: 1922.

Bushy (real name Angelo Geraci) started and ended a long career in American rings. He was a very active fighter for five years before getting a title chance. Challenging Charlie Phil Rosenberg, he lost on points. Then he and his opponent were charged with having made a secret arrangement as to the result. Both were suspended for a year. When he resumed Graham was given an opportunity by the New York Commission to win the title, being matched with Izzy Schwartz in a 15-rounder which he won on points. The following year (1929) he found it

Herol Graham became the British light-middle-weight champion in 1981.

too hard to make bantamweight and gave up the crown. He continued fighting until 1936.
Score 133: *w*107 (39) *d*7 *l*19.

Graham, Herol

British and European Commonwealth Light-Middleweight Champion 1981–

(b. Sheffield, Yorkshire, Sept. 13, 1960). Began pro boxing: Nov. 28, 1978.

Smart and talented, this southpaw won the British title from Pat Thomas on a 15-rounds points verdict in his home town. Five months later he defeated Kenny Bristol (Guyana) to take the Commonwealth crown. In Feb. 1982 he strengthened his grip on his two titles when he stopped Chris Christian, a London challenger, in nine rounds, also in Sheffield.

Retaining his Commonwealth title by outpointing Hunter Clay in Lagos, Graham then won the European light-middleweight title by knocking out Clement Tshinza in two rounds, defended it against Germain LeMaitre, then relinquished it in 1984. His next five bouts he won inside the scheduled distance, then captured the vacant British middleweight title by disposing of Jimmy Price in a single round. He gave up this holding and won the European middleweight crown by stopping Ayub Kalule inside ten rounds, retaining it against Mark Kaylor, who was beaten in eight rounds at Wembley on Nov. 4, 1986. At this point Graham was undefeated in 38 contests, but

he suffered a shock defeat when losing his European crown to Sumbu Kalambay, boxing below form and being well outpointed by the Italian champion. On June 8, 1988 Graham scored a second notch on a Lonsdale Belt by stopping James Cook in five rounds to regain the British middleweight crown.
Score 39: *w*38 (19) *d*0 *l*1.

Rocky Graziano (right) is cut but still stopped Charlie Fusari, in 10 rounds. Few of Rocky's fights lasted the distance.

Gray, Clyde

Canadian and Commonwealth Welterweight Champion 1971–80

(b. Toronto, Canada, March 10, 1947). Began pro boxing: March 13, 1968.

This capable, hard-hitting, Canadian became welterweight champion of his country by outpointing Donato Paduano in Feb. 1971. He kept the crown for six years before losing it to Guerrero Chavez in 11 rounds. Gray also acquired the Commonwealth crown by outpointing Eddie Blay over 15 rounds. He made five successful defences, then lost the crown to Chris Clarke, but won it back in a return bout, holding it until his retirement in 1980. During his lengthy career he also made two attempts to win the world crown, but was outpointed by José Napoles and Ángel Espada.
Score 81: *w*70 (49) *d*1 *l*10.

Graziano, Rocky

World Middleweight Champion 1947–48

(b. New York, Jan. 1, 1922). Began pro boxing: March 31, 1942.

Graziano (real name Rocco Barbella) was a tough street tearaway, constantly in trouble with the law until he turned his ferocity to good purpose in the ring. Proving a savage fighter, relentless and with great hitting power, he had three slugfests with Tony Zale for the middleweight crown, all ending inside the distance. Zale outpunched Rocky in the first to win in six rounds. Then it was Graziano's turn and, on the point of defeat, he produced a vicious counter-attack that gave him victory, also in the sixth. In their third meeting it was Zale who had worn best

and he knocked out Rocky in the third. Four years later Graziano tried to win back the title from Sugar Ray Robinson, but was beaten in three rounds and retired.
Score 83: w67 (52) d6 l10.

Greb, Harry

World Middleweight Champion 1923–26

(b. Pittsburgh, Pennsylvania, June 6, 1894 – d. Atlantic City, New Jersey. Oct. 22, 1926). Began pro boxing: 1913.

Harry Greb ruled the world middleweight division for three years but his most lasting claim to fame is that he was the only man ever to defeat the masterful Gene Tunney. Greb was no gentleman in action: a master of ruthless in-fighting, he used every trick to wear down his opponents. He rarely took a lot of punishment, as his rivals were usually busy defending themselves from the torrent of punches he tossed at them from all angles. Apart from a setback in his first professional year, Greb was never stopped in nearly 300 contests – although, under the rules of the time, many of his fights were 'no decisions'.

He averaged 22 bouts a year, and in 1919 fought 44 times. He kept fit by continuous boxing, rarely entering a gymnasium. And, even more remarkably for a top fighter, for many years he was almost blind in one eye – an injury caused by an opponent's exploring thumb in retaliation against one of Greb's dubious tricks.

When Greb took the American light-heavyweight title from Gene Tunney in 1922

Harry Greb was nicknamed 'The Human Windmill' because of his all-action style.

Emile Griffith (right) defeats Luis Rodriguez to regain the world welterweight crown.

he gave the bigger man such a going-over for 15 rounds that Tunney spent the following week in bed. But Tunney profited from his only defeat and on four subsequent occasions outpointed the rugged Greb. Another indication of just how dangerous Greb could be to the heavier divisions was his victory over top heavyweight Bill Brennan – a fighter who later went 12 rounds with Jack Dempsey for the world title.

Greb won the world middleweight title in 1923 from Johnny Wilson in New York on a points decision. He successfully defended it six times before dropping it in 1926 in a close decision to Tiger Flowers. He lost the return fight, too, and died following an operation after an accident.
Score 299: w264 (49) d12 l23.

Green, Dave 'Boy'

British and European Welter and British and European Light-Welterweight Champion 1976–79

(b. Chatteris, Cambridgeshire, June 2, 1953). Began pro boxing: Dec. 10, 1974.

Green rose rapidly into championship class, first taking the British junior-welterweight title from Joey Singleton in six rounds. Six months later he overcame Jean-Baptiste Piedvache (France) to win the E.B.U. crown. A sensational stoppage (cut eye) of John Stracey gave Green a match with Carlos Palomino for the world title, but despite a gallant attempt he was knocked out in the tenth round. Making another start, he disposed of Henry Rhiney in five rounds to win the British and European welter titles, but was then stopped by the veteran Dane, Jorgen Hansen, who beat him in three rounds. Misguidedly he went to the United States to take on the phenomenal Sugar Ray

Leonard and was knocked cold in four rounds. Still he wanted to keep fighting, but after being stopped in five rounds by the almost unknown Reg Ford (Guyana) he announced his retirement.
Score 41: w37 (29) d0 l4.

Griffith, Emile

World Welter and Middleweight Champion 1961–65

(b. St. Thomas, Virgin Islands, Feb. 3, 1938). Began pro boxing: June 2, 1956.

One of those toughies who seem to be able to go on for ever and a brilliant box-fighter from the start, Griffith opened his career in New York where he quickly became a star box-office attraction. He had three fights with Benny (Kid) Paret for the world welter title and came out the winner in the rubber match, the unfortunate Cuban dying of his injuries. Griffith lost and then regained the title in two matches with Luis Rodriguez. He made three more successful defences before turning his attention to the middleweights and winning the world title from Dick Tiger. Twice he beat challenger Joey Archer, and lost, won and lost again the championship in three battles with Nino Benvenuti. That was the end of Griffith as a champion, but he challenged for both his welter and middleweight crowns, alas unsuccessfully, and kept on fighting regularly as a top-liner until he was coming up to 40. After losing a decision to Alan Minter in Monte Carlo, he announced his retirement.
Score 112: w85 (23) d2 l24 Dnc.1.

Griffo, Young

World Featherweight Champion 1890–93

(b. Sydney, Australia, April 15, 1869 – d. New York, Dec. 7, 1927). Began pro boxing: 1886.

If ever a man was a will-o-the-wisp fighter it was this one. Griffo (real name Albert Griffiths) would stand on a handkerchief and bet that no one could aim blows at him and make him step off. Brilliantly defensive and an astute boxer, he had an amazing career that extended over 30 years, and was still boxing at 42. He won the Australian version of the world title in 1890 by stopping the New Zealander, Billy Murphy, in 15 rounds and he was still claiming the championship when he arrived in America in 1893.

Fighting in all the major fight towns, Griffo met the best feathers in the country and defeated many of them. He had a fondness for a drink and often fought when badly out of condition when, of course, he was beaten. One day he was badly injured in a street accident, yet insisted on going through with a fight that night, but had to retire in the first round. Had Griffo taken his career more seriously, he must surely have been a fully recognized champion.
Score 173: *w*69 (29) *d*43 *l*12 *ND*.48 *Dnc*.1.

Grim, Joe

(b. Avellino, Italy, March 14, 1881 – d. Byberry, Pennsylvania, Aug. 19, 1939).

His real name was Saverio Giannone, and he was known as The Iron Man because of his ability to absorb punishment and persistence in getting off the floor. He is alleged to have taken part in several hundred contests that it is impossible to trace. He fought anywhere there was a chance to earn with his fists, spending most of his time in America, but fighting in many other parts of the world as well. He died in the State Hospital at Byberry.
Known score 134: *w*10 (2) *d*8 *l*34 *ND*.82.

Gumbs, Roy

British and Commonwealth Middleweight Champion 1981–84

(b. Jamaica, Sept. 5, 1954). Began pro boxing: May 18, 1976.

Fighting out of Islington in North London, Gumbs did not show any extraordinary talent until he won the Southern Area title by outpointing Frankie Lucas. He followed this by winning the vacant British title, stopping Howard Mills in three rounds. He then went off to Toronto where he stopped Joe Henry in eight, came back to stop challenger Eddie Burke in six rounds at Glasgow, and four months later made the Lonsdale Belt his own property by stopping Glen McEwan in 13 rounds.

Gumbs stopped Ralph Hollett (twice) in Canada to capture the Commonwealth crown, but lost both his titles to Mark Kaylor on Sept. 14, 1983 in London. He retired the following year.
Score 40: *w*26 (21) *d*3 *l*11.

Gummer, Tom

British Middleweight Champion 1920–21

(b. Rotherham, Yorkshire, Dec. 4, 1894). Began pro boxing: May 5, 1915.

A strong fighter and solid puncher, he had a hazardous career, winning some good fights and losing disastrously in others. He acquired the British title by forcing Jim Sullivan to retire in 14 rounds at the National Sporting Club in London in 1920, but when he tried to add the European crown, he was knocked down in nine rounds by Ercole Balzac in Paris. Almost exactly a year after he had become British champion he lost to Gus Platts, another Yorkshireman, who stopped him in six rounds. Finally a one round kayo defeat by Ted (Kid) Lewis brought his career to an end.
Score 35: *w*22 (20) *d*2 *l*11.

Gushiken, Yoko

World Junior-Flyweight Champion (W.B.A.) 1970–81

(b. Okinawa, Japan, June 26, 1955). Began pro boxing: May 28, 1974.

This hard-hitting southpaw got into the championship range in his ninth pro bout, winning the W.B.A. junior-flyweight title by stopping Juan Guzman, the Dominican holder, in seven rounds. He then made 13 successful title defences in the next four years, finally losing his crown to Pedro Flores, who forced his retirement in 12 rounds, after which he quit boxing.
Score 24: *w*23 (15) *d*0 *l*1.

Guzman, Juan

World Junior-Flyweight Champion (W.B.A.) 1976

(b. Dominican Republic, 1953). Began pro boxing: 1973.

This hard-punching Dominican had an exciting start to a somewhat brief career. He won his first 18 bouts, 13 inside the distance and in his 22nd contest outpointed Jaime Rios in Santo Domingo to become champion according to the W.B.A. His reign was limited to three months, however. He was then knocked out in seven rounds by Yoko Gushiken. After that he won only a single fight and retired when he had lost five fights in a row.
Score 35: *w*26 (20) *d*0 *l*9.

Hagler, Marvin

World Middleweight Champion 1980–87

(b. Newark, New Jersey, May 23, 1952). Began pro boxing: May 18, 1973.

A fine, compact boxer, Hagler was one of the best seen in the division for a long while. He carried a 'killer' punch in both hands, yet when he made his first bid for the world crown in his seventh year as a pro, he had to be content with a draw after 15 rounds with Vito Antuofermo, the Italian holder. Ten months later he went to London and caused a dramatic upset by stopping Alan Minter in three rounds. Hagler made three conclusive defences in 1981, beating Fulgencio Obelmejias, Vito Antuofermo and Mustafa Hamsho, all inside the distance. His next defence, against William 'Caveman' Lee, ended in 67 seconds of the first round on the referee's intervention. On Oct. 13, 1982, he knocked out the Venezuelan challenger, Fulgencio Obelmejias, in five rounds at San Remo, and in Feb. 1983 halted Tony Sibson, British middleweight champion, inside six rounds at Worcester, Massachusetts. Hagler made six more successful title defences after that, beating Wilford Scypion (4 rounds), Roberto Duran (points 15), Juan Roldan (10 rounds), Mustafa Hamsho (3 rounds), Thomas Hearns (3 rounds) and John Mugabi (11 rounds). At Las Vegas in another title fight that aroused world-wide interest, he was very narrowly outpointed over 12 rounds by world welter and light-middleweight champion, Sugar Ray Leonard, who had engaged in only one bout in the previous five years.
Score 67: *w*62 (52) *d*2 *l*3.

Hague, William Ian 'Iron'

British Heavyweight Champion 1908–11

(b. Mexborough, Yorkshire, Nov. 6, 1885 – d. Mexborough, Aug. 18, 1951). Began pro boxing: 1904.

Standing 5 ft. 10 ins., he was handicapped in reach, but carried a knockdown punch in each hand. He became county champion by beating Albert Rodgers and, after he had scored five knockout wins in a row over other contenders, he challenged for the British championship, causing a surprise by knocking out James Moir in the opening round. This earned him a match with Sam Langford, the famous American, who was vastly more experienced and knocked Hague out in four rounds, but not before the Yorkshireman had toppled him over and given him a thick ear. Unfortunately, Hague put on weight and let himself get out of condition. He won five of his next eight bouts, but was kayoed by Billy Wells in six rounds when he made his first title defence. He continued boxing for a while, but gained no further wins.
Score 33: *w*22 (18) *d*1 *l*10.

Halimi, Alphonse

World and European Bantamweight Champion 1957–61

(b. Constantine, Algeria, Feb. 18, 1932). Began pro boxing: Sept. 26, 1955.

Halimi showed great punching power in

his early fights, but had to go the full distance to win the world bantamweight title from Mario d'Agata (Italy) in Paris. He kept the title against Raton Macias (Mexico), but lost it two years later to Joe Becerra, who stopped him in eight. Not satisfied, Halimi tried to get back his crown, but the Mexican was too hard a puncher and this time ended the fight in the ninth. In 1960 the promoter Jack Solomons matched Halimi with Freddie Gilroy in a fight which he advertised as for the world crown. Halimi gained a points verdict and was back on the bantam throne, but not for long. John Caldwell outpointed him, not once but twice, in title fights and, although Halimi won and lost the E.B.U. championship in two fights with Piero Rollo (Italy), it was close to the end of his career. He retired in 1964.
Score 50: *w*41 (21) *d*1 *l*8.

Hall, James

European and British Lightweight Champion 1922–23

(b. Peebles, Scotland, Oct. 15, 1892 – d. Clydebank, Scotland, Nov. 13, 1933). Began pro boxing: 1909

A sailor by profession, he won a number of unrecorded contests while serving in the Royal Navy. A solid, stand-up boxer of the old school, he could box his opponents to a standstill but was not a knockout specialist. After World War I he won six tournaments among men in all branches of the armed forces and then ran up a long list of pro wins that took him to a fight with Ernie Rice for the British and European lightweight titles. Hall won on points and successfully defended his title against his fellow-countryman, Johnny Brown. But against Harry Mason he lost all, being ruled out for an alleged low blow in the 13th round. By that time he was past 30, but continued to box for another two years. He made a comeback some five years later, getting in 20 contests (15 wins) until he decided to retire at the end of 1933.
Score 132: *w*91 (35) *d*10 *l*31.

Hanagata, Susumu

World Flyweight Champion (W.B.A.) 1974

(b. Kanagawa, Japan, Jan. 21, 1946). Began pro boxing: Nov. 1, 1963.

Beginning at 17, he had to wait until his seventh year as a pro before getting a shot at his native title, which he won by outpointing Speedy Hayase over ten rounds. An attempt to win the world crown was thwarted by Elfren Torres in 1969. The following year he had another try, but lost on points to Erbito Salavarria, and when he tried again in 1972, he was beaten on points by Masso Ohba. No one could accuse him of not being a trier, for a year later he was loser to Chartchai Chionoi. In 1974 he got into the ring again

with the Thailander and this time success came his way, the referee stopping the contest in Hanagata's favour in round six. Recklessly he gave first chance to Salavarria, who confirmed his former superiority by gaining a points win. Undaunted, Hanagata turned to the W.B.C. champion, Miguel Canto, but lost the decision.
Score 58: *w*35 (8) *d*7 *l*16.

Harada, Masahiko

World Fly and Bantamweight Champion 1962–68

(b. Setagaya, Tokyo, April 5, 1943). Began pro boxing: Feb. 21, 1960.

One of the very best fighters to come out of Japan, he almost achieved the rare feat of becoming a triple world champion. In his third year of paid boxing he took the flyweight title from Pone Kingpetch by knocking him out in the 11th round, but lost it in a return fight three months later. Setting his sights on the bantam crown, he had to wait more than two years for his chance and then outpointed Eder Joffre to become a world king for the second time. When he finally lost the crown, after four brilliant defences, to Lionel Rose (Australia), he

Masahiko 'Fighting' Harada's greatest assets were his speed and agility and his non-stop whirling punches.

turned his attention to the feathers. Meeting Johnny Famechon in Sydney, he had a terrific fight which the referee declared to have been drawn. On examining his scorecard, however, he changed his verdict, making the Australian the winner, but many thought it should have been Harada. In a second encounter Famechon put the record straight by knocking out his Japanese challenger in the 14th round. Harada then retired.
Score 62: *w*55 (22) *d*0 *l*7.

Hart, Marvin

World Heavyweight Champion 1905–06

(b. Jefferson County, Kentucky, Sept. 16, 1876). Began pro boxing: Dec. 12, 1899.

Hart might never have been a world-beater if it had not been for James J. Jeffries, who decided to retire undefeated as world champion, and named Hart and Jack Root to fight for the vacant title. Root was knocked out in 12 rounds and, before Hart could cash in on his good fortune, he took on Tommy Burns and was outpointed over 20 rounds. Hart had 11 bouts spread over the next four years, and after being stopped by Carl Morris in three rounds, decided to retire.
Score 47: *w*28 (19) *d*4 *l*7 ND.8.

Harvey, Len

World Light-Heavyweight Champion 1939–42, British Middle, Light-Heavy and Heavyweight Champion 1929–42

(b. Stoke Climsland, Cornwall, July 11, 1907 – d. Holloway, London, Nov. 20, 1976). Began pro boxing: Jan. 2, 1920.

Like his fellow-Cornishman, Bob Fitzsimmons, Len Harvey was a collector of titles, and is the only fighter to have won the British middle, light-heavy, and heavyweight titles. In 1926 he almost won the welterweight crown, too, fighting a draw with champion Harry Mason.

In 1929 Harvey took the British middleweight title from Alex Ireland and fought off six challengers until he dropped it to Jock McAvoy in May 1933. But later that year he won both the British light-heavy and heavyweight crowns. Harvey's shock heavyweight victory was probably his finest performance: scaling little more than 12 stone, he outpointed the unbeaten Jack Petersen. Harvey fought two world champions – middleweight Marcel Thil in 1932 and light-heavyweight John Henry Lewis four years later – but lost on points to both. He was to have met Lewis in a return, but the American's eye trouble caused the fight to be cancelled. In 1939 he beat Jock McAvoy on points for the world light-heavyweight title, although this was recognized only by the British Boxing Board of Control. He made one last appearance in

Marvelous Marvin Hagler (right) on the attack against Fulgencio Obelmejias. Hagler swiftly established a fearsome reputation as champion.

1942 to defend his light-heavyeight titles, but Freddie Mills knocked him out in two rounds.

A keen student of the finer points of boxing, Harvey was an accomplished long-range and close-quarter fighter. He fought from an upright stance and was a master of the art of self-defence. Apart from his last fight, he was stopped only once – by a cut eye.
Score 133: *w*111 (51) *d*9 *l*13.

Hearns, Thomas

World Welter (W.B.A.), Light-Middle (W.B.C.), Light-Heavy (W.B.C.) and Middleweight Champion (W.B.C.) 1980–88

(b. Memphis, Tennessee, Oct. 18, 1958). Began pro boxing: Nov. 25, 1977.

A sound boxer and extremely hard puncher, in his first 26 bouts Hearns scored 24 wins inside the distance and became American champion by stopping Angel Espada in four rounds. Three fights later he won the W.B.A. version of the welterweight title by disposing of Pipino Cuevas in two rounds. He kept his crown against Luis Primera (6), Randy Shields (13) and Pablo Baez (4). Then came his much publicized meeting with Sugar Ray Leonard, a fight that produced record television viewing. In the early stages it looked as if Hearns would prove too hard a hitter but Leonard came with a burst in the 14th round to win beyond doubt by causing the referee to save Hearns from being knocked out. On Dec. 3, 1982, he regained world title status by outpointing Wilfredo Benitez at Houston, Texas, for the W.B.C. light-middleweight title.

He defended this title once, outpointing Luigi Minchillo, then won the vacant world light-middleweight crown by knocking out Roberto Duran in two rounds. He made one successful defence, but when attempting to win the world middleweight title was stopped in three rounds by Marvin Hagler. Hearns brought his total of world titles to three with a ten rounds victory over Dennis Andries for the W.B.C. light-heavyweight crown, then took a world title at a fourth weight by disposing a Juan Roldan in four rounds to take the W.B.C. middleweight crown, the first fighter to achieve this feat. Defending this title against Iran Barkley on June 6, 1988, he was knocked out in three rounds by what appeared to be an 'after the bell' punch. Hearns then announced his intention to go after a fifth world crown and claimed to have achieved this, though to the satisfaction of few, when he won a split decision over James Kinchen in Nov. 1988 to win the super-featherweight title recognized by a new body called the World Boxing Organization. Shortly afterwards Sugar Ray Leonard was first to win a fifth title.

Hearns was tall for a welterweight and his all-action style was extremely popular with the fans, who called him the 'Hit Man'. With Hagler and Leonard, he was one of the star attractions of the 1980s.
Score 48: *w*45 (38) *d*0 *l*3.

Heeney, Tom

Heavyweight Title Contender 1928

(b. Gisborne, New Zealand, May 18, 1898). Began pro boxing: 1921.

Heeney began his working life as a blacksmith but, attracted to boxing, turned professional in his early twenties. Weighing 200 pounds and measuring 5 ft. 10½ in. tall, he was, however, handicapped by short arms, making it imperative that he did most of his fighting at close quarters.

Heeney was not a sensation in Australasia, and when he went to England in 1924 he did not captivate the fans, mainly because of his plodding style and lack of a knockdown punch. After two years he decided to go to America and earn enough money to pay for his passage home. Of nine contests there in 12 months, he won six and drew two, but he was not considered to be in the contender class. Consequently, he was a surprise challenger when Tex Rickard brought him in to fight Gene Tunney after Jack Dempsey refused a third title fight with the champion.

The outcome of the fight was predictable, yet Heeney fought so determinedly that, although he was virtually cut to ribbons, he lasted into the 11th round before he was stopped. And even then it was the champion who called a halt to the systematic massacre by dropping his hands and snapping at the referee: 'How much more do you want him to take?' Heeney's purse of $100,000 was as much as he had received in all his other bouts put together, and he continued to campaign in the United States rings for another four years.
Score 70: *w*39 (15) *d*7 *l*22 *ND*.1 *Dnc*.1.

Herman, Pete

World Bantamweight Champion 1916–21

(b. New Orleans, Louisiana, Feb. 12, 1896 – d. New Orleans, April 13, 1973). Began pro boxing: 1912.

One of the most brilliant boxers ever to hold the world's bantamweight title, American Herman (real name Gullota) was stopped only once in ten years of professional boxing, and that was in his very early ring days. He had his first crack at the world title five days before his 20th birthday, and did so well in holding the champion Kid Williams to a 20-round draw that the following year he was given a second chance, becoming champion with a convincing points victory. An orthodox boxer and precision puncher, especially at infighting, Herman remained champion for nearly four years.

In 1920 he contracted to defend his title against the world's flyweight champion, Jimmy Wilde, in London, but conveniently lost it beforehand to his fellow-countryman, Joe Lynch, after a markedly below-form display. This meant that Wilde was forced to meet him in a non-title bout and also give away considerable weight, and it is no

wonder that in their Jan. 1921 fight the famous but ageing Welshman was stopped in 17 rounds. In July Herman then accounted for the British bantamweight champion, Jim Higgins, in 11 rounds, again coming in overweight and paying £300 forfeit.

Two weeks later he had a return fight with Lynch, which Herman won easily on points, but remained champion for only two months, dropping a points verdict to Johnny Buff. He retired from the ring shortly afterwards because of eye trouble and eventually went blind.
Score 144: *w*94 (21) *d*14 *l*26 *ND*.10.

Hernandez, Carlos

World Junior-Welterweight Champion 1965–66

(b. Caracas, Venezuela, April 21, 1940). Began pro boxing: Jan. 25, 1959.

A strong fighter and a big puncher, Hernandez gained his native lightweight title in his 17th pro bout by knocking out Vicente Rivas in eight rounds. He won his way to a title fight with Eddie Perkins, who came to defend his junior-welterweight crown, but had to leave it behind after being outpointed by Hernandez. There were two successful defences the same year, Mario Rissito being stopped in four rounds and Percy Hayles (in Jamaica) in three. The following year, against Sandro Lopopolo in Rome, he was

beaten on points. Continuing his career, he had another chance to regain his lost crown, but was outpointed by Nicolino Loche in Buenos Aires. After a few more fights, mostly wins, he made the mistake of going to London to fight Ken Buchanan and was stopped in eight rounds.
Score 76: *w*60 (43) *d*4 *l*12.

Herrera, Juan

World Flyweight Champion (W.B.A.) 1981–82

(b. Mérida, Mexico, Jan. 12, 1958). Began pro boxing: March 8, 1978.

This young Mexican began by establishing himself as something of a kayo king, but took his state title by outpointing Antonio Benitez over 12 rounds. He got his chance to win world honours 12 fights later and knocked out the Panama holder, Luis Ibarra, in the 11th round. Retaining his crown against Betulio Gonzalez with a seventh-round stoppage, he looked set to remain a champion for some time. But five months later, before his own supporters, he was stopped in 13 rounds by Santos Laciar of Argentina.
Score 48: *w*40 (26) *d*0 *l*8.

Thomas Hearns (facing camera) in a 1986 light-middleweight title defence against Mark Medal.

Herrera, Rafael

World Bantamweight Champion (W.B.C.) 1972–74

(b. Jaliaco, Mexico, Jan. 7, 1945). Began pro boxing: March 20, 1963.

A solid, two-fisted fighter, he campaigned for eight years in his own country and California, where he won the American title by outpointing Rodolfo Martinez over 12 rounds. In March 1972 he caused something of a surprise by knocking out Ruben Olivares to take the world crown. He lost this four months later to Enrique Pinder, but in April 1973 another chance came his way and he won the W.B.C. version of the title by stopping his old enemy, Rodolfo Martinez, in 12 rounds. He twice defended his crown, but a third meeting with Martinez was a disaster, the challenger winning by a knock-out in four rounds. Herrera retired soon afterwards.
Score 60: *w*38 (21) *d*3 *l*9

Higgins, Jim

British and British Empire Bantamweight Champion 1920–22

(b. Hamilton, Scotland, Oct. 25, 1897 – d. Glasgow, Dec. 1964). Began pro boxing: 1919.

When, in his eighth pro bout, this 5 ft. 2 in. Scotsman made his first appearance at the National Sporting club in London, he created a stir by knocking out the experienced Jack (Kid) Doyle in two rounds. The bantam title was vacant at the time, so Higgins was matched with Harold Jones (Wales) and stopped him in 13 rounds. His next appearance at the N.S.C. saw him outpoint Vince Blackburn (Australia) over 20 rounds to capture the British Empire crown. However, he overstretched himself when going for the treble, Charles Ledoux (France) keeping his European title with an 11th round knockout. It was unwise of his supporters to put in with Pete Herman, former world champion, who gave the Scot a bad beating and stopped him in 11 rounds. Higgins never really recovered from that defeat and in his next contest was stopped by Tommy Harrison in 13 rounds and lost his two titles.
Score 36: *w*20 (9) *d*3 *l*13.

Hill, Johnny

World, European and British Flyweight Champion 1927–29

(b. Strathmigloe, Fife, Scotland, Dec. 14, 1905 – d. Edinburgh, Sept. 27, 1929). Began pro boxing: Sept. 30, 1926.

A former amateur champion, he was a neat and accomplished boxer, quick with his leading but not possessed of a damaging punch. He became British champion in his 14th paid bout and ten months later took the

European crown by outpointing Emile Pladner (France). Newsboy Brown was brought to London to defend his title against Hill and was outpointed after a brilliant contest. In a return with Pladner, in Paris, Hill was, surprisingly, stopped in six rounds, but he was already a sick man. He defended his titles twice against Ernie Jarvis, an English flyweight, narrowly winning the first time and gaining the verdict in the second when Jarvis was ruled out in the tenth for an alleged foul blow. To the dismay of all fans, Hill was taken seriously ill and died three months after his last contest.
Score 23: w18 (8) d3 l1 Dnc.1.

Holberg, Waldermar

World Welterweight Champion 1914

(b. Copenhagen, Denmark, 1883 – d. Vienna, Austria, May 18, 1927). Began pro boxing: 1908.

Not many Danes have been world champions and this one had to go to Australia to win title honours. A fierce, but rather wild fighter, unlucky to be short-armed, he was all right when it came to having a close-quarter scrap, although it cost him dearly in disqualifications. An amateur champion of his own country, when he turned pro he had to go abroad to get enough fights. He fought in England, then in Australia where his energetic style was fully appreciated. There was a dispute about the ownership of the world welter crown at that time and an astute Australian promoter matched Holberg with the American star, Ray Bronson, at Melbourne for the championship. Holberg won a convincing points decision and was eager to defend it three weeks later against the Englishman, Tom McCormick. To the Dane's disgust he was ruled out in round six for an alleged low blow and his brief reign was over.
Score (incomplete) 58: w31 (20) d4 l23.

Holmes, Larry

World Heavyweight Champion (W.B.C.) 1978–85

(b. Cuthbert, Georgia, Nov. 3, 1949). Began pro boxing: March 21, 1973.

A sound, upstanding boxer, with a 'killer' punch in each hand, Holmes had to box his way through 26 bouts, winning 20 inside the distance, before getting recognition as a title prospect. He won the W.B.C. version of the heavyweight title by outpointing veteran Ken Norton. He subsequently defeated all comers, including Mike Weaver, the W.B.A. nominee. In his eighth defence he finished off the career of Muhammad Ali, forcing him to quit in 11 rounds. There were three more defences in 1981, all successful, although Trevor Berbick, the rough Canadian, had the satisfaction of putting Holmes on the floor. The much-ballyhooed fight with Gerry Cooney, a white challenger, was a one-sided affair, only Cooney's courage

keeping him in the contest until the 13th round. The same could be said of Holmes' 13th challenger, Randall 'Tex' Cobb, who took heavy punishment in every round.

Holmes defeated four more challengers in 1983, one in 1984 and two the following year. On Sept. 22, 1985, however, he was narrowly outpointed by Michael Spinks, who also won on points in a return bout seven months later. He would have been well advised to have retired, but pride made him meet the formidable and unbeaten Mike Tyson on Jan. 22, 1988 and Holmes was battered into defeat in four rounds. His total of 48 consecutive wins was only one short of Rocky Marciano's record.
Score 51: w48 (34) d0 l3.

Holyfield, Evander

World Cruiserweight Champion 1986–

(b. Atmore, Alabama, Oct. 19, 1962). Began pro boxing: Nov. 15, 1984.

A Golden Gloves winner as an amateur, he missed Olympic Gold in 1984, being ruled out for throwing a punch after the referee had called 'break'. Standing 6 ft. 1 in. and weighing 196 pounds, he made an excellent start in the pro ranks, winning his first ten bouts, seven of them inside the distance. Next time out he defeated Dwight Muhammad Qawi to win the W.B.A. version of the world cruiserweight title. Ten months later he consolidated his championship claim by stopping Rickey Parkey in three rounds to obtain recognition from the I.B.F. On April 9, 1988 he was acknowledged as undisputed champion after disposing of Carlos de Leon in eight rounds at Las Vegas. He is an upstanding boxer with sharp-shooting fists, agility and a knockdown punch.
Score 18: w18 (14) d0 l0.

Honeyghan, Lloyd

British, European, Commonwealth and World Welterweight Champion 1983–

(b. Jamaica, April 22, 1960). Began pro boxing: Dec. 8, 1980.

Starting his career in London, in his first two years Honeyghan won 13 bouts, most of them inside the distance. He became British welterweight champion on April 5, 1983 by outpointing Cliff Gilpin. He retained his title in a return match eight months later with another points win, in between going to America where he stopped Kevin Austin in ten rounds at Chicago. He won the European welterweight crown by knocking out Gianfranco Rossi in three rounds at Perugia, Italy, and successfully defended his two titles, plus the British Commonwealth crown, by stopping Sylvester Mittee in London at the end of 1985. Honeyghan then rose to the heights on Sept. 27, 1986 when he caused a major upset by stopping the hitherto unbeaten Don Curry in six rounds at Atlantic City, to win the undisputed world welterweight title. He gave up the W.B.A.

version to avoid meeting a South African, Harold Volbecht, as a protest against *apartheid*, but defended the other titles successfully against Johnny Bumphus (2 rounds), Maurice Blocker (points) and Gene Hatcher (one round). He lost his W.B.C. title on a technical decision to Jorge Vacca (Mexico), who was unable to continue due to an eye injury and was awarded the decision as he was ahead at the time. The I.B.F. took away their recognition after this defeat. Honeyghan won back his W.B.C. crown, however, by knocking out Vacca in three rounds five months later and defended his title successfully against Yung-Kil Chang (ret 5) at Atlantic City on July 29, 1988.
Score 32: w31 (20) d0 l1.

Hong, Soo-Hwan

World Bantam and Super-Bantamweight Champion 1974–78

(b. Seoul, South Korea, May 26, 1950). Began pro boxing: May 10, 1969.

He won his native bantam title in his 13th pro bout by knocking out Jung-Ho Moon in five rounds. He added the Oriental title by outpointing Al Diaz, and defended it three times before in South Africa outpointing Arnold Taylor to become world champion.

Soo-Hwan Hong kept his crown against

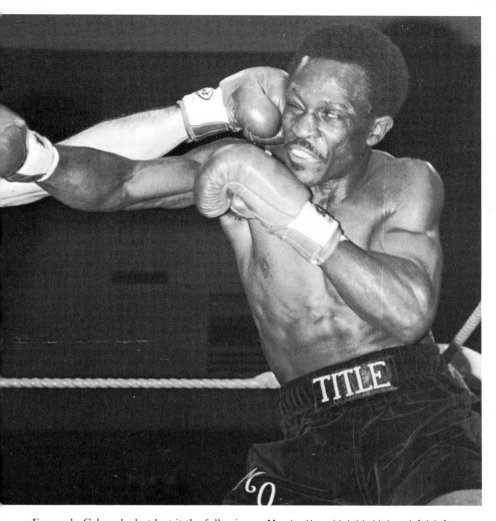

Fernando Cabanels, but lost it the following year to Alfonso Zamora, who stopped him in four rounds. Four fights later he took the W.B.A. version of the super-bantamweight championship by first outscoring Futaro Tanaka in an eliminator and then Hector Carrasquilla, who was stopped in three. He kept the crown against Yutaka Kashara with a points win, but three months later was beaten against Ricardo Cardona (Colombia) in the 12th following the referee's intervention. He retired in 1980.
Score 48: *w*39 (13) *d*4 *l*5.

Hood, Jack

European and British Welterweight Champion 1926–33

(b. Birmingham, Warwickshire, Dec. 17, 1902). Began pro boxing: Oct. 28, 1931.
A superb boxer with a classical stance in the days of the 20 rounders, he set out to win each bout on points, although always ready to end a fight decisively if the opportunity offered. In his fourth year he became British welter king by outpointing Harry Mason. Since the verdict was disputed, they met again two months later when Hood proved his superiority with another win. He defended his title against Alf Mancini, then challenged Len Harvey for the middleweight

Maurice Hope (right) is hit by a left jab from Rocky Mattioli but goes on to stop the challenger and retain his title.

crown. Their three bouts were fine examples of scientific boxing, but the best Hood could get was a draw in one contest. He kept his welter title and, in the twilight of his career, won the European crown when Adrien Anneet, the champion, was disqualified for a low punch. Hood retired in 1935.
Score 77: *w*61 (23) *d*8 *l*6 *ND*.1 *Dnc*.1.

Hope, Maurice

World (W.B.C.), European, British and Commonwealth Light-Middleweight Champion 1974–81

(b. Antigua, West Indies, Dec. 6, 1951). Began pro boxing: June 18, 1973.
An excellent boxer, strong and with a good punch, he started his pro career in England. In seven years he took so many titles that more than a third of his bouts involved a championship of one sort or another. He first won the British crown and was never beaten for it. He next acquired the Commonwealth crown, which in due course he gave up. Winning the European title, he defended it three times, and then relinquished it to go after the world title. In San

Remo he stopped Rocky Mattioli in eight rounds. He defended his title successfully five times in the next four years and then took it to Las Vegas to put it at stake against the highly regarded Wilfred Benitez, who gained his second world crown by knocking out the champion in the 12th round. On March 30, 1982, Maurice was outpointed (on a split decision) by Luigi Minchillo while attempting to regain the E.B.U. title. After the fight Hope announced his retirement.
Score 35: *w*30 (24) *d*1 *l*4.

Hostak, Al

World Middleweight Champion (N.B.A.) 1938–40

(b. Minneapolis, Minnesota, Jan. 7, 1916). Began pro boxing: 1934.
A strong, vigorous fighter, Hostak carried dynamite in his right, winning more than half his contests by stopping his opponents. He created a sensation in his fifth year by knocking out Freddie Steele for the N.B.A. version of the middleweight title in 1 min. 43 sec. of the first round. He kept the title for less than three months, losing it to Solly Krieger on a points verdict, but regained it seven months afterwards by winning in four rounds. He retained the title with a one-round win over Eric Seelig (Germany) and, after dropping a ten-round non-title bout to Tony Zale, was stopped in 13 rounds by him and lost the championship. Attempting to regain it from Zale, he was halted in two rounds and retired in 1943. There was an attempt at a comeback and he finally gave up in 1949.
Score 81: *w*62 (42) *d*10 *l*9.

Humez, Charles

French and European Welter and Middleweight Champion 1950–58

(b. Mericourt, France, May 18, 1927). Began pro boxing: Sept. 26, 1948.
This hard-hitting, competent Frenchman had an extraordinary amateur career for four years prior to turning pro. It is claimed he had about 300 contests and lost only three. As a pro he was even more successful, first as a welterweight, winning both the French and E.B.U. crowns. He eventually relinquished these to box as a middleweight. He starred with Randolph Turpin in London in an eliminator for the vacant world title, but lost on points. He gained the French crown the following year and knocked out Tiberio Mitri (Italy) to add the European title. He defended this successfully against Franco Festucci (Italy), Pat McAteer (G.B.) and Italo Scortichini, another Italian. but in 1958, when he was past 31, he was stopped (for only the second time) by Gustav Scholz (Germany) in 12 rounds, to lose his E.B.U. crown, after which he retired.
Score 102: *w*93 (47) *d*1 *l*7 *ND*.1.

Ibarra, Luis

World Flyweight Champion (W.B.A.)
1979–81

(b. Colon, Panama, Feb. 23, 1953). Began pro boxing: July 20, 1975.

A smart southpaw with a good punch, he took the W.B.A. version of the world flyweight title by outpointing Betulio González over 15 rounds at Maracay in Venezuela. He kept the title for only three months, going to Seoul, South Korea, for his first defence and losing by a knockout in two rounds to Tae-Shik Kim. A little more than a year later he won back the crown by outpointing Santos Laciar at Buenos Aires, but again his tenure of the title was short-lived. In Sept. 1981 he was knocked out in 11 rounds by Juan Herrera at Mérida in Mexico.
Score 30: *w*27 (12) *d*0 *l*3.

Izzard, Ernie

British Lightweight Champion 1924–35

(b. Herne Hill, London, Feb. 25, 1905). Began pro boxing: Nov. 25, 1920.

Standing nearly six feet but weighing only 126 pounds, he was soon called 'The Herne Hill Hairpin'. But he could box well, using a long reach, and when aged 17 won a 112-pound competition. He next won a bantam competition and then one for feathers when he was 18. In 1924, when Champion Harry Mason was campaigning in America, the National Sporting Club matched Izzard with Jack Kirk for what they called the vacant title. Izzard won a 20-rounds points decision and scored similarly when he made his first defence against Teddy Baker. However, when Mason returned home they met at a large skating rink in North London and Mason beat Izzard decisively, the latter being unable to come out for the tenth round. Izzard never had another title chance, but fought on for a further six years.
Score 119: *w*89 (33) *d*9 *l*19 *Dnc*.2.

Jack, Beau

World Lightweight Champion 1943–44

(b. Augusta, Georgia, April 1, 1921). Began pro boxing: May 20, 1940.

Beau Jack (real name Sidney Walker) was a street shoe cleaner who spent all his spare time in a boys' club where he formed a passion for boxing. He proved a busy warrior with a good punch in each hand and was a great favourite in New York where he won that city's version of the world lightweight crown, considered vacant at the time. He

Top left: Larry Holmes (right) finally ended Muhammad Ali's career with an 11th-round stoppage.
Left: Evander Holyfield (left) beating Osvaldo Ocasio at St Tropez in August 1987.

62

Lloyd Honeyghan (left) defending his welterweight title with a win over Maurice Blocker in April 1987.

produced a spectacular three rounds kayo over Tippy Larkin to win the title. Five months later he defended it against Bob Montgomery but lost on points in a return. Inside six months, he regained the crown, also on a points verdict. A third meeting with Montgomery the following year and an adverse decision saw him an ex-champion again. Beau Jack spent over a year inactive and then continued fighting for six years.
Score 112: *w*83 (40) *d*5 *l*24.

Jackson, Peter

World Heavyweight Contender

(b. St. Croix, West Indies, July 3, 1861 – d. Australia, July 13, 1901). Began pro boxing: 1883.

Jackson never won the world title, but some boxing experts consider him the greatest heavyweight of the late 19th century. A Negro, Jackson began boxing in Australia, his adopted home. Jem Mace, the great boxing instructor, had set up a boxing school in Sydney, and in Jackson he found a zealous pupil who quickly developed into a boxer of first-class efficiency. Jackson's early record is obscure but, after one abortive attempt to win the Australian heavyweight title, he stopped Tom Lees in 30 rounds to become champion. Since the best Australian

boxers were seeking their fortunes in American rings, Jackson followed suit and within a year had scored nine wins, most of them inside the distance.

He was now the obvious contender for the world title, but the champion, John L. Sullivan, refused to fight a Negro. In 1891, at the age of 30, Jackson met James J. Corbett in a fight to a finish at San Francisco, it being generally agreed that the winner would be the next challenger. After 61 rounds the decision was a draw, but it was Corbett who got the title contest with Sullivan. The next year Jackson went to London to fight for the Empire title and thrilled the members of the National Sporting Club by the way he handled the rugged Australian, Frank Slavin, who was knocked out in round ten.

Jackson did not fight again for six years, during which time he toured America in *Uncle Tom's Cabin*, a theatrical production in which his colour gave him a leading role. At 37 he took on the rugged James J. Jeffries, but was knocked out in the third round, and a year later returned to Australia where he died of consumption.
Score 41: *w*30 (16) *d*6 *l*3 *ND*.1 *Dnc*.1.

Jadick, Johnny

World Light-Welterweight Champion 1932–33

(b. Philadelphia, Pennsylvania, June 16, 1908 – d. Philadelphia, April 3, 1970). Began pro boxing: 1925.

A lively, hard-working boxer, but without a knockout punch, he fought as often as he got a purse offer. There were some nasty setbacks in his early years, but in his eighth as a pro he took a ten-rounds decision off Tony Canzoneri before his own fans and won the junior-welterweight title, as it was known in those days. When Canzoneri tried to get it back, Jadick again won on points. However, his reign was restricted to just over a year, for he lost his crown to Battling Shaw on a points verdict at New Orleans. He went on fighting for five full years, but never got another title shot and retired after a long sequence of losses in 1937.
Score 151: *w*85 (12) *d*9 *l*57.

Jarvis, Ernie

World Flyweight Contender 1927–29

(b. Millwall, London, Feb. 1904 – d. London, Jan. 21, 1963). Began pro boxing: 1920.

For a man to fight four times for a world title and not even be champion of his own country is something of a record. An apprentice boiler-maker, Jarvis was boxing at the age of 16, a nippy flyweight with busy fists, but not a lot of power in his gloves. He spent a long time in America and Canada where he had his first fling at the world flyweight crown, boxing Frenchie Belanger to a close ten-rounds points verdict in Toronto. Two years later he fought Johnny Hill (Scotland) for the British and European crowns, to a disputed points verdict. Three months later they met again and this time Ernie was ruled out for an alleged low blow in the tenth. Hill was then matched with Frankie Genaro for the world title in London, but the little Scot died suddenly, so Jarvis took his place. He put up the fight of his life, but was not quite good enough, the American winning a close decision. One more year of battling and Jarvis retired in 1930.
Score 155: *w*86 (9) *d*25 *l*44.

Jeannette, Joe

Heavyweight Contender 1911–15

(b. North Bergen, New Jersey, Aug. 26, 1879 – d. Weehawken, New Jersey, July 2, 1956). Began pro boxing: 1904.

One of a great quartet of black boxers (Johnson, McVey and Langford were the others), Jeannette was the lightest, but no less dangerous. By force of circumstances in his day, he spent most of his career fighting men of his own race. He fought Langford 14 times, Johnson ten times and McVey five times. The third meeting with McVey, in Paris, lasted 49 rounds, with McVey being put down 11 times and Jeanette 27 times). It ended with the lighter man taking the full count. He retired at the age of 40 in 1919.
Score 154: *w*72 (56) *d*9 *l*9 *ND*.64.

Jeby, Ben

World Middleweight Champion (New York State title) 1933

(b. New York, Dec. 27, 1909 – d. Brooklyn, New York, July 27, 1949). Began pro boxing: 1927.

A strong, aggressive fighter, Jeby (real name Morris Jebaltowski) was by no means a stylist. Nearly all his fights were in and around New York, starting in the minor clubs and working towards Madison Square Garden where he met Frank Battaglia, a Canadian kayo king, and stopped him in 12 rounds, the bout being advertised as for the world middleweight title. He kept his crown in a drawn bout with Vince Dundee and a points verdict over Young Terry. But, eight months after becoming champion, he lost his title to southpaw Lou Brouillard, who stopped him in seven rounds. He retired after a losing run in 1934.
Score 152: *w*117 (28) *d*13 *l*21 Dnc.1.

Jeffra, Harry

World Bantam and Featherweight Champion 1937–42

(b. Baltimore, Maryland, Nov. 30, 1914). Began pro boxing: Sept. 21, 1933.

Of Italian origin (real name Ignacius Guiffi), he was well into the fight game by the time he was 19. A swarming little fighter with a good punch, he became bantam champion in his fifth pro year by outpointing Sixto Escobar over 15 rounds. The Puerto Rican got the championship back on a points win the following year, so Jeffra turned his attention to the featherweight class, but was outpointed by Joey Archibald. The following year he had another try, and this time was successful on a points win over Archibald. He kept the crown against John Armstrong (Canada), but Archibald turned up again and once more proved his superiority with a points victory. The Maryland State Boxing Commission matched Jeffra with Lou Transparenti and when the former gained a points verdict, they named him champion again. Less than a year later, Jeffra was knocked out in ten rounds by Chalky Wright and that ended his championship status. He boxed on for several years but gradually faded out and finally retired in 1950.
Score 122: *w*94 (28) *d*7 *l*20 Dnc.1.

Jeffries, James J.

World Heavyweight Champion 1899–1905

(b. Carroll, Ohio, April 15, 1875 – d. Burbank, California, March 3, 1953). Began pro boxing: 1896.

This boilermaker's strength and size – he was 6 ft. 2½ in. tall and weighed 220 pounds – led him naturally to the ring, and for several years he acted as sparring partner for leading heavyweights. But after he turned professional in 1896, Jeffries proved he could do more than just absorb heavy punishment. Opponents found it hard to withstand the heavy body punches he delivered from a crouch, and were usually finished off by hooks to the head. In 1899, in only his 13th professional fight, he won the world title by battering the crafty Bob Fitzsimmons to the canvas inside 11 rounds. Six successful title defences followed during the next five years, including a famous 25-round struggle with Tom Sharkey, another win over Fitzsimmons, who broke his right hand trying to knock out the tough champion, and two victories over his ex-employer, Corbett, who exhausted himself in his efforts to regain the championship.

In 1905, having defeated every heavyweight contender worthy of the name, Jeffries retired undefeated as a professional, but five years later was persuaded by public opinion and a purse of £40,000 which included film rights, to challenge the feared Negro fighter, Jack Johnson. Although 35 years old and six years absent from the ring, 'White Hope' Jeffries put up a determined battle against a superior opponent for 15 rounds until the referee intervened to save him from further punishment and humiliation.
Score 21: *w*18 (15) *d*2 *l*1.

Jenkins, Lew

World Lightweight Champion 1940–41

(b. Milburn, Texas, Dec. 4, 1916 – d. Oakland, California, Oct. 30, 1981). Began pro boxing: 1934.

Jenkins (real name Verlin Jenks) was one of the few fighters whose wife, who managed him for a time, was allowed to go into his corner during a fight. Something of a tear-away, with a big punch in his right hand, he sometimes ran into trouble and, in fact was stopped 12 times in a 16-year career. He was a sensation in New York where he knocked out Lou Ambers in three to take the lightweight title. He then took on Henry Armstrong in a battle of champions, but was stopped by the renowned welter king in six rounds. After a two-rounds defence of his crown against Pete Lello, he then tried once again to go in with a welterweight champion, this time losing on points to Freddie Cochrane after a hard fight. Two months later he defended his own crown against Sammy Angott, but was outpointed over 15 rounds. He never got the chance to win back his crown and retired in 1950.
Score 109: *w*65 (47) *d*5 *l*39.

Jofre, Eder

World Bantam and Featherweight Champion 1961–74

(b. São Paulo, Brazil, March 26, 1936). Began pro boxing: March 26, 1957.

James J. Jeffries, world heavyweight champion 1899–1905, was an immensely strong fighter who could absorb heavy punishment and also provide it.

A sturdy two-fisted fighter with a big punch in each hand, he started on his 21st birthday and was soon storming through the bantam ranks, leaving a trail of stopped opponents behind. He won the South American bantam crown in 1960 on a points verdict over Ernesto Miranda and the same year beat Eloy Sanchez in six rounds to win the N.B.A. version of the world title. He made himself universally recognized as title-holder by stopping Piero Rollo (Italy) in ten rounds. He kept the title against a succession of challengers, but in his eighth defence, in Tokyo, he was outpointed by Fighting Harada and announced his retirement. Jofre was out of the ring for over three years, then came back as a feather at the age of 35, and brought off an amazing victory by taking the title from Jose Legra (Spain). He could keep his second world title for only five months, however, losing to Vicente Saldivar on a fourth-round stoppage. Jofre retired in 1976.
Score 78: *w*72 (50) *d*4 *l*2.

Johansson, Ingemar

European and World Heavyweight Champion 1958–62

(b. Göteborg, Sweden, Oct. 16, 1932). Began pro boxing: Dec. 5, 1952.

Ingemar Johansson turned professional after being disbarred from the 1952 Olympics for 'not giving of his best'. He went on to win 21 successive fights before becoming the first European to hold the world heavyweight title since Primo Carnera of Italy 25 years previously. A good boxer, Johansson carried a knockout punch in his right hand that he christened 'Thor's Hammer', a blow that won him the Scandinavian and European titles.

Johansson's manager, Eddie Ahlquist, a newspaper proprietor, imported heavyweights to Sweden as stepping-stones for his protegé and extracted the fullest publicity from Johansson's wins. His boldest move was to snare Eddie Machen, a black Californian rated only second behind the world champion, Floyd Patterson. A sensational first-round knock-out over Machen earned Johansson a crack at the world crown. In June 1959 he astounded the boxing world by stopping Patterson in three rounds after flooring him no fewer than seven times.

In a return with Patterson, however, he fought well below his best form and was himself knocked out in five rounds. But in their third clash he twice had the champion on the canvas before Patterson finally put him away in the sixth round of a thrilling contest. From those three title fights Johansson collected more than $1,500,000.

Johansson regained the European title he had been forced to relinquish when he became world champion. However, after coming perilously close to defeat by Brian London, who had him down and apparently 'out' when the final bell sounded, Johansson decided to retire at the age of 31 to business.
Score 28: *w*26 (17) *d*0 *l*2.

Johnson, Bunny

British and Commonwealth Heavyweight Champion 1974–75, British Light-Heavyweight Champion 1971–81

(b. Jamaica, May 10, 1947). Began pro boxing: Feb 8, 1968.

Brought up in England, Johnson made his pro debut at Bristol, but was based in the Midlands. After knocking out Richard Dunn in ten rounds as an eliminator for the British heavyweight title, he took the championship 15 months later by knocking out Danny McAlinden in nine rounds, the contest involving the Commonwealth crown as well. Surprisingly he lost his two titles to Dunn on points and two years later decided he would box as a light-heavy in future. A lightning one round win over Tim Wood gained him the British championship, but when he tried to add the European crown, he was stopped in 11 rounds by Aldo Traversaro in Genoa. Boxing very infrequently, he managed to keep his British crown against two contenders and win the Lonsdale Belt outright. He had a few fights in Australia and stayed there.
Score 74: *w*57 (34) *d*1 *l*16.

Johnson, Harold

World Light-Heavyweight Champion 1961–63

(b. Manayunk, Pennsylvania, Aug. 9, 1928). Began pro boxing: 1946.

A good, upstanding box-fighter with a knockdown punch, in his early years as a pro he suffered two setbacks – one a points loss to Archie Moore, who five years later was to stop him in 14 rounds in a world title fight, and the other to Jersey Joe Walcott, who

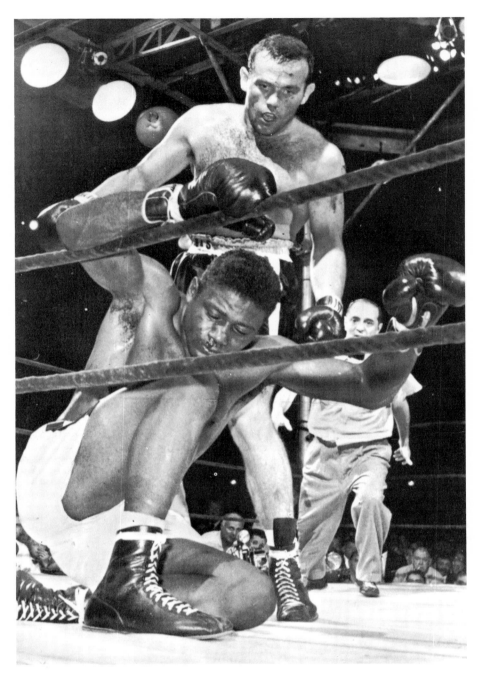

Ingemar Johansson looks on as Floyd Patterson climbs off the canvas for the seventh and last time. His victory was a major upset.

knocked him out in three rounds. Johnson had one more bad reverse in 1955 when he withdrew in the second round of a fight with Julio Medros, complaining that he had been drugged. This incident held him back and it was not until he was 33 that he got another big chance. Paired by the N.B.A. for the vacant world 175-pounds crown, he knocked out Jesse Bowdry in nine rounds to become champion. He made four successful defences in the next two years, then was, surprisingly, outpointed by the light-hitting Willie Pastrano. Johnson gave up boxing in 1971 when an unknown stopped him in three rounds, but by then he was 43.
Score 87: *w*76 (32) *d*6 *l*5.

Johnson, Jack

World Heavyweight Champion 1908–15

(b. Galveston, Texas, March 31, 1878 – d. Raleigh, North Carolina, June 10, 1946). Began pro boxing: 1897.

The career of the Negro fighter, Jack Johnson, is one of the most controversial in boxing history. Much of the attention he attracted came from the fact that he was the first Negro to win the world heavyweight title.

Ironically, Johnson developed the legendary defensive skills that carried him to the top because of the handicap of his colour. When he began boxing, Negro fighters were usually tolerated in America only if they were beaten. When they became dangerous, white fighters drew the 'colour line' and they were forced to fight among themselves. Thus Johnson developed exceptional defensive techniques in order to survive against more experienced white or desperate black rivals. At the same time he perfected the counter-punch, especially a devastating uppercut.

Johnson first fought professionally at the age of 19, and for the next 11 years gradually eliminated various title contenders without any hope of getting a title chance. Then champion Tommy Burns went on a world tour and Johnson followed hot-foot. Eventually, in Dec. 1908, Burns agreed to meet him in Sydney, Australia, for the then huge purse of £6,000 – win, lose, or draw. Johnson cruelly taunted the smaller champion while mercilessly battering him to defeat over 14 rounds.

His arrogance and his relationships with white women (unforgivable in those days) made Johnson many enemies in the United States. Unfortunately for his detractors, there seemed to be no fighter capable of beating him. The famed middleweight, Stanley Ketchel, tried in 1909 and, despite conceding 35 pounds, floored Johnson in the 12th round. Seconds later Johnson knocked him out with such force that two of Ketchel's teeth were later found embedded in Johnson's glove. White hopes soared, however, when the ex-champion, James J. Jeffries, was lured out of a six-year retirement to fight Johnson, who proceeded to dash them by thrashing Jeffries for 15 rounds until the referee stopped the fight.

Johnson jeopardized his career with an infringement of the 'Mann Act', under which he was charged with 'transporting' a white woman for 'immoral purposes'. Found guilty and faced with a year's prison sentence, Johnson fled to Europe in 1913. He defended his title twice in Paris. Then, tired of exile and, he asserted, on the promise that if he defended his title in America the sentence against him would be dropped, he agreed to meet a new hope, Jess Willard.

No one in the United States dared stage the match for fear of race riots, so Johnson met Willard in Havana, Cuba, in 1915. The ageing Negro lost by a knock-out in the 26th round and for the rest of his life claimed that he had 'thrown' the fight, but the claim is usually discounted. Johnson eventually served his prison sentence, then, after his release, boxed spasmodically for several years, and even after he retired in 1924 continued to give exhibition bouts. He died in a car crash.
Score 113: *w*79 (46) *d*12 *l*8 *ND*.14.

Johnson, Len

British Middleweight

(b. Ardwick, Manchester, Oct. 16, 1902). Began pro boxing: Jan. 31, 1921.

But for the fact that he was black, Johnson would undoubtedly have been a British champion, but was never given a title chance. A fine, orthodox boxer, he won the

Jack Johnson (right) and Tommy Burns fought for the world title in Sydney, Australia on Boxing Day, 1908. Johnson gave Burns a severe beating.

majority of his contests with points decisions. The fact that he outpointed Len Harvey, another superlative boxer, gives a clue as to his high standing. In a long career he was stopped only three times, two of these coming when he was on the point of retirement in 1933.
Score 104: *w*77 (27) *d*4 *l*23.

Johnson, Marvin

World Light-Heavyweight Champion 1978–80 and 1986–87

(b. Indianapolis, Indiana, April 12, 1954). Began pro boxing: May 23, 1973.

After a promising amateur career and an unbeaten pro start of 15 wins, he was matched with Matthew Franklin for the American title, but was stopped in 12 rounds. Seventeen months later he won the W.B.C. version of the world crown by halting Mate Parlov (Yugoslavia) in ten rounds at Marsala. He lost this title to Franklin after a four months tenure, being beaten in the eighth round. Later in 1979, however, he won the W.B.A. world crown by stopping Victor Galindez (Argentina) in 11 rounds, but again he was a short-lived champion, losing to Eddie Gregory eight months later on the referee's intervention in the 11th. When in March 1981 he was knocked out in four rounds by Michael

Spinks, it seemed the end, but this remarkable man came back to regain the world crown by halting Leslie Stewart on May 9, 1986, by which time he was in his 32nd year. He defended successfully against Jean-Marie Emebe (stopped 13), but finally lost in a return bout with Leslie Stewart, being saved by the referee in round eight on May 23, 1987.
Score 49: *w*43 (35) *d*0 *l*6.

Jones, Colin

European, British and British Commonwealth Welterweight Champion 1980–84

(b. Gorseinon, Wales, March 21, 1959). Began pro boxing: Oct. 3, 1977.

A tough Welshman with a big left hook, he won a final eliminator for the British title by stopping Joey Mack in ten rounds in his 12th pro bout. Two fights later he stopped Kirkland Laing, the champion, in nine rounds to win the title. Peter Neal was halted in five rounds with an eye wound in Jones' first defence of his crown and he added the Commonwealth title by defeating Mark Harris (Guyana) in seven. To take full possession of the Lonsdale Belt, Jones met his old rival, Laing again, and after seeming to be on the way to a points defeat, produced the punch that counts and again stopped his man in nine rounds. He won the E.B.U. title in Copenhagen on Nov. 5, 1982, stopping Henrik Palm (Denmark) in three rounds. On March 19, 1983 Jones fought the reigning champion, Milton McCrory, in Reno, Nevada for the world welterweight title. The contest ended in a draw after a thrilling fight in which Jones had done all the attacking.

In a return title contest at Las Vegas, on Aug. 13, 1983, Jones was outpointed over 12 rounds. He retired in 1984.
Score 27: w24 (21) d1 l2.

Jones, Percy

World, European and British Flyweight Champion 1914

(b. Porth, Wales, Dec. 26, 1892 – d. Dec. 25, 1922). Began pro boxing: 1911.

The mining areas of Wales are breeding grounds for fighting men and Jones was a worthy product. Fast, with a sizeable punch for a flyweight, he won a competition in his home town that started him on a short but illustrious pro career. He was unbeaten in 27 bouts when he went to London and challenged Bill Ladbury for his three flyweight titles, winning a convincing points victory. Going to Liverpool, he outpointed the French challenger, Eugène Criqui. Seven weeks later, at Plymouth, his run of successes ended when he was knocked out in the 18th round by Joe Symonds. He had been triple champion for just three months. Since he had come in overweight, his title was not at stake. However, he was again overweight when he was called upon to defend his title against Tancy Lee and was forced to give up his holdings. He resumed his career as a bantam, but not for long. Wounded in the legs while serving in the British army in World War I, he could never box again, eventually dying from his injuries.
Score 37: w28 (15) d4 l4 Dnc.1.

Jones, William 'Gorilla'

World Middleweight Champion 1932–37

(b. Memphis, Tennessee, May 4, 1910 – d. Los Angeles, California, Jan. 4, 1982).

Began pro boxing: Jan. 27, 1928.

A hard, swinging southpaw, he kept himself busy with 24 bouts in his first year as a pro and 22 in each of the two following years, but took it easy in 1931 with only 15 contests. In 1932, he knocked out Oddone Piazza (Italy) in six rounds to win the vacant middleweight crown and retained this four months later by outpointing Young Terry. He then went to Paris and lost to Marcel Thil, being ruled out in the 11th round for low hitting. The following year the N.B.A. installed him as world champion again after he had knocked out Sammy Slaughter in four rounds, and he kept a grip on this title for three years, losing it finally to Freddie Steele on a points verdict. He retired in 1940.
Score 140: w98 (55) d13 l21 ND.5 Dnc.3.

Jordan, Ben

World and British Featherweight Champion 1897–99

(b. Bermondsey, London, April 1, 1873 – d. London, Jan. 18, 1945). Began pro boxing: 1892.

One of the hardest hitting featherweights of all time, he won the British title from Fred Johnson in 13 rounds and defended it against Tommy White (19 rounds) and Eddie Curry (17 rounds). After this he went to New York, challenged the world champion, George Dixon, and beat him on points over 25 rounds. Coming home, he made a successful defence of his titles by knocking out Harry Greenfield in nine rounds. Back in America once more, he met his match in Eddie Santry, who stopped the Englishman in 16 rounds to return the world title to American keeping. Jordan made two more defences of his British crown, stopping Jack Roberts in five and outpointing Pedlar Pal-

Colin Jones (left) connects with a left hook to Milton McCrory's cheek in the latter's first title defence which ended in an exciting draw.

mer. By now 31, he decided to retire.
Score 36: w32 (22) d1 l2 ND.1.

Jordan, Don

World Welterweight Champion 1958–60

(b. Los Angeles, California, June 22, 1934). Began pro boxing: April 27, 1953.

A sound boxer, strongly built, but not a devastating hitter, he failed to win his state welter title in his fifth year as a pro, being outpointed over 12 rounds by Charley Tombstone Smith. At the end of the following year, however, he had outpointed Virgil Akins over 15 rounds to take the world crown. He beat off two challengers with a repeat win over Akins and a points verdict over Denny Moyer, but lost his title to Benny (Kid) Paret, of Cuba, who outpointed him. There were 13 bouts after that, but he lost nine of them and so decided to retire.
Score 76: w51 (17) d1 l23 Dnc.1.

Kalambay, Sumbu

European and World Middleweight Champion (W.B.A.) 1987–

(b. Lubunbashi, Zaire, April 10, 1956). Began pro boxing: Oct. 10, 1980.

Kalambay served his apprenticeship in Italian rings, winning all but one of his first 35 bouts, most of them inside the distance. In the early part of 1985 he took a trip to Atlantic City but lost on points over ten rounds to Duane Thomas. Back in Europe he won the Italian middleweight title by outpointing Giovanni DeMarco, a crown he retained in a return contest a year later. Bidding for the European championship he was beaten on points by Ayub Kalule. He made a second attempt 15 months later, going to Wembley where he caused something of a sensation by outpointing Herol Graham, who was almost stopped in the 12th and final round. He next caused another surprise when he won the vacant W.B.A. title by outpointing Iran Barkley over 15 rounds at Liverno, Italy in Oct. 1987 and he went one better when he beat the highly regarded Mike McCullum, the previously unbeaten welterweight champion, at Pesaro on March 5, 1988 in his first defence.
Score 84: w44 (24) d1 l3.

Kalule, Ayub

World Light-Middleweight Champion (W.B.A.) 1979–81, Commonwealth Middleweight Champion 1978, European Middleweight Champion 1985–86

(b. Kampala, Uganda, Jan. 6, 1954). Began pro boxing: April 8, 1976.

A big-hitting southpaw, he began his pro career in Copenhagen, Denmark, where he was living. Unbeaten in 20 starts (12 inside the distance), he stopped Al Korovou (Australia) in 14 rounds to win the Commonwealth middleweight crown and four months later defended it against Reggie Ford (Guyana) with a fifth round kayo. He gave up the title to box as a light-middle and on Oct. 24, 1979 outpointed Masashi Kudo to take the world title. He kept this against Steve Gregory (U.S.A.) w.pts. 15; Emiliano Villa (Colombia) w.ko. 12; Marijan Benes (Yugoslavia) w.pts. 15; and Bushy Bester (South Africa) w.pts 15, but in Jan. 1981 met Sugar Ray Leonard and lost in nine rounds.

In an attempt to win back his crown on July 17, 1982, he was stopped in ten rounds by Davey Moore at Atlantic City. But this amazing man was not finished yet. On June 20, 1985 he won the vacant European middleweight title by stopping Pierre Joly in eight rounds, successfully defended it against Sumbu Kalambay on a points decision, but lost it to Herol Graham, stopped in ten rounds at Sheffield.
Score 50: w46 (23) d0 l4.

Kane, Peter

World Flyweight Champion 1938–43,
European Bantamweight Champion 1947–48

(b. Golborne, Lancashire, Feb. 28, 1918). Began pro boxing: Aug. 19, 1932.

One of the hardest hitters the flyweight division has ever seen, world champion Peter Kane won more than half of his 109 bouts within the distance. His first clash with Benny Lynch, another heavy puncher, has become part of ring lore.

An apprentice blacksmith from Lancashire, Kane had his first fight at Liverpool Stadium at the age of 16, and within three years scored 41 successive wins. After stopping Irish champion Jim Warnock in four rounds he was matched with world titleholder Benny Lynch for the flyweight crown and gave the older and much more experienced champion a torrid time until he was put down for the count in round 13. His great performance earned him a return fight five months later, but Lynch failed to make the weight; the bout was reduced to 12 rounds; and the result was a draw.

Next year the overweight Lynch forfeited his crown, and Kane defeated American Jackie Jurich for the vacant title, but before he could cash in on his laurels World War II intervened and he joined the R.A.F. When eventually he defended his title, almost five years after winning it, he was knocked out in 61 seconds by the Scot Jackie Paterson.

Kane seemed finished, but two years later he surprised the boxing world by coming back to win the European bantamweight title from Theo Medina of France. He defended it successfully against Belgian Joe Cornelis, then lost it to Guido Ferracin of Italy. Following another loss to Ferracin and another defeat he announced his retirement at the age of 30. It was strange that Kane had never been champion of his own country – in fact, he never even fought for the title.
Score 109: w98 (58) d7 l3 Dnc.1.

Peter Kane, world flyweight champion 1938–43.

Kansas, Rocky

World Lightweight Champion 1925–26

(b. Buffalo, New York, April 21, 1895 – d. Buffalo, New York, Jan. 10, 1954). Began pro boxing: 1911.

Success came late in his career to Rocco Tozzo (his real name). A determined two-fisted warrior, he boxed almost exclusively around his home ground for 11 years against the best in the lightweight class before

getting a title bid against the superlative Benny Leonard who won a clear points verdict after being given a stern fight. It was close enough to get Rocky another chance, but this time he was stopped in eight rounds. Three years went by, Leonard retired and Jimmy Goodrich took over the vacant crown. Five months later he defended it against Kansas who, now aged 30, was not considered a real threat. But he outpointed his younger opponent and his dream had at last come true. As champion he had three

bouts before making his first defence against Sammy Mandell in a ten-rounder at Chicago. Unfortunately he was outpointed and Rocky retired after a long innings of 15 years.

Score 164: *w*64 (32) *d*7 *l*12 *ND*.81.

Kaplan, Louis 'Kid'

World Featherweight Champion 1925–27

(b. Russia, 1902 – d. Norwich, Connecticut, Oct. 26, 1970). Began pro boxing: 1921.

Kaplan started in American rings, mainly in New Jersey, and was a clever, well-equipped boxer who scored his many points wins with skill and precision. He took the featherweight title when Johnny Dundee relinquished it by knocking out Danny Kramer in nine rounds in New York. After two defences against Babe Herman, Kaplan gave up the crown in 1927 when he could no longer make the weight. He retired in 1933.

Score 150: *w*108 (26) *d*13 *l*17 *ND*.12.

Keenan, Peter

European, British and Commonwealth Bantamweight Champion 1951–59

(b. Anderston, Glasgow, Aug. 8, 1928). Began pro boxing: Sept. 17, 1948.

A neat precise boxer, who could use a knockdown punch when the opportunity presented itself, Keenan's greatest moment came when he fought in South Africa for the world crown, but was outpointed by Vic Toweel and the adverse altitude. As British champion he won two Lonsdale Belts outright, and he also won the European title by outsmarting Luis Romero (Spain). He lost it to Jean Sneyers (Belgium) by a surprise kayo defeat, but regained it by outpointing Maurice Sandeyron (France). In Australia Keenan won the Commonwealth crown from Bobby Sinn in Sydney, and kept it against Jake Tuli (South Africa), Kevin James (Australia), Graham van de Walt (South Africa) and Pat Supple (Canada). He was finally stopped by Freddy Gilroy (Northern Ireland) in 11 rounds in 1959 and announced his retirement from the ring.

Score 66: *w*54 (23) *d*1 *l*11.

Kelly, Billy 'Spider'

British and Commonwealth Featherweight Champion 1954–56

(b. Londonderry, Northern Ireland, April 21, 1932). Began pro boxing: Feb. 21, 1951.

Taught by his father, it was only natural that he should have a similar cagey style. He also set out to become a dual champion and this he accomplished at the age of 22, first taking the Commonwealth crown from Roy Ankrah (Ghana) on a points verdict and then upsetting the odds by outscoring Sammy McCarthy (London), who was a red-hot favourite to win. Trying to add the

European title, Kelly was outsmarted by Ray Famechon (France) in Dublin and then had a sequence of mishaps, losing his Commonwealth crown to Hogan Bassey (Nigeria) and his British title to Charlie Hill (Scotland). Billy could never regain his fine form after that. He became a lightweight, but was beaten in eliminators. Kelly retired in 1961.

Score 80: *w*54 (15) *d*3 *l*23.

Kelly, Jim 'Spider'

British and British Empire Featherweight Champion 1938–39

(b. Londonderry, Northern Ireland, Feb. 25, 1912). Began pro boxing: 1929.

No doubt called 'Spider' because of his long arms, he was a good defensive fighter with plenty of blarney in his boxing. Kelly fought all the best at his weight and won the Irish title by stopping Frank M'Alorum in 14 rounds on Sept. 2, 1935, and the Northern Ireland crown two years later by stopping Dan M'Allister in three. When the British and British Empire titles fell vacant, he fought Benny Caplan (London) and won a close battle on points to become a dual champion. Kelly did not keep his titles for much more than seven months, being stopped by Johnny Cusick in 12 rounds. It was the third time he had been beaten by the Manchester boy. Jim retired to teach his son, Billy, to follow in his footsteps, which he did most emphatically, winning the same titles as Dad had done 17 years earlier.

Score (incomplete) 64: *w*47 (8) *d*5 *l*12.

Right: Jim 'Spider' Kelly, British and Commonwealth featherweight champion, 1938–9.

Below: Like his father, Billy 'Spider' Kelly (left) was also a British and Commonwealth featherweight champion.

Kelly, Tommy, 'Spider'

World Bantamweight Champion 1887–92

(b. New York City, Sept. 6, 1867 – d. New York, Jan. 4, 1927). Began pro boxing: 1886.

Kelly was one of a number of fighters who claimed the bantam title when the recognized weight was as low as 105 pounds. He

was regarded as American champion only but when he met Chappie Moran (Birmingham, England), the bout was advertised as for the world title. Moran gained a points verdict over ten rounds, but Kelly won a return match in New York the following year, stopping the Englishman in ten rounds. He kept his crown for two years, but in 1892 was beaten on points by another Englishman, Billy Plimmer, over ten rounds and lost his claim. They fought at 110 pounds, the bantam limit having been raised by then. Kelly became American champion again by knocking out Tim Murphy in four rounds, but fought little after that and retired in 1896.

Score 40: *w*24 (15) *d*4 *l*11 *Dnc.*1.

Kenty, Hilmer

World Lightweight Champion (W.B.A.) 1980–81

(b. Austin, Texas, July 30, 1955). Began pro boxing: Oct. 13, 1977.

A colourful box-fighter with a good knockdown punch, Kenty performed mostly in and around Detroit and was unbeaten in 16 contests when he stopped Ernesto Espana to become the W.B.A. world lightweight champion. He defended this three times successfully before losing his crown to Sean O'Grady on a points decision.

Score 24: *w*22 (15) *d*0 *l*2.

Ketchel, Stanley

World Middleweight Champion 1907–10

(b. Grand Rapids, Michigan, Sept. 14, 1886 – d. Conway, Montana, Oct. 15, 1910). Began pro boxing: May 2, 1903.

One of the best and hardest-hitting middleweights of all time, Stanley Ketchel (born Stanislaus Kiecal, the son of a Polish immigrant farmer in America) had his first professional fight at the age of 16. In four years he became a star performer with 35 inside-the-distance wins to his credit and only two defeats.

In 1907 the middleweight title was vacant, Ketchel stopped Joe Thomas, a leading contender, in the 32nd round, beat him again, on points, three months later, and then disposed of Mike 'Twin' Sullivan in a single round: Ketchel was recognized throughout America as the new champion. Because of the destructive way in which he stopped his opponents, he was called 'The Michigan Assassin.'

He made two successful title defences and then gave a championship chance to Bill Papke, whom he had already outpointed over ten rounds. When they came up for the traditional handshake at the start of the contest, Papke threw a vicious right at Ketchel's chin that put him down for a count of 'eight'. The champion took three further counts in round one, but fought on gamely until the 12th round when the referee

stopped the bout. In a return contest, Ketchel knocked out Papke in 11 rounds.

In 1909, he encountered the light-heavyweight champion Jack O'Brien and floored him in the last round; only the final bell saved the heavier man from a knockout defeat in this no-decision contest. Three months later he knocked out O'Brien in three rounds, gave Papke another systematic beating, and then had the temerity to challenge the feared Jack Johnson for the heavyweight title. Although Johnson outweighed Ketchel by 35 pounds the smaller man did all the attacking and floored the champion in round 12 with a swing to the head. But Johnson came up almost immediately and in the same round put Ketchel down for the full count with a powerful right uppercut.

Ketchel had three more knockout wins, then took a holiday on a ranch at Conway, Montana. There, for some elusive reason, he aroused the jealousy of cowhand Walter Dipley, who murdered the 24-year old middleweight champion by firing both barrels of a shotgun into his back as he sat one day at breakfast.

Score 64: *w*55 (49) *d*5 *l*4.

Kilbane, Johnny

World Featherweight Champion 1912–23

(b. Cleveland, Ohio, April 18, 1889 – d. Cleveland, Ohio, May 31, 1957). Began pro boxing: 1907.

He fought in the days when pro fighters made it their sole means of livelihood, thinking nothing of 15-20 fights a year, albeit a big percentage of their bouts were of the no-decision variety in which they had no need to exhaust themselves. Kilbane was a competent workman who preferred to outwit a man rather than try to stop him. He won the world title in 1912, taking it from Abe Attell who had been champion for 12 years.

Johnny did not make any defences in the following 11 years, but stopped George Chaney in three rounds, Alvie Miller in seven and Danny Frush in seven. He was 34 when he finally dropped his crown to Eugene Criqui, a hard-punching Frenchman who knocked him out in the sixth round.

Score 142: *w*114 (25) *d*12 *l*14 *Dnc.*2.

Kim, Chul Ho

World Super-Flyweight Champion (W.B.C.) 1981–82

(b. Ohsan, South Korea, March 3, 1961). Began pro boxing: Oct. 7, 1978.

A busy fighter, he won his native junior-bantam title in his 14th paid fight, outpointing Il-Song Choi over ten rounds. On Jan. 24, 1981 he knocked out Rafael Orono at Caracas, Venezuela to capture the world title and successfully defended it three times

before Orono regained the championship on Nov. 27, 1982, when Kim was stopped in six rounds.

Score 24: *w*19 (9) *d*2 *l*3.

Kim, Hwan-Jin

World Light-Flyweight Champion (W.B.A.) 1981

(b. Kyungnam, South Korea, June 25, 1955). Began pro boxing: June 17, 1981.

The lightest of all the divisions suits Koreans, Thailanders and Japanese fighters and Kim is typical, quickly stepping into championship status by winning the W.B.A. version of the light-flyweight title when he stopped Pedro Flores (Mexico) in 13 rounds. He retained the crown against Alfonso Lopez on a points verdict, but was champion for only two months, losing his crown on points to Katsuo Tokashiki (Japan).

Score 26: *w*22 (8) *d*2 *l*2.

Kim, Ki-Soo

World Light-Middleweight Champion 1966–68

(b. Buk-Chong, South Korea, Sept. 18, 1939). Began pro boxing: Aug. 1961.

He won his native middleweight title early in his career by outpointing Se-Chul Kang and took the Oriental championship by knocking out Fumio Kaizu in six rounds. On June 25, 1966 Ki-Soo Kim surprised the boxing fraternity by outscoring Nino Benvenuti (Italy) and winning the world light-middleweight crown. He defended this against Stan Harrington (w.pts.15) and Freddie Little (w.pts.15), but lost it to Sandro Mazzinghi (Italy) on a points decision on May 25, 1968. He retired the following year.

Score 37: *w*33 (18) *d*2 *l*2.

Kim, Sang-Hyun

World Light-Welterweight Champion 1978–80

(b. Pusan, South Korea, March 15, 1955). Began pro boxing: Sept. 25, 1973.

A southpaw who spent his first three years boxing in his home town – 17 bouts without defeat – he then lost on points in an attempt to win the Oriental title from Wongso Suseno at Jakarta. He built up a big kayo record and on Dec. 27, 1978 knocked out Saensak Muangsurin in 13 rounds at Seoul to become world light-welterweight champion. He retained the title against Fizroy Guisseppi (w.pts.15) and Masahiro Yokai (w.ko. 11), but lost it on a kayo in round 14 to Saoul Mamby on Feb. 23, 1980. After winning the Oriental title from Kyung-Hwan Chae, he defended it successfully against Thomas Americo on Dec. 20, 1981, and Flash Romeo (w.ko.5) at Pusan.

Score 48: *w*41 (24) *d*3 *l*4.

Stanley Ketchel puts down Jack Johnson in the 12th round of their championship contest. However, he was himself knocked out in the same round.

Kim, Tae-Shik

World Flyweight Champion (W.B.A.) 1980–81

(b. Kanwon-Do, South Korea, July 4, 1957). Began pro boxing: Sept. 30, 1977.

Most Korean fighters carry big punches for their small size and this one was no exception. He started off by being put away himself in three rounds by Kap-Chui Shin, but soon got over that sad setback and scored ten inside-the-distance wins out of his next 12 bouts. Next he knocked out Luis Ibarra in two rounds to win the W.B.A. version of the flyweight title; retained it against Arnel Arrozal on points, but then lost it to Peter Mathebula (South Africa) on a points verdict at Los Angeles. Eight months later, in an attempt to recover his crown, he was knocked out in two rounds by the W.B.C. champion, Antonio Avelar.
Score 20: *w*16 (13) *d*0 *l*4.

King, Arthur

Commonwealth and Canadian Lightweight Champion 1948–53

(b. Toronto, Canada, Feb. 28, 1927). Began pro boxing: Jan. 21, 1946.

An excellent, stand-up boxer of great skill, who took the Canadian title from Danny Webb by a knockout in eight rounds in his 18th pro bout. He came to England eight months later to fight for the Commonwealth crown, and stopped British champion Billy Thompson, who retired with a damaged eye in round seven. King campaigned in America, but could not get near a world title shot, although he was worthy of one. He never lost his Canadian or Commonwealth titles and retired in 1954.
Score 69: *w*58 (18) *d*0 *l*11.

King, Johnny

British and British Empire Bantamweight Champion 1932–47

(b. Manchester, Jan. 8, 1912 – d. London, March 10, 1963). Began pro boxing: May 15, 1927.

One of Manchester's great triumvirate of champions in the 1930s, King did everything but win a world title and he tried hard enough to do that, being outpointed by that freak bantam, Al Brown, after 15 exciting rounds with the title at stake in July 1933.

At 15 he won a 7 stone (98 pounds) Belt competition and progressed as he grew. A straightforward boxer, he lacked the imagination that makes for sensation, yet he was a champion for a long while. He won two Lonsdale Belts outright and the Com-

monwealth crown by outpointing Bobby Leitham (Canada). He challenged famous Nel Tarleton for the featherweight title and lost on points, and he went the distance with Freddie Miller, the world featherweight champion, which was something of a performance. World War II interfered with his career, especially when he was serving aboard the *Prince of Wales* when she was sunk by the Japanese, but King came back and returned to the ring for a few more bouts, retiring after he had lost his bantam titles to southpaw Jackie Paterson by a knockout in seven rounds in 1947.
Score 193: *w*139 (66) *d*10 *l*43 *ND*.1.

Kingpetch, Pone

World Flyweight Champion 1960–65

(b. Hui Hui, Thailand, Feb. 12, 1936 – d. Ramanthi, Bangkok, Thailand, May 31, 1982). Began pro boxing: 1955.

One of the first Thailanders to reach world prominence, this capable little boxer did not fight out of Bangkok until he became champion. He won the Oriental flyweight title at the start of his third year as a pro by outpointing Danny Kid over 12 rounds in 1957. He kept this for just over a year and then caused an upset by taking the world crown from brilliant Pascual Perez (Argentina) outpointing him over 15 rounds. Hopeful of getting it back, Perez enticed Kingpetch

to Los Angeles (the first time he had been out of Thailand) and received a shock when Kingpetch knocked him out in eight rounds. Pone then made three trips to Tokyo, with two successful defences, but on the third occasion suffered a knockout in 11 rounds by Fighting Harada to lose his crown. He won it back by outpointing Harada in Bangkok; lost it to Hiroyuki Ebihara by a disastrous one round defeat (2 min. 7 sec.) in Tokyo, and then regained the title by outpointing Ebihara in his home city. Fifteen months later he went to Rome and lost the title to Salvatore Burruni on a points verdict, after which at the age of 30, he retired. Kingpetch died of pneumonia in 1982.
Score 40: *w*33 (11) *d*0 *l*7.

Klaus, Frank

World Middleweight Champion 1912–13

(b. Pittsburgh, Pennsylvania, Dec. 30, 1887 – d. Pittsburgh, Pennsylvania, Feb. 8, 1948). Began pro boxing: 1904.

Klaus was a strong, thick-set, aggressive fighter, who was very dangerous at close range. Except for two ten-rounds points losses, he was unbeaten in his first seven years as a pro, in which he engaged in 73 contests. His ability to absorb punishment and outbox his rivals eventually was extraordinary. In 1912 he went to Paris to fight Georges Carpentier in what was advertised as for the world middleweight title. By the 19th round he had reduced the Frenchman to such a state of weakness that his manager climbed into the ring to stop the fight, whereupon Klaus was given the verdict on a foul. The following year, also in Paris, he won on a foul over Billy Papke (U.S.A.), a strong claimant to the middleweight throne, who hit low and paid the penalty. Seven months later, to general surprise, the tough Klaus was knocked out by George Chip in six rounds. Neither Frank nor his supporters could believe it, but in a return match, two months later, Chip did it again, this time in five. Klaus retired.
Score 88: *w*64 (26) *d*9 *l*11 *ND*.4.

Klick, Frankie

World Junior-Lightweight Champion 1933–35

(b. San Francisco, California, May 5, 1907 – d. San Francisco, May 18, 1952). Began pro boxing: Oct. 29, 1924.

A speedy box-fighter with a knockdown punch when he felt like it, he spent the first nine years of his pro career in and around his home State. Klick went to New York in 1932 and in little more than a year he was matched with Kid Chocolate for his junior-lightweight crown and caused something of a

surprise by stopping the Cuban bonbon in seven rounds. He never defended his title, but instead put on weight and challenged Barney Ross for his light-welterweight title and held him to a draw over ten rounds. They met again ten months later, but this time Ross proved his superiority over 15 rounds. Klick went on boxing for a while, but retired in 1939.
Score 120: *w*81 (24) *d*12 *l*26 *Dnc*.1.

Kobayashi, Hiroshi

World Junior-Lightweight Champion, 1967–71

(b. Isesaki, Japan, July 2, 1962). Began pro boxing: July 2, 1962.

He won his native featherweight title in his third year as a pro, retaining this against five challengers. On Dec. 14, 1967, he knocked out Yoshiaki Numata in 12 rounds to win the

world junior-lightweight title, putting it at stake successfully against Rene Barrientos (draw 15), Jaime Valladares (points 15), Antonio Amaya (points 15), Carlos Canete (points 15), Antonio Amaya (points 15) and Ricardo Arrendondo (points 15). He lost his crown to Alfredo Marcano by a kayo in ten rounds on October 1, 1971. A seven-round defeat by Roberto Duran three months later ended his career.
Score 74: *w*60 (11) *d*4 *l*10.

Kobayashi, Kazuo

World Super-Bantamweight Champion (W.B.C.) 1976

(b. Fukuoka, Japan, Oct. 10, 1949). Began pro boxing: Feb. 25, 1973.

A hard hitter, he boxed exclusively in his own country for three years. His big chance arrived when they brought Alexis Arguello

Pone Kingpetch (right) on his way to a points win over Mitsunori Seki of Japan. He was the first of many Thais to be a world champion.

to Tokyo to defend his W.B.A. version of the world featherweight title, but his Japanese challenger was knocked out in five rounds, whereupon Kobayashi took off a few pounds and went after the super-bantam crown. Stopping Rigoberto Riasco in eight rounds gained him the championship, but only for 45 days, as he lost it on points to Dong-Kyun Yum in Korea. Two months later Kobayashi tried to regain his crown but was knocked out in the third round by Wilfredo Gomez. He had another try a year later and this time was stopped in 13 rounds by Eusebio Pedroza. After that he confined himself to winning the Orient featherweight title and proudly keeping it until Oct. 18, 1981 when Jung-Hwan Hwang took it from him with a one round win.
Score 43: w35 (26) d0 l8.

Kotey, David 'Poison'

World (W.B.C.) and Commonwealth Featherweight Champion 1974–78

(b. Accra, Ghana, Dec. 7, 1950). Began pro boxing: Feb. 5, 1966.

Kotey disposed of so many of his opponents inside the distance that they called him 'Poison'. A strong fighter, he gained the African title on Feb. 2, 1974 with a first round knockout win over Tahar Ben Hassen, then compelled Evan Armstrong (Scotland) to retire in ten rounds with the Commonwealth title at stake. He won the W.B.C. version of the world title by outpointing Ruben Olivares and made two successful defences before losing it on points to Danny Lopez. He regained his native title by outpointing Laurent Bazie in Accra, but in trying to win back the world crown was stopped by Lopez in eight rounds. The same year he was deprived of his Commonwealth crown by Eddie Ndukwu (Nigeria) and with that defeat decided to retire.
Score 45: w38 (23) d1 l6.

Kreiger, Solly

World Middleweight Champion 1938–39

(b. New York, March 28, 1909 – d. Las Vegas, Nevada, Sep. 24, 1965). Began pro boxing: Dec. 22, 1928.

A husky, hard-punching fighter in the true American pattern, he spent most of his career performing in New York rings, but had to go to Seattle, after ten years of hard going, to get his title chance. Opposed to Al Hostak, a noted kayo expert, Solly took a 15 rounds points decision to become holder of the N.B.A. version of the 160 pounds title. He had seven bouts while champion, twice losing to Billy Conn over 12 rounds. Then he returned to Seattle to give Hostak a return fight, found him in his true form and suffered a knockout defeat in four rounds. He had been champion for seven months. After that he competed unsuccessfully among the light-heavies, and retired in 1941.
Score 112: w81 (54) d7 l24.

Kudo, Masashi

World Light-Middleweight Champion 1978–79

(b. Gojonome, Japan, Aug. 24, 1951). Began pro boxing: May 18, 1973.

A strong fighter with a good punch, he won his native middleweight title in his sixth pro bout by outpointing Nubuyoshi over ten rounds. He retained this eight times in the next three years, then reduced to the light-middle limit of 154 pounds and captured the world crown from Eddie Gazo over 15 rounds. After successful defences against Joo-Ho and Manuel Gonzalez, he lost on points to Ayub Kalule (Uganda) and did not box thereafter.
Score 24: w23 (16) d0 l1.

La Barba, Fidel

World Flyweight Champion 1927

(b. New York, Sept. 29, 1905 – d. Los Angeles, California, Oct. 3, 1981). Began pro boxing: Sept. 14, 1924.

A stylish boxer and precise puncher, he was also fast on his feet. He won a gold medal at the Paris Olympic Games 1924 and turning pro the same year was soon mixing with the best at his weight. In his 12th bout he won the American flyweight title by outpointing Frankie Genaro. In 1927, when the death of Pancho Villa made the world title vacant, he fought Elky Clark, the British and European champion, in New York and won on points over 12 rounds. He never defended the title and retired at the end of the year to go to university and continue his education.

La Barba returned to the ring a year later as a featherweight and after four years mixing with top-ranking opponents challenged Battling Battalino, but was beaten on points. Eighteen months later he had another try to win a second world crown, meeting Kid Chocolate for the New York version of the title plus the junior-lightweight crown, but was decisively outpointed, causing him to hang up his gloves for good three bouts later.
Score 95: w73 (16) d7 l15.

LaBlanche, George

World Middleweight Title Claimant 1889

(b. Point Levi, Quebec, Canada, Dec. 17, 1856 – d. Lawrence, Mass., U.S.A., May 3, 1918). Began pro boxing: 1883.

Real name George Blais, LaBlanche was a strong, rugged fighter, with a powerful punch. He had most of his fights in American rings and in 1886 fought Jack Dempsey (The Nonpareil) at Larchmont, New York, and was knocked out in the 13th round of a hard-hitting battle. Three years later they met again in a 'fight to a finish' and Dempsey was knocked out in the 32nd round. But LaBlanche had used the illegal back-hand

swing to gain victory and his claim to the title was not recognized. George did not mind. His popularity had increased as a result and he went on fighting until he was 32.
Score 69: w35 (17) d6 l26 ND.1 Dnc.1.

Laciar, Santos

World Fly (W.B.A.) 1981–85, and Super-Flyweight Champion (W.B.C.) 1987

(b. Cordoba, Argentina, Jan. 31, 1959). Began pro boxing: Dec. 3, 1976.

A busy fighter, Laciar had 48 bouts in his first four years as a pro. He was outpointed by Charlie Magri on Dec. 8, 1980, on a visit to London as the South American flyweight champion, a title he had just won. At Soweto, South Africa, he knocked out Peter Mathebula in seven rounds to win the W.B.A. flyweight championship on March 28, 1981, but was outpointed by Luis Ibarra (Panama) in a defence at Buenos Aires 70 days later. He regained the title by stopping Juan Herrara (Mexico) at Merida, on May 1, 1982. He then successfully defended his crown against nine top-class contenders in the next four years, relinquishing the championship to box for the world super-flyweight title at Cordoba. He was held to a draw by Gilberto Roman in 1986. In a return bout on May 15, 1987 he took the title from Roman, but lost it three months later to Sugar (Baby) Rojas (Colombia) on a points verdict.
Score 82: w63 (24) d12 l7.

Ladbury, Bill

World Flyweight Champion 1913–14

(b. New Cross, London, Oct. 14, 1891 – d. France, July 1916). Began pro boxing: 1912.

A stout-hearted flyweight with a good punch, he was the second boxer to hold the world flyweight crown, knocking out Sid Smith in 11 rounds on June 2, 1913 at the famous Ring at Blackfriars, the promoter advertising the fight as for the world crown. He held the title for seven months, losing on points to Percy Jones in a 20 rounds contest at the National Sporting Club in London. As a soldier in World War I, he did not get much time for training and lost almost as many fights as he won. Being sent to France ended his boxing career, also his life, as he was killed in the frontline in July 1916.
Score 50: w30 (10) d5 l15.

Laguna, Ismael

World Lightweight Champion 1965–70

(b. Colon, Panama, June 28, 1943). Began pro boxing: Jan. 8, 1961.

A tall, immaculate boxer, carrying a knock-down punch, he won his native featherweight title in his 20th paid bout by stopping Pedro Ortiz in seven rounds. Laguna had to

wait nearly three years before he became a title contender, then he outpointed champion Carlos Ortiz. Seven months later, Ortiz regained his title on points at San Juan and a third meeting in New York produced the same result. Three years later Laguna stopped Mando Ramos in nine rounds to become champion once again: he made a successful defence gainst Ishimatsu Suzuki but lost on a points verdict to Ken Buchanan at San Juan, Puerto Rico. Trying to win it back a year later, he was again outpointed by the Scotsman and immediately announced his retirement.
Score 75: w65 (37) d1 l9.

LaMotta, Jake

World Middleweight Champion 1949–51

(b. The Bronx, New York City, July 10, 1921). Began pro boxing: March 3, 1941.

Real name Giacobe LaMotta, he was a tough, strong, two-fisted fighter whose aggressive, attacking methods got him the name of 'The Bronx Bull'. He had to wait so long (nine years) for a title shot that he opened a small arena and became a promoter, putting himself top-of-the-bill when opportunity offered. At last he climbed into the ring with Marcel Cerdan, a fighter like himself. They had a hard brawl until the Frenchman was thrown down and injured his left arm, causing him to retire. There was a return fight clause in the contract, but Cerdan lost his life in an air crash when flying to America, so LaMotta met Tiberio Mitri instead and won on points after 15 rounds. He looked like losing his title to Laurent Dauthuille (France), but brought off a last minute kayo to keep his crown. LaMotta lost it to Ray Robinson five months later and retired in 1952.
Score 106: w83 (30) d4 l19.

Langford, Sam

Heavyweight Contender 1908–11

(b. Weymouth, Nova Scotia, Canada, Feb. 12, 1880 – d. Cambridge, Massachusetts, Jan. 12, 1956). Began pro boxing 1902.

Known as 'Boston Tar Baby', he was one of that famous quartet of black boxers who menaced the heavyweight division prior to World War I. Standing only 5 ft 7½ in., but with a massive pair of shoulders and long arms, he was a danger to anyone. Mostly he had to fight men of his own race. For instance, Harry Wills 23 times; Sam McVey 15; Joe Jeanette 14; Jim Barry 12; Jeff Clark 11 and, of course, such fights did not get him anywhere. Langford went to London in 1909 and knocked out the British champion, 'Iron' Hague, in four rounds. Although only a middleweight he gave weight and a beating to a great many heavies. Only failing eyesight made him give up at the age of 44. He went totally blind and died in 1956.
Score 252: w137 (99) d31 l23 ND.59 Dnc.2.

Laporte, Juan

World Featherweight Champion (W.B.C.) 1982–84

(b. New York City, Nov. 24, 1959). Began pro boxing: Oct. 29, 1977.

A crisp-punching, aggressive feather who worked his way to a title fight with Salvador Sanchez at El Paso, Texas, in his 17th pro bout, but was outpointed over 15 rounds after a strong challenge. He won the American title eight months later by knocking out Rocky Lockridge in two rounds at Las Vegas, and on Sept. 16, 1982 took over the W.B.C. version of the world title, left vacant by the tragic death of the champion Salvador Sanchez, by stopping Mario Miranda (Colombia) in the tenth round. He defended his title successfully by outpointing both Robert Castillo and Johnny de la Rosa in 1983, but lost it on points to Wilfredo Gomez. After being beaten by Barry McGuigan, in Belfast, he made an attempt to win the world super-featherweight crown but lost on points to Julio Chavez in New York on Dec. 12, 1986.
Score 34: w27 (14) d0 l7 Dnc.1.

Larkin, Tippy

World Light-Welterweight Champion 1946

(b. Garfield, New Jersey, Nov. 11, 1917). Began pro boxing: March 14, 1935.

Real name Antonio Pilleteri, he boxed during most of his early career in New Jersey and New York, keeping busy with plenty of bouts and lots of energy. A chance at a title came at the end of his seventh year as a pro when he was paired with Beau Jack for the New York version of the lightweight title. This was followed by a two rounds kayo loss to Henry Armstrong, so it seemed that Tippy was aiming a bit too high for his capabilities. Over three years went by and then he and Willie Joyce were matched to fight for the vacant light-welterweight title; this time he was successful, winning a points decision after 12 fast rounds. Five months later he again defeated Joyce on points, but thereafter lost all interest in being a champion and went on fighting anyone and anywhere until 1952 when he retired.
Score 154: w136 (58) d1 l16 Dnc.1.

Lastra, Cecilio

World Featherweight Champion (W.B.A.) 1977–78

(b. Santander, Spain, Aug. 12, 1951). Began pro boxing: Dec. 20, 1975.

Lastra was a hard, aggressive fighter who rarely fought out of his own country. He became champion of Spain in his second year as a pro, outpointing Isidore Cabeza before his own fans. He lost this on a knockout in 11 rounds to Roberto Castanon within three months, but took the W.B.A.

version of the world crown by outpointing Rafael Ortega (Panama) before the year was out. At his first defence, four months later, he lost his world title to Eusebio Pedroza by a knockout in 13 rounds in Panama City. He became Spanish champion again and then tried for the European title, but was outpointed by Roberto Castanan at Santander, twice defended his native title successfully and had one more shot at the E.B.U. title, again challenging Castanon, but losing, this time in four rounds.
Score 54: w39 (24) d2 l13.

Latzo, Pete

World Welterweight Champion 1926–27

(b. Coloraine, Pennsylvania, Aug. 1, 1902 – d. Atlantic City, New Jersey, July, 1968). Began pro boxing: 1919.

A good all-round fighter with a solid punch who entered the ring at the age of 17 and was rarely out of it for the next 15 years. He had to wait until 1926 before a title chance, then he outpointed Mickey Walker over ten rounds at Scranton, Ohio, to

Laurent Dauthuille (left) slumps into the ropes under the blows of 'Raging Bull' Jake LaMotta in the final round of their championship fight.

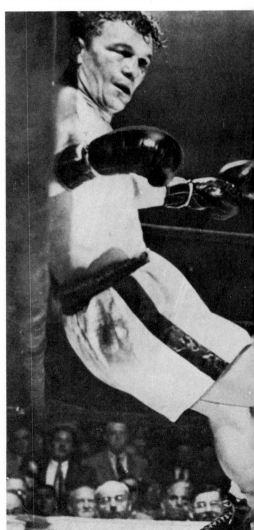

become welter king. The defeated champion did not ask for a return title fight as he moved into the middleweight division. Latzo successfully defended his title against Willie Harmon and George Levine but then came up against Joe Dundee, who outpointed him over 15 rounds. The next year Latzo tried his luck among the light-heavies, but lost twice to champion Tommy Loughran and did not get another title chance. He retired in 1934 after an abortive comeback.

Score 148: w76 (25) d6 l37 ND.28 Dnc.1.

Lavigne, George 'Kid'

World Lightweight Champion 1896–99

(b. Bay City, Michigan, Dec. 6, 1869 – d. Detroit, Michigan, March 9, 1928). Began pro boxing: Sept. 7, 1885.

Known as the 'Saginaw Kid' because he was only 16 when he began battling in this Michigan town, he quickly showed himself to be a smart boxer with a good punch. In 1894 he fought an historic battle with Andy Bowen in New Orleans. It ended with Bowen going down in the 18th round for the full count, but his head struck the boards with such force that he died of concussion. Lavigne went on his winning way and two

years later met Dick Burge, the champion of England, for the world crown in London and won by a knockout in round 17. He defended this title against Jack Everhardt (w.ko.24); Kid McPartland (w.25); Eddie Connolly (w.ko.11); Joe Walcott (w.pts.12); Jack Daly (drew20); Frank Erne (drew20) and Tom Tracey (w.20). He finally lost the title to Erne, who outpointed him over 20 rounds. He had a few occasional bouts after that, the last when he was 40.

Score 55: w35 (19) d10 l6 ND.4.

Ledoux, Charles

World and European Bantamweight Champion 1912–23

(b. Nievre, France, Oct. 27, 1892 – d. France, May 21, 1967). Began pro boxing: 1909.

One of the three musketeers of French boxing (the other two were Eugène Criqui and Georges Carpentier) he was a tireless, attacking, two-fisted fighter who defeated no fewer than seven British champions during his career. Losing on points to Digger Stanley, who claimed the world and European titles, he became French champion by stopping Georges Gaillard in 11 rounds, then halted Stanley in a return bout in seven to gain two more crowns. In 1913 he went to America and there dropped his world title to Kid Williams, who knocked him out in the 15th round. World War I kept him inactive until 1919 when he resumed his career. He was still European champion, but in 1921 lost this temporarily to Tommy Harrison (U.K.) regaining it six months later (w.pts.20). Two years later, however, when he was past 30, he was outpointed by Harry Lake in London and lost his French title to Andre Routis on points over 20 rounds. Ledoux then won and lost the European featherweight title and, at the age of 32, went back to America and challenged Abe Goldstein for the world title in New York but was beaten on points. Coming home he lost his native title to Edouard Mascart over 20 rounds and shortly afterwards retired.

Score 133: w96 (79) d4 l22 ND.11.

Lee, James 'Tancy'

British Fly and Featherweight Champion 1914–19

(b. Glasgow, Scotland, Jan. 31, 1882 – d. Glasgow, Feb. 8, 1941). Began pro boxing: Dec. 10, 1910.

This astonishing Scotsman did not begin a pro career until he was 28 and he was still at it when he was 44. He is one of the very few fighters ever to beat the phenomenal Jimmy Wilde, stopping him in 17 rounds at the National Sporting Club, London, for the British title. He should have been champion three months sooner, but the champion, Percy Jones, came in overweight and Lee

knocked him out in 14 rounds to express his annoyance. He lost his title to Joe Symonds who forced him to retire in 16 rounds and when he fought Wilde again the little Welshman gained revenge by halting him in 11.

By now Tancy was 34, but had no thought of giving up his boxing. Instead he won the British featherweight crown by knocking out Charlie Hardcastle in four rounds; Joe Conn in 17 rounds; and outpointing Danny Morgan to make the Lonsdale Belt his own property, all in the space of 15 months. He lost this crown to Mike Honeyman, 14 years his junior, and that finally brought about his retirement. He was killed in a road accident during an air-raid blackout.

Score 50: w38 (22) d2 l10.

Legra, Jose

World (W.B.C.) and European Featherweight Champion (W.B.C.) 1968–73

(b. Baracoa, Cuba, April 19, 1943). Began pro boxing: Aug. 20, 1960.

Started in Havana, but moved to Spain where he made his home. A busy, two-fisted warrior who loved a fight and carried a knockout punch. He boxed for seven years before getting a title chance and then knocked out Yves Desmarets (France) in three rounds for the European title. Stopping Howard Winstone (Wales) in five rounds gave him the world crown according to the W.B.C., but he lost this after six months to Johnny Famechon (Australia) on a points verdict. He regained the E.B.U. title by outscoring Tommaso Galli (Italy) and never lost it. In 1972 Legra became W.B.C. world champion in ten rounds, but kept the title for less than five months, being outpointed by Eder Jofre over 15 rounds at Brasilia. A knockout defeat in the first round by Alexis Arguello in 1973 brought about his retirement after a marathon career.

Score 148: w132 (49) d4 l12.

Lemos, Richie

World Featherweight Champion (N.B.A.), 1941

(b. Los Angeles, California, Feb. 6, 1920). Began pro boxing: July 2, 1937.

Of Mexican origin, he had all his early fights in Hollywood, the film stars being great fight fans. Although a tough, hard-fighting warrior with a damaging punch, it took five years as a pro to reach the top, knocking out Pete Scalzo for the N.B.A. version of the world featherweight crown. Lemos was champion for only four months, losing the title to Jackie Wilson on a points verdict over 12 rounds. A month later he was given a chance to win it back but was again outpointed. He fought on for another 20 months and then retired.

Score 81: w55 (27) d3 l23.

Leonard, Benny

World Lightweight Champion 1917–24

(b. New York, April 7, 1896 – d. New York, April 18, 1947). Began pro boxing: 1911.

A brilliant boxer with a particularly hard punch in each hand for a lightweight, Benny Leonard (born Benjamin Leiner) began boxing at 15, at a time when the Frawley Law operated in New York. Under this edict, the only way a fighter could gain a definite win was by knocking out or stopping his rival. In 1917 Leonard won the world title from Freddy Welsh in one of these 'no-decision' bouts. The Welshman had twice had the edge on Leonard in earlier no-decision fights, but this time the youngster stopped him in nine rounds.

The new champion took on all challengers, stopping most of them well before the final bell. In 1922 Leonard tried to take the welterweight crown from Jack Britton. But after flooring the champion in the 13th round he struck him while he was down and was promptly disqualified – the first and only time in 210 bouts that he was ruled out. He was never defeated as world lightweight champion.

After seven years in retirement Leonard made a comeback as a welterweight. Although 35 years old, he won 19 fights, but after he was stopped by Jimmy McLarnin he hung up his gloves for good and became a well-respected referee. He died in a New York ring from a heart attack.
Score 213: *w*180 (69) *d*6 *l*21 ND.6.

Leonard, Sugar Ray

World Welter and Light-Middleweight Champion 1979–82, World Middleweight Champion 1987, World Light-heavy and Super-Middleweight Champion (W.B.C.) 1988

(b. Wilmington, South Carolina, May 17, 1956). Began pro boxing: Feb. 5, 1977.

With all the signs of being a great champion, he won a gold medal as a light-welterweight in the 1976 Olympics and started off his pro career with 27 wins without defeat. During this time he became American welterweight champion by stopping Pete Ranzany in four rounds and then won the W.B.C. version of the world title by a surprise last round kayo of another great champion, Wilfred Benitez. Leonard kept his crown against Dave Green (U.K.) with a fourth round knockout, but was beaten on points by Roberto Duran, another famed fighter. Sugar Ray regained this title by the curious retirement of Duran in round eight and defended it successfully against Larry Bonds (U.S.A.). Within three months he gained a second world crown by knocking out Ayub Kalule (Uganda) in nine rounds for the light-middleweight title and then made himself the undisputed welterweight king by halting the W.B.A. champion, Tho-

mas Hearns, in the 14th round of a fight he was on the point of losing. On Feb. 15, 1982 he defended his welter crown by stopping Bruce Finch (U.S.A.) in three rounds and then had to undergo an operation for a detached retina of the eye, which led to his temporary retirement on Nov. 9, 1982. He made a comeback in 1984, stopping Kevin Howard in nine rounds. He retired again, but then created a sensation by making a second come-back in 1987 and securing a close decision over the redoubtable Marvin Hagler to become the W.B.C. middleweight champion of the world. He immediately relinquished the title, but intimated that he might fight yet again. He kept his promise on Nov. 7, 1988 when he stopped Donny Lalonde in the ninth round to take his W.B.C. light-heavyweight title and to add the vacant W.B.C. super-middleweight title, thus becoming the first boxer in history to win world titles at five weights. He then announced he was relinquishing both titles to consider his next career move.

Although having fought only 36 times, Sugar Ray Leonard had proved himself to be not only one of the best champions of the 1980s, but one of the greatest in the history of boxing. His bouts had commanded such fees that he was one of the richest of all sportsmen.
Score 36: *w*35 (25) *d*0 *l*1.

Lesnevich, Gus

World Light-Heavyweight Champion 1941–48

(b. Cliffside, New Jersey, Feb. 22, 1915 – d. New Jersey, Feb. 28, 1964). Began pro boxing: May 5, 1934.

World light-heavyweight champion for almost six years in the 1940s, American Gus Lesnevich was a tough and cagey performer who turned professional at 19 after an outstanding amateur career. He began as a middleweight, then moved up a division after touring Australia. He twice challenged world champion Billy Conn, but was outpointed on both occasions. When Conn relinquished his title, Lesnevich outpointed Anton Christoforidis of Greece in May 1941 for the N.B.A. version of the championship, then defeated Tami Mauriello three months later to become generally regarded as world champion.

In 1946 Lesnevich defended his title against Freddie Mills in London. He dashed British hopes in the opening round by flooring Mills several times, but after that near-disaster Mills fought back. By the end of the ninth round Lesnevich's left eye was in such bad shape that his seconds said they would have to retire him after one more round. Lesnevich came out to throw the winning punch, a long right to the chin that knocked Mills into the ropes where he was subjected to such a hammering that the referee intervened and stopped the fight.

Four months later Lesnevich tackled Brit-

ish heavyweight champion Bruce Woodcock, but was knocked out in the eighth round. Returning to America he stopped Billy Fox, a young undefeated challenger with 43 inside-the-distance wins to his credit, in ten rounds. In a return he belted Fox out in 1 min. 58 sec. of round one to establish the fastest-ever knockout in a light-heavyweight title fight.

In 1948 Lesnevich again met Mills in London. This time he lost his title on a close decision after 15 exciting rounds. The next year Joey Maxim outpointed him for the American title, but the undaunted Lesnevich promptly challenged the younger and heavier Ezzard Charles for the world heavyweight crown but lost in seven rounds. He announced his retirement immediately, and later became a referee.
Score 79: *w*60 (23) *d*5 *l*14.

Benny Leonard, world lightweight champion 1917–24, was a highly skilled boxer with a hard punch in each hand.

Levinsky, Battling

World Light-Heavyweight Champion 1916–20

(b. Philadelphia, Pennsylvania, June 10, 1891 – d. Philadelphia, Feb. 12, 1949). Began pro boxing: 1906.

The true travelling fighter, clever and cagey, his real name was Barney Lebrowitz but for many of his early years he boxed as Barney Williams. He claimed the light heavyweight crown after outpointing Jack Dillon in Oct. 1916, having lost to Dillon in a title fight six months earlier. He did not defend his championship until 1920 when Georges Carpentier (France) knocked him out in four rounds at Jersey City. Although beaten by Gene Tunney for the American title two years later, he continued fighting until 1929 when he retired after a marathon number of bouts.
Score 287: w192 (34) d34 l52 ND.9.

Lewis, Harry

World Welterweight Title Claimant 1908

(b. New York, Sept. 16, 1886 – d. Philadelphia, Pennsylvania, Feb. 22, 1956). Began pro boxing: 1904.

A clever ringster who used every trick in the trade, he fought in the no-decision era, but in 1908, after disposing of Honey Mellody (a former champion) in four rounds, Lewis claimed the world crown and was never beaten for it. In 1910 he met Willie Lewis for the fourth time. Both were in Paris and an ambitious promoter matched them over 25 rounds for the world welter title. Obligingly they travelled the full distance, the referee failed to find a winner, so a draw was declared. Harry did not bother about his half of the crown, boxed a lot in England and France and finished his career after collapsing in the ring at Philadelphia in a bout with middleweight Joe Borrell.
Score 171: w110 (47) d24 l36 Dnc.1.

Lewis, Hedgemon

World Welterweight Champion 1972–74

(b. Greenborough, Alabama, Feb. 25, 1946). Began pro boxing: May 13, 1966.

A good, hard-working, rugged fighter, it took him five years of stiff going to gain a title chance and then he was outpointed by that extremely good champion, Jose Napoles. Six months later the New York State Commission gave him a second chance by pairing him with Billy Backus, and he came out on the right side of the referee's score card: there was a return bout and Lewis again got the verdict. Twenty months later he chanced upon Napoles, who still regarded himself as world champion. Unwisely Lewis took him on to see who was the real king of the welters and found after nine rounds that it was not himself, being

knocked out. In 1975 Napoles lost to John Stracey (U.K.); Lewis challenged him, and was stopped in the tenth round. He retired immediately afterwards.
Score 63: w53 (26) d3 l7.

Lewis, John Henry

World Light-Heavyweight Champion 1935–39

(b. Los Angeles, California, May 1, 1914 – d. Berkeley, California, April 18, 1974). Began pro boxing: 1931.

A fine, upstanding, superlative boxer, he began at the age of 17 and fought his way through the ranks with many inside-the-distance wins until in 1935 he outpointed Bob Olin at St. Louis, Missouri, U.S.A. He kept his title for the rest of his fighting career, warding off challenges from Jock McAvoy (U.K.), Len Harvey (U.K.), Bob Olin, Emilio Martinez and Bob Gainer. At the beginning of 1939 he attempted to take the heavyweight crown from Joe Louis, but lost in 2 min. 29 sec. of the opening round. He never fought again owing to failing eyesight.
Score 117: w103 (60) d6 l8.

Lewis, Ted 'Kid'

World Welterweight Champion 1915–19, European Featherweight Champion 1913–14, British Feather, Welter and Middleweight Champion 1914–24

(b. Aldgate, London, Oct. 24, 1894 – d. London, Oct. 20, 1970). Began pro boxing: Sept. 13, 1909.

Pound for pound, Ted 'Kid' Lewis was probably the greatest fighting machine England has produced. This relentless attacker won nine titles at weights ranging from featherweight to middleweight in his 20-year career. And at the start of the 1970s he was still the only British boxer to win a world title in America this century.

Born Gershon Medeloff in London's East End, he began boxing professionally at 14. In 1914, after winning the British and European featherweight titles, he went to Australia, where he fought five 20-round contests in 63 days, dropping one close decision. Then a heavier Lewis moved on to the United States to fight as a welterweight. In five years in America he twice won the world title, fought 10 championship bouts, and in all won 26 fights, lost 5, and drew 2 – in addition to 63 'no-decision' contests, most of which he was judged to have 'won'. His great rival for welterweight honours was Jack Britton, whom he fought 20 times in various States.

After World War I, Lewis returned to England where he proved too experienced for the local talent in welter, middle, light-heavy, and even heavyweight ranks. He won six more British and European titles, then in 1922 confidently challenged Georges Car-

pentier for the world light-heavyweight crown. Carpentier scored a sensational knock-out in the first round, after Lewis, turning to make a protest to the referee, left his chin open. An attempt to win back his welterweight crown had already been thwarted by his old enemy Jack Britton, and younger fighters slowly stripped him of his remaining titles until he retired at 35.
Score 283: w215 (71) d24 l44.

Limon, Rafael

World Junior-Lightweight Champion (W.B.C.) 1980–82

(b. Mexico City, Jan. 13, 1954). Began pro boxing: Dec. 5, 1972.

Nicknamed 'Bazooka' because of his imposing knockout record, at the start of his sixth year as a pro he stopped Ernest Bing in ten rounds in Los Angeles to win the American junior-lightweight title. He retained this against Bobby Chacon (w.rsf.7) but when he challenged Alexis Arguello for the W.B.C. world crown, he was stopped in 11 rounds. When Arguello relinquished the title to compete as a lightweight, Limon stopped Idelfonso Bethelmi at Los Angeles to become champion. In his first defence Limon was outpointed by Cornelius Boza-Edwards, but regained the crown 14 months later in March 1982 by knocking out Rolando Navarette (w.ko.12) at Las Vegas. He retained the title gainst Chung Il Choi (w.ko.7) at Los Angeles, but then lost it to Bobby Chacon on points in Dec. 1982.
Score 64: w48 (35) d2 l14.

Liston, 'Sonny' Charles

World Heavyweight Champion 1962–64

(b. St. Francis, Arkansas, May 8, 1932 – d. Las Vegas, Nevada, Dec. 30, 1970). Began pro boxing: Sept. 2, 1953.

There was something enigmatic about the fistic career of Sonny Liston, the ponderous, taciturn heavyweight from Arkansas whose 17-month reign as world champion was anything but illustrious. Although his career lasted more than 16 years, he had only 51 contests. And although 36 of his wins were inside the distance, his encounters with Cassius Clay (Muhammad Ali) were decidedly inglorious.

Liston was born in a Negro shanty town from which he ran away at the age of 13 to run wild in St. Louis until the law caught up with him. A reform school directed his energies into boxing. As an amateur he won a Golden Gloves championship, and immediately turned professional. He stood 6 ft. 1 in. with a phenomenal reach of 84 inches and a 15 inch fist – larger than any previous heavyweight champion.

Liston was beaten only once in his first 34 fights, and that defeat was caused by a broken jaw. But those 34 fights were spread

Sugar Ray Leonard (right) taunts Roberto Duran in their second title fight, on Nov. 26, 1980.

over nine years. Two years were lost after he received a nine-month prison sentence for assaulting a policeman and quit the ring for more than a year after his release.

In 1962 Liston was favoured to dethrone Floyd Patterson, who was conceding him 25 pounds. He did so in 2 min. 6 sec. of the first round, and in a return bout ten months later took just four seconds longer to retain his title.

Liston's menacing appearance and his past record, both in and out of the ring, made him seem almost invincible in 1964 when he prepared to defend his title against the rising star Cassius Clay (Muhammad Ali). Their respective chances were reflected in the 7–1 odds laid on the champion. However, at the end of round six, Liston retired (he refused to get up from his stool) with a damaged shoulder. It was an unsatisfactory ending that aroused a storm of controversy. The return fight did nothing to settle it, Liston going down and out in the first round to a 'phantom' right to the chin that few saw, even on a slow-motion television replay. The official time was given as 60 seconds exactly, a record heavyweight title knockout, but television replays showed that the fight lasted 102 seconds with referee Jersey Joe Walcott taking a further 30 seconds to count Liston out.

An attempted comeback that lasted four years and covered 14 wins ended when Liston was knocked out in nine rounds by Leotis Martin in late 1969.
Score 54: *w*50 (39) *d*0 *l*4.

Sonny Liston (right) drives a hard right into Mike DeJohn's jaw.

Little, Freddie

World Light-Middleweight Champion 1969–70

(b. Picayune, Mississippi, April 25, 1936). Began pro boxing: April 5, 1957.

A good fighter with a fine kayo record in his first four years as a paid boxer, then for some reason he laid off from the ring for four years, returning at the age of 29 to start afresh. Going to Korea in 1967 Little was outpointed by Ki-Soo Kim, the reigning champion. In a year's time, however, he got another chance, challenging Sandro Mazzinghi in Rome. To his disgust the bout was declared 'no contest' by the referee after the Italian had failed to come out for the ninth round complaining that he had been injured. Little returned home to find that Mazzinghi had been stripped of his title and he was matched to fight Stan Haywood (USA) for it at Las Vegas. Little won on points, twice successfully defended it, but lost the crown to Carmelo Bossi on a points verdict at Monza. He was now 34 and decided to retire.
Score 58: *w*51 (32) *d*0 *l*6 *Dnc.*1.

Locche, Nicolino

World Light-Welterweight Champion 1968–72

(b. Mendoza, Argentina, Sept. 2, 1939). Began pro boxing: Dec. 11, 1958.

Starting at 19, he soon established himself as a colourful box-office attraction, his speed and variety of punches ensuring that he was never short of work. He won his native lightweight title in his third year as a pro,

then he captured the South American crown. At the end of 1968 he knocked out Paul Fujii in Tokyo to take the world light-welterweight title in ten rounds and successfully defended this five times until finally beaten by Alfonso Frazer on a points verdict in Panama City. An attempt to win back his championship failed when Antonio Cervantes, whom he had already outpointed in a title contest, knocked him out in nine rounds. Locche retired in 1976.
Score 136: *w*117 (14) *d*14 *l*4 *Dnc*.1.

Loi, Duilio

World Junior-Welterweight Champion 1960–62, European Light and Welterweight Champion 1954–62.

(b. Trieste, Italy, April 19, 1929). Began pro boxing: Nov. 1, 1949.

This fine all-round box-fighter seemed to go on for ever. He won his native lightweight title by outpointing Gianni Uboldi in his third year as a pro and was always a champion of one sort or another for the next ten years. In 1954 he won the European crown from Jorgen Johansen on a points verdict and defended it successfully no fewer than eight times over the next five years. He won the F.B.U. welter crown from Emilio Marcini in 1959, and never lost this title, with four defences. Loi gained the world junior-welter title in 1960 by outpointing Carlos Ortiz (U.S.A.). Eddie Perkins (U.S.A.) held him to a draw, then gained a points verdict over him to take the title. But not for long. Three months later Loi outsmarted the American to become world champion again. Without any more fights he announced his retirement, unbeaten for four championships. He was never stopped or knocked out.
Score 126: *w*115 (25) *d*8 *l*3.

Ted 'Kid' Lewis, world welterweight champion 1915–19.

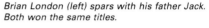
Brian London (left) spars with his father Jack. Both won the same titles.

London, Brian

British and Commonwealth Heavyweight Champion 1958–59

(b. Blackpool, Lancashire, June 19, 1934). Began pro boxing: March 22, 1955.

Real name Brian Harper, he followed his father's example and changed his surname to London, when he turned pro. As an amateur, under his true name, he won the Commonwealth Games heavyweight title and the A.B.A. heavyweight title in 1954. Strong, and hard hitting, he took the British and Commonwealth titles from Joe Erskine by a knockout in eight rounds in his fourth year as a paid fighter. Six months later he lost his crowns to Henry Cooper on points and then took off for Indianapolis, U.S.A. where he challenged Floyd Patterson for the world crown but took the full count in the 11th round. London won a lot of fights after that but never one involving a title. Dick Richardson caused him to retire in eight rounds when they fought for the European crown; Cooper outpointed him again in a triple title bout, while he put up a poor show against Muhammad Ali, who knocked him out in three. Brian retired in 1967.
Score 58: *w*37 (26) *d*1 *l*20.

London, Jack

British and British Empire Heavyweight Champion 1944–45

(b. West Hartlepool, Co. Durham, June 23, 1913). Began pro boxing: July 10, 1931.

Real name John Harper, he changed it because of his admiration for the famous American novelist. Most of his early contests were fought in the depression days of the 1930s when he had to fight hard and often for the poorest wages. It was not until 1944 that he got his big chance. The British and

British Empire titles were vacant and a Manchester promoter paired London with Freddie Mills to find a champion. London outweighed his younger opponent by about 30 pounds and this, plus his extra experience, enabled him to gain a points win. The following year he put his crowns at stake against Bruce Woodcock and was knocked out in the sixth round. Jack was 32 by now, but he continued fighting, finally giving up in 1949.
Score 142: *w*96 (51) *d*5 *l*39 *Dnc.*2.

Lopez, Alfonso

World Flyweight Champion (W.B.A.) 1976

(b. Taimiti, Panama, Jan. 9, 1953). Began pro boxing: April 12, 1971.

In his 23rd paid contest he won the W.B.A. version of the world flyweight title by stopping Erbito Salavarria in the middle of the 15th and last round at Manila. He retained this against Shoji Oguma in Tokyo on a points decision, but lost it to Guty Espadas at Los Angeles, being stopped in the 13th round. An attempt to regain the title six months later produced exactly the same result. Reducing himself by four pounds to make the light-flyweight limit, he challenged the long-reigning Yoko Gushiken in Tokyo, but lost by a knockout in round seven. He made another attempt in 1981 but was outpointed by Hwan-Jin Kim in Korea.
Score 59: *w*40 (21) *d*2 *l*17.

Lopez, Danny

World Featherweight Champion (W.B.C.) 1976–80

(b. Fort Duchesne, Utah, July 6, 1952). Began pro boxing: May 27, 1971.

A fine, aggressive fighter with a damaging punch in each hand, he started his pro career in Los Angeles with a stupendous record of 21 consecutive wins inside the distance. In 1974 he was shaken by two kayo defeats, by Bobby Chacon and Shig Fukuyama, both in nine rounds, but made an astonishing recovery and two years later won the W.B.C. version of the world featherweight title by outpointing David Kotey in Ghana. He beat off five challengers the following year and three the year after, finally losing to Salvador Sanchez, who stopped him in 13 rounds at Phoenix, Arizona. In a return title fight four months later, Sanchez did it again, this time in the 14th round, and Lopez then retired.
Score 47: *w*42 (39) *d*0 *l*5.

Lopopolo, Sandro

World Light-Welterweight Champion 1966–67

(b. Milan, Italy, Dec. 18, 1939). Began pro boxing: March 4, 1961.

Silver medallist at the Rome Olympics in 1960, he turned pro the following year and was soon making his mark among the lightweights, winning his native title in his third year by outpointing Franco Caruso over 12 rounds. He made three successful defences, then took the vacant European light-welterweight crown by outscoring Juan Albornez. The following year he became champion for the third time by gaining a points win over Carlos Hernandez (Venezuela) in Rome for the world title which he defended well against Vicente Rivas, kayoed in eight, but lost six months later to Paul Fujii in Tokyo. He lost his E.B.U. crown three years later to Rene Roque (France). Twice he tried to regain this title, but without success; Roger Zami outpointed him in Paris and Roger Menetrey stopped him in 14 rounds at Grenoble, France. He retired after one more bout, which he won.
Score 76: *w*58 (20) *d*7 *l*10 *Dnc.*1.

Lora, Miguel

World Bantamweight Champion (W.B.C.) 1985–

(b. Monteria, Cordoba, Colombia, 12 April, 1961). Began pro boxing: July 27, 1979.

Lora made a tremendous start by stopping eight of his first 12 opponents as proof of his punching power. After ten more victories, he took the W.B.C. world bantam crown by outpointing Daniel Zaragoza over 12 rounds at Miami on Aug. 9, 1985, a title he successfully defended six times in his first three years as champion, only Wilfredo Vasquez, Albert Davila, Ray Minus and Lucio Lopez staying with him for the scheduled number of rounds.
Score 29: *w*29 (14) *d*0 *l*0.

Loughran, Tommy

World Light-Heavyweight Champion 1927–29

(b. Philadelphia, Pennsylvania, Nov. 29, 1902 – d. Altoona, Pennsylvania, July 7, 1982). Began pro boxing: 1919.

Highly skilful boxer of the old school, with a perfect left lead, he outboxed most of his opponents, only coming to grief when he decided to go after the heavyweight crown. It took him eight years and a hundred contests before he could get a title chance, then he outpointed Mike McTigue, ten years his senior, to win the light-heavyweight crown. He defended this six times successfully against American challengers, then relinquished the title to box as a heavyweight. He did not do too well, but after beating Max Baer, Paolino Uzcudun and Jack Sharkey, he fought for the championship against Primo Carnera at Miami in Florida. It was a case of David v. Goliath, for while Loughran weighed around 180 pounds, the giant Italian scaled 260 pounds and topped Tommy

by 6¾ in. Still Loughran lasted the full 15 rounds to lose on points. He went on boxing for another three years and retired in 1937. He died at a home for former members of the U.S. Forces.
Score 173: *w*123 (17) *d*12 *l*30 *ND.*7 *Dnc.*1.

Louis, Joe

World Heavyweight Champion 1937–50

(b. Lafayette, Alabama, May 13, 1914 – d. Las Vegas, Nevada, April 12, 1981). Began pro boxing: July 4, 1934.

Many boxing critics regard Joe Louis as the greatest of all the modern heavyweight champions. In the first 14 years of his professional career Louis lost only once – in his 28th bout, when he was only 22. As champion he met all-comers, making no fewer than 25 title defences. Only three of his challengers stayed the full distance – Tommy Farr (1937), Arturo Godoy (1940), and Jersey Joe Walcott (1947). Both Godoy and Walcott met him again – and were beaten inside the distance. Five of his title contests ended inside the first round.

Born Joseph Louis Barrow, Louis was of Cherokee Indian stock. When his family moved to Detroit he played truant from violin lessons and spent the money learning to box. In 1934 he won the Golden Gloves title in the heavyweight class, and in total he won 43 of 54 amateur bouts, all his defeats being on points over three rounds.

In July 1934 he turned professional under manager John Roxborough. At 20 he stood 6 ft 1½ in., scaled just over 14 stone (196 pounds), and had a reach of 76 in. – ideal measurements for a young and promising heavyweight. There were 12 wins in his first professional year. Then he made his New York debut at the vast Yankee Stadium, and in June 1935, before 62,000 fans, blasted the giant Primo Carnera into defeat inside six rounds. Only a year earlier Carnera had been world champion. Three months later another former titleholder, Max Baer, succumbed to Louis' fists in four rounds.

Disaster overcame Louis the following year when he took on his third ex-champion, Max Schmeling, who floored the youngster with a right to the chin in the fourth round and finally knocked him out in the 12th. The victor was to challenge James J. Braddock for the world title, but Braddock was persuaded to meet Louis instead. Braddock floored Louis in the early stages of the contest, but Louis came back to knock him out in round eight. Louis, now nicknamed the 'Brown Bomber', defended his title against Tommy Farr of Wales only two months after winning it – the beginning of a long run of title fights that included a 124-second victory over Schmeling. At one stage Louis took on challengers so frequently that his defences were dubbed a 'Bum of the Month' campaign, but despite his conclusive wins some of his challengers were fighters of class. Billy Conn, the former light-heavyweight champion, gave Louis some anxious moments before over confidence led him into a knock-out punch in round 13.

After knocking out Buddy Baer in a single round in 1942, Louis donated his winnings to the Naval Relief Fund. Later in the year he gave his purse from the Abe Simon fight to the Army Relief Fund, then joined the United States Army as a physical training instructor. He entertained soldiers with exhibitions in American and English camps.

In June 1946 Louis returned to the ring with an eight-round win over Billy Conn. Louis was then 32, but still too good for any

Below: *Joe Louis down against 'Two Ton' Tony Galento on June 28, 1939.*

Bottom: *Jersey Joe Walcott down against Joe Louis on June, 25, 1948. Louis won both these bouts.*

ambitious heavyweight – although in Dec. 1947 Jersey Joe Walcott was considered unlucky by some experts when returned the loser of a 15-round title contest in which he twice had the Brown Bomber on the canvas. Six months later Walcott again dropped the champion but was in turn put down – and out – in round 11. Louis immediately retired as undefeated champion but income tax demands forced his return, and in a 1950 attempt to regain the title from Ezzard Charles he was outpointed over 15 rounds. He fought on for another year, until a demoralizing knock-out defeat by rising star Rocky Marciano persuaded him to hang up his gloves for good.

Although a natural boxer, Louis was quick to learn, and easily moulded into the formidable fighting machine he became, because of his ability to assimilate instruction. He owed his success to his perfect physical condition,

his positive advance behind a powerful left jab, his destructive two-fisted punches which he released with accuracy at short range, and his capacity for 'finishing' an opponent who was on the defensive. Louis was the second black heavyweight champion of the world: his exemplary conduct both in and out of the ring sharply raised the prestige of black boxers.
Score 66: w63 (49) d0 l3.

Lujan, Jorge

World Bantamweight Champion (W.B.A.) 1977–80

(b. Colon, Panama, March 18, 1955). Began pro boxing: June 16, 1973.

A capable boxer and good puncher, he was fighting for the W.B.A. world title in his 19th pro bout, winning by ten rounds kayo over Alfonzo Zamora (Mexico) in Los Angeles. He successfully defended his crown against five keen challengers in the next 2½ years, then lost it to Julian Solis on a points decision at Miami Beach. Five months later he challenged Jeff Chandler (U.S.A.) who had beaten Solis, but was outpointed in Philadelphia at the end of 15 stirring rounds.
Score 36: w27 (16) d0 l9.

Lynch, Benny

British and World Flyweight Champion 1935–38

(b. Clydesdale, Scotland, April 12, 1913 – d. Glasgow, Aug. 6, 1946). Began pro boxing: June 11, 1931.

A complete boxer, combining ring artistry with exceptional punching power, Benny Lynch of Scotland gained universal recognition as world flyweight champion when he defeated American claimant Small Montana at Wembley in 1937 after a brilliant display of box-fighting. Yet within 18 months he had forfeited his crown and British and European honours by failing to make the stipulated weight in a title defence, and soon afterwards was out of boxing for good at the age of 25.

A Glasgow newspaper boy, Lynch joined a travelling boxing booth that toured the northern counties, and soon after his 18th birthday became a professional. Right from the start his positive action and precision punching made him the idol of Scottish fight fans. He became Scottish champion at 21, and in March 1935 held Jackie Brown, the world, European, and British titleholder, to a 12-round draw in Glasgow. Six months later at Manchester he stopped him in two rounds – six knock-downs in the second round, four in the first – to become British and world champion.

Lynch won a Lonsdale Belt outright by defeating Pat Palmer (in eight rounds) and Peter Kane (in 13, after a torrid fight), but then began his long battle with the scales.

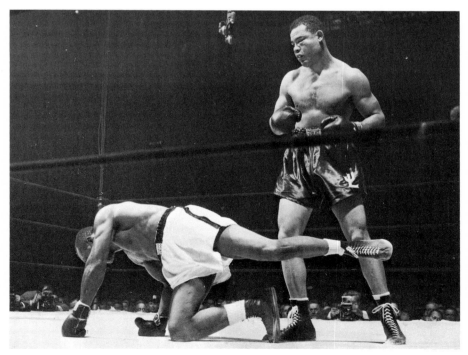

Benny Lynch, world flyweight champion 1935–38.

When he came to defend his title against American Jackie Jurich in 1938 he was 6½ pounds overweight and was stripped of all his honours. He vented his disappointment on Jurich, knocking him out in the 12th round, but afterwards went into a rapid decline.

When Lynch was knocked out for the first and only time by Aurel Toma in Oct. 1938, it was obvious that he was finished as a fighter. And, indeed, he never fought again. He died of malnutrition in Glasgow, on Aug. 6, 1946. *Score 102: w77 (32) d15 l10.*

Lynch, Joe

World Bantamweight Champion 1920–24

(b. New York, Nov. 30, 1898 – d. New York, Aug. 1, 1965). Began pro boxing: 1915.

The true professional, ready to fight wherever there was a chance to earn, his early days were those of the no-decision era, but by 1920 had fought his way close to a title fight. The reigning bantam king was Pete Herman, who was about to go to London and fight the British champion, Jim Higgins. Thinking he might lose his crown in England, Herman conveniently *lost* the title to Lynch, who kept it nice and safe until Pete came home, when he lost it back via a points verdict. Joe had to wait a year before he could be champion again, knocking out Johnny Buff in 14 rounds to do so. He kept his crown for nearly two years, with one defence in which he outpointed Midget Smith. But in 1924 Abe Goldstein proved

too smart for him and the title passed out of his hands. Lynch retired 18 months later and in 1965 was found dead from drowning in Sheepshead Bay, Brooklyn. He was never knocked out or stopped. *Score 133: w42 (29) d15 l13 ND.63.*

McAlinden, Danny

British and British Commonwealth Heavyweight Champion 1972–75

(b. Newry, Northern Ireland, June 1, 1948). Began pro boxing: July 7, 1969.

On the short side, but a heavy puncher at close range. He started his pro career by winning a novice competition, defeating his three opponents by knockouts on the same night. In his third year McAlinden disposed of southpaw Jack Bodell in two rounds at Birmingham to win the British and Commonwealth heavyweight titles and become the first Irishman to do so. However, he had only five bouts in the next two years and when making the first defence of his two crowns was knocked out by Bunny Johnson in nine rounds. A year later Johnson repeated the dose with another nine rounds win, after which Danny boxed very infrequently until another knockout defeat – by Denton Ruddock – caused his retirement in 1981. *Score 45: w31 (28) d2 l12.*

McAteer, Pat

British and Commonwealth Middleweight Champion 1955–58

(b. Birkenhead, Cheshire, March 17, 1932). Began pro boxing: Sept. 11, 1952.

A gifted boxer with a neat style and a good punch, he won his 35 bouts, mostly staged in Liverpool where he defeated Johnny Sullivan for the British title on a low blow foul in round nine. Seeking to add the Commonwealth crown, he went to South Africa and outpointed Mike Holt over 15 rounds. He defended these against Lew Lazer, but when trying for the European title was stopped by Charles Humez (France) in eight rounds. He successfully defended his Commonwealth crown against Jimmy Elliott and both titles against Martin Hansen. After first drawing with Dick Tiger, he then lost both titles to him, being stopped in the ninth. Following an eight rounds loss on points to Terry Downes in 1958, he decided to retire. *Score 56: w48 (23) d2 l6.*

McAuliffe, Jack

World Lightweight Champion 1887–97

(b. Cork, Ireland, March 24, 1866 – d. Forest Hills, New York, Nov. 5, 1937). Began pro boxing: July 1, 1884.

One of the few boxers to go through a career without defeat, he must have left his home for America at an early age because he was fighting in New York when he was 18. Two years later he fought Jack Hopper in what was regarded as for the American lightweight title and he won in 17 rounds. Eight months afterwards he knocked out Bill Frazier in 21 rounds to remain champion and in another defence disposed of Harry Gilmore in 28 rounds. Late in 1887, Jem Carney, the English champion, arrived in the United States and was matched with McAuliffe for the world championship. They fought at Revere in Massachusetts and Carney was getting the better of things when, in the 74th round, the ring was broken into by the American's supporters and the fight came to an end, the referee deciding that the result must be a draw. Both claimed the title and in the next few years McAuliffe made two defences, beating Bill Dacey in 11 rounds and Billy Myer in 15. He retired unbeaten in 1897. *Score 36: w31 (22) d5 l0.*

McAvoy, Jock

British Light-Heavy and Middleweight Champion 1933–37

(b. Burnley, Lancashire, Nov. 20, 1908 – d. Rochdale, Nov. 20, 1971). Began pro boxing: Nov. 6, 1927.

McAvoy's real name was Joseph Bamford, and he changed it so that his widowed mother should not know that he spent Sunday afternoons boxing in a small arena at Royton. A very strong middleweight, with great punching power, he ran up an impressive record as he moved towards a title fight. Outpointed by Len Harvey in an attempt to win the British middleweight title, he succeeded a year later and beat off challenges

from Archie Sexton and Al Burke to make the Lonsdale Belt his own property. He went to America and caused a surprise by knocking out Ed (Babe) Risko, the world champion, in the first of a ten-round non-title bout. He challenged John Henry Lewis for the world light-heavy crown, but lost on points. Back home, he tried to take the British heavyweight title from Jack Petersen, but again was outpointed. He knocked out Eddie Phillips in 14 rounds to win the British light-heavy crown, but lost this to his old enemy Len Harvey on points after a great contest. They had one more meeting, a contest on July 10, 1939 which the B.B.B.C. recognised as for the vacant world light-heavyweight title, and once more Harvey gained a points verdict, although coming close to being knocked out in the 14th round. Fighting Freddie Mills in London, McAvoy injured his back in the first round, which ended his career. There was a comeback in 1945, but after three wins, he did not want any more. He suffered from polio in the last 20 years of his life.
Score 147: w133 (92) d0 l14.

McCallum, Mike

World Junior-Middleweight Champion (W.B.A.) 1984–87

(b. Kingston, Jamaica, Dec. 7, 1956). Began pro boxing: Feb. 19, 1981.
A smart, hard-punching boxer, McCallum won his first 13 bouts, 11 by clean-cut kayos. He continued unbeaten and on Oct. 10, 1984 he won the W.B.A. world junior-middleweight title with a points victory over Sean Mannion in New York. He defended against Juiji Minchillo (stopped 14), David Braxton (stopped 8), Julio Jackson (stopped 2), Said Skouma (stopped 9), Milton McCrory (stopped 10) and Don Curry (stopped 5). He then relinquished the title to box in the middleweight ranks, but his attempt to win the W.B.A. crown failed when he was outpointed by Sumbu Kalambey at Pisaro, Italy, on March 5, 1988, his first defeat.
Score 33: w32 (28) d0 l1.

McCorkindale, Don

South African Heavyweight Champion 1930

(b. Scotland, 1908 – d. Johannesburg, South Africa, Aug. 11, 1970). Began pro boxing: Nov. 17, 1928.
The son of a famous South African athlete, one source suggests he was born in Pretoria in 1905. After an impressive amateur career, he turned pro and won his native title in his eighth bout by beating Johnny Squires in 12 rounds at Johannesburg. He went to England in 1931, won five fights and then, acting as a substitute, boxed a ten rounds draw with Larry Gains. They put up such a terrific fight there was a re-match with the Canadian's British Empire

title at stake. This was even more exciting than the first and Gains won a close decision. Don put up a plucky display against outsize Primo Carnera and stayed the scheduled ten rounds. Then he stopped five opponents in a row, and returned to his own country to drop a decision to Young Stribling in Johannesburg. Back in London he knocked out Gains in ten rounds, then went to America where he had two bouts, beating Patsy Perroni but losing to King Levinsky. In England again he had three further successes, then was badly beaten by Obie Walker in a ten-rounder. This was virtually the end and after World War II he decided to live in South Africa where he died of chronic arthritis.
Score 43: w29 (17) d4 l10.

McCormack, John

European, British and Commonwealth Middleweight Champion 1959

(b. Glasgow, Jan. 9, 1935). Began pro boxing: Feb. 20, 1957.
They called him 'Cowboy' because of his bandy (bent) legs. As an amateur this southpaw had a fine record, being A.B.A. light-middleweight champion in 1956. When he won his first eight bouts inside the distance as a pro, much was expected of him. Then he took a bad beating from Jimmy Lynas, who stopped him in five rounds. However, he won his next 14 contests and then fought Terry Downes for his British and Commonwealth titles. Downes was ruled out in round eight for an alleged low blow, but had his revenge seven weeks later by knocking out the Scot, also in round eight. McCormack continued his career and surprisingly won the European title by outpointing Harko Kokmeyer (Netherlands); he successfully defended it with a points win over Heini Freytag (Germany) but lost it to Chris Christensen (Denmark) on a fourth round foul at Copenhagen. An attempt to regain the British middleweight title, which had fallen vacant, resulted in him being stopped by George Aldridge in six rounds and there were only a few spasmodic fights after that. He retired in 1965.
Score 44: w38 (18) d0 l6.

McCormick, Tom

World, British and British Empire Welterweight Champion 1914–15

(b. Dundalk, Ireland, Aug. 8, 1890 – d. France, June 1916). Began pro boxing: April 10, 1911.
A regular soldier, he was stationed near Plymouth, England where there were plenty of opportunities to box. He learnt the art by reading a book written by Peerless Jim Driscoll. McCormick lost in the final of a lightweight competition held at the National Sporting Club in London and did not lose another bout until the end of 1913 when Gus

Platts outpointed him over 20 rounds at Sheffield. He went to Australia where there were many British, European and American fighters because of a boom in boxing. In his first bout he outpointed Johnny Summers, a fellow-countryman, in a 20 rounds bout advertised as for the British and British Empire titles. A fortnight later, he won over Waldemar Holberg (Denmark) who was claiming the world crown, a title Tom took over. Two months afterwards Matt Wells, another Briton took both his titles on a points decision and with the outbreak of World War 1, McCormick came home to rejoin the army. First he tried to regain the British welterweight title from Johnny Basham, but was surprisingly stopped in 13 rounds. He had four more bouts and was then sent to France where he was killed in action.
Score 45: w37 (19) d2 l6.

McCoy, Al

World Middleweight Champion 1913–17

(b. Rosenhayn, New York, Oct. 23, 1894 – d. Los Angeles, California, Aug. 22, 1966). Began pro boxing: 1908.
Real name Al Rudolph, his southpaw style made him unpopular and after six years, spent mostly by fighting in no-decision contests, he secured a contest in his home town of Brooklyn with George Chip, a good puncher, for the world middleweight title. His father, a poultry farmer, had so little faith in his son's ability to win that he bet a 100 chickens to a cigar that he would be beaten. Instead, McCoy belted out the champion in 1 min. 50 sec. of the opening round. As titleholder McCoy was no more liked, in fact they called him the 'Cheese Champion'. Yet he held this title for over three years, finally losing it to Mike O'Dowd, who got inside his long right lead and knocked him out in four rounds. Trying to win it back, Al was put away in three rounds, after which he retired.
Score 157: w75 (26) d24 l40 ND.18.

McCoy, Charles 'Kid'

World Welterweight Champion 1896, Middleweight Champion 1897

(b. Rush County, Indiana, Oct. 13, 1872 – d. Detroit, Michigan, April 18, 1940). Began pro boxing: June 2, 1891.
American boxer Kid McCoy, real name Norman Selby, is immortalized in the phrase 'the real McCoy'. At times he was a disgrace to the game, but the 'real' McCoy was brilliant. He is credited with the invention of the 'cork-screw' punch – a powerful knock-out blow with the first turned in a half-circle just before impact with the jaw.
McCoy had his first fight in 1891 when he was 18, and retired from the ring in 1916 after a 25-year career. He was a cunning and

skilful boxer, but many of his fights aroused controversy – particularly the one in which he took the world welterweight title from Tommy Ryan in 1896. McCoy is said to have got his title chance by pretending to Ryan that he was dying from consumption and needed a big purse to pay the doctor's bills. Ryan agreed to the contest, for which he did not even bother to train. After the 'sick' McCoy knocked out Ryan in the 15th round, bemused fans realized that with McCoy they never knew whether to expect a poor performance or 'the real McCoy' – the first use of the now-familiar phrase.

Because of increasing weight, McCoy never defended his title. He moved up to the middleweight division, and laid claim to the middleweight title after he had knocked out Dan Creedon in 15 rounds on Dec. 17, 1897. He never defended this title and then fought as a heavyweight. In 1900 he engaged in an unsavoury bout in New York with former world heavyweight champion 'Gentleman' Jim Corbett. McCoy was knocked out in five dull rounds and was generally thought to have thrown the fight. Public boxing was temporarily banned in the city.

When the light-heavyweight class came into being in 1903, McCoy was matched with Jack Root for the title, but lost on points over 15 rounds. After retiring from the ring, McCoy became a successful film actor. He committed suicide in 1940.
Score 107: *w*90 (64) *d*7 *l*7 *Dnc*.3.

McGovern, Terry

World Bantam and Featherweight Champion 1899–1901

(b. Johnstown, Pennsylvania, March 9, 1880 – d. Brooklyn, New York, Feb. 26, 1918). Began pro boxing: April 24, 1897.

The championship career of hardhitting Terry McGovern was short but sensational. When Young Corbett challenged him for the featherweight crown in 1901, 'Terrible Terry' seemed all but invincible – he had won the title the year before by a stunning eight round knock-out of the celebrated negro George Dixon, and had disposed of six challengers within 16 months, all by knockouts. McGovern's only professional loss had been on a foul. But Young Corbett knocked him out, and McGovern was never the same fighter again.

A Brooklyn newspaper boy, McGovern learned to use his fists to protect his 'pitch', and began fighting for pay at 17. He soon punched his way to the top of the bantamweight tree, and when he was 19½ he fought British champion Pedlar Palmer for the vacant world title in New York. McGovern won with almost the first punch, a right to the chin that ended the contest in 75 sec. The next year McGovern moved up a division, won the featherweight crown from George Dixon, then attacked the world's best in and above his division. He put away the reigning lightweight champion Frank Erne in three

'Terrible Terry' McGovern (right) spars with his brother Hugh, who was also a boxer.

rounds and outstanding lightweight Joe Gans in two.

McGovern was expected to repulse Young Corbett's challenge easily but Corbett did not share this view. As he passed the champion's dressing room on his way to the ring, Corbett banged on the door and shouted, 'Come on out, you Irish rat, and take the licking of your life.' McGovern was so incensed that when the bell sounded he tore from his corner to annihilate Corbett, but instead ran into a vicious right to his unguarded chin that dazed him so completely he took the full count in round two. In a return non-title bout 16 months later Corbett proved his victory was no fluke by again knocking out McGovern, this time in the 11th round. McGovern's brilliant career was over, although he fought on intermittently for another four years.
Score 77: *w*59 (34) *d*4 *l*4 *ND*.10.

McGowan, Walter

World Flyweight Champion 1966, British and Commonwealth Fly and Bantamweight Champion 1964–68

(b. Burnbank, Lanarkshire, Scotland, Oct. 13, 1942). Began pro boxing: Aug. 9, 1961.

Among the most brilliant of post-war British boxers, flyweight Walter McGowan restored the world flyweight title to his country in 1966 after an absence of 16 years. It was only a tendency to cut easily that cost him his crown.

McGowan was taught to box at an early age by his father, a former fighter who had adopted the name of the famous lightweight Joe Gans. He had his first contest at the age of ten. As an amateur he lost only two of 124 bouts, winning several Scottish titles and the Amateur Boxing Association championship in 1961. He also represented Scotland in nine international matches.

McGowan turned professional at 18, and in his tenth bout won the British and Commonwealth flyweight titles by knocking out Jackie Brown in the 12th round. An attempt to win the European crown saw him narrowly outpointed by veteran Salvatore Burruni in Rome. The following year he tried to gain the European bantamweight title from Tommaso Galli, again in Rome, but managed only a draw although most ringside critics thought he had won. In a second meeting with Burruni, this time for the world's flyweight title, McGowan won a brilliant points verdict, an achievement that gained him the M.B.E.

McGowan held the title for only six months before he dropped it to Thailand's Chartchai Chionoi in Bangkok. The referee stopped the fight in the ninth round because of McGowan's cut eye, and in a return Wembley bout nine months later the Scot was again stopped with a damaged eye, this time in round seven. Both times he appeared to be in front when the fight was stopped.

Earlier McGowan had scored a surprise points win over British and Commonwealth bantamweight champion Alan Rudkin, but surrendered these titles as well in a 1968 return bout. Both were thrilling, hard-fought battles. McGowan scored six victories over foreign opponents in the next 18 months, but was thwarted in his attempts to win a title

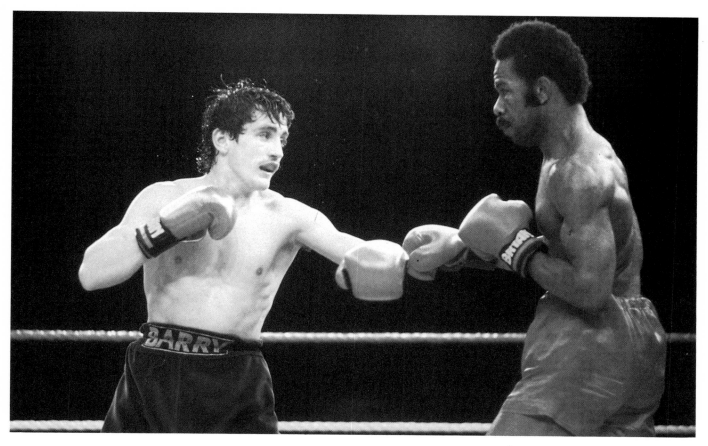

Above: Barry McGuigan (left) attacking Eusebio Pedroza, from whom he won the featherweight title in 1985.
Below: Walter McGowan, a brilliant postwar world flyweight champion, who unfortunately had a tendency to cut.

McGuigan, Barry

World Featherweight Champion (W.B.A.) 1985–86, British and European Featherweight Champion 1983–85

(b. Monaghan, Northern Ireland, Feb. 28, 1961). Began pro boxing: May 10, 1981.

Finbar Patrick McGuigan became an Irish hero from the start of his career, and apart from a six rounds points defeat over six rounds in his third bout, became a great box-office draw thereafter with a continued run of wins, the majority of the conclusive variety. On April 12, 1983 he became British featherweight champion by stopping Vernon Penprase in two rounds and before the year was out he had added the European title by knocking out Valerio Nati in six, a prize he retained against Estaban Eguia, who took the full count in round three. Every time McGuigan fought in Belfast, he filled the King's Hall to capacity. He beat off a challenge for his two titles by halting Clyde Ruan in four rounds and another for the E.B.U. crown by disposing of Farid Gallouze in two rounds. He reached stardom on June 8, 1985 when he outpointed Eusebio Pedroza, from Panama, who had reigned as W.B.A. featherweight champion since 1978 with 19 title defences. Barry confirmed his right to the championship by beating off challenges from Bernard Taylor (stopped 8) and Danio Cabrera (stopped 14), but to the dismay of his followers was outpointed by Steve Cruz, from Fort Worth, Texas, on a heatwave night at Las Vegas on June 23, 1986. McGuigan stayed out of the ring for more than a year because of managerial trouble, then returned with his old zeal and vigour on April 20, 1988 to demolish Nicky Perez of Argentina in four rounds in London.
Score 32: w30 (26) d0 l2.

McKenzie, Clinton

European and British Light-Welterweight Champion 1978–82

(b. Croydon, Surrey, Sept. 15, 1955). Began pro boxing: Oct. 20, 1976.

Exciting boxer, strong puncher and tough with it, he won an eliminator for the British light-welter title in his 12th pro bout and became champion three fights later by stopping Jim Montague in ten rounds at Belfast. He lost his crown to Colin Powers on a points verdict, but regained it from the same fighter seven months later, also on points. Attempts to add to his crown were not successful: he was outpointed by Obisia Nwamkpa in Lagos, Nigeria, for the Commonwealth title and was forced to retire to Giuseppe Martinez for the vacant European title in ten rounds at Senegalia. He won his Lonsdale Belt outright by stopping Des Morrison in 14 rounds and Sylvester Mittee on points, then reached a high point by outpointing Antonio Giunaldo (Italy) on Oct. 13, 1981 for the E.B.U. crown. He lost the title on Oct. 12, 1982 on a foul to Robert Gambini (France) in London.
Score 45: w32 (13) d0 l13.

chance. Even so, his retirement at the early age of 27 came as a surprise.
Score 40: w32 (14) d1 l7.

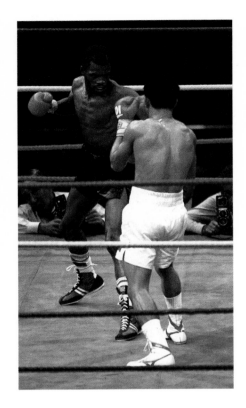

Duke McKenzie (facing camera) on his way to winning the world flyweight title from Rolando Bohol in 1988.

McKenzie, Duke

British and European Flyweight Champion 1985–

(b. Croydon, Surrey, May 5, 1963). Began pro boxing: Nov. 23, 1982.

A lively fighter and strong puncher, he came from a distinguished amateur career and soon proved his worth against the paid boys, winning his first ten bouts, most in conclusive fashion. Among these wins were five gained in American rings, where he was able to add polish to his natural fighting abilities. He gained the British flyweight crown by stopping Danny Flynn in four rounds on June 5, 1985 and retained the title by halting former star Charlie Magri in five, at the same time relieving him of his European title. McKenzie retained his E.B.U. crown with a points win over Giampiero Pinna, going to Italy and fighting at Acqui Terme. Next he defended his European crown against Agapito Gomez, from Spain, who lasted only two rounds at Wembley. *Score* 20: *w*20 (10) *d*0 *l*0.

McLarnin, Jimmy

World Welterweight Champion 1933–35

(b. Inchacore, Ireland, Dec. 19, 1906). Began pro boxing: 1923.

Few world titleholders have been as talented and successful as Jimmy McLarnin. At 18, this fast, hard-punching fighter was among the world's best, and he remained there for another 11 years, accumulating a fortune in the process. McLarnin owed much of his success to his trainer, 'Pop' Foster, an ex-boxer who 'adopted' the young Canadian (McLarnin had moved to Vancouver as a child). It was Foster's guidance that turned McLarnin into a world-class lightweight so quickly.

McLarnin's first attempt to win a world crown was unsuccessful – he dropped a points decision to lightweight champion Sammy Mandell in 1928. It was five years before he got another title shot, mainly because the boxing politics of the day were so dubious in the welterweight division he had moved up to, that Foster refused to involve his fighter in them. Instead McLarnin caused havoc among New York's leading lightweights and welterweights: he put away Sid Terris, a highly rated lightweight, in 1 min. 47 sec., the celebrated Ruby Goldstein lasted only two rounds; and in an overweight clash with lightweight champion Al Singer, he won in three.

In 1933 he won the world welterweight crown from Young Corbett III in just 2 min. 37 sec., and his three great title contests with Barney Ross, in which he lost, retained, and finally dropped the championship, were historic battles that drew enormous gates.

In his last seven years of fighting McLarnin boxed only 16 times, but he earned a small fortune on each occasion. When he retired at the age of 29 he was a wealthy man, with his ring earnings wisely invested. And when 'Pop' Foster died in 1956 he left McLarnin his entire fortune of $200,000. *Score* 77: *w*63 (20) *d*3 *l*11.

McTigue, Mike

World Light-Heavyweight Champion 1923–25

(b. County Clare, Ireland, Nov. 26, 1892 – d. Queens, New York, Aug. 12, 1966). Began pro boxing: 1909.

A true professional, cagey in his fighting, but capable of knocking anyone out. He started as a middleweight and after 12 years of boxing in all parts of America and Canada, was given up by his manager as

Jimmy 'Babyface' McLarnin, world welterweight champion 1933–35.

never likely to get anywhere now that he was 30. So Mike went to England, won four fights with ease to attract attention and found himself matched with Battling Siki, who had just taken the world light-heavyweight title with a surprise win over Georges Carpentier. They fought in Dublin on St. Patrick's Day, 1923, when the 'troubles' were on, so what chance did Siki stand? After a fight void of incident, McTigue was awarded the verdict and returned to America as a world champion. He kept his title against Young Stribling but only because the referee called it a draw. After a two year reign, he was outpointed by Paul Berlanbach in New York and lost his crown. Trying to get it back in 1927, he lost to Tommy Loughran on a points verdict, and when Mickey Walker knocked him out in a single round, most people thought McTigue would retire. But he went on until he was 38 when they took away his licence.
Score 166: w104 (53) d10 l45 ND.6 Dnc.1.

McVey, Sam

World Heavyweight Contender 1910–15

(b. Oxnard, California, May 17, 1885 – d. New York, Dec. 21, 1921). Began pro boxing: 1901.

One of the formidable quartet of black fighters who dominated the scene in their time, McVey stood 5 ft. 10½ ins. and weighed 206 pounds, and was a hard man to beat. His first recorded contest on Feb. 27, 1903, was a 20-rounder with the great Jack Johnson which, not surprisingly, he lost on points. Eight months later they met again with the same result, but a third meeting saw Johnson win by a stoppage in the 20th round. McVey fought Sam Langford 15 times between 1911 and 1920 in France, Australia, America and Argentina, most being drawn or no-decision bouts. He fought Joe Jeannette four times, on one occasion in Paris with the bout ending in the 49th round when Sam was counted out; Jim Johnson, seven times; and Harry Wills four times – these being the days when black boxers had to fight one another to keep in work.
Score 92: w63 (46) d12 l15 Dnc.2.

Mace, Jem

First World Heavyweight Champion 1866–82

(b. Beeston, Norfolk, April 18, 1831 – d. Newcastle, March 3, 1910). Began pro boxing: Oct. 2, 1855.

Regarded as the Father of Boxing, it was Mace, by his scientific approach, who really made it 'The Noble Art'. Having experienced many bare-knuckle encounters he realized that the only way boxing could be accepted lawfully as a sport was by the use of gloves. He was as skilful at teaching others to box as he was himself in the ring and it can be claimed that by his journeyings to South Africa, Australia, New Zealand and America, he taught the world the art of boxing. In Timaru (N.Z.) he discovered Bob Fitzsimmons; in Sydney he tutored Larry Foley among others; in the United States he influenced Jim Corbett, one of the first to apply science to fisticuffs. Mace toured every nook and cranny of England with his travelling show and was still giving exhibitions at the age of 70. He was also very proficient with a violin. His great rival was Tom King whom he beat in 43 rounds in Kent, England on Jan. 28, 1862. They met again ten months later when King stopped Mace in 21 rounds to claim the English title. He died at Newcastle, England, but is buried in Liverpool.
Score (incomplete) 19: w12 (10) d2 l3. Stopped by police: 2.

Macias, Raul 'Raton'

World Bantamweight Champion (N.B.A.) 1955–57

(b. Mexico City, July 28, 1934). Began pro boxing: April, 1953.

Macias had his first 11 bouts in his home city, winning the Mexican and North American bantam titles. His first trip abroad was to San Francisco where he stopped Songkitrat in 11 rounds to win the N.B.A. version of the world crown. Macias defended this in Mexico City against Leo Espinosa with a ten

Charlie Magri (left) and Jose Torres acknowledge the applause of the crowd after their second fight, which Magri won.

rounds kayo, then stopped Dommy Urusa in 11 rounds. In this third defence, however, he lost a 15 rounds decision to Alphonse Halimi (France) and with it his title. He retired in 1959.
Score 38: w36 (22) d0 l2.

Magri, Charlie

World Flyweight Champion (W.B.C.) 1983, European Flyweight Champion 1979–86, British Flyweight Champion 1977–81

(b. Tunisia, July 20, 1956, boxing out of Stepney, London). Began pro boxing: Oct. 25, 1977.

An A.B.A. flyweight champion for three years and with an imposing amateur record, much was expected of Magri and he delighted his followers by winning his first 23 bouts in spectacular fashion. He gained the British flyweight title in 1977 by stopping Dave Smith in seven rounds and the European crown in 1979 by outpointing Franco Udella (Italy) over 12 rounds. He defended this three times successfully, then relinquished his British title to seek world honours.

This ambition seemed shattered in his next fight when Juan Diaz, an unranked Mexican, knocked him out in six rounds. In 1982 he outpointed Cipriano Arreola (10 rds.), beat Ron Cisneros (w.rsf.3) and retained the E.B.U. title against Enrique Rodriguez Cal (w.rsf.2). Although stopped by Jose Torres (Mexico) in 9 rounds, he won the return contest on points.

On March 15, 1983 he finally fought for the world title when he met the reigning

champion, Eleonicio Mercedes (Dominican Republic), at Wembley, London. Magri won in the seventh round when the referee stopped the fight because of a badly cut eye. This made him the first British boxer to win the world flyweight title since Walter McGowan in 1967. Alas, six months later he lost his cherished world crown to Frank Cedeno (Philippines). Magri won and relinquished the European title, then failed in a gallant attempt to regain the world championship from Sot Chitalada, but was stopped in four rounds. On Oct. 30 1985 he regained the E.B.U. title by knocking out Franco Cherchi in two rounds, then seven months later lost both his British and European crowns to Duke McKenzie. He retired and although he had not won a Lonsdale Belt outright, the B.B.B.C. awarded him that on which he had obtained two notches, as a tribute to his great career.
Score 35: w30 (18) d0 l5.

Maher, Peter

World Heavyweight title Contender 1896

(b. Galway, Ireland, March 16, 1869 – d. Baltimore, Maryland, July 22, 1940). Began pro boxing: 1888.

Maher fought in Ireland and England before going to America where his first major engagement was with English-born Bob Fitzsimmons at New Orleans. Put down, he got up to fight back and had Bob's supporters worried until he produced the punch that put Maher down and out in the 12th round. Peter beat George Godfrey in six rounds and Steve O'Donnell in one to put himself in line for a shot at the world title, then regarded as vacant, as James J. Corbett had announced his retirement. His opponent was Fitzsimmons and they met at Langtry in Texas in the open air. It was the first attempt to make a moving picture of a boxing match, but Bob spoiled everything by knocking Maher out in the first round before the cameramen were ready. Peter went on fighting all the heavyweight contenders but never got another championship chance. He retired in 1908.
Score 77: w47 (31) d5 l15 ND.10.

Mamby, Saoul

World Light-Welterweight Champion (W.B.C.) 1980–82

(b. Jamaica, June 4, 1947). Began pro boxing: Sept. 13, 1969.

In his first eight years he did not box with great frequency, averaging less than five bouts a year. In 1977 this New York-based fighter went to Bangkok but failed to take the W.B.C. light-welter title from Saensak Muangsurin, losing on points. In the next two years he had only five contests, but in 1980 went to South Korea and knocked out

Sang-Hyun Kim in the 14th round to become world champion. Defended his title twice that year and three times in 1981 but lost the crown in June 1982, being outpointed by Lercy Haley (U.S.A.) at Cleveland, Ohio. Three attempts to regain his lost laurels – in 1982 and 1983, saw him suffer points defeats. He retired in 1986.
Score 59: w36 (16) d5 l18.

Mancini, Ray 'Boom-Boom'

World Lightweight Champion (W.B.A.) 1982–84

(b. Youngstown, Ohio, March 4, 1961). Began pro boxing: Oct. 18, 1979.

Son of a former fighter who earned the name of 'Boom-Boom', he not only followed in his father's footsteps but won a world title, which his parent never achieved. What is more he did it in his 23rd bout, after suffering a devastating knockout defeat when attempting to take the title from the renowned Alexis Arguello. Undaunted, he came back to win the W.B.A. title in the fast time of 2 min. 34 sec., of the first round against Arturo Frias (U.S.A.) and defended it two months later by stopping Ernesto Espana (Venezuela) in six rounds. On Nov. 13, 1982 he knocked out Duk Koo-Kim (Korea) in 14 rounds of a title defence at Las Vegas. The loser died without regaining consciousness. He went on to retain his title against Orlando Romero (ko 9) in 1983 and Bobby Chacon (rsf. 3) the following year. But on June 4, 1984 he lost his crown to Livingstone Bramble (rsf.14) at Buffalo. After failing to win it back eight months later, he retired.
Score 32: w29 (6) d0 l3.

Mandell, Sammy

World Lightweight Champion 1926–30

(b. Rockford, Illinois, Feb. 5, 1904 – d. Oak Park, Illinois, Nov. 7, 1967. Began pro boxing: 1920.

One of those tough sluggers who seemed to be able to go on for ever. Over a third of his fights were no-decision bouts, which were more in the nature of exhibitions than real fights. He was in his seventh busy year when he met the reigning lightweight champion, Rocky Kansas, and took the title with a points verdict over ten rounds. He kept this nearly two years without defending it, then beat off Jimmy McLarnin in 1928 and Tony Canzoneri the following year. In 1930, however, hard-hitting Al Singer took the title from him in 1 min. 46 sec. of the first round and although Mandell continued boxing for another four years, he never had a chance to be champion again.
Score 187: w147 (33) d13 l26 Dnc.1.

Marcano, Alfredo

World Junior-Lightweight Champion 1971–72

(b. Sucre, Venezuela, Jan. 17, 1947). Began pro boxing: March 4, 1966.

Marcano carried a destructive punch, scoring many inside-the-distance wins, but like all big hitters met with a kayo defeat at times. He won the junior-lightweight title in Japan with a ten rounds knockout win over Hiroshi Kobayashi in 1971, defeated Kenji Iwata at Caracas in four rounds, then lost his crown to Benn Villaflor in Hawaii on a points decision. Two years later he fought Bobby Chacon for the W.B.C. version of the featherweight title which was considered vacant, but was stopped in nine rounds. Following two more disastrous defeats he retired in 1975.
Score 61: w42 (27) d5 l12 Dnc.2.

Marcel, Ernesto

World Featherweight Champion (W.B.A.) 1972–74

(b. Colon, Panama, May 23, 1948). Began pro boxing: April 12, 1966.

One of the few fighters who retired unbeaten as a world champion, this boy carried a knockdown punch and scored many wins inside the distance before meeting fellow-countryman Roberto Duran, who was also fighting his way to the top. Marcel lost in ten rounds, the only time he was ever stopped. He drew with Kuniaki Shibata for the featherweight title in his sixth year as a pro, and ten months later gained the W.B.A. version of the crown by outpointing Antonio Gomez in 15 rounds. He made four successful defences: Enrique Garcia (6), Antonio Gomez (12), Spider Nemoto (pts), and the highly-rated Alexis Arguello with a 15 rounds points verdict. Then he announced his retirement.
Score 47: w41 (24) d2 l4.

Marciano, Rocky

World Heavyweight Champion 1952–56

(b. Brockton, Massachusetts, Sept. 1, 1923 – d. Newton, Iowa, Aug. 31, 1969). Began pro boxing: March 17, 1947.

At 5 ft. 10½ in. and 13 st. 2 lb. (194 pounds) Rocco Francis Marchigiano was not ideally built for competition against the many class heavies of his day. His fists, too, at 11½ in. were much smaller than the average (Liston's were 14), yet 43 of his 49 professional opponents fell before them inside the scheduled distance. Marciano did, however, have the physical assets of a tremendous store of stamina and remarkable durability. His short, thick legs stood their ground against the hardest of hitters, and although twice put down in title fights – by

Rocky Marciano (right) became world champion when he knocked out Jersey Joe Walcott in 13 rounds.

Jersey Joe Walcott and Archie Moore – he bounced up unhurt demoralizingly quickly and won both fights on knock-outs.

Marciano won all his professional contests, took the world title in his 43rd fight, and defended it successfully six times in three years. Only two other men in boxing history had come near his 100% performance. Gene Tunney retired undefeated as champion, but had one defeat on his record. Joe Louis retired unbeaten for his title, but failed in a comeback attempt that ended when Marciano knocked him out in eight rounds.

Massachusetts-born Marciano revelled in several schoolboy sports – boxing, wrestling, baseball, and netball – but his boxing talent emerged above the others during his World War II service in England, where he won a brigade championship and other competitions. On his discharge he wrote to Madison Square Garden for a professional trial. Given an invitation but no fare, Marciano hitchhiked from his home to New York, where matchmaker Weill was decidedly unimpressed, thinking him too small and too easily hit to go far. But in 1951, a winning run of 35 bouts totalling only 146 rounds won him a match with highly rated Rex Layne. When Marciano outpunched his hard-hitting

rival to a six-round defeat, Weill changed his views completely. He paired him with the ageing Joe Louis, and Marciano battered the former titleholder into defeat after being outpointed for most of the fight.

The victory brought him a title chance the following year with Jersey Joe Walcott, who had long forgotten more than his challenger had ever learned about boxing. Those who imagined that Marciano had been over-matched nodded wisely when he was put down in the opening round. They stared unbelievingly, however, when Marciano got straight up at 'two' and continued a relentless two-fisted march forward that eventually destroyed the champion by the 13th round. The return match was all over in 2 min. 25 sec. Then Marciano disposed of Roland LaStarza (rsf.11), Ezzard Charles (w.pts.15 and w.ko.8). Britain's Don Cockell (rsf.9), and Archie Moore (w.ko.9). Moore had the satisfaction of dropping Marciano for four seconds in the second round, but could not do it again and finally was beaten into submission by Marciano's clubbing fists.

Ezzard Charles gave Marciano one of his hardest battles, and in their second fight inflicted a cut on the champion's nose that caused him considerable inconvenience. It took a long time to heal and this injury, plus the Moore knockdown, his age, and the fact that he had earned more than four million dollars, induced Marciano to announce his

retirement, still unbeaten, in April 1956.

In 1967 he emerged the winner of a computerized series of fights between an all-time 'best 16' heavyweights, and in 1969 he 'won' his filmed computerized clash with Muhammad Ali. But it was a film that Marciano never saw. The day before his 46th birthday he died in a plane crash on his way to a public meeting.

Score 49: w49 (43) d0 l0.

Marino, Dado

World Flyweight Champion 1950–52

(b. Honolulu, Hawaii, Aug. 26, 1916). Began pro boxing: June 20, 1941.

Marino spent his first six years boxing in his own country, then went to Scotland where he won over Rinty Monaghan on a foul in nine rounds, but was outpointed by the Irishman in London when they met for the vacant world crown. Two years later, in Honolulu, he tried to take the bantam crown from Manuel Ortiz, but was outpointed. In 1950 he won the undisputed world flyweight title by beating Terry Allen (U.K.) on points in Honolulu, a victory he repeated 15 months later in the same ring. By this time he had become the first grandfather to hold a world crown. After being knocked out in seven rounds by Yoshio Shirai before his own people in a non-title fight, he gave

Dado Marino was nearly 34 when he won the world flyweight championship, and was already a grandfather when he did it.

Shirai a chance at the title in Tokyo and lost on points. In a return title contest six months later, he was again outpointed and then retired.
Score 74: *w*57 (21) *d*3 *l*14.

Marino, Tony

World Bantamweight Champion 1935

(b. Pittsburgh, Pennsylvania, 1912 – d. New York, Feb. 1, 1937). Began pro boxing: 1931.

A lucky, yet very unlucky champion. He came to New York from California and was regarded as just a good club fighter. World champion Baltazar Sangchilli (Spain) had recently arrived in New York and agreed to put his title at stake against Marino at the Dyckman Oval in Brooklyn. It was regarded as a work-out for the titleholder, and he was giving Tony a thorough hiding when suddenly in the 14th round, he was stricken with paralysis and had to retire. Lo and behold, Marino was a world champ. Two months later he met the N.B.A. bantam champion, Sixto Escobar, and suffered a bad beating before being knocked out in the 13th round. He had six more bouts in the next five months, in the last being outpointed by Indian Quintana. He collapsed after the fight and died from a cerebral haemorrhage two days later.
Score 41: *w*27 (7) *d*2 *l*12.

Terry Marsh won the world light-welterweight championship in 1987 but gave up the title undefeated.

Marsh, Terry

British, European and World Light-Welterweight Champion (I.B.F.) 1984–87

(b. Stepney, London, Feb. 7, 1958). Began pro boxing: Oct. 12, 1981.

A London fireman with a flair for boxing, he got off to a successful start by winning his first 15 bouts, capturing the British light-welterweight title by outpointing Clinton McKenzie on Sept. 19, 1984. A non-stop style and a stopping punch enabled him to win the European light-welterweight crown by stopping Alessandro Scepecchi (Italy) in six rounds at Monte Carlo on Oct. 26, 1985. He successfully defended this against Tusi-

koleta Nkalankete (France), who was outpointed over 12 rounds in London. On March 4, 1987 Marsh reached stardom by stopping the I.B.F. world title-holder, Joe Louis Manley, in ten rounds at Basildon, Essex. Six months later he surprisingly relinquished his crown and retired from the ring due to epilepsy soon after he had accounted for Akio Kameda (Japan) in six rounds in London.
Score 27: *w*26 *d*1 *l*0.

Martin, Eddie 'Cannonball'

World Bantamweight Champion 1924–25

(b. Brooklyn, New York, March 3, 1903 – d. Brooklyn, New York, Aug. 27, 1968). Began pro boxing: 1922.

Real name Eduardo Vittorio Martino, he was a hustling fighter, good over short distances, with a fair kayo punch. He boxed with frequency in his first three years as a pro, at the end of which he outpointed Abe Goldstein in New York to win the bantam crown. At his first defence, three months later, he was outpointed by Charlie 'Phil' Rosenburg, also in New York, and lost the championship. Putting on weight he tried to win the junior-lightweight title from Tod Morgan but was outpointed. There were only a few fights after that, and he retired in 1932.
Score 101: *w*82 (30) *d*5 *l*13 *Dnc*.1.

Martinez, Rodolfo

World Bantamweight Champion (W.B.C.) 1974–76

(b. Tepito, Mexico, Aug. 24, 1946). Began pro boxing: Aug. 14, 1965.

Joey Maxim, world light-heavyweight champion 1950–52.

Vigorous and hard-punching, he stormed through his first six years with 29 bouts without defeat, 25 of them wins inside the distance. He lost on points to Rafael Herrera for the American title and when, two years later, he met the same man for the W.B.C. version of the world championship, he was stopped in 12 rounds. The following year in a third meeting with Herrera, he took his revenge and the title with a fourth round stoppage. Martinez defended it successfully three times, then was stopped in nine rounds by Carlos Zarate to lose his crown. A fight with Roberto Rubaldino for the Mexican title resulted in a four rounds defeat and he retired in 1977.
Score 52: w44 (35) d1 l7.

Mason, Harry

European and British Lightweight Champion, British Welterweight Champion 1923–34

(b. London, March 27, 1903 – d. South Africa, Aug. 27, 1977). Began pro boxing: Aug. 23, 1920.

Although born in London's East End he was brought up in Leeds, Yorkshire, and there as a member of the Jewish Lads' Brigade won a six stones (84 pounds) championship. He turned pro at 17 and, eager to fight as often as possible, had 33 bouts in 1922. In his third year he won the British and European lightweight titles from James Hall on a disqualification in round 13. These he defended successfully against Ernie Rice, then went to America where he had eight fights but could win only three of them. In his absence the National Sporting Club installed Ernie Izzard as champion, so Mason met and defeated him in nine rounds. Giving up his titles he went after the welterweight crown and won this by outpointing Johnny Brown, then drew with Len Harvey but was twice outpointed by Jack Hood.

The years went by and Harry kept just as busy, fighting in Australia and South Africa. Then, in 1934, after boxing his way through innumerable eliminators, he won over Len 'Tiger' Smith who was ruled out in the 14th round for an alleged low punch. He had regained the British welter crown, but not for long. Six months later Mason was surprisingly outpointed by Pat Butler and lost his titles. He continued boxing until he was close on 34, then retired, going to South Africa where, sadly he died in a road accident, in his 75th year.
Score 203: w139 (26) d14 l48 ND.2.

Mathebula, Peter

World Flyweight Champion (W.B.A.) 1980–81

(b. Mohlakeng, South Africa, July 3, 1952). Began pro boxing: July 10, 1971.

He fought infrequently at the start and was almost 26 when he won his native title by outpointing Johannes Sithebe over 12 rounds. The following year he won the South African bantam crown by knocking out Leslie Pikoli in eight rounds. He fought for the first time outside his own country when he went to Los Angeles at the end of 1980 to take a 15 rounds points decision off Tai-Shik Kim and with it the W.B.A. version of the world flyweight championship. Three months later, back in South Africa, he dropped his crown to Santos Laciar (Argentina), being stopped in round seven. He fought on for the next three years with mixed success and retired in 1983.
Score 45: w36 (17) d0 l9.

Matthews, Billy

European Featherweight Champion 1922

(b. St. Georges, London, April 13, 1901). Began pro boxing: Feb. 5, 1917.

Elder brother to famous actress, Jessie, he began as a pageboy at the National Sporting Club. He loved boxing, thought he had an iron jaw and went tearing into his opponents from the starting gong. Matthews was fast with his leads and on his feet, but lacked a heavy punch. His big chance came in 1922 when he outpointed Arthur Wyns (Belgium), the European champion, over 15 rounds at Liverpool. Wyns demanded a return over 20 rounds and put his title at stake. Billy won a points verdict and could call himself champion. On the strength of this he went to New York, but dropped a decision to Billy Defoe and came home. He defended his title against Eugène Criqui in Paris and was stopped in 17 rounds. The rot had set in and he did not win another bout, retiring in 1926.
Score 64: w39 (11) d3 l22.

Mattioli, Rocco

World Light-Middleweight Champion (W.B.C.) 1977–79

(b. Ripa Testine, Italy, July 20, 1953). Began pro boxing: March 9, 1970.

Brought up in Australia, he started fighting at 17 and won so many of his bouts inside the distance that they were soon calling him 'Rocky'. He became Australian welter champion by stopping Jeff White in 12 rounds in 1973 and after losing the title to Ali Afakasi in 12 rounds, went home to Italy to continue his boxing career. In two years he became W.B.C. world light-middleweight champion by knocking out Eckhard Dagge in Berlin in five rounds. He went back to Australia and in Melbourne kept his world crown by knocking out Elisha Obed (Bahamas) in seven rounds. Mattioli returned to Italy and at Pescara knocked out Jose Duran (Spain) in five rounds. His next defence, however, brought his downfall, being stopped in eight rounds by Maurice Hope at San Remo in March 1979. The following year he went to London to try to regain his crown, but Hope was again too good for him, this time halting him in 11 rounds. Rocco retired in 1981.
Score 72: w63 (50) d2 l7.

Maxim, Joey

World Light-Heavyweight Champion 1950–52

(b. Cleveland, Ohio, March 28, 1922). Began pro boxing: Jan 13, 1941.

Real name Guiseppe Antonio Berardinelli, his manager changed his surname to Maxim because his rapid left-hand leading was akin to the firing of a Maxim Gun, one

of the earliest machine guns. He used it to good purpose and over a large number of years before it brought him any reward. In 1949 he became American champion by outpointing Gus Lesnevich, then went to London and knocked out Freddie Mills in ten rounds to take the world crown. He kept this for two years, then it passed into the hands of Archie Moore who outpointed him three times in title bouts. Before this, he had made an attempt to win the heavyweight title, but was outpointed by Ezzard Charles in 1951. On June 25, 1952, he had a great fight with Sugar Ray Robinson in defence of his light-heavyweight crown in a New York heat wave that caused first the referee and then the challenger to give in, Robinson being unable to come out for the 14th round. Maxim retired in 1959.
Score 115: *w*82 (21) *d*4 *l*29.

Mazzinghi, Sandro

World Light-Middleweight Champion 1963–65, European Light-Middleweight Champion 1966–68

(b. Pontedera, Italy, Oct. 3, 1938). Began pro boxing: Sept. 15, 1961.

A courageous, aggressive fighter, he lost only one (on points) of his first 30 bouts, then took the world light-middleweight title from Ralph Dupas by a knockout in nine rounds. Three months later he stopped the American in 13. Mazzinghi made two more successful defences, then had to bow the knee to fellow-countryman Nino Benvenuti, who stopped him in six rounds and outpointed him in a return match. Sandro then won the European title with a 12 rounds kayo win over Yolande Leveque (France), beat off four challengers, and then regained the world crown by outscoring Ki-Soo Kim (Korea) who had taken the title from Benvenuti. He retained this against Freddie Little and was never beaten for it, retiring in 1978.
Score 69: *w*64 (42) *d*0 *l*3 *Dnc.*2.

Mellody, Billy 'Honey'

World Welterweight Champion 1906–07

(b. Jan. 15, 1884 – d. Charlestown, Massachusetts, March 15, 1919). Began pro boxing: March 20, 1901.

No doubt they called him 'Honey' because of his sweet boxing, as did Ray Robinson's manager apply the term 'Sugar'. A hardworking, very active fighter, he fought a lot in Boston to begin with then, as his fame spread, went wherever and whenever he was offered a fight. It took him six years to get within title range, then he outpointed the great Joe Walcott to become welter king. At his first defence, six months later, however, he lost the crown on a 20-rounds points decision to Mike 'Twin' Sullivan and never got a chance to regain it during the next six years he was fighting. He retired in 1913.
Score 102: *w*54 (34) *d*20 *l*26 *ND.*2.

Mihara, Tadashi

World Light-Middleweight Champion (W.B.A.) 1981–82

(b. Gumma, Japan, March 3, 1955). Began pro boxing: June 23, 1978.

He came into paid fighting rather later, being 23 when he had his first bout in Tokyo. Mihara started off with five kayo wins, the last making him Oriental champion. He fought off six challengers, then went to Rochester, New York, where he became W.B.A. world light-middleweight champion with a points win over Rocky Fratto (U.S.A.), their fight being for the vacant title. He remained champion for less than three months, losing to Davey Moore (U.S.A.) who stopped him in six rounds. He won the Japanese junior-middleweight title in 1982, defended it six times and was still champion when he retired in 1985.
Score 25: *w*24 (15) *d*0 *l*1.

Miller, Freddie

World Featherweight Champion 1933–36

(b. Cincinatti, Ohio, April 3, 1911 – d. Cincinnati, May 8, 1962). Began pro boxing: 1927.

One of the truly great featherweights, he had an immaculate southpaw style which, added to his remarkable skill, made him a very difficult man to beat. In fact, the majority of his losses occurred in the latter stages of his long career and he was stopped only once, his last bout, when he was 29 and on the point of retirement. He was in the same stable as famous Battling Battalino and in 1932 they met for the world title, it being agreed before hand that the championship should pass to Miller, thus keeping it in the family. They were such poor actors that the referee declared 'no contest' and both were suspended. The following year Miller won over Tommy Paul in a bout recognized for the championship by the N.B.A. and he kept this crown for nearly four long years, in which he engaged in 90 contests, taking his title round the world and defending it ten times. On the last occasion, on May 11, 1936, he was outpointed by Peter Sarron.
Score 246: *w*212 (44) *d*6 *l*27 *Dnc.*1.

Milligan, Tommy

European and British Welter and Middleweight Champion 1924–28

(b. Shieldmuir, Wishaw, Scotland, March 2, 1904 – d. Glasgow, Dec. 17, 1970). Began pro boxing: Oct. 3, 1921.

A sound boxer and hard puncher, his career was brief but he crammed a lot into it. He became Scottish welter champion in 1924 with a points win over Johnny Brown, then took the British and European welter titles from famous Ted 'Kid' Lewis with a fine points win. Seven months later he fought

Bruno Frattini (Italy) for the European middleweight crown and again won on points over 20 rounds. He next won the vacant British middleweight title by stopping George West in 14 rounds on July 12, 1926 and twice stopped Ted Moore in similar manner. Now came his big day – a crack at the world title held by famed Mickey Walker (U.S.A.) who came to London, picked up a fortune and knocked Milligan out in ten rounds after the Scot had fought his heart out to try and force a win. When he defended his middleweight titles against Alex Ireland, he lost disappointingly on an alleged foul in round nine, but he made amends by stopping Maxie Rosenbloom in nine in London. A one round knockout by Frank Moody in 1928 brought his career to a halt.
Score 51: *w*42 (20) *d*0 *l*9.

Mills, Freddie

World, European, British and British Empire Light-Heavyweight Champion 1942–50

(b. Parkstone, Dorset, England, June 26, 1919 – d. London, July 25, 1965). Began pro boxing: March 25, 1936.

A two-fisted, aggressive fighter, Mills was not a clean puncher, but he tossed enough leather to win more than half his contests inside the distance. He could, however, box with classic effect when the occasion demanded it.

Mills picked up the rudiments of the ring in the toughest school of all – a West Country boxing booth. Before his 17th birthday he emerged as a professional by winning a novice competition at Bournemouth and four years and 55 fights later his energetic attacking had made him a local fistic idol. Although Mills was by now serving in the R.A.F. he still managed to meet and beat several outstanding middleweights, light-heavies and even heavyweights. Matched with middleweight champion Jock McAvoy, Mills won sensationally in the first round. This unexpected victory brought Mills a contest in 1942 with Len Harvey for the British and Empire light-heavyweight crowns – plus the British Boxing Board of Control's version of the world title. Mills put Harvey out of the ring in round two, and the champion was unable to get back in time to beat the count.

R.A.F. duties limited Mills's appearances for the next four years. Then, in 1946, he met Gus Lesnevich for the world light-heavyweight crown. Mills had not fought for 15 months so it was not surprising that he was stopped in ten rounds. But he showed that he had learned a lot from the encounter when he met Lesnevich two years later. He outpointed the American and won the world title in his finest performance to become the first British world light-heavyweight champion since Bob Fitzsimmons in 1903. In between the Lesnevich fights, he had picked up the European crown, so Mills now held

Freddie Mills, world light-heavyweight champion 1948–50.

four titles. But when he tried for a fifth and sixth, against British and Empire heavyweight champion Bruce Woodcock in 1949, he found he could not give the weight away, succumbing in round 14 after a tremendous battle. Mills was always ready to take on bigger fighters – in 1946 he had attempted to give away enormous physical advantages to gain American Joe Baksi, and had to be saved by the referee in round six. But he did beat South African heavyweight champion Johnny Ralph by a knock-out in eight rounds.

His last contest was also his first defence of his world title. Challenger Joey Maxim, a fine boxer, checked the 31-year-old champion's determined attacks with left jabs and right uppercuts. Mills fought hard, but in the tenth round went down on his haunches to be counted out.

He announced his retirement immediately, and eventually became a radio and television personality of distinction. His tragic and controversial death from a gunshot wound came as a shock to his many admirers.
Score 97: w74 (52) d6 l17.

Minter, Alan

World, European and British Middleweight Champion 1975–81

(b. Crawley, Sussex, Aug. 17, 1951). Began pro boxing: Oct. 31, 1972.

An attacking southpaw with a good knockdown punch, he won the British title from Kevin Finnegan on a points verdict in his third year as a paid fighter. He retained this twice, winning a Lonsdale Belt outright, and then added the European crown by knocking out Germano Valsecchi in Milan. He won a ten rounds bout with Emile Griffith at Monte Carlo, but lost his E.B.U. title to Gratien Tonna (France) having to retire with a damaged eye in the eighth round. Minter regained it the following year by beating Angelo Jacopucci (Italy) who was knocked out in the fifth. Minter stopped Tonna in the sixth of a return bout, then gave up all his holdings to fight for the world crown.

Going to Las Vegas, he outpointed Vito Antuofermo (Italy), and defended it against the same man in London by stopping him in eight. Three months later he was stopped by Marvelous Marvin Halger in three rounds, which was such a shock to Minter's London admirers that there were ugly scenes when the American was declared the winner. The E.B.U. title had been taken over by fellow-countryman Tony Sibson and when Minter tried to win it back, he was knocked out in the third round, afterwards retiring from the fight game.
Score 49: w39 (23) d0 l9 Dnc.1.

Mitchell, Brian

World Super-Featherweight Champion (W.B.A.) 1986–

(b. Johannesburg, South Africa, Aug. 30, 1961). Began pro boxing: Aug. 15, 1981.

With the current ban on South African boxing by the majority of the boxing associations, Brian Mitchell could not have had a worse start to a fighting career. Yet nothing stops ambition and after five years of very active scrapping, he won his native super-featherweight title (which he retained against no fewer than eight challengers). On Sept. 27, 1986, he captured the W.B.A. super-featherweight title by stopping Alfredo Layne in ten rounds and this he took around the world successfully, defending it in Puerto Rico, Panama, France, Italy and Spain, beating all-comers, and stopping the majority of them.
Score 38: w35 (18) d2 l1.

Mitchell, Charlie

World Heavyweight Title Contender 1888–94

(b. Birmingham, Warwickshire, Nov. 24, 1861 – d. Brighton, Sussex, April 3, 1918). Began pro boxing: (bare knuckles) Jan. 11, 1878; (gloves) April, 1882.

This extraordinary fighter came in the bridging time between bare-knuckle fighting and glove contests. His record has to be studied as a whole to get the full extent of his amazing career. Standing only 5 ft. 9 in. and barely weighing more than a middleweight,

Alan Minter, world middleweight champion 1980.

Brian Mitchell (left) outpointing Jim McDonnell to keep his junior lightweight title in 1988.

he had the courage to go to New York and take up a challenge from mighty John L. Sullivan. Mitchell had the satisfaction of putting the 'Boston Strong Boy' down in the first, the bout being stopped by the police in the third round. Five years later he took on Sullivan again, this time at Chantilly in France where they fought 39 rounds before the bout was stopped when the decision was a draw. But Mitchell had by no means the worst of it. When he was 31 Charlie again went to America to fight the new world heavyweight champion, James J. Corbett, but he was past it now and took the knockout in round three.
Score 27: *w*13 *d*11 *l*3.

Mitchell, Myron (Pinkey)

World Light-Welterweight Champion 1922

(b. Milwaukee, Wisconsin, 1899 – d. Milwaukee, March 11, 1976). Began pro boxing: 1917.

Mitchell must be the only boxer to win a world title by newspaper poll. Quickly making a name for himself he had a chance to win the world welterweight title in 1920, meeting Jack Britton. It was a no-decision bout which meant that Mitchell had to knock out the champion to win. He failed to do this, but stayed the distance. He put on weight and the proprietor of the local boxing magazine, *The Boxing Blade*, proposed that a weight division should be made especially for him and asked his readers to nominate and vote for a champion. Of course they chose Pinkey. Mitchell remained recognized as champion until May 27, 1925 when he lost on a foul (sixth round) to James (Red) Herring at Detroit. He tried to recapture his

crown the following year, but was outpointed by Mushy Callahan at Vernon, California. His elder brother Richie had lost a lightweight title bout with Benny Leonard by a kayo in six rounds and when Pinkey tried to restore the family honour two years later, he was knocked out in the tenth.
Score 79: *w*11 (9) *d*4 *l*12 *ND*.51 *Dnc*.1.

Mitri, Tiberio

European Middleweight Champion 1949–54

(b. Trieste, Italy, July 12, 1926). Began pro boxing: Aug. 1, 1946.

A brilliant boxer, he was unbeaten in his first four years which had 50 contests, in the course of which he won his native title by outpointing Giovanni Manca in 1948 and the European crown by outpointing Cyrille Dellannoit (Belgium), which he defended against Jean Stock (France), also on points. On the strength of this he went to New York and challenged Jake LaMotta for the world title, losing narrowly on points over 15 rounds. He had given up the E.B.U. title, but won this back in dramatic fashion at Rome, knocking out Randolph Turpin in 65 seconds. He finally lost his title to Charles Humez (France), who stopped him in three rounds. Two more years with only one defeat in 19 bouts, then he tired of the ring and retired in 1957.
Score 99: *w*87 (15) *d*5 *l*6 *Dnc*.1.

Moir, Gunner James

British Heavyweight Champion 1906–09

(b. Lambeth, London, April 17, 1879 – d. Sutton, Surrey, June 12, 1939).

In his day many serving men in England were permitted to box professionally and Moir was one of those. He was short for a heavyweight, standing 5 ft. 9½ in. and

weighing 190 pounds, but exceptionally strong and a good puncher when he had the range. He won the British title by knocking out Jack Palmer in nine rounds. He defended it with a one-round kayo of Tiger Smith and could claim to be the first Englishman to fight for the world heavyweight title in his own country. Tommy Burns arrived and was willing to defend his title against Moir, demanding £3,000 for his services. The Gunner was outclassed but proved his gameness by lasting into the tenth round when Tommy knocked him out. In his next fight, two years later, Moir lost his British title to 'Iron' Hague who stopped him in the first round. He caused a sensation by knocking out the 'British Hope', Billy Wells, in three rounds, but when Wells returned the compliment with a five-round win, Moir, now 33, decided to retire.
Score 25: *w*14 (7) *d*0 *l*11.

Monaghan, Rinty

World, European, British and British Empire Flyweight Champion 1947–50

(b. Belfast, Northern Ireland, Aug. 21, 1920 – d. Belfast, March 3, 1984). Began pro boxing: Feb. 17, 1935.

World flyweight champion Rinty Monaghan was a professional fighter at the age of 14, and he never grew any bigger. But the skinny 'Pride of Belfast' carried plenty of punch power in his pipestem arms. Real name John Joseph Monaghan, his speedy footwork earned him the nickname 'Rinty' after the famous dog of silent film days. He was also known as the 'Singing Irishman' for his custom of singing to the crowd after a successful contest. Once, after a split-

decision fight, he quieted a rioting Belfast crowd with an Irish ballad.

Monaghan's first setback came in 1938 when in his 22nd contest he was knocked out by Jackie Paterson, whose southpaw stance posed too many problems. Paterson, who went on to win the world crown, met a different Monaghan in a 1946 non-title fight and was knocked out in six rounds. Victory did not give the Irishman a title shot – Dado Marino of the Philippines became challenger instead. But Paterson came in so much overweight for the 1947 title fight that the out-of-training Monaghan was substituted for him. Monaghan was ruled for persistent holding in round nine.

The British Boxing Board of Control declared the title vacant, and three months later Monaghan again met Marino, this time in a world title bout. Strangely enough, it was the first time in 12 years of boxing – five of which were spent in war service – that Monaghan was seen in London. He gained the admiration of Harringay fans by defeating Marino handsomely on points. Paterson's title was restored to him after he threatened legal action, but after he 'boiled' his weight down to make a title defence against Monaghan, he was pathetically knocked out in seven rounds.

The 28-year-old Monaghan had only five more fights after this, two of them in defence of his crown. In the first of these world title bouts he defeated Maurice Sandeyron of France to add the European title to his world, British, and Empire crowns. But against England's Terry Allen he could manage only a draw, and six months later announced his retirement.
Score 54: w43 (19) d3 l8.

Montana, Small

World Flyweight Champion (N.Y.S.A.C.) 1935–37

(b. Philippines, Feb. 1913 – d. La Carlotta, Philippines, Aug. 4, 1976). Began pro boxing: 1931.

He spent the first four years of his career boxing in and around his country. He then based himself in California, and it was not long before he was involved in a fight for the flyweight title according to the State of California, with the approval of the New York State Athletic Commission. Montana beat Midget Wolgast on points and 16 months later went to London and fought Benny Lynch for the world crown. After a brilliant battle, Lynch was returned a popular winner. Montana (real name Benjamin Gan) continued fighting, losing his Californian title en route to Little Dado in 1938. He retired in 1941.
Score 111: w80 (10) d9 l22.

Montgomery, Bob

World Lightweight Champion (N.Y.S.A.C.) 1943–47

(b. Sumter, South Carolina, Feb 10, 1919). Began pro boxing: 1938.

A fine speedy boxer with a good punch, he was soon an established box-office draw and fought with regularity until he was among the top lightweights in America. The New York State Athletic Commission had installed Beau Jack as world champion when the title had become vacant, but Montgomery outpointed Jack to become champion. Six months later, Beau took his title back, only to lose it again to Montgomery within four months. Bob defended successfully against Allie Stolz and Wesley Mouzon, stopping them in 13 and eight rounds respectively, and went on merrily until the N.B.A. champion, Ike Williams, caught up with him in Philadelphia in 1947 and knocked him out in six rounds to become undisputed world champion. Montgomery retired in 1947, came back three years later to lose four bouts in a row and then gave up.
Score 97: w75 (37) d3 l19.

Monzon, Carlos

World Middleweight Champion 1970–77

(b. Santa Fe, Argentina, Aug. 7, 1942). Began pro boxing: Feb. 6, 1963.

One of the modern greats: Monzon reigned as world middleweight king for seven years, defended his title 14 times in that period, was never knocked out or stopped and lost only three points decisions in his very early days. A magnificent fighting force, he won his native title by outpointing Jorge Fernandez in 12 rounds, adding the South American crown by again outpointing Fernandez in a 12-rounder nine months later. He became world champion by defeating Nino Benvenuti (w.ko.12) and defended his title successfully against Benvenuti, Emile Griffith (twice), Jose Napoles and Rodrigo Valdez. He retired undefeated as world champion in 1977.
Score 102: w89 (61) d9 l3 Dnc.1.

Moody, Frank

British Middle and Light-Heavyweight Champion 1927–28

(b. Pontypridd, Wales, Aug. 27, 1900 – d. Milford Haven, Wales, July 29, 1963). Began pro boxing: Jan. 2, 1915.

One of those who was knocked out in his first fight, four rounds by Charlie Stone, but Moody went on to achieve championship status, not once but twice. Tough and strong and a good puncher, he took on the best in the world at his weight. He went to America in November 1923 and stayed there for three years, during which he met Harry Greb, Tiger Flowers, Maxie Rosenbloom, Jeff Smith and Jack Delaney (all world champions). He came home to win the British middleweight title from Roland Todd and consolidated with a sensational one round win over Tommy Milligan in 2 min. of the first round. Next he defeated Ted Moore for the British light-heavy crown, but Alex Ireland outpointed him for his middleweight crown and Harry Crossley did likewise to take the light-heavyweight title. Just before his 30th birthday, he won the Welsh light-heavyweight title from Billy Daniels and kept it against Tommy Farr with a draw. In his last fight Farr knocked him out in four rounds and that was the finish of a long career.
Score 191: w121 (69) d15 l49 ND.4 Dnc.2.

Beads of sweat are scattered as Carlos Monzon (left) and Rodrigo Valdez clash heads.

Moore, Archie

World Light-Heavyweight Champion 1952–62

(b. Benoit, Mississippi, Dec. 13, 1916). Began pro boxing: 1935.

Most durable of modern fighters, Archie Moore was also one of the most talented. He could jab like Louis, hook like Dempsey, and uppercut like Johnson, even if he was not quite as lethal. Moore won the world light-heavyweight title at the advanced age of 36 and kept it for almost ten years. He was still knocking out opponents in his late 40s.

Moore (born Archibald Lee Wright) opened his professional career in 1935 – rather late for a man who was to achieve so much, especially if his mother's claim that he was born in 1913 is accepted. A welterweight amateur at 16, he moved from middleweight to light-heavyweight as his professional years

went by. Moore developed big hitting muscles by walking on his hands and doing 250 press-ups every day, and this, combined with his technique of punching with maximum power, made him a knock-out specialist.

Moore had a record number of eight managers in his 26 years of professional fighting, mainly because he would not permit himself to be exploited, as were so many black boxers in his day. However, this change of managers was one of the main reasons why he had to wait until 1952 for a title shot. Even after outpointing titleholder Joey Maxim he had to submit to some managerial juggling and meet him twice more in the next two years. Moore defended the title seven more times after that and was never beaten for it. In 1960 the National Boxing Association (N.B.A.) stripped Moore of his title for 'inactivity', but the veteran was still recognized as champion by every other boxing authority when he defeated challenger Giulio Rinaldi in 1961. Next year, however, the New York and European bodies followed suit. He retired in 1963.

To gain publicity and important matches Moore used methods not usually followed by fighting men. He secured his 1955 fight with heavyweight champion Rocky Marciano by writing to every sports editor in the United States, stating his claims so convincingly that he just had to be accepted as challenger. He put the champion down in round two, and always claimed that it was only the referee's assistance to Marciano in the knock-down that cost him the heavyweight crown. Undeterred by his round nine beating by Marciano, he fought Floyd Patterson the next year for the vacant heavyweight championship. But Moore had an 'off' night, and succumbed in five rounds.
Score 215: w183 (129) d9 l22 Dnc.1.

Moore, Davey

World Featherweight Champion 1959–63

(b. Lexington, Kentucky, Nov. 1, 1933 – d. Los Angeles, California, March 23, 1963). Began pro boxing: May 11, 1953.

Moore boxed as a bantam in the amateur ranks winning a national title in 1952. A strong, bustling fighter, he ran up a long sequence of wins and knocked out Ricardo Moreno in a single round to qualify for a world title fight with Hogan Bassey. It was a battle between two vigorous fighters and Moore proved the tougher, forcing the champion to retire in 13 rounds. In a return fight five months later Moore scored a win in 11 rounds. Going to London he knocked out Bobby Neil, the British champion, in 2 min. 55 sec. of the first round. Running short of challengers, Davey took his title wherever he could find one, twice to Japan and then to Finland. Making his sixth defence at Los Angeles against Ultiminio Ramos, he was knocked out in the tenth round, did not regain consciousness and died in hospital two days later.
Score 67: w59 (30) d1 l7.

Moore, Davey

World Light-Middleweight Champion (W.B.A.) 1982–83

(b. New York City, June 9, 1959 – d. Holmdel, New Jersey, June 2, 1988). Began pro boxing: Nov. 1, 1980.

By the way he started his pro career, he looked like being a carbon copy of that other Davey Moore, who ruled the featherweight roost for so long. Carrying a kayo punch, he won his first eight bouts (five inside the distance) then caused a surprise on Feb. 2, 1982 by stopping Tadashi Mihara (Japan) to win the W.B.A. version of the light-middleweight title. Two months later he went to Johannesburg and stopped the South African champion, Charlie Weir, in five and followed this with an astounding ten rounds victory over talented Ayub Kalule (Uganda), a former W.B.A. champion at this weight.

Archie Moore (right) follows through with a right hook to the head of Canadian challenger Yvon Durelle. Moore won by a knockout.

He successfully defended his title against Gary Guiden – a four rounds kayo at Atlantic City, but six months later was stopped in eight by the redoubtable Roberto Duran. He retired in 1984, made a short comeback, finally giving up when beaten in ten rounds by Buster Drayton. The boxing world was shocked when he lost his life in a freak accident at his home in Holmdel, New Jersey.
Score 18: *w*15 (12) *d*0 *l*8.

Moran, Frank

World Heavyweight Contender 1914–16

(b. Pittsburgh, Pennsylvania, March 18, 1887 – d. 1968). Began pro boxing: 1908.
Known as 'The Pittsburgh Dentist', he gave up drawing teeth in favour of knocking them out. He carried a big punch in his right that he christened 'Mary Ann', when she caressed an opponent's chin it was 'goodnight'. At 6 ft. 1½ in. and weighing 205 pounds, he was a menace to all aspiring heavies. Moran fought Jack Johnson for the world's title in Paris in 1914 and was declared a points loser. He met Jess Willard, who succeeded Johnson as champion, in a ten rounds no-decision bout in New York in 1916, but failed to knock the Giant Cowboy out, his only means of winning the championship. In England in 1920 Moran beat all his opponents including Joe Beckett, the British champion, who was knocked out in two rounds. A return with Beckett two years later resulted in one of the best heavyweight bouts ever seen in London, with Beckett getting revenge in seven rounds. Moran retired in 1922.
Score 60: *w*34 (24) *d*2 *l*11 *ND*.13.

Moran, Owen

World Featherweight Title Contender 1908

(b. Birmingham, Warwickshire, Oct. 4, 1884 – d. Birmingham, March 17, 1949). Began pro boxing: 1900.
A sturdy, compact fighter with an attacking style and powerful punch, he became 112 pounds champion of England in his third year and beat Digger Stanley for the 114 pounds title in 1905. (This was before the championship weights were standardised.) Immediately after beating Stanley he went to America where he took on all comers, finally getting a title fight with Abe Attell, the world featherweight champion. The distance was 25 rounds and the verdict a draw. It had been so close that the San Francisco promoter booked them for a return bout. Moran stuck out for 25 rounds, the champion wanted only 20, so they fought 23 rounds, with the result a draw as before. In 1910, Moran caused a stir by knocking out Battling Nelson, former world lightweight champion, in 11 rounds. Another year in America and he came home to challenge Jim Driscoll for the British featherweight title, but again all he could get was a draw after 20 rounds. Two years later, by which time he was past 30, he had a final fling at a title, but was ruled out in the 11th round for an alleged low blow against Llew Edwards for the vacant featherweight crown. He retired in 1916.
Score 110: *w*66 (25) *d*6 *l*17 *ND*.21.

Morgan, Tod

World Junior-Lightweight Champion 1925–29

(b. Seattle, Washington, Dec. 25, 1902 – d. Seattle, Aug. 3, 1953). Began pro boxing: 1920.
You have to be something of a phenomenon to fight continuously for 21 years, reign as a world champion for over four years and get in more than 200 fights. Morgan (real name: Bert Morgan Pilkington) started fighting for pay when 18 and for several years none of his bouts exceeded six rounds, one of the reasons why he lasted so long. It was in his fifth year that he knocked out Mike Ballerino in ten rounds to become world junior-lightweight king and he held on to his title against 12 challengers who included Steve 'Kid' Sullivan, Joe Glick, Johnny Dundee, Carl Duane, Eddie Martin, Joey Sangor and Vic Foley. Eventually he lost his title to Benny Bass, who knocked him out in two rounds in New York. Tod went through the next three years in a vain effort to recapture his crown, then went to Australia where he remained for ten years and had 62 contests there.
Score 206: *w*132 (27) *d*29 *l*44 *Dnc.*1.

Morrison, Des

British Light-Welterweight Champion 1973–81

(b. Jamaica, Feb. 1, 1950. Based in Bedford, England.) Began pro boxing: Jan 27, 1970.
A class boxer with a stopping punch, but he could be hurt. Morrison won the vacant British light-welter title at the end of his fourth year in England, outpointing Joe Tetteh over 15 rounds. He kept it for two years then was outpointed by Joey Singleton. Two more years later, in attempting to regain it, he was stopped in ten rounds by Colin Powers. He had another try in 1979, but lost on points to Clinton McKenzie. Success came his way the following year when he outpointed Sylvester Mittee to become champion again. But only for nine months. Defending against McKenzie he was stopped in 14 rounds. After being stopped in five rounds by Frank Ropis in Australia on Sept. 11, 1982, he announced his retirement.
Score 50: *w*36 (18) *d*2 *l*12.

Moyer, Denny

World Light-Middleweight Champion 1962–63

(b. Portland, Oregon, Aug. 8, 1939). Began pro boxing: Aug. 17, 1957.
A National Amateur Champion in 1957, he made a good start as a pro, getting a fight for the world welter title in his 21st pro bout, but being outpointed by Don Jordan in his

first defeat. He continued to box in the best company for two years, then won the vacant light-middleweight title by gaining a points win over Joey Giambra. Afer two successful defences, he lost to Ralph Dupas on points, and this was repeated when they met in a return match two months later. Moyer became a middleweight and in 1970 won the American middleweight title by outpointing Eddie Pace. He lost and regained this title, then challenged Carlos Monzon for the world crown in Rome, but was stopped in five rounds. Moyer continued to fight for another three years before retiring in 1975.
Score 140: *w*98 (25) *d*4 *l*37 *Dnc*.1.

Muangsurin, Saensak

World Light-Welterweight Champion (W.B.C.) 1975–78

(b. Phetchabun, Thailand, Aug. 13, 1950). Began pro boxing: Nov. 16, 1974.

This hard-hitting Thailander's short record bristles with championship bouts. He took the W.B.C. version of the light-welterweight title in his third recorded bout, stopping Perico Fernandez in ten rounds. He made a successful defence, then lost it to Miguel Velasquez on a fifth round disqualification, but won it back four months later with a second round kayo. He made six successful defences in 1977, going to Japan and even Spain. He started 1978 by stopping challenger Francisco Moreno in 13 rounds, then suffered his first real defeat, being stopped in 13 rounds, by Sang-Hyun Kim in Korea to lose his title. He had five matches in the next three years, winning only one, his worst defeat being by Thomas Hearns who stopped him in three rounds at Detroit.
Score 20: *w*14 *d*0 *l*6.

Muhammad, Eddie Mustafa

World Light-Heavyweight Champion (W.B.A.) 1980–81

(b. Brooklyn, New York, April 30, 1952). Began pro boxing: Sept. 15, 1972.

He started boxing under his first name, Eddie Gregory, but changed it after adopting the Muslim faith. In his first attempt to win the W.B.A. version of the world title in 1977, he was outpointed over 15 rounds by Victor Galindez. Muhammad had to wait 2½ years for another shot and won in 11 rounds from Marvin Johnson. He made two successful defences the same year, but in 1981 lost on points to Michael Spinks at Las Vegas. He retired in 1985.
Score 56: *w*48 (38) *d*1 *l*7.

Muhammad, Matthew Saad

World Light-Heavyweight Champion (W.B.C.) 1979–81

(b. Philadelphia, Pennsylvania, Aug. 5, 1954). Began pro boxing: Jan. 14, 1974.

Born as Maxwell Loach, he started boxing as Matthew Franklin, then switched to Muhammad after adopting the Muslim faith. He won the American light-heavyweight title on July 26, 1977 by knocking out Marvin Johnson in 12 rounds. He defended this three times, then became W.B.C. world champion with an eighth round kayo win over the same Marvin Johnson. After eight successful defences in 17 months, he dropped the title to Dwight Braxton (Dwight Muhammad Qawi), being stopped in the tenth round. In a return bout he was beaten on a stoppage in six rounds. In 1984 he attempted to win the N.A.B.F. light-heavyweight title, but was stopped in 11 rounds by Willie Edwards at Detroit. He retired in 1986.
Score 42: *w*33 (8) *d*2 *l*7.

Mundane, Tony

Commonwealth Middle and Light-Heavyweight Champion 1972–78

(b. Sydney, Australia, June 10, 1975). Began pro boxing: March 5, 1969.

A star attraction because of his great fighting spirit and knockdown punch, he won his native middleweight title by knocking out Billy Choules in four rounds. After drawing with Bunny Sterling (U.K.) for the Commonwealth title in Sydney, he stopped him for it in 15 rounds in Brisbane the following year. Mundine defended this crown three times and then relinquished it to fight as a light-heavyweight. His decision to go up a division was influenced by his gallant attempt at Buenos Aires to win the W.B.A. world middleweight title from Carlos Monzon, but weakened by weight-making he was knocked out in seven rounds. Nevertheless, he became Australian light-heavyweight and heavyweight champion and won the Commonwealth light-heavyweight crown by knocking out Steve Aczek in 12 rounds. Mundine made four successful defences up to Feb. 1978 when Gary Summerhays (Canada) knocked him out in 11 rounds at Melbourne. He has been Australian light-heavyweight champion since 1975.
Score 95: *w*81 (69) *d*1 *l*13.

Murphy, Billy 'Torpedo'

World Featherweight Champion 1890

(b. Auckland, New Zealand, Nov. 3, 1863 – d. Auckland, July 26, 1939). Began pro boxing: 1881.

There were many claimants to the world featherweight crown from the 1860s onwards, but the first man to establish himself as champion was this New Zealander, who learnt his boxing in Australia before going to America in 1889. Before long he was engaged in a fight with Ike Weir, which a San Francisco promoter billed as for the world title. Murphy won by a kayo in round 14, but

returning to his homeland, he lost his crown to Young Griffo, who knocked him out in the 15th round in Sydney. Billy stayed in Australia for nearly two years, then went back to the United States where he fought out the remainder of his long career. His bouts became less frequent after 1900.
Score 114: *w*61 (41) *d*14 *l*32 *ND*.2 *Dnc*.5.

Nakajima, Shigeo

World Light-Flyweight Champion (W.B.C.) 1980

(b. Ibaraki, Japan, Jan. 18, 1954). Began pro boxing: July 12, 1976.

After four years of pro boxing and 15 bouts, he secured a fight with Sung-Jun Kim (Korea) for the W.B.C. world junior-flyweight title and won on points over 15 rounds in Tokyo. He kept his crown for 71 days, then lost it to Hilario Zapata on a points verdict. Attempting to get back his crown he was stopped in 11 rounds by Zapata. Five months later, in his first come-back bout, he was knocked out by Nobuyuki Watanabe in eight rounds and promptly retired from the ring.
Score 19: *w*13 (7) *d*1 *l*5.

Napoles, Jose

World Welterweight Champion, 1969–75

(b. Oriente, Cuba, April 13, 1940). Began pro boxing: Aug. 2, 1958.

The fact that this most competent Cuban reigned as world welter king for over six years and made 15 defences before losing it, gives an idea of his undoubted high class. True, he lost his title to Billy Backus on a fourth round stoppage because of a badly damaged eye, but it was only a temporary loss and six months later he won it back, stopping Backus with cuts after having twice put him down. In successful defences he defeated such big names as Emile Griffith, Curtis Cokes (from whom he took the title), Hedgemon Lewis (twice), Ralph Charles (British champion), Clyde Gray (Canadian champion) and Ernie Lopez (twice). When he went out of his weight class and tried to take the middleweight title from Carlos Monzon in Paris, he was stopped in seven rounds. Finally, when he was in his 36th year, he lost his crown to John H. Stracey (U.K.) who stopped him in six rounds at Mexico City. He retired thereafter.
Score 84: *w*76 (54) *d*0 *l*8.

Navarrete, Rolando

World Junior-Lightweight Champion (W.B.C.) 1981–82

(b. General Santos City, Philippines, Feb. 14, 1957). Began pro boxing: Feb. 17, 1973.

A smart fighter with a good stopping

punch, he was a bantam champion of his own country before he grew heavier. In his eighth year as an pro he boldly challenged Alexis Arguello for the W.B.C. junior-lightweight title, but was stopped in four rounds. A year later he won the American championship by outpointing Johnny Sato and then caused a big surprise by knocking out Cornelius Boza-Edwards in five rounds to take the world crown. In Manila, five months later, he knocked out Choi Chung (South Korea) in 11 rounds, but lost his crown to Rafael 'Bazooka' Limon, being knocked out in 12 rounds on May 29, 1982.
Score 58: *w*45 (24) *d*3 *l*10.

Neil, Frankie

World Bantamweight Champion 1903–04

(b. San Francisco, California, July 25, 1883 – d. Richmond, California, March 6, 1970). Began pro boxing: Nov. 8, 1900.

This hard-hitting Irish-American scored a large number of kayo wins, but was beaten in seven rounds by Harry Forbes when he challenged for the bantam crown in 1902. Eight months later, in a return title contest, he knocked out Forbes in two rounds to become world champion. He defended his crown successfully against Billy DeCoursey (w.ko.15), Johnny Raegan (drew 20) and Harry Forbes (w.ko.3). Going to England he was outpointed over 20 rounds by Joe Bowker in London and lost the title.

Neil challenged Abe Attell for the featherweight crown, but was a loser on points over 20 rounds. He then had two severe setbacks: Owen Moran (U.K.) knocked him out in 16 rounds and Attell stopped him in 13. He fought on for three years, mostly in no-decision bouts, and retired in 1910.
Score 51: *w*29 (18) *d*2 *l*19 *ND*.1.

Nelson, Azumah

Commonwealth and World Feather and Super-Featherweight Champion, 1981–

(b. Accra, Ghana, July 19, 1958). Began pro boxing: Dec. 1, 1979.

Nelson made certain of distinguishing himself by winning his native featherweight title in his second contest, knocking out Henry Saddler in nine rounds. He added the West African crown ten months later by stopping Joe Skipper in five. The Commonwealth title followed with a five-round victory over Brian Roberts, from Australia. In an effort to win the W.B.C. world featherweight title in 1982, he was stopped in the 15th and last round by Salvador Sanchez in New York. Undismayed, he retained his native and Commonwealth crowns and then scored a nine-round victory over Wilfredo Gomez to capture the W.B.C. world title at the second attempt. This he defended successfully against Juvenal Ordenes in five rounds at Miami. Pat Cowdell, the Euro-

Azumah Nelson after retaining his world super-featherweight title in Atlantic City in 1988.

pean super-featherweight champion, was stunningly knocked out in single round when challenging Nelson at Birmingham. Nelson beat off all challengers decisively until 1988, when he relinquished his crown to fight as a super-feather, winning his second world title at the expense of Mario Martinez, of Mexico, on a close decision.
Score 28: *w*27 (19) *d*0 *l*1.

Nelson, Battling

World Lightweight Champion 1908–10

(b. Copenhagen, Denmark, June 5, 1882 – d. Chicago, Illinois, Feb. 7, 1954). Began pro boxing: 1896.

Famed for his abnormal toughness and stamina, world lightweight champion Battling Nelson could absorb the heaviest punishment without noticeable effect. He wore down and knocked out many of his opponents with vicious short-range blows, particularly to the body. Nelson has been credited with the invention of the left hook 'scissors' to the liver – his favourite punch. The thin gloves of his day enabled him to pinch his unfortunate opponent the moment his left hook landed.

Christened – or so he claimed – Oscar Battling Matthew Nelson, in Denmark, he

was brought up in the United States. He had his first fight in a boxing booth soon after his 14th birthday, and he won in the first round. Soon he was bowling over the best lightweights in the business. He knocked out Jimmy Britt in a bout advertised as for the 'white' world championship, and challenged black champion Joe Gans for the title, Nelson was disqualified for low hitting in round 42 (the fight was the longest world title bout ever recorded under Queensbury Rules), but he received $23,000 for the fight – more than twice the amount paid to Gans.

In 1908 he won the title by knocking out Gans in 17 rounds, and defeated him over 21 rounds in a return the same year. Two successful defences followed in 1909, then Nelson met his match in toughness in Ad Wolgast, who floored him in round 40 of their title fight. His only other knockout defeat was at the hands of Owen Moran, the renowned English featherweight, a surprise defeat that knocked Nelson out of the big time. Nelson was nearly 35 when he finally retired from the ring.
Score (incomplete) 131: *w*67 (39) *d*25 *l*31 *ND*.7 *Dnc*.1.

Nichols, George

World Light-Heavyweight Champion 1932

(b. Sandusky, Ohio, July 9, 1908). Began pro boxing: 1927.

A good, workmanlike boxer whom promoters found reliable. Most of his wins were

gained with points decisions. In 1932 the N.B.A. ran an eliminating competition for the light-heavyweight title which was considered vacant and Nichols beat Dave Maier in the final to be recognized as champion. He never defended the crown and went on happily for the next five years. He fought John Henry Lewis in a non-title fight in 1936 and held him to a draw, but in a return bout was outpointed. He kept in top company throughout his career which ended in 1939.
Score 126: w86 (31) d11 l28 ND.1.

Noble, Tommy

British Bantamweight Champion 1918–19, World Featherweight Title Claimant 1920

(b. Bermondsey, London, March 4, 1897). Began pro boxing: 1915.

A courageous box-fighter who would swap punches irrespective of weight or size. He fought as often as he could and had engaged in over a hundred contests before he won the British bantam title by outpointing Joe Symonds over 20 rounds at the National Sporting Club, London, on Nov. 25, 1918. Due to defend this in London against Walter Ross, he went to Paris and fought 20 hard rounds to a draw with Eugene Criqui three days earlier. Small wonder that he had to retire to Ross after ten rounds.

In 1920 he went to America where he became very popular. Promoter Tex Rickard tried hard to get Noble a title fight with Johnny Kilbane, who had not defended his crown for some years, and when this failed he matched Tommy and Johnny Murray over 15 rounds at Madison Square Garden, New York, on Oct. 7, 1920, advertising the contest as for the vacant world title and putting up a diamond belt for the winner. Noble won on points but did not receive recognition as champion. He went to Australia for a series of battles, then back to fight in America and Canada. It is interesting to note that his fight with Murray was the first decision bout in New York under the Walker Law and the first boxers to be issued with licences by the New York State Athletic Commission were: Jack Dempsey, Andy Chaney and Tommy Noble.
Score (incomplete) 132: w74 (25) d13 l39 ND.5 Dnc.1.

Noel, Claude

World Lightweight Champion (W.B.A.) 1981, Commonwealth Lightweight Champion, 1983–84

(b. Port of Spain, Trinidad, July 25, 1948). Began pro boxing: Nov. 13, 1973.

A good puncher himself, but having something of a glass jaw, he won his native title in 1976 by knocking out Fitzroy Guiseppi in ten rounds and retained it in eight rounds when they met a second time. Challenging for the W.B.A. lightweight title, he was knocked

out in 13 rounds by Ernesto Espana, but was more successful against Rodolfo Gonalez in 1981, winning the championship on points over 15 rounds at Atlantic City. His tenure of the title was short, however, as he was knocked out in the eighth by Arturo Frias less than three months later. On Nov. 12, 1982, he lost on points to star American lightweight Howard Davies. It must be recorded, however, that on Dec. 2, 1983 he won the British Commonwealth lightweight title by outpointing Steve Assoon in Trinidad, a crown he kept against Davidson Andeh, but eventually lost to Graeme Brooke in Melbourne, Australia, on Nov. 2, 1984.
Score 41: w31 (18) d0 l10.

Norton, Ken

World Heavyweight Champion (W.B.C.) 1978

(b. Jacksonville, Illinois, Aug. 9, 1945). Began pro boxing: Nov. 14, 1967.

Standing 6 ft. 3in. and weighing 210 pounds, he had all the makings of a world heavyweight champion, especially after his first meeting with Muhammad Ali in 1973 when they fought for the American title. Then he not only gained a points verdict over 12 rounds but broke the former champion's jaw while doing so. He was outpointed by Ali in a return, but this did not stop him from getting his first crack at the world crown. Challenging George Foreman, he was put away in two rounds at Caracas. Two and a half years later, in New York, he failed again – this time being outpointed over 15 rounds by Ali who had regained the world crown. In 1978 the W.B.C. disapproved of Ali defending his title against Leon Spinks and proclaimed Norton champion. But it did him no good as Larry Holmes outpointed him in Las Vegas three months later. Defeats by Earnie Shavers (one round) and Gerry Cooney (also in one) forced his retirement in 1981.
Score 50: w42 (33) d1 l7.

Notice, Horace

British and Commonwealth Heavyweight Champion 1986–

(b. West Bromwich, Aug. 7, 1957). Began pro boxing: Oct. 24, 1983.

Winning the A.B.A. heavyweight title in 1983, the 6 ft. 1 in. Notice won his first nine paid bouts convincingly, then took the British title, combined with the vacant Commonwealth crown, when he stopped Hughroy Currie in six rounds in the Isle of Man, of all places. He strengthened his hold on the Commonwealth title by halting Proud Kilimanjaro, from Zimbabwe, in eight rounds. He successfully defended his twin titles against Dave Garside (stopped 5), Paul Lister (ko.3) and Hughroy Currie (stopped

10). On Dec. 2, 1987 he offset an Australian challenge with a four-round stoppage of Dean Walters. His victory over Lister gained him outright possession of a Lonsdale Belt.
Score 16: w16 (13) d0 l0.

Numata, Yoshiaki

World Junior-Lightweight Champion (W.B.C.) 1967–71

(b. Hokkaido, Japan, April 19, 1945). Began pro boxing: July 26, 1962.

Numata spent most of his fighting life in his own country. He was Oriental champion from 1965 to 1969 when he relinquished the title, but in between he outpointed the very experienced Flash Elorde to win the world crown on June 15, 1967. Six months afterwards he lost it to Hiroshi Kobayashi on a stoppage in 12 rounds, but two years later regained it from Mando Ramos who was knocked out in six. He retained the title against Rene Barrientos, Paul Rojas and Lionel Rose, but eventually lost it to Ricardo Arrendondo in 1971 after which he retired.
Score 55: w44 (14) d3 l8.

Obed, Elisha

World Light-Middleweight Champion 1975–76

(b. Nassau, Bahamas, Feb. 21, 1952). Began pro boxing: Aug. 10, 1967.

Possessing a rugged style plus a good knockdown punch, he won 44 contests inside the distance before knocking out Miguel de Oliveira in Paris to win the W.B.C. version of the world light-middleweight title. He kept this against Sea Robinson in Abidjan on points, but lost it to Eckhard Dagge in Berlin, being stopped in the tenth. He tried to regain the crown in 1979, but was beaten in seven rounds by Rocky Mattioli in Melbourne. He continued in action until 1986, but without any further titular success.
Score 100: w81 (57) d4 l13 Dnc.2.

O'Brien, Philadelphia Jack

World Light-Heavyweight Champion 1905

(b. Philadelphia, Pennsylvania, Jan. 17, 1878 – d. New York, New York, Nov. 12, 1942). Began pro boxing: Dec. 12, 1896.

A talented boxer whose real name was James Francis Hagen, he preferred to fight on the defensive, and his early years as a pro were spent mainly in short distance and no-decision bouts. In 1901 he went to England and spent a year there undefeated. Back in the United States he kept himself busy with 34 bouts in 1902, 26 in 1903 and 20 in 1904. At the end of the following year he knocked out veteran Bob Fitzsimmons in 13

rounds to win the light-heavyweight title. He never defended it, but had two bouts with Tommy Burns for the heavyweight championship, getting a draw first and then being outpointed, both times over 20 rounds. O'Brien almost came to grief in 1909 when that mighty middleweight Stanley Ketchell knocked him cold in the tenth and last round in New York, the bell saving O'Brien from being counted out. He finally retired in 1912.
Score 179: w148 (51) d19 l12.

Ocasio, (Ossie) Ovaldo

World Cruiserweight Champion (W.B.A.) 1982–84

(b. Puerto Rico, Aug. 12, 1955). Began pro boxing: February 20, 1976.

Ocasio built up a good kayo record in his first two years and was unbeaten until March 23, 1979, when Larry Holmes stopped him in seven rounds at Las Vegas in a fight for the W.B.C. heavyweight title. His subsequent career was ruined by being stopped in one round by Michael Dokes and in six rounds by John L. Gardner, the British champion. However, when the W.B.A. decided to recognize a cruiserweight division (195 pounds), Ossie outpointed Robbie Williams (South Africa) at Johannesburg on Feb. 13, 1982 to become their first champion. He made three successful defences, against Young Joe Louis (points 15), Randy Stephens (points 15) and John Odhiambo (stopped 15). When he returned to South Africa to defend the championship, he left it behind, being outscored by Piet Crous at Sun City on Dec. 1, 1986.
Score 26: w21 (11) d1 l14.

O'Dowd, Mike

World Middleweight Champion 1917–20

(b. St. Paul, Minnesota, April 5, 1895 – d. St. Paul, July 28, 1957). Began pro boxing: 1913.

He was so difficult to catch with a solid punch they called him 'The St. Paul Phantom' and it is a fact that in well over a hundred bouts he was stopped only once and that in the final fight of his career. He won the world title in his fifth year by knocking out Al McCoy in six rounds at Brooklyn, New York. The record books claim he defended his crown successfully 11 times, but most of these were no-decision bouts. O'Dowd was finally outpointed by southpaw Johnny Wilson in 1920. He tried to win back his crown the following year, but lost on points. In 1922 the N.Y.S.A.C. staged a world middleweight title fight between O'Dowd and Dave Rosenberg, who was ruled out in the eighth round. Mike retired soon afterwards.
Score 116: w97 (40) d8 l14 ND.7.

O'Grady, Sean

World Lightweight Champion (W.B.A.) 1980–81

(b. Oklahoma City, Oklahoma, Feb. 10, 1959). Began pro boxing: Jan 21, 1975.

A belting lightweight with a big punch who did nearly all his fighting in his native city. Managed by his father who kept him busy with 26 bouts in his first year, but these lasted only 76 rounds. O'Grady won an American version of the world title by outpointing Gonzallo Montellano in Omaha, but lost to Jim Watt in Glasgow where he tried to win the W.B.C. crown, the referee stopping the contest as O'Grady was bleeding badly from a deep cut on his forehead. He won the W.B.A. version of the title by outpointing Hilmer Kenty and when that body withdrew its recognition, he and his father formed the World Athletic Association with Sean as champion. On Oct. 31, 1981, at Little Rock in Arkansas, he lost this crown to Andrew Ganigan (Honolulu), being put down three times in the second round before the referee called a halt.
Score 86: w81 (70) d0 l5.

Oguma, Shoji

World Flyweight Champion (W.B.C.) 1974–81

(b. Fukushima, Japan, July 22, 1951). Began pro boxing: Dec. 26, 1970.

This tough little Japanese warrior won the W.B.C. version of the world flyweight title in his 23rd paid bout, outpointing Betulio Gonzalez in Tokyo. Three months later he lost his crown to Miguel Canto; he made five attempts to regain the title without success in the next four years, but on May 18, 1980 became champion again by knocking out Chan-Hee Park in nine rounds at Sendai, Japan. He retained his crown with points wins over Sung-Jun Kim and Chan-Hee Park (twice), but was knocked out in seven rounds by Antonio Avelar at Mito City on May 12, 1981 to lose his crown. An attempt to become a champion again failed when he was stopped in 12 rounds by Jiro Watanabe (Japan), the W.B.A. junior-bantam champion, the following year.
Score 49: w38 (20) d1 l10.

Ohba, Masao

World Flyweight Champion (W.B.A.) 1970–73

(b. Sumidaku, Japan, Oct. 21, 1949 – d. Tokyo, Jan. 24, 1973). Began pro boxing: Nov. 7, 1966.

Ohba won the W.B.A. version of the world flyweight title in his 28th pro bout by stopping Berkrerk Chartvanchai in 13 rounds in Tokyo. He made five successful defences in the Japanese capital city: Betulio Gonzalez (w.pts.15), Fernando Cabanela (w.pts.15), Susumu Hanagata (w.pts.15), Orlando Amores (w.ko.5) and Chartchai Chionoi (w.ko.12). Twenty-two days after his final defence, he was killed in a car crash.
Score 38: w35 (15) d1 l12.

O'Keefe, Pat

British Middleweight Champion, 1906–18

(b. Bromley-by-Bow, London, March 17, 1883). Began pro boxing: Sept. 20, 1902.

A good strong boxer, O'Keefe was a solid puncher, especially at short range. He won a welterweight competition in 1904 and was recognized as British middleweight champion when he outpointed Mike Crawley and knocked out Charlie Allum in 1906. He lost the title to Tom Thomas on a points verdict two months later. He went to America, where he fought Billy Papke among others, then to Australia where he stayed for nine months. He fought light-heavies and heavies on returning home, staying into the 15th round against Bombardier Billy Wells, the British heavyweight champion. In 1914, he regained the middleweight title by outpointing Harry Reeve, then defended against Nicol Simpson and Jim Sullivan, winning them all on points over 20 rounds. He lost the title to Jack Blake, also on a 20-round points verdict, but he got it back with a two-round knockout to win the Lonsdale Belt outright. He retired soon afterwards.
Score 96: w68 (26) d4 l22 ND.2.

Olin, Bob

World Light-Heavyweight Champion 1934–35

(b. New York, July 4, 1908 – d. New York, Dec. 16, 1956). Began pro boxing: October 8, 1928.

A cagey fighter, with plenty of skill and a good punch who was noted for staying power. He had to wait six years before he could get a title chance and then outpointed the long-reigning Maxie Rosenbloom over 15 rounds in New York to take the world crown. Less than a year later he lost a points verdict to skilful John Henry Lewis and from then on his form deserted him. Making an effort to regain the title, he was stopped by Lewis in eight rounds and at the beginning of 1939 he retired.
Score 85: w54 (25) d4 l27.

Olivares, Ruben

World Bantam and Featherweight Champion 1969–75

(b. Mexico City, Jan 14, 1947). Began pro boxing: Feb. 29, 1964.

The hardest hitter of modern bantams, Ruben Olivares of Mexico was dubbed a 'miniature Marciano' when he took the world title from Australia's Lionel Rose in

August 1969. He battered the talented Aborigine unmercifully for the best part of three rounds before knocking him out.

Unlike most Mexican boxers, Olivares did not go into the fight game because of poverty. His father was a successful businessman in Mexico City, and the independent Ruben took up boxing because he loved it. Local fans quickly realized they had a dynamic knock-out specialist among them: in six years he set up the remarkable record of 50 wins and 1 draw out of 51 bouts, with 49 won inside the distance.

Within four months of winning the world crown, Olivares put it at stake against England's Alan Rudkin. He scored a devastating victory, flooring the British champion three times before the referee called a halt in the second round.

He won, lost and retained the title in three bouts with fellow-countryman Chucho Castillo, retained it against Kazuyoshi Kanazawa and Jesus Pimentel, but dropped it to Rafael Herrera who stopped him in eight rounds in 1972. Two years later he had a seventh round win over Zensuke Utagawa to win the world featherweight crown (W.B.A.); lost it on a 13th round knockout to Alexis Arguello, and won the W.B.C. version by knocking out Bobby Chacon in two rounds. David Kotey took his second crown with a points win in 1975, but Ruben was not done. In 1979 he tried to win back the W.B.A. title, but Eusebio Pedroza was too good for him and won in 12 rounds. He was 32 now and after four more bouts, two of which he lost, he retired in 1981.
Score 102: w87 (77) d3 l12.

Olson, Carl 'Bobo'

World Middleweight Champion 1953–55

(b. Honolulu, Hawaii, July, 1928). Began pro boxing: Nov. 23, 1945.

Strong, with unlimited stamina and no fear of anyone, he was more fighter than boxer. He started professionally in San Francisco, then spent almost five years in his own country. In 1950 he went to Philadelphia to fight Ray Robinson for the State version of the middleweight title but was stopped in 12 rounds. Over the years he had three more bouts with Sugar Ray, but lost each time. In 1953 when the title was vacant he outpointed Paddy Young for the American championship, then assumed the world crown by outpointing Randolph Turpin. He kept the title against Kid Gavilan, Rocky Castellani and Pierre Langlois, then challenged Archie Moore for the light-heavyweight championship. Olson was stopped in three rounds, then Robinson took away his title with a two rounds win, followed by one in four rounds. Bobo (his little sister's way of saying 'Brother') went on fighting for ten years and retired in 1966.
Score 116: w98 (45) d2 l16.

Orono, Rafael

World Super-Flyweight Champion (W.B.C.) 1980–81

(b. Sucre, Venezuela, Aug. 30, 1958). Began pro boxing: Feb. 18, 1979.

He won his native title in his seventh pro bout by outpointing Edgar Roman over 12 rounds. Four bouts later Orono won the W.B.C. version of the world super-flyweight championship by gaining a points win over Seung-Hoon Lee at Caracas. He retained the title three times the same year, but on Jan. 24, 1981, lost his crown to Chul-Ho Kim, being stopped in nine rounds. He then won five bouts in a row, and regained the world title by stopping Chul-Ho Kim in six rounds in Seoul.
Score 40: w33 (16) d1 l6.

Ortego, Rafael

World Featherweight Champion (W.B.A.) 1977

(b. Panama City, Panama, Sept. 25, 1950). Began pro boxing: Jan. 30, 1970.

Ortego started as a flyweight, but was outpointed over 12 rounds by Rigoberto Riasco when he tried to win his native title in 1973. There were only seven bouts in the next three years, but at the start of 1977 he outpointed Francisco Coronado in his home city to win the W.B.A. version of the world featherweight title. Ortego retained it with a points verdict over Flipper Uehera in Japan, but at the end of the year lost his crown on points to Cecilio Lastra at Torrelavega in Spain. He did not fight again.
Score 27: w20 (6) d4 l3.

Ortiz, Carlos

World Light-Welter and Lightweight Champion 1959–68

(b. Ponce, Puerto Rico, Sept. 9, 1936). Began pro boxing: Feb. 14, 1955.

An excellent stand-up boxer, he opened his account in New York, made it his base for a while, won the vacant light-welterweight title by knocking out Kenny Lane in two rounds, then fought wherever boxing was performed. Retained, lost and regained the title in the next two years, then outpointed Joe Brown at Las Vegas to win the lightweight crown on a points decision. He made four defences in Japan, Puerto Rico (twice) and the Philippines, but dropped the title to Ismael Laguna in Panama on points. He won it back in his country, also on points, then held it against challengers in Pittsburgh, Mexico City, New York (twice) and San Juan, finally losing it to Carlos Teo Cruz in Santo Domingo in 1968. He was stopped only once – in six rounds by Ken Buchanan in 1972, his last contest.
Score 70: w61 (30) d1 l7 Dnc.1.

Ortiz, Manuel

World Bantamweight Champion 1942–50

(b. Corona, California, July 2, 1916 – d. San Diego, California, May 31, 1970). Began pro boxing: Feb. 25, 1938.

One of the greatest bantams of all time. He won the world title from Tony Olivera when aged 26 and in his fifth year as a pro. Ortiz kept it for eight years, with a short break of two months in 1946 when he was outpointed by Harold Dade. He regained the title and defended it against 18 more challengers before losing the crown to Vic Toweel (13 years his junior), being outpointed in Johannesburg. He fought on for several years and retired in 1955.
Score 127: w95 (49) d3 l29.

Overlin, Ken

World Middleweight Champion 1937–41

(b. Decator, Illinois, Aug. 15, 1910 – d. Reno, Nevada, July 24, 1969). Began pro boxing: 1932.

A very clever boxer with all the skills and ringcraft, but lacking a 'killer' punch. It took six years as a pro and 75 fights before his title chance came. Then he was knocked out in four rounds by Freddie Steele in an N.B.A. version of the world crown. Three years and 40 bouts had to pass before opportunity knocked again, when he outpointed Ceferino Garcia to win the title. He twice defended this successfully against Steve Belloise on points verdicts, but lost the decision to Billy Soose who took the title. Overlin retired in 1944.
Score 149: w128 (23) d7 l13 Dnc.1.

Owen, Johnny

European, British and Commonwealth Bantamweight Champion 1977–80

(b. Merthyr, Wales, Jan. 7, 1956 – d. Los Angeles, U.S.A., Nov. 4, 1980). Began pro boxing: Sept. 30, 1976.

Very tall for a bantam and with a correspondingly long reach, he became Welsh bantam king in his sixth pro bout, outpointing George Sutton at Ebbw Vale. Three bouts later he was British champion, stopping Paddy Maguire in 11 rounds in London. He won the Lonsdale Belt outright with successful defences against Wayne Evans (w.rsf.10) and Dave Smith (w.rsf.12). Owen won the vacant Commonwealth crown by outpointing Paul Ferreri (Australia) in Wales, but in trying to win the European championship from Juan Francisco Rodriguez at Almeria, Spain, he was outpointed. He defended his two titles against Dave Smith by stopping him in 12 rounds at Caerphilly. Enticing Rodriguez to come to Ebbw Vale he outpointed him to gain a third title. He beat a British challenger, John

Feeney, on points, then went to Los Angeles to try and take the world title from Lupe Pintor. He was putting up a good show until caught on the chin in round 12 and put down heavily for the full count. He failed to regain consciousness and died 46 days later.
Score 28: w25 (10) d1 l2.

Palma, Sergio

World Super-Bantamweight Champion 1980–82

(b. Chaco, Argentina, Jan. 1, 1956). Began pro boxing: Jan 15, 1976.

Strong and tough, with plenty of stamina, he won his country's super-bantam or light-featherweight title in his 16th paid bout by outpointing Arnoldo Aguero at Buenos Aries. He became South American champion seven months later with a points verdict over Hugo Melgarejo. Palma kept both titles for two years and then fought for the W.B.A. version of the world crown, but was outpointed by Ricardo Cardona. On Aug. 9, 1980 he knocked out Leo Randolph in five rounds to become champion, successfully defending his crown five times in the next 17 months. On June 12, 1982, however, he was outpointed by Leo Cruz (Dominica) over 15 rounds at Miami, Florida, and lost the title.
Score 59: w50 (19) d4 l5.

Palmer, Jack

British Heavyweight Champion 1903–06

(b. Benwell, Newcastle, England, March 31, 1878 – d. Newcastle, Feb. 13, 1928). Began pro boxing: Dec. 5, 1898.

He won the title by knocking out Big Ben

Above: Carlos Ortiz in London in 1963, before his points win over Maurice Cullen.

Taylor, defended it against Geoff Thorne but then lost to Gunner James Moir. He then had the audacity to challenge Tommy Burns, the world heavyweight champion, but was knocked out in four at 'Wonderland' in the East End of London and retired in 1909.
Score 29: w20 (5) (2) d6 Dnc.1.

Palmer, Thomas 'Pedlar'

British Bantamweight Champion 1894–99

(b. Canning Town, London, Nov. 19, 1876 – d. Brighton, Sussex, Feb. 13, 1949). Began pro boxing: 1891.

Palmer came of fighting stock. His father was a more than useful prize-ring performer, while his mother could beat any woman in the London suburb of Canning Town – and frequently did. Their son's nickname was one commonly applied at the time to anyone bearing the surname of Palmer. Pedlar was a professional fighter at 15, but his early bare-fist battles are mostly unrecorded. At the age of 19 he won the British title by defeating Billy Plimmer, who was disqualified when his brother climbed into the ring in round 14. In a return bout Plimmer was stopped in 17.

These bouts were held at the National Sporting Club (N.S.C.), scene of many of Palmer's greatest victories. In 1899 members of the club sponsored a trip to America to give their popular champion a chance to win the vacant world title. The little Londoner was knocked out in 75 seconds by 'Terrible Terry' McGovern, who returned Palmer's proferred glove at the start with a swinging

right to the chin. Palmer was given a second chance two years later when the N.S.C. imported an American, Harry Harris, to fight Palmer for the title, vacant once more. But Palmer was beaten on points.

Having lost his British title to Harry Ware, Palmer tried to take the featherweight crown, but lost to Ben Jordan. An attempt to regain his bantamweight title was frustrated by Joe Bowker. In spite of these setbacks he remained a London idol, with polished wins over such celebrities of the time as Digger Stanley, Young Joseph, and Cockney Cohen.

In 1907 he was jailed for five years for manslaughter following a fight in a train. This virtually ended his career, although he did make a comeback after his release. But by this time he was 36, and after eight mediocre performances retired to Brighton.
Score 64: w45 (2) d4 l15.

Palomino, Carlos

World Welterweight Champion (W.B.C.) 1976–79

(b. San Luis, Mexico, Aug. 10, 1949). Began pro boxing: Sept. 14, 1972.

A remarkably skilful boxer with a good punch who had most of his early contests in Los Angles. In his fourth year as a pro, Palomino went to London and stopped John H. Stracey in 12 rounds to win the W.B.C. version of the world welterweight title. In the next two years he successfully defended his crown seven times: Armando Muniz (w.rsf.15), Dave Green (w.ko.11), Everaldo Azevedo (w.pts.15), Jose Palacios (w.ko.13), Ryu Sorimachi (w.ko.7), Mimoun Mohatar (w.rsf.9) and Armando Muniz (w.pts.15). On Jan. 14, 1979, however, he was outpointed by Wilfred Benitez and lost the title. A points loss over ten rounds by Roberto Duran decided his retirement. He was never knocked out or stopped.
Score 34: w28 (16) d3 l3.

Papke, Billy

World Middleweight Champion, 1908–12

(b. Spring Valley, Illinois, Sept. 17, 1886 – d. Newport, California, Nov. 26, 1936). Began pro boxing: Nov. 6, 1905.

A strong, tough, aggressive fighter with a good kayo record who won the world title from the great Stanley Ketchel by some quick thinking. When they advanced to shake hands at the start of the contest Papke slammed a right at the champion's chin and had him so dazed, only his gameness kept him going into the 12th round when the referee called a halt to the slaughter. In a return match Ketchel gave him an unmerciful beating and knocked him out in the 11th round. When Ketchel was murdered in 1910, Papke assumed the championship and, going to London, stopped the British champion,

Jim Sullivan, in the 9th round of a title defence. He lost his claim when outpointed by Frank Mantell over 20 rounds at Sacramento. Fighting Frank Klaus for the vacant title in 1913 he was disqualified for a low punch in the 15th round. He died by his own hand.
Score 62: w42 (30) d7 l13.

Papp, Lazlo

European Middleweight Champion, 1962–65

(b. Hungary, March 25, 1926). Began pro boxing: May 18, 1957.

World middleweight champion Joey Giardello may have been lucky that the Hungarian government denied undefeated Laszlo Papp a shot at his title in 1965. For the Hungarian had disposed of six challengers since he won the European title in 1962 – all but one inside the distance. And as an amateur he had built up an unequalled record, winning gold medals in three consecutive Olympic Games – 1948 (middleweight), 1952 and 1956 (light-middleweight). He also had the distinction of being Hungary's one and only boxer permitted to turn professional, which he did at the age of 31. In his eight professional years he was unbeaten in 29 bouts.

A southpaw, Papp carried tremendous power in his left hook. But he suffered from brittle bones, and a hand injury at times kept him out of the ring. This handicap delayed his chance of a European title fight until 16 May, 1962 when he made short work of Chris Christensen, stopping him in seven

rounds; and in the next 2½ years only Mick Leahy, the British champion, made him travel the full course.

In early 1965 Papp was in line for a world title fight, but was denied permission by the Hungarian authorities to continue to box for financial gain – it was not, they claimed compatible with his country's socialist principles. Papp relinquished his European title and never boxed again professionally.
Score 29: w26 (15) d3 l0.

Paret, Benny 'Kid'

World Welterweight Champion, 1960–62

(b. Santa Clara, Cuba, March 14, 1937 – d. New York, U.S.A. April 3, 1962). Began pro boxing: Aug. 11, 1955.

Smart and fast, but not a big hitter, Paret spent his first three pro years boxing in his own country, going to New York in March 1958. In Las Vegas on May 27, 1960 he won the world welter title by outpointing Don Jordan and defended it against Federico Thompson in New York, but on April 1, 1961 he was knocked out in the 13th round by Emile Griffith. Paret regained the title with a points victory in a return match six months later, then went after the middleweight crown but was stopped by tough Gene Fullmer in ten rounds at Las Vegas. Meeting Griffith again in a rubber contest on March 24, 1962, Paret was battered into unconsciousness before the bout was stopped in the 12th round. He died ten days later.
Score 50: w35 (10) d3 l12.

Park, Chan-Hee

World Flyweight Champion (W.B.C.) 1979–80

(b. Pusan, South Korea, March 23, 1957). Began pro boxing: July 8, 1977.

In his 11th bout as a pro he won the W.B.C. version of the world title by outpointing Miguel Canto over 15 rounds. He retained the crown five times: Riki Igarashi (w.pts.15), Miguel Canto (drew), Guty Espada (w.ko.2), Arnel Arrozal (w.pts.15) and Alberto Morales (w.pts.15). In his next title defence he was knocked out in nine rounds by Shoji Oguma and in a return he was outpointed. They had a third meeting on Feb. 3, 1981 and this also ended in Park losing on points.
Score 23: w17 (6) d2 l4.

Park, Chong-Pal

World Super-Middleweight Champion 1984–88

(b. Chon-Ra, Korea, Aug. 11, 1960). Began pro boxing: Nov. 26, 1977.

A very hard-punching box-fighter, Park was knocked out in the first round in his fifth

paid bout, but this did not deter him and he won the O.P.B.F. middleweight crown on August 22, 1979 by knocking out Cassius Naito in two rounds at Seoul. He defended this successfully on 15 occasions, then lost it to Kyung-Min Nah by a kayo in seven rounds, but regained it in a return bout, winning on a four-round kayo. On July 22, 1984 he won the I.B.F. super-middleweight crown when stopping Murray Sutherland in 11 rounds. He retained this title eight times, and on Dec. 6, 1987 won the vacant W.B.A. crown by knocking out Jesus Gallardo of Mexico in two rounds. He defended this against Polly Pasieron (stopped 5) but dropped it on a points verdict in Fulgencio Obelmejias on May 23, 1988.
Score 52: w46 (40) d2 l4.

Parlov, Mate

World Light-Heavyweight Champion (W.B.C.), 1978. European Light-Heavyweight Champion, 1977

(b. Split, Yugoslavia, Nov. 16, 1948). Began pro boxing: May 31, 1975.

Not many fighters have come out of Yugoslavia, but this Gold Medallist at the 1972 Olympic Games soon made his mark in the pro ranks. He won the European title by outpointing Domenico Adinolfi (Italy) at Belgrade in his 14th paid bout, and defended it successfully three times. He gained the W.B.C. world crown by knocking out Miguel Cuello in nine rounds at Milan. Parlov kept the world title by outpointing John Conteh in Belgrade, but lost to Marvin Johnson at Marsala, Italy, on a stoppage in the tenth. He gained a draw with Marvin Camel when trying to regain the title, but was outpointed in a return contest and retired.
Score 29: w24 (12) d2 l3.

Pastrano, Willie

World Light-Heavyweight Champion 1963–65

(b. New Orleans, Louisiana, Nov. 27, 1935). Began pro boxing: Sept. 10, 1951.

So fond of spaghetti that he had a physique more like a swimmer's than a boxer's, but Pastrano was an extremely clever boxer for all that. He did not carry much of a punch and no one ever thought he would win a world crown. In any case it took him 12 years of fighting all over the place before he got his chance, when he astounded everyone by taking a decision and the title from Harold Johnson. He caused a surprise by stopping his first challenger, Gregorio Peralta in six rounds, and an even greater one when he produced a stopping punch in round 11 of his defence against Terry Downes in Manchester, after looking a loser all the way. Jose Torres got through his defence, however, the bout being stopped in the ninth round and Willie retired.
Score 84: w63 (14) d3 l13.

Right: Lazlo Papp was a great European champion, but never fought for the world title.

Paterson, Jackie

World, British and British Empire Flyweight Champion 1939–48, British and British Empire Bantamweight Champion 1945–49

(b. Springfield, Ayrshire, Scotland, Sept. 5, 1920 – d. South Africa, Nov. 19, 1966). Began pro boxing: May 26, 1938.

The first southpaw to win the world flyweight title, Jackie Paterson was a fast-moving heavy puncher who took the European, Empire, and British bantamweight titles as well. Although he relied principally on a left hook, he could hit hard with either hand.

At the age of 13, Jackie joined the famous Anderston Club in Glasgow. In 1938 he turned professional. Paterson was soon disposing of the leading British flyweight contenders in summary fashion, and in 1939 took the British title by knocking out Paddy Ryan in 13 rounds. After defeating Kid Tanner for the Empire title he met world champion Peter Kane in 1943 and relieved him of his crown in just 61 seconds. Paterson successfully defended his three titles against Joe Curran, but when he failed to make the weight against Hawaiian challenger Dado Marino the British Boxing Board of Control (B.B.B.C.) stripped him of his titles. Rinty Monaghan, one of the few to hold a victory over Paterson, was matched with Marino for the 'vacant' world crown, but a legal move by the Scottish southpaw against the B.B.B.C. restored his titles to him. Paterson then 'boiled' himself down to 8 stone (112 pounds) to meet Monaghan, and was knocked out in seven rounds.

Meanwhile, during his reign as flyweight king, Paterson had acquired the Empire, European, and British bantamweight titles. He lost the European crown back to Theo Medina, but retained the other two by a knockout victory over Norman Lewis. Finally, in 1949, he succumbed to Stan Rowan on points. Paterson was then 29. When he retired in 1951, Paterson had little left of the estimated £100,000 he earned in the ring. Most of the money had gone on losing greyhounds. He moved to South Africa, where he was killed in a street fight.
Score 91: *w*63 (41) *d*3 *l*25.

Patterson, Floyd

World Heavyweight Champion 1956–62

(b. Waco, North Carolina, Jan. 4, 1935). Began pro boxing: Sept. 12, 1952.

Patterson may not rank as a great champion of his division, but he did get several fistic records. He was the first Olympic Games gold medallist to win the world heavyweight championship; and he was the youngest fighter (21 years 11 months) to win that title and the first man to regain it.

An intelligent boxer, Patterson was not ideally built for a heavyweight. He stood barely 6 ft. and weighed only 13 st. 8 lb (190 pounds) with a short reach of 71 inches and a small 12¾-in. fist. His short arms made it imperative for him to leap at his opponents, sometimes with both feet off the floor, in order to land his punches. It was a style that exposed him to counter blows, and in seven of his title bouts he was put down 16 times.

A Golden Gloves champion in 1951 and 1952, Patterson took the Olympic middleweight title at the Helsinki Games and immediately turned professional. In his first 36 contests he was beaten once only, a points defeat by veteran Joey Maxim. In 1956 he fought Archie Moore for the title left vacant by the retirement of Rocky Marciano, and won by a knockout in round five to become the fifth black heavyweight champion.

After he had stopped Tommy Jackson, his

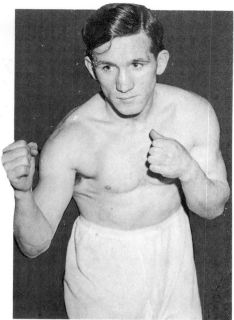

Jackie Paterson was the first southpaw to become world flyweight champion.

leading challenger, Patterson met several 'contenders' such as Pete Rademacher (w.ko.6), Roy Harris (w.ret.12), and Brian London (w.ko.11). But against imported Ingemar Johansson in 1959, Patterson was stopped in three rounds after being floored seven times by the Swede's powerful right. He made history by regaining the title from Johansson by a knockout in five rounds, and completed the rubber with a six-round knockout victory.

He successfully defended his crown against Tom McNeeley, then in his tenth title fight Patterson met the formidable Sonny Liston. He failed miserably, being knocked out in 2 min. 6 sec., of the first round. In the inevitable return bout, he lasted just four seconds longer against his huge Nemesis before being battered to defeat.

Patterson continued boxing for five years and even made another bid to regain his title by challenging Muhammad Ali. He was then 30, and did well to stay 12 rounds before the referee came to his rescue. After Ali had been deprived of his crown Patterson fought the World Boxing Association's champion, Jimmy Ellis, and seemed unlucky to be adjudged a points loser. He was out of the ring for two years, then made a comeback, winning nine fights, but finally was stopped in seven rounds by Muhammad Ali on Sept. 20, 1972.
Score 64: *w*55 (40) *d*1 *l*8.

Paul, Tommy

World Featherweight Champion (N.B.A.) 1932–33

(b. Buffalo, New York, March 4, 1909). Began pro boxing: June 1927.

Paul had a distinguished amateur career,

Willie Pastrano (left) on his way to a points win over Brian London on Feb. 25, 1958.

Mate Parlov (right) dodges a left jab from former champion John Conteh. Parlov was the first Yugoslav world boxing champion.

winning several titles, and turned pro at 18 years of age. He was soon fighting the best at his weight, including Freddie Miller, Bushy Graham, Al Brown, Fidel LaBarba and Archie Bell. When Battling Battalino was under suspension in 1932, Paul was matched by the N.B.A. to fight Johnny Pena for the 'vacant' title and won on points. Eight months later he lost a ten-rounds bout on points to Freddie Miller, which was regarded as carrying the championship. He never had a chance to win back his crown and after a long disappointing run in 1934 and 1935, decided to retire the following year.
Score 117: *w*80 (25) *d*8 *l*29.

Pedroza, Eusebio

World Featherweight Champion (W.B.A.) 1978–85

(b. Panama City, March 2, 1953). Began pro boxing: Dec. 1, 1973.

A hard-punching, aggressive fighter: he began as a bantam and in his 16th pro bout attempted to take the world title from Alfonso Zamora, but was knocked out in the second round. He grew into a featherweight and on April 15, 1978 won the W.B.A. world title by knocking out Cecilio Lastra in the 13th round. Pedroza proved himself a worthy world champion, successfully defending his crown against 19 challengers in his seven year reign, ten of them inside-the-distance wins. At the age of 32, he finally lost his crown to Barry McGuigan in London on June 8, 1985 on a points verdict.
Score 46: *w*39 (24) *d*1 *l*5 *Dnc*.1.

Pender, Paul

World Middleweight Champion 1960–62

(b. Brookline, Massachusetts, June 20, 1930). Began pro boxing: Jan. 28, 1949.

Boxing was more of a hobby than a profession for Pender, who was a fireman by trade. After three years of proficient boxing, he suffered two nasty setbacks and virtually retired. In 1954 he came again, and on Jan. 22, 1960 he caused a surprise by outpointing Ray Robinson for his world title. There were a return championship bout and most people thought Sugar Ray would win back his crown as he had done before. But no, Pender outboxed Robinson to keep the title, defended it against Terry Downes, who was stopped in the seventh, and won a points verdict over Carmen Basilio. In London three months later he was forced to retire to Downes with a cut eye, but in the return in Boston he regained the crown with a fine points win. Later in 1962 he refused to be 'ordered about' by the boxing commissions and announced his retirement. 'It is no real way of living', he said. 'A man is too much away from his family to make it worthwhile.' So a scientist at glove fighting gave it up while still world champion.
Score 48: *w*40 (20) *d*2 *l*6.

Pep, Willie

World Featherweight Champion 1942–50

(b. Middletown, Connecticut, Sept. 19, 1922). Began pro boxing: July 3, 1940.

Boxing fans named featherweight king Willie Pep 'Willie the Wisp' because of his fleet-footed use of every inch of the ring. Unlike many fast boxers, Pep could produce a knock-out punch, but most of his 230 wins (as well as his amateur wins) took him the full distance. He must have boxed thousands of rounds in his 26-year career.

Born William Guiglermo Papaleo in Connecticut, he started his long professional career at the age of 17 after winning the fly and bantam championships of his state as an

Floyd Patterson (left) and Muhammad Ali in their first fight, which Ali won.

Eusebio Pedroza, an outstanding featherweight champion for over seven years.

not fight professionally until he was 26, he was undefeated in his first 50 fights. He won the world title at 28, held it for six years, and made 14 defences of it. He was 34 when he finally dropped it.

To get his big chance Perez had to travel in 1954 to Japan, where he outpointed Yoshio

Pascual Perez, the first Argentinian to win a world boxing title, is carried in triumph after knocking out Japan's Yoshio Shirai in Tokyo.

amateur. When the 20-year-old Pep won the New York State Athletic Commission (N.Y.S.A.C.) version of the world featherweight title in 1942, he became the youngest fighter in 40 years to win a world crown. After consolidating his claim to the crown by beating National Boxing Association champion Sal Bartolo, Pep held it for more than six years before he encountered the lean Sandy Saddler, who sensationally knocked out 'the Wisp' in round four. Before he met Saddler, no one except the heavier Angott (then lightweight champion) had beaten Pep in 136 contests.

Pep confirmed his greatness when he surprisingly outpointed Saddler in their return four months later. Three more successful defences followed, including a points verdict over European champion Ray Famechon. But in the rubber match with Saddler he was forced to retire in round eight after suffering a severe mauling by his long-armed enemy. Pep fought on, but after he had been stopped in two rounds by Lulu Perez in 1954 the N.Y.S.A.C. withdrew his licence on the grounds that, at 32 and with 14 fighting years behind him, he was too old. But elsewhere in America Pep continued as a star performer until 1958 when Hogan 'Kid' Bassey stopped him in nine rounds and Pep retired. Seven years later the 43-year-old Pep made a comeback. After ten bouts – and nine wins – he finally gave up and became a referee.
Score 242: *w*230 (65) *d*1 *l*11.

Perez, Pascual

World Flyweight Champion 1955–60

(b. Mendoza, Argentina, March 4, 1926 – d. Argentina, Jan. 22, 1977). Began pro boxing: Dec. 5, 1952.

The first Argentinian boxer to win a world title, tiny Pascual Perez packed the heaviest punch of modern flyweights. And the 4 ft. 11 in., 7½ stone (105 pounds) champion also possessed seemingly unlimited stamina. His record was remarkable – although he did

Sandy Saddler's face is distorted by a hard right from Willie Pep. Pep won once only in the four times they met.

107

Shirai, who had held the title for 2½ years. Six months later he went back to Tokyo for the return and knocked Shirai out in five rounds. A long run of successful defences followed. It included victories over British champion Dai Dower (round 1), and European titleholder Young Martin of Spain (round 3). In 1960 he lost the title on points in Thailand to Pone Kingpetch. In a return title bout in Los Angeles Perez capitulated in round eight, but continued to box for another four years before he retired at the age of 38.
Score 91: *w*83 (56) *d*1 *l*7.

Perez, Victor

World Flyweight Champion (N.B.A.) 1931–32

(b. Tunis, Tunisia, Oct. 18, 1911 – d. Auschwitz, Poland, Feb. 4, 1943). Began pro boxing: Feb. 4, 1928.

Very fast and clever, with a good punch, he tried to become French champion in 1930 but was knocked out by Kid Oliva in four rounds. The following year he won the title by outpointing Valentin Angelman. Four months later he knocked out Frankie Genaro in two rounds to win the N.B.A. version of the world flyweight title, receiving also I.B.U. recognition for his feat. At his first defence, against Jackie Brown in Manchester, England, a year later, he was surprisingly knocked out in 13 rounds by a supposedly light-hitter. In 1934 he tried to win the world bantam crown from Al Brown in Paris, but was outpointed. Perez went on fighting regularly until after a run on defeats he retired in 1938. He died in a German concentration camp at Auschwitz during World War II.
Score 133: *w*92 (28) *d*15 *l*26.

Perkins, Eddie

World Light-Welterweight Champion 1962–65

(b. Clarksdale, Mississippi, March 3, 1937). Began pro boxing: Dec. 27, 1956.

This good class fighter, strong and with plenty of stamina, fought mainly in Chicago in his early bouts. He went to Milan on Oct. 21, 1961 and fought a draw over 15 rounds with Duilio Loi (Italy) for the world light-welterweight crown. In a return, 11 months later, he beat Loi on points, but lost it back to him (also on points) just three months afterwards. Perkins won the vacant world championship by outpointing Roberto Cruz in Manila, retained it in Tokyo and Kingston, Jamaica, but lost to Carlos Hernandez at Caracas, Venezuela on a points verdict. He went on boxing for over ten years, but never again fought for a world crown, although he won the American welterweight title by out-pointing Amando Muniz in Denver, Colorado. He never defended this and retired in 1975.
Score 98: *w*74 (20) *d*3 *l*20 *Dnc.*1.

Petersen, Jack

British and British Empire Heavyweight Champion 1932–36, British Light-Heavyweight Champion 1932

(b. Cardiff, Wales, Sept. 2, 1911). Began pro boxing: Sept. 28, 1931.

After being A.B.A. light-heavyweight champion he had his father and a syndicate of sportsmen to aid him as a pro. However, he was too light at 13 stone (182 pounds) which meant he had to give weight away more often than not. He won the Welsh light-heavyweight title in one round from Dick Powell in Feb. 1931. On May 23 the same year he outpointed Harry Crossley to win the British championship, and 50 days later knocked out Reggie Meen in two rounds to become British heavyweight king. He defended this against Jack Pettifer (12), Jack Doyle (2), then lost it to Len Harvey on points, but regained the title in a return match, Harvey retiring in the 12th of a bout that also carried the Empire title. He defended the latter against Larry Gains (w.rtd.13), George Cook (w.pts.15), Len Harvey (w.pts.15) and Jock McAvoy (w.pts.15). He was surprisingly beaten for his titles by Ben Foord, and after being stopped in ten rounds by Walter Neusel (with whom he had already fought two terrific battles), he retired.
Score 38: *w*33 (19) *d*0 *l*5.

Phillips, Al

European and British Empire Featherweight Champion 1947

(b. Aldgate, London, Jan. 25, 1920). Began pro boxing: Jan. 20, 1939.

He began as an amateur at the age of 15. In 1938 he toured England's West Country with a travelling booth with Gipsy Daniels and Freddie Mills. He joined the Royal Navy at the outbreak of World War II, but managed to continue his pro career. After winning several eliminators for the British title, he finally met Nel Tarleton at Manchester but was outpointed after a determined challenge. However, he won the British Empire title by outpointing Cliff Anderson (British Guiana), although by a disputed decision. In a return bout Phillips won in eight rounds, the challenger being ruled out for an alleged low punch. Al took the European crown from Raymond Famechon in similar fashion, also in round eight. His reign as a dual champion lasted only four months after which he lost both his titles to Ronnie Clayton, but not before he had put up stout resistance. Al was not done, however. Fighting his way through the featherweight ranks, he again challenged Clayton, this time with only the British title at stake. Phillips fought like the Aldgate Tiger they called him, but it was no use, the verdict going to the champion by a close margin. That was in 1951, when Phillips

retired. A quietly spoken, modest fighter out of the ring, he was liked and respected by all.
Score 77: *w*61 (23) *d*3 *l*3.

Pinder, Enrique

World Bantamweight Champion (W.B.A.) 1972–73

(b. Panama City, Aug. 7, 1947). Began pro boxing: Aug. 20, 1966.

This rapid-punching box-fighter rarely fought out of his own country in his seven years career, winning most of his bouts but occasionally running into trouble. He became W.B.A. world champion by outpointing Rafael Herrera (Mexico) over 15 rounds at Panama City on July 30, 1972. Pinder kept the crown for only six months, being knocked out in three rounds by Romeo Anaya (Mexico). In a return match seven months later the Mexican repeated his victory and after one more losing bout, Pinder retired.
Score 44: *w*37 (15) *d*2 *l*5.

Pintor, Lupe

World Bantam (W.B.C.) 1979–83, Super-Bantamweight Champion (W.B.C.) 1985–86

(b. Cuajimalpa, Mexico, April 13, 1955). Began pro boxing: March 2, 1974.

This strong attacking fighter with a kayo punch in each fist built up a long knockout record before outpointing Carlos Zarate over 15 rounds at Las Vegas to win the W.B.C. world crown on June 3, 1979. He defended against Alberto Sandoval (w.rsf.12), Eijiro Murata (draw), and Johnny Owen (w.ko.12); the British boxer never recovered consciousness and died 46 days later.

Pintor successfully defended his title five more times and relinquished it to go after the W.B.C. super-bantam title. This he won eventually on Aug. 18, 1986 by outpointing Juan Meza at Mexico City, by which time he was 30. He kept his crown for five months, then lost it to Samart Payakaroon in Bangkok on a five rounds kayo.
Score 65: *w*54 (41) *d*2 *l*9.

Pladner, Emile

World Flyweight Champion (N.B.A.) 1929

(b. Clermont-Ferrand, France, Sept. 2, 1906 – d. Auch, France, March 15, 1980). Began pro boxing: Jan. 20, 1926.

This aggressive two-fisted warrior won his native title in his 15th pro bout by outpointing Francois Morracchini in Paris. He was proclaimed European champion by the E.B.U. but lost this title to Johnny Hill (U.K.) on a points defeat in London. Pladner regained the title by stopping the Scot in six rounds in Paris and on May 2, 1929, knocked out Frankie Genaro (U.S.A.) in 56 seconds of the first round to win N.B.A.

recognition as world champion. Seven weeks later he lost the title back to Genaro, being disqualified in the fifth round for hitting low. He went on fighting for the next seven years, all over Europe and in America, but with never a world crown involved. He retired in 1936.
Score 128: *w*101 (36) *d*10 *l*17.

Plimmer, Billy

World Bantamweight Champion 1892–95

(b. Birmingham, Warwickshire, Feb. 6, 1869 – d. Birmingham, Feb. 23, 1929). Began pro boxing: 1888.

A competent boxer with a classical stance, he became bantam champion of England in 1891 by knocking out Jim Stevens in 15 rounds in London. In America the following year he outpointed Tommy Kelly at Coney Island, New York, to win the world title. Plimmer remained in the United States for over three years without defeat, then came home and kept his two titles by knocking out challenger George Corfield in seven rounds. He lost his titles in 1895 to Tom 'Pedlar' Palmer. Plimmer fought once a year for the next five years, then retired in 1900.
Score 46: *w*33 (14) *d*5 *l*5 *ND*.3.

Power, Colin

European and British Light-Welterweight Champion 1977–79

(b. Paddington, London, Feb. 2, 1956). Began pro boxing: June 11, 1975.

A swarming fighter with a good punch who came into the British light-welter title at the end of his third year as a pro, stopping Des Morrison in ten rounds on Oct. 19, 1977. He defended this against Chris Walker, stopping him in the seventh, then went to Paris where he forced Jean Baptiste Piedvache (France) to retire in 11 rounds for the European crown. Three months later he lost his E.B.U. title to Fernando Sanchez (Spain) the referee stopping the contest in the 12th. He made amends by winning the Lonsdale Belt outright by outpointing Clinton McKenzie, thus regaining the crown he had been forced to give up when becoming European champion. In a return bout seven months later McKenzie won back the title on a points verdict and Power retired in 1980, but made a comeback with three wins in 1982.
Score 34: *w*28 (20) *d*1 *l*5.

Pritchett, Johnny

British and Commonwealth Middleweight Champion 1965–69

(b. Nottingham, Feb. 15, 1943). Began pro boxing: Nov. 12, 1963.

Former A.B.A. welter champion, he went up a division when turning pro. A clever boxer with a solid punch, he won 12 of his first 16 paid fights, then took the British title by stopping Wally Swift in 12 rounds on Nov. 8, 1965. He stopped Nat Jacobs (w.rtd.13) and outpointed Wally Swift to make the Lonsdale Belt his own property, then forced Milo Calhoun (Jamaica) to retire in eight rounds to win the Commonwealth crown. He defended both titles against Les McAteer with a points verdict, then on Feb. 20, 1969 went to Milan to challenge Carlos Duran (Italy-Argentina) for the European title. They had a tremendous battle that had a shock ending. For 12 rounds it was hammer and tongs, but in the 13th the champion was hurt and reverted to holding. He was bleeding from a cut eye and the Austrian referee moved between the boxers. It was thought that he was going to stop the contest, but instead he disqualified the British boxer for butting. Pritchett had never been ruled out in over 100 amateur and 35 pro bouts and he was so disgusted that he retired.
Score 34: *w*32 (20) *d*1 *l*1.

Pryor, Aaron

World Light-Welterweight Champion (W.B.A.) 1980–83, (I.B.F.) 1984

(b. Cincinnati, Ohio, Oct. 20, 1955). Began pro boxing: Nov. 12, 1976.

Unbeaten in his first 32 contests. A hard-hitting, aggressive fighter, he boxed mainly around his home town and on Aug. 2, 1980 before his own supporters, won the W.B.A. world light-welter title by knocking out Antonio Cervantes in four rounds. In six successful defences he defeated Gaetan Hart (w.rsf.6), Lennox Blackmore (w.rsf.2), Dujuan Johnson (w.rsf.7), Miguel Montilla (w.rsf.12). Akio Kameda (w.rsf.6), and Alexis Arguello (world lightweight champion) (w.rsf.14) in Miami, Florida on Nov. 12, 1982.

He made two more title defences the following year, then relinquished his world crown. The I.B.F. proclaimed him its junior-welterweight champion in January 1984. Pryor defended this crown against Nick Furlano and Gary Hinton, then retired.
Score 36: *w*36 (32) *d*0 *l*0.

Qawi, Dwight Muhammad

World Light-Heavy 1981–1983 and Cruiserweight Champion, 1985–1986

(b. Baltimore, Maryland, Jan. 5, 1953). Began pro boxing: April 19, 1978.

He never fought as an amateur, but learned to box while serving a prison term. He won his first world crown in his 18th contest by stopping the holder, Matthew Saad Muhammad, in ten rounds. Three months later he defeated Jerry Martin in six rounds in a title defence, and in a return with Muhammad in August 1982, forced the referee to intervene in round six.

Until then he had fought as Dwight Braxton, but he changed his name in 1982 and celebrated by stopping challenger Eddie Davis in 11 rounds. On March 18, 1983 he was outpointed by Michael Spinks for the vacant world light-heavyweight title, but two years later won the W.B.A. junior heavyweight crown by stopping Piet Crous (11 rounds) in South Africa. He successfully defended against Leon Spinks (six rounds) but dropped his title to Evander Holyfield (points 15) at Atlanta, Georgia, on July 12, 1986.
Score 30: *w*26 (15) *d*1 *l*3.

Ramos, Mando

World Lightweight Champion (W.B.C.) 1968–72

(b. Long Beach, California, Nov. 15, 1948). Began pro boxing: Nov. 17, 1965.

A hard-punching, aggressive fighter who made Los Angeles his base. There on Sept. 28, 1968, he fought for the world championship but lost on points to Carlos Teo Cruz. They had a second meeting on Feb. 18, 1969 when he stopped his opponent in the 11th round. Ramos made a successful defence against Yoshiaki Numata eight months later, but was forced to retire in nine rounds to Ismael Laguna. He did not have to try and win it back, as the W.B.C. decided in 1972 that the title was vacant and Mando met Pedro Carrasco in Madrid. Alas, he was disqualified in the 11th round for hitting low after he had floored the Spaniard four times. He got his own back on Feb. 19, 1972, by outpointing Carrasco in Los Angeles and then went back to Madrid to give a repeat performance. Three months later he was stopped in eight rounds by Chango Carmona to lose his crown. Knockouts now began to appear in his record and he retired in 1975.
Score 49: *w*37 (23) *d*1 *l*11.

Ramos, Ultiminio 'Sugar'

World Featherweight Champion 1963–64

(b. Matanzas, Cuba, Dec. 2, 1941). Began pro boxing: Oct. 5, 1957.

A strong, vigorous fighter with a big right-hand punch who spent the early part of his career in his own country before moving on to Panama, Mexico and then America. By that time there were 30 wins by stoppages to his record and on March 21, 1963, he challenged Davey Moore for the world title. He forced the champion to retire after ten rounds. The loser collapsed and died two days later from head injuries. Ramos retained his title against Rafiu King (w.pts.15), Mitsunori Seki (w.rsf.6) and Floyd Robertson (w.pts.15), but against Vicente Saldivar he was forced to retire in the 12th round. He made two attempts to win the lightweight crown from Carlos Oritz, but was stopped each time and retired in 1972.
Score 66: *w*55 (40) *d*4 *l*7.

Randolph, Leo

World Super-Bantamweight Champion 1980

(b. Tacoma, Washington, Feb. 27, 1958). Began pro boxing: June 20, 1978.

Winning an Olympic Gold Medal in 1976, he continued to box as an amateur for two more years, showing good style and respectable punching power. In his third year as a pro and his 18th bout he stopped Ricardo Cardona (Colombia) in the 15th and last round to win the world super-bantam title. He remained champion for only three months, then was knocked out in six rounds by Sergio Palma (Argentina). In the dressing-room after the fight he announced his retirement.
Score 19: w17 (9) d1 l1.

Rea, Des

British Junior-Welterweight Champion 1968–69

(b. Belfast, Northern Ireland, Jan. 8, 1944). Began pro boxing: Nov. 9, 1964.

A busy fighter but no great puncher, he won his native welterweight title in his tenth pro bout and went on to outpoint Vic Andretti to become the first holder of the newly introduced British junior-welterweight title. Trying to add the European crown, he was stopped in six rounds by Bruno Arcari at San Remo. After reigning as British champion for just a year, Rea lost on points in a return match with Andretti and in a third bout between them was knocked out in four. He fought on until 1974, getting in a lot of bouts, but after a losing run decided to retire. Unfortunately the bouts he lost near the end of his career gave him the unusual record for a champion of having lost more contests than he won.
Score 69: w28 (9) d5 l36.

Reeson, Sammy

European and British Cruiserweight Champion 1985–

(b. Battersea, London, Jan. 5, 1963). Began pro boxing: May 19, 1983.

This 6 ft. 1½ in. southpaw became the first holder of the British cruiserweight title by outpointing Stewart Lithgo over 12 rounds on Oct. 31, 1985, when he was unbeaten in 17 bouts as a pro. He added to this honour on April 22, 1987 when he outpointed Manfred Jassmann at London's Albert Hall to become the first European champion of this newly formed weight division. Seven months later he scored a seventh-round kayo victory over Luiji Ricci, his Italian challenger. His sole loss has been to Louis Pergaud when he was forced to retire in round four with a cut eye.
Score 25: w24 (5) d0 l0.

Riasco, Rigoberto

World Super-Bantamweight Champion (W.B.C.) 1976

(b. Panama City, 1948). Began pro boxing: May 10, 1966.

A dashing boxer with fast fists and feet, he never appeared likely to become a champion. Apart from a few trips abroad, all his contests took place in his home city. In 1975 he fought Alexis Arguello for the vacant world featherweight title but was knocked out in two rounds. On April 3, 1976, however, he won the W.B.C. newly-introduced super-bantamweight title by stopping Waruinge Nakayama in nine rounds at Panama City and made three defences the same year, beating off Livio Nolasco in ten rounds and outpointing Dong-Kyun Yum. But against Royal Kobayashi in Tokyo he was stopped in eight rounds to lose his crown.
Score 41: w28 (14) d4 l7.

Rios, Jaime

World Light-Flyweight Champion (W.B.A.) 1975–78

(b. Panama City, Aug. 14, 1953). Began pro boxing: July 28, 1973.

He spent his early years boxing in his home city and there on Aug. 23, 1975, he won the W.B.A. version of the world light-flyweight title by outpointing Rigoberto Marcano. Rios kept the crown against Kazunori Tenryo in Tokyo, but lost it to Juan Jose Guzman after an 11 months reign. He recaptured the title six months later by going back to Japan and outscoring Yoko Gushiken over 15 rounds. Gushiken was granted a return bout the following year and knocked out Rios in 13 rounds, after which defeat he retired.
Score 25: w20 (10) d1 l4.

Risko, Ed 'Babe'

World Middleweight Champion (N.Y.S.A.C.), 1935–36

(b. Syracuse, New York, July 14, 1911 – d. Syracuse, New York, March 7, 1957). Began pro boxing: April 14, 1932.

Real name Henry Pylkowski, of Polish extraction, this strong, vigorous fighter came into the New York State Athletics Commission version of the world championship by outpointing Teddy Yarosz on Sept. 19, 1935. After that he won three non-title bouts on points then met Jock McAvoy, the British champion, in Madison Square Garden. To the astonishment of everyone, Risko was knocked cold in the first round, being floored six times by the Rochdale Thunderbolt. Risko made a good recovery from that disaster, retaining his title against Tony Fisher, who was outpointed. Against Freddie Steele, however, he lost his championship on a points verdict and when they had the inevitable return bout seven months later, the result was the same. In his next 12 contests, Risko was stopped eight times and retired in 1939.
Score 93: w58 (17) d10 l25.

Ritchie, Willie

World Lightweight Champion 1912–14

(b. San Francisco, California, Feb. 13, 1891 – d. Burlingame, California, March 24, 1975). Began pro boxing: 1907.

A superlative boxer in all phases of the business. He spent the first five years of his career in California and in Nov. 1912 at Daly City won the world title from Ad Wolgast, who had ruled out of the fight in the 16th round for low hitting. The following year Ritchie beat off a fierce challenge by Mexican Joe Rivers, knocking him out in the 11th, and nine months later kept his crown by outpointing Tommy Murphy over 20 rounds. He was then tempted to go to London and face Freddie Welsh, the British champion, who narrowly outpointed him. Ritchie did not get a chance to regain his title and virtually retired in 1917 to become a boxing instructor for the army. Later on he was appointed a boxing inspector by the California State Commission.
Score 75: w49 (9) d15 l11.

Roberts, Jack

British Featherweight Champion 1901–02

(b. Broadstairs, Kent, Nov. 11, 1873). Began pro boxing: 1893.

Not much of a boxer, but an outstanding fighter, Roberts was a great favourite of the members of the National Sporting Club, where most of his fights took place. He lost more fights than he won but that did not deter him. On Jan. 21, 1901, he fought Will Curley, who claimed the British featherweight champoinship and was regarded as world champion by his supporters. For seven rounds he cut Roberts to ribbons and one spectator offered £100 to a cigar that Curley would win. Then from out of the blue Jack brought a right-hander that caught Will on the chin and it was all over. Roberts was acclaimed champion and kept the title for nearly two years, then was knocked out in five by the renowned Ben Jordan. Three months after his defeat of Curley, Roberts stopped Billy Smith (real name Murray Livingston) in eight rounds. The loser died two days later and Roberts was charged with manslaughter. Clever advocacy by his counsel, Marshall Hall, secured his freedom, but he was never the same fighter afterwards. However, he did not retire until 1910, by which time he was 37.
Score (incomplete) 68: w36 (8) d2 l30.

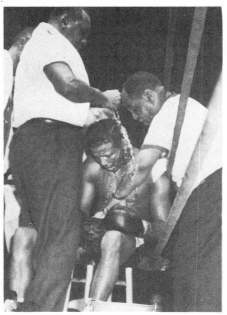

Left: *Sugar Ray Robinson – one of the greatest boxers of all time.*

Above: *Robinson in distress at the end of round 13 of his bout with Joey Maxim. Only a heatwave stopped him becoming a triple world titleholder.*

Robertson, Floyd

Commonwealth Featherweight Champion 1960–67

(b. Accra, Ghana, Jan. 7, 1927). Began pro boxing: Feb. 8, 1958.

A class boxer, he won his native featherweight title in his first pro bout, knocking out Skipping Gilbert in two rounds. Two fights later he won the West African crown by outpointing Ola Michael. He went to Belfast, Northern Ireland and made it his base, outpointing Percy Lewis on Nov. 26, 1960 to win the Commonwealth title. He defended this against Love Allotey (w.pts.15) and Joe Tetteh (w.rsf.11) and then fought Sugar Ramos (Cuba) for the world crown at Accra on May 9, 1964. The British referee, Jack Hart, gave his decision to Robertson, but was over-ruled by the two judges (U.S.A. and Mexico). The Ghanaian Boxing Commission claimed the title for Floyd, but did not get world support. Two years later Robertson tried again to win the world crown, but was knocked out in the second round by Vicente Saldivar. In 1967 he lost his Commonwealth title to John O'Brien and soon afterwards retired.
Score 40: *w*25 (10) *d*4 *l*11.

Robinson, Sugar Ray

World Welter and Middleweight Champion 1946–60

(b. Detroit, Michigan, May 3, 1921). Began pro boxing: Oct. 4, 1940.

Pound for pound, Sugar Ray Robinson must rank as the most skilful boxer of the century, perhaps the most complete ring performer of all time. Consider these facts for some indication of his greatness: he held the world welterweight title for four years and relinquished it undefeated; he was five times middleweight champion; he narrowly missed becoming a triple world titleholder when the extreme heat forced him to retire against world light-heavyweight champion Joey Maxim; he boxed for 25 years and fought 22 world championship contests; he lost only 19 bouts out of 202 professional contests; and he was never knocked out.

Born Walker Smith in Detroit, he was in his teens when his hero Joe Louis was on the rise, and carried the 'Brown Bomber's' kit to and from the gymnasium. As an amateur, Walker Smith won the Golden Gloves title in 1939 and the lightweight title the following year. In all he engaged in 85 amateur bouts, winning 69 inside the distance, and 40 of them in the opening round.

In 1940 he became a professional and acquired a new name – both by accident. Attending a small promotion one day as a spectator he was induced to substitute for a boxer named Ray Robinson who had failed to pass the doctor. He won in two rounds, and looked so promising that he was launched on a professional career that took in 26 straight winning fights in just over a year. He continued to box under his adopted name, and when someone remarked to George Gainsford that he had a 'sweet' fighter in his stable the trainer replied, 'Yes, he's as sweet as sugar'. 'Sugar Ray' was born.

Robinson grew into a welterweight and also moved into the ten-round class. Then,

111

trying for his 41st victory in a row, he dropped a points decision to rugged Jake LaMotta, the 'Bronx Bull'. It was a defeat that Robinson was to avenge four times, on the last occasion stopping LaMotta to relieve him of the middleweight crown. After the defeat by LaMotta, Robinson did not lose a fight for the next eight years. He won the vacant world welterweight title and defended it successfully five times, then reluctantly gave it up when he won his second world title, from LaMotta, on Feb. 14, 1951. In celebration he made a holiday trip to Europe, filling in time by disposing of six Continental middleweights in as many weeks. Then he accepted an offer from promoter Jack Solomons to defend his title against British champion Randolph Turpin in London. Turpin took the title amid scenes of enthusiasm unparalleled in British boxing history. But it was only a temporary loan of the championship. Robinson regained it 64 days later at New York's Polo Grounds by stopping Turpin in ten rounds before a vast crowd of 61,370 – a record for a title fight below the heavyweight class.

After two successful title defences in 1952 came Robinson's attempt to emulate Bob Fitzsimmons and Henry Armstrong and became a triple title holder by challenging Joey Maxim for the light-heavyweight championship. Robinson never tried harder to win a fight than he did this one. Perhaps he tried too hard, for on a heatwave night in June with an outside temperature of 104°F (40°C) he collapsed at the end of round 13. He was unable to come out for the 14th, although well ahead on points and in little danger of defeat. But he did last longer than the referee, who had to be replaced when he left the ring in a state of exhaustion at the end of round ten. After six months of inaction, Robinson announced his retirement from the ring but after almost two years started a comeback campaign that ended with his retaining his old title by knocking out Carl 'Bobo' Olson in spectacular fashion inside two rounds. Although then aged 36, Robinson was to engage in many more world title bouts. He lost and won against both Gene Fullmer and Carmen Basilio, and was twice outpointed by Paul Pender. When Pender was deposed by the National Boxing Association, Robinson had his final flings at the world crown, twice attempting to regain it for one more time. He held Gene Fullmer to a draw, but lost their return match. By then he was nearly 41. Robinson continued to star in the ring for more than four years, retiring for good at the end of 1965.
Score 202: w175 (110) d6 l19 Dnc.2.

Rodak, Leo

World Featherweight Champion (N.B.A.) 1938–39

(b. Chicago, Illinois, June 5, 1913). Began pro boxing: 1933.

After a splendid amateur record, losing only four of over a hundred bouts, he started to fight for pay in his home city and had a good start with a large number of wins. Nearing the end of his sixth year, when he was mingling with the top-notchers, he secured a fight on Dec. 29, 1938 with a Leone Efrati in Chicago which the N.B.A. decided was for the world title. Rodak won on points over ten rounds. Four months later, however, he faced up to Joey Archibald, holder of the New York version of the championship and lost on points over 15 rounds at Providence, Rhode Island. Leo fought on for four more years without getting another title shot, then joined the U.S. Marines. After an unsuccessful comeback he retired in 1946.
Score 115: w77 (6) d11 l27.

Roderick, Ernie

British Welter and Middleweight Champion 1939–48

(b. Liverpool, Lancashire, Jan. 25, 1914). Began pro boxing: June 4, 1931.

One of Britain's greatest fighters, although he failed to win a world crown. This clever boxer and solid puncher had a distinguished career that lasted 19 years, but was interfered with by World War II. Yet it took him into his ninth year as a pro before he got a title chance, then on March 23, 1939 he won the British welterweight title by knocking out Jake Kilrain in eight rounds. In his next bout he had the opportunity of a lifetime, fighting Henry Armstrong in London for the world welterweight title. The champion swarmed over his challenger from first going to last and it must have been a nightmarish encounter for Ernie. But he was there on his feet at the finish, battered but brave. Six years later – on May 29, 1945 – he won the British middleweight crown by outpointing Vince Hawkins, but lost it in a return contest. He went back to the welter class, recovered his title by outpointing Gwyn Williams and beating Eric Boon to win the Lonsdale Belt outright. A year later (1948) when he was 34, he was deprived of his crown by a hotly disputed points loss to Henry Hall. He retired in 1950.
Score 142: w114 (44) d4 l24.

Rodriguez, Luis

World Welterweight Champion 1963

(b. Camaguey, Cuba, June 17, 1937). Began pro boxing: June 2, 1956.

After a quiet start, in which he won his native welter title by outpointing Kid Fighique over 12 rounds at Havana, he found fighting more profitable in America and became something of a kayo specialist. On March 21, 1963 he caused a surprise by outpointing famous Emile Griffith to win the world welter title, but lost it on points in a return bout three months later. The following year he suffered another points loss to

Griffith in an attempt to become champion again. He fought Curtis Cokes for the vacant crown in 1966, but was stopped in 15 rounds. Three years went by before he had another try, this time being stopped in 11 rounds in Rome by Nino Benvenuti. He retired in 1972.
Score 121: w107 (49) d0 l13 Dnc.1.

Rojas, Raul

World Featherweight Champion (W.B.A.) 1968

(b. San Pedro, California, Nov. 5, 1941). Began pro boxing: Jan. 15, 1963.

A strong and vigorous fighter who started off with a long run of kayo wins in the Los Angeles area that in 1966 brought him a contest with Vicente Saldivar for the world title. He did well to stay into the 15th round against a great champion. Two years later he won the W.B.A. version of the featherweight title by outpointing Enrique Higgins (Colombia) on March 28, 1968. He reigned as champion for 70 days, losing his title on points to Shozo Saijyo (Japan). In 1970 he attempted to win the world junior-lightweight title (W.B.C.), but lost in five rounds to Yoshiaki Numata in Tokyo. A final knockout defeat by Mando Ramos brought about his retirement at the end of the year.
Score 47: w38 (24) d2 l7.

Rondon, Vicente Paul

World Light-Heavyweight Champion (W.B.A.) 1971–72

(b. San Jose, Venezuela, July 29, 1938). Began pro boxing: June 28, 1965.

He had his first 13 bouts in Caracas, winning all but one inside the distance. He commuted between his own country and the United States in the next three years with considerable success, then on Feb. 27, 1971, won the W.B.A. version of the world title by stopping Jimmy Dupree in six rounds. He defended against Piero Del Papa (w.ko.1), Eddie Jones (w.pts.15), Gomeo Grennan (w.rsf.13) and Doyle Baird (w.ko.8), but came unstuck against the superlative Bob Foster, who took his title in two rounds. Rondon fought among the heavies until his retirement in 1974.
Score 57: w40 (23) d1 l5 Dnc.1.

Root, Jack

World Light-Heavyweight Champion 1903

(b. Austria, May 26, 1876 – d. Los Angeles, California, June 10, 1963). Began pro boxing: Nov. 12, 1897.

Real name Janos Ruthaly, he was the first holder of the light-heavyweight title, a new division being inspired by his manager Lou Houseman in order to make his man a champion. Root met Kid McCoy in Detroit on April 22, 1903 in a fight advertised for the

light-heavyweight crown and Jack upheld his mentor's faith in him by winning on points over ten rounds. Three months later, however, in a defence against George Gardner, he was knocked out in the 12th round at Fort Erie. Root got another chance to make himself famous, meeting Marvin Hart for the vacant world heavyweight championship. Root was knocked out in 12 rounds on July 3, 1905. He retired the following year.
Score 55: w46 (29) d4 l3 Dnc.2.

Rose, Lionel

World and Commonwealth Bantamweight Champion 1968–69

(b. Drouin, Victoria, Australia, June 21, 1948). Began pro boxing: Sept. 9, 1964.

Australia has produced a number of top-class Aboriginal boxers this century, but Rose was the first to win a world title. He took the crown in an upset over Japan's formidable Fighting Harada in Feb. 1968.

Rose was born near Melbourne, the first child in a family of nine. His fairground fighter father introduced him to boxing from the time he could toddle. As a 15-year-old amateur flyweight, Rose became one of the youngest ever to win a national title. He became bantam champion and turned professional.

In his 20th bout, Rose won the Australian bantam title, and after successfully defending it challenged for the world title in Feb. 1968. It meant travelling to Tokyo to meet a man of far greater experience who had been bantam champion for three years and flyweight titleholder before that. A 4-1 underdog in the betting, Rose boxed brilliantly and, after dropping Harada with a superb right across to the chin in round nine, took a unanimous points verdict. In April 1969 he was awarded an M.B.E. for his contribution to Australian boxing.

Rose proved a busy champion. He returned to Tokyo four months later for a title defence against Takao Sakuri, and before the year was out had travelled to Inglewood, California, to beat off a challenge from Mexico's 'Chuchu' Castillo (the dangerous puncher who was able to take the world title in 1970 from the 'unbeatable' Ruben Olivares). Then in March 1969 Rose defeated Alan Rudkin, the British and Commonwealth champion, in Melbourne after a particularly hard fight. But Rose was doomed to lose his title when he returned to California to take on the dangerous Mexican Ruben Olivares, then undefeated in 53 fights, all but two of which he had ended inside the distance. Weakened by weight reducing. Rose was put down three times and took the full count in round five.

The Australian then put on poundage and boxed as a lightweight, but not very satisfactorily, failing to win a native title from Jeff White in 1971 and the world junior-lightweight title (W.B.C.) from Yoshiaki Numata the same year. He retired in 1976.
Score 53: w42 (12) d0 l11.

Rosenberg, Charley 'Phil'

World Bantamweight Champion 1925–27

(b. New York, Aug. 15,1902 – d.New York, March 12, 1976). Began pro boxing: 1921.

Real name Charles Green, he was a competent box-fighter who quickly got into the top-flight of his class and in his fourth year as a pro outpointed Eddie 'Cannonball' Martin on March 20, 1925 to win the world crown. He defended this four months later by knocking out Eddie Shea in four rounds and subsequently outpointed George Butch over ten to keep the championship. On Feb. 4, 1927 he was due to put up his title against Bushy Graham, but came in overweight. The bout went the full distance of 15 rounds, but afterwards both men were accused of making a 'secret' agreement about it and both were suspended for a year. This was almost the end for Charley. He had one bout in 1928 and one the next year, both of which he won, and then retired.
Score 65: w36 (7) d6 l16 ND.7.

Rosenberg, Dave

World Middleweight Champion (N.Y.S.A.C.) 1922

(b. New York, New York, May 15, 1901). Began pro boxing: 1919.

A strong fighter who could hold his own against the best, he boxed mainly in New York, where he was much liked. In 1922 the New York State Athletic Commission declared the middleweight title to be vacant and Rosenberg was matched with Phil Krug. On Aug. 14 Dave won a 15 rounds points verdict, but his reign was short-lived, Mike O'Dowd taking the crown when Rosenberg was ruled out in round eight for an alleged foul. He boxed on for a few years, but after a losing spell in 1925 decided to retire.
Score 66: w38 (11) d5 l11 Dnc.12.

Rosenbloom, Maxie

World Light-Heavyweight Champion 1930–34

(b. New York City, Sept. 6, 1904 – d. Los Angeles, California, March 6, 1976). Began pro boxing: 1923.

He learnt the art of step-dancing from his pal George Raft and used it to great advantage in his fighting, taking the outer perimeter of the ring and doing all his hitting from long range. Unfortunately he did not always close his gloves and for that they called him 'Slapsie Maxie'.

He fought on an average of once a fortnight for 11 of his 16 years in the ring and was rarely hurt. In 1930 he secured New York recognition as world champion by outpointing Jimmy Slattery on June 25. He defended this title twice, then on July 14, 1932 was internationally accepted as world champion after he had outpointed Lou

Scozza. He made five more defences, his most dangerous challenger being Mickey Walker whom he outpointed in New York. Rosenbloom lost his title in 1934 to Bob Olin on a points verdict. He was knocked out only twice – in 1928 in London by Tommy Milligan in nine rounds and towards the end of his career by Jimmy Adamick at Detroit in two. He retired in 1939.
Score 299: w223 (19) d32 l42 Dnc.2.

Rosi, Gianfranco

European Welterweight Champion 1984, European and World Light-Middleweight Champion (W.B.C.) 1987–

(b. Perugia, Italy, Aug. 5, 1957). Began pro boxing: Sept. 10, 1979.

Rosi suffered only one defeat in his first 30 pro bouts. A strong, resolute fighter, he won the Italian welterweight title on April 16, 1982 by stopping Giuseppe DiPadova in seven rounds. He retained his crown against Antonion Torsello (stopped 2), Everaldo Costa (stopped 7) Pierangelo Pira (stopped 5) and Francesco Gallo (stopped 8). On July 7, 1984, he gained the European title but lost it six months later to Lloyd Honeyghan, who gave him his first kayo defeat (3 rounds). Moving up a weight, he won the European light-middleweight title by outpointing Chris Pyatt (G.B.), kept it against two challengers, then created a surprise by outpointing Lupe Aquino, of Mexico, to gain W.B.C. recognition as world champion. This was on Oct. 2, 1987, and three months later he sealed his title claims by knocking out Duane Thomas in seven rounds at Genoa.
Score 45: w43 (14) d0 l2.

Ross, Barney

World Light, Junior-Light and Welterweight Champion 1933–38

(b. New York City, Dec. 23, 1909 – d. Chicago, Illinois, Jan. 17, 1967). Began pro boxing: Sept. 1, 1929.

The last of a long line of great Jewish boxers, Barney Ross ranks high on the list of welterweight immortals. His three tremendous battles for the world welterweight championship with another great champion, Jimmy McLarnin, have become part of ring lore. Ross's speed and non-stop aggression won him the title in 1934; McLarnin's greater punching power prevailed in their return bout later that year; but in 1935 Ross proved his mastery in the decider.

Ross, born Barnet Rosofsky, turned professional to help support his family after gunmen murdered his grocer father in Chicago. He had been a Golden Gloves champion as an amateur, with a bustling style that proved effective in the paid ranks. In 1933 he won the world lightweight and junior-welterweight titles from the talented Tony

Canzoneri, but increasing weight forced him to relinquish the lightweight crown after only one defence, against Canzoneri.

Ross did not carry a lot of stopping power in his punches, relying on speed instead. But his wide repertoire of deliveries bewildered most opponents. Strong and courageous, he was never beaten inside the distance, and even at the age of 29 he stood up to the phenomenal Henry Armstrong for the full 15 rounds in his last defence of the welterweight title.

After losing his title to Armstrong in this fight, Ross retired from the ring and joined the United States Marines in World War II. He was wounded at Guadalcanal and won the Congressional Medal of Honor. He died in Chicago of cancer after a long illness and a much admired battle against drug addiction which followed medical treatment for his war wounds.

Score 81: w73 (22) d3 l4 ND.1.

Rossman, Mike

World Light-Heavyweight Champion (W.B.A.) 1978–79

(b. Turnersville, New Jersey, July 1, 1956). Began pro boxing: Aug. 10, 1973.

Real name Albert DiPiano, he scored seven knockouts in his first year as a pro and after battling his way through the fight towns of America he was matched to fight Victor Galindez for the W.B.A. version of the world title. They fought at Atlantic City on Sept. 15, 1978 and few gave Rossman much of a chance. But he caught up with the 30-year old champion in the 13th round and was battering him unmercifully on the ropes when the referee intervened. Rossman defended his crown against Aldo Traversaro, stopping him in six, but in a return with Galindez, seven months after their first meeting, the astute Argentinian forced him to retire in the tenth. He retired in 1981.

Score 54: w44 (29) d3 l7.

Roth, Gustave

World Light-Heavyweight Champion (I.B.U.) 1936–38, European Welter and Middleweight Champion 1929–34

(b. Antwerp, Belgium, March 12, 1909 – d. Oakland, California, Sept. 14, 1982). Began pro boxing: Sept. 14, 1927.

A talented boxer, relying on his skill and enterprise to win his contests. His role as champion covered three weight divisions, starting at welter when he won the European crown in his third year as a pro by outpointing Alf Genon in Brussels. He defended his title 11 times and never lost it, going into the middleweight ranks in 1934, and winning the E.B.U. title by outpointing Eric Seelig (Germany). Two months later he lost it to world champion Marcel Thil on a points verdict. He then won his native championship with a points verdict over Charles

Sys, but gave up the title to compete as a light-heavy. On Sept. 1, 1936 he won the I.B.U. version of the world title, plus the E.B.U. crown, by outpointing Heinz Lazek in Vienna. These two titles he defended successfully six times – all bouts going the distance. In March 1938, he was beaten on a stoppage in seven rounds by Adolph Heuser (Germany) and dropped out of the world ratings. He boxed on for five years, winning his country's light-heavy and heavyweight titles, and retired in 1945.

Score 136: w112 (25) d12 l11 Dnc.1.

Routis, Andre

World Featherweight Champion 1928–29

(b. Bordeaux, France, July 16, 1900 – d. Paris, July 16, 1969). Began pro boxing: Feb. 2, 1919.

A strong and determined box-fighter who fought Charles Ledoux three times for the French bantam title, winning on points over 20 rounds on the last occasion. He lost this to Kid Francis, then set off for America where he spent the remaining years of his career. On Sept. 28, 1928, in New York, he captured the world featherweight title by outpointing the renowned Tony Canzoneri. He kept this by knocking out Buster Brown in three rounds, then his luck ran out. He incurred eyesight trouble and this caused him to lose contests including his world crown to Battling Battalino on a points verdict at Hartford, Connecticut. He retired in 1929.

Score 85: w54 (14) d7 l24.

Rudkin, Alan

European, British and Commonwealth Bantamweight Champion 1965–72

(b. Liverpool, Lancashire, Nov. 18, 1941). Began pro boxing: May 15, 1962.

This attacking box-fighter with a good punch won the British and Commonwealth titles when he stopped Johnny Caldwell in ten rounds on March 22, 1965. Eight months later he was in Tokyo attempting to take the world crown from Fighting Harada, but was a points loser. He then lost his pair of titles to Walter McGowan after a fierce fight at Wembley, lost a points decision to Ben Ali when trying to win the European crown, then regained his lost laurels from McGowan with a fine points win at Manchester. He went to Melbourne in another attempt to win the world title, but was outpointed by Lionel Rose and lost his Commonwealth crown. Almost every bout involved a championship now. He won his Lonsdale Belt outright by defeating Evan Armstrong (w.rtd.11), and had a third try at the world title but was stopped in two rounds by Ruben Olivares. He tried to win the British featherweight crown from Jimmy Revie but was outpointed. Rudkin regained the British and Commonwealth bantam titles by stop-

ping Johnny Clark in 12 rounds, then won the European title by stopping Franco Zurlo (Italy) in 11. He lost this to Agustin Senin (Spain) in Bilbao. In 1972 he again outpointed Johnny Clark to keep his two titles and then decided to retire.

Score 50: w42 (16) d0 l8.

Ryan, Tommy

World Welter and Middleweight Champion 1894–1902

(b. Redwood, New York, March 31, 1870 – d. Van Nuys, California, Aug. 3, 1948). Began pro boxing: 1887.

A sterling fighter, he knew every artifice of the game and carried a knockdown punch. He came into the championship picture on July 26, 1894 when he outpointed Mysterious Billy Smith over 20 rounds at Minneapolis to become world welter king. Ryan kept this title for four years with six successful defences, and then gave up the title undefeated and four months later, on Oct. 24, won the vacant middleweight crown by outpointing Jack Bonner over 20 rounds. He kept this championship until the end of his career in 1904, defending it four times. He was stopped only once, being tricked into defeat by the renowned Kid McCoy, who let him believe that he was unfit but needed the purse money, and then became 'the real McCoy' and stopped Ryan in the 15th round.

Score 104: w86 (68) d6 l4 ND.2 Dnc.6.

Saddler, Sandy

World Featherweight Champion 1948–56, World Junior-Lightweight Champion 1949–50

(b. Boston, Massachusetts, June 23, 1926). Began pro boxing: March 7, 1944.

Something of a featherweight freak, Sandy Saddler was tall at 5 ft. 8½ in. and had a correspondingly long reach – a physical advantage he exploited to the full. A firm believer in the use of a left jab, Saddler also perfected the uppercut and hook with his hand. As he also carried crisp punching power in his right, he proved a very destructive fighter indeed.

The son of a West Indian, Saddler was brought up in the Harlem district of New York, and after a brief spell as an amateur turned professional at 17. It took him nearly 100 fights and over four years to get a title bout with Willie Pep, in Oct. 1948, and then only because he guaranteed the champion $25,000. It meant fighting for little more than his training expenses, but he shocked the boxing world by knocking out the hitherto invincible 'Willie the Wisp' in four rounds. Their return early the next year was a featherweight classic. Pep fought brilliantly to regain the crown narrowly on points, although it took 11 stitches to repair the facial damage wrought by the sharp-shooting champion.

Sandy Saddler had a fine corkscrew left jab that helped make him a very destructive fighter who scored over a hundred knockouts.

In 1950 Saddler regained the title by stopping Pep in eight rounds, and in a fourth meeting with him won again, this time in nine. A spell in the army kept him out of boxing for more than three years, but he returned to defeat interim champion Teddy Davis in 1955. One successful title defence followed in 1956, then Saddler badly injured an eye in a car crash and retired from the ring at the age of 30.
Score 162: *w*144 (103) *d*2 *l*16.

Saijyo, Shozo

*World Featherweight Champion (W.B.A.)
1968–71*

(b. Saitama, Japan, Jan. 28, 1947). Began pro boxing: Aug. 13, 1964.

A good fast-moving boxer, but no great puncher, although he could produce a knockdown when the opportunity offered. He won the W.B.A. world featherweight title when he outpointed Raul Rojas over 15 rounds at Los Angeles on Sept. 28, 1968. He defended his crown successfully against Pedro Gomez (w.pts.15), Jose Pimental (w.ko.2), Godfrey Stevens (w.pts.15), and Frankie Crawford (twice w.pts.15). He was knocked out by Antonio Gomez in five rounds at Tokyo on Sept. 2, 1971 and did not fight again.
Score 38: *w*29 (8) *d*2 *l*7.

Salas, Lauro

World Lightweight Champion 1952

(b. Monterrey, Mexico, 1927). Began pro boxing: 1944.

An exceedingly busy fighter, he started at the age of 15 and was in the ring for over 16 years with nearly 200 bouts under his belt. After three years, he made his base in Los Angeles and won the Californian featherweight title in 1951, then moved into the lightweight class to challenge Jimmy Carter for his world crown. Salas was outpointed over 15 rounds, but put up such an aggressive performance that he was granted a second try six weeks later. Then on May 14, 1952 he won a convincing victory over the champion to win the title. There had to be a third meeting and after five months they met again when Carter retrieved his crown as easily as he had lost it. Lauro never had another chance. He went on boxing with great frequency until 1961, when he was 34.
Score (incomplete) 151: *w*85 (41) *d*13 *l*52 ND.1.

Salavarria, Erbito

World Flyweight Champion (W.B.C. and W.B.A.), 1970–76

(b. Manila, Philippines, Jan. 20, 1946). Began pro boxing: Sept. 14, 1963.

This slick Filipino had the distinction of twice being a world champion. He won his native flyweight title in his 21st pro bout and the Oriental crown two years later. On Dec. 7, 1970 he knocked out Chartchai Chionoi in two rounds to become W.B.C. world flyweight king. He defended his title successfully against Susumu Hanagata (w.pts.15) and Betulio Gonzalez (drew 15), but lost it to Venice Borkorsor at Bangkok on Feb. 9, 1973 on a points decision. Salavarria regained the championship via the W.B.A., from Susumu Hanagata on April 1, 1975, twice defended it against the Japanese fighter on points verdicts, but finally lost the crown to Alfonso Lopez (Panama), being stopped in the 15th round at Manila, on Feb. 27, 1976. He retired afterwards.
Score 53: *w*39 (11) *d*3 *l*11.

Saldivar, Vincente

World Featherweight Champion 1964–70

(b. Mexico City, Mexico, May 13, 1943 – d. Mexico, July, 1985). Began pro boxing: Feb. 18, 1961.

'They never come back' was a boxing axiom disproved by Mexican featherweight king Vincente Saldivar. In May 1970, after a 2½ year retirement, he regained his world featherweight crown from Australia's Johnny Famechon.

Born one of a family of nine in the poorest quarter of Mexico City, Vicente Samuel

Saldivar Garcia won a Golden Gloves title as an amateur in 1959. His decisive punching and awkward southpaw stance proved so effective that, apart from an unfortunate disqualification, he was unbeaten in his first 25 paid fights, which included the capture of the Mexican featherweight title in 1964.

His new title earned him a shot at Sugar Ramo's world crown: he stopped the Cuban in 11 rounds, then successfully defended his title eight times in little more than three years. Three of these defences were memorable battles against the brilliant British and European champion Howard Winstone. After stopping Winstone in their third clash he announced his retirement.

However, when he saw Winstone win the now vacant title, Saldivar decided to attempt a comeback. He defeated Jose Legra, who had taken Winstone's title and then dropped it to Famechon. Then Saldivar outpointed the elusive Famechon in Rome.

Saldivar held the crown for little more than seven months. At Tijuana, Mexico, he was surprisingly outpunched and badly cut by Japan's Kuniaka Shibata, the referee calling a halt in round 13 to save Saldivar from further punishment. In 1973, after an absence of over two years, he attempted another comeback but was knocked out in four rounds when trying to take the world featherweight title from Eder Jofre.
Score 41: *w*38 (27) *d*0 *l*3.

Vicente Saldivar, who came from retirement to become world champion a second time.

Salica, Lou

World Bantamwieght Champion (N.B.A.) 1935–42

(b. New York City, July 26, 1913). Began pro boxing: Jan. 5, 1933.

After a truly marvellous amateur career, he started off as a pro by losing only two of his first 30 bouts. His big chance came on Aug. 26, 1935 in New York when he outpointed hard-punching Sixto Escobar to win the N.B.A. version of the world bantam title. In a return match, three months later, he lost on points to Escobar. It took him 15 months to get a third fight with the Peurto Rican, but he was again outpointed. On March 4, 1940 at Toronto, Canada, he drew with Georgie Pace, again for the N.B.A. version of the title, and in a return six months afterwards took the championship for the second time with a points verdict. He defended successfully against Tommy Forte twice (w.pts.15) and Lou Transparenti (w.pts.15), but lost his crown to Manuel Ortiz on a points decision over 12 rounds. An attempt to win back the title failed when Ortiz knocked him out in 11 rounds. There was one more year of boxing, then he retired in 1944.
Score 90: *w*62 (13) *d*11 *l*17.

Sanchez, Clemente

World Featherweight Champion (W.B.C.) 1972

(b. Monterrey, Mexico, July 9, 1947 – d. Monterrey, Dec. 25, 1978). Began pro boxing: March 23, 1963.

Strong and attacking, with a kayo punch, he started at the age of 15 and was soon making a name for himself. He had to wait until his tenth year as a pro before he could secure a championship chance, then on May 19, 1972 he knocked out Kuniaki Shibata (Japan) to win the W.B.C. version of the world featherweight title. At his first defence on Dec. 16 the same year, he was himself knocked out by Jose Legra (Spain) in round ten. Inactive in 1973, Sanchez then made a comeback, but retired after eight fights in 1975. He was murdered on Christmas Day, 1978.
Score 60: *w*46 (29) *d*3 *l*11.

Sanchez, Salvador

World Featherweight Champion (W.B.C.) 1980–82

(b. Santiago, Mexico, Feb. 3, 1958 – d. Queretaro, Mexico, Aug. 12, 1982). Began pro boxing: May 4, 1975.

An exotic two-fisted fighter with tremendous punching power, he lost only one bout in 46 starts, a 12 rounds points decision when he fought for the Mexican bantamweight title in 1977. He won the W.B.C. version of the world featherweight title by knocking

out Danny Lopez at Phoenix, Arizona, on Feb. 2, 1980. Sanchez defended successfully against Ruben Castillo (w.pts.15), Danny Lopez (w.rsf.14), Patrick Ford (w.pts.15), Juan LaPorte (w.pts.15), Roberto Castanon (w.rdf.10), Wilfredo Gomez (w.ko.8), Pat Cowdell (w.pts.15), Jorge Garcia (w.pts.15), and Azumah Nelson (w.rsf.15). He died in a road accident in 1982.
Score 46: *w*44 (32) *d*1 *l*1.

Sands, Dave

Australian and British Empire Middle, Australian Light-Heavy and Heavyweight Champion 1946–52

(b. Burnt Ridge, New South Wales, Australia, Feb. 4, 1926 – d. Australia, Aug. 11, 1952). Began pro boxing: 1943.

Dave Sands ranks with Les Darcy as the greatest of the Australian middleweights. And like Darcy, his life was cut short just when he seemed set to win the world title. Sands, real name Ritchie, was the son of an Aborigine mother and a Puerto Rican father. His four brothers all became main-event fighters, but from the time Sands made his professional debut at the age of 17 he showed himself to be in a class of his own. A good boxer with a knockdown punch in either hand, Sands ended more than half of his bouts within the distance. Within three years he won the Australian middleweight title: in the same year – 1946 – he also took the light-heavyweight crown.

With no one else to beat in Australia, Sands moved to the U.K. He was over-matched against the experienced light-heavy Tommy Yarosz and lost on points, but then began a brilliant series of wins that included a thrilling victory over the redoubtable Robert Villemain of France.

In 1949 Sands met Dick Turpin for the Empire middleweight crown. He knocked Turpin out in 2 min. 35 sec., of the first round. Returning to Australia a national hero, he went on to win the Australian heavyweight crown.

In 1951 Sands moved to London again, lured by the prospect of a big purse from an Empire title bout with Dick Turpin's brother Randolph. But Turpin snatched the chance of a world title bout against Sugar Ray Robinson instead. Sands was left in the cold, so he toured America where he defeated Carl 'Bobo' Olson and Henry Brimm – wins that made him number one contender for the crown.

When Robinson retired in Dec. 1952, British promoter Jack Solomons cabled Sands in Australia to fly to London to fight Randolph Turpin for the vacant world crown. Sands never made the trip. He was driving a 5-ton truck to his training camp when it slipped off the road and rolled down an embankment. He was badly injured and died in hospital.
Score 104: *w*93 (62) *d*1 *l*8 *Dnc*.2.

Sangchilli, Baltazar

World Bantamweight Champion 1935–36

(b. Valencia, Spain, Oct. 15, 1911). Began pro boxing: April 29, 1929.

Real name Hevoas, tough, strong and vigorous, he won his native bantam title in his fifth year as a pro by outpointing Carlos Flix over 12 rounds on April 22, 1933. He kept the title for two years and then, much to the surprise of everyone, took a 15 rounds points decision from veteran Al Brown to win the world bantamweight title. He had two bouts in Britain, losing a ten rounds points verdict to Benny Sharkey at Newcastle, then went on to America. Sangchilli won two club bouts, then engaged in another in which, thinking he had nothing to beat, he put up his world crown. He was beating Tony Marino easily when he was attacked by sudden cramp and was knocked out in the 14th round. He could win only one of his next seven bouts and retired in 1939.
Score 89: *w*68 (30) *d*6 *l*15.

Santry, Eddie

World Featherweight Champion 1899–1900

(b. Aurora, Illinois. Dec. 11, 1878 – d. Chicago, Jan. 28, 1919). Began pro boxing: March 22, 1895.

A strong and attacking box-fighter with a good knockdown punch, he piled up a good kayo record and in his fourth year as a pro challenged George Dixon for the world featherweight title and lost on points over 20 rounds in New York. Just 25 days later, Dixon was outpointed by Ben Jordan in a 25-rounder, also in New York, so Santry promptly challenged the Englishman and knocked him out in 16 rounds on Oct. 10, 1899. Santry's reign was curtailed after four months when he was knocked out in five rounds at Chicago. He was not given the chance to win back his crown. Santry continued boxing until 1909 when he retired. He made a solitary comeback in 1911, knocking out Jack Ryan in four rounds.
Score 82: *w*52 (34) *d*16 *l*14.

Sarron, Petey

World Featherweight Champion 1936–37

(b. Birmingham, Alabama, 1908). Began pro boxing: 1925.

Tough and strong with indomitable pluck, Sarron had his jaw broken in his first pro fight and in the course of his 14-year career suffered a broken nose, several ribs and both hands. He would have been a better fighter had he been taught to close his gloves when punching. His great enemy was southpaw Freddie Miller. They met six times with the score 4-2 to Miller, but Sarron won the third and the last which were title bouts. It was on May 11, 1936 that Sarron first got in front to

win the world crown at Washington D.C. on a points verdict. He then went on a world tour and in Johannesburg, South Africa, they met again, first in a non-title bout which Miller won and then for the championship, when Sarron kept his crown. Almost two months later, however, he was pulverized by Henry Armstrong and had to part with his title on a sixth round knockout. He boxed on for another two years, retiring in 1939.
Score 143: *w*104 (24) *d*11 *l*24 *ND*.4.

Saxton, Johnny

World Welterweight Champion 1954–57

(b. Little Rock, Arkansas, Sept. 9, 1927). Began pro boxing: May 9, 1949.

After a wonderful amateur career, he showed himself a future world champion by losing on points only twice in his first 48 bouts. It took him nearly six years to get a title even with this record, but when he did, he scored a great points victory over Kid Gavilan on Oct. 20, 1954 to win the world welterweight title. His reign lasted only six months, however, then he was surprisingly knocked out by Tony DeMarco in 14 rounds. Eleven months later he regained his crown by outpointing Carmen Basilio. In a return title bout Saxton was knocked out by Basilio in nine rounds and when he attempted to regain his lost crown, Carmen did the trick again, this time in two rounds. One further kayo defeat and Saxton retired in 1958.
Score 66: *w*55 (21) *d*2 *l*9.

Former champion Max Schmeling (right) beats Walter Neusel in eight rounds on Aug. 26, 1934.

Scalzo, Petey

World Featherweight Champion (N.B.A.) 1940–41

(b. New York City, Aug. 1, 1917). Began pro boxing, June 29, 1936.

A fast, strong fighter with a sizzling punch, he had a tremendous career in his first five years, winning 69 bouts out of 75 starts, with three drawn. On May 1, 1940 he stopped Ginger Foran (U.K.) in New York and the N.B.A. declared Scalzo world champion. He defended his title against Bobby 'Poison' Ivy (w.ko.15) and Phil Zwick (w.pts.15), but lost to Richie Lemos at Los Angeles, being knocked out in the fifth round. He boxed on until 1943 when he retired.
Score 111: *w*90 (46) *d*5 *l*15 *ND*.1.

Schmeling, Max

World Heavyweight Champion 1930–32, European Light-Heavyweight Champion, 1927–28

(b. Brandenburg, Germany, Sept. 28, 1905). Began pro boxing: Aug. 2, 1924.

A strong fighter who knew how to box, with a very good right hand punch. He won his native light-heavy title in 1927 and the European crown the following year by stopping Fernand Delarge (Belgium) in 14 rounds. He kept this crown against two challengers and then won the European title by outpointing fellow-countryman Franz

Diener. In the U.S.A. on June 12, 1930 he fought Jack Sharkey for the world championship, left vacant by the retirement of Gene Tunney, and won on a foul in round four, the first time the biggest prize in sport had been decided in this fashion. He defended successfully against Young Stribling, but lost the title on points in a return match with Sharkey. On June 19, 1936 he created a sensation by knocking out Joe Louis in 12 rounds to give the 'Brown Bomber' his first defeat. But in a second fight in 1938 he was knocked out in 2 min. 4 sec., of the first round. Schmeling was inactive in the ring during World War II, then came back for a few fights and retired in 1948.
Score 70: *w*56 (38) *d*4 *l*10.

Schwartz, Izzy

World Flyweight Champion (N.Y.S.A.C.) 1927–29

(b. New York City, Oct. 23, 1902). Began pro boxing: 1922.

A sparkling boxer, fast on his feet but not heavy in punching power. He did not get near a title fight until the end of his sixth year when he outpointed Newsboy Brown over 15 rounds in a bout which the New York authorities recognized as for the world flyweight title. He defended his crown against Routier Parra (w.pts.15), Frisco Grande (w.dis.4), Little Jeff Smith (w.ko.4), and Frenchy Belanger (w.pts.12). In between he tried to win the world bantam title from Bushy Graham, but was outpointed. Finally

Schwartz lost his crown to Willie la Morte on a points verdict and after a spell of inactivity, retired in 1932.
Score 124: *w*69 (7) *d*14 *l*33 *ND*.8.

Scott, Phil

British and British Empire Heavyweight Champion 1926–31

(b. London, Jan. 3, 1900 – d. Sennel Bay, N.S.W. Australia, Dec. 1983). Began pro boxing: March 15, 1919.

He boxed under his real name, Phil Suffling, at the start of his career in which he won several novice competitions. Scott was a better boxer than his critics would admit but failed under pressure, being known in America as 'Phainting Phil' because he won some of his contests by claiming that he had been fouled. He won the British Empire title on Jan. 27, 1926, beating George Cook (Australia) who was ruled out in the 17th round. He knocked out Frank Goddard in three rounds to win the British title on March 8, 1926 and defended both crowns against Boy McCormick (w.rtd.10).

Scott defended the British Empire crown against Tom Heeney (w.pts.20), outpointed Pierre Charles (Belgium) in a bout erroneously advertised as for the European title and went on to America. In eight bouts there he won five: Monte Munn (w.pts.10), Pierre Charles (w.pts.10), Roberto Roberti (w.pts.10), Vittorio Compolo (w.pts.10) and Otto Von Porat (w.dis.2). He lost in one round to Knute Hansen, on points to Johnny Risko and in 1930, in an eliminating bout against Jack Sharkey for the vacant world heavyweight championship, Scott was disqualified in the third round for claiming he had been fouled and refusing to continue the contest. A two rounds knockout defeat by Young Stribling and a similar beating by Larry Gains in 1931 finished his career.
Score 85: *w*65 (29) *d*4 *l*14 *Dnc*.2.

Serrano, Samuel

World Junior-Lightweight Champion (W.B.A.) 1976–

(b. Toa Alta, Puerto Rico, Nov. 7, 1952). Began pro boxing: Nov. 1, 1969.

Serrano won his native featherweight title in his sixth pro bout, by outpointing Francisco Villegas, but lost it in a return contest a fortnight later. He had to wait seven years before getting a W.B.A. world title chance, then drew with Ben Villaflor in Honolulu. In a return match at San Juan on Oct. 16, 1976, Serrano won on points. He successfully defended the title ten times in the next three years, but on Aug. 2, 1980 dropped the championship to Yasatsune Uehara in Japan, being stopped in the sixth round. However, he regained it eight months later with a points decision. There were two more successful defences, then on June 5, 1982, at Santiago he was stopped with an eye injury by Benedict Villablanca (Chile). Before the

winner could realize he was champion, he was not – the W.B.A. deciding that the decision was null and void, so Serrano remained titleholder.
Score 54: *w*49 (17) *d*1 *l*4.

Servo, Marto

World Welterweight Champion 1946

(b. Schenectady, New York, Nov. 3, 1919 – d. Pueblo, Colorado, Feb. 9, 1969). Began pro boxing: August 30, 1938.

Real name Mario Severino; in his first four years he ran up a long string of victories with only two points losses, both against the great Sugar Ray Robinson. He was inactive during most of 1942–45, being on World War II service. In his third fight on his return, Feb. 1, 1946, he knocked out Freddie Cochrane in four rounds to win the world welter title and then foolishly allowed himself to be drawn into a non-title fight with Rocky Graziano, a tough middleweight with devastating punching power. Servo was battered from pillar to post from the start. He had no chance, yet the referee let it continue until Servo was helpless. He announced his retirement the next day.
Score 54: *w*48 (14) *d*2 *l*4.

Sharkey, Jack

World Heavyweight Champion 1932–33

(b. Binghamton, New York, Oct. 26, 1902). Began pro boxing: 1924

Not a huge heavyweight, but a very good boxer. He had to wait five years before getting near a title shot, first winning the American championship by knocking out Tommy Loughran in three rounds, then meeting Max Schmeling in a world title fight that ended in Sharkey's disqualification in the fourth round. Sharkey completely outpointed the German in their return match two years later, but in the following year was knocked out in the sixth round of a title fight with Primo Carnera, the Italian giant. Three years later, at the age of 34, he bravely took on Joe Louis and was knocked out in the third round. He did not fight again.
Score 55: *w*38 (14) *d*3 *l*13 *ND*.1.

Shaw, Battling

World Light-Welterweight Champion 1933

(b. Nuevo Laredo, Mexico, Oct. 21, 1910). Began pro boxing: June 1927.

The early Mexican record of Battling Shaw (real name Jose Perez Flores) is not available, but it must have been imposing as it is claimed that he won around 80 contests with few defeats. In 1932 he based himself in New Orleans and there on Feb. 20, 1933, he outpointed Johnny Jadick over ten rounds to become world light-welter champion. Three months later he lost his title to Tony Canzoneri on a ten rounds points verdict and when he was twice stopped by Willard

Brown (in ten and four rounds) he elected to retire.
Score 66: *w*48 (16) *d*3 *l*15.

Shibata, Kuniaki

World Junior-Lightweight Champion (W.B.C.) 1973–75, World Featherweight Champion 1970–72

(b. Hitachi, Japan, March 28, 1947). Began pro boxing: March 6, 1965.

This hard-punching southpaw won his native featherweight title by knocking out Yasuo Sakurai in ten rounds. Eight months later, on Dec. 11, 1970, he brought off a surprise by knocking out Vicente Saldivar in

Jack Sharkey, world heavyweight champion 1932–33.

Yoshio Shirai was the first Japanese boxer to win a world title when he became world flyweight champion in 1952.

13 rounds to take the W.B.C. world featherweight crown. He beat off two challengers, then lost the title to Clemente Sanchez by a three rounds knockout. Shibata then entered the junior-lightweight class and on March 12, 1973, won his second world title by outpointing Ben Villaflor for the W.B.A. crown. A successful defence against Ricardo Arrendondo (drew 15) was followed by a return fight with Villaflor, who put him away in round one with the first punch he delivered. Within four months Shibata had recovered and on Feb. 28, 1974 took the W.B.C. version of the world junior-lightweight title by outpointing Ricardo Arrendondo. He defended successfully against Antonio Amaya (w.pts.15), Ramiro Bolanos (w.ko.15) and Ouid Makloufi (w.pts.15), but lost the crown eventually to Alfredo Escalera who knocked him out in two rounds. He retired in 1977.
Score 56: *w*46 (25) *d*4 *l*6.

Shirai, Yoshio

World Flyweight Champion 1952–54

(b. Tokyo, Japan, Nov. 23, 1923). Began pro boxing: Nov. 26, 1943.

One of the first Japanese fighters to win a

Tony Sibson (left) fighting Manuel Jiminez, who he stopped, in 1983.

world crown, he did so in his tenth year as a pro, outpointing Dado Marino (Hawaii) over 15 rounds in Tokyo on May 19, 1952. In a return fight six months later, the same result ensued. There were three more successful defences: Tanny Campo (w.pts.15), Terry Allen (w.pts.15) and Leo Espinosa (w.pts.15). He drew with Pascual Perez in a ten rounds non-title event, but when they met for Shirai's crown on Nov. 26, 1954, he was outpointed. A return bout six months later resulted in Shirai being stopped in five rounds, after which he retired.
Score 57: *w*47 (20) *d*2 *l*8.

Sibson, Tony

European, British and Commonwealth Middleweight Champion 1979–88

(b. Leicester, April 9, 1958). Began pro boxing: April 9, 1976.

Strong and tough with a good punch,, his good time started on April 10, 1979 when he stopped Frankie Lucas in four rounds to win the vacant British middleweight title. Seven

119

Battling Siki was a flamboyant character known to have walked around Paris with a lion on a lead.

months later he dropped this to Kevin Finnegan on points, but came back to win the Commonwealth crown by outpointing Chisanda Mutti (Zambia) over 15 rounds in London.

He gained the European title on Dec. 8, 1980 by knocking out Matteo Salvemini (Italy) in seven rounds in London. Sibson defended this title successfully against Andoni Amana (Spain) in Bilbao (w.pts.12), Alan Minter at Wembley (w.ko.3), Nicola Cirelli (Italy) at Wembley (w.ko.10), Jacques Chinon (France) at Wembley (w.rsf.10) and Antonio Garrido (Spain) at Wembley (w.rtd.8). Sibson relinquished the European crown on Sept. 20, 1982 to challenge for the world title but was stopped by Marvin Hagler in six rounds on Feb. 14, 1983.

This did not stop this remarkable fighter. He regained the European title by outscoring Louis Acaries in Paris, successfully defended his three crowns against Mark Kaylor and outpointed Abdul Amoru Sands for the British Commonwealth middleweight title. He next threw out a challenge to Dennis Andries for the W.B.C. and British light-heavyweight titles, but was stopped in nine

rounds in London. Sibson next made a Lonsdale Belt his own property by defending his British middleweight title against Brian Anderson (stopped 8) on Feb. 7, 1987. In attempting to take the I.B.F. middleweight title from Frank Tate (U.S.) on Feb. 7, 1988, he was knocked out in the tenth round, immediately afterwards retiring from the ring.

Score 40: w30 (23) d3 l7.

Siki, Battling

World Light-Heavyweight Champion 1922–23

(b. St. Louis, Senegal, Sept. 16, 1897 – d. New York, Dec. 15, 1925). Began pro boxing: 1913.

Real name Louis Phal, he found his way to France and worked as a dish-washer until someone realized that he was good boxing material. A big swinger with no real defence, he soon attracted the attention of the French fans, even if they came to watch his ring capers. On Sept. 24, 1922 he was put in with famous Georges Carpentier for the Frenchman's world light-heavyweight title. The bout was filmed and the idea was for Carpentier to win by a spectacular knockout. Unfortunately they forgot to give Siki the script and he swept Carpentier off his feet and into a state of collapse in six rounds to become the new titleholder. Six months later he was trapped into going to Dublin to defend his crown against Mike McTigue. The 'troubles' were at their height, McTigue was a cunning opponent, and it happened to be St. Patrick's Day. As a result Siki lost on points over 20 rounds. He went to America, engaged in a number of bouts in the next two years, then was murdered on a New York street.

Score 94: w64 (35) d5 l25.

Singer, Al

World Lightweight Champion 1930

(b. New York City, Sept. 6, 1909 – d. New York, April 20, 1961). Began pro boxing: 1927.

A dashing box-fighter with a knockdown punch whose chance to win the world title came in his fourth pro year after 59 contests. On July 17, 1930 at Madison Square Garden, he caused excitement by knocking out Sammy Mandell, the champion, in 1 min. 46 sec., of the opening round. He looked like proving a world-beater, but 120 days later he too was stopped in a single round, being knocked out by Tony Canzoneri in 66 sec. It is the only case of a world champion winning and losing the title in one round apiece. It must be recorded, however, that in between Singer had been put away in three rounds by hard-hitting Jimmy McLarnin in a non-title fight. He retired in 1935.

Score 72: w61 (25) d2 l9.

Slattery, Jimmy

World Light-Heavyweight Champion (N.B.A. and N.Y.S.A.C.) 1927–30

(b. Buffalo, New York, Aug. 25, 1904 – d. Buffalo, Aug. 30, 1960). Began pro boxing: 1921.

A lively boxer, standing 5 ft. 11 in. with a correspondingly long reach. He impressed by scoring a lot of inside-the-distance wins before getting within reach of a title fight. His first try to win a world crown saw him knocked out in 11 rounds by hard-hitting Paul Berlanbach, then the N.B.A. matched him with Maxie Rosenbloom for their version of the title and he won on points over ten rounds on Aug. 30, 1927. Before the year was out Tommy Loughran had taken over with a points decision and Jimmy had to wait two years before another title chance came his way. Then it was due to the New York Commission, who paired him with Lou Scozza in a world championship bout. Slattery won on points, but again he was not champion for long as Rosenbloom outpointed him four months later. A return with Maxie produced the same result and practically ended Slattery's career. He had six more bouts, but a knockout defeat in four rounds by Jack Gibbons brought about his retirement in 1935.

Score 129: w114 (48) d0 l13 Dnc.2.

Slavin, Frank Paddy

World Heavyweight Contender 1889–92

(b. Maitland, N.S.W., Australia, Jan. 6, 1862 – d. Vancouver, Canada, Oct. 17, 1951). Began pro boxing: 1885.

This tough Aussie fighter fought in the bare-knuckle era before taking to gloves. His outstanding prize ring battles were with Jack Burke in Melbourne (ko2), Bill (Chesterfield) Goode, London (ko1) and Jem Smith, Champion of England, at Bruges in Belgium on Dec. 23, 1889. He was winning when the ring was broken into in round 14, whereupon the outcome was declared a 'draw'. Gamblers who had bet heavily on Smith hit Slavin with sticks during the fight. Although the result was a draw, the promoters insisted on Slavin having the £500-a-side stake money.

With gloves, he knocked out giant Jack McAuliffe in two rounds in London and in America he stopped Jake Kilrain in nine rounds. His greatest battle was with Peter Jackson at the National Sporting Club in London, still rated in England as the best heavyweight battle of all time. Against a superior boxer, Slavin fought his heart out to try and win, but was finally stopped in the tenth round. A year later Slavin was knocked out by fellow-countryman Jim Hall in London and that ended his world title ambitions. He fought occasionally until 1907 when he retired.

Score 37: w25 (16) d4 l6 ND.2.

Smith, Dick

British Light-Heavyweight Champion 1914–18

(b. Woolwich, London, Feb. 10, 1886 – d. Dartford, Kent. Jan. 1950). Began pro boxing: Oct. 27, 1913.

Although only a light-heavy he won the A.B.A. heavyweight title in 1912 and again in 1913. He left it late, at 27, to turn professional, but soon showed his class, being an immaculate boxer with a good straight left. Smith won the new British light-heavy title on Oct. 27, 1913 by outpointing Denis Haugh over 20 rounds. He scored a similar victory over Harry Curzon and then was surprisingly outpointed by Harry Reeve to lose his crown. On Feb. 25, 1918 he made the Lonsdale Belt his own property by outpointing Joe Beckett, setting up a record by doing so in his tenth pro contest. He fought among the heavies after that, but without great success, being unable to give the weight and age away. After a kayo defeat by Jack Bloomfield in 1924 he retired.
Score 21: w7 (1) d1 l13.

Smith, Ed (Gunboat)

World White Heavyweight Champion 1914

(b. Philadelphia, Pennsylvania, Feb. 17, 1887). Began pro boxing: 1906.

Although 6 ft. 2 in. in height, he scaled only 185 pounds, being tall but lean. In the 'White Hope' days he fought all the leading aspirants to the title, beating Frank Moran (points 20), Jess Willard (who became world king in 1915, points 20), Bombardier Billy Wells (stopped 2), Jim Flynn (stopped 5), Carl Morris (stopped 5) and George Rodel (stopped 23). On Jan. 1, 1914 he knocked out Arthur Pelkey in 15 rounds to become 'white champion' at Daly City, California. Going to England on July 16 he fought Georges Carpentier at London's Olympia, with his title at stake. He put the Frenchman down in round six, then brushed his hair with a right-hander as his opponent was still on the floor. It did not strike his opponent, but Carpentier's manager and chief second got into the ring in protest and the fight was over. Smith (they called him Gunboat because he had been in the U.S. Navy and also had big feet) went on fighting for another six years before he retired in 1921.
Score 131: w56 (37) d6 l20 ND.49.

Smith, Jeff

World Middleweight Champion 1914–15

(b. New York City, April 23, 1891 – d. Levittown, New Jersey, Feb. 3, 1962). Began pro boxing: March 7, 1910.

This strong, tough and accomplished box-fighter, who fought in the no-decision era, did not come into fame until he left America to campaign in France and then in Australia where there was a boxing boom in 1914 and 1915. In his first fight there he outpointed fellow-American Eddie McGoorty over 20 rounds in a bout advertised as for the vacant middleweight championship of the world. He defended this title against Pat Bradley (w.ko.16) and Jimmy Clabby (w.pts.20). Smith lost a points decision to Mick King, but regained the crown by outpointing him over 20 rounds in a return bout. He put his crown at stake against Les Darcy, who was ruled out in round five for holding, and then again outpointed King, but lost the world title to Darcy when disqualified in the second round. He came back to America to continue his career for another 12 years, but never again fought in a title bout. Smith retired in 1927.
Score 185: w139 (51) d5 l28 ND.10, Dnc.3.

Smith, Jem

English Heavyweight Champion 1889–95

(b. Cripplegate, London, Jan. 21, 1863 – d. London, Sept. 10, 1931). Began knuckle fighting: Dec. 17, 1885.

Standing only 5 ft. 8½ in. and weighing 180 pounds, he was on the small side for a heavyweight, but was a powerful hitter and possessed unlimited stamina. His outstanding fights with bare fists were with Jack Davis (w.ko.6), Alf Greenfield (drew13), Jake Kilrain in France (drew 106) and Frank Slavin in Belgium (drew14). He was beaten by Ted Pritchard in three rounds for the championship of England, but knocked out Pritchard in two rounds of a return bout on May 9, 1895. Smith had a tremendous fight with Dick Burge at the Bolingbroke Club in Clapham, London, winning on the intervention of the referee in the ninth round. He lost in two rounds to Dan Creedon (Australia) in 1896 and to George Crisp, disqualified in five rounds the following year, after which he retired.
Score (incomplete) 11: w4 (3) d3 l4.

Smith, Mysterious Billy

World Welterweight Champion 1892–1900

(b. Eastport, Maine, May 15, 1871 – d. Portland, Oregon, Oct. 15, 1937). Began pro boxing: 1890.

Real name Amos Smith, he changed it to Billy Smith as more appropriate for a fighting man. The addition of 'Mysterious' came because while still an unknown fighter, he kept coming up with a win here and there until one day a newspaper man wrote: 'I see that Mysterious Billy Smith won again last night – who is he?' From then on the name stuck. Smith knocked out Danny Needham in 14 rounds on Dec. 14, 1892 at San Francisco for the world welterweight title. He defended this against Tom Williams (Australia) with a two rounds win, but lost it over 20 rounds to Tommy Ryan on points. A return fight ended in the 18th round and was declared a draw. When Ryan gave up the title, Smith reclaimed it and defended it successfully against Matty Matthews (w.pts.20), Charlie McKeever (w.pts.25). Joe Walcott (w.pts.20), and Charlie McKeever (drew20). On Jan. 15, 1900 he lost his championship on a foul in the 21st round to Rube Ferns. There was no return bout and in 1902 he retired.
Score 85: w29 (23) d27 l19 ND.7 Dnc.3.

Smith, Sid

World, European and British Flyweight Champion 1911–13

(b. Bermondsey, London, Feb. 2, 1889 – d. Hendon, London, April 28, 1948). Began pro boxing: March 16, 1907.

He had the distinction of being the first boxer to be flyweight champion of the world. Stylish and fast on his feet, he ran up a long list of wins, mostly over short distances, and on Dec. 4, 1911 outpointed Joe Wilson in a memorable bout to win the British title. In 1913 he went to Paris and outpointed the French champion, Eugene Criqui, to add the European and world crown to his holdings.

Sid Smith was the first flyweight champion of the world.

Two months later he went in with Bill Ladbury with all three titles at stake and was knocked out in 11 rounds. Sid went on scrapping for another five years, retiring on Boxing Day, 1919 after being stopped in 11 rounds by Johnny Marshall.
Score 106: *w*82 (11) *d*5 *l*18 *ND*.1.

Smith, Solly

World Featherweight Champion 1897–98

(b. Los Angeles, California, 1871 – d. Culver City, California, Aug. 29, 1933). Began pro boxing: 1888.

A hard puncher with plenty of staying power, he spent his first five years in his home State before going to New York where he soon secured a chance to win the world featherweight crown, but was knocked out in seven rounds by the more experienced and talented George Dixon. He had to wait four years before Dixon would take him on again, on Oct. 4, 1897, and Smith won on points. He defended the title successfully against Billy O'Donnell (w.dis.7) and Tommy White (drew25), but lost it to Dave Sullivan who knocked him out in five rounds at Coney Island, New York on Sept. 26, 1898. There was no return bout and in 1902 Solly retired.
Score 60: *w*24 (18) *d*20 *l*10 *ND*.4 *Dnc*.2.

Smith, Wallace 'Bud'

World Lightweight Champion 1955–56

(b. Cincinatti, Ohio, April 2, 1929 – d. Cincinatti, July 11, 1973). Began pro boxing: Nov. 29, 1948.

A cute box-fighter with a good punch, he spent the first three years in bouts in and around his home town, then went to Australia in 1952 where he had four contests of which he won two. Coming home he made good progress and on Oct. 19, 1955 outboxed Jimmy Carter to win the world lightweight title. The 32-year-old champion had lost and regained his crown several times, but in their return contest Smith again proved his superiority with an undisputed points win. He kept his crown for 14 months, then lost it on a points decision to Joe Brown, who rubbed in his victory by knocking out Smith in 11 rounds of their return bout. Bud went to pieces after that and after he had lost his next six bouts in a row (four by stoppages), he retired in 1958.
Score 60: *w*31 (18) *d*6 *l*23.

Smith, Willie

World Bantamweight Title Claimant 1927

(b. Johannesburg, South Africa, 1905 – d. Roodeport, Transvaal, South Africa, Dec. 20, 1955). Began pro boxing: June 20, 1925.

Although he never won a world title, Willie Smith must be ranked a challenger for the title of greatest South African boxer.

Fast, and a fine exponent of the left hook, he gave his best performance in London when he beat England's Teddy Baldock, who had claimed the world bantamweight crown in 1927.

Smith – who turned professional after winning the bantamweight gold medal at the 1924 Olympics – had chalked up a series of wins over formidable British imports, including British champion Johnny Brown, before he took on Baldock. After his shock win he went to America in search of a title bout with Bud Taylor, another self-styled world bantamweight champion. However, when he lost a close points decision to Dominick Petrone in Cleveland, Smith – disgusted with the racketeering rife in American boxing at the time – returned home. A subsequent Australian campaign proved disastrous. He lost twice to former world flyweight champion Fidel La Barba, and was knocked out by Jack Roberts.

But back in South Africa he staged a remarkable comeback. He won the South African featherweight title, then fought Dick Corbett in London for the vacant British Empire bantamweight crown. But making the weight weakened him, and he lost on points.

Smith continued to draw the crowds in South Africa, even though he was twice knocked out by world featherweight champion Freddie Miller. He closed his 12-year career after Johnny McGrory of Scotland outpointed him for the British Empire featherweight crown on Boxing Day 1936.
Score 55: *w*39 (5) *d*3 *l*13.

Leon Spinks created one of the biggest upsets in ring history when he beat Muhammad Ali in only his eighth professional fight.

Solis, Julian

World Bantamweight Champion (W.B.A.) 1980

(b. Rio Piedras, Puerto Rico, Jan. 7, 1957). Began pro boxing: Nov. 11, 1975.

He secured a world bantamweight title fight after 20 wins and no defeats, outpointing Jorge Lujan at Miami on Aug. 29, 1980. That he had come to championship status too soon seemed evident when at his first defence, three months later, he was stopped in the 14th round by Jeff Chandler (U.S.A.). He won his next bout with a kayo win and qualified for a return with Chandler, but again was beaten, this time by a clean-cut kayo in the seventh. On Nov. 12, 1981 he was stopped by Kiko Bejines at Los Angeles.
Score 41: *w*36 (18) *d*1 *l*4.

Soose, Billy

World Middleweight Champion 1941

(b. Farrell, Pennsylvania, Aug. 2, 1915). Began pro boxing: March 15, 1938.

A strong and determined fighter, he made such a good start that it seemed he must win a world title. At the beginning of 1941 he went to New York for the first time, won three fights in a row and was then matched with Ken Overlin for the world middleweight title on May 9. He won on points over 15 rounds. Soose lost on points in a non-title ten-rounder with Georgie Abrams, then was stopped in eight by Ceferino Garcia, gave up his title and announced his retirement in 1942.
Score 41: *w*34 (13) *d*1 *l*6.

Michael Spinks, world light-heavy champion.

Spinks, Leon

World Heavyweight Champion 1978

(b. St. Louis, Missouri, July 11, 1953). Began pro boxing: Jan. 15, 1977.

He won the light-heavyweight gold medal at the 1976 Olympic Games and gave every indication of being a good professional. Unfortunately he was grossly mismanaged or he had a higher opinion of his prowess than was the case. Lured into the Muhammad Ali web, he was given a shot at the world crown in his eighth pro bout and won a points decision. His reign was restricted to seven months, Ali winning the guaranteed return contest on points.

Spinks was knocked out in 2 min. 3 sec., of the first round by Gerrie Coetzee (South Africa), and after four more bouts challenged Larry Holmes for the W.B.C. heavyweight title – he was saved by the referee in the third round. On Oct. 31, 1982 he won a 12-round points decision over Jesse Burnett to win the N.A.B.F. cruiserweight title.

He retired in 1983 and remained inactive throughout 1984. When he resumed boxing he had a disastrous time but stubbornly continued.
Score 25: w17 (11) d2 l6.

Spinks, Michael

World Light-Heavyweight Champion (W.B.A.) 1981–85, World Heavyweight Champion (I.B.F.) 1985–86

(b. St. Louis, Missouri, July 13, 1956). Began pro boxing: April 17, 1977.

Younger of two fighting brothers, he won the middleweight gold medal at the 1976

Michael Spinks (facing camera) on the way to a gold medal in the 1976 Olympics. Brother Leon also won gold.

Olympic Games. A good box-fighter with a strong punch, he won his first 16 pro bouts (11 inside the distance), and then secured a fight with Eddie Mustafa Mohammad at Las Vegas for the W.B.A. version of the world light-heavyweight title. Spinks won on points over 15 rounds and then defended it periodically against Vonzell Johnson (7), Mustapha Wasajja (6), Murray Sutherland (8) and Jerry Celestine (8).

He disposed of six other challengers in the next three years. On Sept. 22 1985 he outpointed 36-year old Larry Holmes to win the world heavyweight title over 15 rounds at Las Vegas, a feat he repeated seven months later, the last win being a very close thing. He and Leon thereby became the first pair of brothers to win a version of the world heavyweight title. Spinks then challenged the unbeaten Mike Tyson at Atlantic City on June 28, 1988 and was knocked out in 91 sec.
Score 32: w31 (21) d0 l1.

Stanley, George 'Digger'

World and British Bantamweight Champion 1910–13

(b. London [some sources say Norwich], Feb. 28, 1876 – d. London, March 7, 1919). Began pro boxing: 1889.

The story is that his father 'sold' him to a travelling booth proprietor for a sovereign (£1) and a pint of beer. Anyway, he was brought up in a booth and showed extraordinary talent, sweeping all before him when he appeared in public arenas. He knocked out Joe Bowker in eight rounds to win the

world and British titles on Oct. 17, 1910, and defended these against Johnny Condon (w.pts.20) and Ike Bradley (w.pts.20), but going to Dieppe, France, lost his world title to Charles Ledoux. He made a defence of his British title by outpointing Alex Lafferty over 20 rounds, lost the crown to Bill Beynon, but won it back four months later to win a Lonsdale Belt outright. Stanley was beaten for the championship by Curley Walker, being disqualified in the 13th round. He lost his form and after a losing run retired in 1918.
Score 85: w55 (14) d7 l21 ND.2.

Steele, Freddie

World Middleweight Champion (N.B.A.) 1936–38

(b. Tacoma, Washington, Dec. 18, 1912). Began pro boxing: March 1, 1928.

One of the hardest hitting middleweights produced in America. In the first eight years of his career he won a large number of his fights inside the distance and it is surprising that he did not get a world title bid a lot earlier. On July 11, 1936 he outpointed Ed 'Babe' Risko at Seattle to win the N.B.A. version of the world middleweight title.

In two years Steele defended successfully against Gorilla Jones (w.pts.10), Ed 'Babe' Risko (w.pts.15), Frank Battaglia (w.ko.3), Ken Overlin (w.ko.4) and Carmen Barth (w.ko.7). In 1938 he lost the crown to Solly Krieger, who knocked him out in 1 min. 43 sec., of the first round. Steele retired.
Score 133: w119 (57) d8 l5 Dnc.1.

Sterling, Bunny

European, British and Commonwealth Middleweight Champion 1970–76

(b. Jamaica, April 14, 1948). Began pro boxing in England: Sept. 13, 1966.

Resident in Finsbury Park, London, he soon made himself popular with his proficient boxing and won the British title, together with the Commonwealth crown, by stopping (cuts) Mark Rowe in four rounds on Sept. 8, 1970. He kept his Commonwealth title against Kahu Mahanga (w.pts.15), Tony Mundine (drew15) and Johann Louw (w.pts.15). Sterling was knocked out in 14 rounds by Jean-Claude Bouttier when trying to win the European title. In a return with Mundine in Brisbane, he was stopped in 15 rounds.

Beating Phil Matthews (w.ko.5) and Don McMillan (w.rsf.14), he won his Lonsdale Belt outright; outpointed Mark Rowe in a return title bout, then lost his British title to Kevin Finnegan on points. He regained it by stopping Maurice Hope in eight rounds, then relinquished the title to concentrate on the European championship, which he won on Feb. 20, 1976 by stopping Frank Reiche in 13 rounds at Hamburg. Unfortunately, he lost

it four months later to Angelo Jacopucci in Milan on a points verdict and retired in 1977.
Score 57: *w*35 (14) *d*4 *l*18.

Stracey, John H.

World (W.B.C.), European and British Welterweight Champion 1974–76

(b. Bethnal Green, London, Sept. 22, 1950). Began pro boxing: Sept. 17, 1969.

An upstanding skilful boxer with a good punch, he was fighting for a title in his fourth year as a pro, but lost on disqualification to Bobby Arthur in the seventh round of their contest for the vacant British welter title. On May 27, 1974 he knocked out Roger Menetrey (France) to win the European crown, which he retained against Max Hebeisen (Switzerland) by a knockout in round six. On Dec. 6, 1975 he went to Mexico City and pounded Jose Napoles into submission, also in six rounds, to win the W.B.C. world title. Three months later he defended this successfully against Hedgemon Lewis (U.S.A.) with a ten rounds knockout, but that was the end of his successes. Putting his world crown at stake against Carlos Palomino (Mexico) he was stopped in 12 rounds and, following a ten rounds defeat by Dave Green, retired in 1978.
Score 51: *w*45 (37) *d*1 *l*5.

Stribling, Young

Heavyweight Title Contender 1931

(b. Bainbridge, Georgia, Dec. 26, 1904 – d. Oct. 2, 1933). Began pro boxing: Jan. 17, 1921.

His first names were William Lawrence, but he was given the appelation 'Young' because when he first became known he was only 17. He travelled with his parents who were acrobats, and he and his brother 'Babe' formed part of the act as midget boxers. When it was decided that Bill would turn pro, the family concentrated on his career, taking him through the States where he met boxing aspirants of all sorts and sizes, an agent going on in advance to make the selections. In this way Stribling engaged in as many as 36 bouts a year, many going the distance. This went on for ten years. He got into the big time when promoter Jeff Dickson brought him to Europe and he won fights in Paris and London, defeating Phil Scott, the British champion, in two rounds. In America he beat many of the title contenders and then was given a fight with Max Schmeling for the world title on July 3, 1931 at Cleveland, Ohio. Fighting a totally defensive battle he was knocked out in the 15th and last round. He continued his career after that catastrophe, boxing in Canada, Australia and South Africa, and was still a title contender. Riding his motor-cycle home after winning over Maxie Rosenbloom in Houston, however, he ran into a truck on

John L. Sullivan is considered to be the first modern champion although most of his bouts were fought without using gloves.

the highway and died from his injuries.
Score 286: *w*222 (126) *d*14 *l*12 *ND*.36 *Dnc*.2.

Sullivan, Dave

World Featherweight Champion 1898

(b. Cork, Ireland, May 19, 1877 – d. Cork, 1929). Began pro boxing: 1894.

Travelled with his family to America when he was a young lad, and started boxing professionally at the age of 17. In his fifth year as a paid fighter, he knocked out Solly Smith in five rounds at Coney Island, New York on Sept. 26, 1898 to win the world

championship. Just 46 days later he defended the title against clever George Dixon and lost on a foul in the tenth round. His chance to regain his crown came six years later when he challenged Young Corbett II in San Francisco and was stopped in 11 rounds. Sullivan retired in 1905.
Score 59: *w*29 (18) *d*15 *l*12 *ND*.2 *Dnc*.1.

Sullivan, Jim

British Middleweight Champion 1910–14

(b. Bermondsey, London, June 7, 1886 – d. London, July 22, 1949). Began pro boxing: Dec. 22, 1906.

A stylish boxer, he came from a fighting neighbourhood, but made a bad start, being twice knocked out by Charlie Hickman. There were other setbacks, but he really got into his stride by 1909 when he won bouts that led up to a fight for the British middleweight title against Tom Thomas. Jim won a fine points victory and his friends were so delighted they brought over Billy Papke to put his world title at stake against the Londoner. But the tough American knew far too much for his challenger and tore him to pieces with body blows before knocking him out in the ninth round. Worse was to follow. Georges Carpentier put him away in two rounds when they fought for the European crown and later on Pat O'Keefe took away his title with a 20-round points win. Sullivan did not win a fight after that and when he had again been outpointed by O'Keefe and forced to retire to Tom Gummer in 14 rounds, he decided to retire.

Score 27: w12 (5) d1 l14.

Sullivan, John L.

World Heavyweight Champion 1882–92

(b. Roxbury, Massachusetts, Oct. 15, 1858 – d. Abingdon, Massachusetts, Feb. 2, 1918). Began pro boxing: 1878.

Many do not regard Sullivan as being champion of the world, because those fights in which he won the title were fought under Prize Ring rules. However, he did box with gloves, even if it was only in his last fight in which he was knocked out in 21 rounds by James J. Corbett who claimed the world crown thereafter. A virile, stout-hearted fighter, Sullivan was known as 'The Boston Strong Boy' and his favourite saying was that he could lick anyone in the world. Certainly he was never beaten until the end and he had some tough customers to deal with. Among his championship victims were Paddy Ryan (9) and Jake Kilrain (75), but little Charlie Mitchell fought him to a 39 rounds draw in France in 1888. On Aug. 8, 1887, the sportsmen of Boston presented him with a magnificent belt containing 397 diamonds that pricked out his name, emblematic of him being the undisputed champion of the world.

Score 42: w38 (33) d3 l1.

Sullivan, Jack (Twin)

World Heavyweight Contender 1905

(b. Cambridge, Massachusetts, Sept. 23, 1878 – d. Cambridge, Massachusetts, Sept. 4, 1947). Began pro boxing: 1898.

One of twin boxers, he was not much more than a light-heavy, but mingled with the big boys in the last part of his career, which lasted 25 years. His best feat was to win a decision over 20 rounds from Tommy Burns, just before the Canadian took over the heavyweight title. He also fought a draw with Burns, and a draw with Jack O'Brien, who won the world light-heavyweight title five months later. In fact, Jack seemed to thrive on drawn bouts, there being no fewer than 41 in his record, in addition to 26

no-decision contests. Had he been a little heavier and possessed a harder punch, he would have done a lot better, for he was a skilful boxer and knew all the tricks of the ring. Both he and his brother Mike were a credit to the fight game. He retired in 1922 and outlived his twin by ten years.

Score 138: w53 (29) d41 l18 ND.26.

Sullivan, Mike 'Twin'

World Welterweight Champion 1907–08

(b. Cambridge, Massachusetts, Sept. 23, 1878 – d. Cambridge, Massachusetts, Oct. 1937). Began pro boxing: 1901.

A talented boxer, he spent his early career in Boston rings, then extended his range and on April 23, 1907 at Los Angeles, outpointed Honey Mellody over 20 rounds to become world welter king. He gave up the title the following year owing to eye trouble. Came back in 1909 and fought through to 1914 without another title bout and then retired.

In 1908 he was knocked out by Stanley Ketchel in a single round, whereupon his twin brother Jack challenged the 'Michigan Assassin' in order to restore the family honour but was defeated in 20 rounds.

Score 70: w40 (20) d16 l11 ND.21.

Sullivan, Steve 'Kid'

World Junior-Lightweight Champion 1924–25

(b. Brooklyn, New York, May 21, 1897 – date of death unknown). Began pro boxing: 1911.

A smart boxer, his early years were spent in the no-decision era. For seven years he battled through, then laid off during World War I. Returning to the ring in 1921, he fought mainly around Brooklyn and on June 20, 1924 outpointed Johnny Dundee to become the third fighter to win the world junior-lightweight title. He defended this twice successfully, outpointing Vicent 'Pepper' Martin and stopping Mike Ballerino in five rounds. When he met Ballerino for the fourth time (Sullivan w1 l1 ND.1), Steve lost a ten rounds points decision and with it his title. The following year he tried to regain it from Tod Morgan, but was knocked out in six rounds and then retired.

Score 110: w33 (14) d10 l18 ND.49.

Summers, Johnny

British Feather, Light and Welterweight Champion 1906–14, British Empire Welterweight Champion 1913–14

(b. Middlesbrough, Yorkshire, Feb. 1, 1882 – d. New Zealand, March 27, 1946). Began pro boxing: 1900.

This astonishing box-fighter was active for 20 years, becoming a multiple champion. Real name Johnny Somers, he started in

Australia when aged 18. It was a rough school, but the right one for a lad who intended to get to the top in the fight business. It took him six years to get his first title chance, then on Jan. 29, 1906 he outpointed Spike Robson to win the British featherweight crown. He lost this back to Robson on a foul in round four then went to America where he had 17 bouts, winning 15 and losing two on points verdicts.

On Nov. 23, 1908 he won the British lightweight title by stopping Jack Goldswain in 14 rounds, but lost it the following year to Freddie Welsh, who subsequently became world champion. On June 17, 1912, Summers won his third title, beating Arthur Evernden in 13 rounds for the welterweight crown and after one successful defence went back to Australia, where he won the British Empire crown, defeating Sid Burns, Arthur Evernden and Tom McCormick at Sydney, each on points. Coming home, he was knocked out in nine rounds by Johnny Basham. Fighting Harry Stone (U.S.A.) in London in a bout advertised as for the world welterweight title he secured a draw over 20 rounds. He had his last fling at a British title in 1919, when he was 36, but lost to Bob Marriott, being ruled out in the tenth for a low punch. Summers retired in 1920 to become a referee.

Score 191: w108 (53) d34 l35 ND.13 Dnc.1.

Symonds, Joe

World and British Flyweight Champion 1914–16

(b. Plymouth, Devon, Dec. 28, 1894 – d. Plymouth, March 4, 1953). Began pro boxing: Jan. 6, 1911.

In his third year as a pro, he won the world and British flyweight titles by knocking out Percy Jones in 18 rounds. He retained these against Tancy Lee, who was knocked out in the 16th on May 15, 1914, but lost them to the renowned Jimmy Wilde, who stopped him in the 16th. Symonds had a chance to regain his titles when Lee took them from Wilde, but the Scotsman beat him in 17 rounds. Symonds became a featherweight and in 1917 challenged Joe Fox for the British title, but was stopped in the 18th round. He was also outpointed when he tried to take it from Tommy Noble, who outpointed him over 20 rounds. Going to Australia, Joe had 13 bouts, of which he won six and drew two. He boxed on until 1924 but when the losses began to show in his record, he retired.

Score 133: w96 (35) d11 l25 ND.1.

Tarleton, Nel

British Featherweight Champion 1930–45

(b. Liverpool, Lancashire, Jan. 14, 1906 – d. Jan. 12, 1956). Began pro boxing: Jan. 1926.

Liverpool's Nel Tarleton won three British featherweight crowns and lost only 19

Dick Tiger (left) beats Johnny Read at the Café Royal, London, in April 1957.

fights in a 27-year-career – and he did it all on only one sound lung. He went out on a winning note, successfully defending his title in 1945 at the age of 39.

Eldest of eight children, Tarleton began boxing as a schoolboy. He lost his first paid contest, but then quickly developed into a star, first as a bantam, then as world-class featherweight. For 19 years he was the idol of Merseyside.

Very tall for his weight, Tarleton used his long reach to great advantage. He possessed a superb defence and excellent footwork, and also knew how to punch his weight, winning 40 of his 144 bouts inside the distance. However, all Tarleton's title fights went the full distance – he fought ten times in British featherweight title bouts and twice for the world crown: America's Freddie Miller beat him narrowly on points both times. He twice lost his British title, but regained it each time, and won two Lonsdale Belts outright.
Score 144: *w*116 (40) *d*8 *l*20.

Tate, John

World Heavyweight Champion (W.B.A.) 1979–80

(b. Marion City, Arkansas, Jan. 29, 1955).

Began pro boxing: May 7, 1977.

A giant among heavies, he stood 6 ft. 4 in. and weighed 240 pounds. Tate knocked out 15 of his first 19 opponents, then secured a fight with Gerrie Coetzee in Pretoria, South Africa for the W.B.A. version of the world heavyweight title. This took place on Oct. 20, 1979 and Tate gained a points victory. Five months later at Knoxville, Tennessee, he lost the championship to Mike Weaver (U.S.A.), by a knockout in the 15th round. Then a nine rounds knockout by Trevor Berbick, the Canadian champion, put him out of the ratings. He began to make a comeback with four wins in 1981 and another three in 1982.
Score 33: *w*31 (22) *d*0 *l*2.

Taylor, Arnold

World Bantamweight Champion (W.B.A.) 1973–74.

(b. Jeppe, Johannesburg, South Africa, July 21, 1945 – d. Nov. 22, 1981). Began pro boxing: May 20, 1967.

A game and determined fighter and stiff puncher, he won the Transvaal bantam crown in his second pro bout by knocking out Ray Buttle. He stepped out of his class to win the South African feather and light-weight titles, then the bantam championship and was never beaten for them. His big day came on Nov. 3, 1973 when he fought Romeo Anaya (Mexico) for the W.B.A. world bantam title. It was a fierce and gruelling fight with both going all out for victory. This came in the 14th round when a left hook and a straight right put Anaya down for the full count. Taylor's reign came to an end when Soo-Hwan Hong (S.Korea) came to Durban and won a points decision to take the title. Taylor boxed for another two years, but a kayo defeat in London by Vernon Sollas brought about his retirement in 1976. He was killed in a motorcycle accident in 1981.
Score 49: *w*40 (17) *d*1 *l*8.

Taylor, Charles 'Bud'

World Bantamweight Champion (N.B.A.) 1927–28

(b. Terre Haute, Indiana, July 22, 1903 – d. Los Angeles, California, March 8, 1962). Began pro boxing: 1920.

A busy boxer and useful puncher with plenty of stamina. His early career was in the days of the no-decision bouts and he fought on average 13 times a year. He had to wait until 1927 for title recognition, then on March 26 boxed ten rounds to a draw with Tony Canzoneri for the N.B.A. version of the world bantam crown. They met again on June 24 and this time Taylor took a cleancut decision to become champion. He relinquished the title at the end of 1928 to fight as

a featherweight, but never came within range of a championship shot. Taylor retired in 1931.
Score 161: *w*104 (35) *d*12 *l*29 ND.16.

Tendler, Lew

World Light and Welterweight Title Contender 1923–24

(b. Philadelphia, Pennsylvania, Sept. 8, 1898). Began pro boxing: 1913.

Probably the best southpaw of all time. A newsboy when he left school, he had to fight to keep his pitch, so joined a local boys' club to learn how to box and soon was fighting professionally. His early years were in the no-decision era, but he developed a blasting right hook that put many kayo wins in his record. On July 24, 1923 he fought Benny Leonard in New York for the world light-weight crown and almost brought off victory, only the talented champion's cunning saving him from defeat. On June 2, 1924 he challenged the mighty Mickey Walker for the world welterweight title and gave the champion plenty to think about before losing on points over ten rounds. Tendler went on fighting until 1928 when he retired.
Score 168: *w*59 (37) *d*2 *l*11 ND.95 Dnc.1.

Terranova, Phil

World Featherweight Champoin (N.B.A) 1943–44

(b. New York City, Sept. 4, 1919). Began pro boxing: July 14, 1941.

A smart boxer with a respectable punch, he had an in and out career until Aug. 16, 1943 when he met Jackie Callura for the N.B.A. version of the world feathereight title and won on a knockout in round eight. In a return title bout he stopped Callura again, this time in six rounds. On March 10, 1944 in Boston he lost his title on a points decision to Sal Bartolo and in a return contest in the same city two months afterwards, was again outpointed over the full distance. Terranova had an opportunity to regain the crown in New York, but was outpointed by wily Willie Pep. That was his last championship bid, but he went on boxing with considerable success until 1949 when he retired.
Score 99: *w*67 (29) *d*11 *l*21.

Terrell, Ernie

World Heavyweight Champion (W.B.A.) 1965–67

(b. Chicago, Illinois, April 4, 1939). Began pro boxing: May 15, 1957.

Standing 6 ft. 6 in, and scaling 200 pounds, he was big enough to beat anyone, but lacked the 'killer' instinct. He started in his home city and built up a good record in the first six years, then began to meet the rated heavies and beat such as Cleveland Williams (who had once knocked him out), Zora Folley and Jefferson Davis. He was selected by the W.B.A. to box Eddie Machen for its version of the heavyweight title it had taken from Muhammad Ali, and won on points over 15 rounds on March 5, 1965. He retained it against George Chuvalo and Doug Jones, both with points wins, and then had a 'clearing up' fight with Ali, the real champion, who gave him an unmerciful beating for the full 15 rounds. Terrell lost to Thad Spencer in a W.B.A. eliminating tournament and retired in 1967. He made a comeback that ended disastrously in 1973 when he was stopped by unranked Jeff Merritt in New York and retired.
Score 55: *w*46 (21) *d*0 *l*9.

Thil, Marcel

World Middleweight Champion 1932–37, European Middle and Light-Heavyweight Champion 1928–35

(b. Sain-Dizier, France, May 25, 1904 – d. Aug. 14, 1968). Began pro boxing: Nov. 8, 1925.

There was nothing stylish about French middleweight Marcel Thil, but his aggressive body-punching was potent enough to win him the world crown. He was also a hard man to hurt – only twice was he stopped.

Thil was over 21 before he had his first professional fight, and for the first two years he lost almost as many bouts as he won. But he carried on doggedly, then suddenly unleashed exceptional punching power that won him 18 fights in a row. All but one were by the knock-out route, and they included the French championship in a single round. He won and lost the European crown, then had 15 good wins that earned him a match with America's William 'Gorilla' Jones, who had been tempted to Paris to defend his National Boxing Association world title. The coloured American lost on a foul. For the next five years Thil beat off English, Cuban, Spanish, French and American challengers. He also regained the European title and won the European light-heavyweight crown.

In 1939 the hairy chested, bald-headed campaigner moved to New York to meet Fred Apostoli in promoter Mike Jacob's Tournament of Champions; a badly cut eye forced Thil out in round ten. He retired from the ring after that fight.
Score 148: *w*113 (54) *d*13 *l*28.

Thompson, Young Jack

World Welterweight Champion (N.B.A.) 1930–31

(b. Los Angeles, California, Sept. 8, 1904 – d. Los Angeles, April 19, 1946). Began pro boxing: Nov. 20, 1922.

A skilful boxer with a good knockdown punch, he was the second black fighter to win the world welterweight title. The record books show him as starting in 1922 when he was 18, but it is more likely that he began a lot earlier, probably when he was 15. It was 1929 before he could get near a title chance. Then he was outpointed by Jackie Fields over ten rounds in an N.B.A. version of the championship. Thompson won the title on May 9, 1930 by outpointing Fields over 15 rounds at Detroit, but four months later lost it on an adverse points decision to Tommy Freeman at Cleveland. On April 14, 1931 he regained the crown from Freeman with a points victory but again his tenure of the title was short as he lost it to southpaw Lou Brouillard in Boston six months later. Thompson retired in 1932.
Score 104: *w*63 (43) *d*13 *l*28.

Tiger, Dick

World Middle and Light-Heavyweight Champion 1962–68, Commonwealth Middleweight Champion 1958–60

(b. Amaigo, Orlu, Nigeria, Aug. 14, 1929 – d. Nigeria, Dec. 14, 1971). Began pro boxing: 1952.

Hard-hitting Dick Tiger carried off three world crowns in the 1960s: he was twice middleweight champion and once light-heavyweight king. It was a remarkable achievement by an unknown Nigerian fighter who started late – and badly. Born Dick Ihetu, Tiger turned professional at 23 after a short amateur career. For three years he campaigned in Nigera, then decided to try his luck in England. He lost his first four fights – form that won him a 1957 London bout as a trial-horse for up-and-coming Terry Downes. Tiger showed his real class by beating Downes in five rounds. In his 23rd contest he took the Commonwealth middleweight crown from Pat McAteer in nine rounds and headed for America.

Again Tiger made an unimpressive start, even losing his Commonwealth crown in Canada. But he plugged away until his determination – and the right connections – won him a title bout with American Gene Fullmer. He outpointed the tough American in San Francisco, drew with him at Las Vegas, then stopped him in round seven in Nigeria. This last victory won him universal recognition as world champion. In the series of lucrative title bouts that followed he lost and re-won the championship before finally surrendering it to Emile Griffith in 1966.

Tiger promptly moved up a division and took the light-heavyweight crown from Joe Torres in his next fight. Then 37 years old, he retained it for 17 months before Bob Foster defeated him in four rounds – the only time he was knocked out in his long career.
Score 81: *w*61 (3) *d*3 *l*17.

Tiozzo, Christopher

European Middleweight Champion, 1988–

(b. St. Denis, France, June 1, 1963). Began pro boxing: Oct. 29, 1985.

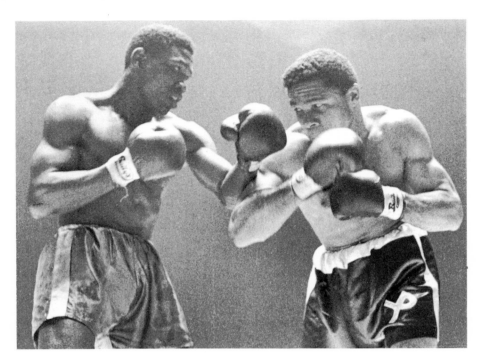

On Oct. 15, 1958 Dick Tiger (left) outpointed Yolande Pompey to retain his Commonwealth title.

Following a remarkable amateur career, during which he won 94 of over a hundred bouts, he turned pro at 22. Topping 6 ft. in height, he made good use of this advantage, and picked up some of his victories during a trip to New York. He won the European middleweight title in Paris on April 18, 1988 by outpointing the titleholder Pierre Joly, but had to sustain a knockdown before gaining a close win. He soon made two successful defences, stopping both Andrea Prox and Alfonso Redondo.
Score 21: w21 (14) d0 l0.

Todd, Roland

European and British Middleweight Champion 1923–27

(b. North Kensington, London, Jan. 9, 1900). Began pro boxing: April 26, 1917.

A strong and clever upstanding boxer, Todd was too lethargic to become a world-beater. In the British Army in 1918, he won an Inter-Allied middleweight competition. From then on he built up a fine record, but it was seven years before he got a championship opportunity. On Nov. 20, 1922, he fought the famous Ted (Kid) Lewis for the British and European crowns and lost very narrowly on points. There had to be a return bout and on Feb. 15 the following year he won a close points decision to take the two titles. In 1924 he lost the Continental crown when losing on points to Bruno Frattini (Italy) in Milan and in the following year the British Boxing Board of Control took away his British title. Todd ignored this and in 1927 lost it to Frank Moody (Wales) on a points verdict. He twice went to America, but his style was not popular there. He met

the best at his weight and of his ten bouts in the U.S. he could only win two and draw one, but was never stopped. He boxed on until 1929 when he retired.
Score 114: w81 (44) d6 l25 ND.2.

Tokashiki, Katsuo

World Light-Flyweight Champion (W.B.A.) 1981–83

(b. Okinawa, Japan, July 29, 1960). Began pro boxing: Dec. 28, 1978.

His first 15 bouts took place in his own country and on Dec. 16, 1981, at Sendai he outpointed Hwan-Jim Kim (S. Korea) in 15 rounds to win the W.B.A. world light-flyweight title. He remained champion, with five successful defences, until July 10, 1983 when he lost his title on a technical verdict to Lupe Madera in Tokyo. In a return contest he was outpointed. In an effort to win the W.B.C. light-flyweight title he was stopped in nine rounds by Jung-Koo Chang.
Score 25: w19 (4) d2 l4.

Tomori, Tadashi

World Light-Flyweight Champion (W.B.C.) 1982

(b. Tokyo, Japan, Dec. 28, 1959). Began pro boxing: May 25, 1978.

He had almost all his fights in the Japanese capital city. Tomori challenged Kanzuori Tenrye for his native title but was outpointed, but in the second try he scored a one round kayo win. He defended his crown successfully, lost it, failed to regain it and finally won it back in the next two years. Then on April 13, 1982 he outpointed Amado Ursua (Mexico) to win the W.B.C. version of the world light-flyweight title. He was champion for only three months, then

was beaten on points by Hilario Zapata (Panama), a former titleholder, on July 20, 1982. In a return contest Tomori was again outpointed, after which he retired.
Score 26: w19 (5) d0 l7.

Torres, Jose

World Light-Heavyweight Champion 1965–66

(b. Playa Ponce, Puerto Rico, May 3, 1936). Began pro boxing: May 24, 1958.

A skilful box-fighter with a good knock-down punch. A silver medallist in the 1956 Olympic Games, he started his pro career in Brooklyn, New York, and built up a good record there with trips to other parts as they came up. His big chance came when he was matched to fight Willie Pastrano for the world light-heavyweight title on March 30, 1965 and won by stopping the champion in round nine. He successfully defended against Wayne Thornton (w.pts.15), Eddie Cotton (w.pts.15) and Chic Calderwood (w.ko.2). Torres lost the title to Dick Tiger on a points verdict after 15 terrific rounds and when they met again, five months later, there was the same result. He fought twice in the next two years, both kayo wins, and retired in 1969 to become a boxing reporter and author.
Score 45: w41 (29) d1 l3.

Toweel, Vic

World Bantamweight Champion 1950–52, Commonwealth Bantamweight Champion 1949–52

(b. Benomi, South Africa, Jan. 12, 1929). Began pro boxing: Jan. 21, 1949.

The first South African boxer to win a world title, bantamweight Vic Toweel had a remarkably quick rise to world fame – and a sensational fall from it. Turning professional at 20, he took little more than a year to win the world crown, and only 2 min. 19 sec., to lose it to Australian underdog Jimmy Carruthers almost 2½ years later.

Second son in a family of eight. Toweel was practically reared in a ring by his father, a former above-average fighter of Lebanese descent. Four other brothers also became prominent fighters. Toweel competed in the 1948 London Olympics, and turned professional on his return to South Africa.

A strong fighter with great punching power for his size and weight, Toweel made a fine start. In his first 11 contests he took the South African bantam and featherweight titles and the Commonwealth bantamweight crown. The following year he won the world title from long-reigning champion Manuel Ortiz, then beat off challenges from the British champions Danny O'Sullivan and Peter Keenan, and European titleholder Luis Romero of Spain. But when he came up against Carruthers he found no answer to the Australian's southpaw style and was completely overwhelmed in round one. By then

Toweel was finding it increasingly difficult to make the 8 st. 6 lb. (118 pounds) limit, and this contributed to his defeat.

Carruthers knocked out Toweel again in their return four months later – this time in ten rounds. So after a few more fights as a featherweight Toweel retired from the ring at the age of 25.

Score 32: w28 (14) d1 l3.

Toweel, Willie

Commonwealth Lightweight Champion 1955–59

(b. Benoni, South Africa, April 6, 1934). Began pro boxing: May 9, 1953.

Willie Toweel came close to emulating his older brother Vic when he tried to win the world bantamweight crown. In his 21st professional fight he held champion Robert Cohen of France to a draw.

The fifth son of the famous fighting Toweel family, Willie represented South Africa at the 1952 Helsinki Olympics. He was outpointed by the eventual winner Nat Brooks and turned professional a year later. Like Vic, he soon captured the South African bantam and featherweight titles. After his 1955 draw with Cohen he grew quickly into a lightweight, and took the Commonwealth crown from fellow-countryman Johnny van Rensburg on his second attempt. Then just 22, Toweel was such a clever boxer and fast, accurate hitter that he seemed destined for world honours. He beat off Commonwealth title challenges from van Rensburg (twice), Dick Howard of Canada, and British champion Dave Charnley. Willie became a crowd-puller in England, where he had nine bouts in eight months and lost only once – stopped in round seven by formidable Frenchman Guy Gracia. But like Vic, Willie was now finding it difficult to make the weight. For his 1959 return title match with Charnley he came to scale 10 ounces over

Right: Gene Tunney is the only world heavyweight champion to retire undefeated while champion. In his whole career he lost only once.

Below: In World War II Tunney was a Navy Commander. Here he is seen next to Brig.-Gen. Jimmy Doolittle (far left).

the lightweight limit. Although he made the weight in time, he was too weak to stand up to the British champion's combination punching and took the full count in round ten.

Willie moved up the scale once again. He fought successfully as a welterweight for another 17 months, until a knock-out defeat by Emile Griffith in New York persuaded him to give it up for good at the age of 26.

Score 54: w46 (23) d2 l6.

Tunney, Gene

World Heavyweight Champion 1926–28

(b. New York City, May 25, 1897 – d. Greenwich, Connecticut, Nov. 7, 1978). Began pro boxing: July 2, 1915.

Some great boxers have related how they were introduced to the game by being given a set of gloves as a birthday present, but not Gene Tunney, the son of comfortably off parents in Greenwich Village, New York. At the age of 11 he himself asked for, and received, a boxing outfit. He had already made up his mind to win the world heavyweight title.

Overcoming initial family opposition, he turned professional at the age of 18. He went through his first dozen contests undefeated, and was then drafted into the U.S. Marine Corps. This involuntary move did not upset his fistic plans. In fact, it enhanced them. Going to France when World War I was on the point of ending, he won the American Expeditionary Force championship at light-heavyweight, and he defeated the heavyweight champion in a special bout.

Returning to America at the end of 1919, Tunney resumed his boxing career, winning 22 contests in two years (17 inside the distance). He then took the American light-heavyweight title from the ageing Battling Levinsky on Jan. 13, 1922. Five months later he lost it to Harry Greb, the notorious 'Human Windmill', after undergoing one of the most brutal beatings in ring history. It was enough to break a young boxer's heart and spirit, but Tunney spent a week in bed while his wounds healed, worked out a way to beat Greb, and did so on four subsequent occasions. This was his only professional defeat in ten years of paid fighting.

Eliminating the heavyweight contenders one by one, Tunney earned the right to challenge the great Jack Dempsey, a man who had been world champion for seven years and who possessed an aggressive, fierce style of fighting and a tremendous killer instinct. But Tunney taught himself to run backwards – to box on the retreat – and did it so well that at the end of the tense ten-rounder the verdict went to him on a unanimous decision.

The return bout was a sell-out, and Tunney, as champion, received $990,445 – the highest pay received by any boxer in the days before television. This contest also produced the famous 'long count' of 14 seconds. Dempsey dropped his rival in the seventh round, but jeopardized his chances of regaining the title by hesitating before going to a neutral corner and thus giving Tunney a chance to recover and go on to win on points and retain the title.

Tunny had one more fight, a title defence against New Zealand's Tom Heeney, who was stopped in 11 rounds. Tunney then retired, an undefeated champion. He refused all offers to make a comeback, and became a wealthy businessman. A literary student, he could also claim the friendship of Bernard Shaw.

Score 83: w77 (45) d3 l1 ND.1 Dnc.1.

129

Randolph Turpin became world champion by defeating the great Sugar Ray Robinson. He is shown wearing his Lonsdale Belt.

Turpin, Dick

British and British Empire Middleweight Champion 1948–50

(b. Leamington Spa, Warwickshire, Nov. 26, 1920). Began pro boxing: Sept. 27, 1937.

A good upstanding boxer, an advocate of the left jab, who won the large majority of his fights in his first four years, but with never a hope of getting a title fight as in those days black men were barred by the boxing authorities in Britain. He was absent for nearly three years due to World War II, but made his presence felt when he resumed in 1946. With the ban against colour finally lifted, he knocked out Bos Murphy (New Zealand) in 2 min. 55 sec., of the opening round to take the British Empire crown. Forty-one days later, June 28, 1948, he outpointed Vince Hawkins to become British champion, and he defended both titles successfully against Albert Finch, who was outpointed.

The following year was disastrous: Finch relieved him of the British crown, while he was relieved of his Empire crown by Dave Sands (Australia) who knocked him out in exactly the same time as he had taken to dispose of Murphy. Turpin lost his British title in March 1950 to Albert Finch and after being stopped twice in subsequent battles, decided to retire. The eldest of three fighting brothers, he was a great help to Randy, but was not allowed to go into his corner for the return bout with Sugar Ray Robinson in New York, otherwise there might have been a different ending.
Score 99: w74 (31) d6 l18 Dnc.1.

Turpin, Randolph

World, European, British and Commonwealth Middleweight Champion, British and Commonwealth Light-Heavyweight Champion 1952–57

(b. Leamington Spa, Warwickshire, June 7, 1928 – d. Leamington Spa, May 17, 1966). Began pro boxing: Sept. 17, 1946.

The most exciting personality to grace the British boxing scene in the 1940s and 1950s, Randolph Turpin was a member of a fighting family. His eldest brother, Dick was the first coloured boxer to fight for and win a Lonsdale Belt, and his other brother, Jackie, was a very passable featherweight. But Randolph was the best of the three. By no means a scientific boxer, but possessed of considerable skill, he relied on his terrific punching powers which were good enough for him to take the world middleweight crown from no less a man than the incomparable Sugar Ray Robinson.

As a cook in the Royal Navy, Randolph enjoyed a sensational amateur career, during which he was A.B.A. weltwerweight champion in 1945 at the age of 17, and middleweight champion the following year. He also won a number of service titles and gained fame helping Great Britain beat the United States in a match at Wembley by knocking out his opponent, Harold Anspach, in 90 seconds. Less than four months later, Turpin turned professional, and began a wonderful career in which he won British, Commonwealth, European, and world titles. Indeed, he might have become British champion earlier than he did but his mother insisted that brother Dick should be given first chance.

In due course, Dick became champion, and then lost his title to Albert Finch, whereupon Randolph redeemed the family honour by stopping Finch in five rounds on Oct. 17, 1950. He followed this success four months later by knocking out Luc Van Dam of the Netherlands in 48 seconds to win the European crown, and then staggered the boxing fraternity by outpointing Sugar Ray Robinson to win the world title – all in the space of nine months.

Victory over Robinson made Turpin a national hero, but his glory was short-lived. The contract called for a return bout within 64 days, and at the New York Polo Grounds Robinson regained the title by stopping Turpin in ten rounds, although an eye injury sustained by the American had seemed destined to give Turpin a second victory. Their contest drew the biggest gate in middleweight history: 61,370 fans paid $767,626 to watch, and Turpin's share, plus the film and television rights, came to over $207,000. Turpin was then 23, and there were seven years of brilliance to come, though he had his setbacks. His next title bout, on June 10, 1952, enabled him to take the British and Commonwealth light-heavyweight titles from Don Cockell, who

was considerably weakened by weight reduction. A year later, after successfully defending his European middleweight title against Charles Humez of France, Turpin again became the leading contender for the world crown, now that Robinson had left it vacant when making a premature retirement from the ring.

Turpin's opponent was Carl 'Bobo' Olsen, a rugged Hawaiian of no great boxing ability whom Turpin at his best should have disposed of easily. But a domestic crisis of major proportions sent Turpin to New York ill-disposed to fight anyone, and his defeat on points was understandable. Worse was to follow. In Rome, defending his European middleweight title against Tiberio Mitri, Turpin was sensationally knocked out in 65 seconds. It seemed to be the end of the road for Turpin, and he stayed out of the ring for almost a year. He then began a comeback in which he regained the British and Commonwealth light-heavyweight titles he had been forced to relinquish when making his bid for the middleweight crown. Turpin gave up these titles for a second time later in 1955, but on Nov. 26, 1956 he fought Alex Buxton for the now vacant British light-heavyweight title, won it and successfully defended it against Arthur Howard in 1957. In 1958 Turpin retired as champion, though he was still a force to be reckoned with until surprisingly beaten by Yolande Pompey in Sept. 1962.

Turpin then faded out of the public eye, trying his hand at various occupations, including wrestling, but all the time disturbed that he had virtually nothing to show for all the money he had earned in the ring. In 1966 he took his own life, a month before his 38th birthday.
Score 75: w66 (45) d1 l8.

Tyson, Mike

World Heavyweight Champion 1986–

(b. Brooklyn, New York, June 30, 1966). Began pro boxing: May 6, 1985.

Shortish for a heavyweight at 5 ft. 11 in., Tyson swept through the amateur ranks, finishing as National Golden Gloves champion in 1984. He turned professional in 1985 and began sensationally by winning his first 15 bouts inside the distance (in a matter of 22 rounds). Few could stay long under his powerful punching, either at short range or long. His speed of punch was devastating, and one on target was usually enough to have his opponent in trouble. A run of 13 wins in his second year forced him into a series of bouts being run to rationalize the heavyweight division. He was matched first with W.B.C. champion Trevor Berbick and destroyed him in two rounds in Nov. 22, 1986. At 20 years and 145 days he became the youngest boxer to claim a version of the heavyweight title. After his victory over Berbick he added the W.B.A. title by beating James 'Bonecrusher' Smith, only the

Mike Tyson (facing camera) in action against Tony Tucker. By beating I.B.F. champion Tucker, Tyson become undisputed world heavyweight champion.

third to take him the distance. Because Michael Spinks had relinquished the I.B.F. title, Tyson had to wait before sealing his claim to be undisputed champion, in the meantime disposing of contenders Pinklon Thomas and Tyrell Biggs.

Tony Tucker emerged as the new I.B.F. champion, and Tyson unified the division by outpointing him on August 1, 1987. He then stopped in quick time former champions Larry Holmes and Tony Tubbs, leaving only the unbeaten Michael Spinks with any pretensions as a challenger. The two met on June 27, 1988 when Tyson completely outclassed Spinks, knocking him out in 91 seconds. He was still younger than Floyd Patterson had been when Patterson had set the record for the youngest undisputed champion.

With no challengers around, Tyson's pri-vate life began to attract the papers, with marriage to an actress, contractual disputes, a public brawl with a former opponent and a car crash which knocked him out for 20 minutes filling the headlines. As a champion, he was as impregnable as any had been before him.
Score 35: w35 (30) d0 l0.

Udella, Franco

World Light-Flyweight Champion (W.B.C.) 1975–76

(b. Cagliari, Italy, Feb. 25, 1947). Began pro boxing: Dec. 4, 1972.

His first championship chance came in his 19th pro bout when he was knocked out by Betulio Gonzalez in the tenth round when trying to win the W.B.C. version of the world flyweight title. Undaunted, in his next bout he won the European crown by stopping Pedro Molledo (Spain) in five rounds. Two winning fights later, on April 4, 1975 he won on a foul over Valentin Martinez (Mexico) to become the first holder of the world light-flyweight title created by the W.B.C. He was stripped of his crown later in the year by the W.B.C. and when he tried to win it back on July 17, 1976, he was knocked out in three rounds by Betulio Gonzalez. Udella continued as European champion, with seven successful defences but finally lost to Charlie Magri in 1979, after which he retired.
Score 43: w37 (18) d0 l5 Dnc.1.

Uehara, Yasutsune

World Junior-Lightweight Champion (W.B.A.) 1980–81

(b. Okinawa, Japan, Oct. 12, 1949). Began pro boxing: Nov. 14, 1972.

He suffered a set-back in his 12th pro bout, being knocked out in two rounds by Ben Villaflor (Philippines) in an attempt to

'Iron' Mike Tyson, the youngest-ever world heavyweight champion.

win the W.B.A. version of the world junior-lightweight title. He won the Japanese championship with a one round kayo win over Susumu Okabe in Tokyo. Uehara successfully defended his title twice, then lost and regained it, made seven successful defences and on Nov. 10, 1980 took the world crown from Samuel Serrano (Peurto Rico) by a knockout in six rounds at Detroit. He successfully defended the world title against Leonel Hernandez (Venezuela) at Caracas. In a return with Serrano on April 9, 1981, he lost his title on a 15 rounds points decision and retired the following year.
Score 32: w27 (21) d0 l5.

Uzcudun, Paolino

European Heavyweight Champion 1926–28, 1933, World Heavyweight Title Contender 1933

(b. Regil, Spain, May 3, 1899). Began pro boxing: 1923.

Short at 5 ft. 11½ in., but weighing over 200 pounds (14 st. 4 lbs), this tough and fierce Basque woodcutter was very belligerent and also carried a powerful punch, nearly half his contests ending inside the distance. He took on every European heavyweight in sight, as well as visiting fighters and although outpointed occasionally by a superior boxer or disqualified, he was never knocked out or stopped until the very last contest in his 12-year career when Joe Louis knocked him out in four rounds – but the Spaniard was 36 by then. Uzcudun won

the European title on May 18, 1926 by beating Erminio Spalla (Italy), forfeited it in 1928 to box in the U.S.A., but regained it by outpointing Pierre Charles (Belgium) on May 12, 1933. In the same year he lost his title in his unsuccessful challenge to Primo Carnera for the world crown on Oct. 22, being outpointed in Rome over 15 rounds. He retired in 1935.
Score 70: w50 (34) d3 l17.

Valdez, Rodrigo

World Middleweight Champion 1974–78

(b. Bolivar, Colombia, Dec. 22, 1946). Began pro boxing: Oct. 25, 1963.

Tough and hard-punching, he did not emerge from his own country until his seventh year as a pro and then enjoyed favour in Los Angeles, New York and Europe. He had three fights with Bennie Briscoe, a veteran Philadelphian middleweight. In the first they fought for the American title and Valdez won on points over 12 rounds. Eight months later, on May 25, 1974, they met for the W.B.C. world title, and this time Valdez scored a knockout in the seventh round. He kept this against Gratien Tonna (w.ko.11), Ramon Mendez (w.ko.8), Rudy Robles (w.pts.15) and Max Cohen (w.ko.4). He lost the title to Carlos Monzon (Argentina) on July 26, 1976, failed to regain it a year later, and when Monzon retired in 1977, Valdez and Briscoe met again for the vacant crown, the Colombian gaining a points win. Hugo Corro (Argentina) took his crown in 1978 and Valdez failed to regain it later in the year, after which he retired in 1980.
Score 73: w63 (41) d2 l8.

Velasquez, Miguel

World and European Light-Welterweight Champion 1976

(b. Santa Cruz, Spain, Dec. 27, 1944). Began pro boxing: Dec. 2, 1966.

This strong, aggressive kayo king won his native lightweight title by beating Serrano II in his 15th pro bout, and retained this four times. Then he tried to win the European title, but was appointed by Pedro Carrasco on a 15 rounds points verdict. When the title became vacant in 1970, he won on points over Ken Buchanan (U.K.) and kept the crown against three challengers, before losing it to Antonio Puddu (Italy) on a knock-out in the fourth round. He was inactive in 1973, but made a comeback the following year. In 1975 he regained his Spanish light-weight title and on June 30, 1976 won the W.B.C. version of the world light-welterweight crown when Saensak Muang-surin (Thailand) was ruled out in the fifth round for a low left hook. There was a return title bout four months later when Velasquez was knocked out in the second. He retired after that disaster.
Score 73: w66 (33) d3 l4.

Villa, Pancho

World Flyweight Champion 1923–25

(b. Illoilo, Philippines, Aug. 1, 1901 – d. U.S.A., July 14, 1925). Began pro boxing: 1919.

Though he had no connection with Mexico, young Francisco Guilledo decided to adopt the name of the Mexican revolutionary Pancho Villa as his professional boxing title. He should have known better, for the real Villa was shot in an ambush in 1923, and the boxing Villa died only two years later in more mundane circumstances.

Villa picked up his boxing at the American base in Manila, and after winning the flyweight and bantamweight championships of the Orient he was taken to New York where he proved an instant sensation. A tireless fighter with a knock-out punch in both fists, he took the American flyweight title from Johnny Buff in only his eighth contest in the United States, and although he lost the title to Frankie Genaro six months later he was chosen by the promoter Tex Rickard to challenge Jimmy Wilde for the world championship because of his colourful style and box-office drawing powers.

Wilde, by then 31, came out of semi-retirement to face Villa in New York and went down like a true champion against the brown-skinned little man who fought like a demon until the Briton lay unconscious at his feet in the seventh round. Money now ran into Villa's pockets and ran out just as fast. During the following two years he engaged in 25 contests without defeat, including two successful defences of his world crown. Then he was injudiciously matched against Jimmy McLarnin, an up-and-coming youngster with considerable promise.

The day before the bout Villa was suffering from toothache and had a wisdom tooth removed. In the fight he took severe punishment to lose on points and the next day had more teeth removed from a badly swollen jaw. Failing to follow his dentist's advice to have more teeth out, Villa developed an abscess in his jaw that required an operation. He died on the operating table just ten days after the McLarnin fight.
Score 105: *w*88 (22) *d*5 *l*9 ND.3.

Villacampo, Bernabe

World Flyweight Champion (W.B.A.)
1969–70

(b. Toledo, Philippines, June 6, 1943). Began pro boxing: April 20, 1963.

In 1968, after 23 pro bouts, he failed twice to become a champion, boxing a draw with Takeshi Nakamura for the Oriental flyweight title and being outpointed by Chartchai Chinonoi in a fight for the world crown. On Oct. 19, 1969, however, he gained the W.B.A. version of the championship by outpointing Hiroyuki Ebihara (Japan) in Osaka. Six months later he lost this in Bangkok to Berkrerk Chartvanchai. Villa-campo was inactive from 1972 to 1974, then made a comeback that lasted four years, but twice failed to win the Filipino flyweight title and retired in 1979.
Score 59: *w*34 (22) *d*4 *l*21.

Villaflor, Ben

World Junior-Lightweight Champion
(W.B.A.) 1972–76

(b. Negros, Philippines, Nov. 10, 1952). Began pro boxing: Feb. 1, 1968.

He started in Manila when he was 15 years old and fought there and in Hawaii for four years. On April 25, 1962 he won the W.B.A. world junior-lightweight title by outpointing Alfredo Marcano (Venezuela) over 15 rounds at Honolulu. He retained this against Victor Echegaray (drew15), but lost it to Kuniaki Shibata (Japan) on a points decision. He regained his crown with a lightning one round win in a return fight on Oct. 17, 1973, and retained it against Apollo Yoshio (drew 15), Yasutsune Uehara (w.ko.2), Hyun-Chi Kim (w.pts.15), Morito Kashiwaba (w.ko.13) and Samuel Serrano (drew15). In a second bout with Serrano on Oct. 15, 1976 he dropped his title on a points verdict and afterwards retired. Villaflor was never knocked out or stopped.
Score 45: *w*35 (20) *d*6 *l*4.

Vorasingh, Netrnoi Sor

World Light-Flyweight Champion (W.B.C.)
1978

(b. Bangkok, Thailand, April 22, 1959 – d. Sakon Nakhon Province, Thailand, Dec. 3, 1982). Began pro boxing: Feb. 12, 1976.

He was chasing championship titles from the start, in his fourth pro bout boxing a draw with Sang II for the Oriental light-flyweight crown. He won the Thailand title in his next bout with a seventh round knockout, but lost in an attempt to win the W.B.C. version of the world championship, being outpointed by Luis Estaba. Vorasingh won the title on May 6, 1978 with a points victory over Freddie Castillo at Bangkok, retained it against Luis Estaba by a fifth round kayo, but lost to Sung-Jun Kim in Korea on Sept. 30, 1978, being knocked out

On July 18, 1951 the veteran fighter Jersey Joe Walcott (left) defeated Ezzard Charles to become the new world heavyweight champion.

in the third round. He made an attempt to regain the title when Hilario Zapata became champion, but was stopped in ten rounds on Nov. 5, 1981 retired. He died in a motorcycle accident.
Score 39: *w*30 (16) *d*2 *l*7.

Wajima, Koichi

World Light-Middleweight Champion
(W.B.A.) 1971–76

(b. Hokkaido, Japan, April 21, 1943). Began pro boxing: June 15, 1968.

A hard hitter, he spent most of his career in fighting for his native title and the W.B.A. version of the world light-middleweight title, engaging in 21 championship fights in his last nine years of battling. He won the Japanese crown by knocking out Noriyasu Yoshimura in four rounds at Tokyo on Sept. 24, 1969, losing and regaining it until May 28, 1971. He then turned his attention to the world title, winning the W.B.A. version on Oct. 31, 1971 from Carmelo Bossi on a points verdict at Tokyo. He retained this against Domenico Tiberia (w.ko.1), Matt Donovan (w.ko.3), Miguel de Oliveira (drew15), Ryu Scrimachi (w.pts.15), Silvano Bertini (w.ko.13), and Miguel de Oliveira (w.pts.15). He lost his crown to Oscar Albarado by a knockout in the 15th round, but regained it with a points verdict. The W.B.C. withdrew its recognition of Wajima and the W.B.A. took over, whereupon he again lost his crown, this time to Jae Do Yuh by a knockout in round seven, but got it back by knocking out the Korean in the 15th round. On May 18, 1976, Jose Duran (Spain) took his title with a kayo in round 14 and when he tried to retrieve it the following year from Eddie Gazo, he was stopped in 11 rounds and promptly retired.
Score 38: *w*31 (25) *d*1 *l*6.

Walcott, Jersey Joe

World Heavyweight Champion 1951–52

(b. Merchantville, New Jersey, Jan. 31, 1914). Began pro boxing: 1930.

Jersey Joe Walcott, whose real name was Arnold Raymond Cream, was distinguished in the boxing world by being the oldest fighter to become heavyweight champion of the world – at 37 years and 5 months. At that time he had been fighting professionally intermittently for 21 years and had made four unsuccessful attempts to win the sport's richest prize. Young Cream adopted the name Joe Walcott from that of a former coloured welterweight champion and schoolboy idol, because his own did not seem to fit a 16-year-old fighter with ambition. And he added the word 'Jersey' to denote his state of birth – New Jersey.

Walcott was by no means a fistic genius, and his early career was very much that of a plodder. By 1944, when he was 30, he decided he would advance no farther. He quit the ring to take a steady job in order to support his wife and family of six.

A local promoter who was anxious to reopen his arena induced Walcott to make a comeback, promising him six well-paid fights. Jersey Joe romped through these, and continued with such success that in three years he had worked himself into a position to challenge Joe Louis for the world title. The referee decided that Walcott was the winner, but was overruled by two judges. Even Louis thought he had lost his title and left the ring before the verdict was announced.

In a return fight, Walcott 'forgot to duck' and was knocked out in 11 rounds, and when Louis retired Ezzard Charles outpointed Walcott to claim the vacant title. They had three further meetings, with Charles winning the first on points. But Walcott produced a pay-off punch in their next meeting to win the world crown. Walcott's reign as champion was restricted to 18 months, during which he again defeated Charles, only to come unstuck against Rocky Marciano, who got up from a first round knockdown to blast out Walcott in the 13th. A return match eight months later lasted only 2 min. 25 sec., and ended Walcott's long boxing career.
Score (early record incomplete) 69: *w*50 (30) *d*1 *l*18.

Walcott, Joe

World Welterweight Champion 1898–1906

(b. Barbados, March 13, 1873 – d. Massillon, Ohio, Oct. 1935). Began pro boxing: Feb. 29, 1890.

Strong and thickset, they called him 'The Barbados Demon' because of his punching power and ability to withstand punishment. In 1906 he was outpointed by George 'Kid' Lavingue in an attempt to win the world lightweight title and the following year he was equally unsuccessful when trying to win the welterweight crown, being held to a 25 rounds draw and then outpointed by Mysterious Billy Smith. It was not until 1901 that he became champion by knocking out Rube Ferns in five rounds on Dec. 18 at Fort Erie. After a successful defence when outpointing Tommy West the following year, he lost the crown to Dixie Kid on a foul in the 20th and last round. In a return bout Walcott was outpointed over 20 rounds. Later in the year Dixie gave up the title, Joe reclaimed it, and when Joe Gans challenged Walcott they drew over 20 rounds. On Oct. 16, 1906, Honey Mellody won the title by outpointing Walcott in a 15-rounder at Chelsea, Massachusetts, and although Joe kept on fighting

for another five years, another title shot did not come his way. He retired in 1911 and was killed in a car accident in 1935.
Score 134: *w*74 (44) *d*22 *l*30 *ND*5 *Dnc.*3.

Walker, Mickey

World Middle and Welterweight Champion 1922–30

(b. Elizabeth, New Jersey, July 13, 1901 – d. Freehold, New Jersey, April 28, 1981). Began pro boxing: Feb. 10, 1919.

Probably the toughest and hardest-hitting middleweight boxer of all time, Mickey Walker was nicknamed 'The Toy Bulldog' because of his aggression and tenacity – yet only one of his 11 world title fights failed to go the distance. A good boxer, Walker did his best work at close-quarters, where he made the body a persistent target.

Walker began fighting for purses as a welterweight before his 18th birthday, and after three years and 45 bouts he took the world title from the veteran champion Jack Britton on a points verdict. He made three defences of his crown in the next two years

Jim Watt (facing camera) fighting Alexis Arguello, who took his title.

before dropping a ten-round decision to Pete Latzo in Scranton, and with it the welter title. It was a home-town decision, but Walker didn't mind; he was fast growing into a middleweight, and had his sights set on winning a second world title.

In fact, he had already had one try, but had been outpointed the previous year by Harry Greb, the notorious human windmill. At his second middleweight title attempt, however, seven months after losing his welterweight laurels, Walker outpointed Tiger Flowers to become middleweight champion. Six months later he went to London and demolished Tommy Milligan, the British titleholder, in ten rounds. Walker made two more title defences, both against Ace Hudkins, and then relinquished the middleweight crown with the object of going after the heavyweight title – a heroic though rash gesture for this 5 ft. 7 in., sub-12-stone (178 pounds) man.

Walker's great feat among the big men was to hold Jack Sharkey, a future world heavyweight champion, to a 15-round draw, but he was punched into oblivion by hard-hitting Max Schmeling in eight rounds. Walker never actually had a heavyweight title fight, and after his attempts to gain the light-heavyweight title had proved abortive, he retired from the ring and took up painting, at which he was very successful.
Score 163: w94 (61) d4 l19 ND.45 Dnc.1.

Walsh, Jimmy

World Bantamweight Champion 1905

(b. Newton, Massachusetts, 1886 – d. Beverley, Mass., Nov. 23, 1964). Began pro boxing: Oct. 23, 1901.

An extremely efficient boxer who fought mainly in Boston in the early years of his career. He made several trips to London, in the second of which he twice met Digger Stanley, who claimed the world crown. The Englishman won the first on points and they drew the second. On Oct. 20, 1905, Stanley went to Chelsea, Massachusetts and lost on points to Walsh over 15 rounds and Walsh claimed the world title. Four years later they were brought together again in London and fought a draw. Walsh gave up the title and challenged Abe Attell for the featherweight crown, but was stopped in nine rounds at Los Angeles on Dec. 7, 1906. Jimmy went on fighting regularly and in 1912 made another attempt to win the featherweight champion but could only get a draw with Johnny Kilbane. He retired in 1915.
Score 118: w77 (16) d24 l13 ND.3 Dnc.1.

Ware, Harry

British Bantamweight Champion 1900–02

(b. Mile End, London, 1875). Began pro boxing: 1893.

More of a fighter than a boxer, determined and gutsy, he had his first fights in Newmarket when he weighed around 98 pounds. His vigorous tactics enabled him to beat Dave Job in 12 rounds and Harry Ashley in six. On Dec. 9, 1895, he had a return fight with Job at the National Sporting Club in London and won a fine points victory over 20 rounds. He went on winning, gradually reducing the number of contenders until on Nov. 12, 1900, he outpointed the skilful Pedlar Palmer to become British bantam champion. He held the title for 15 months, then lost it to Andrew Tokell on a points verdict after 20 rounds, but won it back the same year when the champion was ruled out in round eight. He could keep the title only three months this time, succumbing to clever Joe Bowker, who won on points after 15 rounds. Ware kept going until 1910 when he retired.
Score 52: w30 (8) d9 l13.

Watanabe, Jiro

World Super-Flyweight Champion (W.B.A.) 1982–86

(b. Okayama, Japan, March 16, 1955). Began pro boxing: March 27, 1979.

He showed a kayo punch in his first seven pro bouts which he won in an aggregate of 16 rounds. Four fights later he went to Seoul to contest the W.B.C. super-flyweight world title and was outpointed over 15 rounds by Chul-Ho Kim. He then switched to the W.B.A. camp and after two more kayo wins, won the world super-fly crown by outpointing Rafael Redroza (Panama) at Osaka on April 8, 1982. Watanabe defended this successfully on July 29, 1982 by stopping Gustavo Ballas (Argentina) in nine rounds, also at Osaka. He made five further defences in the next 17 months, then was stripped by the W.B.A. for capturing the vacant world junior-bantamweight title (the W.B.C. version of the same championship) by outpointing Payao Poontarat on July 5, 1984. Four winning defences followed, then on March 30, 1986, he lost his crown to Gilberto Roman on a points verdict at Osaka.
Score 28: w26 (17) d0 l2.

Watt, Jim

World (W.B.C.), European and British Lightweight Champion 1975–81

(b. Glasgow, Scotland, July 18, 1948). Began pro boxing: Oct. 30, 1968.

A fine boxer and stiff puncher: he had only 14 contests in his first four years as a pro, winning all but one which he lost on a cut eye stoppage. Ten of his wins were inside the distance. Competing for the vacant British lightweight title, he lost on a cut eye injury in round ten to Willie O'Reilly, but in a return bout on May 3, 1972, he stopped his fellow Scot in 12 rounds. Eight months later he lost the title to Ken Buchanan on points, but regained it on Jan. 27, 1975 by stopping

Johnny Cheshire in seven rounds.

Going to Nigeria to contest the Commonwealth crown, he was outpointed by Jonathan Dele on May 3, 1975. Watt gave up his British crown and on Aug. 5, 1977 gained the European title by stopping Andre Holyk, the Frenchman being forced to retire in the first round with a damaged eye. Watt made three defences of his E.B.U. title against Spaniards: Jeronimo Lucas (w.rsf.10), Perico Fernandez (w.pts.15), and Antonio Guinaldo (w.rtd.5). On April 17, 1979 in Glasgow he stopped Alfredo Pitalua (Colombia) in 12 rounds to win the vacant W.B.C. lightweight championship, which he defended against Robert Vasquez, U.S.A. (w.ko.9), Charlie Nash, Northern Ireland (w.ko.4), Howard Davis, U.S.A. (w.pts.15) and Sean O'Grady, U.S.A. (w.rsf.12 cut eye). On June 20, 1981 in London, Watt finally lost his world crown to Alexis Arguello (Nicaragua) on a 15 rounds points verdict, and retired.
Score 46: w38 (28) d0 l8.

Weaver, Mike

World Heavyweight Champion (W.B.A.) 1980–82

(b. Gatesville, Texas, June 14, 1952). Began pro boxing: Sept. 14, 1972.

Big and husky, an inch over six feet and scaling 210 pounds, he lost his first pro bout, being knocked out by Howard Smith in three rounds. In fact, in a short career, there are six kayos in his record. He came into the limelight in 1979 when, at the second attempt to win the American title, he knocked out Stan Ward in nine rounds at Las Vegas. Weaver fought Larry Holmes for the W.B.C. version of the world crown, but was stopped in 12 rounds in New York. He kept his American title by outpointing Scott LeDoux over 12 rounds, and won the W.B.A. heavyweight title by knocking out John Tate in the final minute of the 15th round at Knoxville, Tennessee, on March 31, 1980. He made two successful defences – Gerrie Coetzee, the South African champion, by a knockout in round 13 when he looked like losing, and James Tillis (U.S.A.) at Rosemont, Illinois, on a 15 rounds points verdict. However, he lost the title to Michael Dokes at Las Vegas on Dec. 10, 1982 when he was stopped in 63 seconds of the first round – a record time.

A return title match with Dokes ended in a draw and on June 15, 1985, he challenged Pinklon Thomas for the W.B.C. heavyweight title and was knocked out in the eighth round at Las Vegas. Undismayed, he continued to fight on and at the end of 1987 went to South Africa and stopped the Transvaal heavyweight, Johnny Du Plooy, in seven rounds at Johannesburg. However, on April 30, 1988, at Sun City, Weaver sustained a sensational knockout defeat in the second round. He was then in his 37th year.
Score 44: w29 (20) d1 l14.

Wells, Bombardier Billy

British and British Empire Heavyweight Champion 1911–19

(b. Mile End, London, Aug. 31, 1889 – d. Ealing, London, June 11, 1967). Began pro boxing: 1908.

William Thomas Wells – Bombardier was his British Army rank – started his career whilst serving in India where he won several competitions. Standing 6 ft. 3 ins. he did not have corresponding bulk, weighing only 182 pounds (13 stone), which was a big handicap when he came up against heavier opponents. He became British champion on April 24, 1911 by knocking out 'Iron' Hague in six rounds in London.

Wells went to New York as a 'White Hope', but was knocked out in three rounds by Al Palzar and in two by Gunboat Smith. Fighting for the European heavyweight crown he was twice stopped by Georges Carpentier (France) in four and one round respectively. He beat off two challengers to win his Lonsdale Belt outright, but lost his British title to Joe Beckett in five rounds. In a return match he was stopped in three. He won the British Empire title by knocking out Fred Storbeck, South Africa, in 11 rounds in London on Dec. 18, 1911 and defended successfully against Colin Bell, Australia (w.ko.2) and Van Voyles, Ireland, (w.rsf.3). A game fighter, his lack of weight and long torso made him vulnerable. He retired in 1925.

Score 59: *w*48 (40) *d*0 *l*11.

Wells, Matt

World, British and British Empire Welterweight Champion 1914–15, British Lightweight Champion 1911–12

(b. Walworth, London, Dec. 14, 1886 – d. London, June 27, 1953). Began pro boxing: Nov. 4, 1909.

Well-built and strong, but without a great deal of punching power, he relied on his superb fistic skill to see him through. He was A.B.A. lightweight champion for three successive years: 1905–07. After a few pro bouts in London he went to New York, staying there for six months and being unbeaten in eight contests. He challenged Freddie Welsh for the British lightweight title on Feb. 17, 1911, and to the surprise of everyone gained a points verdict after 20 brilliant rounds. He returned to New York for a number of no-decision bouts and then went back to London where he lost his title back to Welsh on a points verdict. He also travelled to Australia where he took part in a number of 20 rounds bouts, one of which was advertised as for the world welterweight title, with the British and British Empire crowns thrown in for good measure. Wells won all three by outpointing Tom McCormick over 20 rounds on March 21, 1914.

Back in America again, he lost his world claim to Mike Glover, who beat him on points over 12 rounds on June 1, 1915. Wells stayed in America for two years and when he returned to London lost his two remaining titles to Johnny Basham on points over 20 rounds. He retired in 1922 to become a referee and boxing coach.

Score 86: *w*34 (11) *d*3 *l*19 *ND*.30.

Welsh, Freddie

British, British Empire and World Lightweight Champion 1914–17

(b. Pontypridd, Wales, March 5, 1886 – d. New York, July 29, 1927). Began pro boxing: 1905.

One of the cleverest lightweight boxers ever, Freddie Welsh started his boxing career in America at the age of 16, but found time to go home to Wales on various occasions to win, lose, and regain the British lightweight title, and pick up the British Empire and world crowns. His real name was Frederick Hall Thomas: he adopted a ring name in order to keep from his mother the fact that he had chosen a career in boxing. He fought for and won the very first Lonsdale Belt to be put into circulation, a trophy that became his own property, and he gained another when he won the British Empire title by defeating Hughie Mehegan of Australia.

Light on his feet, and an excellent long-range boxer, but equally efficient at close-quarters, Welsh met the toughest and best lightweights in the world at a time when the division was at its strongest. He defeated so many top-notchers that neither Joe Gans, Battling Nelson, or Ad Wolgast would give him a title chance during their respective reigns. Eventually it was left to Charles Cochran, the theatrical impresario, to entice Ritchie to London at a fee that left nothing for Welsh beyond his training expenses.

Welsh won by a quarter-of-a-point over 20 tense rounds, and then proceeded to cash in on his title for the next three years. The majority of his contests were no-decision affairs that protected his crown except in the case of an inside-the-distance defeat. This fate overcame him in 1917 when Benny Leonard stopped him in nine rounds.

At this point Welsh was 31 and the loss of his title virtually ended his career. He enlisted to the American army, and when he died in New York he was penniless despite his very busy career. He had put all his money into a health farm which failed.

Score 168: *w*76 (32) *d*7 *l*4 *ND*81.

White, Charlie

World Lightweight Title Contender 1916–20

(b. Liverpool, March 23, 1891). Began pro boxing: 1906.

His real name was Charles Anchowitz, and he was brought to America with his brother, Jack, by his parents who set up

Top: *Jimmy Wilde.*

Above: *Freddie Welsh wearing the first Lonsdale Belt.*

home in Chicago. He picked up his boxing there and was fighting for pay at the age of 15. Developing a left hook that gained him a great many victories, he exploited it to the full. He fought mainly in the no-decision era, but on Sept. 4, 1916 at Colorado Springs, he secured a 20-round fight with Freddie Welsh for the world lightweight title. The Welsh-

man had to produce all of his skill and ringcraft to avoid being knocked out but was a points winner at the finish. Charlie did not get another chance until four years later when, at Benton Harbour, New York, he had Benny Leonard on the verge of a kayo in an early round, but exhausted himself in trying to finish off the groggy champion, who recovered and knocked out his challenger in the ninth round. White fought regularly until 1923 when he retired at the age of 32.
Score 170: w80 (51) d8 l16 ND.65 Dnc.1.

Wilde, Jimmy

World, European and British Flyweight Champion 1916–23

(b. Tylorstown, Wales, May 15, 1892 – d. Cardiff, Wales, March 10, 1969). Began pro boxing: Feb. 18, 1911.

Welsh flyweight boxer Jimmy Wilde was one of the most amazing boxers of all time, and is regarded as being the first world champion of the flyweight division.

Wilde was a physical freak. He stood 5 ft. 2½ in. in height but never weighed more than 7 st. 10 lb. (108 pounds). He had skinny legs and pipe-stem arms, but possessed astonishing punching power that was the envy of most lightweights. Wilde began boxing as a mere boy, fighting in the miners' clubs and Saturday night booths, and in his early days many of his contests went unrecorded. He was a completely unorthodox fighter, with a persistent attacking style, carrying his gloves on a level with his hips. Weaving and bobbing as he came in, he would trap an opponent on the ropes or in a corner and then let loose a stream of shock punches. It was little wonder that he was nicknamed 'the Ghost with a Hammer in his Hand' and 'the Mighty Atom'.

Wilde's first title fight came in 1915, when he challenged Tancy Lee for the British fly-weight championship in London. But it resulted in one of Wilde's very few defeats when Lee had the fight stopped by the referee in round 17. Wilde did not lose another regular flyweight fight for six years.

All Wilde's major successes came during World War I and while he was serving as a physical training instructor in the army. He became British champion by stopping Joe Symonds in 12 rounds on Feb. 14, 1916, and claimed the world championship after knocking out Johnny Rosner in the 11th round two months later. Thereafter he fought and defeated every flyweight of note in Great Britain – and in those days they were plentiful and of a high standard. He beat all the best bantamweights and even took on and beat Joe Conn, one of the outstanding featherweights of the day, in a wartime charity contest. As the army would not permit Wilde to fight for a money purse, his wife was presented with a bag of diamonds worth £3,000 a few days after his great victory.

The little Welshman's claims to the world title were strengthened in Dec. 1916 after he had knocked out Young Zulu Kid in 11 rounds. By the time the war was over, Wilde had won a Lonsdale Belt outright. And he had scored two magnificent wins in 1919 over two American bantams, Joe Lynch and Pal Moore. In 1920 he embarked on a tour of the United States from which he returned undefeated after 12 contests, five of which were won by knock-outs.

However, this enterprise marked the end of Wilde's triumphant career. In 1921, at the age of 29, he was defeated by Pete Herman, one of the great world bantamweight champions, to whom he conceded almost a stone (14 pounds) because the American was overweight. Little Wilde fought gamely into the 17th round, when the referee refused to let him take further punishment.

Wilde retired, but two years later he was tempted to return to the ring to defend his title against the new challenger, the hard-hitting Filipino Pancho Villa. Against the advice of his wife and his friends Wilde made the trip and stood up to a hammering from his younger opponent until he fell flat on his face in round seven. Thereupon he did retire, remaining closely connected with the ring until his death.
Score 153: w132 (101) d2 l6 ND.13.

Willard, Jess

World Heavyweight Champion 1915–19

(b. Pottawatomie, Kansas, Dec. 29, 1881 – d. Los Angeles, California, Dec. 15, 1968). Began pro boxing: Feb. 15, 1911.

Tallest of the heavyweight champs, he stood 6 ft. 6¼ in., and used this and a long reach to win the majority of his fights in his first three years as a pro. In 1915 Jack Johnson was brought out of exile in France to defend his world title against Willard on the racecourse at Havana, Cuba on April 5. The champion was 37 and knew that it was on the cards that he would lose. Yet he stayed into the 26th round when he was thumped down and decided to stay there. A year later in New York, Willard boxed a ten rounds no-decision bout with Frank Moran and did not fight again until July 4, 1919 when Jack Dempsey battered him to defeat in three rounds at Toledo, Ohio. He dropped out of fighting until brought back in 1923 when, after stopping Floyd Johnson in ten rounds, he was himself stopped by Luis Firpo in eight rounds at Jersey City on July 12. Willard never boxed again.
Score 35: w23 (20) d1 l6 ND.5.

Williams, Isiah (Ike)

World Lightweight Champion (N.B.A.) 1945–51

(b. Brunswick, Georgia, Aug. 2, 1923). Began pro boxing: March 15, 1940).

A great boxer, with defensive skill, ringcraft and knockdown power. He had to fight hard because the competition was very strong in the post-World War II years. His first major defeat was in his fifth year as a pro, Bob Montgomery pounding him unmercifully on the ropes until he slid to the floor and stayed there. It was a beating that Ike never forgot. He had to wait until April 18, 1945 to get a title chance, then won the N.B.A. version of the lightweight championship by knocking out Juan Zurita in two rounds at Mexico City. He went to Wales and stopped Ronnie James, the British champion, in nine rounds at Cardiff on Sept. 4, 1946. Williams secured a match with Montgomery, the reigning New York State Athletics Commission champion and returned the treatment he had received three years earlier, the Bobcat being stopped in six rounds. Other successful defences were against Enrique Bolanos (w.pts.15), Beau Jack (w.ko.6), Jesse Flores (w.ko.10), Enrique Bolanos (w.ko.4) and Freddie Dawson (w.pts.15). He finally lost his title to James Carter on May 25, 1951, being knocked out in the 14th round at New York. He retired in 1955.
Score 202: w162 (40) d11 l23 ND.5 Dnc.1.

Williams, Kid

World Bantamweight Champion 1914–17

(b. Copenhagen, Denmark, July 18, 1893 – d. Baltimore, Maryland, U.S.A., Oct. 18, 1963). Began pro boxing: July 18, 1910.

One of the few Danes to win world titles, Williams (real name Johnny Gutenko) was brought up in Baltimore, Maryland. There he had many of his early successes. Very short, at 5 ft. 1 in., he was a compact, two-fisted fighter, who enjoyed his work. He boxed for four years before getting a title chance, then on June 9, 1914 knocked out Johnny Coulon in three rounds to win the world crown.

He kept the title by the skin of his teeth when he lost to Johnny Ertle on a foul in five rounds. The winner claimed the championship, but no one backed him up, so Williams remained titleholder. Both Frankie Burns and Pete Herman held him to draws over 20 rounds in title fights, but on Jan. 9, 1917, he lost a 20 rounds decision to Herman and with it his crown. He continued to box until 1929, when he was 36, but never had another championship chance.
Score 204: w107 (48) d8 l16 ND.73.

Wills, Harry

World Heavyweight Contender 1920–26

(b. New Orleans, Louisiana, May 15, 1889 – d. New York City, Dec. 21, 1958). Began pro boxing: 1907.

Standing 6 ft. 4 in., and weighing 220 pounds, he had exceptional boxing skill and was a menace to the world title for many years; but because he was black, Wills was never given a chance to challenge the reign-

Howard Winstone, world featherweight champion 1968.

ing champion Jack Dempsey. At one point public opinion was so strong in favour of a match between the pair that promoter Tex Rickard signed them for a title bout, but the Governor of New York banned the match and Wills was paid 50,000 dollars as compensation. Most of his fights were against black boxers and he fought some of them many times, in particular Sam Langford. They met 25 times, Wills winning 6, Langford 2, while there were 17 no-decision bouts. He was still boxing occasionally at the age of 40 and retired in 1932.
Score 102: *w*62 (45) *d*2 *l*8 *ND*.27 *Dnc*.3.

Wilson, Jackie

World Featherweight Champion (N.B.A.) 1941–43

(b. Arkansas, 1909 – d. Torrance, Pennsylvania, Dec. 2, 1966). Began pro boxing: 1926.

A speedy featherweight with both fists and feet, but with not a lot of knockdown power. As a boy his fistic hero was Kid Chocolate and when he came to Jackie's home town to box, the boy was paid 15 cents to see him and was so enthralled by the Cuban's ring artistry, he decided there and then to become a professional boxer. The family moved to Pittsburgh and Wilson had his early fights there. He had to be patient and fight his way along for 16 years before a championship chance came his way, then on Nov. 18, 1941, he outpointed Richi Lemos to win the N.B.A. featherweight title. He retained this in a return contest, also by a points verdict, but on Jan. 18, 1943 lost his crown to Jackie Callura on points. Wilson failed to regain it in a return bout and though

boxing for five more years, never again came within range of a title contest. He retired in 1947.
Score 155: *w*102 (19) *d*6 *l*46 *Dnc*.1.

Wilson, Johnny

World Middleweight Champion 1920–23

(b. New York City, March 23, 1893 – d. Boston, Dec. 8, 1985). Began pro boxing: 1911.

A very wily southpaw, with a good knockdown punch when required, he spent his first nine professional years travelling around and indulging in many no-decision bouts. Wilson was not a spectacular fighter, and gained no popularity when on May 6, 1920, he took the world crown away from Mike O'Dowd on a 12 rounds points decision, the boxing fraternity being very suspicious of right-foot forward boxers in those days. He defended his title successfully against George Chip (ND. 10) and Mike O'Dowd (w.pts.15), but when he won over Bryan Downey on a foul in seven rounds in Cleveland, the local Boxing Commission refused to accept the referee's verdict and named Downey as champion. The pair met again in a no-decision bout in New Jersey two months later, which meant that Downey had to knock out the champion to win the title. He failed to do so and Wilson went merrily on his way until on Aug. 31, 1923 he had the worse of a fight with Harry Greb and lost his title on points. A return match had the same result and in 1926 he retired.
Score 123: *w*65 (44) *d*2 *l*21 *ND*.34 *Dnc*.1.

Winstone, Howard

World, European and British Featherweight Champion 1961–68

(b. Merthyr Tydfil, Wales, April 15, 1939).

Began pro boxing: Feb. 24, 1959.

Despite losing the tops of three fingers on his right hand, Howard Winstone was such a brilliant boxer that after winning the British featherweight title in 1961 he remained in championship class until his retirement seven years later. In that time he participated in 17 title contests, involving the British, European and world championships.

As an amateur, Winstone won the Amateur Boxing Association bantamweight title in 1958 and a Commonwealth Games gold medal at the same weight later in the year. He turned professional as a featherweight in 1959 and was unbeaten in his first 34 contests, but in 1962 was stopped in two rounds by the American Leroy Jeffery. It was only a temporary setback and, having already won a Lonsdale Belt outright, Winstone set off after another. En route he picked up the European title which he defended successfully on seven occasions against fellow-countrymen and foreigners alike, even going to Rome and Sardinia to face his challengers. It was a title he never lost in the ring.

Winstone's first attempt to win the world title came in 1965 when he lost on points to Vicente Saldivar, the Mexican southpaw, after a brilliant battle at London's Earls Court. A second match at Cardiff resulted in the Welshman losing so narrowly that a third match was called for in Mexico City in which Winstone was compelled to retire with an eye injury in round 12.

Saldivar then retired and Winstone stopped Mitsunori Seki of Japan in nine rounds to achieve, at last, his life-long ambition and become world featherweight champion. But he was now experiencing difficulty in making the featherweight limit of 9 stone (126 pounds), and when he faced Jose Legra in a world title defence at Porthcawl he went into the ring very much weakened and was stopped in five rounds, a defeat that brought about his retirement aged 29.
Score 67: *w*61 (27) *d*0 *l*6.

Witherspoon, Tim

World Heavyweight Champion (W.B.C.) 1984, (W.B.A.) 1986

(b. Pontiac, Michigan, Dec. 27, 1957). Began pro boxing, Oct. 30, 1979.

Known as Terrible Tim, he won his first 15 bouts in convincing fashion, then challenged Larry Holmes for his W.B.C. heavyweight title and did well to stay the distance, a loser on points. In 1984 he won the vacant W.B.C. title by outpointing Greg Page, but five months later dropped his crown to Pinklon Thomas. On Jan. 17, 1986 he won recognition as W.B.A. champion by outpointing Tony Tubbs, then defended his title in London against Frank Bruno. This went into the 11th round, with Witherspoon trailing on points, but he brought matters to a conclusion by stopping his challenger with a blaze

of big punches. However, he lost his crown in sensational manner on Dec. 12 the same year, being stopped in the first round by James (Bonecrusher) Smith in New York.
Score 28: w25 (17) d0 l3.

Wolfe, Jack 'Kid'

World Super-Bantamweight Champion 1922–23

(b. Cleveland, Ohio, June 11, 1895 – d. Cleveland, Ohio, April 22, 1975). Began pro boxing: 1911.

A clever, defensive boxer, he was the first to hold this title, although when he won it on Sept. 22, 1922 by outpointing Joe Lynch over 15 rounds in New York, it was styled as for the world junior featherweight crown. He had been boxing for ten years prior to becoming champion and he reigned 11 months, being outpointed by Carl Duane over 12 rounds at Long Island, New York, Wolfe retired in 1924.
Score 136: w71 (15) d22 l20 ND.23.

Wolgast, Ad

World Lightweight Champion 1910–12

(b. Cadillac, Michigan, Feb. 8, 1888 – d. Camarillo, California, April 14, 1955). Be-

Tim Witherspoon, who held both the W.B.A. and W.B.C. world heavyweight titles.

gan pro boxing: June 10, 1906.

One of the toughest and roughest lightweights in the early days of the division, equalled only by Battling Nelson. So it can be imagined what sort of scrimmage it was when they met at Port Richmond on Feb. 22, 1910. Nelson was the reigning champion and they were supposed to be fighting to a finish. After a terrific battle Wolgast put his rival down in the 40th round and he was counted out. Wolgast made a defence of his title against Mexican Joe Rivers at Vernon, California, on July 4, 1912. The men landed simultaneous right-handers to the jaw in round 13. Both went down, but the referee picked up the champion and held him under his arm while counting Rivers out. He maintained that Wolgast's right hand had been the first to land. Ad lost his title to Willie Ritchie on a foul in round 16 at Daly City, California, on Nov. 28, 1912. He fought on for four more years and when challenging Freddie Welsh for the championship on July 4, 1916, was disqualified in round 11 for his rough tactics. He retired in 1917.
Score 133: w80 (40) d20 l33.

Wolgast, Midget

World Flyweight Champion (N.Y.S.A.C.) 1930–35

(b. Philadelphia, Pennsylvania, July 18, 1910

– d. Philadelphia, Oct. 19, 1955). Began pro boxing: Nov. 3, 1927.

The fastest boxer in the world in his time, Wolgast (real name Joseph Loscalzo) took the surname of that great lightweight Adolphus, while his small size (5 ft. 2½ in.) accounted for the first name. In his third year as a pro he won the New York version of the world flyweight title by outpointing Black Bill (Cuba) on March 21, 1930. He defended it successfully against Willie LaMorte (w.ko.6), Frankie Genaro (drew15) and Ruby Bradley (w.pts.15) then did not put it at stake for the next four years. On Sept. 16, 1935 he lost on points to Small Montana (Philippines) and became an ex-champion. He did not get another title bout and after a losing sequence retired in 1940.
Score 202: w150 (15) d16 l36.

Woodcock, Bruce

European, British and British Empire Champion 1945–50

(b. Doncaster, Yorkshire, Jan. 18, 1921). Began pro boxing: Jan. 26, 1942.

Not a giant among heavies, Woodcock was, however, big of fighting heart. A former A.B.A. light-heavyweight champion, he won the Northern Area title by knocking out Jack Robinson in three rounds in his seventh pro bout. He met Jack London for the British and British Empire titles in London on July 17, 1945 and won by a knockout in round six. A year later he won the European title by knocking out Albert Renet (France) in six rounds, and retained it against Stephen Olek (Poland) with a 15 rounds points win.

Woodcock won a controversial victory over Lee Savold (U.S.A.), who was ruled out in the fourth round for an alleged low punch. After successfully defending his three titles against Freddie Mills (w.ko.14), he was matched for a return with Savold. However, he suffered injuries when his lorry crashed into a tree and did not meet the American again until July 6, 1950. The bout was advertised as for the world title and Wood-cock was stopped in four rounds in London. On Nov. 14, 1950 he lost his British and British Empire crowns to Jack Gardner, who forced him to retire in the 11th round. Woodcock did not fight again.
Score 39: w35 (32) d0 l4.

Wright, Albert 'Chalky'

World Featherweight Champion 1941–42

(b. Durango, Mexico, Feb. 10, 1912 – d. Los Angeles, California, U.S.A., Aug. 12, 1957). Began pro boxing: Feb. 23, 1928.

Another of the 20-year men; he possessed a long reach and could put plenty of power behind his punches. He spent two years fighting in his own country, then migrated to California. He did not make New York or any of the other big fight cities until 1938; even then he had to wait a further three years before a championship chance came his way. On Sept. 11, 1941 he knocked out Joey Archibald in 11 rounds at Washington to become world featherweight champion.

Wright retained the title twice the following year against Harry Jeffra (w.ko.10) and Lulu Costantino (w.pts.15), but on Nov. 20, 1942 was outpointed by Willie Pep and lost his crown. The following year in New York his attempt to regain the title was thwarted when Pep outpointed him again. Pep seemed to like him as an opponent for they met on two other occasions, and Pep defeated him both times to bring his long career virtually to a close. He retired in 1948 and died from concussion after a slip in his bath.
Score 204: *w*148 (74) *d*16 *l*39 *Dnc*.1.

Yarosz, Teddy

World Middleweight Champion (N.Y.S.A.C.) 1934–35

(b. Pittsburgh, Pennsylvania, June 24, 1910 – d. Monaca, Pennsylvania, March 29, 1974). Began pro boxing: 1929.

A good and clever boxer with great staying power but no real punch, Yarosz fought mainly in his own territory and it was in his home city on Sept. 11, 1934 that he won the New York State version of the world middleweight title by outpointing Vince Dundee over 15 rounds. At his first defence, nine months later (also in Pittsburgh) he lost on points to Ed 'Babe' Risko. Yarosz went on boxing until 1942 when he retired.
Score 127: *w*106 (16) *d*3 *l*18.

Yuh, Jae-Do

World Light-Middleweight Champion (W.B.A.) 1975–76

(b. Chumra-Nam-Do, S. Korea, April 25, 1948). Began pro boxing: Oct. 3, 1968.

A strong puncher with a good kayo record, he was soon winning the South Korean and Oriental titles, retaining the latter against 22 challengers over eight years and never being beaten for it. On June 7, 1975 won the W.B.A. version of the world light-middleweight title by knocking out Koichi Wajima (Japan) in seven rounds at Kitakyushu, Japan. He retained the title with a six rounds kayo win over Mashiro Miasko, but in a return contest with Wajima was knocked out in the 15th and last round on Feb. 17, 1976. He retired in 1978.
Score 55: *w*50 (29) *d*2 *l*3.

Yum, Dong-Kyun

World Super-Bantamweight Champion (W.B.C.) 1976–77

(b. Chung-Buk-Do, S. Korea, Jan. 17, 1952). Began pro boxing: March 7, 1970.

This strong and tough fighter won his native super-bantam title in his 16th pro bout

by outpointing Sung-Jong Hong over ten rounds on Oct. 20, 1971. He made 11 successful defences and then on May 17, 1974, outpointed Kyu-Chul-Chang to gain the Oriental crown. He kept this against five contenders.

Dong-Kyun Yum tried to win the world crown, but lost on points to Rigoberto Riasco (Panama). At his second attempt, on Nov. 24, 1978 he won the title by outpointing Royal Kobayashi (Japan) on points; he kept it against Jose Cervantes (w.pts.15), but on May 21, 1977 lost his crown on a knockout in 12 rounds by Wilfredo Gomez (Puerto Rico). He retired in 1978.
Score 65: *w*52 (21) *d*8 *l*5.

Zale, Tony

World Middleweight Champion 1940–48

(b. Gary, Indiana, May 29, 1913). Began pro boxing: June 11, 1934.

Anthony Florian Zaleski was born in a city noted for its steel output. He worked in the mills there until his 21st birthday, and it seems that some of the metal seeped into his system for as both an amateur and a professional he showed steel-like ability to withstand physical punishment, while his hitting powers were tremendous.

As an amateur, Tony Zale (as he became known) won 50 of his 95 bouts inside the distance and lost only eight times. In his first year as a professional, though, he was over worked, with 28 contests. He lost interest in boxing and went back to the steelworks, staying away from the ring for two years.

In 1937, at the age of 24, he decided to have another try with his fists, and made such progress that he was matched with Al Hostak, the National Boxing Association's middleweight champion, in an overweight contest of ten rounds. Hostak had a big knock-out record – but Zale took his best punches and the decision.

A title fight followed, which Zale won by a knock-out in round 13, but he did not gain universal recognition as world titleholder until he defeated Georgie Abrams, the New York State Athletics commission nominee in 1941. Zale then joined the U.S. Navy and was out of the ring for four years. When he took off his uniform at the end of 1945, he found a dangerous challenger waiting him in the person of Rocky Graziano.

Zale gave himself six warming-up bouts, all of which he won inside the distance. Then came his title defence that produced one of the most savage battles ever seen between middleweights. The champion had to get off the floor to win by a knock-out in six rounds, but Graziano scored revenge in a bitterly fought return. In the inevitable rubber contest, Zale proved his superiority by knocking out Graziano in the third round of another slugging feast, but by this time the pair had punched themselves out. When, three months later, Zale defended his title against rugged Marcel Cerdan of France, he was

battered into subjection after 12 torrid rounds. The 'Man of Steel' was now in his 35th year, and it was not surprising that he chose this moment to hang up his gloves.
Score 87: *w*67 (45) *d*4 *l*18.

Zamora, Alfonso

World Bantamweight Champion (W.B.A.) 1975–77

(b. Mexico City, Feb. 9, 1954). Began pro boxing: April 16, 1973.

A sizzling two-fisted fighter with kayo punching power: Zamora won his first 29 fights inside the distance, then suffered a four rounds defeat by Carlos Zarate, a fellow Mexican. On March 14, 1975 he won the W.B.A. world bantam title by knocking out Soo-Hwan Hong in four rounds. He defended it successfully against Thanomjit Sukbothai (w.ko.4), Socrates Batoto (w.ko.2), Eusebio Pedroza (w.ko.2), Gilberto Illuecoa (w.ko.3) and Soo-Hwan Hong (w.ko.12), but lost the championship to Jorge Lujan (Panama) by a knockout in round ten. After two more bad defeats, he retired in 1980.
Score 38: *w*33 (32) *d*0 *l*5.

Zapata, Hilario

World Light-Flyweight Champion 1980–87

(b. Panama City, Aug. 19, 1958). Began pro boxing: Oct. 28, 1977.

Smart and fast, with a good punch, Zapata won the W.B.C. world light-flyweight championship in his 12th pro fight by outpointing Shigeo Nakajima (Japan) over 15 rounds on March 24, 1980. He retained this title against Chi-Bok Kim, S. Korea (w.pts.15), Hector Melendez, Dominica (w.pts.15), Shigeo Nakajima, Japan (w.rsf.11), Reynaldo Becerra, Venezuela (w.pts.15), Joey Olivo, U.S.A. (w.rtd.13), Rudy Crawford, Nicaragua (w.pts.15), German Torres, Mexico (w.pts.15), and Netrnoi Sor Vorasingh, Thailand (w.rsf.10).

Zapata lost his title by a knockout in two rounds to Amado Urszua (Mexico) on Feb. 6, 1982 at Panama City, but regained it by a points verdict over Tadushi Tomori (Japan) at Tokyo on July 20, 1982. He then retained his title against Jung-Koo Chang (S. Korea) at Seoul by a points verdict and defeated Tadashi Tomori (w.rsf.8) in Tokyo on Nov. 30, 1982. Next time out he lost his crown to Jung-Koo Chang at Seoul, being stopped in three rounds. He lost on points when he tried to take the W.B.A. flyweight title from Santos Lacier at Buenos Aires on December 8, 1984, but captured it when it became vacant by outpointing Alonzo Gonzalez over 15 rounds at Panama city on Oct. 5, 1985. He defended his crown successfully against five challengers, but on Feb. 13, 1987, dropped his title to Fidel Bassa on a points verdict at Barranquilla in Colombia.
Score 40: *w*35 (11) *d*0 *l*5.

Tony Zale (left) flattens Rocky Graziano in their third and last fight.

Zarate, Carlos

World Bantamweight Champion (W.B.C.) 1976–79

(b. Tepito, Mexico, May 23, 1951). Began pro boxing: Feb. 3, 1970.

A mighty puncher, he won his first 23 bouts with knockouts, won a fight on points, then had another long run of 28 inside-the-distance wins. In this glorious period he won the W.B.C. version of the world bantamweight title by knocking out Rodolfo Martinez, a fellow-countryman, on May 8, 1976. He defended his crown successfully against Paul Ferreri, Australia (w.ko.12), Waruinge Nakayama, Japan (w.ko.4), Fernando Cabanela, Philippines (w.ko.3), Danilo Batista (w.ko.6), Juan Rodriguez, Spain (w.ko.5), Alberto Davila, U.S.A. (w.ko.8), Andres Hernandez, Puerto Rico (w.ko.13), Emilio Hernandez (w.ko.4), and Mensah Kpalongo (w.ko.3). Zarate lost the title to Lupe Pintor (Mexico) by a points decision at Las Vegas on June 3, 1979 and retired.

The only time he was stopped (round 5) was by Wilfredo Gomez (Puerto Rico) when Zarate tried to win the world super-bantamweight title at San Juan, Puerto Rico on Oct. 28, 1978.
Score 57: *w*55 (52) *d*0 *l*2.

Zivic, Fritzie

World Welterweight Champion 1940–41

(b. Pittsburgh, Pennsylvania, May 8, 1913). Began pro boxing: 1931.

One of five fighting brothers, he was a rough and tough performer with his own interpretation of the rules. He averaged 18 fights a year during his busy period from 1933 to 1946. Zivic met one of his own kind in Henry Armstrong when they waged war on Oct. 4, 1940 for Homicide Hank's world welterweight title, Zivic winning a hard-won points verdict. In a return fight three months later, Armstrong was battered to defeat in 12 rounds.

On July 20, 1941, Fritzie lost his crown to Freddie 'Red' Cochrane on a points verdict. He never had a chance to retrieve the title although he went on fighting regularly for

the next six years. Things petered out for him after that (five bouts in three years) and he retired in 1949, at the age of 36.
Score 232: *w*157 (81) *d*10 *l*65.

Zurita, Juran

World Lightweight Champion (N.B.A.) 1944–45

(b. Guadalajara, Mexico, 1914 – d. Pittsburgh, May 16, 1984). Began pro boxing: Nov. 22, 1932.

The first Mexican-born boxer to win a world title! It is strange that he had to wait 12 years and 130 fights for his championship chance and by that time he was 30 years old. For more than nine years he did not fight outside his own country, then he fought in Californian rings and became very popular. On March 8, 1944 he won a 15 rounds points decision over Sammy Angott, the reigning N.B.A. lightweight champion, and he kept the title for over a year. Then Ike Williams, a great 135-pounds fighter in his day came to Mexico City on April 18, 1945 and knocked the veteran out in two rounds to take his crown. Zurita never fought again.
Score 137: *w*113 (37) *d*2 *l*22.

Facts and Figures

Amateur Champions

World Amateur Champions

HAVANA–1974 *Heavy:* T. Stevenson (Cuba). *Light-Heavy:* M. Parlov (Yugoslavia). *Middle:* R. Riskiev (U.S.S.R.). *Light-Middle:* R. Garbey (Cuba). *Welter:* E. Correa (Cuba). *Light-Welter:* A. Kalule (Uganda). *Light:* V. Solomin (U.S.S.R.). *Feather:* H. Davis (U.S.A.) *Bantam:* W. Gomez (Puerto Rico). *Fly:* D. Rodriguez (Cuba). *Light-Fly:* J. Hernandez (Cuba).

BELGRADE–1978 *Heavy:* T. Stevenson (Cuba). *Light-Heavy:* S. Soria (Cuba). *Middle:* J. Gomez (Cuba). *Light-Middle:* V. Savachenko (U.S.S.R.). *Welter:* V. Rachkov (U.S.S.R.). *Light-Welter:* V. Lvov (U.S.S.R.). *Light:* A. Davison (Nigeria). *Feather:* A. Herrera (Cuba). *Bantam:* A. Horta (Cuba). *Fly:* H. Srednicki (Poland). *Light-Fly:* S. Muchoki (Kenya).

MUNICH–1982 *Super-Heavy:* T. Biggs (U.S.A.). *Heavy:* A. Iagubkin (U.S.S.R.). *Light-Heavy:* P. Romero (Cuba). *Middle:* B. Comas (Cuba). *Light-Middle:* A. Koshkin (U.S.S.R.). *Welter:* M. Breland (U.S.A.). *Light-Welter:* C. Garcia (Cuba). *Light:* A. Herrera (Cuba). *Feather:* A. Horta (Cuba). *Bantam:* F. Favors (U.S.A.). *Fly:* Y. Alexandrov (U.S.S.R.). *Light-Fly:* 1. Mustafov (Bulgaria).

RENO–1986 *Super-Heavy:* T. Stevenson (Cuba). *Heavy:* F. Savon (Cuba). *Light-Heavy:* P. Romero (Cuba). *Middle:* D. Allen (U.S.A.). *Light-Middle:* A. Espinosa (Cuba). *Welter:* K. Gould (U.S.A.). *Light-Welter:* V. Shishov (U.S.S.R.). *Light:* A. Horta (Cuba). *Feather:* K. Banks (U.S.A.). *Bantam:* Sung Kil Moon (S. Korea). *Fly:* P. Rwywa (Cuba). *Light-Fly:* J. Odelin (Cuba).

European Amateur Champions

PARIS–1924 *Heavy:* O. Von Porat (Norway). *Light-Heavy:* H. J. Mitchell (G.B.). *Middle:* H. W. Mallin (G.B.) *Welter:* J. Delarge (Belgium). *Light:* H. Nielsen (Denmark). *Feather:* R. DeVergnie (Belgium). *Bantam:* J. Ces (France). *Fly:* J. Mackenzie (G.B.).

STOCKHOLM–1925 *Heavy:* B. Persson (Sweden). *Welter:* N. Nielson (Denmark). *Light:* S. Johannsen (Sweden). *Feather:* O. Andren (Sweden). *Bantam:* A. Rule (G.B.). *Fly:* E. Pladner (France).

BERLIN–1927 *Heavy:* N. A. Ramm (Sweden). *Light-Heavy:* Muller (Germany). *Middle:* Christensen (Norway). *Welter:* Cavena (Italy). *Light:* Momgorgen (Germany). *Feather:* Dubbers (Germany). *Bantam:* Dalchow (Germany). *Fly:* Bohman (Sweden).

AMSTERDAM–1928 *Heavy:* N. A. Ramm (Sweden). *Light-Heavy:* E. Pistulla (Germany). *Middle:* P. Toscani (Italy). *Welter:* R. Galataud (France). *Light:* C. Orlandi (Italy). *Feather:* L. van Klaveren (Netherlands). *Bantam:* W. Tamagnini (Italy). *Fly:* A. Kocsis (Hungary).

BUDAPEST–1930 *Heavy:* J. Michaelsen (Denmark). *Light-Heavy:* T. Petersen (Denmark). *Middle:* C. Meroni (Italy). *Welter:* J. Besselmann (Germany). *Light:* M. Bianchini (Italy). *Feather:* G. Szabo (Hungary). *Bantam:* J. Szeles (Hungary). *Fly:* S. Enekes (Hungary).

LOS ANGELES–1932 *Heavy:* L. Rovati (Italy). *Light-Heavy:* G. Rossi (Italy). *Middle:* R. Michelot (France). *Welter:* E. Campe (Germany). *Light:* T. Ahiqvist (Sweden). *Feather:* J. Schleinkofer (Germany). *Bantam:* H. Ziglarski (Germany). *Fly:* S. Enekes (Hungary).

Titles were awarded at Los Angeles to the European boxers who went farthest in the Olympic Games.

BUDAPEST–1934 *Heavy:* G. Baerlund (Finland). *Light-Heavy:* P. Zehetmayer (Australia). *Middle:* S. Szogeto (Hungary). *Welter:* D. McCleave (G.B.). *Light:* E. Facchini (Italy). *Feather:* O. Kaestner (Germany). *Bantam:* S. Enekes (Hungary). *Fly:* P. Palmer (G.B.).

MILAN–1937 *Heavy:* O. Tandberg (Sweden). *Light-Heavy:* Szigeti (Hungary). *Middle:* Chmlelewski (Poland). *Welter:* Murack (Germany). *Light:* Neurnberg (Germany). *Feather:* Polus (Poland). *Bantam:* U. Sergo (Italy). *Fly:* S. Enekes (Hungary).

DUBLIN–1938 *Heavy:* O. Tandberg (Sweden). *Light-Heavy:* L. Musina (Italy). *Middle:* A. Raedck (Estonia). *Welter:* A. Kolczyski (Poland). *Light:* H. Neurnberg (Germany). *Feather:* P. Dowdall (Ireland). *Bantam:* U. Sergo (Italy). *Fly:* J. Ingle (Ireland).

DUBLIN–1947 *Heavy:* G. O'Colmain (Ireland). *Light-Heavy:* H. Quentemeyer (Netherlands). *Middle:* A. Escudie (France). *Welter:* J. Ryan (G.B.). *Light:* J. Vissers (Belgium). *Feather:* K. Kreuger (Sweden). *Bantam:* L. Bogaes (Hungary). *Fly:* L. Martinez Zapata (Spain).

OSLO–1949 *Heavy:* L. Bene (Hungary). *Light-Heavy:* G. di Serni (Italy). *Middle:* L. Papp (Hungary). *Welter:* J. Torma (Czechoslovakia). *Light:* M. McCullagh (Ireland). *Feather:* J. Bataille (France). *Bantam:* G. Zuddas (Italy). *Fly:* J. Kasperczak (Poland).

MILAN–1951 *Heavy:* G. di Serni (Italy). *Light-Heavy:* M. Limage (Belgium). *Middle:* S. Sjolin (Sweden). *Light-Middle:* L. Papp (Hungary). *Welter:* Z. Chychia (Poland). *Light-Welter:* H. Schelling (Germany). *Light:* B. Visintin (Italy). *Feather:* J. Ventaja (France). *Bantam:* Dall'Osso (Italy). *Fly:* A. Pozzali (Italy).

WARSAW–1953 *Heavy:* A. Schotzikas (U.S.S.R.). *Light-Heavy:* U. Nietschke (E. Germany). *Middle:* D. Wemhoner (W. Germany). *Light-Middle:* B. Wells (G.B.). *Welter:* Z. Chychia (Poland). *Light-Welter:* L. Drogosz (Poland). *Light:* V. Jengibarian (U.S.S.R.). *Feather:* J. Kruza (Poland). *Bantam:* Z. Stefaniuk (Poland). *Fly:* H. Kulier (Poland).

WEST BERLIN–1955 *Heavy:* A. Schotzikas (U.S.S.R.). *Light-Heavy:* E. Schoeppner (W. Germany). *Middle:* G. Schatkov (U.S.S.R.). *Light-Middle:* Z. Pietrzykowski (Poland). *Welter:* N. Gargano (G.B.). *Light-Welter:* L. Drogosz (Poland). *Light:* H. Kurschat (W. Germany). *Feather:* T. Nicholls (G.B.). *Bantam:* Z. Stefaniuk (Poland). *Fly:* E. Basel (W. Germany).

PRAGUE–1957 *Heavy:* A. Abramov (U.S.S.R.). *Light-Heavy:* G. Negrea (Romania). *Middle:* Z. Pietrzykov (Poland). *Light-Middle:* G. Benvenuti (Italy). *Welter:* M. Graus (W. Germany). *Light-Welter:* V. Jengibarian (U.S.S.R.). *Light:* K. Pazdior (Poland). *Feather:* D. Venilov (Bulgaria). *Bantam:* O. Grigoryev (U.S.S.R.). *Fly:* M. Homberg (W. Germany).

LUCERNE–1959 *Heavy:* A. Abramov (U.S.S.R.). *Light-Heavy:* Z. Pietrzykowski (Poland). *Middle:* G. Schatkov (U.S.S.R.). *Light-Middle:* G. Benvenuti (Italy). *Welter:* L. Drogosz (Poland). *Light-Welter:* V. Jengbarian (U.S.S.R.). *Light:* O. Maki (Finland). *Feather:* J. Adamski (Poland). *Bantam:* H. Rascher (W. Germany). *Fly:* M. Homberg (W. Germany).

BELGRADE–1961 *Heavy:* A. Abramov (U.S.S.R.). *Light-Heavy:* G. Sarudi (Italy). *Middle:* T. Walasek (Poland). *Light-Middle:* B. Lagutin (U.S.S.R.). *Welter:* R. Tamulis (U.S.S.R.). *Light-Welter:* A. Tamulis (U.S.S.R.) *Light:* R. McTaggart (G.B.). *Feather:* F. Taylor (G.B.). *Bantam:* S. Sivko (U.S.S.R.). *Fly:* P. Vacca (Italy).

Teofilio Stevenson, of Cuba, was the world amateur heavyweight champion in 1974, 1978 and 1986, and Olympic heavyweight gold medalist in 1972, 1976 and 1980 – a brilliant record.

MOSCOW – 1963 *Heavy:* J. Nemee (Czechoslovakia). *Light-Heavy:* Z. Pietrzykowski (Poland). *Middle:* V. Popenchenko (U.S.S.R.). *Light-Middle:* B. Lagutin (U.S.S.R.). *Welter:* R. Tamulis (U.S.S.R.). *Light-Welter:* J. Kulej (Poland). *Light:* J. Kajdi (Hungary). *Feather:* S. Stepashkin (U.S.S.R.). *Bantam:* O. Grigoryev (U.S.S.R.). *Fly:* Bystrov (U.S.S.R.).

EAST BERLIN – 1965 *Heavy:* A. Isosimov (U.S.S.R.). *Light-Heavy:* D. Poznyak (U.S.S.R.). *Middle:* V. Popenchenko (U.S.S.R.). *Light-Middle:* V. Ageyev (U.S.S.R.). *Welter:* R. Tamulis (U.S.S.R.). *Light-Welter:* J. Kulej (Poland). *Light:* V. Barranikov (U.S.S.R.). *Feather:* S. Stepashkin (U.S.S.R.). *Bantam:* O. Grigoryev (U.S.S.R.). *Fly:* H. Freidstadt (W. Germany).

ROME – 1967 *Heavy:* M. Baruzzi (Italy). *Light-Heavy:* D. Poznyak (U.S.S.R.). *Middle:* M. Casati (Italy). *Light-Middle:* V. Ageyev (U.S.S.R.). *Welter:* B. Nemecek (Czechoslovakia). *Light-Welter:* V. Frolov (U.S.S.R.). *Light:* J. Grudzien (Poland). *Feather:* R. Petek (Poland). *Bantam:* N. Gijuc (Romania). *Fly:* H. Skrzyczak (Poland).

BUCHAREST – 1969 *Heavy:* I. Alexe (Romania). *Light-Heavy:* D. Poznyak (U.S.S.R.). *Middle:* V. Tarasenkov (U.S.S.R.). *Light-Middle:* V. Tregubov (U.S.S.R.). *Welter:* G. Mier (W. Germany). *Welter:* V. Frolov (U.S.S.R.). *Light:* C. Cutov (Romania). *Feather:* L. Orban (Hungary). *Bantam:* A. Dumitrescu (Romania). *Fly:* C. Ciuca (Romania). *Light-Fly:* G. Gedo (Hungary).

MADRID – 1971 *Heavy:* V. Tchernishev (U.S.S.R.). *Light-Heavy:* M. Parlov (Yugoslavia). *Middle:* J. Juotsiavitchus (U.S.S.R.). *Light-Middle:* V. Tregubov (U.S.S.R.). *Welter:* J. Kajdi (Hungary). *Light-Welter:* U. Beyer (E. Germany). *Light:* J. Sczepanski (Poland). *Feather:* R. Tomczyk (Poland). *Bantam:* T. Badari (Hungary). *Fly:* J. Rodriguez (Spain). *Light-Fly:* G. Gedo (Hungary).

BELGRADE – 1973 *Heavy:* V. Ulyanich (U.S.S.R.). *Light-Heavy:* M. Parlov (Yugoslavia). *Middle:* V. Lemechev (U.S.S.R.). *Light-Middle:* A. Kilmanov (U.S.S.R.). *Welter:* S. Csjef (Hungary). *Light-Welter:* M. Benes (Yugoslavia). *Light:* S. Cutov (Romania). *Feather:* S. Forster (E. Germany). *Bantam:* A. Cosentino (France). *Fly:* C. Gruescu (Romania). *Light-Fly:* V. Zasipko (U.S.S.R.).

KATOWICE – 1975 *Heavy:* A. Biegalski (Poland). *Light-Heavy:* A. Kilmanov (U.S.S.R.). *Middle:* V. Lemeschev (U.S.S.R.). *Light-Middle:* W. Rudknowski (Polnad). *Welter:* K. Marjaama (Finland). *Light-Welter:* V. Limasov (U.S.S.R.). *Light:* S. Cutov (Romania). *Feather:* T. Badari (Hungary). *Bantam:* V. Rybakov (U.S.S.R.). *Fly:* W. Zasypko (U.S.S.R.). *Light-Fly:* A. Tkachenko (U.S.S.R.).

HALLE – 1977 *Heavy:* E. Gorstkov (U.S.S.R.). *Light-Heavy:* D. Kvadchadze (U.S.S.R.). *Middle:* I. Shaposhnikov (U.S.S.R.). *Light-Middle:* B. Shevchenko (U.S.S.R.). *Welter:* V. Limassov (U.S.S.R.). *Light-Welter:* B. Gajda (Poland). *Light:* A. Rusevski (Yugoslavia). *Feather:* R. Nowakowski (E. Germany). *Bantam:* S. Forster (E. Germany). *Fly:* L. Blazynski (Poland). *Light-Fly:* H. Srednicki (Poland).

COLOGNE – 1979 *Super-Heavy:* P. Hussing (W. Germany). *Heavy:* E. Gorstkov (U.S.S.R.). *Light-Heavy:* A. Nikolyan (U.S.S.R.). *Middle:* T. Unsivirta (Finland). *Light-Middle:* M. Perunovic (Yugoslavia). *Welter:* E. Muller (W. Germany). *Light-Welter:* S. Konokbaev (U.S.S.R.). *Light:* V. Demkanenko (U.S.S.R.). *Feather:* V. Rybakov (U.S.S.R.). *Bantam:* N. Khrapzov (U.S.S.R.). *Fly:* H. Srednicki (Poland). *Light-Fly:* S. Sabirov (U.S.S.R.).

TAMPERE – 1981 *Super-Heavy:* F. Damiani (Italy). *Heavy:* A. Jagubkin (U.S.S.R.). *Light-Heavy:* A. Krupin (U.S.S.R.). *Middle:* J. Torbek (U.S.S.R.). *Light-Middle:* A. Koshkin (U.S.S.R.). *Welter:* S. Konaknaev (U.S.S.R.). *Light-Welter:* V. Shishev (U.S.S.R.). *Light:* V. Rybakov (U.S.S.R.). *Feather:* R. Nowakowski (E. Germany). *Bantam:* V. Miroshinichenko (U.S.S.R.). *Fly:* P. Lessov (Bulgaria). *Light-Fly:* I. Mustafov (Bulgaria).

VARNA – 1983 *Super-Heavy:* F. Damiani (Italy). *Heavy:* A. Jagubkin (U.S.S.R.). *Light-Heavy:* V. Kokhanovski (U.S.S.R.). *Middle:* V. Melnik (U.S.S.R.). *Light-Middle:* V. Laptev (U.S.S.R.). *Welter:* P. Galkin (U.S.S.R.). *Light-Welter:* V. Shishov (U.S.S.R.). *Light:* E. Ychuprenski (Bulgaria). *Feather:* S. Nurkazov (U.S.S.R.). *Bantam:* Y. Alexandrov (U.S.S.R.). *Fly:* P. Lessov (Bulgaria). *Light-Fly:* I. Mustafov (Bulgaria).

BUDAPEST – 1985 *Super-Heavy:* F. Somodi (Hungary). *Heavy:* A. Jagubkin (U.S.S.R.). *Light-Heavy:* N. Shanavasov (U.S.S.R.) *Middle:* H. Maske (E. Germany). *Light-Middle:* M. Timm (E. Germany). *Welter:* I. Akopokhian (U.S.S.R.). *Light-Welter:* S. Mehnert (E. Germany). *Light:* E. Chuprenski (Bulgaria). *Feather:* S. Khachatrian (U.S.S.R.). *Bantam:* L. Simic (Yugoslavia). *Fly:* D. Berg (E. Germany). *Light-Fly:* R. Breitbarth (E. Germany).

TURIN – 1987 *Super-Heavy:* U. Kaden (E. Germany). *Heavy:* A. Vanderlijde (Netherlands). *Light-Heavy:* V. Vaulin (U.S.S.R.). *Middle:* H. Maske (E. Germany). *Light-Middle:* E. Richter (E. Germany). *Welter:* V. Shishov (U.S.S.R.) *Light-Welter:* B. Abadjier (Bulgaria). *Light:* G. Nazarov (U.S.S.R.). *Feather:* M. Kazaryan (U.S.S.R.). *Bantam:* A. Hristov (Bulgaria). *Fly:* A. Tews (E. Germany). *Light-Fly:* N. Munchyan (U.S.S.R.).

European Amateur Junior Champions

MISKOLC – 1970 *Heavy:* Reder (Hungary). *Light-Heavy:* Sache (E. Germany). *Middle:* Anfimov (U.S.S.R.). *Light-Middle:* Lemischev (U.S.S.R.). *Welter:* Davidov (U.S.S.R.). *Light-Welter:* Nemecz (Hungary). *Light:* Jujasz (Hungary). *Feather:* Andrianov (U.S.S.R.). *Bantam:* Levitschev (U.S.S.R.). *Fly:* Kismeneth (Hungary). *Light-Fly:* Gluck (Hungary).

BUCHAREST – 1972 *Heavy:* Subotin (U.S.S.R.). *Light-Heavy:* Mirounik (U.S.S.R.). *Middle:* Lemeschev (U.S.S.R.). *Light-Middle:* Babescue (Romania). *Welter:* Zorov (U.S.S.R.). *Light-Welter:* Pierwieniecki (Poland). *Light:* Cutov (Romania). *Feather:* Lvov (U.S.S.R.). *Bantam:* Solomin (U.S.S.R.). *Fly:* Condurat (Romania). *Light-Fly:* Turei (Romania).

KIEV – 1974 *Heavy:* K. Mashev (Bulgaria). *Light-Heavy:* K. Dafinoiu (Romania). *Middle:* D. Jende (E. Germany). *Light-Middle:* V. Danshin (U.S.S.R.). *Welter:* M. Bychkov (U.S.S.R.). *Light-Welter:* N. Sigov (U.S.S.R.). *Light:* V. Limasov (U.S.S.R.). *Feather:* V. Sorpkin (U.S.S.R.). *Bantam:* C. Andreikovski (Bulgaria). *Fly:* V. Rybakav (U.S.S.R.). *Light-Fly:* A. Tkaschenko (U.S.S.R.).

IZMUR – 1976 *Heavy:* B. Wnjenyan (U.S.S.R.). *Light-Heavy:* I. Yantchauskas (U.S.S.R.). *Middle:* H. Lenhart (W. Germany). *Light-Middle:* W. Lauder (Scotland). *Welter:* K. Ozoglouz (Turkey). *Light-Welter:* V. Zverev (U.S.S.R.). *Light:* M. Puzovic (Yugoslavia). *Feather:* V. Demaneko (U.S.S.R.). *Bantam:* M. Navros (U.S.S.R.). *Fly:* G. Khratsov (U.S.S.R.). *Light-Fly:* C. Seican (Romania).

DUBLIN – 1978 *Heavy:* P. Stomenov (Bulgaria). *Light-Heavy:* I. Jolta (Romania). *Middle:* G. Zinkovitch (U.S.S.R.). *Middle:* A. Beliave (U.S.S.R.). *Welter:* R. Filimanov (U.S.S.R.). *Light-Welter:* V. Laptev (U.S.S.R.). *Light:* O. Patrizio (Italy). *Feather:* H. Loukmanov (U.S.S.R.). *Bantam:* S. Khatchatrian (U.S.S.R.). *Fly:* D. Radu (Romania). *Light-Fly:* R. Marx (E. Germany).

RIMINI – 1980 *Super-Heavy:* S. Kormilitsine (U.S.S.R.). *Heavy:* V. Tioumentsev (U.S.S.R.). *Light-Heavy:* V. Dolgoun (U.S.S.R.). *Middle:* S. Laptiev (U.S.S.R.). *Light-Middle:* N. Wilshire (England). *Welter:* T. Holonies (E. Germany). *Light-Welter:* R. Lomski (Bulgaria). *Light:* V. Shishov (U.S.S.R.). *Feather:* J. Gladychev (U.S.S.R.). *Bantam:* F. Rauschning (E. Germany). *Fly:* J. Varadi (Hungary). *Light-Fly:* A. Mikoulin (U.S.S.R.).

SCHWERIN – 1982 *Super-Heavy:* V. Aldoshin (U.S.S.R.). *Heavy:* A. Popov (U.S.S.R.). *Light-Heavy:* Y. Waulin (U.S.S.R.). *Middle:* E. Cristie (G.B.). *Light-Middle:* B. Shararov (U.S.S.R.). *Welter:* T. Schmitz (E. Germany). *Light-Welter:* S. Mehnert (E. Germany). *Light:* E. Chakimov (U.S.S.R.). *Feather:* B. Blagoev (Bulgaria). *Bantam:* M. Stecca (Italy). *Fly:* L. Filchev (Bulgaria). *Light-Fly:* R. Kabirov (U.S.S.R.).

TAMPERE – 1984 *Super-Heavy:* L. Kamenov (Bulgaria). *Heavy:* R. Draskovic (Yugoslavia). *Light-Heavy:* G. Pescov (U.S.S.R.). *Middle:* R. Ryll (E. Germany). *Middle:* O. Volkov (U.S.S.R.). *Welter:* K. Oinov (Bulgaria). *Light:* C. Furnikov (Bulgaria). *Feather:* O. Nazarov (U.S.S.R.). *Bantam:* K. Khdrian (U.S.S.R.). *Fly:* D. Berg (E. Germany). *Light-Fly:* R. Breitbart (E. Germany).

BRONDBY – 1986 *Super-Heavy:* A. Prianichnikov (U.S.S.R.). *Heavy:* A. Golota (Poland). *Light-Heavy:* A. Schultz *Middle:* A. Kurnabka (U.S.S.R.). *Light-Middle:* E. Elibaev (U.S.S.R.). *Welter:* S. KaravaYev (U.S.S.R.). *Light-Welter:* F. Vastag (Romania). *Light:* G. Akopian (U.S.S.R.). *Feather:* K. Dziu (U.S.S.R.). *Bantam:* D. Drumm (E. Germany). *Fly:* S. Galotian (U.S.S.R.). *Light-Fly:* S. Todorov (Bulgaria).

The age limit of the Junior Championship was reduced from 21 to 19 in 1976.

British A.B.A. Champions

Super Heavyweight
1982 A. E. Elliott
1983 K. Ferdinand
1984 R. Wells
1985 G. Williamson
1986 J. Oyebola
1987 J. Oyebola
1988 D. Crawford

Heavyweight
1881 R. Frost Smith
1882 H. Dearsley
1883 H. Dearsley
1884 H. Dearsley
1885 W. West
1886 A. Diamond
1887 E. White
1888 W. King
1889 A. Bowman
1890 J. Steers
1891 V. Barker
1892 J. Steers
1893 J. Steers
1894 H. King
1895 Capt. W. Edgeworth Johnstone
1896 Capt. W. Edgeworth Johnstone
1897 G. Townsend
1898 G. Townsend
1899 F. Parks
1900 W. Dees
1901 F. Parks
1902 F. Parks
1903 F. Dickson
1904 A. Horner
1905 F. Parks
1906 F. Parks
1907 H. Brewer
1908 S. Evans
1909 C. Brown

1910 F. Storbeck
1911 W. Hazell
1912 R. Smith
1913 R. Smith
1914 E. Chandler
1919 H. Brown
1920 R. Rawson
1921 R. Rawson
1922 T. Evans
1923 E. Eagan
1924 A. Clifton
1925 Lt. D. Lister
1926 T. Petersen
1927 Lt. C. Capper
1928 J. L. Driscoll
1929 H. P. Floyd
1930 V. Stuart
1931 M. Flanaghan
1932 V. Stuart
1933 C. O'Grady
1934 H. P. Floyd
1935 H. P. Floyd
1936 V. Stuart
1937 V. Stuart
1938 G. Preston
1939 A. Porter
1944 M. Hart
1945 D. Scott
1946 H. P. Floyd
1947 G. Scriven
1948 J. Gardner
1949 A. Worrall
1950 P. Toch
1951 A. Halsey
1952 E. Hearn
1953 J. Erskine
1954 B. Harper
1955 D. Rowe
1956 D. Rent
1957 D. Thomas
1958 D. Thomas
1959 D. Thomas
1960 L. Hobbs
1961 W. Walker
1962 R. Dryden
1963 R. Sanders

1964 C. Woodhouse
1965 W. Wells
1966 A. Brogan
1967 P. Boddington
1968 W. Wells
1969 A. Burton
1970 J. Gilmour
1971 L. Stevens
1972 T. Wood
1973 G. McEwan
1974 N. Meade
1975 G. McEwan
1976 J. Rafferty
1977 G. Adair
1978 J. Awome
1979 A. Palmer
1980 F. Bruno
1981 A. Elliott
1982 H. Hylton
1983 H. Notice
1984 D. Young
1985 H. Hylton
1986 E. Cardouza
1987 J. Moran
1988 H. Akinwande

Light-Heavyweight
1920 H. Franks
1921 L. Collett
1922 H. Mitchell
1923 H. Mitchell
1924 H. Mitchell
1925 H. Mitchell
1926 D. McCorkindale
1927 A. Jackson
1928 A. Jackson
1929 J. Goyder
1930 J. Murphy
1931 J. Petersen
1932 J. Goyder
1933 G. Brennan
1934 G. Brennan
1935 R. Hearns
1936 J. Magill
1937 J. Wilby
1938 A. S. Brown

1939 B. Woodcock
1944 E. Shackleton
1945 A. Watson
1946 J. Taylor
1947 A. Watson
1948 D. Scott
1949 Declared no contest
1950 P. Messervy
1951 G. Walker
1952 H. Cooper
1953 H. Cooper
1954 A. Madigan
1955 D. Rent
1956 D. Mooney
1957 T. Green
1958 J. Leeming
1959 J. Ould
1960 J. Ould
1961 J. Bodell
1962 J. Hendrickson
1963 P. Murphy
1964 J. Fisher
1965 E. Whistler
1966 R. Tighe
1967 M. Smith
1968 R. Brittle
1969 J. Frankham
1970 J. Rafferty
1971 J. Conteh
1972 W. Knight
1973 W. Knight
1974 W. Knight
1975 M. Heath
1976 G. Evans
1977 C. Lawson
1978 V. Smith
1979 A. Straughn
1980 A. Straughn
1981 A. Straughn
1982 G. Crawford
1983 A. Wilson
1984 A. Wilson
1985 J. Beccles
1986 J. Moran
1987 J. Beccles

1988 H. Lawson

Middleweight
1881 T. Bellhouse
1882 A. Curnick
1883 A. Curnick
1884 W. Brown
1885 M. Salmon
1886 W. King
1887 R. Hair
1888 R. Hair
1889 G. Skyes
1890 J. Hoare
1891 J. Steers
1892 J. Steers
1893 J. Steers
1894 W. Sykes
1895 G. Townsend
1896 W. Ross
1897 W. Dees
1898 G. Townsend
1899 R. Warnes
1900 E. Mann
1901 R. Warnes
1902 E. Mann
1903 R. Warnes
1904 E. Mann
1905 J. Douglas
1906 A. Murdock
1907 R. Warnes
1908 W. Child
1909 W. Child
1910 R. Warnes
1911 W. Child
1912 E. Chandle
1913 W. Bradley
1914 H. Brown
1919 H. Mallin
1920 H. Mallin
1921 H. Mallin
1922 H. Mallin
1923 H. Mallin
1924 J. Elliott
1925 J. Elliott
1926 F. P. Crawley
1927 F. P. Crawley

1928 F. Mallin
1929 F. Mallin
1930 F. Mallin
1931 F. Mallin
1932 F. Mallin
1933 A. Shawyer
1934 J. Magill
1935 J. Magill
1936 A. Harrington
1937 M. Dennis
1938 H. Tiller
1939 H. Davies
1944 J. Hockley
1945 R. Parker
1946 R. Turpin
1947 R. Agland
1948 J. Wright
1949 S. Lewis
1950 P. Longo
1951 E. Ludlam
1952 T. Gooding
1953 R. Barton
1954 K. Phillips
1955 F. Hope
1956 P. Redrup
1957 P. Burke
1958 P. Hill
1959 F. Elderfield
1960 R. Addison
1961 J. Caiger
1962 A. Matthews
1963 A. Matthews
1964 W. Stack
1965 W. Robinson
1966 C. Finnegan
1967 A. Ball
1968 P. McCann
1969 D. Wallington
1970 J. Conteh
1971 A. Minter
1972 F. Lucas
1973 F. Lucas
1974 D. Odwell
1975 D. Odwell
1976 E. Burke
1977 R. Davies

1978 H. Graham
1979 N. Wiltshire
1980 M. Kaylor
1981 B. Schumacher
1982 J. Price
1983 T. Forbes
1984 B. Shumacher
1985 D. Cronin
1986 N. Benn
1987 R. Douglas
1988 M. Edwards

Light-Middleweight
1951 A. Lay
1952 B. Foster
1953 B. Wells
1954 B. Wells
1955 B. Foster
1956 J. McCormack
1957 J. Cunningham
1958 S. Pearson
1959 S. Pearson
1960 W. Fisher
1961 J. Gamble
1962 J. Lloyd
1963 A. Wyper
1964 W. Robinson
1965 P. Dwyer
1966 T. Imrie
1967 A. Edwards
1968 E. Blake
1969 T. Imrie
1970 D. Simmonds
1971 A. Edwards
1972 L. Paul
1973 R. Maxwell
1974 R. Maxwell
1975 A. Harrison
1976 W. Lauder
1977 C. Malarkey
1978 E. Henderson
1979 D. Brewster
1980 J. Price
1981 E. Christie
1982 D. Milligan
1983 R.Douglas
1984 R. Douglas
1985 R. Douglas
1986 T. Velinor
1987 N. Brown
1988 W. Ellis

Welterweight
1920 F. Whitbread
1921 A. Ireland
1922 E. White
1923 P. Green
1924 P.O'Hanrahan
1925 P. O'Hanrahan
1926 B. Marshall
1927 H. Dunn
1928 H. Bone
1929 T. Wigmore
1930 F. Brooman
1931 J. Barry
1932 D. McCleave
1933 P. Peters
1934 D. McCleave
1935 D. Lynch
1936 W. Pack
1937 D. Lynch
1938 C. Webster
1939 R. Thomas
1944 H. Hall
1945 R. Turpin
1946 J. Ryan
1947 J. Ryan
1948 M. Shacklady

1949 A. Buxton
1950 T. Ratcliffe
1951 J. Maloney
1952 J. Maloney
1953 L. Morgan
1954 N. Gargano
1955 N. Gargano
1956 N. Gargano
1957 R. Warnes
1958 B. Nancurvis
1959 J. McGrail
1960 C. Humphries
1961 A. Lewis
1962 J. Pritchett
1963 J. Pritchett
1964 M. Varley
1965 P. Henderson
1966 P. Cragg
1967 D. Cranswick
1968 A. Tottoh
1969 T. Henderson
1970 T. Waller
1971 D. Davies
1972 T. Francis
1973 T. Waller
1974 T. Waller
1975 W. Bennett
1976 C. Jones
1977 C. Jones
1978 E. Byrne
1979 J. Frost
1980 T. Marsh
1981 T. Marsh
1982 C. Pyatt
1983 R. McKenley
1984 M. Hughes
1985 E. McDonald
1986 D. Dyer
1987 M. Elliott
1988 M. McCreath

Light-Welterweight
1951 W. Conner
1952 P. Waterman
1953 D. Hughes
1954 G. Martin
1955 F. McQuillan
1956 D. Stone
1957 D. Stone
1958 R. Kane
1959 R. Kane
1960 R. Day
1961 B. Brazier
1962 B. Brazier
1963 R. McTaggart
1964 R. Taylor
1965 R. McTaggart
1966 W. Hiatt
1967 B. Hudspeth
1968 E. Cole
1969 J. Stacey
1970 D. Davies
1971 M. Kingwell
1972 T. Waller
1973 N. Cole
1974 P. Kelly
1975 J. Zeraschi
1976 C. McKenzie
1977 J. Douglas
1978 D. Williams
1979 E. Copeland
1980 A. Willis
1981 A. Willis
1982 T. Adams
1983 D. Dent
1984 D. Griffiths
1985 I. Mustafa
1986 J. Alsop

1987 A. Holligan
1988 A. Hall

Lightweight
1881 F. Hobday
1882 A. Bettinson
1883 A. Diamond
1884 A. Diamond
1885 A. Diamond
1886 G. Roberts
1887 J. Hair
1888 A. Newton
1889 W. Neale
1890 A. Newton
1891 E. Dettmer
1892 E. Dettmer
1893 W. Campbell
1894 W. Campbell
1895 A. Randall
1896 A. Vanderhout
1897 A. Vanderhout
1898 H. Marks
1899 H. Brewer
1900 G. Humphries
1901 A. Warner
1902 A. Warner
1903 H. Fergus
1904 M. Wells
1905 M. Wells
1906 M. Wells
1907 M. Wells
1908 H. Holmes
1909 F. Grace
1910 T. Tees
1911 A. Spenceley
1912 R. Marriott
1913 R. Grace
1914 R. Marriott
1919 F. Grace
1920 F. Grace
1921 G. Shorter
1922 G. Renouf
1923 G. Shorter
1924 W. White
1925 Signr. Viney
1926 T. Slater
1927 W. Hunt
1928 F. Webster
1929 W. Hunt
1930 J. Waples
1931 D. McCleave
1932 F. Meacham
1933 H. Mizler
1934 J. Rolland
1935 F. Frost
1936 F. Simpson
1937 A. Danahar
1938 T. McGrath
1939 H. Groves
1944 W. Thompson
1945 J. Williamson
1946 E. Thomas
1947 C. Morrissey
1948 R. Cooper
1949 A. Smith
1950 R. Latham
1951 R. Hinson
1952 F. Reardon
1953 D. Hinson
1954 G. Whelan
1955 S. Coffey
1956 R. McTaggart
1957 J. Kidd
1958 R. McTaggart
1959 P. Warwick
1960 R. McTaggart
1961 P. Warwick
1962 B. Whelan

1963 B. O'Sullivan
1964 J. Dunne
1965 A. White
1966 J. Head
1967 T. Waller
1968 J. Watt
1969 H. Hayes
1970 N. Cole
1971 J. Singleton
1972 N. Cole
1973 T. Dunn
1974 J. Lynch
1975 P. Cowdell
1976 S. Mittee
1977 G. Gilboby
1978 T. Marsh
1979 G. Gilbody
1980 G. Gilbody
1981 G. Gilbody
1982 Jim McDonnell
1983 K. Willis
1984 A. Dickson
1985 E. McAuley
1986 J. Jacobs
1987 M. Ayers
1988 C. Kane

Featherweight
1881 T. Hill
1882 T. Hill
1883 T. Hill
1884 E. Hutchings
1885 J. Pennell
1886 T. McNeil
1887 J. Pennell
1888 J. Taylor
1889 G. Belsey
1890 G. Belsey
1891 F. Curtis
1892 F. Curtis
1893 T. Davidson
1894 R. Gunn
1895 R. Gunn
1896 R. Gunn
1897 N. Smith
1898 P. Lunn
1899 J. Scholes
1900 R. Lee
1901 C. Clarke
1902 C. Clarke
1903 J. Godfrey
1904 C. Morris
1905 H. Holmes
1906 A. Miner
1907 C. Morris
1908 T. Ringer
1909 A. Lambert
1910 C. Houghton
1911 H. Bowers
1912 G. Baker
1913 G. Baker
1914 G. Baker
1919 G. Baker
1920 J. Fleming
1921 G. Baker
1922 E. Swash
1923 E. Swash
1924 A. Beavis
1925 A. Beavis
1926 R. Minshull
1927 F. Webster
1928 F. Meachem
1929 F. Meachem
1930 J. Duffield
1931 B. Caplan
1932 H. Mizler
1933 J. Walters
1934 J. Treadway

1935 E. Ryan
1936 J. Treadaway
1937 A. Harper
1938 C. Gallie
1939 C. Gallie
1944 D. Sullivan
1945 J. Carter
1946 P. Brander
1947 S. Evans
1948 P. Brander
1949 H. Gilliland
1950 P. Brander
1951 J. Travers
1952 P. Lewis
1953 P. Lewis
1954 D. Charnley
1955 T. Nicholls
1956 T. Nicholls
1957 M. Collins
1958 M. Collins
1959 G. Judge
1960 P. Lundgren
1961 P. Cheevers
1962 B. Wilson
1963 A. Riley
1964 R. Smith
1965 R. Buchanan
1966 H. Baxter
1967 K. Cooper
1968 J. Cheshire
1969 A. Richardson
1970 D. Polak
1971 T. Wright
1972 K. Laing
1973 J. Lynch
1974 G. Gilbody
1975 R. Beaumont
1976 P. Cowdell
1977 P. Cowdell
1978 M. O'Brien
1979 P. Hanlon
1980 M. Hanif
1981 P. Hanlon
1982 H. Henry
1983 P. Bradley
1984 K. Taylor
1985 F. Havard
1986 P. Hodkinson
1987 P. English
1988 D. Anderson

Bantamweight
1884 A. Woodward
1885 A. Woodward
1886 T. Isley
1887 T. Isley
1888 H. Oakman
1889 H. Brown
1890 J. Rowe
1891 E. Moore
1892 F. Godbold
1893 E. Watson
1894 P. Jones
1895 P. Jones
1896 P. Jones
1897 C. Lamb
1898 F. Herring
1899 A. Avent
1900 J. Freeman
1901 W. Morgan
1902 A. Miner
1903 H. Perry
1904 H. Perry
1905 W. Webb
1906 T. Ringer
1907 E. Adams
1908 H. Thomas
1909 J. Condon

1910 W. Webb
1911 W. Allen
1912 W. Allen
1913 A. Wye
1914 W. Allen
1919 W. Allen
1920 G. McKenzie
1921 L. Tarrant
1922 W. Boulding
1923 A. Smith
1924 L. Tarrant
1925 A. Goom
1926 F. Webster
1927 E. Warwick
1928 J. Garland
1929 F. Bennett
1930 H. Mizler
1931 F. Bennett
1932 J. Treadaway
1933 G. Johnston
1934 A. Barnes
1935 L. Case
1936 A. Barnes
1937 A. Barnes
1938 J. Pottinger
1939 R. Watson
1944 R. Bissell
1945 P. Brander
1946 C. Squire
1947 D. O'Sullivan
1948 T. Profit
1949 T. Miller
1950 T. Nicholls
1951 T. Nicholls
1952 T. Nicholls
1953 J. Smillie
1954 J. Smillie
1955 G. Dormer
1956 O. Reilly
1957 J. Morrissey
1958 H. Winstone
1959 D. Weller
1960 F. Taylor
1961 P. Benneyworth
1962 P. Benneyworth
1963 B. Packer
1964 B. Packer
1965 R. Mallon
1966 J. Clark
1967 M. Carter
1968 M. Carter
1969 M. Piner
1970 A. Oxley
1971 G. Turpin
1972 G. Turpin
1973 P. Cowdell
1974 S. Ogilvie
1975 S. Ogilvie
1976 J. Bambrick
1977 J. Turner
1978 J. Turner
1979 R. Ashton
1980 R. Gilbody
1981 P. Jones
1982 R. Gilbody
1983 J. Hyland
1984 J. Hyland
1985 S. Murphy
1986 S. Murphy
1987 J. Sillitoe
1988 K. Howlett

Flyweight
1920 H. Groves
1921 W. Cuthbertson
1922 E. Warwick
1923 L. Tarrant
1924 E. Warwick

145

1925 E. Warwick	1969 D. Needham		
1926 J. Hill	1970 D. Needham		
1927 J. Roland	1971 P. Wakefield		
1928 C. Taylor	1972 M. O'Sullivan		
1929 T. Pardoe	1973 R. Hilton		
1930 T. Pardoe	1974 M. O'Sullivan		
1931 T. Pardoe	1975 C. Magri		
1932 T. Pardoe	1976 C. Magri		
1933 T. Pardoe	1977 C. Magri		
1934 P. Palmer	1978 G. Nickels		
1935 G. Fayaud	1979 R. Gilbody		
1936 G. Fayaud	1980 K. Wallace		
1937 P. O'Donaghue	1981 K. Wallace		
1938 A. Russell	1982 J. Kelly		
1939 D. McKay	1983 S. Nolan		
1944 J. Clinton	1984 P. Clinton		
1945 J. Bryce	1985 P. Clinton		
1946 R. Gallacher	1986 J. Lyon		
1947 J. Clinton	1987 J. Lyon		
1948 H. Carpenter	1988 J. Lyon		
1949 H. Riley			
1950 A. Jones	*Light-Flyweight*		
1951 G. John	1971 M. Abrams		
1952 D. Dower	1972 M. Abrams		
1953 R. Currie	1973 M. Abrams		
1954 R. Currie	1974 C. Magri		
1955 D. Lloyd	1975 M. Lawless		
1956 T. Spinks	1976 P. Fletcher		
1957 R. Davies	1977 P. Fletcher		
1958 J. Brown	1978 J. Dawson		
1959 M. Gushlow	1979 J. Dawson		
1960 D. Lee	1980 T. Barker		
1961 W. McGowan	1981 J. Lyon		
1962 M. Pye	1982 J. Lyon		
1963 M. Laud	1983 J. Lyon		
1964 J. McCluskey	1984 J. Lyon		
1965 J. McCluskey	1985 M. Epton		
1966 P. Maguire	1986 M. Epton		
1967 S. Curtis	1987 M. Epton		
1968 J. McGonigle	1988 M. Cantwell		

America's Boxing Associations

At one time, particularly 1920–40, almost all the world championship titles were in American hands, but after World War II, with the advent of fighters from Mexico, Japan, Thailand, the Philippines, and the South American countries, the United States' dominance gradually disappeared and only in the heavyweight division has the monopoly been maintained.

It was then considered necessary to create American champions in all weight divisions, if only to give promoters additional means of attracting the public. There had been American champions in the past, when a world title had been in the possession of a foreigner. Gene Tunney and Harry Greb were U.S. light-heavyweight kings in 1922, as was Joey Maxim in 1949. When Jimmy Wilde ruled the flyweight class, Frankie Genaro and Fidel LaBarba were nominated as champions of America.

Then, at the end of 1969 there appeared the (North American Boxing Federation) N.A.B.F. which began setting up its own titleholders in every weight division. In 1979 the (United States Boxing Association) U.S.B.A. came into being, so once again there were two conflicting champions which, added to the duplicate set created by the W.B.A. and the W.B.C. gave American fight fans, at least, four boxers holding prominent titles in each of the 15 divisions.

To add to the complexity – undoubtedly to the joy of fight promoters universally – the International Boxing Federation was formed in 1983 and issued its own World Champions in due course. Thus, at the present time boxers throughout the world have three world titles at 15 different weights (plus the recent addition of a mini-flyweight (straw-weight) class (under 105 pounds) at which to aim their endeavours.

Furthermore, the W.B.C. introduced its World 'International' titles in 1987, aimed at giving the holders of its championships the right to challenge for a W.B.C. title proper without having to be rated in the Top Ten of each division.

Belts

Prize Ring Belts

The first Belt awarded in the Prize Ring went to Tom Cribb after he had beaten Tom Molineaux, a former American slave, at Copthall Common, Sussex, on Dec. 18, 1810. It was presented to the winner by no less a personage than George III of England. Another Belt was presented to Jem Ward when he became champion by defeating Tom Cannon at Stanfield Park, Warwick, on July 19, 1825. Ward retained it until 1835 and then gave it to Bold Bendigo who succeeded him; it was never seen again. Other famous Belts were presented to Dick Burge, Jem Mace and Tim 'Pedlar' Palmer by their admirers.

Just before the contest between Nick Ward (Jem's younger brother) and Benjamin Caunt at Long Marsden, on May 11, 1841 a new Champion's Belt, provided by public subscription, was exhibited to be presented to the winner. In the centre were a pair of clasped hands surrounded by a wreath of the rose, thistle and shamrock. On each side were three shields of bright silver on which were inscribed the names of the former champions of England with space for the name of the winner of the contest. The Belt was to be held by the winner so long as he was the champion. On taking it into his hands Caunt remarked to Ward: 'This is mine, Nick' to which Ward replied: 'I hope the best man may win it and wear it.' The 'best man' was Caunt, who won it after 35 rounds that lasted 47 minutes. The Belt was officially presented to him on May 31, 1841.

When Tom Sayers of England and John C. Heenan of America fought their famous international battle at Farnborough, Hampshire in 1860 the Englishman put up the handsome silver Belt which had been presented to him by his friends after beating Billy Percy, the Tipton Slasher. The fight was declared a draw after 42 rounds when the ropes were cut by the Englishman's supporters. It was decided to award each man a special silver Belt to commemorate their great contest, and they were presented at the Alhambra Theatre in London's Leicester Square on May 30, 1860.

American Championship Belts

It was Richard K. Fox, proprietor of the *Police Gazette*, a weekly pictorial newspaper dealing with most sports, particularly boxing, who raised the idea of presenting Belts emblematic of World Championships. His trophies were worth fighting for and provided him with plenty of publicity.

Fox, a great boxing enthusiast, had a special Belt made for the world heavyweight championship. It cost him 5,000 dollars and he first put it up for a contest between John L. Sullivan, who claimed the title, and Jem Smith, the reigning British champion. Sullivan refused to fight the Englishman, so the Belt was handed to Jake Kilrain, from Ireland, on condition that he defended it against Smith. This he did in France: the bout went to 106 rounds and was a 'draw'.

The Irishman returned to America, collected the Belt and challenged Sullivan. On August 8, 1889 he was knocked out in 75 rounds at Richburg, Mississippi but the winner sneered at the *Police Gazette* Belt and refused to accept it. In the meantime the sporting citizens of Boston, Sullivan's home city, had subscribed for a magnificent Belt that outdid the one provided by Mr Fox. Holding the *Police Gazette* Belt aloft, Sullivan declared that in contrast to his Boston trophy, this was nothing more than a dog collar.

The Boston belt also cost 5,000 dollars. It was 48 inches long and in design had eight posts to represent a ring, through which ran three gold ropes. Between the posts were gold plates. There were 351 diamonds in the belt, 291 of them being used to spell out Sullivan's name. On the trophy were the flags of America, England and Ireland, with portraits of John L. Sullivan and his manager, Pat Sheedy.

However, the *Police Gazette* Belt was accepted by Gentleman Jim Corbett when in 1892 he knocked out Sullivan in 21 rounds for the world title. He carried it about with him when on a vaudeville tour and one day, in

John L. Sullivan's famous Boston Belt.

Indianapolis, was persuaded to put it on show in a jeweller's window. That night someone smashed the plate glass that shielded the trophy and made off with it. It was never seen again.

When Terry McGovern won the world bantam title by knocking out Pedlar Palmer, the British champion, in a single round in 1899 the *Police Gazette* proprietor awarded Terrible Terry a valuable Belt. He either lost it, sold it or had it stolen, so Mr Fox provided him with another. In 1949 it turned up when the National Boxing Association staged a world heavyweight title bout between Ezzard Charles and Jersey Joe Walcott at Chicago. Charles won, was proclaimed champion and presented with this ancient Belt. It was advertised by the promoter as being the original 'Dog Collar', but in fact it was McGovern's duplicate.

Another heavyweight Belt was put up by friends of Charlie Mitchell of England when he met John L. Sullivan on the Rothschild Estate near Chantilly in France in 1887. After 39 rounds the bout was abandoned as a 'draw' but Mitchell was regarded as the winner by his backers and given the trophy. Thirty-seven years later it came into the possession of Ted Broadribb who sold it to Nat Fleischer and it now reposes in his boxing museum at the office of *The Ring Magazine*.

Ring Magazine Belts

When Nat Fleischer launched his famous monthly boxing magazine *The Ring*, in February 1922, he presented a most attractive Belt to every world champion at the time and continued to do so until his death in 1972. During all those years he must have awarded something in the region of 300 trophies and towards the end of the number must have accelerated. When he began there were only eight reigning champions. Now with the addition of seven more classes – the in-between championships, plus dual title-holders in many instances, due to the activities of the W.B.A. and the W.B.C. to say nothing of the I.B.F., N.A.B.F. and the U.S.B.A. – it would have been very expensive to keep pace.

Emile Griffiths won six *Ring* Belts, Nino Benvenuti four, while Jimmy Carter, Carmen Basilio, Pone Kingpetch and Dick Tyler each won three of these trophies.

When in 1920 England's Tommy Noble defeated Johnny Murray at Madison Square Garden, New York, in a bout which promoter Tex Rickard advertised as for the Featherweight Championship of the world, he was

Rocky Marciano with the *Ring Magazine* Belt awarded to him as world heavyweight champion.

presented with a diamond-studded Belt. Thirty years later he was asked if he still had it and replied: 'Of course, would you like to see it?' When it was produced, however, only the punctured leather was to be seen, the gems having long since been taken out and sold.

Lonsdale Belts

In 1909 the National Sporting Club of London, which since its inauguration in 1891 had controlled the official championships of Great Britain, made two major innovations in an effort to maintain its monopoly against the growing competition that was coming from other promoters of boxing, who used far bigger arenas and consequently could outbid the N.S.C. for the services of the champions.

First it was stipulated that there should be eight weight classes, from flyweight to heavyweight and that at the weigh-in of boxers for title bouts these specified poundages should operate.

It was also announced that an official championship Belt for each weight class would be put into circulation and that Lord Lonsdale, the President of the Club, had consented to lend his name to the new trophies which would be known as Lonsdale Belts, the Earl providing the first one.

From 1909 until 1935, when the power of the N.S.C. had been handed over to the British Boxing Board of Control, 22 of these Belts, made of gold and bearing a central panel in enamel depicting two boxers in fighting stance (with additional panels for recording the names of the winners), were issued under the following conditions:

1 Any boxer holding a championship must defend his title within six months after the receipt of a challenge, for a minimum stake of £100 a side, excepting the heavyweight, when the minimum is to be £200 a side, the challenge to be accompanied by a deposit of £50 and approved by the Committee of the N.S.C.

2 The Belt to become the absolute property of the holder if he is declared the winner of same at three contests, whether consecutive or not, held to decide such Championship under the control of the N.S.C., or be the undisputed holder of same for three consecutive years. Provided that in the event of a *bona fide* challenge in accordance with the terms of condition being made before the expiration of the said three years, it shall be necessary for the holder to win such contest before the Belt becomes his absolute property, although the said contest may not be determined within the said three years.

3 The holder shall deposit such Belt with the manager of the Club previous to any contest taking place in reference to such Championship.

4 The holder shall be held responsible for any damage done to the Belt during such time as he is qualified holder, and shall insure it against loss or damage by larceny and fire in the sum of £200.

5 The holder of the Belt shall deposit as security the sum of £200 with the N.S.C., which shall be returned when the Belt becomes his absolute property in accordance with the above conditions, or on his returning same.

Of the 22 Belts circulated by the N.S.C., 20 were won outright, as follows: Heavy 2, Light-Heavy 1, Middle 3, Welter 2, Light 1, Feather 4, Bantam 5, Fly 2. The second Light-Heavyweight Belt was not awarded to Len Harvey, the rightful winner, but put up for a Heavyweight Novices Competition and won by Jack Smith, of Worcester. The second Lightweight Belt, on which Al Foreman had scored two wins and a 'draw', was sold by him privately. Jim Higgins (bantam) held the record for making a Belt his own property in 11 months and eight days; Jim Driscoll (feather) took 11 months and 16 days; Jack Petersen (heavy) a year to the day. Len Harvey (middle) took 371 days, but fought four Belt contests in that time, one of them being declared a 'draw'.

The British Boxing Board of Control took over the issue of its own Belts. These bear a portrait of Lord Lonsdale on the centre panel and if not containing as much gold as the original Belts, they have a resplendent and glittering appearance. To date more than 60 of these trophies have been won outright since the first was won by Benny Lynch when he successfully defended his flyweight title against Pat Palmer at Glasgow on September 16, 1936.

Record for the quickest outright win is held by Robert Dickie (feather) in 200 days. Others within a year have been: Pat Cowdell (feather) 205 days; Bunny Sterling (middle) 224 days; Dennis Andries (light-heavy) 258 days; Horace Notice (heavyweight) 287 days; Alan Minter (middle) 295 days; Lloyd Christie (light-welter) 295 days; Howard Winstone (feather) 312 days; Brian Curvis (welter) 344 days; and Tom Collins (light-heavy) 359 days.

Outright winners of two Belts have been: Brian Curvis (welter), Peter Keenan (bantam), Ronnie Clayton (feather) and Howard Winstone (feather). Both Nel Tarleton (feather) and Johnny King (bantam) won an N.S.C. and a B.B.B. of C. Belt outright. Freddie Welsh (light) and Johnny King (bantam) were each awarded special Lonsdale Betls after winning the Commonwealth title.

Henry Cooper is the only boxer to make three Lonsdale Belts his own property. This achievement will never be repeated or surpassed as on June 10, 1981 the following amendment was made to the B.B.B. of C. Rules and Regulations: 'The Board shall supply a Lord Lonsdale Championship Challenge Belt or similar belt for every championship of Great Britain and such Belt shall become the property of any boxer who shall win a championship on three occasions in the same weight division, but no boxer shall receive more than one belt as his own property, in any one weight division. In the event of a champion not being called upon to defend his title or not having defended his title in a contest ordered or approved by the Board for a period of three years from winning the title, the Board may, at its discretion, authorize the Belt to become the property of such champion.'

Boxing Families

Fathers and Sons

Barnes, Frank (Burns) and son §George.
Cerdan, *Marcel and son Marcel (Jun.).
Famechon, Andre and son *Johnny.
Fitzsimmons, *Bob and son Young Bob.
Frazier, *Joe, and sons Marvis and Hector.
Hyer, Jacob and son Tom (*both U.S. heavyweight champions*).
London, †Jack and sons †Brian and Jack.
Johnson, Phil and son *Harold.
Kelly, †Jim (Spider) and son †Billy (Spider).
Sullivan, Battling Sam and sons †Johnny and Sammy.
Swift, †Wally and son Wally.

Brothers

Arrendondo, *Ricardo, Rene, Roberto.
Attell, *Abe, Monte.
Baer, *Max, Buddy.
Belloise, *Mike, Steve.
Bird, Billy, Sonny.
Buxton, †Alex, Alan, Joe, Laurie.
Canizales, *Gaby, *Orlando.
Cardona, *Roberto, *Prudencio.
Cattouse, †Ray, Trevor.
Chip, *George, Joe.
Corbett, †Dick, †Harry.
Curry, *Bruce, *Donald.
Curvis, †Brian, †Cliff, Ken.
Dundee, *Joe, *Vince.
Famechon, ‡Ray, Andre, Emile.
Feeney, George, †John.
Finnegan, †Chris, †Kevin.
Galaxy, *Kaosai, *Kaokow.
Gibbons, Tom, Mike.
Hagler, *Marvin, Robbie Sims (half-brother).
Johnson, †Frank, *Braddock*, Jackie.
(*Real surname: Williamson*)
Jones, †Colin, Peter.
La Motta, *Jake, Joey.
Laing, †Kirkland, †Tony.
Leonard, *Benny, Charlie, Joey.
Leonard, *Sugar Ray, Roger.
McKenzie, †Clinton, †Duke, Dudley
Marchant, Albert, Benny, Jack, Teddy.
Mitchell, †Pinkey, Richie.
Moody, †Frank, Glen, Jackie.
Moyer, *Denny, Phil.
Norris, Olin, Terry.
O'Sullivan, †Danny, Dickie, Mickey.
Patterson, *Floyd, Ray.
Rocchigland, Graciano, Rolf.
Sands, §Dave, Clem, Ritchie, Alfie, Russell.
Spinks, *Leon, *Michael.
Stribling, Young Bill, Babe.

Max (left) and Buddy Baer were famous boxing brothers. Max was a world heavyweight champion: Buddy twice fought Joe Louis for the same title.

Toweel, *Vic, §Willie, Jimmy, Frazer.
Turpin, *Randolph, †Dick, Jackie.
Waters, Dean, Troy.
Woodcock, †Bruce, Billy.
Yarosz, *Teddy, Tommy.
Zivic, *Fritzie, Pete, Joe, Jack, Eddie.

Twins

Cooper, ‡Henry, George (Jim).
O'Sullivan, *Mike, Jack.

*World Champion   †British Champion
‡E.B.U. Champion   §Commonwealth Champion

Boxing Firsts on Film, Radio, and Television

Sept. 2, 1894: Thomas Edison filmed an exhibition bout in a studio between James J. Corbett, world heavyweight champion, and Peter Courteney. By arrangement Corbett scored a knockout in round six.
Feb. 21, 1896: Abortive attempt to film a fight in the open air. Bob Fitzsimmons knocked out Peter Maher, at Langtry, Texas, U.S.A. in the first round before the cameraman could get started.
March 17, 1897: First film of a championship fight outdoors, Bob Fitzsimmons w.ko.14 v. James J. Corbett, at Carson City, Nevada, U.S.A., for the world heavyweight title.
Nov. 3, 1899: First film of a championship fight under artificial light. James J. Jeffries w.pts.25 Tom Sharkey, Coney Island, New York, U.S.A. for the world heavyweight championship.
July 2, 1921: First radio broadcast of a world title fight. Jack Dempsey w.ko.4 Georges Carpentier at Jersey City, U.S.A.
Jan. 24, 1927: First radio broadcast in England. Johnny Curley w.pts.20 Johnny Cuthbert for the British featherweight title at the N.S.C. London, England.

Bob Fitzsimmons (right) and Peter Maher, Feb. 21, 1896. The bout ended before filming could begin.

Aug. 22, 1933: First televised boxing. This was an exhibition bout between Archie Sexton and Laurie Rateri at B.B.C. Broadcasting House, London, England.

April 4, 1938: First televised title fight. Len Harvey w.pts.15 Jock McAvoy, Harringay Arena, London, England.
This was not publicly screened.

Feb. 23, 1939: First publicly screened and theatre tele-cast contest. Eric Boon w.rsf14 Arthur Danahar at Harringay Arena for the British lightweight title, London, England.

June 1, 1939: First important bout televised in America. Lou Nova w.ko.11 Max Baer at Yankee Stadium, New York, U.S.A.

Dec. 5, 1947: First world heavyweight championship contest televised. Joe Louis w.pts.15 Jersey Joe Walcott, Madison Square Garden, New York, U.S.A.

Sept. 29, 1952: First three-dimensional TV world championship fight: Rocky Marciano w.ko.13 Jersey Joe Walcott, at Philadelphia Stadium, U.S.A.

Dec. 10, 1965: First colour TV of a world title bout, Emile Griffith w.pts.15 Manuel Gonzalez (welter) at Madison Square Garden, New York, U.S.A.

1967: First computerized boxing for the 'All-Time Heavyweight Championship of the World' in America. Sixteen past world champions were selected from John L. Sullivan to Muhammad Ali, but the winner was Rocky Marciano who 'knocked out' Jack Dempsey in the final.

Aug. 1968: Marciano and Ali sparred 70 rounds which was afterwards computerised for public screening in Jan. 1970. Different endings to the 'fight' were made, each being a winner, but in the version televised Marciano won by a knock-out.

Boxing for Cups and Medals

In Great Britain the annual Amateur Boxing Association Championships gloriously end the amateur season. Held annually, they were started in 1881 and ran without a break until 1914. The years of World War I saw no A.B.A. Championships, but they were resumed in 1919 and were staged without a break until 1939, then World War II intervened. There have been no interruptions from 1944 onwards. They are conducted by the Amateur Boxing Association which was founded in 1880, and a boy from the remotest part of the country who belongs to a recognised amateur club can box his way to the finals that have been staged over the years at such large arenas as Alexandra Palace, the Albert Hall and Wembley Arena.

Not all the amateur champions automatically turn professional, but a lot do and many of them have fought their way to become British champions, as follows. *Heavyweight:* Jack Bodell, Henry Cooper, Joe Erskine, Jack Gardner, Brian London (boxing as Jack Harper), Neville Meade, Bruce Woodcock. *Light-Heavyweight:* Ron Barton, Alex Buxton, Chic Calderwood, John Conteh, Chris Finnegan, Johnny Frankham, Jack Petersen, Dick Smith, Randolph Turpin, Tim Wood. *Middleweight:* Anthony Diamond, Alex Ireland, John McCormack, Alan Minter, Johnny Pritchett, Randolph Turpin, Mark Kaylor, Herol Graham. *Light-Middleweight:* Herol Graham, Larry Paul. *Welterweight:* Henry Hall, Colin Jones, Kirkland Laing, Dave McCleave, John Stracey, Eddie Thomas, Peter Waterman, Matt Wells, Terry Marsh. *Light-Welterweight:* Clinton McKenzie, Joey Singleton. *Lightweight:* Ken Buchanan, Dave Charnley, Bob Marriott, Harry Mizler, Billy Thompson, Jim Watt, Fred Webster. *Featherweight:* Pat Cowdell, Charlie Hill, George McKenzie, Dave Needham, Alan Richardson, Howard Winstone. *Bantamweight:* Freddie Gilroy, Peter Keenan, Walter McGowan, Danny O'Sullivan. *Flyweight:* Dai Dower, Johnny Hill, Walter McGowan, Johnny McCluskey, Charlie Magri. *For a complete list of the A.B.A. champions, see p. 000.*

British Title Fights

British Heavyweight Title Fights

1882	Dec. 22	Charlie Mitchell w.pts.3 Jack Knifton, London. *Competition to decide Heavyweight Championship of England.*
1885	Dec. 17	Jem Smith w.ko.6 Jack Davies, in Surrey, England. *This was fought with bare fists and Smith claimed title.*
1889	Sept. 30	Jem Smith w.pts.10 Jack Wannop, London.
1890	Feb. 7	Charlie Mitchell w.rsf.3 Jem Mace, Edinburgh.
1891	July 27	Ted Pritchard w.ko.3 Jem Smith, London.
1895	May 10	Jem Smith w.ko.2 Ted Pritchard, London.
	Nov. 26	Jem Smith w.dis.9 Dick Burge, London.
1897	Feb. 19	George Crisp w.dis.5 Jem Smith, Newcastle.
1901	Jan. 7	Jack Scales w.ko.2 Cloggy Saunders, London.
	Sept. 23	Jack Scales w.ko.4 Jack Palmer, Newcastle.
1902	June 25	Jack Scales w.pts.10 Ben Taylor, London.
	Oct. 13	Jack Scales w.ko.7 Harry 'Slouch' Dixon, London.
	Nov. 8	Charlie Wilson w.ko.3 Jack Scales, London.
1903	May 2	Jack Palmer w.ko.12 Ben Taylor, Newcastle.
1905	Dec. 18	Jack Palmer w.ko.4 Geoffrey Thorne, London.
1906	Oct. 29	Gnr. James Moir w.dis.9 Jack Palmer, London.
1907	Feb. 25	Gnr. James Moir w.ko.1 James 'Tiger' Smith, London.
1909	April 19	William 'Iron' Hague w.ko.1 Gnr. James Moir, London.
1910	Feb. 11	William 'Iron' Hague w.ko.15 P.O. 'Nutty' Curran, Plymouth.
	Feb. 21	William 'Iron' Hague w.pts.20 Jewey Smith, Sheffield.
	May 26	William 'Iron' Hague w.pts.20 Sgt. Sunshine, Liverpool.
	Aug. 15	William 'Iron' Hague w.pts.20 Pte. W. Smith, Sheffield.
	Nov. 7	William 'Iron' Hague w.ko.18 Cpl. Brown, Sheffield.
	Dec. 5	William 'Iron' Hague w.pts.20 Jewey Smith, Sheffield.
1911	Jan. 2	William 'Iron' Hague w.ko.9 Sgt. Sunshine, Mexborouigh.
	Jan. 30	William 'Iron' Hague w.ko.6 Bill Chase, London.
	April 24	‡Bombardier Billy Wells w.ko.6 William 'Iron' Hague, N.S.C. London.
1913	June 30	Bombardier Billy Wells w.ko.13 Packey Mahoney, N.S.C. London.
	Aug. 4	Bombardier Billy Wells w.ko.15 Pat O'Keefe, London.
	Sept. 10	Bombardier Billy Wells w.ko.10 Gnr. James Moir, London.
1914	Jan. 14	Bombardier Billy Wells w.ret.10 Gnr. Rawles, Belfast.
	March 3	Bombardier Billy Wells w.ko.4 Bandsman Jack Blake, London.
	April 30	Bombardier Billy Wells w.pts.20 Bandsman Dick Rice, Liverpool.
1915	Feb. 24	Bombardier Billy Wells w.ko.6 Bandsman Dick Rice, Belfast.
	May 31	Bombardier Billy Wells w.ko.9 Dick Smith, London.
	Dec. 27	Bombardier Billy Wells w.ko.1 Bandsman Dick Rice, Liverpool.
1916	Feb. 21	Bombardier Billy Wells w.ko.3 Dick Smith, London.
	March 31	Bombardier Billy Wells w.ko.5 P. O. 'Nutty' Curran, Plymouth.
	Aug. 26	Bombardier Billy Wells w.ret.9 Dick Smith, Newcastle.
	Dec. 18	*Bombardier Billy Wells w.rsf.2 Dan Voyles, London.
1919	Feb.27	Joe Beckett w.ko.5 Bombardier Billy Wells, London.
	May 26	Frank Goddard w.ret.10 Jack Curphey, London.
	June 17	Joe Beckett w.ko.2 Frank Goddard, London.
1920	March 5	Joe Beckett w.ko.5 Dick Smith, London.
	May 10	Joe Beckett w.ko.3 Bombardier Billy Wells, London.
1921	Sept. 12	Joe Beckett w.rsf.2 Noel 'Boy' McCormick, London.
1923	March 14	Joe Beckett w.ko.17 Dick Smith, London.
	Nov. 21	Frank Goddard w.dis.2 Jack Bloomfield, London.
1924	April 29	Frank Goddard w.ko.6 Jack Stanley, London.
1926	March 18	Phil Scott w.ko.3 Frank Goddard, London.
	April 30	Phil Scott w.ret.10 Noel 'Boy' McCormick, Manchester.
1931	Nov. 16	Reggie Meen w.pts.15 Charlie Smith, Leicester.
1932	July 12	Jack Petersen w.ko.2 Reggie Meen, London.
1933	Jan. 26	Jack Petersen w.ko.12 Jack Pettifer, London.
	July 12	*Jack Petersen w.dis.2 Jack Doyle, London.
	Nov. 30	Len Harvey w.pts.15 Jack Petersen, London.
1934	June 4	Jack Petersen w.ret.12‖ Len Harvey, London.
	Dec. 17	Jack Petersen w.pts.15 George Cook, London.
1936	Jan. 29	Jack Petersen w.pts.15 Len Harvey, London.
	April 23	Jack Petersen w.pts.15 Jock McAvoy, London.
	Aug. 17	Ben Foord w.rsf.3 Jack Petersen, Leicester.
1937	March 15	§Tommy Farr w.pts.15 Ben Foord, London.
1938	Dec. 1	Len Harvey w.dis.4 Eddie Phillips, London.
1944	Sept. 15	Jack London w.pts.15 Freddie Mills, Manchester.
1945	July 17	Bruce Woodcock w.ko.6 Jack London, London.
1949	June 2	Bruce Woodcock w.ko.14 Freddie Mills, London.
1950	Nov. 14	Jack Gardner w.ret.11 Bruce Woodcock, London.
1952	March 11	Johnny Williams w.pts.15 Jack Gardner, London.
1953	May 12	Don Cockell w.pts.15 Johnny Williams, London.
1956	Aug. 27	Joe Erskine w.pts.15 Johnny Williams, Cardiff.
1957	Sept. 17	Joe Erskine w.pts.15 Henry Cooper, London.
1958	June 3	Brian London w.ko.8 Joe Erskine, London.
1959	Jan. 12	Henry Cooper w.pts.15 Brian London, London.
	Nov. 17	Henry Cooper w.rsf.12 Joe Erskine, London.
1961	March 21	*Henry Cooper w.rsf.5‖ Joe Erskine, London.
1962	April 2	Henry Cooper w.rsf.9‖ Joe Erskine, Nottingham.
1963	March 26	Henry Cooper w.pts.5 Dick Richardson, London.
1964	Feb. 24	†Henry Cooper w.pts.15 Brian London, Manchester.
1965	June 15	Henry Cooper w.ret.10 Johnny Prescott, Birmingham.
1967	June 13	Henry Cooper w.rsf.2 Jack Bodell, Wolverhampton.
	Nov. 7	Henry Cooper w.rsf.6‖ Billy Walker, London. *Won 3 Lonsdale Belts outright.*
1969	Oct. 13	Jack Bodell w.pts.15 Carl Gizzi, Nottingham.
1970	March 24	Henry Cooper w.pts.15 Jack Bodell, London.
1971	March 16	Joe Bugner w.pts.15 Henry Cooper, London.
	Sept. 27	Jack Bodell w.pts.15 Joe Bugner, London.
1972	June 27	Danny McAlinden w.ko.2 Jack Bodell, Birmingham.
1975	Jan. 13	Bunny Johnson w.ko.9 Danny McAlinden, London.
	Sept. 30	Richard Dunn w.pts.15 Bunny Johnson, London.
	Nov.3	Richard Dunn w.ko.2 Danny McAlinden, London.
1976	Oct. 12	Joe Bugner w.ko.1 Richard Dunn, London.
1978	Oct. 24	John L. Gardner w.ret.5 Billy Aird, London.
1979	June 26	John L. Gardner w.rsf.6 Paul Sykes, London.
1981	March 30	Gordon Ferris w.pts.15 Billy Aird, Birmingham.
	Oct. 12	Neville Meade w.ko.1 Gordon Ferris, Birmingham. *Won Lonsdale Belt outright.*

Beckett, Scott, Farr, Cooper and Bugner relinquished title. Harvey, Cockell and John L. Gardner retired, Pearce disqualified from boxing.

1983	Sept. 22	David Pearce, w.rsf.9 Cardiff.
1985	Sept. 18	Hughroy Currie w.pts.12 Funso Banjo, London.
1986	April 12	Horace Notice w.rsf.6 Hughroy Currie, Isle of Man.
1987	May 26	Horace Notice w.rsf.5 Dave Garside, London.
1987	Nov. 3	Horace Notice w.ko.3 Paul Lister, Sunderland.
1988	March 9	Horace Notice w.rsf.10 Hughroy Currie, London.

British Cruiserweight Title Fights
(195 pounds: 13 stone 13 pounds)

1985	Oct. 31	Sammy Reeson w.pts.12 Stewart Lithgo, Wandswoth.
1986	Oct. 25	Andy Straughan w.pts.12 Tee Jay, Stevenage.
1987	Feb. 17	Roy Smith w.pts.12 Andy Straughan, Alfreton.
	May 9	Tee Jay w.rs.f.1 Roy Smith, Wandsworth.
1988	Jan. 21	Glenn McCrory w.pts.12 Tee Jay, Battersea.
	April 23	Glenn McCrory w.ret. 8 Lou Gent, Gateshead.

Reeson relinquished title.

British Light-Heavyweight Title Fights
(175 pounds: 12 stone 7 pounds)

1913	June 9	Dennis Haugh w.ko.1 Sid Ellis, London.
	Nov. 10	Dennis Haugh w.rsf.8 Pte. Dan Voyles, London.
1914	Jan. 19	Dennis Haugh w.pts.15 Dick Smith, London.
	March 9	‡Dick Smith w.pts.20 Dennis Haugh, London.
1916	June 5	Dick Smith w.pts.20 Harry Curzon, London.
	Oct. 10	Harry Reeve w.pts.20 Dick Smith, London.
1918	Feb. 25	*Dick Smith w.pts.20 Joe Beckett, London.
1919	April 28	Noel 'Boy' McCormick w.dis.11 Harold Rolph, London.
1922	May 1	Jack Bloomfield w.ret.9 Harry Drake, London.
1925	March 9	Tom Berry w.pts.20 Sid Pape, London.
1927	April 25	Billy 'Gipsy' Daniels w.pts.20 Tom Berry, London.
	Nov. 27	Frank Moody w.pts.20 Ted Moore, London.
1929	Nov. 25	Harry Crossley w.pts.15 Frank Moody, London.

1932 May 23 Jack Petersen w.pts.15 Harry Crossley, London.
1933 June 13 Len Harvey w.pts.15 Eddie Phillips, London. *Billed for June 12 but began after midnight.*
1935 Feb. 4 Eddie Phillips w.pts.15 Tommy Farr, Mountain Ash.
1937 April 27 §Jock McAvoy w.ko.14 Eddie Phillips, London.
1938 April 7 Len Harvey w.pts.15 Jock McAvoy, London.
1939 July 10 Len Harvey w.pts.15 Jock McAvoy, London.
1942 June 20 Freddie Mills w.ko.2 Len Harvey, London.
1950 Oct. 17 Don Cockell w.ko.14 Mark Hart, London.
1951 Oct. 16 Don Cockell w.ko.7 Albert Finch, London.
1952 June 10 Randolph Turpin w.rsf.11 Don Cockell, London.
1953 March 26 Dennis Powell w.ret.11 George Walker, Liverpool.
Oct. 26 Alex Buxton w.rsf.10‖ Dennis Powell, Nottingham.
1954 Nov. 9 Alex Buxton w.ko.8 Albert Finch, Birmingham.
1955 April 26 Randolph Turpin w.ko.2 Alex Buxton, London.
1956 March 13 Ron Barton w.ret.8‖ Albert Finch, London.
Nov. 26 *Randolph Turpin w.rsf.5 Alex Buxton, Leicester.
1957 June 11 Randolph Turpin w.pts.15 Arthur Howard, Leicester.
1960 Jan. 28 Chic Calderwood w.rsf.13 Arthur Howard, Paisley.
1962 Feb. 12 Chic Calderwood w.ko.4 Stan Cullis, London.
1963 July 30 *Chic Calderwood w.ret.11 Ron Redrup, Blackpool.
1964 Nov. 11 Chic Calderwood w.ret.7 Bob Nicolson, Paisley.
1967 June 19 John 'Young' McCormack w.rsf.7‖ Eddie Avoth, London.
Nov. 22 John 'Young' McCormack w.ko.7 Derek Richards, Solihull.
1969 Jan. 13 Eddie Avoth w.ret.11‖ John 'Young' McCormack, London.
1970 April 6 Eddie Avoth w.dis.8 John 'Young' McCormack, Nottingham.
1971 Jan. 24 Chris Finnegan w.rsf.15 Eddie Avoth, London.
1973 March 13 Chris Finnegan w.pts.15 Roy John, London.
May 22 John Conteh w.pts.15 Chris Finnegan, London.
1974 May 21 John Conteh w.rsf.6‖ Chris Finnegan, London.
1975 June 3 Johnny Frankham w.pts.15 Chris Finnegan, London.
Oct. 14 *Chris Finnegan w.pts.15 Johnny Frankham, London.
1976 April 28 Tim Wood w.pts.15 Phil Martin, London.
1977 March 8 Bunny Johnson w.ko.1 Tim Wood, Wolverhampton.
1979 May 13 Bunny Johnson w.ko.4 Rab Affleck, Glasgow.
1980 Feb. 27 *Bunny Johnson w.pts.15 Dennis Andries, Burslem.
1982 March 15 Tom Collins w.pts.15 Dennis Andries, London.
May 26 Tom Collins w.ko.4 Trevor Cattouse, Leeds.
1983 March 9 Tom Collins, w.rsf.6 Antonio Harris, Solihull. *Won Lonsdale Belt outright.*
1984 Jan. 26 Dennis Andries w.pts.12 Tom Collins, London.
April 6 Dennis Andries w.pts.12 Tom Collins, Watford.
Oct. 10 Dennis Andries w.ko.12 Devon Bailey, London. *Won Lonsdale Belt in record time for the light-heavyweight division (258 days).*
1986 Feb. 13 Dennie Andries w.rsf.6 Keith Bristol, Longford.
Sept. 10 Dennis Andries w.rsf.9 Tony Sibson, London.
1987 March 11 Tom Collins w.rsf.10 John Moody, London.
1987 Dec. 15 Tony Wilson w.rsf.6 Blaine Longsden, Cardiff.
1988 May 10 Tony Wilson w.rsf.6 Brian Schumacher, Tottenham.

Reeve, Smith, McCormack, Bloomfield, Daniels, Petersen, Harvey (first time), Turpin (thrice), Conteh, Johnson, Andries and Collins relinquished title. Mills, Barton and Finnegan retired. Calderwood was killed in a car accident.

British Middleweight Title Fights
(160 pounds: 11 stone 6 pounds)

1882 April Charlie Mitchell won competition at Chelsea, London, to decide British title.
1890 Feb. 7 Toff Wall w.pts.12 Bill 'Chesterfield' Goode, London.
1891 March 12 Ted Pritchard w.ko.3 Jack Burke, London.
1894 Nov. 26 Ted Pritchard w.ko.2 Dick Burge, London.
1898 Feb. 25 Anthony Diamond w.pts.12 Dido Plumb, Birmingham.
1900 March 17 Dido Plumb w.ko.8 Australian Jem Ryan, London.
1902 April 14 Jack Palmer w.ko.11 Joe White, Newcastle.
June 2 Jack Palmer w.ko.3 Dave Peters, Merthyr.
Sept. 13 Jack Palmer w.ko.5 Harry 'Slouch' Dixon, Newcastle.
1906 March 19 Pat O'Keefe w.pts.15 Mike Crawley, London.
April 23 Pat O'Keefe w.ko.6 Charlie Allum, London.
May 28 Tom Thomas w.pts.15 Pat O'Keefe, London.
1908 April 30 Tom Thomas w.ko.5 Mike Crawley, London.
June 1 Tom Thomas w.ko.4 James 'Tiger' Smith, London.
Nov. 17 Tom Thomas w.ko.6 Jack Costello, Swansea.

1909 Oct. 5 Tom Thomas w.ret.11 Jack Kingsland, Pontypridd.
Dec. 20 ‡Tom Thomas w.ko.2 Charlie Wilson, London.
1910 Nov. 14 Jim Sullivan w.pts.20 Tom Thomas, London.
1912 May 20 Jack Harrison w.pts.20 Pte. Pat McEnroy, London.
1914 Feb. 23 Pat O'Keefe w.pts.20 Harry Reeve, London.
April 27 Pat O'Keefe w.pts.20 Nichol Simpson, London.
May 25 Pat O'Keefe w.pts.20 Jim Sullivan, London.
1916 Feb. 21 Pat O'Keefe w.pts.20 Jim Sullivan, London.
May 22 Bandsman Jack Blake w.pts.20 Pat O'Keefe, London.
1918 Jan. 28 *Pat O'Keefe w.ko.2 Bandsman Jack Blake, London.
1920 March 11 Ted 'Kid' Lewis w.ko.4 Johnny Bee, London.
March 29 Tom Gummer w.ret.14 Jim Sullivan, London.
1921 March 28 Gus Platts w.ret.6 Tom Gunner, Sheffield.
May 31 Johnny Basham w.pts.20 Gus Platts, London.
June 27 Ted 'Kid' Lewis, p.ts.20 Jack Bloomfield, London.
Oct. 14 Ted 'Kid' Lewis w.ret. 12 Johnny Basham, London.
1922 Nov. 20 Ted 'Kid' Lewis w.pts.20 Roland Todd, London.
1923 Feb. 15 Roland Todd w.pts.20 Ted 'Kid' Lewis, London.
1926 July 12 Tommy Milligan w.rsf.14 George West, London.
Oct. 7 Tommy Milligan w.rsf.14 Ted Moore, London.
1927 Jan. 27 Tommy Milligan w.rsf.14 Ted Moore, London.
Feb. 16 Frank Moody w.pts.15 Roland Todd, London.
1928 March 14 Alex Ireland w.dis.9 Tommy Milligan, Edinburgh.
Aug. 6 Frank Moody w.ko.1 Tommy Milligan, Glasgow.
Sept. 17 Alex Ireland w.pts.15 Frank Moody, Edinburgh.
1929 May 16 Len Harvey w.ko.7 Alex Ireland, London.
Oct. 21 Len Harvey w.pts.15 Jack Hood, London.
Dec. 18 Len Harvey drew 15 Jack Hood, London.
1930 May 22 *Len Harvey w.rsf.9 Steve McCall, London.
1931 June 22 Len Harvey w.pts.15 Jack Hood, London.
1932 March 21 Len Harvey w.pts.15 Jock McAvoy, Manchester.
Dec. 12 Len Harvey w.pts.15 Jack Casey, Newcastle.
1933 April 10 Jock McAvoy w.pts.15 Len Harvey, Manchester.
Oct. 9 Jock McAvoy w.ko.10 Archie Sexton, Manchester.
1935 June 24 *Jock McAvoy w.pts. 15 Al Burke, Manchester.
1937 Oct. 25 §Jock McAvoy w.ret.11 Jack Hyams, Manchester.
1939 May 22 Jock McAvoy w.pts.15 Arthur 'Ginger' Sadd, Manchester.
1945 May 29 Ernie Roderick w.pts. 15 Vince Hawkins, London.
1946 Oct. 28 Vince Hawkins w.pts.15 Ernie Roderick, London.
1948 June 28 Dick Turpin w.pts.15 Vince Hawkins, Birmingham.
1949 June 20 Dick Turpin w.pts.15 Albert Finch, Birmingham.
1950 April 24 Albert Finch w.pts.15 Dick Turpin, Nottingham.
Oct. 17 Randolph Turpin w.ko.5 Albert Finch, London.
1954 Sept. 14 Johnny Sullivan w.ko.1 Gordon Hazell, London.
1955 June 16 Pat McAteer w.dis.9 Johnny Sullivan, Liverpool.
1956 Oct. 8 Pat McAteer w.rsf.4 Lew Lazar, Nottingham.
1957 Sept. 5 *Pat McAteer w.pts.15 Martin Hansen, Liverpool.
1958 Sept. 30 Terry Downes w.rsf.13 Phil Edwards, London.
1959 Sept. 15 John McCormack w.dis.8 Terry Downes, London.
Nov. 3 Terry Downes w.rsf.8 John McCormack, London.
1960 July 5 *Terry Downes w.ret.12 Phil Edwards, London.
1962 Nov. 26 George Aldridge w.ko.6 John McCormack, Manchester.
1963 May 28 Mick Leahy w.rsf.1 George Aldridge, Nottingham.
1964 Dec. 14 Wally Swift w.pts.15 Nick Leahy, Nottingham.
1965 Nov. 8 Johnny Pritchett w.rsf.12 Wally Swift, Nottingham.
1966 March 21 Johnny Pritchett w.ret.13 Nat Jacobs, Nottingham.
1967 Feb. 20 *Johnny Pritchett w.pts. 15 Wally Swift, Nottingham.
1968 Feb. 26 Johnny Pritchett w.pts.15 Les McAteer, Nottingham.
1969 July 14 Les McAteer w.ret.11‖ Wally Swift, Nottingham.
1970 May 12 Mark Rowe w.rsf.14 Les McAteer, London.
Sept. 8 Bunny Sterling w.rsf.4‖ Mark Rowe, London.
1972 Sept. 19 Bunny Sterling w.ko.5 Phil Matthews, Manchester.
1973 Jan. 17 *Bunny Sterling w.rsf.11 Don McMillan, Solihull.
April 17 Bunny Sterling w.pts.15 Mark Rowe, London.
1974 Feb. 11 Kevin Finnegan w.pts.15 Bunny Sterling, London.
1975 June 10 Bunny Sterling w.rsf.8 Maurice Hope, London.
Nov. 4 Alan Minter w.pts.15 Kevin Finnegan, London.
1976 April 27 Alan Minter w.rsf.2 Billy Knight, London.
Sept. 14 *Alan Minter w.pts.15 Kevin Finnegan, London.
1977 May 31 Kevin Finnegan w.rsf.11‖ Frankie Lucas, London.
Nov. 8 Alan Minter w.pts.15 Kevin Finnegan, London.
1979 April 10 Tony Sibson w.rsf.5 Frankie Lucas, London.
Nov. 6 *Kevin Finnegan w.pts.15 Tony Sibson, London.
1981 Feb. 2 Roy Gumbs w.rsf.3 Howard Mills, London.
Oct. 29 Roy Gumbs w.rsf.6 Eddie Burke, Glasgow.
1982 Feb. 18 *Roy Gumbs w.rsf.13 Glen McEwan, Liverpool. *Won Lonsdale Belt outright.*

Palmer, Sullivan (Jim), Harrison, O'Keefe, McAvoy, Turner (Randolph), Sterling, Finnegan, Sibson and Graham relinquished title. Todd, Downes and Minter (twice) forfeited title. McAteer (Pat), Pritchett and Finnegan retired.

1983	Sept. 14	Mark Kaylor w.ko.5 Roy Gumbs, Wembley.
1984	Nov. 27	Tony Sibon w.pts.12 Mark Kaylor, Wembley.
1985	April 24	Herol Graham w.ko.1 Jimmy Price, London.
1986	Oct. 29	Brian Anderson w.rsf.8 Tony Burke, Belfast.
1987	Sept. 16	Tony Sibson w.rsf.7 Brian Anderson, London.
		Won Lonsdale Belt outright.
1988	June 8	Herol Graham w.rsf.5 James Cook, Sheffield.

British Light-Middleweight Title Fights
(154 pounds: 11 stone)

1973	Sept. 25	Larry Paul w.ko.10 Bobby Arthur, Wolverhampton
1974	April 24	Larry Paul w.pts.15 Kevin White, Wolverhampton.
	Nov. 5	Maurice Hope w.ko.8 Larry Paul, Wolverhampton.
1975	Sept. 30	Maurice Hope w.rsf.4 Larry Paul, London.
1976	April 20	*Maurice Hope w.rsf.12‖ Tony Poole, London. *Hope relinquished title.*
1977	Feb. 1	Jimmy Batten w.ret.7 Albert Hillman, London.
	Oct. 25	Jimmy Batten w.rsf.4 Larry Paul, London.
1978	Sept. 12	Jimmy Batten w.ret.13 Tony Poole, London.
1979	Sept. 11	Pat Thomas w.rsf.9 Jimmy Batten, London.
	Dec. 11	Pat Thomas w.ko.7 Dave Proud, Milton Keynes.
1980	Sept. 16	*Pat Thomas w.rsf.15 Steve Hopkin, London.
1981	March 24	Herol Graham w.pts.15 Pat Thomas, Sheffield.
1982	Feb. 24	Herol Graham w.rsf.9 Chris Christian, Sheffield.
		Graham relinquished title.
1983	Oct. 11	Prince Rodney w.rsf.6 Jimmy Batten, London.
1984	Feb. 22	Jimmy Cable w.pts.12 Nick Wilshire, London.
1985	Feb. 20	Jimmy Cable w.pts.12 Gary Cooper, London.
	May 11	Prince Rodney w.ko.1 Jimmy Cable, Hasting.
	Sept. 7	Prince Rodney w.pts.12 Mick Courtney, Isle of Man.
		Won Lonsdale Belt outright.
1986	Feb. 19	Chris Pyatt w.ko.10 Prince Rodney, London.
1987	March 11	Lloyd Hibbert w.pts.12 Nick Wilshire, London.
1988	Feb. 3	Gary Cooper w.pts.12 Michael Harris, Wembley.
		Rodney (in 1983), Pyatt and Hibbert relinquished title.

British Welterweight Title Fights
(147 pounds: 10 stone 7 pounds)

1903	Jan. 2	Pat O'Keefe outpointed Jack Kingsland in final of 10 st. 7 lbs. Competition recognised as for the British welterweight title, at Olympia, London.
	Nov. 16	Charlie Allum w.ko.9 Charlie Knock, London.
1906	May 21	Charlie Knock w.rsf.17 Robert 'Curley' Watson, London.
	Dec. 17	Robert 'Curley' Watson w.pts.10 Charlie Knock, London.
1907	Feb. 11	Robert 'Curley' Watson w.pts.20 Andrew Jephtha, London.
	March 25	Andrew Jephtha w.ko.4 Robert 'Curley' Watson, London.
	Aug. 8	Joe White w.pts.15 Andrew Jephtha, Cardiff.
	Nov. 18	Robert 'Curley' Watson w.pts.15 Andrew Jephtha, London.
1908	April 18	Robert 'Curley' Watson w.pts.10 Charlie Knock, London.
	May 21	Joe White w.pts.20 Robert 'Curley' Watson, Liverpool.
	Oct. 19	Aschel 'Young' Joseph w.pts.15 L/Cpl. Baker, London.
1910	March 21	‡Aschel 'Young' Joseph w.dis.11 Jack Goldswain, London.
1911	Jan. 23	Arthur Evernden w.dis.3 Aschel 'Young' Joseph, London.
1912	April 11	Johnny Summers w.pts.20 Aschel 'Young' Joseph, Liverpool.
	June 17	Johnny Summers w.rsf.13 Arthur Evernden, London.
	Dec. 9	Johnny Summers w.pts.20 Sid Burns, London.
1914	Jan. 10	Tom McCormick w.pts.20 Johnny Summers, Sydney, Australia.
	Feb. 14	Tom McCormick w.ko.1 Johnny Summers, Sydney, Australia.
	March 21	Matt Wells w.pts.20 Tom McCormick, Sydney, Australia.
	Dec. 14	Johnny Basham w.ko.14 Johnny Summers, London.
1915	May 10	Johnny Basham w.rsf.13 Tom McCormick, London.
1916	May 1	*Johnny Basham w.rsf.19 Eddie Beattie, London.
1919	Nov. 13	Johnny Basham w.pts.20 Matt Wells, London.
1920	June 9	Ted 'Kid' Lewis w.ko.9 Johnny Basham, London.
	Nov. 19	Ted 'Kid' Lewis w.ko.19 Johnny Basham, London.
1924	July 3	Ted 'Kid' Lewis w.pts.20 Hamilton Johnny Brown, London.

	Nov. 26	Tommy Milligan w.pts.20 Ted 'Kid' Lewis, Edinburgh.
1925	Oct. 8	Hamilton Johnny Brown w.pts.20 Harry Mason, London.
	Nov. 19	Harry Mason w.pts.20 Hamilton Johnny Brown, London.
1926	April 29	Harry Mason drew 20 Len Harvey, London.
	May 31	Jack Hood w.pts.20 Harry Mason, London.
	July 22	Jack Hood w.pts.20 Harry Mason, London.
1928	June 25	Jack Hood w.pts.15 Alf Mancini, Birmingham.
1933	March 13	*Jack Hood w.ko.9 Stoker George Reynolds, Birmingham.
1934	June 11	Harry Mason w.dis.14 Len 'Tiger' Smith, Birmingham.
	Dec. 17	Pat Butler w.pts.15 Harry Mason, Leicester.
1936	April 23	Dave McCleave w.pts.15 Chuck Parker, London.
	June 2	Jake Kilrain w.ko.8 Dave McCleave, Glasgow.
1938	Feb. 21	§Jake Kilrain w.pts.15 Jack Lord, Manchester.
1939	March 23	Ernie Roderick w.ko.7 Jake Kilrain, Liverpool.
1940	July 13	Ernie Roderick w.pts.15 Norman Snow, Northampton.
1941	Sept. 29	*Ernie Roderick w.pts.15 Arthur Danahar, London.
1947	Sept. 8	Ernie Roderick w.pts.15 Gwyn Williams, London.
	Dec. 9	Ernie Roderick w.pts.15 Eric Boon, London.
1948	Nov. 8	Henry Hall w.pts.15 Ernie Roderick, London.
1949	Nov. 15	Eddie Thomas w.pts.15 Henry Hall, London.
1950	Sept. 13	Eddie Thomas w.pts.15 Cliff Curvis, Swansea.
1951	Oct. 16	Wally Thom w.pts.15 Eddie Thomas, London.
1952	July 24	Cliff Curvis w.ko.9 Wally Thom, Liverpool.
1953	Sept. 24	Wally Thom w.pts.15 Peter Fallon, Liverpool.
1954	Oct. 19	*Wally Thom w.ko.6 Lew Lazar, London.
1956	June 5	Peter Waterman w.ret.5‖ Wally Thom, London.
	Dec. 17	Peter Waterman w.ret.10‖ Frank Johnson, Birmingham.
1958	July 15	Tommy Molloy w.pts.15 Jimmy Newman, London.
1959	Oct. 14	Tommy Molloy w.rsf.12 Albert Carroll, Liverpool.
1960	Feb. 1	Wally Swift w.pts.15 Tommy Molloy, Nottingham.
	Nov. 21	Brian Curvis w.pts.15 Wally Swift, Nottingham.
1961	May 8	Brian Curvis w.pts.15 Wally Swift, Nottingham.
	Oct. 31	*Brian Curvis w.ko.8 Mick Leahy, London.
1962	Feb. 20	Brian Curvis w.rsf.5 Tony Mancini, London.
1963	Feb. 12	Brian Curvis w.rsf.10 Tony Smith, London.
1964	July 28	†Brian Curvis w.ret.5 Johnny Cooke, Porthcawl.
1965	Nov. 25	Brian Curvis w.rsf.12 Sammy McSpadden, Cardiff.
1967	Feb. 13	Johnny Cooke w.pts.15 Brian McCaffrey, Manchester.
	May 9	Johnny Cooke w.pts. 15 Shaun Doyle, Liverpool.
1968	Feb. 20	Ralph Charles w.pts.15 Johnny Cooke, London.
1969	Nov. 11	Ralph Charles w.ko.5 Chuck Henderson, London.
1971	Dec. 7	*Ralph Charles w.rsf.8 Bernie Terrell, London.
1972	Oct. 31	Bobby Arthur w.dis.7 John H. Stracey, London.
1973	June 5	John H. Stracey w.ko.4 Bobby Arthur, London.
1975	Dec. 15	Pat Thomas w.ko.13 Pat McCormack, London.
1976	Sept. 23	Pat Thomas w.pts.15 Trevor Francis, London.
	Dec. 7	Henry Rhiney w.rsf.8 Pat Thomas, Luton.
1978	Feb. 13	Henry Rhiney w.pts.15 Billy Walth, Barnsley.
1979	April 4	Kirkland Laing w.rsf.10 Henry Rhiney, Birmingham.
1980	April 1	Colin Jones w.rsf.9 Kirkland Laing, London.
	Aug. 12	Colin Jones w.rsf.5 Peter Neal, Gowerton.
1981	April 28	*Colin Jones w.rsf.9 Kirkland Laing, London.
		Won Lonsdale Belt outright.
1983	April 5	Lloyd Honeyghan w.pts.12 Cliff Gilpin, London.
	Dec. 6	Lloyd Honeyghan w.pts.12 Cliff Gilpin, London.
1985	April 13	Kostas Petrou w.rsf.9 Rocky Kelly, Darlington.
	Sept. 18	Sylvester Mittee w.pts.12 Kostas Petrou, London.
	Nov. 1	Lloyd Honeyghan w.rsf.8 Sylvester Mittee, London.
1987	March 14	Kirkland Laing w.rsf.5 Sylvester Mittee, London.
	Nov. 26	Kirkland Laing w.rsf.5 Rocky Kelly, London.

Milligan, Hood, Curvis (Cliff), Waterman, Charles, Stracey, Jones and Honeyghan (twice) relinquished title. Curvis (Brian) retired.

British Junior-Welterweight Title Fights
(140 pounds: 10 stone)

1968	Feb. 27	Des Rea w.pts.15 Vic Andreetti, London.
1969	Feb. 17	Vic Andreetti w.pts.15 Des Rea, Nottingham.
	Oct. 13	Vic Andreetti w.ko.4 Des Rea, Nottingham.
		Division abolished

British Light-Welterweight Title Fights
(140 pounds: 10 stone)

1973	Nov. 27	Des Morrison w.pts.15 Joe Tetteh, London.
1974	March 26	Pat McCormack w.ko.11 Des Morrison, London.
	Nov. 21	Joey Singleton w.pts.15 Pat McCormack, Liverpool.
1975	Sept. 30	Joey Singleton w.rsf.9 Alan Salter, London.

	Nov. 11	*Joey Singleton w.pts.15 Des Morrison, Manchester.
1976	June 1	Dave Green w.rsf.6 Joey Singleton, London.
1977	Oct. 19	Colin Power w.rsf.10 Des Morrison, London.
1978	Feb. 27	Colin Power w.rsf.7 Chris Walker, Sheffield.
	Oct. 11	Clinton McKenzie w.rsf.10 Jim Montague, Belfast.
1979	Feb. 6	*Colin Power w.pts.15 Clinton McKenzie, London.
	Sept. 11	Clinton McKenzie w.pts.15 Colin Power, London.
1981	Jan 6	*Clinton McKenzie w.rsf.14 Des Morrison, London.
	March 31	Clinton McKenzie w.pts.15 Sylvester Mittee, London.
1982	Feb. 16	Clinton McKenzie w.rsf.4 Steve Early, London.
1983	Aug. 4	Clinton McKenzie w.pts.12 Alan Lamb, Liverpool.
	Sept. 19	Terry Marsh w.pts.12 Clinton McKenzie, London.
1986	May 7	Tony Laing w.pts.12 Clinton McKenzie, London.
1986	Sept. 20	Tony McKenzie w.rsf.3 Clinton McKenzie, Hemel Hempstead.
	Oct. 25	Tony McKenzie w.ko.10 Michael Harris, Stevenage.
1987	Jan. 28	Lloyd Christie w.rsf.3, Tony McKenzie, Croydon
	Jun. 17	Lloyd Christie w.rsf.12, Mo Hussein, London. *Won Lonsdale Belt outright.*
	Nov. 19	Lloyd Christie w.ko.1 Chris Blake, London.

Marsh and Laing relinquished title.

British Lightweight Title Fights

(135 pounds: 9 stone 9 pounds)

1884	Dec. 20	Jem Carney w.ko.45 Jake Hyams, London.
1891	May 25	Dick Burge w.dis.11 Jem Carney, London.
1892	June 27	Dick Burge w.ko.2 Jackie Thompson, London.
1894	May 4	Dick Burge w.ko.28 Harry Nickless, London.
1897	May 31	Tom Causer w.ret.7 Dick Burge, London.
	Oct. 8	Dick Burge w.ko.1 Tom Causer, London.
1898	April 25	Johnny Hughes w.pts.20 Jim Curran, London.
1899	Nov. 20	Jabez White w.ko.8 Harry Greenfield, London.
1901	Dec. 23	Jabez White drew 20 Jim Curran, Birmingham.
1902	April 21	Jabez White w.ko.6 Bill Chester, London.
1906	April 23	Jack Goldswain w.pts.20 Jabez White, London.
1907	Feb. 11	Jack Goldswain w.ko.5 Pat Daly, London.
1908	Nov. 23	Johnny Summers w.rsf.14 Jack Goldswain, London.
1909	Nov. 8	‡Freddie Welsh w.pts.20 Johnny Summers, London.
1911	Feb. 27	Matt Wells w.pts.20 Freddie Welsh, London.
1912	Nov. 11	*Freddie Welsh w.pts.20 Matt Wells, London.
1919	June 23	Bob Marriott w.dis.10 Johnny Summers, London.
1921	April 11	Ernie Rice w.ko.7 Ben Callicott, London.
1922	Sept. 18	Seaman James Hall w.pts.20 Ernie Rice, Liverpool.
1923	Jan. 2	Seaman James Hall w.pts.20 Hamilton Johnny Brown, Edinburgh.
	May 17	Harry Mason w.dis.13 Seaman James Hall, London.
	Nov. 21	Harry Mason w.pts.20 Ernie Rice, London.
1924	Nov. 24	Ernie Izzard w.pts.20 Jack Kirk, London.
1925	April 27	Ernie Izzard w.pts.20 Teddy Baker, London.
	June 22	Harry Mason w.rsf.9 Ernie Izzard, London.
1926	Feb. 11	Harry Mason w.dis.5 Ernie Rice, London.
1928	Sept. 17	Sam Steward w.ko.12 Ernie Rice, London.
1929	May 2	Fred Webster w.pts.15 Sam Steward, London.
1930	May 21	Al Foreman w.ko.1 Fred Webster, London.
	Oct. 20	Al Foreman w.ko.6 George Rose, Manchester.
	Dec. 15	Al Foreman drew 15 Johnny Cuthbert, London. *Foreman absconded with 2nd N.S.C. Lonsdale Belt.*
1932	Aug. 11	Johnny Cuthbert w.rsf.10 Jim Hunter, Glasgow.
1934	Jan. 18	Harry Mizler w.pts.15 Johnny Cuthbert, London.
	Aug. 4	Harry Mizler w.pts.15 Billy Quinlan, Swansea.
	Oct. 29	Jack 'Kid' Berg w.rsf.10 Harry Mizler, London.
1936	April 24	Jimmy Walsh w.rsf.9 Jack 'Kid' Berg, Liverpool.
	Oct. 19	§Jimmy Walsh w.pts.15 Harry Mizler, London.
1938	June 26	Dave Crowley w.pts.15 Jimmy Walsh, Liverpool.
	Dec. 15	Eric Boon w.ko.13 Dave Crowley, London.
1939	Feb. 23	Eric Boon w.rsf.14 Arthur Danahar, London.
	Dec. 9	*Eric Boon w.ko.7 Dave Crowley, London.
1944	Aug. 12	Ronnie James w.ko.10 Eric Boon, Cardiff.
1947	Oct. 16	Billy Thompson w.rsf.3 Stan Hawthorne, Liverpool.
1949	May 18	Billy Thompson w.rsf.5 Harry Hughes, Glasgow.
1950	July 11	*Billy Thompson w.pts.15 Tommy McGovern, Hanley.
1951	Aug. 28	Tommy McGovern w.ko.1 Billy Thompson, London.
1952	July 25	Frank Johnson w.pts.15 Tommy McGovern, Manchester.
1953	Sept. 29	Joe Lucy w.pts.15 Tommy McGovern, London.
1955	April 26	Frank Johnson w.pts.15 Joe Lucy, London.
1956	April 13	Joe Lucy w.rsf.8‖ Frank Johnson, Manchester.
	June 26	*Joe Lucy w.rsf.13 Sammy McCarthy, London.
1957	April 9	Dave Charnley w.pts.15 Joe Lucy, London.
1961	Nov. 20	Dave Charnley, w.ko.1 David 'Darkie' Hughes, Nottingham.
1963	May 20	*Dave Charnley w.pts.15 Maurice Cullen, Manchester.
1965	April 8	Maurice Cullen w.pts.15 Dave Coventry, Liverpool.
	Nov. 30	Maurice Cullen w.pts.15 Vic Andreetti, Wolverhampton.
1966	June 6	*Maurice Cullen w.rsf.5 Terry Edwards, Newcastle.
1967	April 25	Maurice Cullen w.pts.15 Vic Andreetti, Newcastle.
1968	Feb. 19	Ken Buchanan w.ko.11 Maurice Cullen, London.
1970	May 12	Ken Buchanan w.ko.5 Brian Hudson, London.
1972	Feb. 1	Willie Reilly w.rsf.10 Jim Watt, Nottingham.
	May 3	Jim Watt w.rsf.12 Tony Riley, Solihull.
1973	Jan. 29	*Ken Buchanan w.pts.15 Jim Watt, Glasgow.
1975	Jan. 27	Jim Watt w.rsf.7 Johnny Cheshire, Glasgow.
1977	Feb. 21	*Jim Watt w.rsf.10 Johnny Claydon, Glasgow.
1978	Feb. 28	Charlie Nash w.rsf.12 Johnny Claydon, Londonderry.
1980	March 24	Ray Cattouse w.rsf.8 Dave McCabe, Glasgow.
1981	March 23	Ray Cattouse w.rsf.15 Dave McCabe, Glasgow.
1982	Oct. 12	George Feeney w.rsf.14 Ray Cattouse, London.
1983	Dec. 3	George Feeney w.rsf.11 Tony Willis, London.
1984	Feb. 10	George Feeney w.pts.12 Paul Chance, Dudley. *Won Lonsdale Belt outright and relinquished title.*
1985	May 16	Tony Willis w.pts.12 Ian McLeod, Digbeth.
	Nov. 14	Tony Willis w.rsf.5 Paul Chance, Dudley.
1986	May 24	Tony Willis w.rsf.9 Steve Boyle, Manchester. *Won Lonsdale Belt outright.*
1987	Sept. 24	Alex Dickson w.pts.12 Tony Willis, Glasgow.
1988	Feb. 24	Steve Boyle w.ko.2 Alex Dickson, Glasgow.

Welsh, Marriott, Mason (second time), Foreman, Buchanan (twice), Watt and Nash relinquished title. Mason (first time), James, Johnson (first time), and Reilly forfeited title. Charnley retired.

British Junior-Lightweight Title Fights

(130 pounds: 9 stone 4 pounds)

1968	Feb. 20	Jimmy Anderson w.rsf.9 Jimmy Revie, London.
	Oct. 8	Jimmy Anderson w.pts.15 Brian Cartwright, London.
1969	Feb. 25	Jimmy Anderson w.rsf.7 Colin Lake, London.

Division abolished

British Super-Featherweight Titles

1986	Jan. 16	John Doherty w.pts.12 Pat Doherty, Preston.
1986	April 17	Pat Cowdell w.rsf.6 John Doherty, Bradford.
	May 24	Najib Daho w.ko.1 Pat Cowdell, Manchester.
1987	Oct. 26	Pat Cowdell w.rsf.8 Najib Daho, Birmingham.
1988	May 18	Floyd Harvard w.rsf.8 Pat Cowdell, Aberavon.

British Featherweight Title Fights

(126 pounds: 9 stone)

1895	April 29	Fred Johnson w.ko.4 Charlie Beadling, Newcastle.
1897	Feb. 22	Ben Jordan w.rsf.13 Fred Johnson, London.
1899	May 29	Ben Jordan w.ko.9 Harry Greenfield, London.
1900	Jan. 22	Will Curley w.pts.20 Nat Smith, Newcastle.
1901	Jan. 21	Jack Roberts w.ko.7 Will Curley, London.
1902	Oct. 20	Ben Jordan w.ko.5 Jack Roberts, London.
1904	Dec. 12	Ben Jordan w.pts.15 Tom 'Pedlar' Palmer, London.
1905	March 20	Joe Bowker w.ko.12 Tom 'Pedlar' Palmer, London.
	Oct. 23	Joe Bowker w.pts.20 Frank 'Spike' Robson, London.
1906	Jan. 29	Johnny Summers w.pts.20 Frank 'Spike' Robson, London.
	March 19	Johnny Summers w.pts.20 Seaman Arthur Hayes, London.
	May 28	Jim Driscoll w.pts.15 Joe Bowker, London.
	Oct. 1	Johnny Summers w.pts.20 Boss Edwards, London.
	Dec. 17	Frank 'Spike' Robson w.dis.4 Johnny Summers, London.
1907	June 1	Jim Driscoll w.ko.17 Joe Bowker, London.
1910	Feb. 14	‡Jim Driscoll w.rsf.6 Seaman Arthur Hayes, London.
	April 18	Jim Driscoll w.ko.15 Frank 'Spike' Robson, London.
1911	Jan. 30	*Jim Driscoll w.rsf.11 Frank 'Spike' Robson, London.
1913	Jan. 27	Jim Driscoll drew20 Owen Moran, London.
	Oct. 6	Ted 'Kid' Lewis w.rsf.17 Alec Lambert, London.
1915	May 31	Llew Edwards w.dis.10 Owen Moran, London.
1917	June 4	Charlie Hardcastle w.ko.1 Alf Wye, London.
	Nov. 5	James 'Tancy' Lee w.ko.4 Charlie Hardcastle, London.
1918	Oct. 21	James 'Tancy' Lee w.ko.7 Joe Conn, London.
1919	Feb. 24	*James 'Tancy' Lee, w.pts.20 Danny Morgan, London.
1920	Jan. 26	Mike Honeyman w.pts.20 Billy Marchant, London.
	Oct. 25	Mike Honeyman w.ret.19 James 'Tancy' Lee, London.

1921	Oct. 31	Joe Fox w.pts.20 Mike Honeyman, London.
1924	June 2	George McKenzie w.pts.20 Harry Leach, London.
	Dec. 15	George McKenzie w.pts.20 Harry Leach, London.
1925	March 30	Johnny Curley w.pts.20 George McKenzie, London.
1926	March 29	Johnny Curley w.pts.20 Harry Corbett, London.
	Nov. 1	Johnny Curley w.pts.20 Billy Hindley, Manchester.
1927	Jan. 24	Johnny Cuthbert w.pts.20 Johnny Curley, London.
1928	March 12	Harry Corbett w.pts.20 Johnny Cuthbert, London.
1929	March 18	Harry Corbett drew 15 Johnny Cuthbert, London.
	May 16	Johnny Cuthbert w.pts.15 Harry Corbett, London.
1930	May 22	*Johnny Cuthbert w.pts.15 Dom Volante, London.
	Nov. 6	Johnny Cuthbert drew 15 Nel Tarleton, Liverpool.
1931	Oct. 1	Nel Tarleton w.pts.15 Johnny Cuthbert, Liverpool.
1932	Nov. 10	Seaman Tommy Watson w.pts.15 Nel Tarleton, Liverpool.
1934	March 21	Seaman Tommy Watson w.pts.15 Johnny McMillan, Glasgow.
	July 26	Nel Tarleton w.pts.15 Seaman Tommy Watson, Liverpool.
	Dec. 12	*Nel Tarleton w.pts.15 Dave Crowley, London.
1936	May 6	Nel Tarleton w.pts.15 Johnny King, Liverpool.
	Sept. 24	§Johnny McCrory w.pts.15 Nel Tarleton, Liverpool.
1938	Nov. 23	Jim 'Spider' Kelly, w.pts. 15 Benny Caplan, Belfast.
1939	June 28	Johnny Cusick w.rsf.12 Jim 'Spider' Kelly, Belfast.
1940	Feb. 1	Nel Tarleton w.pts.15 Johnny Cusick, Liverpool.
	Nov. 2	Nel Tarleton w.pts.15 Tom Smith, Liverpool.
1945	Feb. 23	†Nel Tarleton w.pts.15 Al Phillips, Manchester.
1947	Sept. 11	Ronnie Clayton w.pts.15 Al Phillips, Liverpool.
1949	April 11	Ronnie Clayton w.pts.15 Johnny Molloy, Nottingham.
1950	Nov. 28	*Ronnie Clayton w.pts.15 Jim Kenny, London.
1951	Feb. 26	Ronnie Clayton w.pts.15 Al Phillips, Nottingham.
1952	June 30	Ronnie Clayton w.rsf.5 Dai Davies, Abergavenny.
1953	May 12	†Ronnie Clayton w.ko.4 Freddie King, London.
1954	June 1	Sammy McCarthy w.ret.8 Ronnie Clayton, London.
1955	Jan. 22	Billy 'Spider' Kelly w.pts.15 Sammy McCarthy, Belfast.
1956	Feb. 4	Charlie Hill w.pts.15 Billy 'Spider' Kelly, Belfast.
1957	Oct. 7	Charlie Hill w.ko.10 Jimmy Brown, Nottingham.
1958	July 2	*Charlie Hill w.ret.11 Chic Brogan, Glasgow.
1959	April 13	Bobby Neill w.rsf.9 Charlie Hill, Nottingham.
1960	Sept. 27	Terry Spinks w.rsf.7‖ Bobby Neill, London.
	Nov. 22	Terry Spinks w.ko.14 Bobby Neill, London.
1961	May 2	Howard Winstone w.ret.10 Terry Spinks, London.
1962	April 10	Howard Winstone w.rsf.14‖ Derry Treanor, London.
	May 30	*Howard Winstone w.ret.6 Harry Carroll, Cardiff.
1963	Jan. 31	Howard Winstone w.rsf.11 Johnny Morrissey, Glasgow.
	Aug. 20	Howard Windstone w.pts.15 Billy Calvert, Porthcawl.
	Dec. 9	†Howard Winstone w.pts.15 John O'Brien, London.
1966	Dec. 7	Howard Winstone w.rsf.8 Lennie Williams, Aberavon.
1969	March 24	Jimmy Revie w.rsf.5 John O'Brien, London.
1970	Sept. 8	Jimmy Revie w.pts.15 Alan Rudkin, London.
1971	July 5	Evan Armstrong w.ko.12 Jimmy Revie, London.
1972	April 18	Evan Armstrong w.rsf.6 Howard Hayes, Nottingham.
	Sept. 25	Tommy Glencross w.pts.15 Evan Armstrong, London.
1973	Sept. 17	*Evan Armstrong w.rsf.3‖ Tommy Glencross, Glasgow.
1974	July 8	Evan Armstrong w.rsf.11 Alan Richardson, London.
1975	March 25	Vernon Sollas w.ko.4 Jimmy Revie, London.
1977	March 15	Alan Richardson w.rsf.3 Vernon Sollas, Leeds.
	Oct. 3	Alan Richardson w.pts.15 Les Pickett, Aberavon.
1978	April 20	Dave Needham w.pts.15 Alan Richardson, London.
1979	Sept. 18	Dave Needham w.pts.15 Pat Cowdell, Wolverhampton.
	Nov. 6	Pat Cowdell w.pts.15 Dave Needham, London.
1980	Feb. 19	Pat Cowdell w.ret.11 Jimmy Flint, London.
	May 29	*Pat Cowdell w.ret.12 Dave Needham, Wolverhampton.
		Cowdell won Lonsdale Belt outright.
1982	Sept. 29	Steve Sims w.ko.12 Terry McKeown, Glasgow.
1983	April 12	Barry McGuigan w.rsf.2 Vernon Penprase, Belfast.
1984	Dec. 19	Barry McGuigan w.ko.4 Clyde Ruan, Belfast.
1986	April 9	Robert Dickie w.pts.12 John Feeney, London.
	July 30	Robert Dickie w.ko.5 Steve Simms, Ebbw Vale.
	Oct. 29	Robert Dickie w.pts.12 John Feeney, Ebbw Vale.
		Dickie won Lonsdale Belt outright in record time – 203 days.
1988	Feb. 24	Peter Harris w.pts.12 Kevin Taylor, Aberavon.
	May 18	Paul Hodkinson w.rsf.12 Peter Harris, Aberavon.

Bowker, Driscoll, Lewis, Edwards, Lee, Fox, McCrory, Tarleton, Cowdell, Sims and McGuigan relinquished title. Dickie forfeited title through inability to defend owing to road accident. Winstone and Armstrong retired.

British Bantamweight Title Fights
(118 pounds: 8 stone 8 pounds)

1891	April 2	Billy Plimmer w.ret.15 Jem Stevens, London.
1895	May 28	Billy Plimmer w.ko.7 George Corfield, London.
	Nov. 25	Tom 'Pedlar' Palmer w.dis.14 Billy Plimmer, London.
1898	Feb. 25	Joe Barrett w.pts.12 Joe Elms, Birmingham.
	Dec. 12	Tom 'Pedlar' Palmer w.rsf.17 Billy Plimmer, London.
1900	May 28	Tom 'Pedlar' Palmer w.pts.15 Harry Ware, London.
	Nov. 12	Harry Ware w.pts.20 Tom 'Pedlar' Palmer, London.
1902	Feb. 13	Andrew Tokell w.pts.20 Harry Ware, London.
	May 12	Andrew Tokell w.pts.20 Jim Williams, London.
	Sept. 8	Harry Ware w.dis.8 Andrew Tokell, London.
	Dec. 15	Joe Bowker w.pts.15 Harry Ware, London.
1903	May 25	Joe Bowker w.pts.15 Andrew Tokell, London.
	Oct. 3	Joe Bowker w.pts.15 Bill King, London.
1904	May 30	Joe Bowker w.pts.20 Owen Moran, London.
1910	Oct. 17	‡George 'Digger' Stanley w.ko.8 Joe Bowker, London.
	Dec. 5	George 'Digger' Stanley w.pts.20 Johnny Condon, London.
1911	Sept. 14	George 'Digger' Stanley w.pts.20 Ike Bradley, Liverpool.
1912	Oct. 21	George 'Digger' Stanley w.pts.20 Alex Lafferty, London.
1913	June 2	Bill Beynon w.pts.20 George 'Digger' Stanley, London.
	Oct. 27	*George 'Digger' Stanley w.pts.20 Bill Beynon, London.
1914	April 20	Con 'Curley' Walker w.dis.13 George 'Digger' Stanley, London.
1915	Nov. 22	Joe Fox w.rsf.16 Jimmy Berry, London.
1916	April 17	Joe Fox w.pts.20 Tommy Harrison, London.
1917	June 25	*Joe Fox w.rsf.18 Joe Symonds, London.
1918	Nov. 25	Tommy Noble w.pts.20 Joe Symonds, London.
1919	June 30	Walter Ross w.rsf.10 Tommy Noble, London.
1920	Feb. 23	Jim Higgins w.rsf.13 Harold Jones, London.
	Nov. 29	Jim Higgins w.pts.20 Billy Eynon, London.
1921	Jan. 31	*Jim Higgins w.pts.20 Ernie 'Kid' Symonds, London.
1922	June 26	Tommy Harrison w.ko.13 Jim Higgins, Liverpool.
1923	Feb. 26	Bugler Harry Lake w.pts.20 Tommy Harrison, London.
	Nov. 26	Johnny Brown w.pts.20 Bugler Harry Lake, London.
1925	Feb. 23	Johnny Brown w.ret.16 Harry Corbett, London.
	Oct. 19	*Johnny Brown w.ko.12 Mick Hill, London.
1928	June 4	Alf 'Kid' Pattenden w.ko.12 George 'Kid' Nicholson, London.
	Aug. 29	Teddy Baldock w.rsf.2 Johnny Brown, London.
	Nov. 25	Alf 'Kid' Pattenden w.ret.12 Young Johnny Brown, London.
1929	May 16	Teddy Baldock w.pts.15 Alf 'Kid' Pattenden, London.
1931	Dec. 21	Dick Corbett w.pts.15 Johnny King, Manchester.
1932	Oct. 10	Johnny King w.pts.15 Dick Corbett, Manchester.
1934	Feb. 12	Dick Corbett w.pts.15 Johnny King, Manchester.
	Aug. 20	Dick Corbett drew 15 Johnny King, London.
1935	May 27	*Johnny King w.pts.15 Len Hampston, Manchester.
1937	May 31	§Johnny King w.ko.13 Jackie Brown, Manchester.
1938	June 22	†Johnny King w.dis.3 Len Hampston, Leeds.
1947	Feb. 10	Jackie Paterson w.ko.7 Johnny King, Manchester.
	Oct. 20	Jackie Paterson w.ko.5 Norman Lewis, London.
1949	March 24	Stan Rowan w.pts.15 Jackie Paterson, Liverpool.
	Dec. 13	Danny O'Sullivan w.ret.9‖ Teddy Gardner, London.
1951	May 9	Peter Keenan w.ko.6 Danny O'Sullivan, Glasgow.
	June 27	Peter Keenan w.rsf.12 Bobby Boland, Glasgow.
1953	Jan. 28	*Peter Keenan w.rsf.7 Frank Williams, Paisley.
	Oct. 3	John Kelly w.pts.15 Peter Keenan, Belfast.
1954	Sept. 21	Peter Keenan w.ko.6 John Kelly, Paisley.
	Dec. 11	Peter Keenan w.pts.15 George O'Neill, Belfast.
1957	May 22	†Peter Keenan w.rsf.6 John Smillie, Glasgow.
1959	Jan. 10	Freddie Gilroy w.rsf.11 Peter Keenan, Belfast.
1960	Mar. 19	Freddie Gilroy w.rsf.13‖ Billy Rafferty, Belfast.
1962	Mar. 3	*Freddie Gilroy w.ko.12 Billy Rafferty, Belfast.
	Oct. 20	Freddie Gilroy w.ret.9‖ John Caldwell, Belfast.
1964	March 5	John Caldwell w.rsf.7‖ George Bowes, Belfast
1965	March 22	Alan Rudskin w.rsf.10‖ John Caldwell, London.
1966	Sept. 6	Walter McGowan w.pts.15 Alan Rudkin, London.
1968	May 13	Alan Rudkin w.pts.15 Walter McGowan, Manchester.
1969	June 9	*Alan Rudkin w.ret.11 Evan Armstrong, Manchester.
1970	April 21	Alan Rudkin w.rsf.12 Johnny Clark, London.
1972	Jan. 25	Alan Rudkin w.pts.15 Johnny Clark, London.
1973	Feb. 20	Johnny Clark w.pts.15 Paddy Maguire, London.
1974	Dec. 10	Dave Needham w.pts.15 Paddy Maguire, Nottingham.
1975	Oct. 20	Paddy Maguire w.rsf.14 Dave Needham, London.
1977	Nov. 29	Johnny Owen w.rsf.11 Paddy Maguire, London.

1978	April 6	Johnny Owen w.rsf.10 Wayne Evans, Ebbw Vale.
1979	June 13	*Johnny Owen w.ret.12 Dave Smith, Caerphilly.
1980	June 28	Johnny Owen w.pts.15 John Feeney, London.
1981	Sept. 22	John Feeney w.rsf.8 Dave Smith, London.
1983	Jan. 25	Hugh Russell w.dis.13 John Feeney, Belfast.
	March 2	Dave Larmour w.pts.12 Hugh Russell, Belfast.
	Nov. 16	John Feeney w.rsf.3 Dave Larmour, Belfast.
1985	June 13	Ray Gilbody w.rsf.8 John Farrell, London.
1987	Feb. 19	Bill Hardy w.rsf.3 Ray Gilbody, St. Helens.
1988	March 17	Bill Hardy w.ko.2 John Hyland, Sunderland.

Walker, Fox, Ross, Baldock, Corbert (Dick), Rowan, Gilroy, and Clark relinquished title, Rudkin retired. Owen died following contest for world title.

British Flyweight Title Fights
(112 pounds: 8 stone)

1897	March 7	Jack Walker won 8 stone Competition at Holloway Baths, London.
1898		Charlie Exall w.pts.20 Jack Walker.
	April 4	Charlie Exall w.dis.17 Harry Brodigan, Gateshead.
1899		Mike Riley w.pts.20 Charlie Exall, London.
1900	Jan 29	Matt Precious w.ko.9 Mike Riley, London.
1903	May 25	Owen Moran w.pts.15 Jack Walker, London.
	Dec. 14	George 'Digger' Stanley w.pts.15 Jack Walker, London.
1911	Sept. 25	Sid Smith w.pts.20 Stoker Hoskyne, London.
	Oct. 19	Sid Smith w.pts.20 Louis Ruddick, Liverpool.
	Dec. 4	‡Sid Smith w.pts.20 Joe Wilson, London.
1912	Sept. 19	Sid Smith w.pts.20 Con 'Curley' Walker, London.
1913	June 2	Bill Ladbury w.rsf.11 Sid Smith, London.
1914	Jan. 26	Percy Jones w.pts.20 Bill Ladbury, London.
	May 15	Joe Symonds w.ret.18 Percy Jones, Plymouth.
	Oct. 19	James 'Tancy' Lee w.ret.14 Percy Jones, London. *Jones was overweight so the title was not at stake, but Lee was regarded as the new champion.*
	Jan. 25	James Lee w.rsf.17 Jimmy Wilde, London.
	Oct. 18	Joe Symonds w.rsf.16 James Lee, London.
1916	Feb. 14	Jimmy Wilde w.rsf.12 Joe Symonds, London.
	June 26	Jimmy Wilde w.rsf.11 James 'Tancy' Lee, London.
	July 31	Jimmy Wilde w.ko.10 Johnny Hughes, London.
1917	March 11	*Jimmy Wilde w.rsf.4 George Clark, London.
	April 29	Jimmy Wilde w.rsf.2 Dick Heasman, London.
1924	March 31	Elky Clark w.rsf.20 Joe 'Kid' Kelly, London.
1926	April 19	Elky Clark w.rsf.20 George 'Kid' Socks, London.
1927	May 23	Johnny Hill w.rsf.14 Alf Barber, London.
1929	March 31	Johnny Hill w.pts.15 Ernie Jarvis, London.
	June 29	Johnny Hill w.dis.10 Ernie Jarvis, Glasgow.
	Oct. 13	Jackie Brown w.ko.3 Bert Kirby, Birmingham.
1930	March 3	Bert Kirby w.ko.3 Jackie Brown, London.
1931	Feb. 2	Jackie Brown w.pts.15 Bert Kirby, Manchester.
1932	Sept. 19	Jackie Brown w.dis.8 Jim Maharg, Manchester.
1933	Dec. 11	*Jackie Brown w.pts.15 Chris 'Ginger' Foran, Manchester.
1935	Sept. 9	Benny Lynch w.ret.2 Jackie Brown, Manchester.
1936	Sept. 16	§Benny Lynch w.ko.8 Pat Palmer, Glasgow.
1937	Oct. 3	Benny Lynch w.ko.13 Peter Kane, Glasgow.
1939	Sept. 30	Jackie Paterson w.ko.13 Paddy Ryan, Glasgow.
1941	Feb. 3	Jackie Paterson w.ko.8 Paddy Ryan, Nottingham.
1943	June 19	*Jackie Paterson w.ko.1 Peter Kane, Glasgow.
1946	July 10	Jackie Paterson w.pts.15 Joe Curran, Glasgow.
1948	March 23	John 'Rinty' Monaghan w.ko.7 Jackie Paterson, Belfast.
1949	Sept. 30	John 'Rinty' Monaghan drew 15 Terry Allen, Belfast.
1951	June 11	Terry Allen w.pts.15 Vic Herman, Leicester.
1952	March 17	Teddy Gardner w.pts.15 Terry Allen, Newcastle.
	Oct. 21	Terry Allen w.rsf.6∥ Eric Marsden London.
1954	Feb. 16	Terry Allen w.dis.5 Eric Marsden, London.
1955	Feb. 7	Dai Dower w.pts.15 Eric Marsden, London.
1957	July 31	Frankie Jones w.ko.11 Len Reece, Porthcawl.
1959	Feb. 5	Frankie Jones w.pts.15 Alex Ambrose, Glasgow.
1960	Oct. 8	John Caldwell w.ko.3 Frankie Jones, Belfast.
1962	Feb. 27	Jackie Brown w.pts.15 Brian Cartwright, Birmingham.
1963	May 2	*Walter McGowan w.ko.12 Jackie Brown, Paisley.
1967	Jan. 16	John McCluskey w.ko.8 Tony Barlow, Manchester.
1969	May 7	John McCluskey w.rsf.13 Tony Barlow, Solihull.
1974	Oct. 14	*John McCluskey w.rsf.1 Tony Davies, Swansea.
1977	Dec. 6	Charlie Magri w.rsf.7 Dave Smith, London.
1982	Sept. 14	Kevin Smart w.ko.6 Dave George, Wembley.
1984	Jan. 25	Hugh Russell w.ret.7 Kevin Smart, Belfast.

	Nov. 13	Hugh Russell w.rsf.8 Danny Flynn, Belfast.
1985	Feb. 23	Hugh Russell w.rsf.12 Charlie Brown, Belfast. *Won Lonsdale Belt outright.*
	June 5	Duke McKenzie w.rsf.4 Danny Flynn, London.
1986	May 20	Duke McKenzie w.ret.5 Charlie Magri, Wembley. *Charlie Magri awarded Lonsdale Belt by B.B.B.C.*
	Oct. 20	Dave McAuley w.rsf.9 Joe Kelly, Glasgow.
1988	March 9	Pat Clinton w.pts.12 Joe Kelly, London.

Wilde, Clarke, Lynch, Monaghan, Allen, Dower, Caldwell, McGowan, Magri, Russell, McKenzie and McAuley relinquished title. Gardner retired. Johnny Hill died 27.9.29.

Empire and Commonwealth Games Gold Medallists: 1930–82

Canada–1930

Heavyweight: V. A. Stuart (E); *Light-heavyweight:* J. W. Goyder (E.); *Middleweight:* F. Mallin (E.); *Welterweight:* L. Hall (S.A.); *Lightweight:* J. Rolland (S); *Featherweight:* F. R. Meachem (E.); *Bantamweight:* H. Mizler (E.); *Flyweight:* W. Smith (S.A.)

England–1934

Heavyweight: H. P. Floyd (E.); *Light-heavyweight:* G. J. Brennan (E.); *Middleweight:* A. Shawyer (E.); *Welterweight:* D. McCleave (E.); *Lightweight:* L. Cook (Aust.); *Featherweight:* C. Catterall (S.A.); *Bantamweight:* F. Ryan (E.); *Flyweight:* P. Palmer (E.).

Australia–1938

Heavyweight: T. Osborne (Can.); *Light-heavyweight:* N. Wolmarans (S.A.); *Middleweight:* D. P. Reardon (W.); *Lightweight:* H. Groves (E.); *Featherweight:* A. W. Henricus (Ceylon); *Bantamweight:* W. H. Butler (E.); *Flyweight:* J. S. Joubert (S.A.).

New-Zealand–1950

Heavyweight: F. Creagh (N.Z.); *Light-heavyweight:* D. Scott (E.); *Middleweight:* T. van Schalkwyk (S.A.); *Welterweight:* T. Ratcliffe (E.); *Lightweight:* R. Latham (E.); *Featherweight:* H. Gilliland (S.); *Bantamweight:* J. van Rensburg (S.A.); *Flyweight:* H. Riley (S.).

Canada–1954

Heavyweight: B. Harper (E.); *Light-heavyweight:* P. van Vuuren (S.A.); *Middleweight:* J. van de Kolff (S.A.); *Light-middleweight:* W. Greaves (Can.); *Welterweight:* N. Gargano (E.); *Light-welterweight:* M. Bergin (Can.); *Lightweight:* P. van Staden (S.A.); *Featherweight:* L. Leisching (S.A.); *Bantamweight:* J. Smillie (S.); *Flyweight:* R. Currie (S.).

Wales–1958

Heavyweight: D. Bekker (S.A.); *Light-heavyweight:* Madigan (Aust.); *Middleweight:* T. Milligan (N.I.); *Light-middleweight:* G. Webster (S.A.); *Welterweight:* J. Greyling (S.A.); *Light-welterweight:* H. Loubscher (S.A.); *Lightweight:* R. McTaggart (S.); *Featherweight:* W. Taylor (Aust.); *Bantamweight:* H. Winstone (W.); *Flyweight:* J. Brown (S.).

Australia–1962

Heavyweight: G. Oywello (U.); *Light-heavyweight:* A. Madigan (Aust.); *Middleweight:* C. Colquhoun (Jam.); *Light-middleweight:* H. Mann (Can.); *Welterweight:* W. Coe (N.Z.); *Light-welterweight:* C. Quartey (Gha.) *Lightweight:* E. Blay (Gha.); *Featherweight:* J. McDermott (S.); *Bantamweight:* J. Dynevor (Aust.); *Flyweight:* R. Mallon (S.).

Jamaica–1966

Heavyweight: W. Kini (N.Z.); *Light-heavyweight:* R. Tighe (E.); *Middleweight:* J. Darkey (Gha.); *Light-middleweight:* M. Rowe (E.); *Welterweight:* E. Blay (Gha.); *Light-welterweight:* J. McCourt (N.I.); *Lightweight:* A. Andeh (Nig.); *Featherweight:* P. Waruinge (Kenya); *Bantamweight:* E. Ndukwu (Nig.); *Flyweight:* S. Shittu (Gha.).

Edinburgh–1970

Heavyweight: B. Masanda (U.); *Light-heavyweight:* F. Ayinia (Nig.); *Middleweight:* J. Conteh (E.); *Light-Middleweight:* T. Imrie (S.); *Welterweight:* Flash Emma Ankudey (Gha.); *Light-welterweight:* M. Muruli (U.); *Lightweight:* A. Adeyemi (Nig.); *Featherweight:* P. Waruinge (Kenya); *Bantamweight:* S. Shittu (Gha.); *Flyweight:* D. Needham (E.) *Light-flyweight:* J. Odwori (U.).

Christchurch–1974

Heavyweight: N. Meade (E.); *Light-heavyweight:* W. Knight (E.);

Middleweight: F. Lucas (St. Vincent); *Light-middleweight:* L. Mwale (Z.); *Welterweight:* M. Muruli (U.); *Light-welterweight:* O. Nwankpa (Nig.); *Lightweight:* A. Kalule (U.); *Featherweight:* E. Ndukwu (Nig.); *Bantam-weight:* P. Cowdell (E.); *Flyweight:* D. Larmour (N.I.); *Light-flyweight:* J. Odwori (U.).

Edmonton–1978
Heavyweight: J. Awome (E.); *Light-heavyweight:* R. Fortin (Can.); *Middleweight:* P. McElwaine (Aust.); *Light-Middleweight:* K. Perlette (Can.); *Welterweight:* M. McCallum (Jam.); *Light-welterweight:* W. Braithwaite (Gu.); *Lightweight:* G. Hamill (N.I.); *Featherweight:* N. Azumah (Gha.); *Bantamweight:* F. McGuigan (N.I.); *Flyweight:* M. Irunga (Kenya); *Light-flyweight:* S. Muchoki (Kenya).

Brisbane–1982
Heavyweight: W. Dewitt (Can.): *Light-heavyweight:* F. Sani (Fiji); *Middleweight:* J. Price (E.); *Light-middleweight:* S. O'Sullivan (Can.); *Welterweight:* C. Pyatt (E.); *Light-welterweight:* C. Ossai (Nig.); *Lightweight:* H. Khalili (Kenya); *Featherweight:* P. Konyegwachie (Nig.); *Bantamweight;* J. Orewa (Nig.); *Flyweight:* M. Mutua (Kenya); *Light-flyweight:* I. Bilale (Kenya).

Edinburgh–1986
Super-Heavyweight: L. Lewis (Can.); *Heavyweight:* J. Peau (N.Z.) *Light-Heavyweight:* J. Moran (E.). *Middleweight:* R. Douglas (E.). *Light-Middleweight:* D. Sherry (Can.). *Welterweight:* D. Dyer (E.). *Light-Welterweight:* H. Grant (Can.). *Lightweight:* A.Dar (Can.). *Featherweight:* B. Downey (Can.). *Bantamweight:* S. Murphy (E.). *Flyweight:* J. Lyon (E.). *Light-Flyweight:* S. Olson (Can.).

Empire and Commonwealth Professional Boxing

For many years these bouts were known as British Empire Championships and were open to any professional boxer living in Great Britain or any part of the British Empire: in the first such bout Jim Driscoll, the British featherweight champion, outpointed Charlie Griffin (Australia) at the National Sporting Club, London, in 1908. Fights for Empire titles were few, and apart from the home countries it was mainly South Africa and Australia which took part. In 1950 a Commonwealth Committee was formed in London to maintain control of the newly-named Commonwealth Championship, and consequently there are considerably more of these title fights, which have spread to the smallest member country of the Commonwealth. The rules governing these titles are similar to those that govern British championships. There are 24 countries affiliated to the Commonwealth Committee: Australia, Bahamas, Barbados, Bermuda, Canada, Eire (naturalized British subjects), England, Fiji, Ghana, Guyana, Jamaica, New Zealand, Nigeria, Northern Ireland, Papua, Samoa, Scotland, South Africa, Tonga, Trinidad, Uganda, Wales, Zambia and Zimbabwe.

Commonwealth Heavyweight Title Fights

1910	April 7	Tommy Burns (Can.) w.pts.20 Bill Lang (Aust.), Sydney, Australia.
1911	Jan. 18	P.O. 'Nutty' Curran (E.) w.dis.I. Bill Lang (Aust.), London.
	Dec. 18	Bombardier Billy Wells (E.) w.ko.11 Fred Storbeck (S.A.), London.
1912	Dec. 6	Bombardier Billy Wells (E.) w.ko.2 George Rodel (S.A.) London.
1914	June 30	Bombardier Billy Wells (E.) w.ko.2 Colin Bell (Aust.). London.
1919	Feb. 27	Joe Beckett (E.) w.ko.5 Bombardier Billy Wells (E.), London.
1920	July 17	Joe Beckett (E.) w.ret.7 Tommy Burns (Can.), London.
1922	April 10	Joe Beckett (E.) w.dis.6 George Cook (Aust.), London.
1926	Jan. 27	Phil Scott (E.) w.dis.17 George Cook (Aust.), Edinburgh.
	July 10	Phil Scott (E.) w.pts.20 Tom Heeney (N.Z.), Southampton.
1931	June 13	Larry Gains (Can.) w.ko.2 Phil Scott (E.), Leicester.
1932	Jan. 28	Larry Gains (Can.) drew 15 Don McCorkindale (S.A.), London.
	March 3	Larry Gains (Can.) w.pts.15 Don McCorkindale (S.A.), London.

1933	May 18	Larry Gains (Can.) w.pts.15 George Cook (Aust.), London.
1934	Feb. 8	Len Harvey (E.) w.pts.15 Larry Gains (Can.), London
	June 4	Jack Petersen (W.) w.ret.12‖ Len Harvey (E.). London.
	Sept. 10	Jack Petersen (W.) w.ret.13 Larry Gains (Can.), London.
	Dec. 17	Jack Petersen (W.) w.pts.15 George Cook (Aust.), London.
1936	Jan. 29	Jack Petersen (W.) w.pts.15 Len Harvey (E.), London.
	April 23	Jack Petersen (W.) w.pts.15 Jock McAvoy (E.) London.
	Aug. 17	Ben Foord (S.A.) w.rsf.3 Jack Petersen (W.), Leicester.
1937	March 15	Tommy Farr (W.) w.pts.15 Ben Foord (S.A.), London.
1939	March 10	Len Harvey (E.) w.ret.13 Larry Gains (Can.), London.
1944	Sept. 15	Jack London (E.) w.pts.15 Freddie Mills (E.), Manchester.
1945	July 17	Bruce Woodcock (E.) w.ko.6 Jack London (E.), London
1949	March 26	Bruce Woodcock (E.) w.ko.3 Johnny Ralph (S.A.), Johannesburg, South Africa.
	June 2	Bruce Woodcock (E.). w.ko.14 Freddie Mills (E.), London.
1950	Nov. 14	Jack Gardner (E.) w.ret.11 Bruce Woodcock (E.), London.
1952	March 11	Johnny Williams (W.) w.pts.15 Jack Gardner (E.), London.
	Oct. 13	Johnny Williams (W.) w.ret.7 Johnny Arthur (S.A.). Johannesburg, South Africa.
1953	May 12	Don Cockell (E.) w.pts.15 Johnny Williams, (W.), London.
1954	Jan. 30	Don Cockell (E.) w.pts.15 Johnny Arthur (S.A.), Johannesburg, South Africa.
1956	June 26	Joe Bygraves (Jam.) w.pts.15 Kitione Lave (To.), London.
1957	Feb. 19	Joe Bygraves (Jam.) w.ko.9 Henry Cooper (E.), London.
	May 27	Joe Bygraves (Jam.) drew 15 Dick Richardson (W.), Cardiff.
	Nov. 25	Joe Erskine (W.) w.pts. 15 Joe Bygraves (Jam.), Leicester.
1958	June 3	Brian London (E.) w.ko.8 Joe Erskine (W.), London.
1959	Jan. 12	Henry Cooper (E.) w.pts. 15 Brian London (E.), London.
	Aug. 26	Henry Cooper (E.) w.rsf.5 Gawie De Klerk (S.A.), Porthcawl.
	Nov. 17	Henry Cooper (E.) w.rsf.12 Joe Erskine (W.), London.
1961	March 21	Henry Cooper (E.) w.ret.5‖ Joe Erskine (W.), London.
1962	April 2	Henry Cooper (E.) w.rsf.9‖ Joe Erskine (W.), Nottingham.
1963	March 26	Henry Cooper (E.) w.ko.5 Dick Richardson (W.), London.
1964	Feb. 24	Henry Cooper (E.) w.pts.15 Brian London (E.), Manchester.
1965	June 15	Henry Cooper (E.) w.ret.10 Johnny Prescott (E.), Birmingham.
1967	June 13	Henry Cooper (E.) w.rsf.2 Jack Bodell (E.), Wolverhampton.
	Nov. 7	Henry Cooper (E.) w.rsf.6‖ Billy Walker (E.), London.
1970	March 24	Henry Cooper (E.) w.pts.15 Jack Bodell (E.), London.
1971	March 16	Joe Bugner (E.) w.pts.15 Henry Cooper (E.), London.
	Sept. 27	Jack Bodell (E.) w.pts.15 Joe Bugner (E.), London.
1972	July 27	Danny McAlinden (N.I.) w.ko.2 Jack Bodell (E.), Birmingham.
1975	Jan. 13	Bunny Johnson (E.) w.ko.9 Danny McAlinden (N.I.), London.
	Sept. 30	Richard Dunn (E.) w.pts.15 Bunny Johnson (E.), London.
	Nov. 4	Richard Dunn (E.) w.ko.2 Danny McAlinden (N.I.), London.
1976	Oct. 12	Joe Bugner (E.) w.ko.1 Richard Dunn (E.), London.
1978	Oct. 24	John L. Gardner (E.) w.ret.5 Billy Aird (E.), London.
1979	June 26	John L. Gardner (E.) w.rsf.6 Paul Sykes (E.), London.
1981	July 22	Trevor Berbick (Can.) w.ko.2 Conroy Nelson (Can.), Halifax, Nova Scotia.
1982	March 5	Trevor Berbick (Can.) w.rsf.11 Gord Racette (Can.), Nanaimo, British Columbia. *Fought over 12 rounds.*
1983	Sept. 9	Trevor Berbick (Can.) w.ko.10 Ken Lakusta (Can.) Edmonton, Canada.
1984	Sept. 1	Trevor Berbick (Can.) w.rsf.4 Ernie Barr (Bah), Nassau, Bahamas.
1986	April 12	Horace Notice (E.) w.rsf.6 Hughroy Currie (E.), Isle of Man.
1987	March 4	Horace Notice (E.) w.rsf.8 Proud Kilimanjaro (Zim), Dudley, England.
	May 26	Horace Notice (E.) w.rsf.5 Dave Garside (E.), Wembley, England.

	Dec. 2	Horace Notice (E.) w.rsf.4 Dean Waters (Aust.) Wembley, England.
1988	March 9	Horace Notice (E.) w.rsf.10 Hughroy Currie (E.) London, England.

Commonwealth Cruiserweight Title fights
(195 pounds: 13 stone 13 pounds)

1984	May 14	Stewart Lithgo (E.) w.rsf.11 Steve Aczel (Aust.), Brisbane, Australia.
	Dec. 1	Chisanda Mutti (Zam) w.rsf.9 Stewart Lithgo (E.), Dusseldorf, Germany.
1986	May 9	Chisanda Mutti (Zam.) w.ko.11 Dave Russell (Aust.), Melbourne, Australia.
1987	Sept. 4	Glen McCrory (E.) w.pts.12 Chisanda Mutti (Zam.), Gateshead, England.
1988	Jan. 21	Glen McCrory (E.) w.pts.12 Tee Jay (E.) London, England.
	April 22	Glen McCrory (E.) w.ret.8 Lou Gent (E.) Gateshead, England.

Commonwealth Light-Heavyweight Title Fights
(175 pounds: 12 stone 7 pounds)

1923	March 26	Jack Bloomfield (E.) w.ret.5 Horace 'Soldier' Jones (Can.), London.
	May 17	Jack Bloomfield (E.) w.ret.13 Dave Magill (N.I.), London.
1927	Jan. 31	Tom Berry (E.) w.pts.20 Dave Magill (N.I.), Manchester.
	April 25	Billy 'Gipsy' Daniels (W.) w.pts.20 Tom Berry (E.), London.
1939	July 10	Len Harvey (E.) w.pts.15 Jock McAvoy (E.), London
1942	June 20	Freddie Mills (E.) w.ko.2 Len Harey (E.), London.
1952	June 10	Randolph Turpin (E.) w.rsf.11 Don Cockell (E.), London.
1955	April 26	Randolph Turpin (E.) w.ko.2 Alex Buxton (E.), London.
1956	June 19	Gordon Wallace (Can.) w.pts. 15 Ron Barton (E.), London.
1957	May 30	Yvon Durelle (Can.) w.ko.2 Gordon Wallace (Can.), Monoton, Canada.
1958	July 16	Yvon Durelle (Can.) w.ret.8 Mike Holt (S.A.), Montreal, Canada.
1960	April 25	Mike Holt (S.A.) drew 15 Johnny Halafihi (To.), Nottingham.
	June 9	Chic Calderwood (S.) w.rsf.12‖ Johnny Halafihi (To.), Glasgow.
1962	Feb. 12	Chic Calderwood (S.) w.ko.4 Stan Cullis (E.), London.
1963	Jun 30	Chic Calderwood (S.) w.pts.15 Johnny Halafihi (To.), Newcastle.
1968	Feb. 12	Bob Dunlop (Aust.) w.rsf.7 John 'Young' McCormack (Ei.), Sydney, Australia.
1969	Jan. 1	Bob Dunlop (Aust.) w.pts.15 Al Sparks (Can.), Melbourne, Australia.
1970	Oct. 23	Eddie Avoth (W.) w.ret.6 Trevor Thornberry (Aust.), Brisbane, Australia.
1971	Jan. 24	Chris Finnegan (E.) w.rsf.15 Eddie Avoth (W.), London.
1973	March 13	Chris Finnegan (E.) w.pts.15 Roy John (W.), London.
	May 22	John Conteh (E.) w.pts.15 Chris Finnegan (E.), London.
	Oct. 23	John Conteh (E.), w.pts.15 Baby Boy Rolle (Bah), Nottingham.
1974	May 21	John Conteh (E.) w.rsf.6‖ Chris Finnegan (E.), London.
1975	Feb. 19	Steve Aczel (Aust.), w.rsf.3 Maxie Smith (E.), Manchester.
	Oct. 30	Tony Mundine (Aust.) w.ko.12 Steven Aczel (Aust.), Blacktown, Australia.
	Dec. 4	Tony Mundine (Aust.) w.rsf.2 Victor Attivor (Gha.) Blacktown, Australia.
1976	March 26	Tony Mundine (Aust.) w.ko.3 Baby Boy Rolle (Bah.), Brisbane, Australia.
	Sept. 4	Tony Mundine (Aust.) w.rsf.9 Victor Attivor (Gha.), Accra, Ghana.
1977	July 8	Tony Mundine (Aust.) w.pts.15 Ernie Barr (Bah.), Brisbane, Australia.
1978	Feb. 27	Gary Summerhays (Can.) w.ko.11 Tony Mundine (Aust.), Melbourne, Australia.
1979	March 31	Lottie Mwale (Z.) w.rsf.5 Gary Summerhays (Can.), Lusaka, Zambia.
1982	May 7	Louis Mwale (Zam). w.rsf.13 Chisanda Mutti (Zam.) Lusaka, Zambia.

	Dec. 5	Louis Mwale (Zam). w.ko.13 Kid Power (Zim.), Lusaka, Zambia.
1983	Jan. 30	Louis Mwale (Zam.) w.rsf.2 Billy Savage (Nig.), Lusaka, Zambia.
	March 12	Louis Mwale (Zam.) w.rsf.3 Mustafa Wasajja (Uganda), Lusaka, Zambia.
1983	Oct. 8	Louis Mwale (Zam.) w.pts.12 Chisanda Mutti (Zam.), Lusaka, Zambia.
1985	Aug. 4	Leslie Stewart (Trin.) w.pts.12 Louis Mwale (Zam.), Port of Spain, Trinidad.
1986	Sept. 18	Leslie Stewart (Trin.) w.rsf.5 Gary Hubble (Aust.), Sydney, Australia.
1987	Sept. 12	Willy Featherstone (Can.) w.pts.12 Enoch Charles (Zam.), Nova Scotia, Canada.
	Dec. 8	Willy Featherstone (Can.) w.pts.12 Danny Lindstrom (Can.), Toronto, Canada.
1988	May 27	Willy Featherstone (Can.) w.pts.12 Dave Fiddler (Can.) Port Hawksbury, Canada.

Commonwealth Middleweight Title Fights
(160 pounds: 11 stone 6 pounds)

1922	June 19	Ted 'Kid' Lewis (E.) w.ko.11 Frankie Burns (Aust), London.
1923	Feb. 15	Roland Todd (E) w.pts.20 Ted 'Kid' Lewis (E.), London.
1926	July 12	Tommy Milligan (S.) w.rsf.14 George West (E.), London.
	Oct. 7	Tommy Milligan (S.) w.rsf.14 Ted Moore (E.), London.
1927	Jan. 27	Tommy Milligan (S.) w.rsf.14 Ted Moore (E.), London.
1928	March 14	Alex Ireland (S.) w.dis.9 Tommy Milligan (S.), Edinburgh.
	Sept. 17	Alex Ireland (S.) w.pts.15 Frank Moody (W.), Edinburgh.
1929	May 16	Len Harvey (E.) w.ko.7 Alex Ireland (S.), London.
	Oct. 21	Len Harvey (E.) w.pts.15 Jack Hood (E.), London.
	Dec. 19	Len Harvey (E.) drew 15 Jack Hood (E.), London.
1930	May 22	Len Harvey (E.) w.rsf.9 Steve McCall (S.), London.
1931	June 22	Len Harvey (E.) w.pts.15 Jack Hood (E.), London.
1932	March 21	Len Harvey (E.) w.pts.15 Jock McAvoy (E.), Manchester.
	Dec. 12	Len Harvey (E.) w.pts.15 Jack Casey (E.), Newcastle.
1933	April 10	Jock McAvoy (E.) w.pts. 15 Len Harvey (E.), Manchester.
	Oct. 9	Jock McAvoy (E.) w.ko.10 Archie Sexton (E.), Manchester.
1935	June 24	Jock McAvoy (E.) w.pts.15 Al Burke (Aust.), Manchester.
1937	Oct. 25	Jock McAvoy (E.) w.ret.11‖ Jack Hyams (E.), Manchester.
1939	May 22	Jock McAvoy (E.), w.pts.15 Arthur 'Ginger' Sadd (E.), Manchester.
1940	Feb. 26	Ron Richards (Aust.), w.dis.11 Fred Henneberry (Aust.), Sydney, Australia.
	Dec. 16	Ron Richards (Aust.) w.dis.12 Fred Henneberry (Aust.), Sydney, Australia.
1941	Nov. 27	Ron Richards (Aust.) w.dis.13 Fred Henneberry (Aust.), Sydney, Australia.
1948	Jan. 26	Bos Murphy (N.Z.) w.pts.15 Vince Hawkins (E.), London.
	May 18	Dick Turpin (E.) w.ko.1 Bos Murphy (N.Z.), Coventry.
	June 26	Dick Turpin (E.) w.pts.15 Vince Hawkins (E.), Birmingham.
1949	June 20	Dick Turpin (E.) w.pts. 15 Albert Finch (E.), Birmingham.
	Sept. 6	Dave Sands (Aust.) w.ko.1 Dick Turpin (E.), London.
1952	May 9	Dave Sands (Aust.), w.ko.5 Al Burke (Aust.), Melbourne, Australia.
	Oct. 21	Randolph Turpin (E.), w.pts.15 George Angelo (S.A.), London.
1954	Sept. 14	Johnny Sullivan (E.) w.ko.1 Gordon Hazell (E.), London.
1955	June 16	Pat McAteer (E.) w.dis.9 Johnny Sullivan (E.), Liverpool.
	Nov. 12	Pat McAteer (E.) w.pts.15 Mike Holt (S.A.), Johannesburg, South Africa.
1956	Oct. 8	Pat McAteer (E.) w.rsf.4 Lew Lazar (E.), Nottingham
1957	May 4	Pat McAteer (E.) w.ko.6 Jimmy Elliott (S.A.), Johannesburg, South Africa.
	Sept. 5	Pat McAteer (E.) w.pts.15 Martin Hansen (E.), Liverpool.
1958	March 27	Dick Tiger (Nig.) w.ko.9 Pat McAteer (E.), Liverpool.
1960	June 22	Wilf Greaves (Can.) w.pts.15 Dick Tiger (Nig.), Edmonton, Canada.
	Nov. 30	Dick Tiger (Nig.) w.rsf.9 Wilf Greaves (Can.), Edmonton, Canada.
1963	Oct. 22	Gomeo Brennan (Bah.) w.pts.15 Mick Leahy (E.), London.

1964	March 14	Tuna Scanlan (N.Z.) w.pts.15 Gomeo Brennan (Bah.), Auckland, New Zealand.
	Nov. 12	Gomeo Brennnan (Bah.) w.pts.15 Earl Nikora (N.Z.), Auckland, New Zealand.
1965	June 15	Gomeo Brennan (Bah.) w.pts.15 Earl Nikora (N.Z.), Auckland, New Zealand.
	Sept. 25	Gomeo Brennan (Bah.) w.ko.11 Blair Richardson (Can.), Glace Bay, Canada.
1966	March 26	Blair Richardson (Can.) w.pts.15 Gomeo Brennan (Bah.), Glace Bay, Canada.
1967	July 28	Milo Calhoun (Jam.) w.pts.12 Johnny Meilleur (Can.), Glace Bay, Canada.
	Oct. 9	Johnny Pritchett (E.) w.ret.8 Milo Calhoun (Jam.), Manchester.
1968	Feb. 26	Johnny Pritchett (E.) w.pts.15 Les McAteer (E.), Nottingham.
1969	July 14	Les McAteer (E.) w.ret.11‖ Wally Swift (E.), Nottingham.
1970	May 12	Mark Rowe (E.) w.rsf.14 Les McAteer (E.), London.
	Sept. 8	Bunny Sterling (Jam.) w.rsf.4 Mark Rowe (E.), London.
	Nov. 13	Bunny Sterling (Jam.) w.pts.15 Kahu Mahanga (N.Z.), Melbourne, Australia.
1971	Jan. 21	Bunny Sterling (Jam.) drew 15 Tony Mundine (Aust.), Sydney, Australia.
	March 22	Bunny Sterling (Jam.) w.pts.15 Johann Louw (Can.), Edmonton, Canada.
1972	April 14	Tony Mundine (Aust.) w.rsf.15 Bunny Sterling (Jam.), Brisbane, Australia.
1973	Feb. 7	Tony Mundine (Aust.) w.rsf.3 Matt Donovan (Tr.), Sydney, Australia.
	Aug. 20	Tony Mundine (Aust.) w.ko.1 Fred Etuati (Sam.), Auckland, New Zealand.
	Sept. 28	Tony Mundine (Aust.) w.pts.15 Carlos Mark (Tr.), Brisbane, Australia.
1975	July 24	Monty Betham (N.Z.) w.pts.15 Carlos Mark (Tr.), Wellington, New Zealand.
1976	Jan. 19	Monty Betham (N.Z.) w.rsf.9 Semi Bula (Aust.), Port Kembla, Australia.
	March 11	Monty Betham (N.Z.) w.pts.15 Alipate Korovou (Fiji), Wellington, New Zealand.
	June 5	Monty Betham (N.Z.) w.ko.7 Jone Mataitini (Fiji), Suva, Fiji.
	July 30	Monty Betham (N.Z.) w.pts.15 Carlos Mark (Tr.), Port of Spain, Trinidad.
	Sept. 23	Monty Betham (N.Z.) w.ko.11 Wally Carr (Aust.), Wellington, New Zealand.
1978	March 17	Al Korogou (Aust.), w.ko.12 Monty Betham (N.Z.), Suva, Fiji.
	May 25	Ayub Kalule (U.) w.rsf.14 Al Korovou (Aust.), Copenhagen, Denmark.
	Sept. 14	Ayub Kalule (U.) w.ko.5 Reggie Ford (Gu.), Randers, Denmark.
1980	March 4	Tony Sibson (E.) w.pts.15 Chisanda Mutti (Z.), London.
1983	Feb. 8	Roy Gumbs (E.) w.rsf.5 Ralph Hollett (Can.). Dartmouth, Nova Scotia.
	March 29	Roy Gumbs (E.) w.rsf.4 Ralph Hollett (Can.), Halifax, Nova Scotia.
	Sept. 14	Mark Kaylor (E.) w.ko.4 Roy Gumbs (E.), London, England.
1984	Nov. 27	Tony Sibson (E.) w.pts.12 Mark Kaylor (E.), Wembley, England.
1986	March 19	Tony Sibson (E.) w.pts.12 Abdul Amaru Sanda (Ghana), London, England.
1987	Sept. 16	Tony Sibson (E.) w.rsf.7 Brian Anderson (E.) London, England.
1988	April 20	Nigel Benn (E.) w.rsf.2 Abdul Amura Sanda (Ghana), London, England.

Commonwealth Light-Middleweight Title Fights
(154 pounds: 11 stone)

1972	Oct. 30	Charkey Ramon (Aust.) w.rsf.8 Pat Dwyer (E.), Melbourne, Australia.
1973	June 7	Charkey Ramon (Aust.) w.rsf.11 Donato Paduano (Can.), Sydney, Australia.
1976	April 20	Maurice Hope (E.) w.rsf.12 ‖ Tony Poole (E.), London.
1979	July 29	Kenny Bristol (Gu.) w.pts.15 Pat Thomas (W.), Georgetown, Guyana.

1980	Feb. 24	Kenny Bristol (Gu.) w.pts.15 Eddie Marcelle (Tr.), Georgetown, Guyana.
1981	Nov. 25	Herol Graham (E.) w.pts.15 Kenny Bristol (Gu), Sheffield.
1982	Feb. 24	Herol Graham (E.) w.rsf.9 Chris Christian (E.), Sheffield.
	Sept. 30	Herol Graham (E.) w.pts.15 Hunter Clay (Nigeria), Lagos, Nigeria.
1984	Aug. 21	Ken Salisbury (Aust.) w.pts.12 Nelson Bosso (Zim.), Sydney, Australia.
1985	June 5	Nick Wilshire (E.) w.rsf.2 Ken Salisbury (Aust.), London, England.
1987	March 11	Lloyd Hibbert (E.) w.pts.12 Nick Wilshire (E.), London, England.
	Aug. 5	Troy Waters (Aust.) w.rsf.4 Lloyd Hibbert (E.), Hobart, Tasmania.

Commonwealth Welterweight Title Fights
(147 pounds: 10 stone 7 pounds)

1913	June 11	Johnny Summers (E.) w.pts.20 Sid Burns (E.), Sydney, Australia.
	Oct. 11	Johnny Summers (E.) w.pts.20 Arthur Evernden (E), Sydney, Australia.
1914	Jan. 10	Tom McCormick (E.) w.pts.20 Johnny Summers (E.), Sydney, Australia.
	Feb. 14	Tom McCormick (E.) w.ko.1 Johnny Summers (E.), Sydney, Australia.
	March 21	Matt Wells (E.) w.pts.20 Tom McCormick (E.), Sydney, Australia.
1919	Nov. 13	Johnny Basham (W.) w.pts.20 Matt Wells (E.), London.
1920	April 12	Johnny Basham (W.) w.pts.20 Fred Kay (Aust.), London.
	June 9	Ted 'Kid' Lewis (E.) w.ko.9 Johnny Basham (W.), London.
1924	Nov. 26	Tommy Milligan (S.) w.pts.20 Ted 'Kid' Lewis (E.), Edinburgh.
1951	Jan. 27	Eddie Thomas (W.) w.ko.13 Pat Patrick (S.A.), Johannesburg, South Africa.
	Oct. 16	Wally Thom (E.) w.pts.15 Eddie Thomas (W.), London.
1952	July 24	Cliff Curvis (W.) w.ko.9 Wally Thom (E.), Liverpool.
	Dec. 8	Gerald Dreyer (S.A.) w.pts.15 Cliff Curvis (W.), Johannesburg, South Africa.
1954	Jan. 15	Barry Brown (N.Z.) w.rsf.7 Gerald Dreyer (S.A.), Wellington, New Zealand.
	Nov. 24	George Barnes (Aust.) w.ko.11 Barry Brown (N.Z.), Sydney, Australia.
1955	Nov. 28	George Barnes (Aust.) w.pts.15 Attu Clottey (Ghana), Sydney, Australia.
1956	April 14	George Barnes (Aust.) w.rsf.13 Benny Nieuwenhuizen (S.A.), Johannesburg, South Africa.
	Aug. 6	Darby Brown (Aust.) w.pts.15 George Barnes (Aust.), Sydney, Australia.
	Nov. 12	George Barnes (Aust.) w.pts.15 Darby Brown (Aust.), Sydney, Autralia.
1957	Aug. 12	George Barnes (Aust.) w.pts.15 Attu Clottey (Gha.), Sydney, Australia.
1958	May 17	Johnny van Rensburg (S.A.) w.pts.15 George Barnes (Aust.), Salisbury, Rhodesia.
	Aug. 18	George Barnes (Aust.) w.rsf.13 Johnny van Rensburg (S.A.), Sydney, Australia.
1959	Aug. 7	George Barnes (Aust.) w.pts.15 Billy Todd (Aust.), Brisbane, Australia.
	Dec. 7	George Barnes (Aust.) w.rsf.6 Billy Todd (Aust.), Sydney, Australia.
1960	May 9	Brian Curvis (W.) w.pts.15 George Barnes (Aust.), Swansea.
	Nov. 21	Brian Curvis (W.) w.pts.15 Wally Swift (E.), Nottingham.
1961	May 8	Brian Curvis (W.) w.pts.15 Wally Swift (E.), Nottingham.
	Oct. 31	Brian Curvis (W.) w.ko.8 Micky Leahy (Ei.), London.
1962	Feb. 20	Brian Curvis (W.) w.rsf.5 Tony Mancini (E.), London.
1963	Feb. 12	Brian Curvis (W.) w.rsf.10 Tony Smith (E.), London.
1964	July 28	Brian Curvis (W.) w.ret.5 Johnny Cooke (E.), Porthcawl.
1965	Nov. 25	Brian Curvis (W.) w.rsf.12 Sammy McSpadden (E.), Cardiff.
1967	Oct. 16	Johnny Cooke (E.) w.pts.15 Lennox Beckles (Gu.), Liverpool.
1968	Feb. 20	Ralph Charles (E.) w.pts.15 Johnny Cooke (E.), London.
1969	Nov. 11	Ralph Charles (E.) w.ko.5 Chuck Henderson (E.), London.

1971	Dec. 7	Ralph Charles (E.) w.rsf.8 Bernie Terrell (E.), London.
1973	Feb. 12	Clyde Gray (Can.) w.pts.15 Eddie Blay (Gha.), Toronto, Canada.
1974	Feb. 18	Clyde Gray (Can.) w.ret.8 Bunny Grant (Jam.), Toronto, Canada.
1975	March 3	Clyde Gray (Can.) w.ko.5 Mare Gervais (Can.), Calgary, Canada.
	Dec. 1	Clyde Gray (Can.) w.rsf.8 Lawrence Hafey (Can.), Halifax, Nova Scotia, Canada.
1976	Nov. 23	Clyde Gray (Can.) w.rsf.5 Kevin Odus (Nig.), Halifax, Nova Scotia, Canada.
1977	Dec. 9	Clyde Gray (Can.) w.pts.15 Vernon Lewis (Gu.), Port of Spain, Trinidad.
1978	Aug. 19	Clyde Gray (Can.) w.rsf.8 Sakaria Ve (Fiji), Suva, Fiji.
	Dec. 15	Clyde Gray (Can.) w.ko.9 Sakaria Ve (Fiji), Lautoka, Fiji.
1979	Aug. 28	Chris Clarke (Can.) w.rsf.10‖ Clyde Gray (Can.), Halifax, Nova Scotia, Canada.
	Nov. 13	Clyde Gray (Can.) w.rsf.10 Chris Clarke (Can.), Halifax, Nova Scotia, Canada.
1981	March 3	Colin Jones (E.) w.rsf.9 Mark Harris (Gu.), London.
1981	April 28	Colin Jones (W.) w.rsf.9 Kirkland Laing (E.), London, England.
1982	Sept. 14	Colin Jones (W.) w.ko.2 Sakari Ve (Fiji), Wembley, England.
1984	Oct. 10	Sylvester Mittee (E.) w.rsf.11 Fighting Romanus (Nig.), London, England.
1985	April 13	Sylvester Mittee (E.) w.pts.12 Martin McGough (E.) Darlington, England.
	Sept. 18	Sylvester Mittee (E.) w.pts.12 Kostas Petrou (E.) London, England.
	Nov. 27	Lloyd Honeyghan (E.) w.rsf.8 Sylvester Mittee (E.) London, England.
1987	April 6	Brian Jansen (Aust.) w.pts.12 Judas Clottey (E.), Brisbane, Australia.
	Aug. 28	Wilf Gentzen (Aust.) w.pts.12 Brian Jensen (Aust.), Melbourne, Australia.
1988	April 19	Gary Jacobs (S.) w.pts.12 Wilf Gentsen (Aust.), Glasgow, Scotland.

Commonwealth Light-Welterweight Title Fights

(140 pounds: 10 stone)

1972	Sept. 21	Joe Tetteh (Gha.) w.rsf.10 Joey Santos (N.Z.), Wellington, New Zealand.
1973	March 26	Hector Thompson (Aust.) w.pts.15 Joe Tetteh (Gha.), Brisbane, Australia.
	July 16	Hector Thompson (Aust.) w.pts.15 Joe Tetteh (Gha.), Brisbane, Australia.
1975	May 19	Hector Thompson (Aust.) w.rsf.10 Ali Afakasi (N.Z.), Brisbane, Australia.
1976	Aug. 16	Hector Thompson (Aust.) w.ko.6 Andy Broome (Aust.), Tweed Heads, Australia.
	Dec. 3	Hector Thompson (Aust.) w.rsf.15 Ross Eadie (Aust.), Wollongong, Australia.
	Dec. 16	Hector Thompson (Aust.) w.rsf.10 Martin Beni (P.N.G.), Broad Meadow, Australia.
1977	April 28	Baby Cassius Austin (Aust.) w.rsf.15‖ Hector Thompson (Aust.), Perth, Australia.
	June 16	Hector Thompson (Aust.), w.pts.15 Baby Cassius Austin (Aust.), Perth, Australia.
	Sept. 15	Baby Cassius Austin (Aust.) w.pts.15 Hector Thompson (Aust.), Perth, Australia.
1978	April 21	Baby Cassius Austin (Aust.) w.ko.4 Tony Aba (P.N.G.), Boroko, Papua New Guinea.
	Sept. 24	Jeff Malcolm (Aust.) w.pts.15 Baby Cassius Austin (Aust.), Melbourne, Australia.
1979	March 3	Obisia Nwankpa (Nig.) w.pts.15 Jeff Malcolm (Aust.), Lagos, Nigeria.
1980	July 4	Obisia Nwankpa (Nig.) w.pts.15 Clinton McKenzie (E.), Lagos, Nigeria.
	Nov. 7	Obisia Nwankpa (Nig.) w.rsf.2 Derrick McKenzie (Gu.), Lagos, Nigeria.
1982	June 11	Obisia Nwankpa (Nig.) w.rsf.10 Des Morrison (E.), Aba, Nigeria.
1983	May 28	Billy Famous (Nig.) w.pts.12 Obisia Nwankpa (Nig.), Lagos, Nigeria.
1984	March 17	Billy Famous (Nig.) w.ko.5 Obisia Nwankpa (Nig.), Lagos, Nigeria.
1985	June 28	Billy Famous (Nig.) w.ret.11 Langton Tinago (Zim.), Lagos, Nigeria.
1987	Oct. 24	Tony Laing (E.) w.rsf.11 David Chibuye (Zam.), London, England.
1988	Aug. 4	Lester Ellis (Aust.) w.pts.15 Tony Laing (E.) Adelaide, Australia.

Commonwealth Lightweight Title Fights

(135 pounds: 9 stone 9 pounds)

1912	Dec. 16	Freddie Welsh (W.) w.pts.20 Hughie Mehegan (Aust.), London.
1930	May 21	Al Foreman (Can.) w.ko.1 Fred Webster (E.), London.
	Oct. 20	Al Foreman (Can.) w.ko.6 George Rose (E.), Manchester.
	Dec. 15	Al Foreman (Can.) drew 15 Johnny Cuthbert (E.), London.
1933	April 24	Jimmy Kelso (Aust.) w.pts.15 Al Foreman (Can.), Sydney, Australia.
	May 22	Al Foreman (Can.) w.dis.3 Jimmy Kelso (Aust.), Sydney, Australia.
1936	Jan. 11	Laurie Stevens (S.A.) w.pts.12 Jack 'Kid' Berg (E.), Johannesburg, South Africa.
1948	Oct. 1	Arthur King (Can.) w.ret.7 Billy Thompson (E.), Manchester.
1953	Jan. 23	Frank Johnson (E.) w.rsf.10 Frank Flannery (Aust.), Melbourne, Australia.
	Aug. 28	Pat Ford (Aust.) w.pts.15 Frank Johnson (E.), Melbourne, Australia.
	Oct. 9	Pat Ford (Aust.) w.ko.13 Frank Johnson (E.), Melbourne, Australia.
1954	April 9	Ivor Germain (Bah.) w.pts.15 Pat Ford (Aust.), Melbourne, Australia.
	July 2	Pat Ford (Aust.) w.pts.15 Ivor Germain (Bah.), Melbourne, Australia.
1955	Feb. 12	Johnny van Rensburg (S.A.) w.pts.15 Joe Jucy (E.), Johannesburg, South Africa.
	June 11	Johnny van Rensburg (S.A.) w.pts.12 Louis Klopper (S.A.), Johannesburg, South Africa.
	Aug. 20	Johnny van Rensburg (S.A.) w.rsf.8 Roy Louw (S.A.), Cape Town, South Africa.
	Dec. 10	Johnny van Rensburg (S.A.) w.ret.9‖ Willie Toweel (S.A.), Johannesburg, South Africa.
1956	June 16	Willie Toweel (S.A.) w.pts.15 Johnny van Rensburg (S.A.), Johannesburg, South Africa.
	Aug. 11	Willie Toweel (S.A.) drew 15 Johnny van Rensburg (S.A.), Johannesburg, South Africa.
	Nov. 10	Willie Toweel (S.A.) w.pts.15 Richard Howard (Can.), Johannesburg, South Africa.
1957	Feb. 14	Willie Toweel (S.A.) w.ret.4 Johnny van Rensburg (S.A.), Johannesburg, South Africa.
	July 9	Willie Toweel (S.A.) w.pts.15 Dave Charnley (E.), London.
1959	May 12	Dave Charnley (E.) w.ko.10 Willie Toweel (S.A.), London.
1961	Nov. 20	Dave Charnley (E.) w.ko.1 David 'Darkie' Hughes (W.), Nottingham.
1962	Aug. 4	Bunny Grant (Jam.) w.pts.15 Dave Charnley (E.), Kingston, Jamaica.
1967	March 15	Mancel Santos (N.Z.) w.pts.15 Bunny Grant (Jam.), Wellington, New Zealand.
	Oct. 7	Love Allotey (Gha.) w.pts.15 Bunny Grant (Jam.), Accra, Ghana.
1968	July 27	Percy Hayles (Jam.) w.pts.15 Love Allotey (Gha.), Kingston, Jamaica.
1970	Aug. 14	Percy Hayles (Jam.) w.pts.15 Jeff White (Aust.), Brisbane, Australia.
1971	July 10	Percy Hayles (Jam.) w.pts.15 Al Ford (Can.), Kingston, Jamaica.
1973	Jan. 22	Percy Hayles (Jam.) w.rsf.12 Al Ford (Can.), Kingston, Jamaica.
1974	July 22	Percy Hayles (Jam.) w.pts.15 Manny Santos (N.Z.), Kingston, Jamaica.
1975	May 31	Jonathan Dele (Nig.) w.pts.15 Jim Watt (S.), Lagos, Nigeria.

1976	July 16	Jonathan Dele (Nig.) w.pts.15 Percy Hayles (Jam.), Lagos, Nigeria.
1977	March 4	Jonathan Dele (Nig.) w.pts.15 Hogan Jimoh (Nig.), Lagos, Nigeria.
	Sept. 30	Lennox Blackmore (Gu.) w.pts.15 Jonathan Dele (Nig.), Lagos, Nigeria.
1978	Oct. 25	Hogan Jimoh (Nig.) w.ko.5 Lennox Blackmore (Gu.), Lagos, Nigeria.
1979	Nov. 30	Hogan Jimoh (Nig.) w.rsf.8 Johnny Claydon (E.), Lagos, Nigeria.
1980	Dec. 7	Langton Tinago (Zim.) w.rsf.7 Hogan Jimoh (Nig.), Lagos, Nigeria.
1981	May 6	Barry Michael (Aust.) w.pts.15 Langton Tinago (Zim.), Melbourne, Australia.
	Dec. 11	Barry Michael (Aust.) w.rsf.10 Willie Tarika (Fiji), Melbourne, Australia.
1982	July 20	Barry Michael (Aust.) w.rsf.7 Dave McCabe (E.), Melbourne, Australia.
	July 22	Claude Noel (Trin.) w.pts.15 Barry Michael (Aust.), Melbourne, Australia.
1983	Dec. 2	Claude Noel (Trin.) w.pts.12 Steve Assoon (Trin.), Port of Spain, Trinidad.
1984	March 16	Claude Noel (Trin.) w.ko.7 Davidson Andeh (Nig.), Port of Spain, Trinidad.
	Nov. 2	Graeme Brooke (Aust.) w.pts.12 Claude Noel (Trin.), Melbourne, Australia.
1985	Feb. 22	Barry Michael (Aust.) w.pts.12 Graeme Brooke (Aust.), Melbourne, Australia.
1986	Aug. 23	Langton Tinago (Zim.) w.rsf.5 Graeme Brooke (Aust.), Manchester, England.
1987	April 3	Mo Hussein (E.) w.ko.12 Langton Tinago (Zim.), Basildon, England.
1988	Jan. 27	Mo Hussein (E.) w.ko.1 Bright Spider (Zam.), London, England.
	March 29	Mo Hussein (E.) w.ret.5 Brian Roche (E.), London, England.

Commonwealth Junior-Lightweight Title Fights
(130 pounds: 9 stone 4 pounds)

1975	May 13	Billy Moeller (Aust.) w.pts.15 Jimmy Bell (S.), Sydney, Australia.
1976	May 25	Billy Moeller (Aust.) w.pts.15 Mama Clay (Nig.), Lagos, Nigeria.
	Dec. 22	Billy Moeller (Aust.) w.pts.15 Barry Michael (Aust.), Orange, Australia.
1977	Dec. 1	Johnny Aba (P.N.G.) w.pts.15 Billy Moeller (Aust.), Boroko, Papua-New Guinea.
1978	May 5	Johnny Aba (P.N.G.) w.ko.12 Brian Roberts (Aust.) Port Moresby, Papua-New Guinea.
	Aug. 11	Johnny Aba (P.N.G.) w.rsf.2 Billy Moeller (Aust.), Rabaul, New Britain.
1979	Oct. 20	Johnny Aba (P.N.G.) w.pts.15 Willie Tarika (Fiji), Suva, Fiji.
1980	March 21	Johnny Aba (P.N.G.) w.pts.15 Willie Tarika (Fiji), Port Moresby, Papua-New Guinea.
1981	Oct. 28	Johnny Aba (P.N.G.) drew 15 Billy Moeller (Aust.), Orange, Australia.
1982	Sept. 17	Johnny Aba (P.N.G.) w.pts.15 Gary Williams (Aust.), Port Moresby, Papau New Guinea.
1983	May 7	Langton Tinago (Zim.) w.pts.15 Safiu Okebadan (Nig.), Harare, Zimbabwe.
1984	Feb. 4	John Sichula (Zam.) w.ko.5 Langton Tinago (Zim.) Harare, Zimbabwe.
	Nov. 16	Lester Ellis (Aust.) w.pts.12 John Sichula (Zam.), Melbourne, Australia.
1985	June 8	John Sichula (Zam.) w.ko.3 Hans Sankisa (Zam.), Lusaka, Zambia.
1986	Oct. 25	Sam Akromah (Gha.) w.pts.12 John Sichula (Zam.), Accra, Ghana.
1987	Aug. 29	John Sichula (Zam.) w.pts.12 Sam Akromah (Gha.), Lusaka, Zambia.

Commonwealth Featherweight Title Fights
(126 pounds: 9 stone)

| 1908 | Feb. 24 | Jim Driscoll (W.) w.pts.15 Charlie Griffin (Aust.), London. |

1915	Dec. 18	Llew Edwards (W.) w.ret.13 Jimmy Hill (Aust.), Sydney, Australia.
1936	Dec. 26	Johnny McGrory (S.) w.pts.12 Willie Smith (S.A.), Johannesburg, South Africa.
1938	Nov. 23	Jim 'Spider' Kelly (N.I.) w.pts.15 Benny Caplan (E.), Belfast.
1939	June 28	Johnny Cusick (E.) w.pts.15 Jim 'Spider' Kelly (N.I.), Belfast.
1940	Feb. 1	Nel Tarleton (E.) w.pts.15 Johnny Cusick (E.), Liverpool.
	Nov. 2	Nel Tarleton (E.) w.pts.15 Tom Smith (E.), Liverpool.
1945	Feb. 23	Nel Tarleton (E.), w.pts.15 Al Phillips (E.), Manchester.
1947	March 18	Al Phillips (E.) w.pts.15 Cliff Anderson (B.G.), London.
	July 1	Al Philips (E.) w.dis.8 Cliff Anderson (B.G.), London.
	Sept. 11	Ronnie Clayton (E.) w.pts.15 Al Phillips (E.), Liverpool.
1949	April 11	Ronnie Clayton (E.) w.pts.15 Johnny Molloy (E.), Nottingham.
	Aug. 11	Ronnie Clayton (E.) w.ko.12 Eddie Miller (Aust.), Liverpool.
1950	Nov. 28	Ronnie Clayton (E.) w.pts.15 Jim Kenny (S.), London.
1951	Feb. 26	Ronnie Clayton (E.) w.pts.15 Al Phillips (E.), Nottingham.
	April 30	Roy Ankrah (Gha.) w.pts 15 Ronnie Clayton (E.), London.
1952	Feb. 25	Roy Ankrah (Gha.) w.ret.13 Ronnie Clayton (E.), Nottingham.
1954	Oct. 2	Billy 'Spider' Kelly (N.I.) w.pts.15 Roy Ankrah (Gha.), Belfast.
1955	Jan. 22	Billy 'Spider' Kelly (N.I.) w.pts.15 Sammy McCarthy (E.) Belfast.
	Nov. 19	Hogan Bassey (Nig.) w.ko.8 Billy 'Spider' Kelly (N.I.), Belfast.
1957	April 1	Hogan Bassey (Nig.) w.pts.15 Percy Lewis (Tr.), Nottingham.
	Dec. 9	Percy Lewis (Tr.) w.rsf.10 Charlie Hill (S.), Nottingham.
1959	Dec. 7	Percy Lewis (Tr.) w.ko.2 John O'Brien (S.), Nottingham.
1960	Nov. 26	Floyd Robertson (Gha.) w.pts.15 Percy Lewis (Tr.), Belfast.
1962	Aug. 4	Floyd Robertson (Gha.) w.pts.15 Love Allotey (Gha.), Accra, Ghana.
1963	Oct. 5	Floyd Robertson (Gha.) w.rsf.11 Joe Tettch (Gha.), Accra, Ghana.
1967	Feb. 3	John O'Brien (S.) w.ret.12 Floyd Robertson (Gha.), Accra, Ghana.
	Nov. 24	Johnny Famechon (Aust.) w.rsf.11 John O'Brien (S.), Melbourne, Australia.
1968	Sept. 13	Johnny Famechon (Aust.) w.rsf.12 Billy McGrandle (Can.), Melbourne, Australia.
1970	Dec. 12	Toro George (N.Z.) w.rsf.6 Ken Bradley (Aust.), Canberra, Australia.
1971	Sept. 6	Toro George (N.Z.) w.pts.15 Evan Armstrong (S.), Melbourne, Australia.
1972	Nov. 3	Bobby Dunne (Aust.) w.pts.15 Toro George (N.Z.), Melbourne, Australia.
1974	April 5	Evan Armstrong (S.) w.rsf.8 Bobby Dunne (Aust.), Brisbane, Australia.
	July 8	Evan Armstrong (S.) w.rsf.11 Alan Richardson (E.), London.
	Dec. 7	David 'Poison' Kotey (Ghana) w.ret.10‖ Evan Armstrong (S.), Accra, Ghana.
1977	June 17	Eddie Ndukwu (Nig.) w.rsf.12 Alan Richardson (E.), Lagos, Nigeria.
	Dec. 9	Eddie Ndukwu (Nig.) w.ret.8‖ Alan Richardson (E.), Lagos, Nigeria.
1978	Oct. 3	Eddie Ndukwu (Nig.) w.pts.15 David Kotey (Gha.), Lagos, Nigeria.
1979	Sept. 28	Eddie Ndukwu (Nig.) w.ret.8 Henry Saddler (Gha.), Lagos, Nigeria.
1980	Aug. 1	Pat Ford (Gu.) w.ret.9 Eddie Ndukwu (Nig.), Lagos, Nigeria.
1981	Sept. 26	Aguma Nelson (Gha.) w.rsf.5 Bryan Roberts (Aust.), Accra, Ghana.
	Dec. 4	Azumah Nelson (Gha.) w.ko.6 Kabiru Akindele (Nig.), Freetown, Sierre Leone.
1982	Feb. 28	Azumah Nelson (Gha.) w.rsf.10 Charm Chiteule (Zam.) Lusaka, Zambia.
1983	Nov. 2	Azumah Nelson (Gha.) w.ko.9 Kabiru Akindele (Nig.), Lagos, Nigeria.

| 1986 | Feb. 28 | Tyrone Downes (Trin.) w.pts.12 Snake Mandeya (Zim.) Port of Spain, Trinidad. |
| 1987 | May 23 | Tyrone Downes (Trin.) w.ret.5 Ray Akwaye (Zim.) Port of Spain, Trinidad. |

Commonwealth Bantamweight Title Fights
(118 pounds: 8 stone 6 pounds)

1920	April 26	Jim Higgins (S.) w.pts.20 Vince Blackburn (Aust.), London.
1922	June 26	Tommy Harrison (E.) w.ko.13 Jim Higgins (S.), Liverpool.
1923	Feb. 26	Bugler Harry Lake (E.) w.pts.20 Tommy Harrison (E.), London.
	Nov. 26	Johnny Brown (E.) w.pts.20 Bugler Harry Lake (E.), London.
1925	Feb. 23	Johnny Brown (E.) w.ret.16 Harry Corbett (E.), London.
	Oct. 19	Johnny Brown (E.) w.ko.12 Mick Hill (E.), London.
1928	Aug. 29	Teddy Baldock (E.) w.rsf.2 Johnny Brown (E.), London.
1929	May 16	Teddy Baldock (E.) w.pts.15 Alf 'Kid' Pattenden (E.), London.
1930	May 22	Dick Corbett (E.), w.pts.15 Willie Smith (S.A.), London.
1931	Dec. 21	Dick Corbett (E.) w.pts.15 Johnny King (E.), Manchester.
1932	Oct. 10	Johnny King (E.) w.pts.15 Dick Corbett (E.), Manchester.
1933	June 12	Johnny King (E.) w.pts.15 Bobby Leitham (Can.), London.
1934	Feb. 12	Dick Corbett (E.) w.pts.15 Johnny King (E.), Manchester.
	Aug. 20	Dick Corbett (E.) drew 15 Johnny King (E.), London.
1941	Jan. 1	Jim Brady (S.) w.pts.15 Ritchie 'Kid' Tanner (B.G.), Dundee.
	Aug. 5	Jim Brady (S.) w.pts.15 Jackie Paterson (S.), Glasgow.
1945	Sept. 12	Jackie Paterson (S.) w.pts.15 Jim Brady (S.), Glasgow.
1947	Oct. 20	Jackie Paterson (S.) w.ko.3 Norman Lewis (W.), London.
1949	March 24	Stan Rowan (E.) w.pts.15 Jackie Paterson (S.), Liverpool.
	Nov. 12	Vic Toweel (S.A.) w.pts.15 Stan Rowan (E.), Johannesburg, South Africa.
1950	April 8	Vic Toweel (S.A.) w.pts.15 Fernando Gagnon (Can.), Johannesburg, South Africa.
	Dec. 2	Vic Toweel (S.A.) w.ret.10 Danny O'Sullivan (E.), Johannesburg, South Africa.
1952	Jan. 26	Vic Toweel (S.A.) w.pts.15 Peter Keenan (S.), Johannesburg, South Africa.
	Nov. 15	Jimmy Carruthers (Aust.) w.ko.1 Vic Toweel (S.A.), Johannesburg, South Africa.
1953	March 21	Jimmy Carruthers (Aust.) w.ko.10 Vic Toweel (S.A.) Johannesburg, South Africa.
1955	March 28	Peter Keenan (S.) w.pts.15 Bobby Sinn (Aust.), Sydney, Australia.
	Sept. 14	Peter Keenan (S.) w.ko.14 Jake Tuli (S.A.), Glasgow.
1956	Oct. 22	Peter Keenan (S.) w.rsf.2 Kevin James (Aust.), Sydney, Australia.
1957	May 22	Peter Keenan (S.) w.rsf.6 John Smillie (S.), Glasgow.
1958	April 2	Peter Keenan (S.) w.pts.15 Graham van de Walt (S.A.), Paisley.
	Oct. 16	Peter Kennan (S.) w.pts.15 Pat Supple (Can.), Paisley.
1959	Jan. 10	Freddie Gilroy (N.I.) w.rsf.11 Peter Keenan (S.), Belfast, Northern Ireland.
	Dec. 5	Freddie Gilroy (N.I.) w.ko.5 Bernie Taylor (S.A.), Belfast, Northern Ireland.
1960	March 19	Freddie Gilroy (N.I.) w.rsf.13 Billy Rafferty (S.), Belfast, Northern Ireland.
1962	March 3	Freddie Gilroy (N.I.) w.ko.12 Billy Rafferty (S.), Belfast, Northern Ireland.
	Oct. 20	Freddie Gilroy (N.I.) w.ret.9‖ John Caldwell (N.I.), Belfast, Northern Ireland.
1964	March 5	John Caldwell (N.I.) w.rsf.7‖ George Bowes (E.) Belfast, Northern Ireland.
1965	March 22	Alan Rudkin (E.) w.rsf.10‖ John Caldwell (N.I.), Nottingham.
1966	Sept. 6	Walter McGowan (S.) w.pts.15 Alan Rudkin (E.), London.
1968	May 13	Alan Rudkin (E.) w.pts.15 Walter McGowan (S.) Manchester.
1969	March 8	Lionel Rose (Aust.) w.pts.15 Alan Rudkin (E.), Melbourne, Australia.
1970	April 21	Alan Rudkin (E.) w.rsf.12 Johnny Clark (E.), London.

1972	Jan. 25	Alan Rudkin (E.) w.pts.15 Johnny Clark (E.), London.
	Sept. 16	Paul Ferreri (Aust.) w.pts.15 John Kellie (S.), Melbourne, Australia.
1973	April 26	Paul Ferreri (Aust.) w.pts.15 Fred Burns (Aust.), Carlton, Australia.
1975	March 7	Paul Ferreri (Aust.) w.rsf.8 Paddy Maguire (N.I.), Melbourne, Australia.
1976	March 25	Paul Ferreri (Aust.) w.pts.15 Brian Roberts (Aust.), Blacktown, Australia.
1977	Jan. 29	Sulley Shittu (Gha.) w.pts.15 Paul Ferreri (Aust.), Accra, Ghana.
1978	Nov. 2	Johnny Owen (W.) w.pts.15 Paul Ferreri (Aust.), Ebbw Vale, Wales.
1979	June 13	Johnny Owen (W.) w.ret.12‖ Dave Smith (E.), Caerphilly, Wales.
1980	June 28	Johnny Owen (W.) w.pts.15 John Feeney (E.), London.
	Dec. 11	Paul Ferreri (Aust.) w.rsf.12 Steve McLeod (Z.), Sydney, Australia.
1982	April 2	Paul Ferreri (Aust.) w.rsf.13 John Feeney (E.), Sydney, Australia.
	Sept. 24	Paul Ferreri (Aust.) w.rsf.12 Francis Musankabala (Zam.), Melbourne, Australia.
1983	May 7	Paul Ferreri (Aust.) w.ko.9 Stix Macloud (Zim.), Harare, Zimbabwe.
1986	April 18	Paul Ferreri (Aust.) w.rsf.5 Junior Thompson (Aust.) Canberra, Australia.
	Sept. 27	Ray Minus (Bah.) w.ret.10 Paul Ferreri (Aust.), Naussau, Bahamas.
1987	July 1	Ray Minus (Bah.) w.rsf.5 Sean Murphy (E.) London, England.

Commonwealth Flyweight Title Fights
(112 pounds: 8 stone)

1924	Sept. 6	Elky Clark (S.) w.rsf.10 Jim Hanna (N.I.), Glasgow.
1926	April 19	Elky Clark (S.) w.rsf.20 George 'Kid' Socks (E.), London.
1940	March 11	Jackie Paterson (S.) w.pts.15 Ritchie 'Kid' Tanner (B.G.), Manchester.
1941	Feb. 3	Jackie Paterson (S.) w.ko.8 Paddy Ryan (E.), Nottingham.
1943	June 19	Jackie Paterson (S.) w.ko.1 Peter Kane (E.), Glasgow.
1946	July 10	Jackie Paterson (S.) w.pts.15 Joe Curran (E.), Glasgow.
1948	March 23	John 'Rinty' Monaghan (N.I.) w.ko.7 Jackie Paterson (S.), Belfast.
1949	Sept. 30	John 'Rinty' Monaghan (N.I.) drew 15 Terry Allen (E.), Belfast.
1952	March 17	Teddy Gardner (E.) w.pts.15 Terry Allen (E.), Newcastle.
	Sept. 8	Jake Tuli (S.A.) w.rsf.12 Teddy Gardner (E.), Newcastle.
1954	Oct. 19	Dai Dower (W.) w.pts.15 Jake Tuli (S.A.), London.
1955	Feb. 8	Dai Dower (W.) w.pts.15 Eric Marsden (E.), London.
	Dec. 6	Dai Dower (W.) w.pts.15 Jake Tuli (S.A.), London.
1957	July 31	Frankie Jones (S.) w.ko.11 Len Reece (W.), Porthcawl.
	Oct. 23	Dennis Adams (S.A.) w.ko.3 Frankie Jones (S.), Glasgow.
1958	Jan. 24	Dennis Adams (S.A.) w.ko.2 Warner Batchelor (Aust.), Durban, South Africa.
1960	July 16	Dennis Adams (S.A.) w.ko.1 Les Smith (S.A.), Durban, South Africa.
1961	May 13	Dennis Adams (S.A.) dnc.9 John Mtimkulu (S.A.), Luanskya, Northern Rhodesia (Zambia).
1962	Dec. 10	Jackie Brown (S.) w.pts.15 Orizu Obilaso (Nig.), London.
1963	May 2	Walter McGowan (S.) w.ko.12 Jackie Brown (S.), Paisley.
	Sept. 12	Walter McGowan (S.) w.rsf.9 Kid Solomon (Jam.), Paisley.
1970	July 16	John McCluskey (S.) w.pts.15 Harry Hayes (Aust.), Melbourne, Australia.
1971	Aug. 6	Henry Nissen (Aust.) w.ret.8 John McCluskey (S.), Melbourne, Australia.
1974	March 14	Big Jim West (Aust.) w.ret.4‖ Henry Nissen (Aust.), Melbourne, Australia.
1976	July 3	Patrick Mambwe (Z.) w.rsf.9 Gwyn Jones (Aust.), Lusaka, Zambia.
1980	Feb. 8	Ray Amoo (Nig.) w.pts.15 Neil McLaughlin (N.I.), Lagos, Nigeria.
	Oct. 17	Stephen Muchoki (Kenya) w.rsf.12 Ray Amoo (Nig.), Copenhagen, Denmark.
1983	Feb. 3	Keith Wallace (E) w.rsf.9 Stephen Muchoki (Ken.), London, England.

1986	April 26	Richard Clarke (Jam.) w.ko.4 Wayne Mulholland (Aust.), Kingston, Jamaica.
1987	Oct. 10	Nana Yew Koradu (Gha.) w.ko.6 Alberto Musamkabala (Zam.), Accra, Ghana.
	Dec. 22	Nana Yew Koradu (Gha.) w.ko.2 Pat Nkwo (Nig.), Accra, Ghana.

European Professional Boxing

France was the first European country to adopt boxing professionally; dropping the national sport of *La Savatte* (using the feet) for the fast coming trend, *La Boxe Anglais*. This was in the very early days of the century and it spread rapidly, until French boxers advanced to such an extent that they became worthy opponents for their British counterparts. There was no control over European championships as such, except for the laws laid down by the British, but in 1911 the International Boxing Union (I.B.U.), situated in Paris to begin with, formed itself not only for the control of championship titles but also generally to supervise the sport in all its departments. It continued to function in World War II.

Following World War II its name was changed to the European Boxing Union (E.B.U.) from 1946 and it has continued ever since, issuing Belts for the winners of European titles. At the present time there are 20 countries affiliated to the E.B.U.: Austria, Belgium, Denmark, Finland, France, Great Britain, Greece, Hungary, Italy, Luxemburg, Netherlands, Norway, Portugal, Romania, Senegal, Spain, Switzerland, Turkey, West Germany and Yugoslavia.

The E.B.U. is affiliated to the World Boxing Council.

European Heavyweight Title Fights

International Boxing Union

1913	June 1	Georges Carpentier (F.) w.ko.4 Billy Wells (U.K.) Ghent.
	Dec. 8	Georges Carpentier (F.) w.ko.1 Billy Wells (U.K.), London.
1914	Jan. 19	Georges Carpentier (F.) w.ko.2 Pat O'Keefe (U.K.), Nice.
	July 16	Georges Carpentier (F.) w.dis.6 Gunboat Smith (U.K.), London.
1919	July 19	Georges Carpentier (F.) w.ko.8 Dick Smith (U.K.), Paris.
	Dec. 4	Georges Carpentier (F.) w.ko.1 Joe Beckett (U.K.), London.
1922	May 11	Georges Carpentier (F.) w.ko.1 Ted 'Kid' Lewis (U.K.), London.
	Sept. 24	Battling Siki (Sen.) w.ko.6 Georges Carpentier (F.), Paris.
1923	Feb. 17	Erminio Spalla (I.) w.pts.20 Piet van der Veer (Nl.), Rome.
	Sept. 22	Erminio Spalla (I.) drew 20 Jack Humbeck (B.), Milan.
1924	Sept. 28	Erminio Spalla (I.) w.pts.20 Piet van der Veer (Nl.), Milan.
1926	May 18	Paolino Uzcudun (Sp.) w.pts.15 Erminio Spalla (I.), Barcelona.
	June 14	Harry Persson (Swe.) w.ko.11 Phil Scott (U.K.), London.
1928	July 8	Paolino Uzcudun (Sp.) w.ko.11 Ludwig Haymann (G.), San Sebastian.
1929	Feb. 3	Pierre Charles (B.) w.pts.15 Ludwig Haymann (G.), Dortmund.
	June 30	Pierre Charles (B.) w.pts.15 Jose Santa (P.), Lisbon.
	July 31	Pierre Charles (B.) w.dis.5 Giacomo Panfilo (I), Brussels.
	Sept. 7	Pierre Charles (B.) w.rsf.11 Franz Diener (G.), Berlin.
1930	May 31	Pierre Charles (B.) w.pts.15 Roberto Roberti (I.), Brussels.
	July 20	Pierre Charles (B.) w.ko.2 Piet van der Veer (Nl.), Antwerp.
1931	July 8	Pierre Charles (B.) w.pts.15 Maurice Griselle (F.), Brussels.
	Aug. 30	Hein Muller (G.) w.pts.15 Pierre Charles (B.), Berlin.
1932	May 28	Pierre Charles (B.) w.pts.15 Hein Muller (G.), Brussels.
1933	May 13	Paolino Uzcudun (Sp.) w.pts.15 Pierre Charles (B.), Madrid.
	Oct. 22	Primo Carnera (I.), w.pts.15 Paolino Uzcudun (Sp.), Rome. (*This fight was also for the world heavyweight crown*).
1935	June 21	Pierre Charles (B.) w.pts.15 Vincenz Hower (G.), Berlin.

	Nov. 26	Pierre Charles (B.) w.pts.15 Robert Limousin (B.), Charleroi.
1937	March 17	Arno Kolblin (G.) w.pts.15 Pierre Charles (B.), Berlin.
1938	March 4	Heinz Lazek (A.) w.dis.2 Arno Kolblin (G.), Berlin.
	Aug. 10	Heinz Lazek (A.) w.pts.15 Santo De Leo (I.), Vienna.
	Sept. 16	Heinz Lazek (A.) w.pts.15 Walter Neusel (G.), Vienna.
1939	Jan. 20	Heinz Lazek (A.) w.pts.15 Karel Sys (B.), Berlin.
	March 17	Adolf Heuser (G.) w.ko.5 Heinz Lazek (A.) Berlin.
	July 2	Max Schmeling (G.) w.ko.1 Adolf Heuser (G.) Stuttgart.
1943	May 30	Olle Tandberg (Swe.) w.pts.15 Karel Sys (B.), Stockholm.
	Nov. 14	Karel Sys (B.) w.pts.15 Olle Tandberg (Swe.), Brussels.

European Boxing Union

1946	July 29	Bruce Woodcock (U.K.) w.ko.6 Albert Renet (F.), Manchester.
1947	March 17	Bruce Woodcock (U.K.) w.pts.15 Stephane Olek (F.), Manchester.
1949	June 2	Bruce Woodcock (U.K.) w.ko.14 Freddie Mills (U.K.), London.
1950	June 3	Jo Weidin (A.) w.pts.15 Stephane Olek (F.), Vienna.
1951	March 27	Jack Gardner (U.K.) w.pts.15 Jo Weidin (A.), London.
	Sept. 23	Hein ten Hoff (W.G.) w.pts.15 Jack Gardner (U.K.), Berlin.
1952	Jan. 12	Karel Sys (B.) w.pts.15 Hein ten Hoff (W.G.), Brussels.
	March 9	Heinz Neuhaus (W.G.) w.pts.15 Karel Sys (B.), Dortmund.
	July 20	Heinz Neuhaus (W.G.) w.ko.1 Hein ten Hoff (W.G.), Dortmund.
	Nov. 2	Heinz Neuhaus (W.G.) w.ko.4 Wilson Kohlbrecher (W.G.), Dortmund.
1953	Aug. 2	Heinz Neuhaus (W.G.) w.pts.15 Karel Sys (B.), Dortmund.
1954	Oct. 9	Heinz Neuhaus (W.G.) w.ko.3 Kurt Schiegl (A.), Frankfurt.
1955	June 26	Franco Cavicchi (I.) w.pts.15 Heinz Neuhaus (W.G.), Bologna.
1956	July 21	Franco Cavicchi (I.) w.ko.11 Heinz Neuhaus (W.G.), Bologna.
	Sept. 30	Ingemar Johansson (Swe.) w.ko.13 Franco Cavicchi (I.), Bologna.
1957	May 19	Ingemar Johannson (Swe.) w.ko.5 Henry Cooper (U.K.), Stockholm.
1958	Feb. 21	Ingemar Johansson (Swe.) w.ret.13 Joe Erskine (U.K.), Gothenburg.
1960	March 27	Dick Richardson (U.K.) w.rsf.13 Hans Kalbfell (W.G.), Dortmund.
	Aug. 29	Dick Richardson (U.K.) w.ret.8 Brian London (U.K.), Porthcawl.
1961	Feb. 18	Dick Richardson (U.K.) w.pts.15 Hans Kalbfell (W.G.), Dortmund.
1962	Feb. 24	Dick Richardson (U.K.) w.ko.1 Karl Mildenberger (W.G.), Dortmund.
	June 17	Ingemar Johansson (Swe.) w.ko.8 Dick Richardson (U.K.), Gothenburg.
1964	Feb. 24	Henry Cooper (U.K.) w.pts.15 Brian London (U.K.), Manchester.
	Oct. 17	Karl Mildenberger (W.G.) w.ko.1 Sante Amonti (I.), Berlin.
1965	May 14	Karl Mildenberger (W.G.) w.pts.15 Piero Tomasoni (I.), Frankfurt.
	Nov. 26	Karl Mildenberger (W.G.) w.pts.15 Gerhard Zech (W.G.), Frankfurt.
1966	June 15	Karl Mildenberger (W.G.) w.pts.15 Yvan Prebeg (Yugo.), Frankfurt.
1967	Feb 1	Karl Mildenberger (W.G.) w.pts.15 Piero Tomasoni (I.), Frankfurt.
	March 21	Karl Mildenberger (W.G.) w.rsf.8 Billy Walker (U.K.), London.
	Dec. 30	Karl Mildenberger (W.G.) w.pts.15 Gerhard Zech (W.G.), Berlin.
1968	Sept. 18	Henry Cooper (U.K.) w.dis.8 Karl Mildenberger (W.G.), London.
1969	March 13	Henry Cooper (U.K.) w.ko.5 Piero Tomasoni (I.), Rome.
	Dec. 6	Peter Weiland (W.G.) w.ko.1 Bernard Thebault (F.), Kiel.
1970	April 3	Jose Manuel Ibar Urtain (Sp.) w.ko.7 Peter Weiland (W.G.), Madrid.
	June 22	Jose Manuel Ibar Urtain (Sp.) w.pts.15 Jurgen Blin (W.G.) Barcelona.

	Nov. 10	Henry Cooper (U.K.) w.rsf.9 Jose Manuel Ibar Urtain (Sp.), London.
1971	March 16	Joe Bugner (U.K.) w.pts.15 Henry Cooper (U.K.), London.
	May 11	Joe Bugner (U.K.) w.pts.15 Jurgen Blin (W.G.), London.
	Sept. 27	Jack Bodell (U.K.) w.pts.15 Joe Bugner (U.K.), London.
	Dec. 17	Jose Manuel Ibar Urtain (Sp.) w.rsf.2 Jack Bodell (U.K.), Madrid.
1972	June 9	Jurgen Blin (W.G.) w.pts.15 Jose Urtain (Sp.) Madrid.
	Oct. 10	Joe Bugner (U.K.) w.ko.8 Jurgen Blin (W.G.), London.
1973	Jan. 16	Joe Bugner (U.K.) w.pts.15 Rudi Lubbers (Nl.), London.
	Oct. 2	Joe Bugner (U.K.) w.pts.15 Bepi Ros (I.), London.
1974	May 29	Joe Bugner (U.K.) w.ret.9 Mario Baruzzi (I.), Copenhagen.
1975	March 1	Joe Bugner (U.K.) w.rsf.4 Dante Cane (I.), Bologna.
1976	April 6	Richard Dunn (U.K.) w.rsf.3 Bernd August (W.G.), London.
	Oct. 12	Joe Bugner (U.K) w.ko.1 Richard Dunn (U.K.), London.
1977	March 12	Jean-Pierre Coopman (B.) w.ko.4 Jose Manuel Ibar Urtain (Sp.), Antwerp.
	May 7	Lucien Rodriguez (F.) w.pts.15 Jean-Pierre Coopman (B.), Antwerp.
	Sept. 7	Alfredo Evangelista (Sp.) w.rsf.11 Lucien Rodriguez (F.), Madrid.
	Nov. 26	Alredo Evangelista (Sp.) w.ko.1 Jean-Pierre Coopman (B.), Madrid.
1978	March 3	Alfredo Evangelista (Sp.) w.pts.15 Billy Aird (U.K.), Leon.
	Dec. 26	Alfredo Evangelista (Sp.) w.ko.4 Dante Cane (1.), Bologna.
1979	March 2	Alfredo Evangelista (Sp.) w.ko.2 Lucien Rodriguez (F.), Liege.
	April 18	Lorenzo Zanon (I.) w.pts.12 Alfredo Evangelista (Sp.), Turin.
	July 11	Lorenzo Zanon (I.) drew 12 Alfio Righetti (I.) Rimini.
	Oct. 10	Lorenzo Zanon (I.) w.pts.12 Felipe Rodriguez (Sp.). Turin.
1980	April 22	John L. Gardner (U.K.) w.ret.9 Rudi Gauwe (B.), London.
	Nov. 28	John L. Gardner (U.K.) w.ko.5 Lorenzo Zanon (I.), London.
1981	Nov. 26	Lucien Rodriguez (F.) w.pts.15 Felipe Rodriguez (Sp.), Paris.
1982	March 6	Lucien Rodriguez (F.) w.pts.12 Albert Syben (B.), Paris.
	April 2	Lucien Rodriguez (F.) w.pts.12 Mikan Popovic (Yugo.), Pau.
	June 7	Lucien Rodriguez (F.) w.pts.12 Alfredo Evangelista (Sp.), Paris.
1982	Nov. 11	Lucien Rodriguez (F.) w.pts.12 Domenico Adinolfi (I.), Paris, France.
1983	Aug. 5	Lucien Rodriguez (F.) w.ret.8 Al Syben (B.), Nimes, France.
1984	March 30	Lucien Rodriguez (F.) w.pts.12 David Pearce (U.K.) Limoges, France.
	Nov. 9	Steffan Tangstad (Nor.) w.pts.12 Lucien Rodriguez (F.), Copenhagen, Denmark.
1985	March 9	Anders Ekland (Swe.) w.rsf.4 Steffan Tamgstad (Nor.), Copenhagen, Denmark.
	Oct. 1	Frank Bruno (U.K.) w.ko.4 Anders Ekland (Swe.) Wembley, England.
1986	April 18	Steffan Tangstad (Nor.) w.pts.12 John Westgarth (U.K.) Randers, Denmark.
1987	Aug. 1	Alfredo Evangelista (Sp.) w.rsf.5 Andre van den Oetalaar (Nl.), Bilbao, Spain.
	March 28	Anders Ekland (Swe.) w.ko.7 Alfredo Evangelista (Sp.), Copenhagen, Denmark.
	Oct. 9	Francesco Damiana (I.) w.rsf.6 Anders Ekland (Swe.), Copenhagen, Denmark.
1988	April 22	Francesco Damiana (I.) w.rsf.3 John Emmin (Nl.), Milan, Italy.

European Cruiserweight Title Fights
(195 pounds: 13 stone 13 pounds)

1987	April 22	Sammy Reeson (U.K.) w.pts.12 Manfred Jassman (W.G.) London, England.
	Nov. 28	Sammy Reeson (U.K.) w.ko.7 Luiji Ricci (B.), Windsor, England.

European Light-Heavyweight Title Fights
(175 pounds: 12 stone 7 pounds)

International Boxing Union

1913	Feb. 12	Georges Carpentier (F.) w.ko.2 Bandsman Rice (U.K.), Paris.
1922	Sept. 24	Battling Siki (Sen.) w.ko.6 Georges Carpentier (F.), Paris.
1923	Feb. 26	Emile Morelle (F.) w.dis.6 Battling Siki (Sen.), Paris.
	Dec. 1	Raymond Bonnel (F.) w.ko.3 Emile Morelle (F.), Paris.
1924	April 27	Louis Clement (Sw.) w.pts.20 Raymond Bonnel (F.), Geneva.
1926	Jan. 5	Herman Van T'Hof (Nl.) w.ret.6 Louis Clement (Sw), Rotterdam.
	July 25	Fernand Delarge (B.) w.pts.15 Herman van T'Hof (Nl.), Rotterdam.
	Dec. 31	Fernand Delarge (B.) w.pts.15 Herman van T'Hof (Nl.), Brussels.
1927	June 19	Max Schmeling (G.) w.ko.14 Fernand Delarge (B.), Dortmund.
	Nov. 6	Max Schmeling (G.) w.ko.7 Hein Dormgorgen (G.), Leipzig.
1928	Jan. 6	Max Schmeling (G.) w.ko.1 Michele Bonaglia (I.), Berlin.
1929	Feb. 10	Michele Bonaglia (I.) w.pts.15 Jack Etienne (B.), Milan.
	June 27	Michele Bonaglia (I.) w.ret.4 Helm Miller (G.), Turin.
1930	Feb. 26	Michele Bonaglia (I.) w.pts.15 Jack Etienne (B.), Milan.
1931	March 18	Ernst Pistulla (G.) w.pts.15 Martinez de Alfara (Sp.), Valencia.
	Sept. 5	Ernst Pistulla (G.) drew Adolf Heuser (G.), Hamburg.
1932	June 25	Adolf Heuser (G.) w.ko.1 Martinez de Alfara (Sp.), Valencia.
1933	April 1	John Anderson (Swe.), w.pts.15 Jack Etienne (B.), Brussels.
1934	Feb. 7	Martinez de Alfara (Sp.) w.pts.15 Leon Steyaert (B.), Barcelona.
	March 26	Marcel Thil (F.) w.dis.13 Martinez de Alfara (Sp.), Paris.
	June 17	Marcel Thil (F.) w.ko.8 Adolf Witt (G.), Paris.
1935	Jan. 14	Marcel Thil (F.) w.pts.15 Jock McAvoy (U.K.), Paris.
	Aug. 9	Merlo Preciso (I.) w.pts.15 Adolf Witt (G.), Munich.
	Sept. 17	Heinz Lazek (A.) w.dis.13 Merlo Preciso (I.), Vienna.
1936	Feb. 25	Heinz Lazek (A.) w.ret.5 Renus de Boer (Nl.), Vienna.
	Aug. 3	Heinz Lazek (A.) w.ko.9 Emile Ollive (F.), Vienna.
	Sept. 1	Gustave Roth (B.) w.pts.15 Heinz Lazek (A.), Vienna.
	Oct. 29	Gustave Roth (B.) w.pts.15 Adolf Witt (G.), Berlin.
1937	March 24	Gustave Roth (B.) w.pts.15 Merlo Preciso (I.), Brussels.
	May 1	Gustave Roth (B.) w.pts.15 John Andersson (Swe.), Antwerp.
	Dec. 1	Gustave Roth (B.) drew 15 Karel Sys (B.), Brussels.
1938	Jan. 21	Gustave Roth (B.) w.pts.15 Josef Besselmann (G.), Berlin.
	March 25	Adolf Heuser (G.) w.ret.7 Gustave Roth (B.), Berlin.
	Sept. 9	Adolf Heuser (G.) w.pts.13 Merlo Preciso (I.), Berlin.
1939	Aug. 11	Adolf Heuser (G.) w.ko.2 Merio Preciso (I.), Berlin.
1942	April 5	Luigi Musina (I.) w.pts.15 Richard Bogi (G.), Berlin.
1934	May 10	Luigi Musina (I.) w.ko.3 Jack Nielson (D.), Milan.

European Boxing Union

1947	Sept. 8	Freddie Mills (U.K.) w.ret.4 Paul Goffaux (B.), London.
1938	Feb. 17	Freddie Mills (U.K.) w.ko.2 Paco Bueno (Sp.), London.
1950	July 9	Albert Yvel (F.) w.dis.10 Renato Tontini (I.), Algiers.
1951	March 27	Don Cockell (U.K.) w.rsf.9 Albert Yvel (F.), London.
	Oct. 16	Don Cockell (U.K.) w.ko.7 Albert Finch (U.K.), London.
1952	July 26	Conny Rux (W.G.) w.ko.12 Willy Schagen (Nl.), Berlin.
1953	July 12	Jacques Hairabedian (F.) w.pts.15 Renato Tontini (I.), Rome.
1954	April 9	Gerhard Hecht (W.G.) w.pts.15 Jacques Hairabedian (F.), Hamburg.
	Sept. 23	Gerhard Hecht (W.G.) w.pts.15 Wim Shoeck (Nl.), Hamburg.
1955	March 11	Willi Hoepner (W.G.) w.ret.3 Gerhard Hecht (W.G.), Hamburg.
	June 12	Gerhard Hecht (W.G.) w.ko.13 Willi Hoepner (W.G.), Dortmund.
1956	Feb. 25	Gerhard Hecht (W.G.) w.ret.13 Charles Colin (F.), St. Nazaire.
1957	July 12	Artemio Calzavara (I.) w.pts.15 Gerhard Hecht (W.G.), Milan.

1958	May 30	Willie Hoepner (W.G.) w.dis.6 Artemio Calzavara (I.), Hamburg.
	Dec. 12	Erich Schoppner (W.G.) w.ko.5 Willie Hoepner (W.G.) Hamburg.
1959	April 11	Erich Schoppner (W.G.) w.pts.15 Rocco Mazzola (I.), Dortmund.
	Nov. 7	Erich Schoppner (W.G.) w.pts.15 Sante Amonti (I.), Dortmund.
1960	April 9	Erich Schoppner (W.G.) w.pts.15 Helmut Ball (W.G.), Frankfurt.
1961	Feb. 5	Erich Schoppner (W.G.) w.rsf.13 Paul Roux (F.), Dortmund.
1962	Sept. 28	Giulio Rinaldi (I.) w.pts.15 Chic Calderwood (U.K.), Rome.
1963	May 23	Giulio Rinaldi (I.) w.pts.15 Erich Schoppner (W.G.), Rome.
1964	April 4	Gustav Scholz (W.G.) w.dis.8 Giulio Rinaldi (I.) Dortmund.
1965	July 8	Giulio Rinaldi (I.) w.ret.13 Peter-Klaus Gumpert (W.G.), Rome.
1966	March 11	Piero del Papa (I.) w.pts.15 Giulio Rinaldi (I.), Rome.
	Aug. 17	Piero del Papa (I.) d.n.c.6 (*rain*) Chic Calderwood (U.K.), Lignano
	Nov. 19	Piero del Papa (I.) w.dis.11 Wilhelm von Homburg (W.G.), Berlin.
1967	April 6	Piero del Papa (I.) w.pts.15 Pekka Kokkonen (Fin.), Helsinki.
	Aug. 9	Piero del Papa (I.) w.ko.4 Vittorio Saraudi (I.), San Benedetto del Tronto.
	Dec. 2	Lothar Stengel (W.G.) w.ko.5 Piero del Papa (I.), Frankfurt.
1968	Sept. 12	Tom Bogs (D.) w.ko.1 Lothar Stengel (W.G.), Copenhagen.
1969	Jan. 28	Tom Bogs (D.) w.pts.15 Peiro del Papa (I.), Copenhagen.
	June 28	Yvan Prebeg (Yugo.) w.pts.15 Eddie Avoth (U.K.), Zagreb.
1970	Feb. 6	Piero del Papa (I.) w.pts.15 Yvan Prebeg (Yugo.), Milan.
	Sept. 11	Piero del Papa (I.) w.pts.15 Rudiger Schmidtke (W.G.), Frankfurt.
	Nov. 27	Piero del Papa (I.) w.rsf.15 Horst Benedens (W.G.), Berlin.
1971	Jan. 22	Conny Velensek (W.G.) w.pts.15 Pierro del Papa (I.), Berlin.
	May 5	Conny Velensek (W.G.) drew 15 Chris Finnegan (U.K.), Berlin.
1972	Feb. 1	Chris Finnegan (U.K.) w.pts.15 Conny Velensek (W.G.), Nottingham.
	June 6	Chris Finnegan (U.K.) w.ko.8 Jan Lubbers (Nl.), London.
	Nov. 14	Rudiger Schmidtke (W.G.) w.rsf.12 Chris Finnegan (U.K.), London.
1973	March 13	John Conteh (U.K.) w.rsf.12 Rudiger Schmidtke (W.G.), London.
	May 22	John Conteh (U.K.) w.pts.15 Chris Finnegan (U.K.), London.
1974	March 12	John Conteh (U.K.) w.ret.6 Tom Bogs (D.), London.
	May 21	John Conteh (U.K.) w.rsf.6 Chris Finnegan (U.K.), London.
	Dec. 4	Domenico Adinolfi (I.) w.rsf.1 Karl-Heinz Klein (W.G.), Campione, Italy.
1975	April 19	Domenico Adinolfi (I.) w.ret.11 Freddy Dekerpel (B.), Wieze, Belgium.
	Oct. 31	Domenico Adinolfi (I.) w.ko.2 Rudi Lubbers (Nl.), Turin.
1976	May 14	Domenico Adinolfi (I.) w.rsf.8 Leo Kakolewiez (W.G.), Rome.
	July 10	Mate Parlov (Yugo.) w.rsf.11 Domenico Adinolfi (I.), Belgrade.
	Oct. 15	Mate Parlov (Yugo.) w.pts.15 Aldo Traversaro (I.), Milan.
1977	April 29	Mate Parlov (Yugo) w.pts.15 Francois Foil (Sw.), Morges.
	July 9	Mate Parlov (Yugo.) w.pts.15 Harald Skog (N.), Basle.
	Nov. 26	Aldo Traversaro (I.) w.rsf.11 Bunny Johnson (U.K.), Genoa.
1978	Feb. 16	Aldo Traversaro (I.) drew 15 Rudi Koopmans (Nl.), Rotterdam.
	April 28	Aldo Traversaro (I.) w.ret.5 Francois Fiol (Sw.), Geneva.
	Sept. 5	Aldo Traversaro (I.) drew 15 Avenemar Peralta (Sp.), Bibione.
1979	March 7	Rudi Koopmans (Nl.) w.ret.6 Aldo Traversaro (I.), Rotterdam.

	May 28	Rudi Koopmans (Nl.) w.rsf.10 Robert Amory (F.), Amsterdam.
	Oct. 30	Rudi Koopmans (Nl.) drew 12 Hocine Tafer (F.), Rotterdam.
1980	Jan. 28	Rudi Koopmans (Nl.) w.pts.12 Ennio Cometti (I.), Rotterdam.
	July 9	Rudi Koopmans (Nl.) w.pts.12 Fred Serres (Lux.), Differdange.
1981	Feb. 26	Rudi Koopmans (Nl.) w.ret.9 Hocine Tager (F.), Paris.
	Oct. 5	Rudi Koopmans (Nl.) w.rsf.1 Fred Serres (W.G.), Rotterdam.
1982	June 2	Rudi Koopmans (Nl.) w.ko.1 Christiano Cavina (I.), Chianiano.
	Nov. 15	Rudi Koopmans (Nl.) w.rsf.8 Alex Blanchard (Nl.), Amsterdam, Holland.
1983	July 10	Rudi Koopmans (Nl.) w.ko.8 Manfred Jassman (W.G.), Frankfurt, W. Germany.
	Nov. 21	Rudi Koopmans (Nl.) w.pts.12 Ruffino Augulo (F.), Paris, France.
1984	Feb. 2	Richard Caramanolis (F.) w.ret.8 Rudi Koopmans (Nl.), Marseilles, France.
	May 28	Alex Blanchard (Nl.) w.rsf.6 Richard Caramanolis (F.), Amsterdam, Holland.
	Sept. 15	Alex Blanchard (Nl.) w.ret.4 Manfred Jassman (W.G.), Dortmund, Germany.
1985	April 22	Alex Blanchard (Nl.) drew 12 Richard Caramanolis (F.), Rotterdam, Holland.
	Dec. 11	Alex Blanchard (Nl.) drew 12 Dennis Andries (U.K.), London, England.
1986	Oct. 3	Alex Blanchard (Nl.) w.pts.12 Ralf Rocchigiani (W.G.), Berlin, West Germany.
1987	Aug. 15	Alex Blanchard (Nl). w.ret.8 Enrico Scacchia (I.), Berne, Switzerland.
	Nov. 11	Tom Collins (U.K.) w.ko.2 Alex Blanchard (Nl.), Usk, Wales.
1988	May 20	Tom Collins (U.K.) w.ko.9 Mark Taylor (U.K.), Wembley, England.

European Middleweight Title Fights
(160 pounds: 11 stone 6 pounds)

International Boxing Union

1912	Feb. 29	Georges Carpentier (F.) w.ko.2 Jim Sullivan (U.K.), Monte Carlo.
1920	Dec. 7	Ercole Balzac (F.) w.ko.9 Tom Gummer (U.K.), Paris.
1921	Jan. 13	Ercole Balzac (F.) w.dis.10 Jim Tyncke (B.), Paris.
	Feb. 21	Gus Platts (U.K.) w.ret.7 Ercole Balzac (F.), Sheffield.
	May 31	Johnny Basham (U.K.) w.pts.20 Gus Platts (U.K.), London.
	Oct. 14	Ted 'Kid' Lewis (U.K.) w.ko.12 Johnny Basham (U.K.), London.
1923	Feb. 15	Roland Todd (U.K.) w.pts.20 Ted 'Kid' Lewis (U.K.), London.
1924	Nov. 30	Bruno Frattini (I.) w.pts.20 Roland Todd (U.K.), Milan.
	Dec. 16	Bruno Frattini (I.) drew 20 Francis Charles (F.), Paris.
1925	June 8	Tommy Milligan (U.K.) w.pts.20 Bruno Frattini (I.), London.
1926	Jan. 31	Rene Devos (B.) w.pts.15 Bruno Frattini (I.), Milan.
	March 19	Rene Devos (B.) w.pts.15 Hein Domgorgen (G.), Berlin.
1927	March 31	Rene Devos (B.) w.pts.20 Jack Etienne (B.), Brussels.
1928	April 1	Mario Basisio (I.) w.pts.15 Barthelemy Molina (F.), Milan.
	June 24	Leone Lacovacci (I.) w.pts.15 Mario Bosisio (I.), Rome.
	Dec. 16	Leone Jacovacci (I.) w.pts.15 Hein Domgorgen (G.), Milan.
1929	March 27	Marcel Thil (F.) w.pts.15 Leone Jacovacci (I.), Paris.
	Nov. 1	Marcel Thil (F.) w.ko.7 Motzi Spakow (R.), Bucharest.
1930	March 17	Marcel Thil (F.) w.pts.15 Alfredo Pegazzano (I.), Paris.
	Nov. 23	Mario Biosisio (I.) w.pts.15 Marcel Thil (F.), Milan.
1931	March 1	Mario Biosisio (I.) w.pts.15 Enzo Fiermonto (I.), Milan.
	June 19	Poldi Steinbach (A.) w.pts.15 Mario Biosisio (I.), Vienna.
	Aug. 30	Hein Domgorgen (G.) w.pts.15 Poldi Steinbach (A.), Berlin.
1932	May 9	Ignacio Ara (Sp.) w.ko.11 Karl Neubauer (A.), Vienna.
1933	June 24	Gustave Roth (U.K.) w.pts.15 George Axiotti (R.), Bucharest.

1934	May 3	Marcel Thil (F.) w.pts.15 Gustave Roth (B.), Paris.
	Oct. 16	Marcel Thil (F.) drew 15 Carmelo Candel (F.), Paris.
1935	May 4	Marcel Thil (F.) w.ret.14 Kid Jaks (Czc.), Paris.
	June 1	Marcel Thil (F.), w.pts.15 Ignaclo Ara (Sp.), Valencia.
1938	April 7	Edouard Tennet (F.) w.ret.12 Josef Besselmann (G.), Berlin.
	July 17	Bep van Kalveren (Nl.) w.pts.15 Edouard Tenet (F.), Rotterdam.
	Nov. 14	Anton Christoforidis (Gr.) w.pts.15 Bep van Klaveren (Nl.), Rotterdam.
1939	Jan. 14	Edouard Tenet (F.) w.pts.15 Anton Christoforidis (Gr.), Paris.
1942	May 23	Josef Besselmann (G.) w.pts.15 Mario Casadei (I.), Stuttgart.
1943	Jan. 20	Josef Besselmann (G.) w.pts.15 Luc van Dam (Nl.), Hamburg.

European Boxing Union

1947	Feb. 2	Marcel Cerdan (F.) w.ko.1 Leon Fouguet (B.), Paris.
1948	Jan. 26	Marcel Cerdan (F.) w.ko.2 Giovanni Manca (I.), Paris.
	May 23	Cyrille Delannoit (B.) w.pts.15 Marcel Cerdan (F.), Brussels.
	July 10	Marcel Cerdan (F.) w.pts.15 Cyrille Delannoit (B.), Brussels.
	Nov. 6	Cyrille Delannoit (B.) w.pts.15 Luc van Dam (Nl.), Brussels.
1949	May 7	Tiberio Mitri (I.) w.pts.15 Cyrille Delannoit (B.), Brussels.
	Dec. 12	Tiberio Mitri (I.) w.pts.15 Jean Stock (F.), Paris.
1951	Feb. 27	Randolph Turpin (U.K.) w.ko.1 Luc van Dam (Nl.), London.
1953	June 9	Randolph Turpin (U.K.) w.pts.15 Charles Humez (F.), London.
1954	May 2	Tiberio Mitri (I.) w.rsf.1 Randolph Turpin (U.K.), Rome.
	Nov. 13	Charles Humez (F.) w.rsf.3 Tiberio Mitri (I.), Milan.
1956	Oct. 13	Charles Humez (F.) w.rsf.12 Franco Festucci (I.), Milan.
1957	Feb. 4	Charles Humez (F.) w.rsf.8 Pat McAteer (U.K.), Paris.
	May 29	Charles Humez (F.) w.pts.15 Italo Scortichini (I.), Milan.
1958	Oct. 4	Gustav Scholz (W.G.) w.ret.12 Charles Humez (F.), Berlin.
1959	July 4	Gustav Scholz (W.G.) w.pts.15 Hans-Werner Wohlers (W.G.), Berlin.
	Nov. 14	Gustav Scholz (W.G.) w.ret.1 Peter Muller (W.G.), Berlin.
	Dec. 5	Gustav Scholz (W.G.) w.rsf.14 Andre Drille (F.), Berlin.
1961	Oct. 17	John McCormack (U.K.) w.pts.15 Harko Kokmeyer (Nl.), London.
1962	Jan. 6	John McCormack (U.K.), w.pts.15 Heini Freytag (W.G.), Frankfurt.
	Feb. 8	Chris Christensen (D.) w.dis.4 John McCormack (U.K.), Copenhagen.
	May 16	Lazlo Papp (Hun.) w.rsf.7 Chris Christensen (D.), Vienna.
	Nov. 19	Lazlo Papp (Hun.) w.ko.9 Hippolyte Annex (F.), Paris.
1963	Feb. 6	Lazlo Papp (Hun.) w.rsf.15 George Aldridge (U.K.), Vienna.
	March 30	Lazlo Papp (Hun.) w.rsf.4 Peter Muller (W.G.), Dortmund.
	Dec. 6	Lazlo Papp (Hun.) w.rsf.8 Luis Folledo (Sp.), Madrid.
1964	July 2	Lazlo Papp (Hun.) w.ko.4 Chris Christensen (D.), Copenhagen.
	Oct. 9	Lazlo Papp (Hun.) w.pts.15 Mick Leahy (U.K.), Vienna.
1965	Oct. 15	Nino Benvenuti (I.) w.rsf.6 Luis Folledo (Sp.), Rome.
1966	May 14	Nino Benvenuti (I.) w.rsf.14 Jupp Elze (W.G.), Berlin.
	Oct. 21	Nino Benvenuti (I.) w.ret.10 Pascal Di Benedetto (F.), Rome.
1967	Nov. 17	Juan Carlos Duran (I.) w.rsf.12 Luis Folledo (Sp.), Turin.
1968	March 26	Juan Carlos Duran (I.) w.dis.10 Wally Swift (U.K.), Birmingham.
	June 12	Juan Carlos Duran (I.) w.rsf.15 Jupp Elze (W.G.), Cologne.
1969	Feb. 20	Juan Carlos Duran (I.) w.dis.13 Johnny Pritchett (U.K.), Milan.
	June 25	Juan Carlos Duran (I.) w.rsf.14 Hans-Dieter Schwartz (W.G.), Montecantini.
	Sept. 11	Tom Bogs (D.) w.pts.15 Juan Carlos Duran (I.), Copenhagen.
	Dec. 7	Tom Bogs (D.) w.ret.5 Luigi Patruno (I.), Aarhus.
1970	April 2	Tom Bogs (D.) w.ret.11 Les McAteer (U.K.), Aarhus.

	Aug. 27	Tom Bogs (D.) w.pts.15 Chris Finnegan (U.K.), Copenhagen.
	Dec. 4	Juan Carlos Duran (I.) w.pts.15 Tom Bogs (D.), Rome.
1971	June 9	Jean-Claude Bouttier (F.) w.pts.15 Juan Carlos Duran (I.), Paris.
	Dec. 20	Jean-Claude Bouttier (F.) w.ko.14 Bunny Sterling (U.K.), Paris.
1973	Jan. 18	Tom Bogs (D.) w.pts.15 Fabio Bettini (F.), Copenhagen.
	Nov. 7	Elio Calcabrini (I.) w.pts.15 Bunny Sterling (U.K.), San Remo.
1974	March 2	Jean-Claude Bouttier (F.) w.ret.12 Elio Calcabrini (I.), Paris.
	May 25	Kevin Finnegan (U.K.) w.pts.15 Jean-Claude Bouttier (F.), Paris.
1975	May 7	Gratien Tonna (F.) w.pts.15 Kevin Finnegan (U.K.), Monte Carlo.
1976	Feb. 23	Bunny Sterling (U.K.) w.rsf.13 Frank Reiche (W.G.), Hamburg.
	June 4	Angelo Jacopucci (I.) w.pts.15 Bunny Sterling (U.K.), Milan.
	Oct. 1	Germano Valsecchi (I.) w.pts.15 Angelo Jacopucci (I.), Milan.
	Nov. 19	Germano Valsecchi (I.) w.ko.7 Poul Knudsen (D.), Randers.
1977	Feb. 4	Alan Minter (U.K.) w.ko.5 Germano Valsecchi (I.), Milan.
	Sept. 21	Gratien Tonna (F.) w.rsf.8‖ Alan Minter (U.K.), Milan.
1978	July 19	Alan Minter (U.K.) w.ko.6 Angelo Jacopucci (I.), Bellaria.
	Nov. 7	Alan Minter (U.K.) w.ret.6 Gratien Tonna (F.), Wembley.
1980	Feb. 7	Kevin Finnegan (U.K.) w.pts.12 Gratien Tonna (F.), Paris.
	May 4	Kevin Finnegan (U.K.) drew 12 George Steinerr (W.G.), Munich.
	Sept. 10	Matteo Salvemini (I.) w.pts.12 Kevin Finnegan (U.K.), San Remo.
	Dec. 8	Tony Sibson (U.K.) w.ko.7 Matteo Salvemini (I.), London.
1981	May 14	Tony Sibson (U.K.) w.pts.12 Andoni Amana (Sp.), Bilbao.
	Sept. 15	Tony Sibson (U.K.) w.ko.3 Alan Minter (U.K.), London.
	Nov. 24	Tony Sibson (U.K.) w.ko.10 Nicola Cirelli (I.), London.
1982	May 4	Tony Sibson (U.K.), w.rsf.10 Jacques Chinon (F.), London.
	Dec. 3	Louis Arcaries (F.) w.rsf.6 Frank Wissenbach (W.G.), Paris, France.
1983	March 25	Louis Arcaries (F.) w.ko.4 Frank Wintersetein (W.G.), Paris, France.
	Aug. 5	Louis Arcaries (F.) w.pts.12 Stephane Ferrers (F.), Nimes, France.
1984	Feb. 25	Tony Sibson (U.K.) w.pts.12 Louis Arcaries (F.), Paris, France.
	Nov. 27	Tony Sibson (U.K.) w.pts.12 Mark Kaylor (U.K.), Wembley, England.
1985	June 20	Ayub Kalule (D.) w.rsf.8 Pierre Joly (F.), Copenhagen, Denmark.
	Dec. 19	Ayub Kalule (D.) w.pts.12 Sumbu Kalambay (I.), Ancona, Italy.
1986	Feb. 5	Herol Graham (U.K.) w.rsf.10 Ayub Kalule (D.), Sheffield, England.
	Nov. 4	Herol Graham (U.K.) w.ret.8 Mark Kaylor (U.K.), Wembley, England.
1987	May 26	Sumbu Kalambay (I.) w.pts.12 Herol Graham (U.K.), Wembley, England.
	Dec. 18	Pierre Joly (F.) w.pts.12 Miguel Angel (Sp.), Pointe-a-Pitre, France.
1988	April 18	Christophe Tiozzo (F.), w.pts.12 Pierre Joly (F.), Paris, France.

European Light-Middleweight Title Fights
(154 pounds: 11 stone)

European Boxing Union

| 1964 | May 22 | Bruno Visintin (I.) w.pts.15 Yolande Leveque (F.), Turin. |
| | Aug. 20 | Bruno Visintin (I.) w.pts.15 Cesareo Barrera (Sp.), San Remo. |

	Nov. 23	Bruno Visintin (I.) w.ko.14 Souleymane Diallo (F.), Paris.
1965	March 12	Bruno Visintin (I.) w.rsf.11 Chris Christensen (D.), Copenhagen.
	June 28	Bruno Visintin (I.) w.pts.15 Ray Philippe (Lux.), Luxemburg.
	Oct. 16	Bruno Visintin (I.) w.pts.15 Peter Muller (W.G.), Dortmund.
1966	Jan. 1	Bo Hogberg (Swe.) w.ret.7 Bruno Visintin (I.), Copenhagen.
	Feb. 11	Yolande Leveque (F.) w.pts.15 Bo Hogberg (Swe.), Stockholm.
	June 17	Sandro Mazzinghi (I.) w.ko.12 Yolande Leveque (F.), Rome.
	Nov. 11	Sandro Mazzinghi (I.) w.ret.14 Bo Hogberg (Swe.), Stockholm.
1967	Feb. 3	Sandro Mazzinghi (I.) w.rsf.10 Jean-Baptiste Rolland (F.), Milan.
	Sept. 9	Sandro Mazzinghi (I.) w.ret.6‖ Wally Swift (U.K.), Milan.
	Dec. 1	Sandro Mazzinghi (I.) w.ko.4 Joseph Gonzales (F.), Rome.
1968	Nov. 29	Remo Golfarini (I.) w.pts.15 Joseph Gonzales (F.), Rome.
1969	May 6	Remo Golfarini (I.) w.ret.10 Peter Marklewitz (A.), Vienna.
	July 16	Gerhard Piaskowy (W.G.) w.pts.15 Remo Golfarini (I.), Vibo Valentia.
1970	Jan. 24	Gerhard Piaskowy (W.G.) w.ko.8 Jean-Baptiste Rolland (F.), Berlin.
	Sept. 11	Jose Hernandez (Sp.) w.rsf.14 Gerhard Piaskowy (W.G.), Barcelona.
	Nov. 27	Jose Hernandez (Sp.) w.pts.15 Peter Markletwitz (A.), Berlin.
1971	June 18	Jose Hernandez (Sp.) w.pts.15 Domenico Tiberia (I.), Barcelona.
1972	March 24	Jose Hernandez (Sp.) drew 15 Jacques Kechichian (F.), Barcelona.
	July 5	Carlos Duran (I.) w.pts.15 Jose Hernandez (Sp.), San Remo.
	Nov. 15	Carlos Duran (I.) w.dis.14 Jacques Kechichian (F.), Schio.
1973	March 15	Carlos Duran (I.) w.pts.15 Johann Orsolics (A.), Vienna.
	July 4	Jacques Kechichian (F.) w.rsf.9 Carlos Duran (I.), Lignano.
1974	Feb. 1	Jacques Kechichian (F.) w.rsf.9 Johann Orsolics (A.), Vienna.
	June 7	Jose Duran (Sp.) w.pts.15 Jacques Kechichian (F.), Madrid.
	Sept. 3	Jose Duran (Sp.) w.rsf.11 Eckhard Dagge (W.G.), Berlin.
	Nov. 5	Jose Duran (Sp.) w.rsf.14 Johann Orsolics (A.), Berlin.
1975	Jan. 7	Jose Duran (Sp.) w.pts.15 Franz Csandl (A.), Vienna.
	June 24	Eckhard Dagge (W.G.) w.ret.9 Jose Duran (Sp.), Berlin.
	Nov. 4	Eckhard Dagge (W.G.) w.rsf.7 Franz Csandl (A.), Vienna.
1976	Jan. 16	Vito Antuofermo (I.) w.pts.15 Eckhard Dagge (W.G.), Berlin.
	March 26	Vito Antuofermo (I.) w.ret.13 Jean-Claude Warusfel (F.), Milan.
	Oct. 1	Maurice Hope (U.K.) w.rsf.15 Vito Antuofermo (I.), Rome.
1977	March 15	Maurice Hope (U.K.) drew 15 Eckhard Dagge (W.G.), Berlin.
	May 7	Maurice Hope (U.K.) w.pts.15 Frank Wissenbach (W.G.), Hamburg.
	Nov. 8	Maurice Hope (U.K.) w.ko.5 Joel Bonnetaz (F.), London.
1978	Nov. 21	Gilbert Cohen (F.) w.ko.3 Jimmy Batten (U.K.), London.
1979	March 17	Marijan Benes (Yugo.) w.ko.4 Gilbert Cohen (F.), Banja Luka.
	June 6	Marijan Benes (Yugo.) w.rsf.8 Andoni Amana (Sp.), Bilbao.
	Oct. 30	Marijan Benes (Yugo.) w.rsf.3 Aarde Huussen (Nl.), Rotterdam.
1980	Feb. 13	Marijan Benes (Yugo.) drew 12 Damiano Lassandro (I.), Pesaro.
	Oct. 6	Marijan Benes (Yugo.) w.rsf.5 Georges Warusfel (F.), Paris.
1981	March 19	Louis Acaries (F.) w.pts.12 Marijan Benes (Yugo.), Paris, France.
	July 1	Luigi Minchillo (I.) w.pts.12 Louis Arcaries (F.), Fornia, Italy.

	Nov. 28	Luigi Minchillo (I.) w.ko.1 Claude Martin (F.), St. Malo, France.
1982	March 30	Luigi Minchillo (I.) w.pts.12 Maurice Hope (U.K.), Wembley, England.
	Aug. 22	Luigi Minchillo (I.) w.rsf.4 Jean-Andre Emmerich (W.G.), Praia, Italy.
	Oct. 28	Luigi Minchillo (I.) w.pts.12 Marijan Benes (Yugo.), San Servero, Italy.
1983	May 23	Herol Graham (U.K.) w.rsf.2 Clemente Tshinza (B.), Sheffield, England.
	Dec. 9	Herol Graham (U.K.) w.rsf.8 Germain LeMaitre (F.), St.Nazaire, France.
1984	May 25	Jimmy Cable (U.K.) w.rsf.11 Said Skouma (F.), Toulouse, France.
	Sept. 28	Georg Steinherr (W.G.) w.pts.12 Jimmy Cable (U.K.), Munich, West Germany.
	Nov. 30	Said Skouma (F.) w.rsf.6 Enrico Scacchia (Sw.), Geneva, Switzerland.
1986	April 10	Said Skouma (F.) w.rsf.8 Angelo Liquori (I.), Antibes, France.
	May 23	Said Skouma (F) w.rsf.4 Alfonso Redondo (S.), Bordeaux, France.
	Sept. 17	Chris Pyatt (U.K.) w.ko.1 John van Elteren (Nl), London, England.
1987	Jan. 28	Gianfranco Rossi (I.) w.pts.12 Chris Pyatt (U.K.), Perugia, Italy.
	May 6	Gianfranco Rossi (I.) w.rsf.2 Emilo Sole (Sp.), Lucca, Italy.
	May 27	Gianfranco Rossi (I.) w.dis.5 Marc Ruocco (F.), Cannes, France.
1988	Jan. 2	Rene Jacquot (F.) w.rsf.4 Luigi Minchillo (I.), Rimini, Iraly.
	April 9	Rene Jacquot (F.) w.rsf.12 Eric Taton (B.), Echirolles, France.
	June 29	Rene Jacquot (F.) w.ko.11 Erwin Heiber (W.G.), Hamburg, W. Germany.

European Welterweight Title Fights
(147 pounds: 10 stone 7 pounds)

International Boxing Union

1910	Dec. 19	Young Joseph (U.K.) w.pts.20 Battling Lecroix (F.), Paris.
1911	May 5	Young Joseph (U.K.) w.pts.15 Robert Eustache (F.), Paris.
	Oct. 23	Georges Carpentier (F.) w.ret.10 Young Joseph (U.K.), London.
1915	April 20	Albert Badoud (Sw.) w.ko.9 Johnny Basham (U.K.), Liverpool.
1917	Aug. 31	Ted 'Kid' Lewis (U.K.) w.ko.1 Albert Badoud (Sw.), New York.
1919	Aug. 17	Albert Badoud (Sw.) w.pts.20 Francis Charles (F.), Paris.
1920	June 9	Ted 'Kid' Lewis (U.K.) w.ko.9 Johnny Basham (U.K.), London.
	Nov. 19	Ted 'Kid' Lewis (U.K.) w.ko.19 Johnny Basham (U.K.), London.
1921	June 25	Piet Hobin (B.) w.ret.7 Francis Charles (F.), Paris.
1922	Sept. 12	Piet Hobin (B.) w.pts.15 Fred Davies (U.K.), Brussels.
1923	March 6	Piet Hobin (B.) w.pts.15 Billy Porcher (U.K.), Paris.
	April 23	Billy Mack (U.K.) w.dis.11 Piet Hobin (B.), Liverpool.
	Aug. 26	Piet Hobin (B.) w.pts.20 Leo Darton (B.), Antwerp.
	Sept. 18	Piet Hobin (B.) w.pts.12 Billy Mack (U.K.), Antwerp.
1924	Feb. 3	Piet Hobin (B.) w.pts.15 Ricardo Alis (Sp.), Barcelona.
	Dec. 28	Piet Hobin (B.) drew20 Mario Bosisio (I.), Milan.
1925	April 7	Piet Hobin (B.) drew15 Barthelemy Molina (F.), Paris.
	Sept. 27	Mario Bosisio (I.) drew15 Piet Hobin (B.), Milan.
	Nov. 28	Mario Bosisio (I.) w.pts.15 Nol Steenhorst (Nl.), Rome.
1926	May 23	Mario Bosisio (I.) w.pts.15 Rene Devos (B.), Milan.
	July 21	Mario Bosisio (I.) w.pts.15 Emile Romerio (I.), Milan.
1927	June 12	Mario Bosisio (I.) w.pts.15 Van Vliet (Nl.), Milan.
1928	Nov. 26	Alf Genon (B.) w.pts.15 Leo Darton (B.), Charleroi.
1929	June 2	Alf Genon (B.) w.pts.15 Van Vliet (Nl.), Brussels.
	Oct. 19	Gustave Roth (B.) w.pts.15 Alf Genon (B.), Brussels.
	Dec. 17	Gustave Roth (B.) w.pts.15 Leo Darton (B.), Charleroi.
1930	Feb. 5	Gustave Roth (B.) w.pts.15 Camille Desmedt (B.), Charleroi.
	May 11	Gustave Roth (B.) drew15 Vittorio Venturi (I.), Rome.

	Oct. 15	Gustave Roth (B.) w.pts.15 Aime Raphael (F.), Brussels.
	Dec. 3	Gustave Roth (B.) w.pts.15 Gustav Eder (G.), Brussels.
1931	Jan. 14	Gustave Roth (B.) w.pts.15 Hans Holdt (D.), Copenhagen.
	March 6	Gustave Roth (B.) drew15 Franta Nekoiny (Cze.), Prague.
	June 27	Gustave Roth (B.) w.pts.15 Vittorio Venturi (I.), Brussels.
	Aug. 30	Gustave Roth (B.) w.pts.15 Gustav Eder (G.), Berlin.
	Nov. 18	Gustave Roth (B.) w.pts.15 Huib Huizenaar (Hun.), Brussels.
1932	April 26	Gustave Roth (B.) w.pts.15 Camille Desmedt (B.), Charleroi.
	June 24	Gustave Roth (B.) w.pts.15 George Aciotti (F.), Brussels.
	Oct. 26	Adrien Aneet :B.) w.dis.6 Gustave Roth (B.), Brussels.
1933	Jan. 4	Adrien Aneet (B.) w.pts.15 Vittorio Venturi (I.), Brussels.
	May 22	Jack Hood (U.K.) w.dis.3 Adrien Aneet (B.), Birmingham.
1934	June 8	Gustave Eder (G.) w.ko.11 Nestor Charlier (B.), Berlin.
	Sept. 2	Gustave Eder (G.) drew15 Vittorio Venturi (I.), Zurich.
	Oct. 5	Gustave Eder (G.) w.pts.15 Francois Sybile (B.), Berlin.
1935	Jan. 11	Gustave Eder (G.) w.ko.2 Elnar Aggerholm (D.), Copenhagen.
	March 23	Gustave Eder (G.) w.ko.5 Karl Blaho (A.), Berlin.
	June 29	Gustave Eder (G.) w.pts.15 Vittorio Venturi (I.), Hamburg.
	Nov. 11	Gustave Eder (G.) w.ko.9 Felix Wouters (B.), Berlin.
	Dec. 9	Gustave Eder (G.) w.pts.15 Hilario Martinez (Sp.), Berlin.
1936	July 23	Felix Wouters (B.) w.pts.15 Len Saunder (Nl.), Brussels.
	Nov. 25	Felix Wouters (B.) w.pts.15 Al Baker (U.K.), Brussels.
1937	Nov. 3	Felix Wouters (B.) w.pts.15 Cleto Locatelli (I.), Brussels.
1938	Feb. 16	Felix Wouters (B.) w.pts.15 Gustave Eder (G.), Brussels.
	Aug. 26	Felix Wouters (B.) drew15 Gustave Eder (G.), Berlin.
	Dec. 26	Saverio Turiello (I.) w.pts.15 Felix Wouters (B.), Milan.
1939	June 3	Marcel Cerdan (F.) w.pts.15 Saverio Turiello (I.), Milan.
1941	May 4	Marcel Cerdan (F.) w.ret.8 Omar Kouidri (F.), Oran.
1942	May 23	Marcel Cerdan (F.) w.pts.15 Felix Wouters (B.), Brussels.
	Sept. 30	Marcel Cerdan (F.), w.ret.1 Jean Ferrer (F.), Paris.

European Boxing Union

1946	June 4	Ernie Roderick (U.K.) w.pts.15 Omar Kouidri (F.), London.
1947	Feb. 1	Robert Villemain (F.) w.ret.9 Ernie Roderick (U.K.), Paris.
	June 1	Robert Villemain (F.) w.pts.15 Kid Marcel (F.), Marseilles.
	Nov. 24	Robert Villemain (F.) w.ret.9 Egisto Peyre (I.), Paris.
	Dec. 17	Robert Villemain (F.) w.pts.15 Omar Kouidri (F.), Paris.
1949	March 4	Livio Minelli (I.) w.rsf.11 Giel de Roode (Nl.), The Hague.
	Nov. 10	Livio Minelli (I.) w.pts.15 Omar Kouidri (F.) Algiers.
1950	July 14	Michele Palermo (I.) w.pts.15 Livio Minelli (I.) Milan.
1951	Feb. 19	Eddie Thomas (U.K.) w.pts.15 Michele Palermo (I.), Carmarthen.
	June 13	Charles Humez (F.) w.pts.15 Eddie Thomas (U.K.), Porthcawl.
	May 29	Charles Humez (F.) w.ko.7 Emile Delmine (B.), Paris.
1953	March 22	Gilbert Lavoine (F.) w.dis.10 Cliff Curvis (U.K.), Paris.
	Aug. 6	Gilbert Lavoine (F.) w.ko.4 Kid Dussart (B.), Nice.
1954	Aug. 26	Wally Thom (U.K.) w.rsf.10 Gilbert Lavoine (F.), Liverpool.
	Oct. 19	Wally Thom (U.K.) w.ko.6 Lew Lazar (U.K.), London.
1955	June 23	Idrissa Dione (F.) w.pts.15 Wally Thom (U.K.), Liverpool.
	Nov. 28	Idrissa Dione (F.) w.pts.15 Bep van Klaveren (Nl.), Rotterdam.
1956	Feb. 12	Emilio Marconi (I.) w.pts.15 Idrissa Dione (F.), Grosseto.
	Oct. 29	Emilio Marconi (I.) w.dis.13 Valere Benedetto (F.), Bologna.
1957	May 30	Emilio Marconi (I.) drew15 Peter Waterman (U.K.), Rome.
1958	Jan. 28	Peter Waterman (U.K.) w.rsf.15 Emilio Marconi (I.), London.
	Dec. 26	Emilio Marconi (I.) w.pts.15 Jacques Herbillon (F.), Milan.
1959	April 19	Duilio Loi (I.) w.pts.15 Emilio Marconi (I.), Milan.
1960	Feb. 13	Duilio Loi (I.) w.pts.15 Bruno Visintin (I.), Milan.
	Nov. 25	Duilio Loi (I.) w.pts.15 Maurice Auzei (F.), Rome.
1961	Aug. 5	Duilio Loi (I.) w.pts.15 Chris Christensen (D.), St. Vincent.

1962	July 15	Duilio Loi (I.) w.pts.15 Fortunato Manca (I.), Cagliari.
1964	Oct. 9	Fortunato Manca (I.) w.ret.6 Francois Pavilla (F.), Rome.
1965	June 2	Fortunato Manca (I.) w.ko.3 Carmelo Garcia Gancho (Sp.), Madrid.
1966	April 25	Jean Josselin (F.) w.ret.13 Brian Curvis (U.K.), Paris.
1967	May 17	Carmelo Bossi (I.) w.pts.15 Jean Josselin (F.), San Remo.
	Aug. 15	Carmelo Bossi (I.) w.rsf.12 Johnny Cooke (U.K.), San Remo.
1968	May 3	Carmelo Bossi (I.) w.pts.15 Jean Josselin (F.), Rome.
	Aug. 14	Fighting Mack (Nl.) w.ret.9 Carmelo Bossi (I.), Lignano Sabbiadoro.
1969	Jan. 13	Silvano Bertini (I.) w.ko.13 Fighting Mack (Nl.), Bologna.
	May 5	Jean Josselin (F.) w.ret.8 Silvano Bertini (I.), Paris.
	Sept. 25	Johann Orsolics (A.) w.ko.4 Josselin (F.), Vienna.
1970	Jan. 26	Johann Orsolics (A.) w.ret.9 Klaus Klein (W.G.), Vienna.
	April 9	Johann Orsolics (A.) w.pts.15 Carmelo Bossi (I.), Vienna.
	Nov. 20	Ralph Charles (U.K.) w.ko.12 Johann Orsolics (A.), Vienna.
1971	June 4	Roger Menetrey (F.) w.ko.7 Ralph Charles (U.K.), Geneva.
	Nov. 26	Roger Menetrey (F.) w.ret.13 Silvano Bertini (I.), Geneva.
1972	March 13	Roger Menetrey (F.) w.ko.5 Robert Gallios (F.), Paris.
	June 22	Roger Menetrey (F.) w.ko.10 Jorgen Hansen (D.), Copenhagen.
	Dec. 9	Roger Menetrey (F.) w.ret.13 Sandro Lopopolo (I.), Grenoble.
1973	Nov. 5	Roger Menetrey (F.) w.pts.15 Gonzalez Dolpico (Sp.), Paris.
1974	May 27	John H. Stracey (U.K.) w.rsf.8 Roger Menetrey (F.), Paris.
1975	April 29	John H. Stracey (U.K.) w.rsf.6 Max Hebeisen (Sw.), London.
1976	April 9	Marco Scano (I.) w.ko.2 Pat Thomas (U.K.), Cagliari.
	Nov. 10	Marco Scano (I.) w.rsf.14 Luciano Borracio (I.), Cagliari.
1977	June 2	Jorgen Hansen (D.) w.ko.5 Marco Scano (I.), Randers.
	Aug. 6	Jorg Eipel (W.G.) w.dis.13 Jorgen Hansen (D.), Randers.
	Dec. 17	Alain Marion (F), w.ko.15 Jorg Eipel (W.G.), Creil.
1978	April 27	Jorgen Hansen (D.) w.ko.6 Alain Marion (F.), Randers.
	Aug. 18	Josef Pachler (A.) w.dis.8 Jorgen Hansen (D.), Villach.
	Dec. 2	Henry Rhiney (U.K.) w.ko.10 Josef Pachler (A.), Dornbirn.
1979	Jan. 23	Dave Green (U.K.) w.rsf.5 Henry Rhiney (U.K.), London.
	June 28	Jorgen Hansen (D.), w.ko.3 Dave Green (U.K.), Randers.
1980	Feb. 7	Jorgen Hansen (D.) w.ko.5 Alois Carmeliet (B.), Randers.
	April 17	Jorgen Hansen (D.) w.pts.12 Joey Singleton (U.K.), Randers.
	Sept. 6	Jorgen Hansen (D.) w.ko.7 Horace McKenzie (U.K.), Aarhus.
	Oct. 17	Jorgen Hansen (D.) w.ko.9 Henrik Palm (D.), Copenhagen.
	Dec. 4	Jorgen Hansen (D.) w.pts.12 Giuseppe Di Padova (I.), Randers.
1981	May 21	Jorgen Hansen (D.) w.pts.12 Richard Rodriguez (F.), Copenhagen.
	Sept. 10	Jorgen Hansen (D.) w.pts.12 Hans Henrik Palm (D.), Copenhagen.
1982	Feb. 26	Hans Henrik Palm (D.) w.rsf.2 Georges Wariesfel (F.), Copenhagen.
	April 30	Hans Henrik Palm (D.) w.pts.12 Pierangelo Pirc (I.), Copenhagen.
	Nov. 5	Colin Jones (U.K.) w.rsf.2 Hans Henrik Palm (D.), Copenhagen, Denmark.
1983	Oct. 10	Giles Elbilia (F.) w.pts.12 Frankie Decaestecker (B.), Paris, France.
1984	Feb. 18	Giles Elbilia (F.) w.rsf.6 Nino La Rocca (I.), Capo D'Orlando, Italy.
	July 7	Gianfranco Rossi (I.) w.pts.12 Perico Fernandez (Sp.), Perugia, Italy.
1985	Jan. 5	Lloyd Honeyghan (U.K.), w.ko.3 Gianfranco Rossi (I.), Perugia, Italy.
	Nov. 27	Lloyd Honeyghan (U.K.) w.rsf.8 Sylvester Mittee (U.K.), London, U.K.
1986	Oct. 10	Jose Varela (W.G.) w.rsf.5 Brahim Messoudi (F.), Russelheim, W. Germany.
1987	April 4	Alfonso Ronondo (Sp.) w.ret.10 Jose Varela (W.G.), Dusseldorf, W. Germany.

June 26	Mauro Martelli (Sw.) w.pts.12 Alfonso Ronondo (Sp.) Geneva, Switzerland.	
Oct. 9	Mauro Martelli (Sw.) w.pts.12 Erwin Heiber (W.G.), Morges, Switzerland.	
Dec. 27	Mauro Martelli (Sw.) w.pts.12 Jean-Marie Touati (F.), Martigny, Switzerland.	
1988 March 4	Mauro Martelli (Sw.) w.pts.12 Antoine Fernandez (F.), Geneva, Switzerland.	
June 4	Mauro Martelli (Sw.) w.pts.12 Efisio Galaci (I.), Cagliari, Italy.	

European Light-Welterweight Title Fights
(140 pounds: 10 stone)

European Boxing Union

1964	Feb. 14	Olli Maki (Fin.) w.pts.15 Conny Rudhof (W.G.), Helsinki.
	Oct. 5	Olli Maki (Fin.) w.ret.8 Aissa Hashas (F.), Helsinki.
1965	July 17	Juan Sombrita Albornoz (Sp.) w.pts.15 Sandro Lopopolo (I.), Tenerife.
	Dec. 26	Willi Quartuor (W.G.) w.pts.15 Juan Sombrita Albornoz (Sp.), Berlin.
1966	May 18	Willi Quartour (W.G.) w.ko.8 Piero Brandi (I.), Arezzo.
1967	Feb. 1	Conny Rudhof (W.G.) w.pts.15 Olli Maki (Fin.), Frankfurt.
	June 6	Johann Orsolics (A.) w.pts.15 Conny Rudhof (W.G.), Vienna.
	Sept. 12	Johann Orsolics (A.) w.rsf.11 Juan Sombrita Albornoz (Sp.), Vienna.
	Dec. 5	Johann Orsolics (A.) drew15 Juan Sombrita Albornoz (Sp.), Vienna.
1968	May 5	Bruno Arcari (I.) w.rsf.12 Johann Orsolics (A.), Vienna.
	Aug. 21	Bruno Arcari (I.) w.rsf.6 Des Rea (U.K.), San Remo.
1969	Jan. 24	Bruno Arcari (I.) w.ko.7 Willi Quartuor (W.G.), Rome.
	Aug. 13	Bruno Arcari (I.) w.ko.6 Juan Sombrita Albornoz (Sp.), San Remo.
	Dec. 1	Bruno Arcari (I.) w.ko.5 Jose Luis Torcida (Sp.), Bologna.
1970	March 21	Rene Roque (F.) w.pts.15 Sandro Lopopolo (I.), Montecatini.
	Aug. 27	Rene Roque (F.) w.pts.15 Borge Krogh (D.), Copenhagen.
	Nov. 16	Rene Roque (F.) w.pts.15 Roger Zami (F.), Paris.
	Dec. 27	Rene Roque (F.) w.pts.15 Romano Fanali (I.), Lyons.
1971	March 16	Rene Roque (F.) drew15 Cemal Kamaci (Turkey), Vienna.
	May 21	Pedro Carrasco (Sp.) w.pts.15 Rene Roque (F.), Madrid.
1972	Feb. 28	Roger Sami (F.) w.pts.15 Sandro Lopopolo (I.), Paris.
	Oct. 1	Cemal Kamaci (Turkey) w.pts.15 Roger Zami (F.), Istanbul.
1973	June 16	Toni Ortiz (Sp.) w.pts.15 Cemal Kamaci (Turkey), Istanbul.
1974	April 30	Toni Ortiz (Sp.) w.rsf.7 Roger Zami (F.) Barcelona.
	July 26	Perico Fernandez (Sp.) w.ko.12 Toni Ortiz (Sp.), Madrid.
	Aug. 24	Perico Fernandez (Sp.) w.rsf.2 Piero Ceru, (I.), Viareggio.
1975	March 8	Jose Ramon Gomez Fouz (Sp.) w.pts.15 Walter Blaser (Sw.), Zurich.
	June 18	Jose Ramon Gomez Fouz (Sp.) w.pts.15 Ramano Fanali (I.), Barcelona.
	Oct. 31	Cemal Kamaci (Turkey) w.rsf.7 Jose Ramon Gomez Fouz (Sp.), Cologne.
1976	June 4	Cemal Kamaci (Turkey) w.pts.15 Jean Saadi (F.), Istanbul.
	Dec. 7	Dave Green (U.K.) w.ret.9 Jean-Baptiste Piedvache (F.), London.
1977	Aug. 10	Primo Bandini (I.) w.dis.6 Jean-Baptiste Piedvache (F.), Rimini.
	Dec. 5	Jean-Baptiste Piedvache (F.) w.ko.2 Primo Bandini, (I.), Paris.
1978	June 5	Colin Powers (U.K.) w.ret.11 Jean-Baptiste Piedvache (F.) Paris.
	Sept. 9	Fernando Sanchez (Sp.) w.rsf.12 Colin Powers (U.K.), Miranda.
	Dec. 2	Fernando Sanchez (Sp.) w.pts.12 Giuseppe Martinese (I.), Bilbao.
1979	Mar. 3	Jose Luis Heredia (Sp.) w.pts.12 Fernando Sanchez (Sp.), Malago.

	May 19	Jo Kimpuani (F.) w.rsf.3 Jose Luis Heredia (Sp.), Dunkirk.
1980	Aug. 27	Giuseppe Martinese (I.) w.ret.10 Clinton McKenzie (U.K.), Senegalia.
	Dec. 17	Antonio Guinaldo (Sp.) w.ko.3 Giuseppe Martinese (I.), Senegalia.
1981	March 13	Antonio Guinaldo (Sp.) w.rsf.8 Andre Holyk (F.), Villeurbame, France.
	Oct. 13	Clinton McKenzie (U.K.) w.pts.12 Antonio Guinalso (Sp.), London, U.K.
1982	Oct. 12	Robert Gambini (F.) w.dis.2 Clinton McKenzie (U.K.) London, U.K.
1983	Jan. 5	Patrizio Oliva (I.) w.pts.12 Robert Gambini (F.), Forio D'Ishia, Italy.
	March 19	Patrizio Oliva (I.) w.ret.11 Francisco Leon (Sp.), Naples, Italy.
	May 25	Patrizio Oliva (I.) w.rsf.6 Jean-Marie Touati (F.), Santo Margherita, Italy.
	July 31	Patrizio Oliva (I.) w.pts.12 Antonio Guinaldo (Sp.), Rapallo, Italy.
	Oct. 14	Patrizio Oliva (I.) w.pts.12 Juan Giminez (Sp.), Milan, Italy.
1984	April 28	Patrizio Oliva (I.) w.rsf.4 Ramon Gom-Fouz (Sp.) Naples, Italy.
	Sept. 4	Patrizio Oliva (I.) w.pts.12 Tusikoleta Nkalankete (F.), Acciaroli, Italy.
	Dec. 15	Patrizio Oliva (I.) w.ret.7 Michel Giroud (Sw.), Cantanzaro, Italy.
1985	March 27	Patrizio Oliva (I.) w.pts.12 Alessandro Scapecchi (I.), Monte Carlo.
	Oct. 26	Terry Marsh (U.K.) w.ko.6 Alessandro Scapecchi (I.), Monte Carlo.
1986	Jan. 22	Terry Marsh (U.K.) w.pts.12 Tusikoleta Nkalankete (F.), London, U.K.
	April 12	Terry Marsh (U.K.) w.pts.12 Francesco Prezioso (I.), Isle of Man.
1987	Feb. 6	Tusikoleta Nkalankete (F.) w.rsf.9 Tony Laing (U.K.), Antibes, France.
	April 22	Tusikoleta Nkalankete (F.) w.rsf.6 Alessandro Scapecchi (I.), Canatania, Italy.
1988	May 26	Tusikoleta Nkalankete (F.) w.ko.6 Lloyd Christie (U.K.), Paris, France.

European Lightweight Title Fights
(135 pounds: 9 stone 9 pounds)

International Boxing Union

1909	Aug. 23	Freddie Welsh (U.K.) w.ret.12 Henri Piet (F.), Mountain Ash.
1911	Feb. 27	Matt Wells (U.K.) w.pts.20 Freddie Welsh (U.K.), London.
1912	Nov. 11	Freddie Welsh (U.K.) w.pts.20 Matt Wells (U.K.), London.
1913	Feb. 10	Freddie Welsh (U.K.) w.ret.13 Raul Brevieres (F.), Cardiff.
	March 3	Freddie Welsh (U.K.) w.rsf.10 Raymond Vittet (F.), Sheffield
1919	April 10	Bob Marriott (U.K.) w.dis.3 Raymond Vittet (F.), London.
1920	May 17	Georges Papin (F.) w.pts.20 Bob Marriott (U.K.), Paris.
1921	May 9	Ernie Rice (U.K.) w.ko.10 Georges Papin (F.), London.
1922	Sept. 18	Seaman Hall (U.K.) w.pts.20 Ernie Rice (U.K.), Liverpool.
1923	Jan. 8	Seaman Hall (U.K.) w.pts.20 Johnny Brown (U.K.), Edinburgh.
	May 17	Harry Mason (U.K.) w.dis.13 Seaman Hall (U.K.), London.
	Nov. 21	Harry Mason (U.K.) w.pts.20 Ernie Rice (U.K.), London.
1924	Feb. 27	Fred Bretonnel (F.) w.pts.20 Juliard Baudry (U.K.), Lyon.
	June 24	Fred Bretonnel (F.) w.ret.8 Danny Frush (U.K.), Paris.
	Oct. 7	Lucien Vinez (F.) w.pts.20 Fred Bretonnel (F.), Paris.
1925	Sept. 16	Lucien Vinez (F.) w.pts.15 Van Vliet (Nl.), Paris.
1926	April 2	Lucien Vinez (F.) w.pts.15 Van Vliet (Nl.), Paris.
1927	June 19	Lucien Vinez (F.) w.pts.15 Thomas Cola (Sp.), Barcelona.
	Aug. 3	Luis Rayo (Sp.) w.pts.15 Lucien Vinez (F.), Barcelona.
	Oct. 20	Luis Rayo (Sp.) w.pts.15 Thomas Cola (Sp.), Barcelona.

1928	Dec. 22	Alme Raphael (F.) w.ko.11 Otto Czirson (G.), Paris.
1929	April 14	Francois Sybille (B.) w.pts.15 Alme Raphael (F.), Marseilles.
1930	Jan. 16	Alf Howard (U.K.) w.dis.8 Francois Sybille (B.), Liverpool.
	June 10	Francois Sybille (B.) w.ko.9 Alf Howard (U.K.), Brussels.
	Oct. 11	Francois Sybille (B.) w.pts.15 Henry Vullamy (F.), Leige.
1931	July 19	Bep van Klaveren (Nl.) w.ko.2 Francois Sybille (B.), Amsterdam.
	Oct. 10	Bep van Klaveren (Nl.) w.pts.15 Harry Corbett (U.K.), Bristol.
	Nov. 17	Bep van Klaveren (Nl.) w.pts.15 Henry Scillie (U.K.), The Hague.
1932	March 26	Bep van Kalveren (Nl.) drew15 Francois Sybille (B.), Brussels.
	July 17	Cleto Locatelli (I.) w.dis.15 Bep van Klaveren (Nl.), Rotterdam.
	Dec. 7	Francois Sybille (B.) w.dis.3 Cleto Locatelli (I.), Brussels.
1933	Oct.22	Cleto Locatelli (I.) w.pts.15 Francois Sybille (B.), Rome.
1934	Feb. 10	Francois Sybille (B.) w.pts.15 Gustave Humery (F.), Brussels.
	March 17	Carlo Orlandi (I.) w.pts.15 Francois Sybille (B.), Milan.
	Dec. 9	Carlo Orlandi (I.) w.pts.15 Richard Stegemann (G.), Milan.
1935	Oct. 12	Enrico Venturi (I.) w.pts.15 Henri Ferret (F.), Rome.
1936	Oct. 10	Vittorio Tamagnini (I.) w.ret.7 Raymond Renard (B.), Rome.
	Dec. 7	Vittorio Tamagnini (I.) w.ret.5 Gustave Humery (F.), Paris.
1937	Jan. 22	Vittorio Tamagnini (I.) w.pts.15 Rudolf Kretzschmer (G.), Berlin.
	April 22	Maurice Arnault (F.) w.rsf.11 Vittorio Tamagnini (I.), Paris.
	May 27	Gustave Humery (F.) w.rsf.3 Maurice Arnault (F.), Paris.
1938	Sept. 2	Aldo Spoldi (I.) w.pts.15 Carl Anderson (D.), Copenhagen.
1940	Oct. 26	Karl Blaho (A.) w.pts.15 Otello Abbruciati (I.), Vienna.
1941	Feb. 16	Karl Blaho (A.) w.pts.15 Carl Andersen (D.), Berlin.
	May 31	Bruno Bisterzo (I.) w.pts.15 Karl Blaho (A.), Munich.
	Nov. 26	Ascenzo Botta (I.) w.ko.1 Bruno Bisterzo (I.), Rome.
	Dec. 31	Bruno Bisterzo (I.) w.pts.15 Ascenzo Botta (I.), Rome.
1942	May 14	Ascenzo Botta (I.) w.pts.15 Bruno Bisterzo (I.), Rome.
	Sept. 20	Roberto Proietti (I.) w.pts.15 Ascenzo Botta (I.), Rome.
1943	May 8	Bruno Bisterzo (I.) w.pts.15 Roberto Proietti (I.), Lucca.

European Boxing Union

1946	May 26	Roberto Proietti (I.) w.ret.6 Bruno Bisterzo (I.), Rome.
	Dec. 4	Emile Dicristo (F.) w.pts.15 Joseph Preys (B.), Brussels.
1947	March 29	Kid Dussart (B.) w.pts.15 Emile Dicristo (F.), Brussels.
	May 21	Roberto Proietti (I.) w.ret.13 Kid Dussart (B.), Brussels.
	July 6	Roberto Proietti (I.) w.pts.15 Joseph Preys (B.), Tournai.
1948	Feb. 17	Billy Thompson (U.K.) w.pts.15 Roberto Proietti (I.), London.
	July 26	Billy Thompson (U.K.) drew15 Pierre Montane (F.), London.
1949	Jan. 17	Billy Thompson (U.K.) w.pts.15 Joseph Preys (B.), Birmingham.
	May 18	Billy Thompson (U.K.) w.rsf.5 Harry Hughes (U.K.), Glasgow.
	July 5	Kid Dussart (B.) w.dis.6 Billy Thompson (U.K.), London.
	Dec. 17	Roberto Prioetti (I.) w.pts.15 Kid Dussart (B.), Brussels.
1950	Jan. 11	Roberto Proietti (I.) w.pts.15 Billy Thompson (U.K.), London.
	June 20	Roberto Prioetti (I.) w.pts.15 Joseph Preys (B.), Milan.
1951	Feb. 23	Pierre Montane (F.) w.ko.12 Billy Thompson (U.K.), Manchester.
	Aug. 17	Elis Ask (Fin). w.ko.12 Pierre Montane (F.), Helsinki.
1952	Jan. 4	Jorgen Johansen (D.) w.pts.15 Alis Ask (Fin.), Copenhagen.
	March 20	Jorgen Johansen (D.) drew15 Tommy McGovern (U.K.), Copenhagen.
	Aug. 18	Jorgen Johansen (D.) w.pts.15 Duilio Loi (I.), Copenhagen.
1953	May 7	Jorgen Johansen (D.) w.pts.15 Jacques Prigent (F.), Copenhagen.
	Sept. 3	Jorgen Johansen (D.) drew15 Werner Handke (W.G.), Copenhagen.

1954	Feb. 6	Duilio Loi (I.) w.pts.15 Jorgen Johansen (D.), Milan.
	May 13	Duilio Loi (I.) w.pts.15 Bruno Visintin (I.), Milan.
	July 16	Duilio Loi (I.) w.pts.15 Jacques Herbillon (F.), Milan.
1955	July 2	Duilio Loi (I.) w.pts.15 Giancarlo Garbelli (I.), Milan.
	Nov. 26	Duilio Loi (I.) w.pts.15 Serephin Ferrer (F.), Milan.
1956	May 12	Duilio Loi (I.) drew15 Jose Hernandez (Sp.), Milan.
	Dec. 26	Duilio Loi (I.) w.pts.15 Jose Hernandez (Sp.), Milan.
1957	Dec. 26	Duilio Loi (I.) w.pts.15 Felix Chiocca (F.), Milan.
1958	Sept. 5	Duilio Loi (I.) drew15 Mario Vecchiatto (I.), Milan.
1959	Oct. 24	Mario Vecchiatto (I.). w.dis.8 Laouari Godih (F.), Milan.
1960	March 29	Dave Charnley (U.K.) w.ret.10 Mario Vecchiatto (I.), London.
1961	Feb. 21	Dave Charnley (U.K.) w.pts.15 Fernand Nollet (F.), London.
	July 5	Dave Charnley (U.K.) w.ret.4 Ray Nobile (I.), Rome.
	Nov. 20	Dave Charnley (U.K.) w.ko.1 Darkie Hughes (U.K.), Nottingham.
1963	Sept. 29	Conny Rudholf (W.G.) w.pts.15 Giordani Compari (I.), Russelshelm.
1964	May 8	Willi Quatuor (W.G.) w.ko.14 Michele Gullotti (I.), Berlin.
1965	March 13	Franco Brondi (I.) w.ret.3 Leon Zadourian (F.), Cannes.
	June 18	Franco Brondi (I.) ret.11 Kid Tano (Sp.), Milan.
	Oct. 9	Maurice Tavent (F.) w.ko.3 Franco Brondi (I.), Lyon.
1966	Feb. 5	Maurice Tavent (F.) w.ko. Lothar Abend (W.G.), Kiel.
	April 16	Maurice Tavent (F.) w.pts.15 Aldo Pravisani (I.), Lyon.
	Nov. 3	Borge Korgh (D.) w.pts.15 Maurice Tavent (F.), Copenhagen.
1967	June 30	Pedro Carrasco (Sp.) w.rsf.8 Borge Krogh (D.), Madrid.
1968	May 10	Pedro Carrasco (Sp.) w.ko.8 Kid Tano (Sp.), Madrid.
	Sept. 13	Pedro Carrasco (Sp.) w.ret.3 Bruno Melissano (I.), Barcelona.
	Oct. 18	Pedro Carrasco (Sp.) w.pts.15 Olli Maki (Fin.), Valencia.
1969	March 6	Pedro Carrasco (Sp.) w.ko.3 Tore Magnussen (N.), Barcelona.
	June 14	Pedro Carrasco (Sp.) w.pts.15 Miguel Velazquez (Sp.), Madrid.
1970	Jan. 29	Miguel Velazquez (Sp.) w.pts.15 Ken Buchanan (U.K.), Madrid.
	June 26	Miguel Velazquez (Sp.) w.ret.11 Carmelo Coscia (I.), Madrid.
1971	Jan. 29	Miguel Velazquez (Sp.) drew15 Antonio Puddu (I.), Barcelona.
	July 31	Antonio Puddu (I.) w.ko.4 Miguel Velazquez (Sp.), Cagliari.
	Oct. 27	Antonio Puddu (I.) w.pts.15 Pierre Claude Thomias (F.), San Remo.
1972	Jan. 28	Antonio Puddu (I.) w.pts.15 Jean-Pierre Le Jaouen (F.), Milan.
	Sept. 13	Antonio Puddu (I.) w.ret.11 Enzo Petriglia (I.), Cagliari.
1973	April 4	Antonio Puddu (I.) w.rsf.1 Dominique Azzaro (F.), Cagliari.
1974	May 1	Ken Buchanan (U.K.) w.ko.6 Antonio Puddu (I.), Cagliari.
	Dec. 16	Ken Buchanan (U.K.) w.rsf.14 Leonard Taverez (F.), Paris.
1975	July 25	Ken Buchanan (U.K.) w.rsf.12 Giancario Usai (I.), Cagliari.
1976	Feb. 6	Fernand Roelands (B.) w.pts.15 Andre Holyk (F.), Bruges.
	July 9	Perico Fernandez (Sp.) w.rsf.1 Fernand Roelands (B.), Zaragoza.
	Nov. 13	Perico Fernandez (Sp.) w.pts.15 Giancario Usai (I.), Bilbao.
1977	Aug. 5	Jim Watt (U.K.) w.rsf.1 (*cut eye*) Andre Holyk (F.), Glasgow.
	Nov. 16	Jim Watt (U.K.) w.rsf.10 Jeromino Lucus (Sp.), Solihull.
1978	Feb. 17	Jim Watt (U.K.) w.pts.15 Perico Fernandez (Sp.), Madrid.
1978	Oct. 18	Jim Watt (U.K.) w.ret.5 Antonio Guinaldo (Sp.), Glasgow.
1979	June 27	Charlie Nash (U.K.) w.pts.12 Andre Holyk (F.), Londonderry.
	Dec. 6	Charlie Nash (U.K.) w.pts.12 Ken Buchanan (U.K.), Copenhagen.
1980	June 1	Francisco Leon (Sp.) w.rsf.9 Giancario Usai (I.), Tarras.
	Dec. 14	Charlie Nash (U.K.) w.pts.12 Francisco Leon (Sp.), Dublin.
1981	May 10	Joey Gibilisco (I.) w.ko.6 Charlie Nash (U.K.), Dublin.

	Oct. 21	Joey Gibilisco (I.) w.ko.9 Jose Luis Heredia (Sp.), Sicily, Campobasso.
1982	Nov. 11	Joey Gibilisco (I.) w.ko.4 Jose Garcia (Sp.), Sassari, Italy.
1983	March 17	Lucio Cusma (I.) w.ret.11 Joey Gibilisco (I.), Capo D'Orlando, Italy.
	June 29	Lucio Cusma (I.) drew 12 Rene Weller (W.G.), Brolo, Italy.
	Sept. 30	Lucio Cusma (I.) w.pts.12 Aldo d'Benedetto (I.), Modena, Italy.
1984	March 9	Rene Weller (W.G.) w.pts.12 Lucio Cusma (I.), Frankfurt, West Germany.
	April 13	Rene Weller (W.G.) w.rsf.9 Jose Garcia (Sp.), Hagen, West Germany.
	May 26	Rene Weller (W.G.) w.pts.12 Daniel Londas (F.), Dusseldorf, West Germany.
	Oct. 5	Rene Weller (W.G.) w.pts.12 George Feeney (U.K.), Frankfurt, West Germany.
1985	April 26	Rene Weller (W.G.) w.ko.11 Frederick Geoffrey (F.), Frankfurt, West Germany.
1986	Jan. 1	Gert Bo Jacobsen (D.) w.rsf.8 Rene Weller (W.G.), Randers, Denmark.
	April 18	Gert Bo Jacobsen (D.) w.pts.12 Alfredo Raininger (I.), Randers, Denmark.
	Oct. 17	Gert Bo Jacobsen (D.) w.pts.12 Fernando Blanco (Sp.), Randers, Denmark.
1987	Feb. 27	Gert Bo Jacobsen (D.) w.pts.12 Jose A. Hernandez (Sp.) Randers, Denmark.
	June 8	Gert Bo Jacobsen (D.) w.rsf.8 Alain Simoes (F.), Merignac, France.
	Oct. 2	Gert Bo Jacobsen (D.) w.rsf.4 Claudio Nitti (I.), Copenhagen, Denmark.
1988	March 4	Rene Weller (W.G.) w.pts.12 Jose Maillot (F.), Karlsruhe, West Germany.

European Junior-Lightweight Title Fights
(130 pounds: 9 stone 4 pounds)

European Boxing Union

1971	Jan. 13	Tommaso Galli (I.) w.pts.15 Luis Aisa Marin (Sp.), Ladispoli.
	July 14	Tommaso Galli (I.) w.pts.15 Lothar Abend (W.G.), Ligano.
1972	March 9	Tommaso Galli (I.) w.ret.11 Jean De Keers (B.), San Remo.
	May 10	Tommaso Galli (I.) w.rsf.11 Luis Aisa (Sp.), Rimini.
	Oct. 13	Lothar Abend (W.G.) w.pts.15 Domenico Chiloiro (I.), Hamburg.
1973	Feb. 3	Lothar Abend (W.G.) w.rsf.1 Jean De Keers (B.,), Kiel.
	May 13	Lothar Abend (W.G.) w.ret.10 Felix Brami (F.), Kiel.
	Dec. 7	Lothar Abend (W.G.) w.pts.15 Ugo Poli (I.), Hamburg.
1974	May 7	Svein-Erik Paulsen (N.) w.rsf.3 Lothar Abend (W.G.), Oslo.
	Oct. 8	Svein-Erik Paulsen (N.) w.pts.15 Giovanni Girgenti (I.), Oslo.
1975	Jan. 23	Svein-Erik Paulsen (N.) w.pts.15 Domingo Jiminez (Sp.), Oslo.
	June 19	Svein-Erik Paulsen (N.) w.pts.15 Antonio Puddu (I.), Oslo.
	Sept. 25	Svein-Erik Paulsen (N.) w.pts.15 Antonio Guinaldo (Sp.), Oslo.
1976	Feb. 27	Roland Cazeaux (F.) w.pts.15 Rudi Haeck (B.), St. Nazaire.
	June 16	Roland Cazeaux (F.) drew15 Ramon Garcia Marichal (Sp.) Santa Cruz.
	Sept. 24	Natale Vezzoli (I.) w.rsf.11 Roland Cazeaux (F.), Milan.
	Nov. 12	Natale Vezzoli (I.) w.rsf.12 Domingo Jiminez (Sp.), Milan.
1977	April 1	Natale Vezzoli (I.) w.rsf.11‖ Albert Amatler (F.), Brescia.
	May 27	Natale Vezzoli (I.) w.rsf.12‖ George Cotin (F.), Brescia.
	July 6	Natale Vezzoli (I.) w.ko.11 Ethem Ozakalin (Turkey), Viesta.
	Dec. 13	Natale Vezzoli (I.) w.pts.15 Salvatore Liscapade (I.), Taurisano.
1978	March 8	Natale Vezzoli (I.) w.pts.15 Elio Cotena (I.), Brescia.
	Aug. 11	Natale Vezzoli (I.) w.pts.15 Isidoro Cabeza (Sp.), Lepe.
	Dec. 13	Natale Vezzoli (I.) drew12 Charley Jurietti (F.), Brescia.

1979	March 10	Carlos Hernandez (Sp.) w.rsf.4 Natale Vezzoli (I.), Valladolid.
	June 3	Rodolfo Sanchez (Sp.) w.pts.12 Carlos Hernandez (Sp.), Miranda de Ebro.
	Dec. 21	Carlos Hernandez (Sp.) w.pts.12 Rodolfo Sanchez (Sp.), Valladolid.
1980	April 30	Carlos Hernandez (Sp.) w.rsf.6 Salvatore Liscapade (I.), Nepi.
	Sept. 6	Carlos Hernandez (Sp.) w.pts.12 Ramon Marichal (Sp.), Santa Cruz.
	Nov. 12	Carlos Hernandez (Sp.) w.ko.7 Aristide Pizzo (I.), Marsala.
1981	Jan. 31	Carlos Hernandez (Sp.) w.ko.10 Amalio Galan (Sp.), Valladoid.
	Feb. 14	Carlos Hernandez (Sp.) drew12 Jose Luis Vicho (Sp.), Palma de Mallorca.
	Dec. 5	Carlos Hernandez (Sp.) drew Roberto Castanon (Sp.), Valladolid.
1982	March 23	Cornelius Boza-Edwards (U.) w.ret.4 Carlos Hernandez (Sp.), London.
	Nov. 6	Roberto Castanon (Sp.) w.ret.9 Daniel Londas (F.), Leon, Spain.
1983	Feb. 4	Roberto Castanon (Sp.) w.pts.12 Carlos Rodriguez (Sp.), Leon, Spain.
	April 29	Roberto Castanon (Sp.) w.ko.4 Michele Siracusa (F.), Aix en Provence, France.
	Sept. 21	Alfredo Raininger (I.) w.pts.12 Roberto Castanon (Sp.), Caserta, Italy.
	Dec. 14	Alfredo Raininger (I.) w.rsf.6 Francis Tripp (F.), Loano, Italy.
1984	April 12	Jean-Marc Renard (B.) w.pts.12 Alfredo Raininger (I.), Casavatore, Italy.
	July 7	Pat Cowdell (U.K.) w.pts.12 Jean Marc Renard (B.), Aston Villa, U.K.
	Oct. 24	Pat Cowdell (U.K.) w.rsf.5 Robert Castanon (Sp.), Birmingham, U.K.
1985	March 16	Pat Cowdell (U.K.) w.pts.12 Carlos Hernandez (Sp.), Birmingham, U.K.
1986	Jan. 29	Jean-Marc Renard (B.) w.rsf.8 Marco Gallo (I.), Catanzaro, Italy.
	April 18	Jean-Marc Renard (B.) w.ko.8 Fernando Rodriguez (Sp.), Brustem, Belgium.
	Oct. 31	Jean-Marc Renard (B.) w.ret.5 Najib Daho (U.K.), Kortrijk, Belgium.
	Dec. 20	Jean-Marc Renard (B.) drew12 Daniel Londas (F.), St. Quen, France.
1987	March 11	Jean-Marc Renard (B.) w.rsf.8 Antonio Renzo (I.), Cosenza, Italy.
	May 16	Salvatore Curcetti (I.) w.rsf.1 Daniel Londas (F.), Reims, France.
1988	Feb. 17	Pierre Morello (I.) w.pts.12 Salvatore Curcetti (I.), Brescia, Italy.
	June 4	Pierre Morello (I.) w.pts.12 Raymond Armand (F.), Villabate, Italy.

European Featherweight Title Fights
(126 pounds: 9 stone)

International Boxing Union

1912	June 3	Jim Driscoll (U.K.) w.ko.12 Jean Poesy (F.), London.
1913	Jan. 27	Jim Driscoll (U.K.) drew 20 Owen Moran (U.K.), London.
	Oct. 6	Ted 'Kid' Lewis (U.K.) w.ret.17 Alec Lambert (U.K.), London.
1914	Feb. 2	Ted 'Kid' Lewis (U.K.) w.dis.12 Paul Til (F.), London.
1919	Dec. 24	Louis De Ponthieu (F.) w.ko.17 Tancy Lee (U.K.), Paris.
1920	May 13	Arthur Wyns (B.) w.ret.10 Mike Honeyman (U.K.), London.
	July 26	Arthur Wyns (B.) w.ret.14 Joe Conn (U.K.), London.
1921	Dec. 5	Arthur Wyns (B.) w.ko.17 Ben Callicot (U.K.), London.
1922	June 12	Billy Mathews (U.K.) w.pts.20 Arthur Wyns (B.), Liverpool.
	July 7	Eugene Criqui (F.) w.ko.12 Arthur Wyns (B.), Paris.
	Sept. 9	Eugene Criqui (F.) w.ret.6 Arthur Wyns (B.), Paris.
	Nov. 4	Eugene Criqui (F.) w.ko.1 Walter Rossi (I.), Paris.
	Dec. 12	Eugene Criqui (F.) w.ret.17 Billy Matthews (U.K.), Paris.

1923	Dec. 20	Edouard Mascart (F.) w.pts.20 Eugene Criqui (F.), Paris.
1924	Feb. 9	Charles Ledoux (F.) w.pts.20 Edouard Mascart (F.), Paris.
	May 8	Henry Hebrans (B.) w.pts.15 Charles Ledoux (F.), Brussels.
	Dec. 17	Henry Hebrans (B.) drew 10; Arthur Wyns (B.), Brussels.
1925	Oct. 30	Antonio Ruiz (Sp.) w.ret.9 Henry Hebrans (B.), Madrid.
1928	Jan. 7	Luigi Quadrini (I.) w.pts.15 Antonio Ruiz (Sp.), Barcelona.
1929	Jan. 11	Knud Larsen (D.) w.pts.15 Luigi Quadrini (I.), Copenhagen.
	April 12	Knud Larsen (D.) w.pts.15 Henry Scillie (B.), Copenhagen.
	Dec. 1	Jose Girones (Sp.) w.pts.15 Knud Larsen (D.), Barcelona.
1930	May 7	Jose Girones (Sp.) w.ret.9 Julien Verbist (B.), Barcelona.
1931	June 10	Jose Girones (Sp.) w.rsf.12 Vittorio Tamagnini (I.), Barcelona.
	Aug. 30	Jose Girones (Sp.) w.ret.8 Guy Buonagure (F.), Monte Carlo.
1932	Jan. 26	Jose Girones (Sp.) w.ko.4 Paul Noack (G.), Barcelona.
	Nov. 23	Jose Girones (Sp.) w.rsf.12 Otello Abbruciati (I.), Barcelona.
1933	June 7	Jose Girones (Sp.) w.pts.15 Georges Laperson (F.), Barcelona.
	Nov. 22	Jose Girones (Sp.) w.pts.15 Lucien Popescu (R.), Barcelona.
1935	March 26	Maurice Holtzer (F.) w.pts.15 Vittorio Tamagini (I.), Paris.
1936	Jan. 11	Maurice Holtzer (F.) w.ret.13 Georges Laperson (F.), Paris.
1937	Jan. 11	Maurice Holtzer (F.) w.pts.15 Joseph Parisis (F.), Paris.
	Oct. 5	Maurice Holtzer (F.) w.pts.15 Phil Dolhelm (B.), Algiers.
1938	Feb. 19	Maurice Holtzer (F.) drew 15 Maurice Dubois (Sw.), Geneva.
	Sept. 6	Phil Dolhelm (B.) w.ko.11 Maurice Dubois (Sw.), Liege.
1939	Jan. 19	Phil Dolhelm (B.) w.pts.15 Joe Preys (B.), Brussels.
	June 3	Lucien Popescu (R.) w.pts.15 Phil Dolhelm (B.), Bucharest.
1941	May 30	Ernst Weiss (A.) w.pts.15 Lucien Popescu (R.), Vienna.
	June 30	Gino Bondavalli (I.) w.pts.15 Ernst Weiss (A.), Vienna.
1942	May 30	Gino Bondavalli (I.) w.pts.15 Lucien Popescu (R.), Reggio Emilia.
	Oct. 4	Gino Bondavalli (I.) w.pts.15 Georges Popescu (R.), Bucharest.
1945	Nov. 11	Ermanno Bonetti (I.) w.pts.15 Gino Bondavalli (I.), Modena.

European Boxing Union

1947	May 27	Al Phillips (U.K.) w.dis.8 Ray Famechon (F.), London.
	Sept. 11	Ronnie Clayton (U.K.) w.pts.15 Al Phillips (U.K.), Liverpool.
1948	March 22	Ray Famechon (F.) w.pts.15 Ronnie Clayton (U.K.), Nottingham.
	Nov. 20	Ray Famechon (F.) w.pts.15 Jean Machterlinek (B.), Charleroi.
1949	Nov. 18	Ray Famechon (F.) w.pts.15 Ronnie Clayton (U.K.), Manchester.
1950	July 29	Ray Famechon (F.) w.ko.3 Luis De Santiago (Sp.), Madrid.
1951	June 28	Ray Famechon (F.) w.rsf.13 Alvaro Cerasani (I.), Milan.
1952	April 21	Ray Famechon (F.) w.ret.5 Ronnie Clayton (U.K.), Nottingham.
	Oct. 9	Ray Famechon (F.) w.ko.4 Nello Barbadoro (I.), Milan.
1953	Oct. 17	Jean Sneyers (B.) w.pts.15 Ray Famechon (F.), Brussels.
1954	Feb. 16	Jean Sneyers (B.) w.pts.15 Sammy McCarthy (U.K.), London.
	Sept. 20	Ray Famechon (F.) w.ret.3 Jean Sneyers (B.), Paris.
1955	Jan. 29	Ray Famechon (F.) w.pts.15 Sergio Milan (I.), Milan.
	May 27	Ray Famechon (F.) w.pts.15 Billy Kelly (U.K.), Dublin.
	Nov. 3	Fred Galiana (Sp.) w.ret.6 Ray Famechon (F.), Paris.
1956	May 3	Fred Galiana (Sp.) w.ret.12 Jules Touan (F.), Abidjan.
1957	Jan. 21	Cherif Hamia (F.) w.pts.15 Jean Sneyers (B.), Paris.
1958	Aug. 18	Sergio Caprari (I.) w.ret.11 Jean Sneyers (B.), San Remo.
1959	Sept. 15	Gracieux Lamperti (F.) w.pts.15 Sergio Caprari (I.), San Remo.
1960	March 27	Gracieux Lamperti (F.) w.pts.15 Manolo Garcia (Sp.), Marseilles.
	Oct. 15	Gracieux Lamperti (F.) w.pts.15 Pierre Cossemyns (B.), Brussels.

1962	July 22	Gracieux Lamperti (F.) drew15 Lino Mastellaro (I.), Rome.
	Aug. 19	Alberto Serti (I.) w.pts.15 Gracieux Lamperti (F.), San Remo.
1963	July 9	Howard Winstone (U.K.) w.ret.14 Alberto Serti (I.), Cardiff.
	Aug. 20	Howard Winstone (U.K.) w.pts.15 Billy Calvert (U.K.), Porthcawl.
	Dec. 9	Howard Winstone (U.K.) w.pts.15 John O'Brien (U.K.), London.
1964	May 12	Howard Winstone (U.K.) w.ret.8 Lino Mastellaro (I.), London.
1965	Jan. 22	Howard Winstone (U.K.) w.pts.15 Yves Desmarets (F.), Rome.
1966	March 7	Howard Winstone (U.K.) w.rsf.15 Andrea Silanos (I.), Sassari.
	Sept. 6	Howard Winstone (U.K.) w.rsf.3 Jean de Keers (B.), London.
	Dec. 7	Howard Winstone (U.K.) w.rsf.8 Lennie Williams (U.K.), Aberavon.
1967	Dec. 22	Jose Legra (Sp.) w.rsf.3 Yves Desmaret (F.), Barcelona.
1968	Dec. 17	Manuel Calvo (Sp.) w.pts.15 Nevio Carbi (I.), Barcelona.
1969	Aug. 20	Tommaso Galli (I.) w.rsf.15 Manuel Calvo (Sp.), Barcelona.
1970	Feb. 19	Tommaso Galli (I.) w.pts.15 Manuel Calvo (Sp.), Barcelona.
	June 26	Jose Legra (Sp.) w.pts.15 Tommaso Gali (I.), Madrid.
1971	Jan. 25	Jose Legra (Sp.) w.pts.15 Jimmy Revie (U.K.), London.
	Aug. 14	Jose Legra (Sp.) w.ko.9 Giovanni Girgenti (I.), Alicante.
1972	Feb. 15	Jose Legra (Sp.) w.pts.15 Evan Armstrong (U.K.), London.
	May 17	Jose Legra (Sp.) w.pts.15 Tommy Glencross (U.K.), Birmingham.
	Oct. 6	Jose Legra (Sp.) w.pts.15 Daniel Vermandere (F.), Madrid.
1973	May 12	Gitano Jiminez (Sp.) w.pts.15 Tommy Glencross (U.K.), Gijon.
1974	Jan. 11	Gitano Jiminez (Sp.) w.pts.15 Daniel Vermandere (F.), Madrid.
	April 17	Gitano Jiminez (Sp.) w.ko.15 Elio Cotena (I.), Zaragoza.
1975	Feb. 12	Elio Cotena (I.) w.rsf.11 Gitano Jiminez (Sp.), Naples.
	April 30	Elio Cotena (I.) w.pts.15 Rodolfo Sanchez (Sp.), Naples.
	Oct. 22	Elio Cotena (I.) w.ret.11 Michel Lefebvre (F.), Cefalu.
1976	Feb. 25	Elio Cotena (I.) w.ko.14 Vernon Sollas (U.K.), London.
	May 26	Elio Cotena (I.) w.rsf.12 Nevio Carbi (I.), Trieste.
	Dec. 3	Pedro 'Nino' Jimenez (Sp.) w.ret.12 Elio Cotena (I.), Madrid.
1977	May 13	Nino Jiminez (Sp.) w.pts.15 Michele Siracusa (F.), Madrid.
	Sept. 16	Manuel Masso (Sp.) w.rsf.10 Nino Jimenez (Sp.), Madrid.
	Dec. 16	Roberto Castanon (Sp.) w.ko.11 Manuel Masso (Sp.), Barcelona.
1978	July 15	Roberto Castanon (Sp.) w.rsf.5 Albert Amatler (F.), La Coruna.
	Sept. 23	Roberto Castanon (Sp.) w.rsf.10 Mariano Rodriguez (Sp.), Leon.
	Dec. 16	Roberto Castanon (Sp.) w.ret.5 Dave Needham (U.K.), Leon.
1979	Feb. 3	Roberto Castanon (Sp.) w.rsf.7 Gerard Jacob (F.), Criel.
	Sept. 29	Roberto Castanon (Sp.) w.pts.12 Cecilio Lastra (Sp.), Santander.
1980	March 8	Roberto Castanon (Sp.) w.pts.12 Emilio Barcala (Sp.), Leon.
	April 12	Roberto Castanon (Sp.) w.pts.12 Modesto Gomez (Sp.), Santander.
	May 18	Roberto Castanon (Sp.) w.dis.9 Salvatore Melluzzo (I.), Leon.
	June 28	Roberto Castanon (Sp.) w.rsf.6 Laurent Grimbert (F.), Leon.
	Oct. 7	Roberto Castanon (Sp.) w.rsf.8 Ethem Oezakalim (W.G.), Barcelona.
	Nov. 29	Roberto Castanon (Sp.) w.rsf.4 Cecilio Lastra (Sp.), Leon.
1981	July 23	Salvatore Melluzzo (I.) w.rsf.9 Laurent Grimbert (F.), Marsala.
1982	March 30	Pat Cowdell (U.K.) w.rsf.10 Salvatore Melluzo (I.), London.
	Oct. 30	Pat Cowdell (U.K.) w.rsf.12 Sepp Iten (Sw.), Zurich, Switzerland.

1983	April 7	Loris Stecca (I.) w.rsf.5 Steve Sims (U.K.), Sassari, Italy.
	Aug. 5	Loris Stecca (I.) w.pts.12 Valerio Nati (I.), Camaiore, Italy.
	Nov. 16	Barry McGuigan (U.K.) w.ko.6 Valerio Nati (I.), Belfast, N. Ireland.
1984	June 5	Barry McGuigan (U.K.) w.ko.3 Esteban Eguia (Sp.) London, U.K.
	Dec. 12	Barry McGuigan (U.K.) w.ko.4 Clyde Ruan (U.K.), Belfast, N. Ireland.
1985	March 26	Barry McGuigan (U.K.) w.ret.2 Farid Gallouze (F.), Wembley, U.K.
	Nov. 5	Jim McDonald (U.K.) Jose Luis Vicho (Sp.), Wembley, U.K.
1986	July 19	Jim McDonald (U.K.) w.pts.12 Salvatore Bottiglieri (I.), Wembley, U.K.
1987	March 13	Valerio Nati (I.) w.rsf.2 Marc Amand (F.), Forli, Italy.
	July 24	Valerio Nati (I.) w.dis.7 Vicenzo Limarolo (I.), Silvi Mariani, Italy.
1988	June 25	Jean-Marc Renard (B.) w.pts.12 Farid Benredjeb, (F.) Compiegne, France.

European Bantamweight Title Fights
(118 pounds: 8 stone 6 pounds)

International Boxing Union

1910	March 7	Joe Bowker (U.K.) w.ko.8 Jean Audony (F.), London.
	Oct. 17	Digger Stanley (U.K.) w.ko.8 Joe Bowker (U.K.), London.
1912	April 22	Digger Stanley (U.K.) w.pts.20 Charles Ledoux (F.), London.
	June 23	Charles Ledoux (F.) w.ko.7 Digger Stanley (U.K.), Dieppe.
1919	Oct. 20	Charles Ledoux (F.) w.ret.16 Jim Driscoll (U.K.), London.
1920	May 31	Charles Ledoux (F.) w.ko.11 Jim Higgins (U.K.), London.
1921	Oct. 24	Tommy Harrison (U.K.) w.pts.20 Charles Ledoux (F.), Hanley.
1922	April 24	Charles Ledoux (F.) w.pts.20 Tommy Harrison (U.K.), Liverpool.
	June 18	Charles Ledoux (F.) w.pts.15 Andre Routis (F.), Casablanca.
	Oct. 9	Charles Ledoux (F.) w.rsf.18 Tommy Harrison (U.K.), Hanley.
1923	Feb. 27	Charles Ledoux (F.) w.ko.11 Michel Montreuil (B.), Paris.
	May 6	Charles Ledoux (F.) w.pts.20 Andre Routis (F.), Paris.
	July 30	Harry 'Bugler' Lake (U.K.) w.pts.20 Charles Ledoux (F.), London.
	Nov. 26	Johnny Brown (U.K.) w.pts.20 Harry 'Bugler' Lake (U.K.), London.
1924	Feb. 24	Johnny Brown (U.K.) w.ret.16 Harry Corbett (U.K.), London.
1925	May 11	Henri Scillie (B.) w.pts.20 Andre Routis (F.), Brussels.
1926	Sept. 11	Henri Scillie (B.) w.pts.15 Kid Francis (F.), Brussels.
	Oct. 25	Henri Scillie (B.) w.pts.15 Domenico Bernasconi (I.), Milan.
1929	March 10	Domenico Bernasconi (I.) w.pts.15 Nicholas Biquet (B.), Milan.
	June 3	Domenico Bernasconi (I.) w.ko.9 Rinaldo Castellenghi (I.), Bologna.
	Sept. 26	Carlos Flix (Sp.) w.pts.15 Domenico Bernasconi (I.), Barcelona.
1930	June 4	Carlos Flix (Sp.) w.pts.15 Nicholas Biquet (B.), Barcelona.
1931	Sept. 19	Lucien Popescu (R.) w.pts.15 Carlos Flix (Sp.), Bucharest.
1932	March 19	Domenico Bernasconi (I.) w.ko.3 Lucien Popescu (R.), Milan.
	Dec. 7	Nicholas Biquet (B.) w.pts.15 Carlos Flix (Sp.), Brussels.
1933	July 15	Nicholas Biquet (B.) drew 15 Balthasar Sangchilli (Sp.), Valencia.
1934	March 17	Nicholas Biquet (B.) w.pts.15 Domenico Bernasconi (I.), Milan.
	July 5	Joseph Decico (F.) w.pts.15 Nicholas Biquet (B.), Lyon.
	July 28	Nicholas Biquet (B.) drew15 Joseph Decico (F.), Lyon.
	Dec. 28	Nicholas Biquet (B.) drew15 Frank Harsene (F.), Lille.
1935	Jan. 22	Nicholas Biquet (B.) w.pts.15 Carlos Flix (Sp.), Antwerp.
	May 11	Maurice Dubois (Sw.) w.pts.15 Nicholas Biquet (B.), Geneva.

	Oct. 6	Maurice Dubois (Sw.) w.pts.15 Emile Pladner (F.), Geneva.
1936	Feb. 19	Joseph Decico (F.) w.ko.4 Maurice Dubois (Sw.), Lyon.
	July 26	Aurel Toma (R.) w.ret.11 Joseph Decico (F.), Bucharest.
1937	Feb. 3	Nicholas Biquet (B.) w.rpts.15 Maurice Huguenin (F.), Brussels.
1938	June 4	Aurel Toma (R.) w.pts.8 Gino Cattaneo (I.), Bucharest.
1939	Aug. 11	Ernst Weiss (A.) w.ko.12 Aurel Toma (R.), Berlin.
	Nov. 25	Gino Cattaneo (I.) w.pts.15 Ernst Weiss (A.), Berlin.
1941	May 31	Gino Cattaneo (I.) drew15 Hermann Remscheid (G.), Munich.
	Sept. 27	Gino Bondavalli (I.) w.pts.15 Gino Cattaneo (I.), Reggio Emilia.

European Boxing Union

1946	March 19	Jackie Paterson (U.K.) w.dis.8 Theo Medina (F.), London.
	Oct. 30	Theo Medina (F.) w.ko.4 Jackie Paterson (U.K.), Glasgow.
1947	Sept. 19	Peter Kane (U.K.) w.pts.15 Theo Medina (F.), Manchester.
	Dec. 15	Peter Kane (U.K.) w.pts.15 Joe Cornelis (B.), Manchester.
1948	Feb. 20	Guido Ferracin (I.) w.pts.15 Peter Kane (U.K.), Manchester.
	July 16	Guido Ferracin (I.) w.ret.5 Peter Kane (U.K.), Manchester.
1949	Aug. 10	Luis Romero (Sp.) w.ko.7 Guido Ferracin (I.), Barcelona.
1950	April 25	Luis Romero (Sp.) w.rsf.13 Danny O'Sullivan (U.K.), London.
	Sept. 22	Luis Romero (Sp.) w.pts.15 Marcel Mathieu (F.), Barcelona.
1951	June 20	Luis Romero (Sp.) w.pts.15 Alvaro Nuvoloni (I.), Barcelona.
	Sept. 5	Peter Keenan (U.K.) w.pts.15 Luis Romero (Sp.), Glasgow.
1952	May 21	Jean Sneyers (B.) w.ko.5 Peter Keenan (U.K.), Glasgow.
1953	June 16	Peter Keenan (U.K.) w.pts.15 Maurice Sandeyron (F.), Glasgow.
	Oct. 3	John Kelly (U.K.) w.pts.15 Peter Keenan (U.K.), Belfast.
1954	Feb. 27	Robert Cohen (F.) w.ko.3 John Kelly (U.K.), Belfast.
1955	Oct. 29	Mario D'Agata (I.) w.dis.5 Andre Valignat (F.) Milan.
1957	Oct. 27	Mario D'Agata (I.) w.ko.8 Federico Scarponi (I.), Cagliari.
1958	Oct. 15	Piero Rollo (I.) w.pts.15 Mario D'Agata (I.), Cagliari.
1959	May 30	Piero Rollo (I.) drew 15 Juan Cardenas (Sp.), Cagliari.
	Oct. 3	Piero Rollo (I.) w.dis.5 Federico Scarponi (I.), Cagliari.
	Nov. 3	Freddie Gilroy (U.K.) w.pts.15 Piero Rollo (I.), London.
1960	March 19	Freddie Gilroy (U.K) w.rsf.13 Billy Rafferty (U.K.), Belfast.
1961	May 27	Pierre Cossemyns (B.) w.ret.9 Freddie Gilroy (U.K.), Brussels.
	Nov. 4	Pierre Cossemyns (B.) w.pts.15 Piero Rollo (I.), Cagliari.
1962	April 13	Piero Rollo (I.) w.ko.5 Pierre Cossemyns (B.), Brussels.
	June 26	Alphonse Halimi (F.) w.pts.15 Piero Rollo (I.), Tel Aviv.
	Oct. 28	Piero Rollo (I.) w.pts.15 Alphonse Halimi (F.,), Cagliari.
1963	July 19	Mimoun Ben Ali (Sp.) w.pts.15 Piero Rollo (I.), Madrid.
	Dec. 9	Risto Luukkonen (Fin.) w.pts.15 Mimoun Ben Ali (Sp.), Helsinki.
1964	May 22	Risto Luukkonen (Fin.) w.pts.15 Pierre Vetroff (F.), Helsinki.
1965	Feb. 4	Limoun Ben Ali (Sp.) w.pts.15 Pierre Vetroff (F.), Barcelona.
	Aug. 19	Tommaso (I.) w.pts.15 Mimoun Ben Ali (Sp.), San Remo.
	Dec. 3	Tommaso Galli (I.) drew 15 Walter McGowan (U.K.), Rome.
1966	March 6	Tommaso Galli (I.) w.pts.15 Pierre Vetroff (F.), Marseilles.
	June 17	Mimoun Ben Ali (Sp.) w.pts.15 Tommaso Galli (I.), Barcelona.
	Sept. 22	Mimoun Ben Ali (Sp.) w.pts.15 Jose Arranz (Sp.), Barcelona.
1967	April 27	Mimoun Ben Ali (Sp.) w.pts.15 Alan Rudkin (U.K.), Barcelona.
1968	Jan. 10	Salvatore Burruni (I.) w.pts.15 Mimoun Ben Ali (Sp.), Naples.
	July 31	Salvatore Burruni (I.) w.pts.15 Franco Zuro (I.), San Benedetto del Trento.

1969	April 9	Salvatore Burruni (I.) w.ret.9 Pierre Vetroff (F.), Reggio Calabria.
	Dec. 17	Franco Zurlo (I.). w.pts.15 Mimoun Ben Ali (Sp.), Taurianova.
1970	March 11	Franco Zurlo (I.) w.ret.4 Francisco Martinez (Sp.), Caserta.
	April 4	Franco Zurlo (I.) w.pts.15 John McClusky (U.K.), Zurich.
	June 24	Franco Zurlo (I.) w.pts.15 Enzo Farinelli (I.), Naples.
1971	Feb. 16	Alan Rudkin (U.K.) w.ret.11 Franco Zurlo (I.), London.
	Aug. 10	Agustin Senin (Sp.) w.pts.15 Alan Rudkin (U.K.), Bilbao.
1972	Feb. 2	Agustin Senin (Sp.) w.pts.15 Guy Caudron (F.), Barcelona.
	Sept. 27	Agustin Senin (Sp.) w.ret.6 Antonio Sassarini (I.), La Spezia.
1973	April 17	Johnny Clark (U.K.) w.pts.15 Franco Zurlo (I.), London.
1974	Jan. 15	Johnny Clark (U.K.) w.pts.15 Salvatore Fabrizio (I.), London.
	Oct. 4	Bob Allotey (Sp.) w.pts.15 Guy Caudron (F.), Madrid.
1975	Feb. 9	Daniel Trioulaire (F.) w.rsf.9 Bob Allotey (Sp.), Notre Dame de Bondeville.
	April 11	Daniel Trioulaire (F.) drew 15 Dave Needham (U.K.), Barentin.
1976	Jan. 16	Daniel Trioulaire (F.) drew 15 Paddy Maguire (U.K.), Cluses.
	April 7	Daniel Trioulaire (F.) drew 15 Fernando Bernandez (Sp.), Vigo.
	Aug. 14	Salvatore Fabrizio (I.) w.pts.15 Daniel Trioulaire (F.), Ospedaletti.
1977	Feb. 23	Franco Zurlo (I.) w.pts.15 Salvatore Fabrizio (I.), Fasano.
	June 15	Franco Zurlo (I.) w.rsf.7‖ Jacky Bihin (F.), Cagliari.
	Sept. 28	Franco Zurlo (I.) w.ret.8 Paddy Maguire (U.K.), Cagliari.
1978	April 20	Franco Zurlo (I.) drew 15 Esteban Eguia (Sp.), Via Reggio.
	July 7	Franco Zurlo (I.) drew 15 Alfredo Mulas (I.), Rome.
	Aug. 20	Franco Zurlo (I.) w.ret.10 Franco Buglione (I.), Rocco Monfina.
	Sept. 16	Juan Francisco Rodriguez (Sp.) w.pts.15 Franco Zurlo (I.), Vigo.
1979	March 3	Juan Francisco Rodriguez (Sp.) w.pts.15 Johnny Owen (U.K.), Almeria.
	Aug. 10	Juan Francisco Rodriguez (Sp.) w.pts.12 Laurent Grimbert (F.), Lepe.
1980	Feb. 28	Johnny Owen (U.K.) w.pts.12 Juan Francisco Rodriguez (Sp.), Ebbw Vale.
	Dec. 3	Valerio Nati (I.) w.pts.12 Juan Francisco Rodriguez (Sp.) Forli.
1981	April 1	Valerio Nati (I.) w.ko.5 Vicente Rodriguez (Sp.), Cenenatico.
	June 17	Valerio Nati (I.) w.pts.12 John Feeney (U.K.), Cervi.
	Aug. 31	Valerio Nati (I.) w.ko.2 Jean-Jacques Souris (F.), Roccaruji.
	Nov. 19	Valerio Nati (I.) w.pts.12 Jose Luis de la Sagra (I.), Mazara.
1982	Jan. 27	Valerio Nati (I.) w.ret.5 Esteban Egula (Sp.), Castrocito.
	April 29	Guiseppe Fossati (I.) w.pts.12 Valerio Nati (I.), Lignano.
	June 30	Guiseppe Fossati (I.) w.pts.12 John Feeney (U.K.) , Campobello.
	Oct. 14	Guiseppe Fossati (I.) w.pts.12 Luis de la Sagra (Sp.), Marino Vicentino, Italy.
1983	Feb. 24	Guiseppe Fossati (I.) drew Valerio Nati (I.), Bologna, Italy.
	July 9	Walter Giorgetti (I.) w.pts.12 Guiseppe Fossati (I.), Sciacca, Italy.
	Sept. 22	Walter Giorgetti (I.) w.rsf.7 Jose Antunez (Sp.), Roseto, Italy.
	Dec. 28	Walter Giorgetti (I.) w.pts.12 John Feeney (U.K.) Campobasso, Italy.
1984	April 17	Walter Giorgetti (I.) w.rsf.5 Kamel Djadda (F.), Treviso, Italy.
	Nov. 14	Ciro de Leva (I.) w.pts.12 John Feeney (U.K.), Salerno, Italy.
1985	March 13	Ciro de Leva (I.) w.pts.12 Jose Antunez (Sp.), Caserta, Italy.
	May 2	Ciro de Leva (I.) w.rsf.8 Walter Giorgetti (I.), Messina, Italy.
	July 6	Ciro de Leva (I.) w.rsf.7 Enrique Rodriguez Cal (Sp.), Lerici, Italy.

	Aug. 10	Ciro de Leva (I.) w.pts.12 Alain Limarola (F.), Eboli, Italy.
1986	Feb. 26	Ciro de Leva (I.) w.pts.12 Ray Gilbody (U.K.) Cosenza, Italy.
	Oct. 27	Antoine Montero (F.) w.rsf.1 Ray Gilbody (U.K.), Paris, France.
1987	May 22	Louis Gomis (F.) w.pts.12 Antoine Montero (F.), La Seine Sur Mer, France.
	Oct. 14	Louis Gomis (F.) w.pts.12 Maurizio Lupino (I.), Calgiari, Italy.
1988	Jan. 20	Fabrice Venichou (F.) w.pts.12 Antoine Montero (F.), La Seine du Mer, France.
	April 13	Vincenzo Belcastro (I.) w.ko.3 Fabrice Benichou (F.), Busalia, Italy.
	June 1	Vincenzo Belcastro (I.) w.rsf.9 Lorenzo Martinez Pacheco (Sp.), Campione, Italy.

European Flyweight Title Fights
(112 pounds: 8 stone)

International Boxing Union

1913	April 11	Sid Smith (U.K.) w.pts.20 Eugene Criqui (F.), Paris.
	June 2	Billy Ladbury (U.K.) w.ko.11 Sid Smith (U.K.), London.
1914	Jan. 26	Percy Jones (U.K.) w.pts.20 Billy Ladbury (U.K.), London.
	March 26	Percy Jones (U.K.) w.pts.20 Eugene Criqui (F.), Liverpool.
	March 30	Jimmy Wilde (U.K.) w.ko.6 Eugene Husson (F.), London.
	April 16	Jimmy Wilde (U.K.) w.ko.6 Albert Bouzonnie (F.), Liverpool.
	May 11	Jimmy Wilde (U.K.) w.ko.9 Georges Gloria (F.), London.
	May 15	Joe Symonds (U.K.) w.ret.18 Percy Jones (U.K.), Plymouth.
	Oct. 19	Tancy Lee (U.K.) w.ret.14 Percy Jones (U.K.), London.
1915	Jan. 25	Tancy Lee (U.K.) w.ret.17 Jimmy Wilde (U.K.), London.
1916	June 26	Jimmy Wilde (U.K.) w.ret.11 Tancy Lee (U.K.), London.
	July 31	Jimmy Wilde (U.K.) w.ko.4 Johnny Hughes (U.K.), London.
1917	March 12	Jimmy Wilde (U.K.) w.ret.4 George Clark (U.K.), London.
1923	Sept. 29	Michel Montreuil (B.) w.pts.20 Andre Gleizes (F.), Brussels.
1924	Nov. 21	Michel Montreuil (B.) w.pts.20 Elky Clark (U.K.), Glasgow.
1925	Jan. 31	Elky Clark (U.K.) w.pts.20 Michel Montreuil (B.), Glasgow.
	April 30	Elky Clark (U.K.) w.rsf.20 Young Johnny Brown (U.K.), London.
1926	April 19	Elky Clark (U.K.) w.rsf.20 George 'Kid' Socks (U.K.), London.
	Oct. 7	Elky Clark (U.K.) w.pts.20 Francois Morrachini (I.), London.
1927	Sept. 15	Victor Ferrand (Sp.) drew 20 Nicholas Biquet (B.), Barcelona.
1928	Feb. 14	Emile Pladner (F.) w.pts.20 Victor Ferrand (Sp.), Paris.
	March 19	Johnny Hill (U.K.) w.pts.15 Emile Pladner (F.), London.
1929	Feb. 7	Emile Pladner (F.) w.ko.6 Johnny Hill (U.K.), Paris.
	June 20	Eugene Huat (F.) w.ret.15 Emile Pladner (F.), Paris.
1930	March 5	Kid Oliva (F.) w.pts.15 Emile Degand (B.), Lyon.
	June 7	Lucien Popescu (R.) w.ret.10 Kid Oliva (F.) Bucharest.
	Aug. 16	Lucien Popescu (R.) w.pts.15 Henry Challenge (F.), Bucharest.
1931	May 4	Jackie Brown (U.K.) w.pts.15 Lucien Popescu (R.), Manchester.
	June 15	Jackie Brown (U.K.) w.pts.15 Emile Degand (B.), London.
	July 6	Jackie Brown (U.K.) w.pts.15 Vinzenzo Savo (I.), Manchester.
1932	Sept. 19	Jackie Brown (U.K.) w.dis.8 Jim Maharg (U.K.), Manchester.
	Nov. 1	Praxile Gyde (F.) w.ret.8 Willy Metzner (G.), Lille.
1933	Feb. 18	Praxile Gyde (F.) drew15 Kid Oliva (F.), Nice.
	May 25	Praxile Gyde (F.) w.pts.15 Emile Degand (B.), Valenciennes.
	Nov. 1	Praxile Gyde (F.) w.pts.15 Kid Oliva (F.), Lille.

1934	Jan. 21	Praxile Gyde (F.) drew 20 Mariano Arilla (Sp.), Lille.
	July 1	Praxile Gyde (F.) w.pts.15 Pedriot Ruiz (Sp.) Nimes.
	Oct. 14	Praxile Gyde (F.) w.pts.15 Francois Antenica (F.), Aix en Provence.
1935	Jan. 27	Praxile Gyde (F.) w.pts.15 Maurice Huguenin (F.), Lille.
	June 23	Kid David (B.) w.pts.15 Praxile Gyde (F.), Lille.
1936	Oct. 5	Ernst Weiss (A.) w.pts.15 Fortunato Ortega (Sp.), Paris.
	Dec. 12	Valentin Angelmann (F.) w.pts.15 Ernst Weiss (A.), Paris.
1938	Dec. 4	Enrico Urbinati (I.) w.pts.15 Pierre Louis (F.), Rome.
1939	Apr. 3	Enrico Urbinati (I.) w.pts.15 Raoul Degryse (B.), Rome.
1940	Jan. 12	Enrico Urbinati (I.) w.ret.11 Gavino Matta (I.), Rome.
1942	Jun. 28	Enrico Urbinati (I.) w.ret.13 Fortunato Ortega (Sp.), Rome.

European Boxing Union

1946	Oct. 9	Raoul Degryse (B.) w.pts.15 Emile Famechon (F.), Brussels.
1947	May 21	Maurice Sandeyron (F.) w.pts.15 Raoul Degryse (B.), Brussels.
1948	July 6	Maurice Sandeyron (F.) drew 15 Dickie O'Sullivan (U.K.), London.
	Nov. 8	Maurice Sandeyron (F.) w.pts.15 Dickie O'Sullivan (U.K.), London.
1949	April 5	Rinty Monaghan (U.K.) w.pts.15 Maurice Sandeyron (F.), Belfast.
	Sept. 30	Rinty Monaghan (U.K.) drew 15 Terry Allen (U.K.), Belfast.
1950	April 25	Terry Allen (U.K.) w.pts.15 Honore Pratesi (F.), London.
	Oct. 30	Jean Sneyers (B.) w.pts.15 Terry Allen (U.K.), Nottingham.
	Nov. 18	Jean Sneyers (B.) w.ret.3 Honore Pratesi (F.), Brussels.
1952	Feb. 18	Teddy Gardner (U.K.) w.ko.6 Louis Skena (F.), Newcastle.
	Mar. 17	Teddy Gardner (U.K.) w.pts.15 Terry Allen (U.K.), Newcastle.
	June 30	Teddy Gardner (U.K.) w.pts.15 Otello Belardinelli (I.), West Hartlepool.
1953	June 12	Louis Skena (F.) w.ret.14 Young Martin (Sp.) Madrid.
	Dec. 18	Louis Skena (F.) w.pts.15 Nazzarena Giannelli (I.), Geneva.
1954	Sept. 10	Nazzareno Giannelli (I.) w.pts.15 Terry Allen (U.K.), Milan.
1955	March 8	Dai Dower (U.K.) w.pts.15 Nazzareno Giannelli (I.), London.
	Oct. 3	Young Martin (Sp.) w.ko.12 Dai Dower (U.K.), Nottingham.
1956	May 30	Young Martin (Sp.) w.pts.15 Guy Schatt (F.), Madrid.
1957	March 2	Young Martin (Sp.) w.ko.4 Aristide Pozzali (I.), Milan.
1958	July 23	Young Martin (Sp.) w.pts.15 Robert Pollazon (I.), Madrid.
1959	Sept. 3	Risto Luukkonen (Fin.), w.pts.15 Young Martin (Sp.), Helsinki.
1961	June 29	Salvatore Burruni (I.) w.pts.15 Risto Luukkonen (Fin.), Alghero.
	Aug. 13	Salvatore Burruni (I.) w.rsf.6 Derek Lloyd (U.K.), San Remo.
1962	Jun. 30	Salvatore Burruni (I.) w.pts.15 Mimoun Ben Ali (Sp.), St. Vincent.
	Sept. 14	Salvatore Burruni (I.) w.pts.15 Piero Rossi (I.), Milan.
1963	July 5	Salvatore Burruni (I.) w.pts.15 Rene Libeer (F.), Alessandria.
1964	April 24	Salvatore Burruni (I.) w.pts.15 Walter McGowan (U.K.), Rome.
1965	June 13	Rene Libeer (F.) w.ret.15 Paul Chervet (Sw.), Lille.
	Sept. 18	Rene Libeer (F.) w.ko.5 Joseph Horney (B.), Armentiers.

1966	Jan. 22	Rene Libeer (F.) w.ko.2 Dionisio Bisbal (Sp.), Tourcoing.
	March 12	Rene Libeer (F.) w.pts.15 Antoine Porcel (F.), Lyon.
1967	Jan. 25	Fernando Atzori (I.) w.pts.15 Rene Libeer (F.), Florence.
	Aug. 2	Fernando Atzori (I.) drew15 Rene Libeer (F.), Levico Terme.
	Dec. 15	Fernando Atzori (I.) w.,ko.14 Fritz Chervet (Sw.), Berne.
1968	June 26	Fernando Atzori (I.) w.ko.4 John McClusky (U.K.) Naples.
	Dec. 20	Fernando Atzori (I.) w.ret.9 Franco Sperati (I.), Turin.
1969	Sept. 3	Fernando Atzori (I.) w.pts.15 Kamara Diop (F.), Cosenza.
1970	May 1	Fernando Atzori (I.) w.ko.12 Franco Sperati (I.), Calgliari.
	Dec. 18	Fernando Atzori (I.) w.ret.12 Kid Romero (Sp.), Madrid.
1971	March 19	Fernando Atzori (I.) w.pts.15 John McCluskey (U.K.), Zurich.
	Aug. 4	Fernando Atzori (I.) w.pts.15 Gerard Macrez (F.), Ascona.
1972	March 3	Fritz Chervet (Sw.) w.ret.11 Fernando Atzori (I.), Berne.
	June 23	Fritz Chervet (Sw.) w.pts.15 Kid Romero (Sp.), Berne.
	Oct. 13	Fritz Chervet (Sw.) w.pts.15 Mariano Garcia (Sp.), Geneva.
	Dec. 26	Fritz Chervet (Sw.) w.pts.15 John McClusky (U.K.), Zurich.
1973	June 28	Fernando Atzori (I.) w.ko.12 Dominique Cesari (F.), Novara.
	Dec. 26	Fritz Chervet (Sw.) w.ko.6 Fernando Atzori (I.), Zurich.
1974	Oct. 25	Franco Udella (I.) w.ko.5 Pedro Molledo (Sp.), Milan.
1975	May 31	Franco Udella (I.) d.n.c.2 Fritz Chervet (Sw.), Zurich.
1976	Jan. 14	Franco Udella (I.) w.pts.15 Fritz Chervet (Sw.), Campione.
	June 12	Franco Udella (I.) w.rsf.9 Franco Sperati (I.), Santa Teresa.
1977	June 10	Franco Udella (I.) w.ko.5 Jose Cantero (Sp.), Milan.
	Oct. 26	Franco Udella (I.) w.ret.9 Nessim Zebelini (F.), Vigevano.
	Dec. 24	Franco Udella (I.) w.pts.15 Emilio Pireddu (I.), Cagliari.
1978	March 24	Franco Udella (I.) w.rsf.6 Mariano Garcia (Sp.), Cagliari.
	Nov. 15	Franco Udella (I.) w.pts.15 Manuel Carrasco (Sp.), Bellaria.
1979	May 1	Charlie Magri (U.K.) w.pts.12 Franco Udella (I.), London.
	Dec. 4	Charlie Magri (U.K.) w.pts.12 Manuel Carrasco (Sp.), London.
1980	June 28	Charlie Magri (U.K.) w.rsf.3 Giovanni Camputaro (I.), London.
1981	Feb. 24	Charlie Magri (U.K.) w.rsf.2 Enrique Rodriguez Cal (Sp.), London, U.K.
1982	Sept. 18	Charlie Magri (U.K.) w.ko.2 Enrique Rodriguez Cal (Sp.), Aviles, Spain.
1983	June 17	Antoine Montero (F.) w.ret.8 Mariano Garcia (Sp.), La Roche, France.
	Aug. 4	Antoine Montero (F.) w.rsf.8 Giovanni Camputaro (I.), Nimes, France.
	Dec. 7	Antoine Montero (F.) w.ko.8 Keith Wallace (U.K.), London, U.K.
1984	Aug. 24	Charlie Magri (U.K.) w.rsf.1 Franco Cherchi (I.), Cagliari, Italy.
1985	Feb. 27	Franco Cherchi (I.) w.pts.12 Alain Limarola (F.), Lucca, Italy.
	Aug. 4	Franco Cherchi (I.) w.pts.12 Lorenzo Pacheco (Sp.), Palau, Italy.
	Oct. 30	Charlie Magri (U.K.) w.ko.2 Franco Cherchi (I.),. Alessandria, Italy.
1986	May 20	Duke McKenzie (U.K.) w.ret.5 Charlie Magri (U.K.), Wembley. U.K.
	Dec. 17	Duke McKenzie (U.K.) w.pts.12 Piero Pinna (I.), Auqui Terme. Italy.

Glossary of Boxing Terms

Terms that originated in the days of the prize ring are in bold italic (e.g. **Block**): terms originating in modern boxing are in bold (e.g. **Below the belt**).

Bag, Big A long, suspended, padded bag used for striking practice and power of punch, both at long and short range.

Bag, Platform A small leather bag hanging from an overhead platform and used for obtaining rhythm in punching.

Bag, Swinging A bag mounted on a flexible spring stand. It is used for hitting and avoiding a dodging object, to perfect aim and the judging of distance, and for counter-punching.

Bell This is rung at the start of a contest, to end each round or to silence the spectators before an announcement is made from the ring. Sometimes a gong or a whistle is used instead. The bell is solely for the use of the timekeeper.

Below the belt The body from the top of the hips downward. Any punch here is a foul.

Block To use the arms, elbows, hands and wrists in order to minimize the effects of a blow and cause the opponent to waste most of his punches and energy.

Bobbing and weaving Ducking and dodging intended blows. Some fighters weave into an attack, i.e. they crouch slightly and move the shoulders as they advance, usually in an effort to get to close range.

Boxing Fighting using a clenched fist, with the thumb laid across the fingernails to form a box, and using the bare knuckles for solid hitting. Comes from the Latin *boxus* – a box.

Break A command by the referee for the men to end a prolonged clinch; it is universally used by referees. It is an offence to 'hit on the break', i.e. to sneak over a punch when parting from an opponent after being ordered to do so. A clean 'break' occurs when the men step back and momentarily lower their hands. To ignore a command to break can lead to instant disqualification.

Butt To place the head beneath an opponent's chin and jerk upwards: a foul.

Button Point of the jaw, or chin. A straight blow to it is capable of putting a man down. A left hook or right cross properly delivered to the button often results in a knock-out. *Also known as* the point.

Clinch To go into a hold, usually after a mishit from one or both fighters. The object of a clinch is to trap the opponent's arms so that he cannot use them. Prolonged holding or clinching and ignoring an instruction from the referee to break may result in disqualification.

Counter The move made after an opponent has delivered a punch or been made to miss with one. A *cross-counter* is the answer to a straight left lead or jab: the right is brought over the left arm of the opponent and is aimed at his chin. A *counter attack* is an answer to an opponent's attack.

Cross The breaking of an agreement by one of the two boxers making it. Usually the agreement is to arrange the result of their contest in advance.

Double-cross The breaking of an agreement by both people making it. There is a boxing joke that whereas an illiterate boxer may sign with a cross, a manager uses a double-cross.

Draw A decision that both boxers are equal in points scoring at the end of their contest, i.e. that one man has not won more rounds than his opponent. It comes from prize fighting days when the *drawing* or pulling out of the stakes holding the ring-rope terminated a contest, the referee deciding to end the contest early, with the two men equal in scoring, either because it was becoming too dark, the police were arriving, the ground was becoming too slippery, both men were too exhausted to continue or spectators were intruding into the ring.

Elbowing Using the elbows as weapons: a foul.

Feint To deceive an opponent by making him expect one sort of punch and then catching him with another, e.g. to threaten a blow to the head to make a rival put up his guard, and then to catch him with a body blow and vice versa. *See also* nod.

Fix An arrangement to ensure a specific outcome of a contest in advance, usually made by the two contestants but something involving instead the promoter, referee, managers, seconds, etc. Fixing a fight was prevalent in prize ring days and has occurred in the modern ring, but there are strict penalties if fixing is discovered.

Fox To act as if hurt or in distress, usually by going back into the ropes in order to lure an opponent into a counter attack. The famous Kid McCoy was noted for this form of trickery.

Gate The paying spectators at a boxing match. The term derives from the time when the public were allowed into an enclosure to watch a contest. Each person passed through a gate, either to pay for admission or to present a ticket. The idea was inspired by Daniel Mandoza, who was averse to giving his services for free. Subsequently boxers would often 'box on the gate', i.e. they would share the takings with each other and the promoter on an agreed percentage. The size of the 'gate money' depended on the drawing power of the contestants and public interest in the fight.

Glass jaw Mocking epithet for a boxer who cannot withstand a blow to the chin or suffers repeatedly from punches to the jaw; a man who can be put down by a jaw punch or is repeatedly staggered by one. Usually attributed to a man who has been knocked out a number of times.

Gong See Bell.

Haymaker A swinging punch, usually a right (left for southpaw), which is inaccurately directed: a wild delivery that comes a long way and is usually used in desperation. It should be easy to avoid.

Hitting and holding Hitting with one hand whilst holding with the other: a foul.

Hitting on the break See Break.

Holding See Clinch.

Hook A short-arm punch delivered with the wrist turned at the point of impact, the arm being curved rather than bent. Attributed to Kid McCoy, who used it to considerable effect after it was explained to him that the bore in a rifle spun a bullet, sending it faster, truer and with more devastating results.

Infighting Fighting close together so as to use short-arm punches, hooks or uppercuts to the body and head. Both hands must be free, it being an offence to hold with one hand and hit with the other. When there is a deadlock between the men, the order comes to break.

Kidney punch A blow to the area of the kidneys: a foul.

Knockout There was no such term in prize ring days, and in any case it is a misnomer. A man unable to come to 'scratch' or 'toe the line' was counted out of time. No count was made over a man put down: if he fell or was thrown, his seconds entered the ring to carry or help him to his corner. When 'time' was called, he had a bare eight seconds to get up and walk to the centre of the ring. If he was incapable of walking there were times, in those brutal days, when his seconds carried him there and stood him up to face his opponent in order to prolong the fight. The term is used in modern boxing, but is widely misunderstood – see page 178.

Mark, The A blow to the solar plexus, the nerve centre just below the navel and under the ribs. It was a favourite punch of John Broughton, and was known as 'Broughton's Mark'. In 1897 Bob Fitzsimmons used it to win the world heavyweight title from James J. Corbett.

Milling Boxing, fighting or exchanging blows.

Milling on the retreat: Backing off and drawing an advancing opponent on to your own punches so that they have a double effect. Although attack is considered the best form of defence, a retreating boxer can wear a rival down and then set up an attack of his own.

Muffers Wrappings once tied around the hand to minimize the damaging power of a punch. These were the earliest form of boxing glove, and were introduced by John Broughton in 1743. The modern glove has a leather grip on the inside and a separate thumb cover. (Efforts are being made to introduce a thumbless glove to prevent eye damage.)

Neutral corner The corners of a ring unoccupied by the boxers and their seconds. A referee usually goes to one of them to add up his score card.

Nobbins The money thrown into the ring by spectators in appreciation for an exciting contest. The word is still used in modern boxing and derives from the collections made by the 'whips' after a contest. The hat was thrust under a spectator's nose, a stick threatened, and if nothing was forthcoming there was a tap on the 'nob' (head). This was the method used by travelling circuses and shows where the public was admitted free for the first half of the programme and then called upon to subscribe in order to be allowed to see the second half.

No contest A verdict the referee can make if he thinks that the two men are not trying and are engaged more in a sparring match than a fight, or if there is anything suspicious about their intentions, he is at liberty to stop the affair and declare 'no contest'. The boxers are then in danger of losing their purse or being put under suspension.

No decision A verdict that could be delivered in American bouts only. When boxing got out of hand in New York, the Horton Law was introduced in 1900. It permitted boxing contests to take place in New York State but only by club membership. In 1911 the Frawley Law took over. This enabled the public to witness bouts, but these were limited to ten rounds and no decision could be given as to the winner. They were called 'No Decision Bouts' and this spread to practically every other State. It left the ringside reporter to make his own decision as to the winner and led to the term 'newspaper decision'. The Frawley Law lasted until 1917 and three years later the Walker Law (after Jim Walker, Mayor of New York) came into being. This allowed for a decision to be rendered, the licensing of boxers, promoters and all those connected with the sport. The principles of this law have remained in effect ever since.

Nod To deceive an opponent by moving the head slightly to imply one type of punch is coming and then delivering another. *See also* feint.

One-two punches 1. A right instantly followed by a left to the same target or vice versa. Sometimes referred to as 'The Postman's Knock' (rat tat). Two quickly delivered punches, usually to the same spot and the second coming before the opponent has recovered from the first.

Open glove punch Hitting with the inside of the glove or slapping with the open glove: a foul.

Palming To rub an opponent's face upwards with the palm of the hand when in a clinch: a foul.

Parry To push away an aimed blow or misdirect a punch, either by turning a delivery out of its intended course by hitting at the glove or arm, or coming inside the offensive arm and turning it away from its target.

Pivot punch A backwards swing whereby an opponent is hit by the back knuckles: a foul.

Pugilism Fighting with the fists. *Pugilist* (contracted to *pug*) One who takes part in pugilism. From the Greek *puxos* – box, *pugme* a fist doubled for fighting.

Pulling Dragging a rival forward into a punch: a foul.

Pulling a punch To contract a blow so that it loses some force. A boxer might do this when he feels compassion for an opponent who is being outclassed. Punches are, of course, also pulled in sparring. There have been instances when the favourite to win a contest has deliberately held back his blows to minimize their effect and to enable him to lose gracefully. When both men 'pull' their punches an observant referee can stop the bout and it is recorded as 'No contest'. It is an offence that can lead to disqualification.

Purse The money paid to the boxers. In the prize rings days, the purse would contain as many guineas (a gold coin valued at £1.05) as the particular fighters merited. However, from the beginning of glove-fighting, the contestants would fight for a guaranteed purse, and usually the winner took all of it or the purse was shared 60/40 by prior agreement. Nowadays, every boxer knows how much he will receive win, lose or draw.

Rabbit punch A hit on the back of the neck: a foul.

Referee The person appointed to see fair play and to keep the fight active. He could break up prolonged spells of holding, hugging or wrestling and prevent one man from choking the other, kicking him when he was down or falling on him and remaining there for too long. It was in his power to terminate a contest if it became too dark or the ground was too slippery because of rain. He could then render a decision as to the winner or order the pair to meet the next day or on a subsequent date by arrangement. On rare occasions he might disqualify one of the contestants for an emphatic breach of the rules.

Ring The circle of ropes used in the earliest days of bare-knuckle fighting. It was held by the spectators, who in moments of excitement would close in around the fighters. Eventually, to avoid interference, stakes were driven into the ground to form a square in which the contestants would fight but it retained the name of the ring, which is still used.

Scratch A mark drawn on the ground or turf to denote the halfway mark that in prize-fighting days divided the ring into two parts, one for each boxer, and his seconds. Each boxer was called to 'scratch', came up to the 'mark' or had to 'toe the line' for the start of the contest and for the commencement of each round. If he was 'not up to scratch' or 'not up to the mark' (present-day terms for feeling unwell) he lost the contest. Today, if told to conform to accepted practices, one must 'toe the line'. If it is necessary to start all over again, one must 'go back to scratch'. If there is no advantage at the outset then one 'starts from scratch'.

Seconds The men who stay outside the ring by their boxer's corner and enter it at the end of each round to refresh him, attend to any injuries, and to see if he is fit to continue the contest. In the days of the prize ring, these attendants were always boxers themselves,

trained and ready to go into the ring and fight an opponent's second if a contest ended quickly or to give the spectators more for their money. They were called 'seconds' because they were of secondary importance or were engaged in a secondary bout, and the name has stuck.

Shadow boxing Solitary training by a boxer to sharpen up his movements and punches. In the ring by himself he fights an imaginery opponent, concentrating on footwork and speed, varying his actions both for attack and defence.

Southpaw A boxer with an unorthodox stance, i.e. right foot forward and leading with the right hand, rather than left foot forward and leading with the left. Usually a southpaw carries more destructive force in his left hand, whereas the orthodox fighter has more power in his right. The term originates from baseball. On most baseball grounds the pitcher (ball thrower) pitches from east to west: therefore his throwing arms is on the north side of the baseball ground. If he is a left-handed pitcher, then his throwing arm is to the south – hence the name.

Spar To box in a friendly contest. *Sparring partner* A person who boxes in a make-believe contest in the gymnasium, when either punches are 'pulled' or large sparring gloves are used to minimize hitting power.

Spikes Spiked shoes. In order to secure a safe footing, most essential in the prize ring, pugilists were allowed to use spiked shoes, as do modern track athletes. Apart from sash, breeches and hose, shoes were the only items worn. Of course, men were sometimes 'spiked' by their opponents but this was against the rules; another infringement was to carry a bullet or short piece of brass in a clenched hand in order to add more power to a punch. In America this was known as 'Irishman's Confetti'. The American ex-slave Tom Molineaux was accused of carrying a bullet in his palm when fighting Tom Cribb in 1811. This was untrue, but the time taken up in proving so gave the Englishman extra minutes in which to recover from the punishment he had taken the previous round and he won the fight.

Stakes Posts driven into the ground to form the 'ring'. The fighters would tie their colours (a scarf or a neckpiece) to a stake to show who they were and to denote their corner. To a corner stake would be hung the purse for which they were fighting: a square of soft leather, bunched together into a bag and closed with a brass ring. This held the 'stake money' which usually went to the winner. In horse-racing today, some races are known as the '–Stakes'.

Sucker punch Any blow that should have been avoided: often a chance blow against a confident opponent that comes when least expected. Sensational endings to many contests have been caused by sucker punches.

Swing A sweeping delivery that comes with the full curve of the arm. Only an expert can achieve success with this punch – it is an easy delivery with which to miss.

Umpire An official who looked after the interests of his own boxer. There were always two, one for each fighter. They occupied initially the 'neutral' corners of the ring, but when an outer ring was introduced, they patrolled this to keep an observant eye of the proceedings in the interest of their own competitors. They had no powers except to protest if they disagreed with the referee's actions,

which they very often did, but they also were there to see that the best sort of order was kept, both by the contestants and the onlookers. The cry of 'police' would cause them to help the principals to escape and carry off the equipment with the aid of the seconds and others involved in the proceedings. They could come to a mutual agreement with the referee as to the outcome of the contest if there was any doubt about it and determine when or if an unfinished fight should be continued. Today there are referees in boxing, football, and similar sports, with umpires for baseball, cricket and other such games.

Uppercut A punch delivered with the front knuckle portion of the glove towards the boxer, so that his back-knuckles (where lies all the power) meet the target with upward force. It can be used both at long and short range and during infighting. It is a most destructive delivery, aimed at either the solar plexus or the chin.

Whip A man, armed with short but efficient whip, who was employed to walk around the 'outer ring' during prize ring days to keep order, prevent the fighters being interfered with or molested, and to keep the space clear. After a contest they would go round, cap in one hand and the whip in the other and beg money for the loser or for any 'second boxer' who had no purse to fight for. This was called 'making a whip round', a phrase used currently to describe providing a monetary benefit for someone in distress or as a present to someone who may have achieved athletic prowess of some sort. Today, at a boxing tournament the Whip's place is in the dressing-room before the start of the show. He checks the occupants to see all are present, gives any aid that may be required, especially in the case of novice boxers, keeps a timetable, and while one fight is in progress makes sure that he has the next pair ready in case of an early closure. He is responsible for the smooth running of the show.

Golden Gloves

Many future world professional champions have emerged from the Golden Gloves championships, the most famous of all the amateur boxing tournaments held in the United States. Class winners of this annual event are awarded a gold medal and a diamond-studded Golden Gloves trophy.

The championships begin with a series of elimination bouts in every major American city where amateur boxing is established. There are city titles to be won, followed by State and Inter-State tournaments, the semi-finals and finals of the National Championships being distributed among the cities of the United States.

The Golden Gloves tournament was the idea of Arch Ward, sports editor of the *Chicago Tribune*, and the newspaper staged the first championships in Chicago in 1926. Next year Paul Gallico, sports editor of the *New York Daily News*, organized the Golden Gloves in New York. The first inter-city Golden Gloves championships were held in 1928 and the tournaments then became an annual national event.

The tournaments soon proved a testing

ground for the professional ring. In 1929 Barney Ross won the Golden Gloves featherweight title, then turned professional and took the world lightweight and welterweight crowns. Joe Louis (who lost only 4 out of 58 amateur bouts) won the light-heavyweight Golden Gloves title in 1934 at the age of 20. He turned professional the same year and won the world heavyweight championship in 1937.

Ray Robinson, Golden Gloves featherweight champion in 1939 and lightweight champion in 1940, scored 69 knock-outs in 85 amateur bouts – 40 of them in the first round. As a professional 'Sugar' Ray Robinson became one of the greatest world welterweight and middleweight champions in ring history. Tony Zale and

Rocky Graziano were two Golden Gloves champions of the 1930s who clashed three times for the world middleweight crown in the 1940s.

In 1938 Ezzard Charles won both the Golden Gloves welterweight title and the national A.A.U. (Amateur Athletic Union) title at the same weight. Next year he moved up a division and took the Golden Gloves and A.A.U. middleweight titles. Charles never lost an amateur fight. He turned professional in 1940 and became world heavyweight titleholder in 1950 by defeating Joe Louis over 15 rounds.

Muhammad Ali (then known as Cassius Clay) won six Golden Gloves titles – the first at the age of 14 in the Junior division – before he dazzled the world as a professional champion.

In 1959 he stepped up to the heavyweight division to avoid a clash with his light-heavyweight brother Rudy and took the Golden Gloves title with a sensational knock-out.

Floyd Patterson, twice world heavyweight king, and Emile Griffith, holder of both the welter and middleweight world titles, were two outstanding Golden Gloves winners. The world light-heavyweight kings that have come from these top-rated competitions have been: Jose Torres, Marvin Johnson, Melio Bettina, Joey Maxim and Gus Lesnevich. Other Golden Gloves world titleholders have been Solly Krieger, Pete Scalzo, Harold Dade and Lou Salica.

The Greats

Boxers Who Won The Same World Title More Than Once

Five Times

Ray Robinson	Middleweight	1951, 1951, 1955, 1957, 1958

Three Times

Ali, Muhammad	Heavyweight	1964, 1974, 1978
Chionoi, Chartchai	Flyweight	1966, 1970, 1973
Gonzalez, Betulio	Flyweight	1971, 1973, 1978
Kingpetch, Pone	Flyweight	1960, 1963, 1964
Wajima, Koichi	Light-Middleweight	1971, 1975, 1976
De Leon, Carlos	Cruiserweight	1980, 1983, 1986
Griffith, Emile	Welterweight	1961, 1962, 1963

Twice

Basilio, Carmen	Welterweight	1955, 1956
Britton, Jack	Welterweight	1915, 1919
Cervantes, Antonio	Light-Welterweight	1972, 1977
Ebihara, Hiroyuki	Flyweight	1963, 1969
Herrara, Rafael	Bantamweight	1972, 1973
Honeyghan, Lloyd	Welterweight	1985, 1988
Ibarra, Luis	Flyweight	1979, 1981
Johnson, Marvin	Light-Heavyweight	1978, 1986
Ketchel, Stanley	Middleweight	1908
Leonard, Sugar Ray	Welterweight	1979, 1980
Loi, Duilio	Light-Welterweight	1960, 1962
Mazzinghi, Sandro	Light-Middleweight	1963, 1968
Muangsurin, Saensak	Light-Welterweight	1975, 1976
Napoles, Jose	Welterweight	1969, 1971
Numata, Yoshiaki	Junior-Lightweight	1967, 1970
Oguma, Shoji	Flyweight	1974, 1980
Olivares, Ruben	Bantamweight	1969, 1971
Patterson, Floyd	Heavyweight	1956, 1960
Perkins, Eddie	Light-Welterweight	1962, 1963
Pical, Ellyas	Super-Featherweight	1985, 1986
Roman, Gilberto	Super-Featherweight	1986, 1988
Salavarria, Erbito	Flyweight	1970, 1975
Saldivar, Vicente	Featherweight	1964, 1970
Serrano, Samuel	Junior-Lightweight	1976, 1981
Valdez, Rodrigo	Middleweight	1974, 1977
Villaflor, Ben	Junior-Lightweight	1972, 1973
Wajima, Koichi	Light-Middleweight	1971, 1975

Boxers Who Won More Than One World Title

Three

Arguello, Alexis	Featherweight, Junior-Lightweight, Lightweight
Armstrong, Henry*	Featherweight, Lightweight, Welterweight
Benitez, Wilfred	Light-Welterweight, Welterweight, Light-Middleweight
Canzoneri, Tony	Featherweight, Junior-Lightweight, Lightweight
Duran, Roberto	Lightweight, Welterweight, Light-Middleweight
Fenech, Jeff	Bantamweight, Featherweight, Super-Featherweight
Fitzsimmons, Bob	Middleweight, Light-Heavyweight, Heavyweight
Hearns, Thomas	Welterweight, Light-Middleweight, Light-Heavyweight
Leonard, Sugar Ray	Welterweight, Light-Middleweight, Middleweight
Ross, Barney	Lightweight, Light-Welterweight, Welterweight

Two

Basilio, Carmen	Welterweight, Middleweight
Bass, Benny	Featherweight, Junior-Lightweight
Benvenuti, Nino	Light-Middleweight, Middleweight
Brouillard, Lou	Welterweight, Middleweight
Castillo, Freddie	Light-Flyweight, Flyweight
Chacon, Bobby	Featherweight, Junior-Lightweight
Chavez, Julio Cesar	Super-Featherweight, Lightweight
Chocolate, Kid	Featherweight, Junior-Lightweight
De Leon, Carlos	Cruiserweight, Light-Heavyweight
Dixon, George	Bantamweight, Featherweight
Dundee, Johnny	Featherweight, Junior-Lightweight
Griffith, Emile	Welterweight, Middleweight
Harada, Masahiko	Flyweight, Bantamweight
Hong, Soo-Hwan	Bantamweight, Super-Bantamweight
Jeffra, Harry	Bantamweight, Featherweight
Jofre, Eder	Bantamweight, Featherweight
Lacier, Santos	Featherweight, Super-Featherweight
McGovern, Terry	Bantamweight, Featherweight
Olivares, Ruben†	Bantamweight, Featherweight
Pintor, Lupe	Bantamweight, Super-Bantamweight
Robinson, Ray‡	Welterweight, Middleweight
Ryan, Tommy	Welterweight, Middleweight
Saddler, Sandy	Featherweight, Junior-Lightweight
Shibata, Kuniaki	Featherweight, Junior-Lightweight
Spinks, Michael	Light-Heavyweight, Heavyweight
Tiger, Dick	Middleweight, Light-Heavyweight
Walter, Mickey	Welterweight, Light-Middleweight
Zapata, Hilario	Light-Flyweight, Flyweight

*Also fought for the world middleweight title. †Won each title twice. ‡Also fought for the world light-heavyweight title.

Vicente Saldivar was a Mexican southpaw who was twice world featherweight champion.

British Boxers Who Won The Same National Title More Than Once

Three Times

Turpin, Randolph	Light-Heavyweight	1952, 1955, 1956

Twice

Allen, Terry	Flyweight	1951, 1952
Armstrong, Evan	Featherweight	1971, 1973
Bodell, Jack	Heavyweight	1969, 1971
Brown, Jackie*	Flyweight	1929, 1931
Buchanan, Ken	Lightweight	1968, 1973
Bugner, Joe†	Heavyweight	1971, 1976
Cooper, Henry†	Heavyweight	1959, 1970
Cowdell, Pat	Super-Featherweight	1986, 1987
Feeney, John	Bantamweight	1981, 1983
Finnegan, Chris	Light-Heavyweight	1971, 1975
Finnegan, Kevin	Middleweight	1977, 1979
Harvey, Len†	Heavyweight	1933, 1938
Harvey, Len†	Light-Heavyweight	1933, 1938
Keenan, Peter†	Bantamweight	1954, 1957
King, Johnny†	Bantamweight	1932, 1935
McKenzie, Clinton	Light-Welterweight	1978, 1979
Mason, Harry	Welterweight	1925, 1934
Petersen, Jack†	Heavyweight	1933, 1934
Power, Colin	Light-Welterweight	1977, 1979
Rudkin, Alan†	Bantamweight	1965, 1968
Sibson, Tony	Middleweight	1984, 1986
Stanley, George*	Bantamweight	1910, 1913
Thom, Wally	Welterweight	1951, 1953

British Boxers Who Won More Than One Title

Three

Harvey, Len*	Middleweight†, Light-Heavyweight†, Heavyweight†
Lewis, Ted 'Kid'*	Featherweight, Welterweight†, Middleweight
Summers, Johnny	Featherweight, Lightweight, Welterweight†

Two

Basham, Johnny	Welterweight†, Middleweight
Bowkers, Joe*	Bantamweight, Featherweight
Cowdell, Pat	Featherweight, Super-Featherweight
Cuthbert, Johnny	Featherweight, Lightweight
Graham, Herol	Light-Middleweight, Middleweight
Lee, Tancy	Flyweight, Featherweight
McAvoy, Jock	Middleweight, Light-Heavyweight
McGowan, Walter	Flyweight, Bantamweight
Mason, Harry	Lightweight, Welterweight
Moody, Frank	Middleweight, Light-Heavyweight
Paterson, Jackie*	Flyweight†, Bantamweight†
Petersen, Jack	Light-Heavyweight, Heavyweight†
Roderick, Ernie	Welterweight†, Middleweight
Swift, Wally	Welterweight, Middleweight
Thomas, Pat	Welterweight, Light-Middleweight
Turpin, Randolph	Middleweight, Light-Heavyweight

*World Champion † Empire or Commonwealth Champion

The Knock-out

The average fight enthusiast misconstrues the term 'knock-out' to mean that a boxer has been knocked unconscious or so dazed that he cannot get up inside ten seconds, whereas in fact it implies that he has been knocked or counted out of time. When there is a knock-down the fallen boxer is given ten seconds in which to get up and continue the contest. If he fails to do so he is counted out of time by the timekeeper. The referee in the ring takes up time from the timekeeper and calls out the seconds over the man on the canvas, standing close enough for him to hear if he is capable of hearing.

There is a rest of one minute between each round (in Prize Ring days it was 30 seconds). At the end of this interval the timekeeper calls for 'seconds out', then rings his bell for the start of the next round. If a boxer fails or is unable to come up to the centre of the ring to resume fighting (to 'toe-the-line' or come up to 'scratch') he is regarded as out of time and his opponent is declared the winner. Apart from losing on retirement from a bout, a boxer can also lose on the intervention of a referee who may consider he is not in a fit state to defend himself, or has sustained a cut on the face or any injury that makes it impossible for him to continue in his own interests. In America all contests that end up inside the scheduled distance of a contest (apart from 'fouls') are regarded as knockouts, but in Great Britain and the rest of Europe a truer definition exists, the record being marked RET when a boxer has retired or RSF when the bout is stopped by the referee.

Should a boxer retire or be retired when in his corner during an interval between the rounds, it is generally regarded that he has been beaten in the round that follows. Thus if a bout ends after the 13th round it is recorded as a win for his opponent in the 14th round, it being argued that the 13th round has ended and that the interval belongs to the following round.

Longest-Reigning Champions

Longest-Reigning World Champions

DIVISION	PERIOD	YEARS
Heavyweight		
Joe Louis	1937–49	12*
Larry Holmes	1978–85	8
Muhammad Ali	1964–71	7
	1974–78	5
Jack Johnson	1908–15	7
Light-Heavyweight		
Archie Moore	1952–62	10
Gus Lesnevich	1941–48	7*
Bob Foster	1968–74	6
Victor Galindez (W.B.A.)	1974–78	4
Michael Spinks	1981–85	4
Super-Middleweight		
Chong-Pal Park (I.B.F.)	1984–87	3
Middleweight		
Ray Robinson	1951–60	9†
Carlos Monzon	1970–77	7
Marvin Hagler	1980–87	7
Tony Zale	1940–47	7*
Light-Middleweight		
Koichi Wajima	1971–76	5‡
Alessandro Mazzinghi	1963–65	2
	1968–71	3
Nino Benvenuti	1967–70	3

Referee Buck McTiernan bends over a kayoed Ezzard Charles as Jersey Joe Walcott looks on.

Welterweight		
Jose Napoles	1969–75	6
Freddie Cochrane	1941–46	4⅔*
Pipino Cuevas (W.B.A.)	1976–80	4
Jack Britton	1919–22	3
Carlos Palomino	1976–79	3
Donald Curry	1983–86	3
Sugar Ray Leonard	1979–82	3‡

Light-Welterweight		
Saoul Mamby (W.B.C.)	1977–82	5
Aarön Pryor	1980–85	5‡
Bruno Arcari (W.B.C.)	1970–76	4
Antonio Cervantes (W.B.A.)	1972–76	3
Nicolino Locche (W.B.A.)	1968–72	3
Saensak Muangsurin (W.B.C.)	1975–78	3

Lightweight		
Benny Leonard	1917–25	7
Roberto Duran	1972–79	6
Joe Gans	1902–08	6

Junior-Lightweight		
Gabriel Elorde	1960–67	7
Tod Morgan	1925–29	4
Hiroshi Kobayashi	1967–71	4
Ben Villaflor	1972–76	4
Ricardo Arredondo (W.B.C.)	1971-74	3
Alfredo Escalera (W.B.C.)	1975–78	3
Samuel Serrano (W.B.A.)	1976–80	3
Julio Cesar Chavez (W.B.C.)	1984–87	3

Featherweight		
Johnny Kilbane	1912–23	11
Abe Attell	1904–12	8
Eusebio Pedrosa	1978–85	7
Sandy Saddler	1950–57	7‡
Davey Moore	1958–63	4
Vicente Saldivar	1964–67	3
Shozo Salivo (W.B.A.)	1968–71	3

Super-Bantamweight		
Wilfredo Gomez (W.B.C.)	1977–84	6½
Carl Duane	1923–26	3
Victor Callejas (W.B.A.)	1984–86	2
Ricardo Cardona (W.B.A.)	1978–80	2
Sergio Victor Palma (W.B.A.)	1980–82	2
Leonardo Cruz (W.B.A.)	1982–84	2

Bantamweight		
Panama Al Brown	1929–35	6
Manuel Ortiz	1942–47	5
	1947–50	4
Jimmy Barry	1894–99	5

Super-Flyweight		
Jiro Watanabe (W.B.A.)	1982–86	4‡
Kaosai Galaxy (W.B.A.)	1984–	4

Flyweight		
Jimmy Wilde	1916–23	7
Midget Wolgast	1930–35	5
Pascual Perez	1954–60	5
Yoko Gushiken (W.B.A.)	1976–81	5
Jung-Koo Chang (W.B.C.)	1983–88	5
Miguel Canto (W.B.C.)	1975–79	4
Sot Chitalada (W.B.C.)	1984–88	4
Santos Lacier (W.B.A.)	1982–85	3

Light-Flyweight		
Yoko Gushiken (W.B.A.)	1976–81	5
Yuh Mysung-Woo (W.B.A.)	1985–	3

*Includes World War II years. ‡Won title five times. ‡Twice won title.

Longest Reigning British Champions

DIVISION	PERIOD	YEARS
Heavyweight		
Cooper, Henry	1959–69	10
Wells, Billy	1911–19	8
Woodcock, Bruce	1945–50	5

Light-Heavyweight		
Calderwood Chic	1960–66	6
Harvey, Len	1938–42	4
Bunny Johnson	1977–80	3
Dennis Andries	1984–87	3

Middleweight		
McAvoy, Jock	1933–39	6
Thomas, Tom	1906–10	4
Bunny, Sterling	1970–75	5
Harvey, Len	1929–33	4
Pat McAteer	1855–58	3
Johnny Pritchett	1965–68	3

Light-Middleweight		
Hope, Maurice	1974–77	3
Batten, Jimmy	1977–79	2
Thomas, Pat	1979–81	2

Welterweight		
Roderick, Ernie	1939–48	9
Hood, Jack	1926–34	8
Curvis, Brian	1960–67	7
Basham, Johnny	1914–20	6
Ralph Charles	1968–71	3

Light-Welterweight		
McKenzie, Clinton	1979–82	3
Singleton, Joey	1974–76	2

Lightweight		
Welsh, Freddie	1912–21	9
Charnley, Dave	1957–65	8
White, Jabez	1899–06	7
Boon, Eric	1938–44	6
Watt, Jim	1972–77	5
Thompson, Billy	1947–51	4
Buchanan, Ken	1968–72	4
Feeney, George	1982–85	3

Featherweight		
Winstone, Howard	1961–69	8
Tarleton, Nel	1940–47	7
Clayton, Ronnie	1947–54	7
Driscoll, Jim	1907–13	6
Armstrong, Evan	1971–72	2
	1973–74	2

Bantamweight		
King, Johnny	1935–47	12*
Keenan, Peter	1951–53	3
Rudkin, Alan	1965–66	2
Gilroy, Freddie	1959–64	5
Stanley, George	1910–14	4
Palmer, Tom	1895–1900	5
Brown, Johnny	1923–28	5
†Owen, Johnny	1977–80	3

Flyweight		
McCluskey, Johnny	1967–77	10
Paterson, Jackie	1939–48	9
Wilde, Jimmy	1916–23	7

*Includes War Service years. †Owen died while still champion

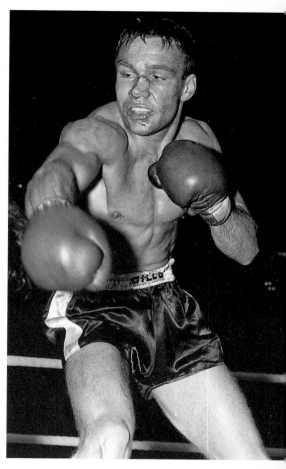

Dave Charnley, seen here in his second unsuccessful bid to take Joe Brown's world title, was Britain's lightweight champion in 1957–65.

Madison Square Garden

Most American cities have a large entertainments arena in which boxing tournaments can be staged, with the additional use of the baseball parks during the summer months. The most famous, however, is New York's Madison Square Garden, situated just off Broadway. There have, in fact, been four Gardens, the first being a derelict railway building, converted into a sports arena by William K. Vanderbilt in 1879. It was also used for concerts, political meetings, circuses and religious meetings.

In 1889 this was pulled down and a new Garden erected. It covered a city block bounded by Madison and Fourth Avenues. It was dominated by a 340ft. tower and cost 1,575,000 dollars to build. In 1906 its designer, Stafford White, was murdered by Harry Thaw, a jealous husband, in the roof garden of his own creation.

In May 1925 this building was demolished and a new one erected by promoter Tex Rickard. It was nicknamed 'The House That Tex Built'. It cost 5,500,000 dollars and was capable of seating 23,000. It opened with a Six-Day Bike Race, the first boxing show being on Dec. 11 when Paul Berlanbach successfully defended his world light-heavyweight title against Jack Delaney. The principal promoters at the 'House That Tex Built', the most famous of the four Gardens were: 1925–29, Tex Rickard; 1932–37, James J. Johnston; 1937–49, Mike Jacobs; 1949–58, James Norris (I.B.C.); 1958–68, Various promoters.

The fourth and present day Madison Square Garden was built in 1968 over and around Penn Station on Seventh Avenue. It cost 130,000,000 dollars and had a seating capacity of 20,000. The first main events staged in this modern arena saw Joe Frazier k.o. Buster Mathis in 11 rounds, while Nino Benvenuti regained the world middleweight title by outpointing Emile Griffith.

At the present time, M.S.G. promotions are staged in the newly appointed Felt Stadium.

179

Marathon Fights: 1892–1915

	DATE	ROUNDS
Andy Bowen drew Jack Burke, New Orleans.	6.4.1893	110 (7hrs 19min)
Jake Kilrain drew Jem Smith, Isle de Souveraines, France.	19.12.1887	106 (2hrs 30min)
Danny Needham v. Patsy Sheridan, San Francisco.	27.2.1890	100 (6hrs 39min)
Tommy White drew Dan Daly	1891	91
Andy Bowen beat Jack Everhardt, New Orleans.	31.5.1893	85
Alec Greggrains drew Buffalo Costello, San Francisco.	28.11.1892	80
Ike Weir drew Frank Murphy, Kous, Indiana.	31.3.1889	80
Harry Sharpe w.ko. Frank Crosby, Nameski, Illinois.	2.2.1892	77 (5hrs 8min)
George 'Kid' Lavigne drew George Siddons, Saginaw, Michigan.	1.3.1887	77
Cal McCarthy drew Jimmy Readen, Staten Is.	4.7.1888	76
William Sheriff drew Jack Welch, Philadelphia.	20.4.1884	76
Tommy Ryan w.ko. Danny Needham, Minneapolis.	16.2.1891	76
Dal Hawkins drew Fred Brogan, San Francisco.	3.6.1889	75
Fred Brogan w.ko. Dal Hawkins, San Francisco. *No result decided, fight continued the next day.*	4.6.1889	15 75
John L. Sullivan w.ko. Jake Kilrain, Richburg, Miss.	8.7.1889	75 (2hrs 16min)
Jack McAuliffe drew Jem Carney, Revere, Mass.	16.11.1887	74
George Dixon drew Cal McCarthy, Boston.	7.2.1890	70
Young Griffo drew Young Pluto, Melbourne, Australia.	12.12.1889	70
Jack McAuliffe drew Billy Myer, N. Judson, Illinois.	13.2.1889	64
James J. Corbett drew Peter Jackson, San Francisco.	21.5.1891	61
Ike Weir drew Jack Havlin, Warwick, Rhode Island.	20.7.1887	61
Tommy Ryan drew Jimmy Murphy, Grand Rapids, Mich.	10.8.1889	57
Solly Smith drew George Siddons, San Francisco.	29.9.1892	56
George 'Kid' Lavagne drew George Siddons, Grand Rapids, Mich.	26.4.1887	55
Alec Greggrains drew Buffalo Costello, San Francisco.	30.8.1892	50
Joe Jeanette w.ko. Sam McVey, Paris, France.	17.4.1909	49
Austin Gibbons w.ko. Andy Bowen, New York.	29.12.1891	48 (3hrs 41min)
Tommy Ryan w.ko. Mo Shaunessy, Detroit.	18.6.1889	46
Jack Dempsey w.ko. Johnny Reagan, Long Island, New York.	13.12.1887	45 (1hr 13min)
Jake Kilrain w.ko. George Godfrey, San Francisco.	13.3.1891	44
Andy Bowen drew Charley Johnson, Abita, Springs, L.A.	9.2.1890	43
Frankie Conley w.ko. Monte Attell, Los Angeles.	22.2.1910	42
Young Gardiner w.ko. Charley Goldman, Brooklyn.	1.6.1904	42
Joe Gans w.dis. Battling Nelson, Goldfield, Nev.	3.9.1906	42
Dick Hyland w.ko. Leach Cross, Colma, Cal.	26.1.1909	41
Ad Wolgast w.ko. Battling Nelson, Pt. Richmond.	22.2.1910	40
George Dixon w.pts. Johnny Murphy, Providence.	23.10.1890	40

Jack Johnson (left) and Jess Willard met in the last title contest scheduled for 45 rounds.

	DATE	ROUNDS
Billy Murphy drew Johnny Murphy, Boston.	31.3.1892	40
Jess Willard w.ko. Jack Johnson, Havana, Cuba. *Last scheduled 45 rounds championship contest.*	5.4.1915	26
Abe Attell drew Owen Moran, San Francisco.	1.1.1908	25
Abe Atell drew Owen Moran, San Francisco, *Moran wanted 25 rounds, Attell 20, so Promoter Jim Coffroth decided on 23*	7.9.1908	23

Measurements of the Heavyweight Champions

	HEIGHT	WEIGHT	REACH	CHEST (nor)	CHEST (exp)	FIST
Sullivan, John L.	5ft. 10½in.	196lb	74in.	43in.	48in.	14in.
Corbett, James J.	6ft. 1in.	178lb.	73in.	38in.	42in.	12¾in.
Fitzsimmons, Bob	5ft. 11¾in.	167lb.	71¾in.	41in.	44in.	12½in.
Jeffries, James J.	6ft. 2½in.	206lb.	76½in.	43in.	48½in.	13½in.
Burns, Tommy	5ft. 7in.	180lb.	74½in.	40in.	43¾in.	12in.
Johnson, Jack	6ft. 1¼in.	192lb.	74in.	37½in.	42¾in.	14in.
Willard, Jess	6ft. 6¼in.	230lb.	83in.	46in.	49½in.	14in.
Dempsey, Jack	6ft. ¾in.	187lb.	77in.	42in.	46in.	11¼in.
Tunney, Gene	6ft. ½in.	189½lb.	77in.	42in.	45in.	11¼in.
Schmeling, Max	6ft. 1in.	188lb.	76in.	43in.	47in.	12in.
Sharkey, Jack	6ft.	205lb.	74½in.	40½in.	45½in.	12¾in.
Carnera, Primo	6ft. 5¾in.	260½lb.	85½in.	48in.	54in.	14¾in.
Baer, Max	6ft. 2½in.	209½lb.	81in.	44in.	47½in.	12in.
Braddock, Jimmy	6ft. 2½in.	193¾lb.	75in.	41in.	44in.	11½in.
Louis, Joe	6ft. 1½in.	197¼lb.	76in.	42in.	45in.	11¾in.
Charles, Ezzard	6ft.	181¾lb.	74in.	39in.	42in.	12in.
Walcott, Joe	6ft.	194lb.	74in.	40in.	43in.	12in.
Marciano, Rocky	5ft. 10¼in.	184lb.	68in.	39in.	42in.	11½in.
Patterson, Floyd	6ft.	182¼lb.	71in.	40in.	42in.	12¾in.
Johannson, Ingemar	6ft. ½in.	196lb.	72½in.	43in.	45in.	13½in.
Liston, Sonny	6ft. 1in.	214lb.	84in.	44in.	46½in.	15in.
Ali, Muhammad	6ft. 3in.	210½lb.	82in.	43in.	45½in.	12½in.
Frazier, Joe	5ft. 11½in.	205lb.	73½in.	42in.	44in.	13in.
Foreman, George	6ft. 3in.	217½lb.	82in.	42in.	44½in.	12in.
Spinks, Leon	6ft. 2in.	196lb.	76in.	40½in.	42in.	12½in.
Norton, Ken	6ft. 3in.	215½lb.	80in.	45in.	48in.	13in.

Holmes, Larry	6ft. 4in.	209lb.	81in.	43½in.	45½in.	13½in.
Tate, John	6ft. 4in.	240lb.	80in.	42in.	44in.	13in.
Weaver, Mike	6ft. 1in.	207½lb.	78½in.	44½in.	46½in.	13½in.
Dokes, Michael	6ft. 3in.	216lb.	78in.	44in.	46in.	12½in.
Coetzee, Gerrie	6ft. 2½in.	215lb.	81in.	43in.	46½in.	13in.
Witherspoon, Tim	6ft. 3in.	220lb.	80in.	43in.	46in.	12½in.
Thomas, Pinklon	6ft. 3in.	216lb.	78in.	44in.	46in.	12½in.
Page, Greg	6ft. 3in.	239lb.	81in.	45in.	47in.	13in.
Tubbs, Tony	6ft. 3in.	239lb.	80in.	46in.	49in.	14in.
Berbick, Trevor	6ft. 2in.	239lb.				
Smith, James	6ft. 4in.	238lb.				
Tyson, Mike	5ft. 11in.	221lb.				

Oldest and Youngest Champions

Age when winning World Championship

DIVISION	CHAMPION	YRS: MNTHS	CHAMPION	YRS: MNTHS
	Oldest		*Youngest*	
Heavyweight:	Jersey Joe Walcott	37:6	Floyd Patterson	21:10
Light-Heavyweight:	Bob Fitzsimmons	40:6	John Henry Lewis	21:5
Middleweight:	Joey Giardello	33:5	Al McCoy	19:6
Light-Middleweight	Freddy Little	32:11	Denny Moyer	23:2
Welterweight:	Jack Britton	29:8	Pipino Cuevas	18:7
Light-Welterweight:	Saoul Mamby	32:8	Wilfred Benitez	17:3
Lightweight:	Claude Noel	30:11	Armando Ramos	19:10
Junior-Lightweight:	Yasutsune Uehara	30:10	Ben Villaflor	19:5
Featherweight:	Jackie Wilson	32:6	Tony Canzoneri	19:3
Super-Bantamweight:	Soo-Hwan Hong	27:5	Harold Gomez	20:7
Bantamweight:	Johnny Buff	33:3	Pedlar Palmer	19:0
Super-Flyweight:	Jiro Watanabe	27:1	Cesar Polano	18:3
Flyweight:	Dado Marino*	33:11	Midget Wolgast	19:9
Light-Flyweight:	Luis Estaba	34:1	Netrnoi Vorasingh	19:1

*Was a Grandfather

Cassius Clay (M. Ali) won the 1960 Olympic Games light-heavyweight gold medal. C. Pietrzykowski (Poland) was second; A. Madigan (Australia) and G. Saraudi (Italy) were third.

Frank Tate, light middleweight gold medallist in the 1984 Olympics, took the I.B.F. middleweight title by beating Michael Olajide in 1987.

Olympic Games

Gold Medal Winners Who Became World Professional Boxing Champions

DIVISION	MEDALLIST	YEAR	PRO TITLE
Flyweight	Frankie Genaro (U.S.A.)	1920	1928 (Fly)
	Fidel La Barba (U.S.A.)	1924	1925 (Fly)
	Pascual Parez (Argentina)	1948	1954 (Fly)
Bantamweight	Willie Smith (South Africa)	1924	1927 (Bantam)
Super-Bantam-weight	Leo Randolph (U.S.A.)	1976	
Featherweight	Jackie Fields (U.S.A.)	1924	1929 (Welter)
Light-Welterweight	Ray Leonard (U.S.A.)	1976	1979 (L.M.)
			1981 (Welter)
Welterweight	Nino Benvenuti (Italy)	1960	1965 (L.M.)
			1967 (Middle)
Light-Middleweight	Frank Tate (U.S.A.)	1984	
Featherweight	Jackie Fields (U.S.A.)	1924	1929 (Welter)
Light-Welterweight	Ray Leonard (U.S.A.)	1976	1979 (L.M.)
			1981 (Welter)
Welterweight	Nino Benvenuti (Italy)	1960	1965 (L.M.)
			1967 (Middle)
Light-Middleweight	Frank Tate (U.S.A.)	1984	1987 (Middle)
Middleweight	Floyd Patterson (U.S.A.)	1952	1956 (Heavy)
	Michael Spinks (U.S.A.)	1976	1981 (L.Heavy)
Light-Heavyweight	Cassius Clay (U.S.A.)	1960	1964 (Heavy)
	Mate Parlov (Yugoslavia)	1972	1978 (L.Heavy)
Light-Heavyweight	Leon Spinks (U.S.A.)	1976	
	Kacar Slobodan (Yugo)	1980	
Heavyweight	Joe Frazier (U.S.A.)	1964	1968 (Heavy)
	George Foreman (U.S.A.)	1968	1973 (Heavy)

European Titles

Flyweight	Fernando Atzori (Italy)	1964	1967 (Fly)
Welterweight	Nino Benvenuti (Italy)	1960	1965 (Middle)
Middleweight	Lazlo Papp (Hungary)	1948/52 56	1962 (Middle)
	Chris Finnegan (U.K.)	1968	1971 (L. Heavy)

Commonwealth Titles

Lightweight	Laurie Stevens (S. Africa)	1932	1936 (Light)
	Gerald Dreyer (S. Africa)	1948	1952 (Welter)

British Titles

Flyweight	Terry Spinks (U.K.)	1956	1960 (Feather)
Middleweight	Chris Finnegan (U.K.)	1968	1971 (L.Heavy)

The Prize Ring

Self-preservation being the first law of nature and fighting with the bare fists a basic instinct, the Prize Ring was the first step towards making contests between accomplished men a profitable form of entertainment, starting from the 17th century or even earlier when men would fight one another, not for possessions, revenge over a slight or a family feud, but for a purse plus, of course, the satisfaction of proving their superiority and the sheer joy of swapping punches.

The Prize Ring – it gets its name from the fact that the contestants fought in a circular enclosure and were rewarded for their efforts by gifts of money subscribed for or given by the onlookers – was introduced into Western civilization by the British. The exact date is unknown, but it was one of the sports taken up by young men of athletic nature and prowess, such as wrestling, weight-lifting, running and swimming. We know that Henry VIII played tennis and there is a hint that his son, Edward VI, was taught to box as a youth, probably because, being delicate, he needed exercise.

Of course, men have fought with their fists, either in anger or competition, since they first stood upright and fighting for money has been the natural outcome. Competing in front of an audience was included in the original Olympic Games devised in Greece and then introduced into the Roman circus where men fought for their lives, wearing the *cestus*, a form of the illegal knuckle-duster. Both Homer in the *Iliad* and Virgil in *Aeneid* make references to notable contests in which there were rules of a sort. There is recorded one instance where a fighter allowed his finger nails to grow, sharpened them and during a contest thrust his open hand into his opponent's midriff and damaged his entrails to earn instant disqualification.

Only in Britain did the sport find a foothold. There fists came to be used in preference to any additional equipment and the sporting element was developed. Men would pick up a beaten opponent, a loser would shake hands with the man who had beaten him; the onlookers were indignant when any form of foul was observed, the general theme was for fair play.

Boxing as a professional public entertainment began in England when strongly built men, proud of their prowess with their fists and seeking employment for which they had an inborn desire and aptitude, would travel the countryside in pairs or as a small party, one of them carrying a full length of stout rope. They would travel from one village fair to another, which took place at seasonable times, saints' days and public holidays. Arriving, they would select a level pitch and attired in breeches, held up by a coloured scarf, hose and perhaps spiked shoes would start sparring to attract a crowd quickly. Their spokesman would then announce that one of them, so-and-so, champion of somewhere or the other, would fight anyone to a knockdown or fall, and offer a guinea to anyone who fancied his chances. The challenge was answered by throwing a hat into the ring which had been formed by the spectators holding the length of rope into a circle. If no challenger was forthcoming, the men would indulge in a sparring match or a fake contest to keep the attention of the audience, afterwards

going around with a hat to reap some reward for their efforts. The pugilists would then try again at intervals for the duration of the fair and then move on.

Sometimes the village would boast a blacksmith, farm-hand, butcher or strongman who was their local champion and pit him against the visiting pugs. The squire might produce his coachman or some member of his working household to take up the challenge, even offering to put up a 'purse' containing a guinea or two. The earliest known report of a bare-knuckle fight appeared in the *Protestant Mercury* in 1681. It concerns a match between a gentleman's footman and a butcher, but does not state who won. So it appears that the Prize Ring was a notable form of public entertainment in the days of Charles II.

The rules were simple. One had to be prepared for anything as wrestling was an essential part of the encounter and the thrower was permitted to fall on top of the thrown. Kicking, biting and gouging were barred, also the use of spikes (if they were being worn) except for ensuring a foothold, otherwise anything was allowable. There was no need for a referee or umpire, the round ended when one man was down or was forced to quit. The

An etching of a prize fight by Thomas Rowlandson.

An encounter between Broome and Hannan on March 4, 1818: Broome won after 79 mins. The picture gives a good idea of what a prize fight was like; the 'stake money', 'whip', 'bottle-holders' and 'seconds' can all be seen.

onlookers voiced their disapproval if they thought their man was being unfairly dealt with. From this very primitive form of Prize Fighting there developed an improved method of presentation. The circle or ring of rope was abandoned as it proved unworkable when the onlookers surged one way or the other in their excitement or partisanship. Then stakes were introduced, set up in a square with the rope wound round them. The contestants each occupied a corner diagonally opposed, and a line was scratched midway across the enclosure to divide it into two equal halves. The boxer was aided and abetted by his supporters, usually two: one to provide him with a seat on his return at the end of a round, the other to revive or clean him up in readiness for the next. The latter was known as the bottle-holder. The bouts were fought until one of the men was unable to continue.

At the blow of a whistle, the ringing of a bell or the clanging of a gong to signify the start of the fight or another round, each man would come from his corner and put his left foot on the scratch mark to show that he was ready. The round then continued until one or the other was knocked or thrown down. Rounds could occupy considerable time or could be concluded in a matter of seconds. Each man then returned to his corner and was given thirty seconds in which to 'come up to scratch'. If he failed to do so within this time he was automatically declared the loser. Each fighter had his own timekeeper and his own umpire to see that he was fairly dealt with.

When there was a big pugilistic event, such as a match between the champion of one part of

the country and an equally important fighter from elsewhere, it was found necessary to set up a roped enclosure outside the one in which the fighting took place. This outer 'ring' was occupied by the timekeepers and umpires, also by the 'whips' (tough individuals armed with short whips who kept order and prevented the onlookers from breaking into the area of combat). It also became a secluded place for the gentlemen who had put up the money for the fight to stand and watch without fear of being molested. The men usually fought for a purse containing the prize money and to make sure that they knew they were being paid for their efforts, the purse or purses were tied to the stakes, thus becoming 'stake money', a term used in horse-racing circles to this day. The men who attended to the boxers in their corners were usually fighters themselves. There might be a second fight advertised to take place after the main event or one could be hastily arranged if the principal bout ended very quickly, as was always a possibility. These supplementary fighters became known as 'seconds', because they were secondary in importance, and the word 'seconds' has remained as the name of those who attend to boxers and refresh them during the intervals between the rounds and, of course, before and after the contest has ended. The principal timekeeper used a whistle, a bell or a gong *not* to indicate the ending of a round, but to inform all and sundry that the half-minute respite had expired and the men should leave their corners and come up to toe the line for the next round. If a man was physically incapable of doing this, being injured, too dazed or even unconscious,

James Figg, the earliest of the prize ring champions.

he was regarded as the loser because he had been counted out of time. The timekeeper would call out from one to eight seconds, this being considered sufficient time for a man to reach the centre of the ring.

Bets were made on who would cause the first knockdown or produce first blood. There was no limit to the number of rounds or the time the contest would last. It ended when one man was incapable of continuing or both were too spent to go any longer. Some fights ended when it was too dark for the contestants to see one another and then they would start again the next morning. Sometimes an angry crowd might break into the ring and end a fight; there were occasions when a hired gang would break up the assembly in order to save the wagers put on a man who seemed in danger of being defeated. Those who came to watch in carts and coaches drew these as close as possible.

It was a rough, tough and very often a disgraceful affair, but it had a great attractive hold on people, giving them an opportunity to let loose their basic instincts. Ruffians of every description flocked along: thieves, vagabounds and tricksters of every type found such events very remunerative. In time it became illegal to promote or take part in a Prize Fight, even as an onlooker. In fact, to this day, boxing in Great Britain has never been legalized, the law having shifted its responsibility on to the willing shoulders of the British Boxing Board of Control. Tickets for forthcoming knuckle fights were hawked in taverns and inns, the date, time and place being kept secret until the last moment. Often the would-be spectators would have to cross fields, go through woods, cross streams and other natural obstacles to reach the site chosen for the encounter. Sometimes there was a 'decoy' fight in another area altogether intentionally meant to put the forces of the law on a false scent. There was an occasion when a fight was arranged to take place at a point where three countries met, so that in the event of the arrival of the Sheriff and his men, there was ample time to cross the borders and escape. With the advent of steam trains, prize fighting could be conducted in out-of-the-way places. Ticket holders would embark on a special train, only the driver knowing where to stop. The trains would leave at dawn and put its travellers down at a place between stations. There they would find guides to take them to the combat.

Similar evasive tactics had to be employed in America when the allure of Prize Fighting reached there with the arrival of the first English settlers, and later the soldiers who manned the forts and took part in the War of Independence. In the 18th century professional pugilists were arising and illegal battles taking place in many parts of the United States. By the early part of the 19th century Tom Molineaux, a former slave, came to England to challenge Tom Cribb, the English champion. Famous fights in America took place on barges, on islands and in no-man's-land between two States, the performers and the onlookers always risking arrest, which doubtless added to the excitement. Bare knuckle fighting was a regular form of entertainment in the lumber camps, the mining areas, the wharves and anywhere where intense effort was required in employment.

Eventually the travelling pugilist disappeared with the advent of the boxing booth that travelled from one fairground to the next, carrying its quota of fighting men, ready to take on all comers. Next came the established arenas in the larger cities, usually run by the fighting men themselves or ex-pugilists and which were attended by the sporting gentry who liked to call this rough sport 'The Fancy' and themselves 'The Corinthians'. It was they who named pugilism 'The Noble Art'. It was their money and support that enabled the Prize Ring to survive until the coming of glove-fighting which brought the era of bare-fist battling to an end.

Some of the terms that evolved in the Prize Fight era and which have seeped into the English language and become commonplace words will be found in the *Glossary* (p. 150).

In 1723 King George I had a 'Ring' set up in Hyde Park for the use of the populace for boxing and other forms of athletics, used principally by the link-men and chair-men of that era, plus anyone else who sought a fight. It was dismantled by the Bow Street police in 1820, so for nearly a hundred years boxing was encouraged – in fact, it was only when there were 'big' fights that attracted enormous crowds, including the riff-raff of the community, that the law intervened to prevent a 'disturbance of the peace' or the incentive to cause a riot. When pugilistic entertainment was presented to the public in the cities, especially London, indoor arenas were set up, with boxes and balconies for those who could afford to pay for the best viewpoints, the others sitting on benches or standing up. The sporting members of royalty, the aristocracy and the upper classes were frequent visitors. Naturally this helped to bring boxing out of its early disreputable state into a more acceptable place in society.

Prize Ring Championship Fights: 1719–1889

In the early days of bare-knuckle fighting there were no recognized weight divisions and men fought for the Championship, irrespective of their weight, some of them being as light as ten stone (140 pounds). In later years a lightweight class was recognized at 140 pounds and a middleweight class at 154 pounds. There were, of course, many contests between men and lower poundages, but these were not thought of sufficient importance to warrant their recording.

The following shows the principal Prize Ring battles from the time of James Figg who is universally recognized as the first of the Bare Knuckle Champions.

1719		James Figg (or Fig) opened his theatre on Oxford Road, London, and was generally recognized as the Champion.
1720		James Figg defeated Sutton (Gravesend pipe-maker).
1734		George Taylor erected his 'great booth' in Tottenham Court Road, London and claimed the Championship.
1740		Jack Broughton beat George Taylor in 20 min. at the Tottenham Court Road 'Booth', London.
1741	April 24	Jack Broughton beat George Stevenson in 39 mins. at Taylor's Booth, Tottenham Court Road, London.
1750	April 10	Jack Slack beat Jack Broughton in 14 mins. at a theatre in Oxford Street, London.
1760	June 17	Jean Stevens (The Nailer) beat Jack Slack at the Tennis Court, Haymarket, London.
1761	March 2	George Meggs beat Jem Stevens at the Tennis Court, Haymarket, London.
1762	July	George Millsom beat George Meggs at Calne, Wiltshire.
1765	Aug. 27	Tom Juchau (The Pavior) beat George Millsom near St. Albans.
1766	May	Bill Darts beat Tom Juchau at Guildford.
1769	June 27	Tom Lyons (The Waterman) beat Bill Darts at Kingston.
1771	May 10	Peter Corcoran beat Bill Darts in 1 round and claimed the Championship.
1775	Oct. 16	Harry Sellers beat Peter Corcoran, 100 guineas, 38 rounds, Crown Inn, Staines.
1779	Sept. 25	Duggan Fearns beat Harry Sellers at Slough. (Said to be a 'cross').
1789	Feb. 11	Tom Johnson beat Michael Ryan, 300 guineas, 33 mins., near Rickmansworth.
	Oct. 22	Tom Johnson beat Isaac Perrins, 50 guineas, 62 rounds, 1 hr. 15 mins., Banbury.
1791	Jan. 17	Big Ben (Benjamin Brain or Bryan) beat Tom Johnson, 500 guineas, 18 rounds, 21 min., Wrotham, Kent.
1794	Nov. 12	Daniel Mendoza beat Bill War, small stakes, 17 mins., Bexley Heath, Kent.
1795	April 15	Gentleman John Jackson beat Daniel Mendoza, 200 guineas, 10½ mins., Hornchurch, Essex.
1800	Dec. 22	Jem Belcher beat Andrew Gamble, 50 guineas, 5 rounds, 7 mins., Wimbledon.
1803	April 12	Jem Belcher beat Jack Fearby (The Young Ruffian), 100 guineas, 11 rounds, 20 mins., near Linton, Essex.
1805	March 11	Henry Pearce (The Game Chicken) beat Elias Spray, 50 guineas, 29 rounds, 35 mins., Moulsey Hurst.
	Oct. 8	Henry Pearce beat John Gully, 600 guineas to 400 guineas, 64 rounds, 1 hr. 17 min., Hailsham, Sussex.
	Dec. 6	Henry Pearce beat Jem Belcher, 500 guineas, 18 rounds, 35 mins., Blythe, Notts.
1807	Oct. 14	John Gully beat Bob Gregson, 200 guineas, 26 rounds, near Newmarket.
1808	May 10	John Gully beat Bob Gregson, 200 guineas, 28 rounds, 1 hr. 15 mins., near Market Street, Herts.
	Oct. 25	Tom Cribb beat Bob Gregson, 500 guineas, 23 rounds, Moulsey Hurst.
1809	Feb. 1	Tom Cribb beat Jem Belcher, 200 guineas, 31 rounds, 40 mins., Epsom Downs.
1810	Dec. 10	Tom Cribb beat Tom Molineaux (The Black), 200 guineas a side, and 100 guineas, 39 rounds, 55 mins., Copthall Common.
1811	Sept. 28	Tom Cribb beat Tom Molineaux, £600, 11 rounds, 20 mins., Thistleton Gap, Leicester.

1821	Dec. 11	Bill Neat beat Tom Hickman (The Gas Man), 100 guineas, 18 rounds, 23½ mins., Hungerford Downs, Newbury.
1823	May 20	Tom Spring (Thomas Winter) beat Bill Neat, £200, 8 rounds, 37 mins., near Andover.
1824	Jan. 7	Tom Spring beat Jack Langan, £300 a side, 77 rounds, 2 hrs. 20 mins., Worcester.
	June 8	Tom Spring beat Jack Langan, 500 guineas a side, 77 rounds, 1 hr. 48 mins., Birdham Bridge, near Chichester.
	Nov. 23	Tom Cannon (The Great Gun of Windsor) beat Josh Hudson, £500 a side, 16 rounds, 20 mins., stage, at Warwick.
1825	July 19	Jem Ward (The Black Diamond) beat Tom Cannon, £500 a side, 10 rounds, 10 mins., Warwick.
1827	Jan. 2	Peter Crawley (Young Rump Steak) beat Jem Ward, £200, 11 rounds, 26 mins., Royston Heath.
1831	July 12	Jem Ward beat Simon Byrne, £200 a side, 33 rounds, 1 hr. 17 mins., Willeycuts.
	July 14	Jem Ward was given a Champion's Belt at Harry Holt's benefit.
1833	May 30	Deaf (James) Burke beat Simon Byrne, £100 a side, 99 rounds, 3 hrs. 6 mins., No-Man's Land.
1839	Feb. 12	Bendigo (William Thompson) beat Deaf Burke, who fought £100 to £80, 10 rounds, 24 mins., Heather, Leicestershire. Burke was disqualified for butting.
1840	Sept. 22	Nick Ward (brother of Jem Ward) beat Deaf Burke, £50 a side, 17 rounds, Lillingstone Level, Oxfordshire.
1841	Feb. 2	Nick Ward beat Ben Gaunt, £100 a side, 7 rounds, 12 mins. (foul blow), Crookham Common.
	May 11	Ben Caunt beat Nick Ward, £100 a side, 35 rounds, 47 mins., Long Marsden.
1845	Sept. 9	Bendigo beat Ben Caunt, £200 a side, 93 rounds, 2 hrs. 10 mins., near Sutfield Green, Oxon.
1850	June 5	Bendigo beat Tom Paddock, £200 a side, 49 rounds, 59 mins. (foul blow), Mildenhall, Staffs. Title claimed by Tom Paddock.
	Dec. 17	William Perry (Tipton Slasher) beat Tom Paddock £100 a side, 27 rounds, 42 mins. (foul blow), Woking, Surrey.
1851	Sept. 29	Harry Broome beat William Perry, £200 a side, 15 rounds, 33 mins. (foul blow), Mildenhall, Staffs.
1853	April 18	Harry Broome beat Harry Orme, £250 a side, 31 rounds, 2 hrs. 18 mins., near Brandon.
1856	Oct. 2	Tom Paddock beat Harry Broome, £200 a side, 51 rounds, 1 hr. 3 mins., near Bentley, Suffolk.
1857	Feb. 19	Tom Sayers beat Aaron Jones, £100 a side, and a bet of £100 a side, 85 rounds, 2 hrs. Banks of Medway.
	June 16	Tom Sayers beat William Perry, £200 a side, 10 rounds, 1 hr. 42 mins., Isle of Grain.
1858	June 16	Tom Sayers beat Tom Paddock, £150 a side, 21 rounds, 1 hr. 20 mins., Canary Island.
1860	April 17	Tom Sayers (U.K.) drew with John Camel Heenan (U.S.A.), £200 a side, 37 rounds, 2 hrs. 6 mins., Farnborough Common, Hampshire.
	Nov. 5	Sam Hurst beat Tom Paddock, £200 a side, 5 rounds, 9 mins., 30 secs., Berkshire.
1861	June 13	Jem Mace beat Sam Hurst, £200 a side, 8 rounds, 40 mins., Home Circuit.
1862	Jan. 28	Jem Mace beat Tom King, £200 a side, 43 rounds, 1 hr. 8 mins., Home Circuit.
	Nov. 26	Tom King beat Jem Mace, £200 a side, 21 rounds, 38 mins., Home Circuit.
1863	May 5	Joe Coburn beat Mick M'Coole, £200 a side, and the Championship of America, 1 hr. 10 mins., Charlesworth, Maryland, U.S.A.
	Sept. 1	Jem Mace beat Jose Goss, allegedly for £1,000, 19 rounds, 1 hr. 55½ mins. near the River Thames, London.
	Dec. 10	Tom King beat John C. Heenan, £1,000 a side, 24 rounds, 35 mins., Wadhurst, Kent.
1864	Oct. 4	Jem Mace drew with Joe Coburn, £500 a side, the latter receiving £100 for expenses, Ireland. No referee appointed.
1865	Jan. 4	Joe Wormald beat Andrew Marsden, £200 a side, 18 rounds, 37 mins., Horley, Surrey.
1866	May 24	Jem Mace drew with Joe Gross, £200 a side, 1 round, 1 hr. 5 mins., Longfield Court, near Meopham, Kent.
	Aug. 6	Jem Mace beat Joe Goss, £200 a side, 21 rounds, 31 mins., in a 16ft. ring. London District.
	Sept. 19	Mick M'Coole beat W. Davis, £200 a side and the Championship of America, 34 rounds, 35 mins., Rhoails's

		Point, Choulton Island, near St. Louis, U.S.A.
1867	Aug. 31	Mick M'Coole beat Aaron Jones, £250 a side, 34 rounds, 26 mins., Ohio, U.S.A.
	Oct. 15	Jeam Mace drew with Ned Baldwin, £200 a side.
1868	Oct. 29	Ned Baldwin fought Joe Wormald, 1 round, lasting 10 mins., after which the police intervened, Lynnfield, Mass., U.S.A.
1869	Jan. 12	Tom Allen beat Bill Davis, $2,000 and the Championship of America, 43 rounds, Choteau Island, U.S.A.
	June 12	Mike M'Coole beat Tom Allen, $2,000 and the Championship of America, 9 rounds, Foster's Island, Mississippi, U.S.A.
1870	May 10	Jem Mace beat Tom Allen, 10 rounds, Kennerville, Louisiana, U.S.A.
1871	Nov. 30	Jem Mace drew with Joe Coburn, 12 rounds, St. Louis, U.S.A. Mace was winning but the referee stopped the fight and called it a draw because of the crowd.
1873	Sept. 23	Tom Allen beat Mike M'Coole, 7 rounds, 20 mins., near St. Louis, U.S.A.
1876	Sept. 7	Joe Goss beat Tom Allen, 21 rounds (foul), fought in two rings at Kenton and Boone countries, Kentucky, U.S.A.
1880	May 30	Paddy Ryan beat Joe Goss, 87 rounds, Collier Station, West Virginia, U.S.A.
1882	Feb. 7	John L. Sullivan beat Paddy Ryan, 9 rounds, 10 mins. 30 secs., $5,000 and Championship, Mississippi City, Miss., U.S.A.
1885	Dec. 17	Jem Smith beat Jack Davis, 6 rounds, borders of Surrey and Sussex.
1886	Feb. 16	Jem Smith drew with Alf Greenfield, 13 rounds, Maison Lafite, France.
1887	Dec. 19	Jake Kilrain drew with Jem Smith, 106 rounds, 2 hrs. 30 mins., at Isle des Souverains, River Seine, France.
1888	March 10	John L. Sullivan (U.S.A.) drew with Charlie Mitchell (U.K.), 39 rounds, 3 hrs. 10 mins., 55 secs., Chantilly, France.
1889	July 8	John L. Sullivan beat Jake Kilrain, $10,000 a side and Championship of America, 75 rounds, Richburg, Mississippi, U.S.A.
	Dec. 23	Jem Smith drew with Frank Slavin, 14 rounds, Bruges, Belgium. (Last Prize Ring fight of Championship standard in Europe.)

John L. Sullivan (left) and Jake Kilrain fought the last prize ring world title bout.

Prize Ring Fighters

Allen, Tom *Champion*

(b. Birmingham, April 1840 – d. April 5, 1903). Height 5 ft. 11 ins. Weight 175 lbs.

Allen won his first fight by defeating Posh Price in 50 mins; in a second bout Price was beaten in 2 hrs 5 mins. Allen beat Bingy Ross and Jack Garkinson, but lost to Bob Smith in 50 rounds (2 hrs 49 mins.). He drew with Joe Goss (34 rounds), then went to America and met Goss again, losing on a foul. He was unsuccessful against Charley Gallagher and Mike McCoole, but went ten rounds with the redoubtable Jem Mace for the World's Heavyweight Title, at Kennerville, Louisiana, on May 10, 1870. When Mace retired, Allen fought Goss for the Championship on Sept. 23, 1873, and won in seven rounds (20 mins.). He defended his title successfully against Ben Hogan, but lost it to Goss in 21 rounds on Sept. 7, 1876 in Kentucky. Allen never fought again.

Belcher, Jem *Champion*

(b. Bristol, April 15, 1781 – d. Soho, London, July 30, 1811). Height 5 ft. 11 ins. Weight 166 lbs.

Belcher was not much more than a middleweight. He came of renowned fighting stock and on his arrival in London was regarded as a phenomenal boxer. This was borne out when he defeated Jack Britton in 33 mins. on May 15, 1798, after which he fought once a year. He defeated Paddington Jones (33 mins.), and drew with Jack Bartholomew over 55 rounds, both men being too exhausted to continue. In a return bout Belcher won in 17 rounds, Andrew Gamble lasted only five rounds, then came three battles with Joe Berks, all of which Jem won, followed by a win over Jack Firley in 11 rounds. An unfortunate accident marred the rest of his career. Whilst playing rackets, he was struck in the eye and lost the sight of it. He retired, but returned two years later and on Dec. 6, 1805 his long run of successes came to an end, being beaten by Hen Pearce in 18 rounds. He twice lost to Tom Cribb, the second fight taking place on Epsom Downs on Feb. 1, 1809 and lasting 31 rounds. He died, aged 30, 'universally regretted by all who knew him'.

'Bendigo' *Champion*

(b. Nottingham, Oct. 11, 1811 – d. Beeston, Aug. 11, 1880). Height 5 ft. 9¼ ins. Weight 165 lbs.

Real name William Thompson, he was one of triplets in a family of 21. Nicknamed Abednego from the Bible, this became '(Bold) Bendigo' in his fighting life. One of the most colourful of the Champions, he was a veritable box-of-tricks both in and out of the ring. He was taught to box by his mother, and after winning all his early battles, he met Bill Caunt at Hucknall in Nottinghamshire on July 21, 1835. There was a great disparity in size, Caunt at 6 ft. 2½in. and 210 lbs. towering over Bendigo. The fight went 22 rounds with the smaller man tantalizing his rival so much that Caunt lost his temper and was disqualified when he rushed across the ring to strike Bendigo while he was seated in his corner.

Bendigo then fought John Brassey near Sheffield and again won on a foul in the 52nd round of which he had all the best of matters. Charles Langan was beaten in 92 rounds (1 hr. 33 mins.) and Bill Looney in 99 rounds (2 hr. 24 mins.). Next came a return with Caunt at Shelby on April 3, 1838. Again Bendigo did well against his giant rival, but was adjudged the loser in the 75th round (1 hr. 20 mins.), being disqualified for going down without taking a punch.

On Feb. 12, 1839 he met Deaf Burke at Heather in Leicestershire. The bout went into the tenth round (24 mins.) and ended with Burke being ruled out for butting. Caunt and Bendigo had a third meeting, at Stony Stratford on Sept. 9, 1845, this time with the Championship at stake. It went 93 rounds (2 hrs. 10 mins.) with Caunt losing through dropping from a threatened punch. In Bendigo's final bout he beat Tom Paddock at Mildenham on June 5, 1850 in 49 rounds (59 mins.), who was disqualified for striking the Champion when down. Bendigo, who was in prison 28 times for various offences, eventually became a preacher; there is a huge memorial in Nottingham in his honour.

Brain, Benjamin *Champion*

(b. Bristol, 1753 – d. London, April 8, 1794). Height 5 ft. 10 ins. Weight 196 lbs.

A collier by profession, he was not as large as his nickname of Big Ben Brain suggested. He was celebrated for his straight and severe right-hand punching, although remarkably good with both fists. After a few local victories he proceeded to London where, on Oct. 31, 1786 he defeated a soldier known as 'The Fighting Grenadier' in a few minutes. He next beat an Irishman named Corbally, then a Birmingham man named Jacombs, who stayed 86 mins. before being conquered. Tom Tring, a porter, went down in 12 rounds that lasted less than 20 mins. and this was followed by an easy victory over Bill Hooper, a tinman, after 3½ hours in which Hooper spent most of the time in running away or going down. Then came his great fight with Tom Johnson which aroused keen interest all over the country. They met at Wrotham in Kent, England, on Jan. 17, 1791, the Duke of Hamilton wagering 500 guineas that Big Ben would win. He was on a good thing for the size and power of Brain were too much for the Champion, who was beaten in 18 rounds that occupied 21 mins. Although Brain appeared to have suffered little hurt, he never fought again, dying from liver disease in 1794.

Broughton, Jack *Champion*

(b. Cirencester, 1704 – d. Lambeth, London, Jan. 8, 1789). Height 5 ft. 11½ ins. Weight 200 lbs.

Known as the 'Father of Boxing', he took over Figg's place and then built one of his own behind it. He brought more art into boxing, introducing scientific moves and the delivery of punches, especially 'milling on the retreat', i.e. moving backwards and drawing an opponent into punches, so their effectiveness is doubled. He became Champion of England by defeating George Taylor, of Norfolk, and kept the title against Tom Pipes and Bill Gretting. George Stevenson, a Yorkshire coachman, was brought to meet him, backed by Frederick, Prince of Wales, while his brother, the infamous Duke of Northumberland, supported Broughton. Stevenson was game but found the Champion too good for him and after 40 mins. it was all over with the Yorkshireman in a dreadful state. He died several days later and Broughton was so grieved at what he had done, he wrote a set of rules to try and prevent such a tragedy happening again. Broughton's Rules were the basis of all Prize Fighting for almost a century.

Broughton was eventually beaten by Jack Slack and retired, using his boxing premises as a warehouse for furniture and antiques. He became a Yoeman of the Guard at the Tower of London and is buried in Lambeth church. A large paving stone bearing his name and description can be seen today in Westminster Abbey, London.

Broughton was responsible for the introduction of gloves or 'mufflers' as they were called in his day. Among the pupils were many of the aristocracy and it was to avoid damaging their features that inspired him to cover the hands and so minimize the effect of a punch. He announced his new invention to the sporting public by means of an advertisement in a Feb. 1747 issue of *The Daily Advertiser*. It reads as follows: 'Mr. Broughton proposes, with proper assistance, to open an academy at his house in the Haymarket, for the instruction of those who are willing to be initiated in the mystery of boxing, where the whole theory and practice of that truly British art, with all the various stops, blows, cross-buttocks, etc. incident to combatants, will be fully taught and explained; and that persons of quality and distinction may not be debarred from entering into a course of these lectures, they will be given with the utmost tenderness and regard to the delicacy of the frame and constitution of the pupil; for which reason mufflers are provided, that will effectually secure them from the inconveniency of black eyes, broken jaws and bloody noses.'

Burke, James *Champion*

(b. London, Dec. 8, 1809 – d. Jan. 8, 1845). Height 5 ft 8½ ins. Weight 178 lbs.

Known as 'The Deaf 'Un' because he was hard of hearing, this River Thames waterman began fighting for prize money at 18, but his first important contest took place at Harpenden against Bill Fitzmaurice on June 9, 1829 when he won in 166 rounds (3 hrs). He lost to Bill Cousins 2½ months later, in 111 rounds (2 hrs. 50 mins.). In the next three years he disposed of eight more rivals and on May 30, 1833 took on Simon Byrne on the outskirts of London. Byrne was a much bigger man and put up a terrific fight for 99 rounds (3 hrs. 16 min.), but was so badly beaten by a superior boxer that he died three days later. Burke skipped off to America where he fought Sam O'Rourke at New Orleans on May 6, 1836. He was well beating the American when thugs broke into the ring armed with knives and the Deaf 'Un had to run for his life. In New York he beat Tom O'Connell in ten rounds and then returned to England. On Feb. 12, 1839, at Heather in Leicestershire, he challenged Bold Bendigo for the Championship, but was ruled out in the tenth round for butting. The following year, on Sept. 22, 1840, he was easily defeating Nick Ward when friends of his rival broke into the ring to save their man and the bout ended after 17 rounds (2 hrs.). A claim of foul was made by Ward's seconds, which was allowed two days later. Burke retired but returned to face Bob Castles on June 13, 1843. They fought for 70 mins., completing 37 rounds, when Burke was declared the winner. He died of tuberculosis in 1845.

Cannon, Tom *Champion*

(b. 1790 – d. July 11, 1858). Height 5 ft. 11¾ ins. Weight 165 lbs.

Son of a Windsor bargee, he did not feature in the Prize Ring until he was 27 and seven more years were to elapse before he was taken seriously. His first notable win was over Josh Hudson on June 23, 1824 in a field near Everfield churchyard. It went 17 rounds (20½mins.), Tom finishing it with a terrific blow to the head. Five months later (Nov. 23) they met again, when Hudson was beaten in 16 rounds (20 mins.). Cannon backed himself and won close on a thousand pounds.

He now claimed the Championship, and on July 19, 1825 was challenged by Jem Ward, who beat him at Warwick in 10 mins. on sheer boxing superiority. Cannon's last contest was with Ned Neale at Warfield in Berkshire on Feb. 20, 1827. He was doing well until thrown so heavily he injured a shoulder and had to give up after 22 rounds (30 mins.). In retirement he suffered badly from rheumatics and died by his own hand.

Caunt, Ben *Champion*

(b. Hucknall Torkard, Nottinghamshire, March 22, 1815 – d. London, Sept. 10, 1861). Height 6 ft. 2½ ins. Weight 210 lbs.

Noted for his three historic battles with Bendigo. This big man won a number of unrecorded contests in his local vicinity before agreeing to meet Bendigo for the Championship at Appleby House on July 21, 1835. With 4¾ ins. advantage in height and 46lbs. in weight, Ben seemed a sure winner, but the crafty tactics and greater experience of his rival were too much for his ability and his temper. After being punished for 22 rounds, he rushed across the ring and struck a blow at Bendigo as he was sitting in his corner, thus earning instant disqualification.

Caunt then beat William Butler in 14 rounds and Bill Boneford in six rounds. On April 3, 1838 he had his second meeting with Bendigo and this time got his own back, the Champion being ruled out in the 75th round (1 hr. 20 mins.) for falling without taking a punch and the title changed hands. Caunt defended his crown against Bill Brassey on Oct. 26, 1840, winning after 101 rounds (1 hr. 30 mins.); lost on a foul to Nick Ward (low blow) on Feb. 2, 1841 and three months later beat him over 35 rounds (47 mins.). After the contest Caunt was

presented with the 'Champion's Belt' produced by public subscription. He then went to America but failing to find a challenger, came home again. Then came the third fight with Bendigo on Sept. 9, 1845 at Stony Stratford. This went into the 93rd round (2 hr. 10 mins.) when Caunt was ruled out for dropping without taking a punch and had to hand over the cherished Belt to his hated rival. Ben retired, but came back 12 years later when he was 42 and fought a drawn battle with Nat Langham that lasted 60 rounds.

Coburn, Joe

(b. Middletown, County Armagh, Ireland, July 29, 1835 – d. New York, U.S.A. Dec. 6, 1890). Height 5 ft. 9 ins. Weight 190 lbs.

All his Prize Fighting took place in America. His first important bout was with Ned Price at Boston, May 1, 1856, which lasted 3 hrs. 20 mins. and ended in a draw when it became too dark for them to see one another. He beat Mike McCoole at Cecil County, Maryland, in 70 mins. on May 5, 1863. On Oct. 4, 1864 he fought Jem Mace for the world title when the Englishman was turned 40. They gave what resembled an exhibition for 77 mins. when the police intervened. Meeting again six months later they fought 12 rounds to another draw.

Corcoran, Peter

Active 1769–76.

An Irishman of no great ability but tremendous courage, he was credited with a number of wins in his own country before going to England. He claimed the Championship after his disgraceful 'cross' with Bill Darts, but did not receive recognition by the sporting public. His bouts with Ned Turner and Sam Peters were also suspect. Corcoran was finally beaten by Harry Sellers in 28 mins. at Staines, Middlesex on Oct. 10, 1776.

The second bout between Tom Cribb (left) and Tom Molineaux. Cribb won after 11 rounds.

Crawley, Peter *Champion*

(b. Newington Green, London, Dec. 5, 1799 – d. London, March 12, 1865). Height 6 ft. Weight 164 lbs.

He has the distinction of retiring from the ring one week after winning the Championship. The son of a butcher, Crawley was fighting at 17 and gained his first major success against Dick Acton who was defeated in 13 rounds (16 mins.) at Blindley Heath on May 6, 1823. On the strength of this win Crawley challenged Jem Ward for the Championship but had to wait until Jan. 2, 1827 before getting his chance. They met at Royston Heath and after a hard battle that went 11 rounds and lasted 26 mins., the Champion was beaten and had to be carried from the ring in an insensible state. Ward's friends sought a return fight, but Crawley declined, having decided to go into business, and gave up the title. Only one defeat mars his great record. On March 16, 1819, he met Tom Hickman at Mousley Hurst and was beaten in 13 rounds (13½mins.). It was not surprising as Peter was only 19, whereas his opponent was much older and more experienced. Crawley died in London, where he had taught the art of self-defence to amateurs, in 1865.

Cribb, Tom *Champion*

(b. Hansham, Gloucestershire, July 8, 1781 – d. London, May 11, 1848). Height 5 ft. 10 ins. Weight 199 lbs.

He came to fame at the age of 24 when he defeated George Maddox (76 rounds), Tom Blake (20 rounds) and Ikey Pigg (11 rounds). In his next battle, however, he was forced to surrender to George Nicholls, a hard hitting warrior from Bristol, after 52 rounds. Cribb regained high prestige when he beat Bill Richmond, a former American slave, in 90 mins. at Hailsham in Sussex – a win that secured him a Championship fight with the renowned Jem Belcher at Mousley Hurst on April 8, 1807. Cribb won in 41 rounds (35 mins.). He de-

fended his Belt successfully against George Horton (25 rounds) and Bob Gregson (23 rounds), then beat Belcher again, this time on Epsom Downs in 31 rounds (40 mins.). Next came Cribb's two great historic battles with Tom Molineaux, another ex-slave, brought to England by Bill Richmond. They fought first on Copthall Common in Sussex on Dec. 18, 1810 and the black fighter had the better of matters until tricked by Cribb's second in the 28th round and finally beaten in the 33rd. They met again the following year, but this time Cribb proved far superior and stopped the American in 11 rounds (19 mins. 10 secs.) at Thistleton Gap, Leicestershire on Sept. 28, 1811. Tom did not fight again, except in a private bout with Jack Carter in 1820 which he won in less than a minute. For many years Cribb kept *The Union Arms* in Panton Street, Piccadilly, London. He was liked and respected by everyone: on his death Cribb was buried in Woolwich churchyard where a huge memorial was erected to him by public subscription.

Curtis, Dick *Champion*

(b. Southwark, London, Feb. 1, 1802 – d. Southwark, Sept. 16, 1843). Height 5 ft. 6 ins. Weight 126 lbs.

For skill, finish, straight and swift hitting, he was incomparable. As Champion of the Light-weights, he has no superior in the annals of pugilism.

He came of a fighting family and his brothers (John and George) had figured in the Prize Ring. He had his first bout against Watson from Westminster at Moulsey Hurst on June 27, 1820, winning in 25 mins. On Wimbledon Common on Aug. 28, 1820, he beat Ned Brown in 15 rounds (57 mins.) of sheer boxing. Then followed wins over Lenney in 29 rounds (38½ mins.); The Gipsy, 7 rounds (10 mins.); Dick Hares, 3 rounds (20 mins.); Barney Aaron, 9 rounds (50 mins.); Jack Tisdale, 17 rounds (58 mins.); George Phillips, in 20 mins. and again in 27 mins. Curtis was undefeated for eight years, then at the age of 26 and innumerable bouts, he was beaten in 11 rounds (23½ mins.) by Jack Perkins, to whom he conceded considerable weight.

Darts, Bill *Champion*

(b. 1741.) Height 5 ft. 10 ins. Weight 187 lbs.

Darts held a high reputation for courage and hard hitting. One of his best battles was with Tom Juchau at Guildford in Surrey in May 1766. They fought for a thousand guineas and Darts won in 40 mins. He claimed the Championship which he held for three years until beaten in 45 mins. by a River Thames waterman named Lyons. Darts blotted his copybook when he was paid to lose to Peter Corcoran in 1771.

Dogherty, Dan

Active 1807–11.

He first appeared in the Prize Ring in June 1806 when he defeated a Jew at Willesden Green, London. At Golders Green he disposed of a Scotsman named Pentiken in 45 mins. Dogherty twice beat George Cribb, but lost to

Tom Belcher. His most famous contest was a return with Belcher on April 23, 1813 on the Curragh of Kildare. The Irishman fought with great courage for 33 rounds (45 mins.) before having to give in. He retired soon afterwards.

Figg (or Fig), James *Champion*

(b. Thame, Oxfordshire, 1695 – d. London, Dec. 8, 1734).

Figg is generally regarded as the earliest of the Prize Ring Champions; the first bare-fist fighter to receive any publicity. He came into prominence in 1719 as an all-round exponent of such competitive sports as quarter-staff, small backsword and cudgel fighting, but was best known as a pugilist. Figg not only engaged in fighting but taught it. He visited the annual fairs to set up his booth and is featured in William Hogarth's *Southwark Fair*. This great artist also drew a card for Figg which the boxer distributed among interested parties. He set up an amphitheatre in Oxford Road, London, where he instructed in various sports and staged contests.

Figg defeated such men as Timothy Buck, Tom Stokes, Bill Flanders and Chris Clarkson, his bout with the latter lasting 30 mins. He also defeated Ned Sutton three times; on the first occasion they fought with cudgels before using their fists.

Gallagher, Charley *American Champion*

(b. Canada, March 10, 1849 – d. 1871). Height 6 ft 1 in. Weight 196 lbs.

His first bout was in Detroit on Oct. 5, 1867 and Gallagher won in 45 rounds. He lost to Jim Elliott at Detroit, 23 rounds (77 mins.). He won the American Championship by defeating Tom Allen at St. Louis on Feb. 23, 1869, in two rounds (3 mins.). In a return title bout he lost to Allen at St. Louis on Aug. 17, 1869 in 12 rounds, but the referee declared the contest drawn. Gallagher died from tuberculosis in 1871.

Goss, Joe

(b. Northampton, Nov. 5 1838 – d. Boston, Lincolnshire, March 24, 1885). Height 5 ft. 8½ ins. Weight 150 lbs.

Goss mingled with men much bigger and heavier than himself. His first recorded fight was with Jack Rooke who was beaten in 64 rounds on Sept. 20, 1859. In the next three years he beat Tom Price (25 mins.), Rodger Critchley (120 rounds), Bill Ryall (37 rounds) with Posh Price (66 rounds). A second bout with Ryall ended in a draw after 36 rounds. Goss fought Jem Mace for the Championship on Sept. 1, 1863 in London and lost in 19 rounds (1 hr. 55 mins.). He was beaten by Mace twice more: on May 24, 1866 at Farningham in 19 rounds (65 mins.) and on Aug. 6 the same year over 21 rounds in London. He beat Ike Baker in 80 mins. and fought a 34-round draw with Tom Allen at Bristol on March 5, 1867. Goss went to America and beat Allen on a foul at Cincinnati six months later. In a third match with Allen on Sept. 7, 1876 at Kentucky, he won in 21 rounds, Allen being ruled out. On May 30, 1880, he fought Paddy Ryan for the Championship at West Vancouver and lost in

87 rounds (84 mins.). He also twice lost to John L. Sullivan over three rounds in Boston.

Gully, John *Champion*

(b. Bristol, Aug. 21, 1783 – d. March 9, 1863). Height 6 ft. Weight 190 lbs.

Gully became a champion prize fighter almost by accident. He was in a debtors' prison on behalf of his father, a butcher, when he received a visit from Hen Pearce, who was seeking a challenger for the Championship. He had heard that Gully was both big and proficient with his fists and after sparring with him in the prison courtyard, had his debt paid and release obtained. Gully was now honour-bound to fight Pearce for the title.

They met at Hailsham, Sussex on Oct. 8, 1805 and Gully put up a gallant battle that lasted 64 rounds before he was forced to admit defeat. When Pearce retired, Gully twice defeated Bob Gregson (from Oct. 14, 1807; May 10, 1808) to be acknowledged as Champion and never fought again. He then became interested in horse racing, becoming a bookmaker and owner. Twice he won The Derby and once The Oaks. In 1832 he was elected a Member of Parliament for Pontefract, Yorkshire. He also owned coal mines and died a wealthy man.

Heenan, John Camel

(b. West Troy, New York, U.S.A., May 2, 1833 – d. Green River; Wyoming, U.S.A., Nov. 2, 1873). Height 6 ft. 2 ins. Weight 195 lbs.

Known as 'The Benicia Boy', Heenan had fistic skill and plenty of punching power. Despite this, he lost his first major battle (to John Morrisey in 11 rounds) at Long Point. Canada on Oct. 20, 1858, for the American title but broke his right hand early in the bout. He rose to international fame when he went to England and fought Tom Sayers for the World Championship at Farnborough, Hampshire on April 17, 1860: an historic date in ring events. The bout ended in the 42nd round (2 hrs. 20 mins.) when Heenan had Sayers over the ropes and in danger of strangling him; the crowd broke into the ring and a 'draw' was declared. It had been evenly fought until then. Heenan came to England again and on Dec. 8, 1863 met Tom King for the title at Wadhurst, Kent. The British Champion won in 24 rounds (35 mins.). Heenan never fought again.

Jackson, John *Champion*

(b. Sept. 25, 1769 – d. London, Oct. 7, 1845). Height 5 ft. 11 ins. Weight 202 lbs.

A cut above the average pugilist of his day: well-spoken, well-dressed, and so much at home with his 'betters' that he was known as 'Gentleman' Jackson. Apart from his fistic ability, which was considerable, he was a renowned boxing instructor and ran a well-ordered establishment at No. 13 Old Bond Street in London, one of his outstanding pupils being the renowned poet, Lord Byron, who mentioned in several letters that he had been sparring with Jackson, 'The Emperor of Pugilism'. Gloves were always used in Jackson's Rooms and he did much in their development.

On June 15, 1814, at the house of Lord Lowther in Pall Mall, London, a pugilistic fête was arranged by Gentleman John for the Emperor of Russia. It was so well received that similar entertainment was provided at which the King of Prussia, the Prince Royal, the Prince of Mecklenburgh and other royalty assembled. At the 1821 Coronation of George IV, Jackson was instructed to furnish a company of pugilists to act as a guard to prevent followers of Queen Charlotte from entering Westminster Abbey and disturbing the ceremony. Those in the corps were Tom Cribb, Tom Spring, Tom Belcher, Jack Carter, Bill Richmond, Ben Burn, Henry Harmer, Harry Lee, Tom Owen, Josh Hudson, Tom Oliver, Harry Holt, Peter Crawley, Dick Curtis, Medley, Purcell and Eales, with Jackson at the head, all dressed as royal pages. One medal was awarded to them and this was raffled and won by Belcher.

Jackson's great battle with Mendoza, from whom he won the Championship, was the epic event in his career. They met at Hornchurch, Essex, on April 15, 1795, and Jackson, the taller by 4 ins. and the heavier by 42 lbs. was not having the best of matters when, in the ninth round, he seized the Jew by his long hair and held his head down while he pounded him into insensibility. Jackson beat William Fewterell in 1 hr. 7 mins. at Smitham Botton, Surrey, on June 9, 1788, but lost to George Ingleston on May 12, 1789, in 20 mins., due to breaking his leg in a fall. He is buried in Brompton Cemetery where there is a magnificent memorial to him.

Johnson, Tom *Champion*

(b. Derbyshire, England, 1750 – d. Cork, Ireland, Jan. 21, 1797). Height 5 ft. 10 ins. Weight 200 lbs.

Real name Thomas Jackling, this thickset fighter changed his surname to Johnson for fighting purposes. 'His strength, science and astonishing 'bottom' (pluck and durability) gave him rank superior to all his contemporaries, but his greatest excellence was his surprising coolness and judgment,' says *Pugilistica*. In June 1783 he had his first fight of importance, beating a carman named Jarvis in 15 mins. at Walworth, London. Success followed success. In March 1784 he stopped 'The Croydon Driver' in 27 mins. and three months later, Stephen Oliver in 35 mins. In Feb. 1786, Jack Towers was beaten in less than 15 mins. In June of the same year Bill Fry was crushed in half-an-hour, while in the same month Bill Love lasted only four mins. On Jan. 18, 1787, Bill Warr lasted 1 hr. and 40 mins.; and on Dec. 19, the Irish Champion, Michael Ryan, went to defeat in half-an-hour. Two months later Ryan succumbed in 33 mins.

Johnson's greatest victory was on Oct. 22, 1789, when he fought Isaac Perrins, a coppersmith from Birmingham. He was the same age as Johnson, but towered over him, standing 6 ft. 2 in., and scaling 328 lbs. They fought at Banbury, Oxfordshire on Oct. 22, 1789 for 250 guineas a side and after a desperate contest that lasted 62 rounds, Perrins gave in. Johnson's victory had taken him 80 mins. He had one more fight, losing the Championship to Ben Brain in 1791.

King, Tom *Champion*

(b. Stepney, London, Aug. 14, 1835 – d. Stockbridge, Hampshire, Oct. 3, 1888). Height 6 ft. 2 ins. Weight 175 lbs.

The last legitimate Champion of the British Prize Ring. His youth was spent in the Royal Navy, and on leaving the Service he became a dockyard worker where he was able to practise the natural talent he had for boxing. Befriended by Jem Ward, he had his first major bout with Tom Truckle of Portsmouth, and King showed his superiority by halting his opponent in 49 rounds (1 hr. 2 mins.). Young Broome (William Evans) was his next opponent. They met at Farnborough, Hampshire on Oct. 21, 1861. They had fought 17 rounds (20 mins.) when a cry of 'Police' went up. Hastily the ring was dismantled, the party crossed the country border into Surrey, and the battle was resumed, King winning in the 43rd round after fighting for 42 mins. in two rings.

King challenged Jem Mace for the Championship and they met at Godstone, Surrey on Jan. 28, 1862. Mace was the shorter and lighter man, but was four years older and had that extra experience. King fought gamely for 43 rounds (68 mins.) then could not come up for any more. He had earned a second try, however, and they met again on Nov. 26 the same year, this time at Medway, Kent. King turned the tables completely by stopping the Champion in 21 rounds (38 mins.).

He then announced that he would not defend the title, but when John C. Heenan made his second trip to England from America, King was induced out of retirement by the offer of a thousand pounds purse and he agreed to meet Heenan for the World Championship at Wadhurst, Kent on Dec. 8, 1863. The American was the heavier by 23 lbs. but while strong and determined, had not the class of King and the fight ended after 24 rounds (35 mins.) with King as conqueror. He became interested in horse racing and made a considerable fortune.

Meggs, George

Active 1761–62.

A Bristol collier, he claimed the Championship after his suspicious win over Bill Stevens on March 2, 1761. Not a class fighter, he was twice beaten by a Bath baker named Millsom in the summer of 1762. Any other fights he may have had are lost in obscurity.

Mendoza, Daniel *Champion*

(b. Whitechapel, London, July 5, 1763 – d. London. Sept. 3, 1836). Height 5 ft. 7 ins. Weight 168 lbs.

One of the most accomplished and scientific of the bare-knuckle boxers, he was also one of the brainiest; the first man to manage himself and take a hand in the promotion of his own contests. This Jewish boxer's first encounter was with a coalheaver, a man much bigger than himself, and he beat him in 40 mins. On April 17, 1787, on Barnet racecourse, he defeated Sam Martin, a butcher from Bath, in 20 mins. for 25 guineas. This victory brought him into such prominence that he claimed the Championship of England. Then came his three

clashes with Richard Humphries, 1788–90, with Mendoza, with his great skill and ring cleverness, triumphing in the last two. (In their last contest, at Doncaster in Yorkshire, Mendoza, keen to earn as much as he could, had a stage erected in a barn and the onlookers for the first time in prize ring history had to pass through a gate to pay for admission [see *gate* p. 000].)

Other notable wins were against Squire Fitzgerald in Ireland (20 mins.); Bill Warr at Croydon, Surrey (23 rounds) and at Bexley Heath, Kent (15 mins.). In 1795 he took on John Jackson – five years younger, 4 ins. taller and 42 lbs. heavier. They met for the Championship at Hornchurch, Essex and the bigger man won in nine rounds, paving the way to victory by seizing Mendoza by his long hair and holding him with one hand while he pounded his head with the other.

Mendoza retired and opened a school for boxing and like sports. He also wrote his *Memoirs*, which make absorbing reading. In a comeback 11 years later, he beat Harry Lee in 53 rounds, and his last contest, when he was 57, saw him lose to Tom Owen in 12 rounds on Banstead Downs, Surrey.

Molineaux, Tom

(b. Georgetown, South Carolina, U.S.A., 1784 – d. Galway, Ireland, Aug. 4, 1818). Height 5 ft 8½ ins. Weight 198 lbs.

A former slave, he followed the example of his fellow-countryman, Bill Richmond, and came to England in 1809 to continue his fistic career. He started off by defeating Bill Burrows of Bristol in an hour, then stopped Tom Blake in eight rounds on Aug. 21, 1810. On Dec. 10, 1810 he had the first of his two famous fights with Tom Cribb. In the 28th round, with the Englishman on the verge of defeat, Joe Ward (one of Cribb's seconds) went over to Molineaux's corner and falsely accused him of carrying a bullet in his right hand to increase his punching power. This was strenuously denied and a prolonged argument ensued, giving Cribb time to recover so well that he caused Molineaux to retire in 33 rounds (55 mins.).

On May 21, 1811 Molineaux was successful over Jim Rimmer in 21 rounds, then came his eagerly awaited return bout with Cribb. They fought at Thistleton Gap on Sept. 28, 1811 and this time Cribb was definitely the master and won in 11 rounds of a savage fight in which the American's jaw was broken. Jack Carter and Bill Fuller were beaten by Molineaux, but George Cooper stopped him in 14 rounds (20 mins.) in Edinburgh, Scotland on March 11, 1815. He went down rapidly after that defeat and died in 1818.

Neat, Bill *Champion*

(b. Bristol, March 11, 1791 – d. Bristol, March 23, 1858). Height 5 ft. 11½ ins. Weight 196 lbs.

Neat had many local fights before, at the age of 27, he ventured to London. His first important bout was against Tom Oliver on July 10, 1818 at Rickmansworth, Buckinghamshire and Neat won in 28 rounds (1 hr. 31 secs.). The formidable Tom Hickman came next. They met at Newbury, Berkshire, on Dec. 11, 1821 and Neat won in 18 rounds (23½ mins.), thousands of pounds being lost by Hickman's backers.

Daniel Mendoza was one of the most accomplished of the prize ring boxers. (From a print by James Gillray.)

Neat now claimed the Championship and was challenged by Tom Spring. They met at Hinckley Down, Hampshire on May 17, 1823 and Neat was outclassed and beaten in eight rounds (37 mins.). He had broken his left arm and retired to become a butcher in Bristol.

Paddock, Tom *Champion*

(b. Redditch, Herefordshire, 1824 – d. June 30, 1863). Height 5 ft. 8 ins. Weight 166 lbs.

Noted for the famous men he met over a period of 16 years, and for the fact that most of his battles were of long duration. His first important bout was at the age of 20 when he beat Elijah Parsons in 23 rounds (22 mins.) at Sutton Coldfield. On Jan. 27, 1846 he beat Nobby Clarke in 42 rounds and 16 months later beat him in 55 rounds. His victory run was halted by Bold Bendigo at Mildenham on June 5, 1850, Paddock losing on a foul after 49 rounds when he seemed on the point of winning the Championship. Six months later he lost to William Perry at Woking and again threw a fight by being disqualified, this time in the 27th round.

Then came three bouts in a row with Harry Poulson. He lost the first on Sept. 23, 1851 at Sedgebrook in 71 rounds (95 mins.); won the next at Cross End, Derbyshire in 86 rounds (95 mins.) in Dec. 1852; and won the third bout in London on Feb. 14, 1854 in 102 rounds (2 hrs. 32 mins.) – the gap in time between the second and third fights being spent by both men in jail for disturbing the peace by fighting.

Paddock twice beat Aaron Jones in 121 rounds (2 hrs. 24 mins.) and a year later in 61 rounds (1 hr. 29 mins.). After beating Harry Broome in 51 rounds (63 mins.) on May 19, 1856, Paddock was presented with a new Belt and could style himself as Champion. Two years later he lost the title to Tom Sayers in 21 rounds, but was not his true self. He died in 1863 after a long illness.

Pearce, Hen *Champion*

(b. Bristol, 1777 – d. London, April 30, 1809). Height 5 ft. 9 ins. Weight 175 lbs.

His full first name was Henry, but they shortened it to Hen and then, because of his bravery in the ring, they named him 'The Game Chicken'. His career, like his life, was short, only seven bouts being recorded. His prowess at sparring brought him to London where he was matched with Joe Berks who claimed the Championship. On June 3, 1803, Pearce

stopped Jack Firley in ten rounds. Two months later he defeated Berks in 15 rounds and on Jan. 23, 1804 Berks was again beaten, this time in 24 rounds. Pearce had four wins in 1805; Elias Spray (29 rounds), Stephen Carte (25 rounds), John Gully (64 rounds) and Jem Belcher (18 rounds). Pearce died suddenly in 1809.

Perry, William

(b. Tipton, Staffordshire, March 21, 1819 – d. Wolverhampton, Staffordshire, Jan. 18, 1881). Height 6 ft. ½ in. Weight 185 lbs.

Known as 'The Tipton Slasher' after his birthplace, this renowned and determined battler threw his hat into the ring at Chelsea on Nov. 3, 1835 at the age of 16 and beat Barney Dougherty in seven rounds. The same distance was enough for Ben Spilsbury at Oldbury, while Jem Scunner was stopped in 31 rounds (1 hr.) at Wolverhampton.

Perry next took on a veritable giant in Charles Freeman, who had been brought from America by Ben Caunt. He measured 6 ft. 10½ ins. and scaled 276 lbs. but The Slasher was undaunted and they met at Sawbridgeworth on Dec. 10, 1842 and contested 70 rounds until darkness forced them to withdraw. Ten days later they met at Cliffe Marshes by the River Thames and in the 37th round (39 mins.) Perry fell without taking a blow and was ruled out. There followed three fights with Tass Parker: a draw (67 rounds/94 mins.) and wins for Perry in 133 rounds and 23 rounds (27 mins.). Tom Paddock was beaten in 22 rounds (42 mins.) at Woking on Dec. 17, 1850, but Perry lost to Tom Sayers on June 16, 1857; being halted in ten rounds but making the fight last 1 hr. 42 mins.

Richmond, Bill *Champion*

(b. Staten Island, New York, U.S.A. – d. London, England, Dec. 28, 1829). Height 5 ft. 9 ins. Weight 152 lbs.

Born in slavery, he picked up his boxing skills while sparring with British soldiers and was taken to England by the Duke of Northumberland. His first fight in England saw him defeat George Moore in 25 mins. at York. Wins over Paddy Green and Frank Myers followed, then he lost to George Maddox in five rounds. There were three victories in 1809: Jack Carter (25 mins.), Jim Atkinson (20 mins.), Ike Wood (23 rounds). In a second fight with Maddox, on Aug. 9, 1809, he won in 52 mins. after a hectic battle.

The following year he beat Young Powers in 15 mins. and did not fight again until 1814 when he stopped Tom Davis in 13 rounds. In the next year he won over Tom Shelton in 23 rounds and in his last bout on Nov. 12, 1818, he beat Jack Carter in three rounds.

Ryan, Paddy

(b. Thurles, Tipperary, Ireland, March 15, 1853 – d. Troy, New York, U.S.A., 1901). Height 5 ft. 11 ins. Weight 200 lbs.

All his fighting took place in America. There is no clear record of his early contests, but he won the American Championship on May 30, 1880 by beating Joe Goss at Collier Station,

West Vancouver in 87 rounds (1 hr. 24 mins.). He did not keep his title very long, being beaten by John L. Sullivan on Feb. 7, 1882 at Mississippi City in nine rounds (10½ mins.) for a purse of 5,000 dollars. He fought Sullivan again on Jan. 19, 1885 in New York, losing in only 50 seconds.

Sayers, Tom *Champion*

(b. Brighton, Sussex, May 25, 1826 – d. Camden Town, London, Nov. 8, 1865). Height 5 ft. 8½ ins. Weight 152 lbs.

One of the most renowned and respected of the Prize Ring heroes, he was not much more than a welterweight yet met opponents of all sizes and poundages and lost only once in a long career.

His career began when he was working as a bricklayer on a roadway bridge. There was an argument with a fellow workman that resulted in an impromptu scrap that was halted by the foreman. 'If you want to fight, go to London', he said and Tom took him at his word. He was then 22, his first match being with Abe Couch at Greenhythe on March 19, 1849 who was beaten in 13 mins. News of his ability spread and 19 months passed before he could induce Dan Collins to fight on Oct. 22, 1850. They fought nine rounds (27 mins.) at Edenbridge, then the police arrived so they continued the contest at Redhill and fought another 39 rounds (1 hr. 52 mins.) before darkness fell and a draw was declared.

His next four bouts covered three years: Dan Collins was beaten at Long Reach in 44 rounds (84 mins.); Jack Grant lasted 64 rounds (2½ hrs.); Jack Martin was stopped in 23 rounds (55 mins.). On Oct. 18, 1853 he was outsmarted by Nat Langham at Lakenheath, who closed both his eyes causing him to give in after 61 rounds (2 hrs. 2 mins.). It was Sayers' only loss and he was soon back in favour, beating George Sims in four rounds (5 mins.). On Jan. 29, 1856 he defeated Harry Poulson at Appledore, Kent, in 109 rounds (3 hrs. 8 mins.), and he kept busy the following year with four bouts, beating Aaron Jones, 85 rounds (2 hrs.); Bill Perry, ten rounds (1 hr. 42 mins.) for the Championship of England, and Bob Brett, seven rounds (15 mins.). He also boxed a 62-rounds (3 hrs.) draw with Aaron Jones. Sayers continued victoriously, stopping Bill Benjamin in three rounds (6½ mins.), Tom Paddock, 21 rounds (1 hr. 20 mins.) and Benjamin again, in 11 rounds (22 mins.).

A year went by during which time arrangements were made for the staging of a great international match with John C. Heenan, of America. It attracted enormous public interest in England as it was announced that they would fight for the Championship of the world. Heenan had all the advantages. He was the younger man by seven years, taller by 5½ ins. and heavier by 43 lbs. On paper it was no match, but Sayers had ten times more ring 'know-how' which made up for everything else. They met at Farnborough, Kent before an estimated 12,000 people, with many distinguished personages among the assembly and newspaper reporters from both sides of the Atlantic.

They fought for 2 hrs. 20 mins. but after the 37th round the fight became a shambles due to the ring being broken into. After five more rounds it ended with Heenan having his opponent over the ropes and in danger of strangling him, the crowd surged into the ring and the fight was abandoned. It was declared a draw and both men received a silver belt emblematic of the title. Sayers did not fight again and on his death was buried in Highgate cemetery beneath a magnificent memorial.

Sellers, Harry *Champion*

(b. England, Aug. 10, 1753). Height 5 ft. 11½ ins. Weight 178 lbs.

He was recognized as Champion after defeating Peter Corcoran at Staines, Middlesex on Oct. 10, 1776 in 28 mins. Other wins were over Joe Hood (twice) and Bill Stevens in 10 mins. He was beaten by Duggan Fearns at Slough in 90 secs. in 1779 and by William Harvey in London in 20 mins. Details of his death are not known.

Slack, Jack *Champion*

(b. 1720 – d. 1778). Height 5 ft. 8 ins. Weight 200 lbs.

This Norfolk butcher came to fame in London when he performed at Broughton's arena and there defeated Daniel Smith (for the second time) in less than 20 mins. on Nov. 12, 1744. He challenged Broughton, who gave him ten guineas to meet him which the butcher promptly bet on himself at the prevailing odds of 100–1. They fought on April 11, 1750 and although the Champion was on top from the start, Slack landed heavy punches that closed both Broughton's eyes and in a blinded state he was forced to defeat after 14 mins. The Duke of Cumberland lost £10,000. Afterwards Slack had several important fights. On July 8, 1751, he stopped a Frenchman named Pettitt in 25 mins.; stopped Cornelius Harris in 20 mins. on March 13, 1755 and on Oct. 20, 1759 defeated Goerge Moreton in 35 mins. He lost his title to Bill Stevens in 1760. Slack opened a shop in Chandos Street, London and remained there until his death.

Spring, Tom *Champion*

(b. Fownhope, Herefordshire, Feb. 23, 1795 – d. London, Aug. 26, 1851). Height 5 ft. 11½ ins. Weight 186 lbs.

Born Thomas Winter at Fownhope, Herefordshire, on Feb. 33, 1795, he changed his name to one he thought more suitable for prize fighting. Spring, who won most of his fights with steadiness and science, began at the age of 17. His first bout of note was against a Yorkshireman named Stringer at Mousley Hurst on Sept. 9, 1817; Spring won in 29 rounds (39 mins.). Then came two bouts with Ned Painter: the first at Mickleham Downs in Surrey, on April 1, 1818 which Spring won in 31 rounds (89 mins.), and the second on Aug. 7, 1818 at Russia Farm, Kingston, which he lost in 42 rounds (64 mins.) being put down and out from a blow to the ear.

Tom claimed the Championship after beating Jack Carter at Crawley Downs in 71 rounds (1

hrs. 55 mins.), on May 4, 1819. He was never beaten for the title, Ben Burn being stopped in 18 rounds; Tom Oliver in 25 rounds (55 mins.); Bill Neat in eight rounds (37 mins.), and Jack Langan in a terrific battle on Worcester race-course on Jan. 17, 1724 that lasted 77 rounds (2 hrs.). They met again on June 8 the same year, at Warwick, when Spring was again successful, this time beating the Irish Champion in 76 rounds (1 hr. 49 mins.). In a year he had defended his Championship three times.

He retired to become a publican and died on Aug. 26, 1851, an impressive memorial being erected over his grave in Norwood cemetery in South London.

Stevens, Bill *Champion*

Active 1760–78.

Known as 'The Nailer' because of his tremendous hitting powers with the right, was also impervious to punishment and might have been one of the great Champions but for the fact that he fell in with those who persuaded him to 'fix' his fights for the benefit of the gamblers. His battle with Slack (1760) was suspect, while his contest with George Meggs (1761) was so obviously a sham that the Prize Ring fell into disrepute until Tom Johnson's arrival in 1783.

Meggs met Stevens for his Championship title on March 2, 1761 at the Tennis Court in St. James's Street, London. With the first punch from Meggs, the Champion went down and there was scarcely a blow struck for the 17 mins. the affair lasted and which ended with Stevens giving in. Meeting him one day a friend expressed his surprise at his defeat to which Stevens replied: 'Why, Lord bless you, the day I fought Jack Slack I got 90 guineas; but I got 50 guineas more that I should otherwise have done by letting George beat me; and, damme, ain't I the same man still?'

Stevens did have some straight fights. In Feb. 1760 he defeated Jacob Taplin in a few rounds, knocking him flat with some tremendous blows. His last bout, in June 1778, was with Harry Sellers who defeated him easily in one-sided contest. The date of 'The Nailer's death is as unknown as his date of birth.

Taylor, George *Champion*

(b. 1714 – d. London, 1758).

On the retirement of Figg, he claimed the Championship of England. He had been a performer at Figg's amphitheatre and built one for himself nearby in Tottenham Court Road, London. Here he had his retinue of pugilists and fought there himself on special occasions.

Taylor could never forgive Broughton for beating him for the Championship and was always his deadly rival, even seeking challengers to beat the Champion, but none succeeded until George Slack appeared on the scene. Taylor beat Slack in 25 mins. on Jan. 31, 1750, then trained him to challenge Broughton.

Taylor's last contest of any significance was a meeting with Tom Faulkner, whom he had already twice beaten some years earlier. They met for 200 guineas-a-side and the 'gate' money on Aug. 5, 1758 outside St. Albans, Hertfordshire. The betting was 3–1 on Taylor to win, but after a vicious contest that lasted an hour and a quarter, he was forced to give in and was so badly hurt that he died four months later on his home at Deptford, London.

Ward, Jem *Champion*

(b. London, Dec. 26, 1800 – d. London, April 3, 1884). Height 5 ft. 10 ins. Weight 175 lbs.

Whether being born on Boxing Day had anything to do with him taking up the fistic profession is mere conjecture. The oldest of seven, he was born in London's East End, and at 16 was working in a coal yard. His prowess with his fists soon attracted attention and at the age of 21 he was introduced to The Fancy as 'The Black Diamond'. At that time he had beaten George Robinson (45 mins.); Bill Wall (2 hrs.), George Webb (3 mins.), Jack Murray (45 mins.), Nick Murphy (35 mins.), Mike Hayes (40 mins.) and John Delaney (35 mins.), all in the space of four years. At Mousley Hurst on June 12, 1822 he beat Dick Acton in six rounds (14½ mins.).

He had a big chance to gain fame against Bill Abbott at the same place four months later but was paid to fix the fight and would not come up after the 22nd round. When he lost to Josh Hudson in 15 rounds a year later suspicion again fell on him. Ward regained some prestige by twice beating Phil Sampson (in 26 and 27 rounds), then came his winning of the Championship and Belt by defeating Tom Cannon in Warwickshire on July 19, 1825 in ten rounds (10 mins.). He remained out of the ring for 18 months, then defended his title against Peter Crawley at Royston on Jan. 2, 1827, and lost in 11 rounds (26 mins.). There were two more contests. Jack Carter was beaten in 17 rounds (32 mins.) at Shepperton on May 27, 1828 and Simon Byrne at Willeycutt, Stratford-on-Avon, on July 12, 1831 – a disgraceful affair that ended in 17 rounds (77 mins.). Ward died at the Licensed Victuallers Home in the Old Kent Road, London at the age of 83.

Ward, Nick *Champion*

(b. London, April 1, 1811 – d. London, Feb. 17, 1850).

Younger brother to Jem and also from London's East End. His first real try-out was at Mousley Hurst on Feb. 1833 when he accounted for John Lockyer in 18 rounds. Next he retired against an unknown black boxer in London in 12 rounds. Another match was made but it fell through. On Oct. 18, 1839 he won over Jem Bailey who lost to Ward through striking him when he was down.

So far Nick showed no signs of attaining the heights, then he was paired with Deaf Burke at Stony Stratford on Sept. 22, 1840, when Ward brought off a surprise by halting the veteran in 17 rounds. This brought a challenge from Ward to Ben Caunt for the Championship. The bout took place at Crookham Common on Feb. 2, 1841 and Nick was lucky to win, his rival being ruled out in the seventh round for striking Ward when he was down. So Nick was Champion, but only for three months. In a return fight with Caunt on May 11, 1841, he was well beaten in 35 rounds (47 mins.). He did not fight again.

Publicizing Pugilism

Broadsheets Where would boxing be without the media? In the early days of the Prize Ring the reporting of famous fights was carried to the country by way of broadsheets: single page accounts, very often in verse, that gave highly descriptive accounts of important contests, often with lurid drawings depicting the decisive moments of the encounter. These were carried by travelling salesmen to the fairs and festivals and sold to those who could read, together with sensational stories of the big events of the day.

Newspapers These fistic reports were distributed in the very earliest days of printing, later being taken up by the newspapers and periodicals. Almost every newspaper carried the events of the Prize Ring, from *The Daily Courant* in 1702 onward. Celebrated boxing historian Pierce Eagan claimed that 'the most fashionable daily paper of the day (probably *The Times*, which was first published in 1785) enjoyed a happy increase in sales in respect of its containing the genuine correspondence between Humphries and Mendoza', who had their first three encounters in 1788.

Boxiana Eagan brought out the first edition of his famous *Boxiana* in 1818: it was subtitled *Sketches of Ancient and Modern Pugilism* and covered the Prize Ring from its earliest days. It was based on an earlier work printed and published by his employer, George Smeeton, at St. Martin's Lane, London, in 1812. Also he derived much of his information from *Pancratia – A History of Pugilism* attributed to J. B. In reviewing Eagan's *Boxiana* in an 1820 issue *Blackwood's Magazine* stated: 'It is sufficient justification of Pugilism to say Mr. Eagan is its historian. His style is perfectly his own, and likely to remain so, for it is inimitable as it is excellent. The man who has not read *Boxiana* is ignorant of the power of the English language.' Many editions of *Boxiana* have been forthcoming, the last appearing in the 1970s.

First Boxing Book Books on boxing were next to appear and the first notable one was *A Treatise upon the useful Science of Defence* by Captain Godfrey in 1747, who dedicated his work to the Duke of Cumberland, an ardent supporter of the Noble Art.

Mendoza's Memoirs In 1789 appeared *The Memoirs of the Life of Daniel Mendoza* by that famous Prize Ring Champion. Its title page under the top heading is worth repeating: 'Containing a faithful narrative of the various vicissitudes of the numerous Contests in which he has been engaged with observations on each; comprising also Genuine Anecdotes of many Distinguished Characters, to which are added Observations on the art of Pugilism; Rules to be observed with regard to Training, etc.' It was printed for Mendoza by G. Hayden of Brydges St., Covent Garden, London. A new edition was published in 1816 and one as late as 1951.

Bell's Life In 1824 Eagan was responsible for *Eagan's Life in London and Sporting Guide* which was eventually taken over by John Bell who amalgamated it with his own *Bell's Life in London* which had begun publication two years earlier and ran daily until 1886. It was the forerunner of the present *Sporting Life* which saw off such rivals as *The Sporting Times, The*

Sportsman, and *The Sporting Telegraph*.

Pugilistica Henry Downes Miles, editor of the *Sportsman's Magazine*, brought out *Pugilistica* in 1880. It was claimed to be a more accurate history of the Prize Ring than Eagan's and ran to three volumes. This, too, went to several editions, the last being in 1906, and can be regarded as more authentic and detailed than Eagan's work, at which it scoffs.

Fistiana Fistiana or the Oracle of the Ring was published by the editor of *Bell's Life in London*. It was a pocket-sized book that gave a list of Prize Fights in chronological order, plus the current set of rules, and the duties of referees, umpires and seconds. It went into several editions, the last being in 1864. He also produced *Fights for the Championship* in a single volume.

Fights for the Championship In 1910 Fred Hemming, editor of the *Licensed Victuallers' Gazette* that gave a lot of support to boxing, brought out his own version of *Fights for the Championship*, sub-titling it *The Men and Their Times*. The contents had been serialized in his paper beforehand, now it appeared in two volumes. Other books by Hemming were *Recollections of the Prize Ring* and *Trips to our Training Quarters*.

Sayers v. Heenan When Tom Sayers fought his historic battle with John Camel Heenan at Farnborough in 1860, practically every newspaper in the country devoted maximum space to it, both before and after the contest, while *The Times* issued a complete special edition to this international event the day after, which had to be reprinted several times to meet the demand.

Police Gazette Richard Kyle Fox, a man devoted to the Prize Ring as well as a keen supporter of all competitive sports, plus the Stage and the Turf, produced in New York in 1873 his world-famous *Police Gazette*. He termed it *The Leading Illustrated Sporting Journal of America*. In the earlier edition the pictures were drawn by artists with vivid imaginations, in fact the whole contents bordered on the lurid. A great deal of its space was devoted to boxing and it was so successful that a British edition was published in London on October 3, 1896. The *Police Gazette* ceased publication in America in 1932 and attempts to revive it in later years were only partially successful.

Mirror of Life The success of the *Police Gazette* prompted the appearance of a rival publication in London – *The Mirror of Life* which adopted the same style and lay-out, but devoted an even greater percentage of its space to the professional side of boxing. It started on January 1, 1900 and ran until March 1, 1924. Frank Bradley, a former amateur boxer of repute, was its editor for most of its life, and in fact it folded up after his death in 1923.

Boxing In 1909 Frank Bradley also published *Boxing World*, a weekly rival to the more popular *Boxing* which the Berry Brothers launched on September 11, 1909, after the historic battle between Jack Johnson and Tommy Burns in Sydney, Australia, on December 26, 1908, had convinced them there was a market for ringside descriptions of boxing contests and stories about the leading personalities of the roped arena. When *Boxing World* finally proved a liability, its name was incorporated with the *Mirror of Life* heading, but in no way did this stop its eventual demise.

Boxing under the editorship of the celebrated John Murray, continued as The Bible of Boxing through two World Wars, but its name was changed to Boxing News.

Boxing News This weekly succeeded Boxing during World War II. It is to this day a weekly of considerable popularity and renown throughout the fistic world, noted for its detailed reporting and action illustrations.

Ring Magazine In February 1922 Nat Fleischer, former sports editor of the New York Telegram, launched his now famous Ring Magazine, a full-sized monthly that has not missed an issue in 60 years. It is devoted to stories about past and present heroes of the ring, plus reports from correspondents from all over the world, with monthly ratings and reviews. After a spasmodic start it proved a highly successful venture. When Fleischer died in 1972 the magazine was taken over by his son-in-law, Nat Loubert, and is now under the personal direction of Bert Randolph Sugar. There have been many rival publications. Boxing and Wrestling, Boxing Illustrated, World Boxing and other periodicals devoted to the sport, but The Ring has been the most lasting.

Record books

Police Gazette In conjunction with his Police Gazette, Richard Fox produced an annual record book dealing with all sports, but devoted largely to boxing. First published in January 1896, it gave the records of 45 prominent boxers, plus lists of champions, the Police Gazette rules of boxing and a collection of fistic facts, plus portraits of the leading fighters and other personalities of athletics and the stage. It continued publication until 1918 when a disastrous fire destroyed the Police Gazette office and all the records.

Innes' Ring Record One of the earliest record books was published at Boston, U.S.A., in 1895 by Nelse Innes, sports editor of the Boston Herald in conjunction with Don Saunders, sports writer for the Boston Globe. It was pocket-sized, its illustrations being wood-block engravings. It sold as Innes' Ring Record, priced at 10 cents, and copies could be obtained in almost every bar in America.

Andrews Tom Andrews of Milwaukee, Wisconsin, next came into the record book picture. In 1903 he produced his famous Ring Battles of Centuries, which gave not only a multitude of boxers' individual records, but also facts and figures relating to the history of the sport. His books went into several editions, being reprinted and brought up to date as required. After a few years he resorted to a smaller size, and continued until opposition from other record books forced him out of business in 1937.

Everlast In 1922 the Everlast Sports Equipment Company issued the first of a series of annual pocket-sized record books that ran until 1937. They contained a mixture of prominent boxers, past and present, with illustrations, and a number of articles by sports writers of the day. They were priced at 35 cents a copy.

Post In 1930 a rival record book, on very similar lines and size, was produced by Max Post,

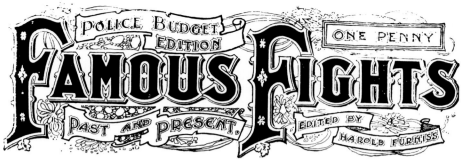

The front page of an early boxing periodical supposedly illustrating the bout between Fitzsimmons (right) and Maher, but compare it with page 149!

President of Post Sports, and edited by John L. Romano. The records given in these two productions were disappointing as in many instances they gave no details as to the exact date or place where the contests took place.

Sporting Life The daily Sporting Life issued a boxing record book in 1909 and again in 1921, but these, too, lacked full details except for the current year and were small in size.

Boxing The weekly periodical Boxing issued record books in 1914 and again in 1921, but both were unsatisfactory, lacking the fullest information and leaving out some fighters of importance. From 1937–1939 a Handbook of

Boxing was published, but this merely gave lists of world and British champions up to and from the turn of the century.

Boxing News Annual The year 1944 saw the birth of the Boxing News Annual a record book that contained every possible detail and listed the full records of early reigning world, British, European and British Empire champions, together with a photo portrait, plus the record of many other boxers for the past year. There were listed all the championship changes and a special section devoted to the amateur side of the sport. This invaluable work is indispensable for sport writers as well as avid boxing fans.

Ring Record Book In 1942 Nat Fleischer brought off his major triumph in record books, producing a hardbacked volume that has grown bigger and bigger as the years have passed. It contains not only complete lists of all world championship fights in each weight division, but the full individual records of every past world champion, plus the annual records of every boxer of note. It also contains a huge chronicle of facts and figures about the fight game and is rightly sub-titled *Boxing Encyclopedia*.

Annuaire Du Ring From 1909 to 1939 Victor Breyer, a Paris journalist and boxing referee, was responsible for the appearance of the *Annuaire Du Ring*, a record book mainly devoted to French boxers but including other European fighters of note and lists of champions and title changes. It was valuable because it contained the records of Continental boxers not obtainable elsewhere. It was re-issued in 1945 by Georges Denis, owner-editor of *La Boxe*, a weekly that did not live up to expectations. When it ceased publication in 1959 the *Annuaire Du Ring* did too.

Pugilato The only annual record book to compare with those issued by *The Ring* and *Boxing News* is the massive, comprehensive *Pugilato* first published by Guiseppe Bellarati in Rome in 1972 and which has continued to grow in size and contents since. Invaluable to students of European boxing, it includes a vast number of individual records in its 700 pages. Although printed in Italian, the publisher, himself a great follower of fisticuffs, provides his information in a simple form that creates no problems for foreign readers.

Minor Record Books Persuaded by L. N. 'Bill' Bailey, boxing correspondent to the now defunct evening paper *The Star*, Jack Solomons published a record book under his own name. This was issued annually from 1948 and 1953 when high production costs caused it to cease. It was a meritorious effort, edited by a dedicated recorder of fistic facts. Geoffrey Bardsley, a devout fan, brought out an excellent pocket-sized record book of his own in 1939, at a time when one was sorely needed. In 1956 and again in 1958, Charlie Parish brought out a *Continental Boxing Guide* which contained the

individual records of all the important European boxers of the day, plus such details as age, place of birth, etc. – an invaluable contribution to a boxing library.

In 1985 Barry Hugman produced his *British Boxing Yearbook*, an extensive volume containing records and facts covering British fighters and their contests since the turn of the century. A comprehensive and invaluable volume for all connected with the fight game in a world-wide capacity. This has become an annual volume, subsequent editions having appeared each year since.

Scoring Fights in American Rings

Whereas in Great Britain the winner of a contest is determined solely on the referee's score card, under the rules of the European Boxing Union there is the Three-Judges system of finding the winner, the referee taking no part in rendering the verdict, being there solely to control the boxers in the ring.

In the United States of America, in all its various Associations, the judging of a contest is decided by two judges with the referee giving the casting vote. Both round-by-round and points scoring is used. If the contest ends in a draw on the round-by-round system, then the points scoring system comes into effect. This system was introduced in 1945 by Eddie Eagan, Olympic Games light-heavyweight champion in 1920, who for many years was Chairman of the New York State Athletic Commission. In most of the States five points is the maximum that can be earned in a round, in others it is ten. One point is scored for the boxer winning the round by a shade, nothing for the loser. When a round has been clearly won, the boxer in question receives two points, none going to the loser. If one boxer is by far the superior of the other, he receives three points, while a knock-

down also scores three points, with none for the loser in either case. When a round is one sided in one man's favour and he also scores a knockdown, he is entitled to four points.

Where the judging by rounds system prevails, the winner of a round receives five points (or ten) and the loser gets four, while a clean knockdown makes the score 5–3. An even round is scored 0–0. If a fighter is put down and the bell sounds signifying the ending of a round, the referee must continue counting and if the boxer rises before the count of ten seconds has ended, he can return to his corner and continue the contest. If he fails to rise inside ten seconds, he is regarded as having been counted out in that particular round. In America the announcement of the verdict has changed from former times when the referee merely held up the right arm of the winner at the conclusion of the contest or spread his arms to indicate a draw. Nowadays the announcer tells the spectators the findings of each judge and the referee separately. The first time this occurred was at Madison Square Garden, New York on Feb. 9, 1944, when it was decided that Tippy Larkin was a unanimous winner over Lulu Constantino in a ten rounds bout, the referee and one judge awarding him 9–1, and the other judge making it 8–2.

Rules for Championship Contests

1. Both champion and challenger must make the specified weight.

2. If the champion makes the weight, but his challenger does not, the title is not at stake if the fight takes place.

3. If the challenger is unable to make the weight, he forfeits his chance of winning the championship.

4. If the champion does not make the weight, he forfeits his title and if the fight proceeds, the challenger cannot win the championship.

Shortest-Reigning Champions

Shortest-Reigning World Champions

CHAMPION	DAYS
Heavyweight	
John Tate (W.B.A.)	163
Leon Spinks (W.B.C.)	212
Marvin Hart	235
Light-Heavyweight	
Bob Godwin	23
Jimmy Slattery (N.Y.A.C.)	106
Anton Christoforidis (N.B.A.)	129
Middleweight	
Randolph Turpin	64
Gene Fullmer	119
Emile Griffith	157
Light-Middleweight	
Ralph Dupas	131
Jose Duran (W.B.C.)	143
Miguel Castellini (W.B.A.)	148
Welterweight	
Johnny Bratton	65
Tony DeMarco	70

Virgil Akins	75
Light-Welterweight	
Roberto Cruz (W.B.A.)	86
Battling Shaw	90
Miguel Valesquez (W.B.C.)	120
Lightweight	
Erubey Carmona (W.B.A.)	56
Claude Noel (W.B.A.)	84
Al Singer	120
Junior-Lightweight	
Rafael Limon (W.B.C.)	88
Cornelius Boza-Edwards (W.B.C.)	174
Yoshiaki Numata	182
Featherweight	
Dave Sullivan	46
Eugene Criqui	54
Ruben Olivares (W.B.A.)	54
Super-Bantamweight	
Kazuo Kobayashi (W.B.C.)	45
Leo Randolph (W.B.A.)	97
Rigoberto Riasco (W.B.C.)	190
Bantamweight	
Pete Herman	60
Harold Dade	64
Julian Solis (W.B.A.)	77

Super-Flyweight	
Gustavo Ballas (W.B.A.)	84
Rafael Pedroza (W.B.A.)	124
Rafael Orono (W.B.C.)	226
Flyweight	
Emile Pladner (N.B.A.)	47
Santos Lacier (W.B.A.)	70
Luis Ibarra (W.B.A.)	91
Light-Flyweight	
Amado Ursua (W.B.C.)	67
Freddy Castillo (W.B.C.)	76
Shigeo Nakajima (W.B.C.)	81

Shortest-Reigning British Champions

CHAMPION	DAYS
Heavyweight	
Frank Goddard	23
Len Harvey	186
Joe Bugner	195
Light-Heavyweight	
Dennis Powell	85
Ron Barton	98
Johnny Frankham	133

Middleweight	
Gus Platts	92
Kevin Finnegan	139
Albert Finch	176
Welterweight	
Dave McCleave	40
Johnny Brown	42
Harry Mason	190
Light-Welterweight	
Des Morrison	119
Lightweight	
Willie Reilly	92
Tom Causer	130
Dave Crowley	172
Featherweight	
Johnny Summers	77
Charlie Hardcastle	152
John Kelly	218
Bantamweight	
Harry Ware	98
Bill Beynon	116
Tommy Noble	217
Flyweight	
Joe Symonds	58
Percy Jones	110
Jackie Brown	141

Shortest Title Fights (One Round Was Enough)

Shortest World Title Fights

CONTESTANTS: WINNER NAMED FIRST	DATE	TIME
Heavyweight		
Muhammad Ali v. Sonny Liston, Lewiston, Maine.	25. 5.65	*1.00
Michael Dokes v. Mike Weaver, Las Vegas.	12.12.82	1.03
Tommy Burns v. Jem Roche, Dublin.	17. 3.08	1.28
Mike Tyson v. Michael Spinks, Atlantic City.	28. 6.88	1.31
Joe Frazier v. Dave Zyglewicz, Houston.	22. 4.69	1.36
George Foreman v. Jose 'King' Roman, Tokyo.	9. 1.73	2.00
Joe Louis v. Max Schmeling, New York.	22.6.38	2.04
Sonny Liston v. Floyd Patterson, Chicago.	25.9.62	2.06
Tommy Burns v. Bill Squires, Colma, Calif.	4. 6.07	2.09
Joe Louis v. Tami Mauriello, New York.	18.9.46	2.09
Sonny Liston v. Floyd Patterson, Las Vegas.	22. 7.63	2.10
James Smith v. Tim Witherspoon, New York.	12.12.86	2.12
Joe Louis v. Jack Roper, Los Angeles.	17. 4.39	2.20
Rocky Marciano v. Jersey Joe Walcott, Chicago.	15. 5.53	2.25
Joe Louis v. John Henry Lewis, New York.	25. 1.39	2.29
Joe Louis v. Buddy Baer, New York.	9. 1.42	2.56

*Official time, but Liston was put down at 1.42 and Referee Walcott stopped fight at 2.12.

Light-Heavyweight		
Gus Lesnevich v. Billy Fox, New York.	5. 3.48	1.58
Bob Foster v. Frankie DePaula, New York.	23. 1.69	2.17
Georges Carpentier v. Ted 'Kid' Lewis, London.	11. 5.22	2.30
Vicente Rondon v. Piero Del Papa, Caracas.	7. 6.71	2.35
Middleweight		
Al McCoy v. George Chip, Brooklyn, N.Y.	6. 4.14	0.45
Marvin Hagler v. William 'Caveman' Lee, Atlantic City.	7. 3.82	1.07
Al Hostak v. Freddie Steele, Seattle.	26. 7.38	1.43
Stanley Ketchel v. Mike 'Twin' Sullivan, Colma.	22. 2.08	1.48
Light Middleweight		
Koichi Wajima v. Domencio Tiberia, Fukuoka City.	7. 5.72	1.40
Welterweight		
Lloyd Honeyghan v. Gene Hatcher, Marbella.	30. 8.87	0.45
Henry Armstrong v. Lew Feldman, St. Louis.	16. 3.39	2.12
Jimmy McLarnin v. Young Corbett III, Los Angeles.	29. 5.33	2.37
Ted 'Kid' Lewis v. Albert Badoud, New York.	31. 8.17	2.45
Pipino Cuevas v. Billy Backus, Los Angeles.	20. 5.78	3.00
Light-Welterweight		
Nil		
Lightweight		
Tony Canzoneri v. Al Singer, New York.	14.11.30	1.06
Joe Gans v. Frank Erne, Fort Erie, Canada.	12. 5.02	1.40
Roberto Duran v. Massataka Takayama, San Jose.	21.12.74	1.40
Al Singer v. Sammy Mandell, New York.	17. 7.30	1.46
Edwin Rosario v. Roberto Elizondo, San Juan.	17. 3.84	1.56
Roberto Duran v. Alvaro Rojas, Hollywood.	15.10.76	2.17
Ray 'Boom-Boom' Mancini v. Arturo Filas, Las Vegas.	8. 5.82	2.54
Junior-Lightweight		
Gabriel 'Flash' Elorde v. Harold Gomez, San Francisco.	17. 8.60	1.20
Rocky Lockridge v. Roger Mayweather, Beaumont.	26. 2.84	1.31
Ben Villaflor v. Kuniaki Shibata, Honolulu.	18.10.73	1.56
Alexis Arguello v. Diego Alcala, San Juan.	3. 6.78	1.56
Gabriel 'Flash' Elorde v. Sergio Caprari, Manila.	16.12.61	2.03
Roger Mayweather v. Benedicto Villablanco, Las Vegas.	17. 8.83	*3.04

*Final bell sounded at 3.00, but referee continued to count out Villablanco.

Featherweight		
Azumah Nelson v. Pat Cowdell, Birmingham.	12.10.85	2.24
Freddie Miller v. Jose Girones, Barcelona.	17. 2.35	2.30
Davey Moore v. Danny Valdez, Los Angeles.	8. 4.61	2.48
Kuniaki Shibata v. Raul Cruz, Tokyo.	3. 6.71	*3.04

*Final bell sounded at 3.00. but referee continued to count out Cruz.

Super-Bantamweight		
Juan (Kid) Meza v. Jaime Garza, New York.	3.11.84	2.54
Bantamweight		
Terry McGovern v. Tom 'Pedlar' Palmer, Luckahoe, New York.	12. 9.1899	1.15
Sixto Escobar v. Indian Quintana, New York.	13.10.36	1.49
Jimmy Carruthers v. Vic Toweel, Johannesburg, South Africa.	15.11.52	2.19
Panama Al Brown v. Emile Pladner, Toronto, Canada.	19. 9.32	2.21
Super-Flyweight		
Nil		
Flyweight		
Emile Pladner v. Frankie Genaro, Paris, France.	2. 3.29	0.58
Jackie Paterson v. Peter Kane, Glasgow, Scotland.	19. 6.43	1.01
Santos Lacier v. Hi-Sup Shin, Cheju, S. Korea.	17. 7.83	1.19
Pascual Perez v. Dai Dower, Buenos Aires, Argentina.	30. 3.57	2.00
Prudencio Cardona v. Antonio Avelar, Tampico.	20. 3.82	2.04
Hiroyuki Ebihara v. Pone Kingpetch, Tokyo.	18. 9.63	2.07
Light-Flyweight		
Nil		

Shortest European Title Fights

CONTESTANTS: WINNER NAMED FIRST	DATE	TIME
Heavyweight		
Georges Carpentier v. Joe Beckett, London.	1.10.23	0.15
Heinz Neuhaus v. Hein Ten Hoff, Dortmund.	20. 7.52	0.50
Max Schmeling v. Adolf Heuser, Stuttgart.	2. 7.39	1.11
Georges Carpentier v. Billy Wells, London.	8.12.13	1.13
Georges Carpentier v. Joe Beckett, London.	4.12.19	1.14
Karl Mildenberger v. Sante Amonti, Berlin.	17.10.64	1.32
Georges Carpentier v. Ted 'Kid' Lewis, London.	11. 5.22	2.30
Dick Richardson v. Karl Mildenberger, Dortmund.	24. 2.62	2.35
Peter Weiland v. Bernard Thebault, Kiel.	6.12.69	2.35
Alfredo Evangelista v. Jean-Pierre Coopman, Brussels.	26.11.77	2.40
Light-Heavyweight		
Domenico Adinolfi v. Karl-Heinz Klein, Campione.	4.12.74	1.47
Max Schmeling v. Michel Bonaglia, Berlin.	6. 1.28	1.50
Adolf Heuser v. Martinez de Alfara, Valencia.	25. 6.32	2.10
Rudi Koopman v. Fred Serres, Rotterdam.	4.10.81	2.12
Tom Bogs v. Lother Stengel, Copenhagen.	12. 9.68	2.43
Middleweight		
Randolph Turpin v. Luc Van Dam. London.	27. 2.51	0.48
Tiberio Mitri v. Randolph Turpin, Rome.	2. 5.54	1.05
Gustav Scholz v. Peter Mueller, Berlin.	14.11.59	1.22
Marcel Cerdan v. Leon Fouquet, Paris.	2. 1.47	2.06
Light-Middleweight		
Chris Pyatt v. John van Elteren	17. 9.86	1.30
Luigi Minchillo v. Claude Martin, Rennes.	28.11.81	1.51
Welterweight		
Marcel Cerdan v. Jean Ferrer, Paris.	30. 9.42	2.27
Lightweight		
Jim Watt v. Andre Holyk, Glasgow.	5. 8.77	1.22
Antonio Puddu v. Dominique Azzaro, Cagliari.	4. 4.73	1.55
Ascenzo Botta v. Bruno Bisterzo, Rome.	26.11.41	2.00
Perico Fernandez v. Fernand Roelands, Saragosa.	9. 7.76	2.15
Junior-Lightweight		
Lothar Abend v. Jean de Keers, Kiel.	3. 2.73	2.25
Featherweight		
Eugene Criqui v. Walter Rossi, Paris.	4.11.22	2.30
Bantamweight		
Antoine Montero v. Ray Gilbody	27.10.86	1.55

Shortest Empire or Commonwealth Title Fights

CONTESTANTS: WINNER NAMED FIRST	DATE	TIME
Heavyweight		
Matthew Curran v. Bill Lang, London.	18. 1.11	*0.55
*Disqualification		
Middleweight		
Tony Mundine v. Fred Etuati, Auckland.	20. 8.73	1.44
Dick Turpin v. Bos Murphy, London.	18. 5.48	2.55
Dave Sands v. Dick Turpin, London.	6. 9.49	2.55
Lightweight		
Mo Hussein v. Bright Spider	27. 1.88	1.14
Bantamweight		
Jimmy Carruthers v. Vic Toweel, Johannesburg.	15.11.52	2.19
Flyweight		
Dennis Adams v. Les Smith, Durban.	16. 7.60	1.54

Shortest British Title Fights

CONTESTANTS: WINNER NAMED FIRST	DATE	TIME
Heavyweight		
Joe Bugner v. Richard Dunn, London.	12.10.76	2.14
Neville Meade v. Gordon Ferris, Birmingham.	12.10.81	2.45
William 'Iron' Hague v. James Moir, London.	19. 4.09	2.47
James Moir v. Tiger Smith, London.	25. 2.07	2.49
Cruiserweight		
Tee Jay v. Roy Smith	9. 5.87	1.30
Light-Heavyweight		
Bunny Johnson v. Tim Wood, Wolverhampton.	8. 3.77	1.43
Middleweight		
Herol Graham v. Jimmy Price, London.	24. 4.85	1.40
Mick Leahy v. George Aldridge, Nottingham.	28. 5.63	1.45
Frank Moody v. Tommy Milligan, Glasgow.	6. 8.28	2.00
Johnny Sullivan v. Gordon Hazell, London.	14. 9.54	2.22
Light-Middleweight		
Prince Rodney v. Jimmy Cable, Hastings.	11. 5.85	2.00
Welterweight		
Tom McCormick v. Johnny Summers, Sydney.	14. 2.14	2.30
Lightweight		
Dave Charnley v. Dave Hughes, Nottingham.	20.11.61	0.40
Tommy McGovern v. Billy Thompson, London.	28. 8.51	0.55
George Feeney v. Tony Willis, London.	3.12.83	1.00
Dick Burge v. Tom Causer, London.	8.10.1897	1.01
Al Foreman v. Fred Webster, London.	21. 5.30	1.43

	DATE	TIME
Junior-Lightweight		
Najib Daho v. Pat Cowdell, Manchester.	24. 5.86	3.00
Featherweight		
Charlie Hardcastle v. Alf Wye, London	4. 6.17	2.22
Flyweight		
Jackie Paterson v. Peter Kane, Glasgow.	19. 6.43	1.01
Johnny McCluskey v. Tony Davis, Swansea.	14.10.74	2.05

The Undefeated
World Champions who retired undefeated throughout their entire career

NAME	NATION	DIVISION	PERIOD	BOUTS	DRAWS
Barry, Jimmy	(U.S.A.)	Bantamweight	1891–99	70	9
McAuliffe, Jack	(U.S.A.)	Lightweight	1884–96	52	9
Marciano, Rocky	(U.S.A.)	Heavyweight	1947–56	49	–
Marsh, Terry	(E.)	Light-Welterweight	1981–87	27	1

World Champions who retired while holding title

NAME	NATION	DIVISION	PERIOD	BOUTS	DRAWS
Accavallo, Horacio	(Arg.)	Flyweight	1966–68	10	–
Ali, Muhammad†	(U.S.A.)	Heavyweight	1964–70	10	–
Angott, Sammy†	(U.S.A.)	Lightweight	1940–42	22	2
Arcari, Bruno	(Italy)	Junior-Welterweight	1970–74	28	–
Armstrong, Henry	(U.S.A.)	Featherweight	1937–38	17	–
Beccerra, Joe	(Mex.)	Bantamweight	1959–61	9	1
Darcy, Les§	(Aus.)	Middleweight	1915–17	22	–
Duran, Roberto	(Pan.)	Lightweight	1972–79	39	–
Jeffries, James J.†	(U.S.A.)	Heavyweight	1899–1905	8	–
Ketchel, Stanley‡	(U.S.A.)	Middleweight	1908–10	10	–
Leonard, Benny†	(U.S.A.)	Lightweight	1917–25	83	–
Louis, Joe†	(U.S.A.)	Heavyweight	1937–49	26	–
Marcel, Ernesto	(Pan.)	Featherweight	1972–74	8	–
Monaghan, Rinty	(U.K.)	Flyweight	1947–50	7	1
Monzon, Carlos	(Arg.)	Middleweight	1970–77	20	–
Ohba, Masao‖	(Japan)	Flyweight	1970–73	10	–
Robinson, Ray	(U.S.A.)	Welterweight	1946–50	48	1
Rosenberg, Charley	(U.S.A.)	Bantamweight	1925–27	22	2
Saddler, Sandy†	(U.S.A.)	Featherweight	1950–57	39	9
Saldivar, Vicente†	(Mex.)	Featherweight	1964–67	9	–
Sanchez, Salvador‖	(Mex.)	Featherweight	1980–81	8	–
Servo, Marty†	(U.S.A.)	Weltwerweight	1946	2	–
Tunney, Gene	(U.S.A.)	Heavyweight	1926–28	3	–
Walker, Mickey	(U.S.A.)	Middleweight	1926–31	36	–

Several boxers lost bouts while not champion (see 'A–Z'). Ali was defeated in his 2nd spell as champion.

†Made comeback ‡Murdered §Died ‖Killed in car crash

World Boxing Association (W.B.A.)

One of the two major controlling bodies of boxing, it was formed at a Convention in Tacoma, Washington in Aug. 1962, its first Chairman being Emile Bruneau, Chairman of the Louisiana State Athletic Commission. It succeeded the National Boxing Association (N.B.A.) which was set up in 1921, but did not start creating its own world champions until 1927. Its object was to try and break the monopoly of championship titles and contests assumed by the Boxing Department of the New York State Athletic Commission. Other states in which boxing flourished resented the preference given to boxers licensed in New York and a number of them banded together to form the N.B.A.

This meant, of course, that whenever a championship fell vacant through a universally recognized world champion relinquishing his title, both the New York body and the N.B.A.

set up a titleholder of their own, and sometimes years elapsed with the two men claiming an identical title. This unsatisfactory situation was righted only when the two champions or their successors could be brought together or when one of them surrendered his claim, leaving the other to assume full rights. There were also occasions when one controlling body declared a title vacant because the reigning champion failed to meet a challenger nominated by them, while the opposing body continued to recognize the legal titleholder, with the result that again there were two claimants in one division. At its inauguration, the W.B.A. had the allegiance of 51 State and City Boxing ·Commissions or authorities.

World Boxing Council (W.B.C.)

The World Boxing Council (W.B.C.), founded in Mexico on Feb. 14, 1963 was set up in response to the move made by the National

Boxing Association to claim universal coverage by altering its title to the World Boxing Association (W.B.A.). It was the outcome of a World Boxing Committee formed by the British Boxing Board of Control and other interested controlling bodies anxious to place the ownership of world titles in a single champion. The membership of the W.B.C. comprises those American States not affiliated to the W.B.A., the Mexican Federation of Boxing Commissions, the European Boxing Union, the British Boxing Board of Control, Commonwealth countries, South Africa, several Far Eastern countries, and the Caribbean countries. Some Central and South American countries are also affiliated.

With so many countries affiliated to it, the W.B.C. can be said to hold sway over the largest area of the world, and it also has strong support from the Boxing Department of the New York State Athletic Commission, with which it has a working agreement. In fact, the W.B.C. takes up the old-time feud between

New York and the N.B.A. that covered 44 years, during which there were long periods of duplicate champions in most of the weight divisions. Attempts have been made on a number of occasions to form one controlling body for world boxing championships, but without success. And it will never come about until New York State changes its regulations which do not permit its Athletic Commission to affiliate itself with any other similar authority.

It is generally agreed by the many controlling bodies throughout the world that a champion should defend his title at six-monthly intervals. When, for some reason or another, he fails to meet a challenger nominated by either the W.B.A. or the W.B.C. (on rare occasions there is unison on this) then either one of these controlling bodies will set up a new champion – with the result that there are dual claimants to one championship. Only on rare occasions has

there been total agreement between the two world controlling bodies as to a rightful title-holder, and the situation now exists where there could be 30 world champions, one for each of the 15 titles that can be won at the present time.

In Dec. 1982, the W.B.C. reduced the number of rounds for championship contests from 15 to 12 in a move to safeguard boxers. In due course the other Boxing Commissions followed suit.

World Champions: The First in Each Country
(Under Marquess of Queensberry Rules)

COUNTRY	CHAMPION	DATE	DIVISION
ALGERIA	Marcel Cerdan	1948	Middleweight
ARGENTINA	Pascual Perez	1954	Flyweight
AUSTRALIA	Young Griffo	1890	Featherweight
AUSTRIA	Johnny Ertle	1915	Bantamweight
BAHAMAS	Elisha Obed	1975	Light-Middleweight
BARBADOS	Joe Walcott	1901	Welterweight
BRAZIL	Eder Jofre	1961	Bantamweight
CANADA	Lou Broulliard	1933	Welterweight
CHILE	Benedicto Villablanca	1980	*Junior-Lightweight
COLOMBIA	Antonio Cervantes	1972	Light-Welterweight
CUBA	Kid Chocolate	1931	Junior Lightweight
DENMARK	Battling Nelson	1908	Lightweight
DOMINICA	Carlos Teo Cruz	1968	Lightweight
FRANCE	Charles Ledoux	1912	Bantamweight
GERMANY	Max Schmeling	1930	Heavyweight
GHANA	David Kotey	1975	Featherweight
GT. BRITAIN	Bob Fitzsimmons	1897	Heavyweight
GREECE	Anton Christoforidis	1941	Light-Heavyweight
HAWAII	Dado Marino	1950	Flyweight
IRELAND	Dave Sullivan	1898	Featherweight
ITALY	Johnny Dundee	1923	Featherweight
JAPAN	Yoshio Shirai	1952	Flyweight
JAMAICA	Mike McCullum	1984	Light-Middleweight
KOREA	Ki-Soo Kim	1966	Light-Middleweight
MEXICO	Chalky Wright	1941	Featherweight
NICARAGUA	Eddie Gazo	1977	Light-Middleweight
NIGERIA	Hogan Bassey	1957	Featherweight
PANAMA	Al Brown	1929	Bantamweight
PHILIPPINES	Pancho Villa	1923	Flyweight
PUERTO RICO	Sixto Escobar	1934	Bantamweight
SOUTH AFRICA	Vic Toweel	1950	Bantamweight
SOUTH KOREA	Min-Keun Oh	1984	Flyweight
SPAIN	Balthazar Sangechilli	1935	Bantamweight
SWEDEN	Angemar Johannson	1959	Heavyweight
THAILAND	Pone Kingpetch	1960	Flyweight
TRINIDAD	Claude Noel	1981	Lightweight
UGANDA	Ayub Kalule	1979	Light-Middleweight
UNITED STATES	James J. Corbett	1892	Heavyweight
U.S.S.R.	Louis 'Kid' Kaplan	1925	Featherweight
VENEZUELA	Alfredo Marcano	1971	Junior-Lightweight
YUGOSLAVIA	Mate Parlov	1979	Light-Heavyweight

Joe Walcott, the first Barbadian world boxing champion.

World Champions

World Champions who had the most fights

WEIGHT		BOUTS IN CAREER
Heavyweight	Ezzard Charles (U.S.A.)	122
Light-Heavyweight	Maxie Rosenbloom (U.S.A.)	299
Middleweight	Harry Greb (U.S.A.)	299
Light-Middleweight	Denny Moyer (U.S.A.)	140
Welterweight	Jack Britton (U.S.A.)	299
Light-Welterweight	Jack 'Kid' Berg (U.K.)	192
Lightweight	Benny Leonard (U.S.A.)	213
Junior-Lightweight	Tod Morgan (U.S.A.)	206
Featherweight	Johnny Dundee (U.S.A.)	337
Super-Bantamweight	Jack 'Kid' Wolfe (U.S.A.)	136
Bantamweight	Kid Williams (U.S.A.)	204
Flyweight	Valentin Angelmann (France)	176
Light-Flyweight	Freddy Castillo (Mexico)	69

World Champions who had the most wins inside the distance

WEIGHT		WINS INSIDE DISTANCE
Heavyweight	Primo Carnera (Italy)	69
Light-Heavyweight	Archie Moore (U.S.A.)	129
Middleweight	Sugar Ray Robinson (U.S.A.)	110
Light-Middleweight	Elisha Obed (Bahamas)	57
Welterweight	Henry Armstrong (U.S.A.)	100
Light-Welterweight	Jack 'Kid' Berg (U.K.)	57
Lightweight	Benny Leonard (U.S.A.)	69
Junior-Lightweight	Ricardo Arrendondo (Mexico)	57
Featherweight	Sandy Saddler (U.S.A.)	103
Super-Bantamweight	Wilfredo Gomez (Puerto Rico)	40
Bantamweight	Charles Ledoux (France)	79
Flyweight	Jimmy Wilde (U.K.)	101
Light-Flyweight	Luis Estaba (Ven)	27

The World Champions and Their Title Fights

The world champions in all weight divisions carried almost indisputable universal recognition until the advent of the National Boxing Association, a body formed in 1921 by the fusion of those State Athletic Commissions in America that refused any longer to give supreme dominance to the New York State Athletic Commission and its satellites in the authorizing and matchmaking of world title contests, the deposition of champions and the setting up of others in their stead.

As a result there were times when two claimants to a world crown received recognition of some sort, and on occasions even three, when an individual State or a European controlling body decided to produce a champion of its own, in what it considered justice to a boxer under its jurisdiction.

In assessing the tables of world championship holders, all boxers with a legitimate claim have been included in chronological order, the authority for each being denoted by the following code: *World Boxing Association, †World Boxing Council, ‡International Boxing Federation. World champions created by other bodies before the formation of the W.B..A and W.B.C. are also listed, but the organization awarding the title is not shown – this information can be found in each fighter's biography. Wherever possible, the nationality of each fighter has been listed. If a nationality is not given, then that fighter is American. From the lightweight division onward, only those fights in which the title changed hands are listed.

Prior to the setting up of the B.B.B. of C. (1929) boxing in the British Isles was governed to a great extent by the National Sporting Club, which formed a so-styled British Boxing Board of Control in 1918 and from which grew the present day authority. In 1962 the National Boxing Association changed its name to the World Boxing Association, and to give itself equal authority, the New York body and its associated States, together with most of the European countries, the European Boxing Union and the British Boxing Board of Control, formed the World Boxing Council.

At the time of compiling this work, only two of the 15 weight divisions boast a champion recognized by both authorities, this having been brought about by the meeting of two rival champions. It is hoped that there will be more such meetings, as it is ludicrous for two boxers to be able to style themselves as world titleholders, when they have not met to decide who really is the best. Of course, the more championships there are the better it is for the promoters and it is this very commercial side of boxing that has brought about the present unsatisfactory state.

World Heavyweight Title Fights
Under Marquess of Queensberry Rules

The biggest prize in boxing is the heavyweight championship of the world, and big fighters always attract the fans in search of excitement and sensation. Throughout its history the giants of the ring have commanded most attention and it can be said that the health of the sport depends on the quality of its heavyweight champion.

From the days of James J. Corbett – regarded as the first titleholder under Marquess of Queensberry Rules in 1892, up to the time of Muhammad Ali's forfeiture of the crown in 1967, there was one indisputable heavyweight champion. But from then on both the W.B.A.

and the W.B.C. have set up their own man, except for the time Ali returned to regain the title he had never lost in the ring.

Before his penultimate retirement in 1979, the W.B.C. matched Ken Norton with Larry Holmes and the former was outpointed over 15 rounds at Las Vegas on June 9: to counter this the W.B.A. blessed a contest between John Tate and Gerrie Coetzee, South Africa, as being for the world crown. Tate won on points, but was knocked out in the 15th round by Mike Weaver on Oct. 3, 1981, and in his turn Weaver was knocked out by Michael Dokes on Dec. 10, 1982.

Of the 32 men who have claimed the heavyweight championship of the world, all have been of American origin with the exception of one each from Canada, Germany, Italy, Sweden and the U.K.

1892	Sep. 7	James J. Corbett w.ko.21 John L. Sullivan, New Orleans, U.S.A.
1894	Jan. 25	James J. Corbett w.ko.3 Charlie Mitchell (U.K.), Jacksonville, U.S.A.
1896	Feb. 21	Bob Fitzsimmons (U.K.) w.ko.1 Peter Maher (Ireland), Langtry, U.S.A.
1897	March 17	Bob Fitzsimmons (U.K.) w.ko.14 James J. Corbett, Carson City, U.S.A.
1899	June 9	James J. Jeffries w.ko.11 Bob Fitzsimmons (U.K.), Coney Island, U.S.A.
	Nov. 3	James J. Jeffries w.pts.25 Tom Sharkey (Eire), Coney Island, U.S.A.
1900	May 11	James J. Jeffries w.ko.23 James J. Corbett, Coney Island, U.S.A.
1901	Nov. 15	James J. Jeffries w.ret.5 Gus Ruhlin, San Francisco, U.S.A.
1902	July 25	James J. Jeffries w.ko.8 Bob Fitzsimmons (U.K.), San Francisco, U.S.A.
1903	Aug. 14	James J. Jeffries w.ko.10 James J. Corbett, San Francisco, U.S.A.
1904	Aug. 26	James J. Jeffries w.ko.2 Jack Munro, San Francisco, U.S.A.
1905	July 3	Marvin Hart w.rsf.12 Jack Root, Reno, U.S.A.
1906	Feb. 23	Tommy Burns (Can.) w.pts.20 Marvin Hart, Los Angeles, U.S.A.
	Oct. 2	Tommy Burns (Can.) w.ko.15 Jim Flynn, Los Angeles, U.S.A.
	Nov. 28	Tommy Burns (Can.) drew20 Philadelphia Jack O'Brien, Los Angeles, U.S.A.
1907	May 8	Tommy Burns (Can.) w.pts.20 Philadelphia Jack O'Brien, Los Angeles, U.S.A.
	July 4	Tommy Burns (Can.) w.ko.1 Bill Squires (Aust.), Colma, U.S.A.
	Dec. 2	Tommy Burns (Can.) w.ko.10 Gunner James Moir (U.K.), London, U.K.
1908	Feb. 10	Tommy Burns (Can.) w.ko.4 Jack Palmer (U.K.), London, U.K.
	Mar. 17	Tommy Burns (Can.) w.ko.1 Jem Roch (Ireland), Dublin, Ireland.
	April 18	Tommy Burns (Can.) w.ko.5 Jewey Smith (U.K.), Paris, France.
	June 13	Tommy Burns (Can.) w.ko.8 Bill Squires (Aust.), Paris, France.
	Aug. 24	Tommy Burns (Can.) w.ko.13 Bill Squires (Aust.), Sydney, Australia.
	Sept. 2	Tommy Burns (Can.) w.ko.6 Bill Lang (Aust.), Sydney, Australia.
	Dec. 26	Jack Johnson w.rsf.14 Tommy Burns (Can.), Sydney, Australia.
1909	Sep. 9	Jack Johnson ND10 Al Kaufman, San Francisco, U.S.A.
	Oct. 16	Jack Johnson w.ko.12 Stanley Ketchel, Colma, U.S.A.
1910	July 4	Jack Johnson w.rsf.15 James J. Jeffries, Reno, U.S.A.
1912	July 4	Jack Johnson w.ko.9 Jim Flynn, Las Vegas, U.S.A.
1913	Dec. 19	Jack Johnson drew10 Jim Johnson, Paris, France.
1914	June 27	Jack Johnson w.pts.20 Frank Moran, Paris, France.
	Dec. 15	Jack Johnson w.ko.3 Jack Murray, Buenos Aires, Argentina.
1915	April 5	Jess Willard w.ko.26 Jack Johnson, Havana, Cuba.
1916	March 25	Jess Willard ND10 Frank Moran, New York, U.S.A.
1919	July 4	Jack Dempsey w.ret.3 Jess Willard, Toledo, U.S.A.
1920	Sep. 6	Jack Dempsey w.ko.3 Billy Miske, Benton Harbor, U.S.A.
	Dec. 14	Jack Dempsey w.ko.12 Bill Brennan, New York, U.S.A.
1921	July 2	Jack Dempsey w.ko.4 Georges Carpentier (F.), New Jersey, U.S.A.
1923	July 4	Jack Dempsey w.pts.15 Tom Gibbons, Selby, U.S.A.
	Sept. 14	Jack Dempsey w.ko.2 Luis Firpo (Arg.), New York, U.S.A.
1926	Sep. 23	Gene Tunney w.pts.10 Jack Dempsey, Philadelphia, U.S.A.
1927	Sep. 22	Gene Tunney w.pts.10 Jack Dempsey, Chicago, U.S.A.
1928	July 23	Gene Tunney w.rsf.11 Tom Heeney (N.Z.), New York.
1930	June 12	Max Schmeling (G) w.dis.4 Jack Sharkey, New York, U.S.A.
1931	July 3	Max Schmeling (G.) w.rsf.15 Young Stribling, Cleveland, U.S.A.
1932	June 21	Jack Sharkey w.pts.15 Max Schmeling (G.), Long Island, U.S.A.

1933	June 29	Primo Carnera (I.) w.ko.6 Jack Sharkey, Long Island, U.S.A.
	Oct. 22	Primo Carnera (I.) w.pts.15 Paulino Uzcudun (Sp.), Rome, Italy.
1934	March 1	Primo Carnera (I.) w.pts.15 Tommy Loughran, Miami, U.S.A.
	June 14	Max Baer w.ko.11 Primo Carnera (I.), Long Island, U.S.A.
1935	June 13	James J. Braddock w.pts.15 Max Baer, Long Island, U.S.A.
1937	June 22	Joe Louis w.ko.8 James J. Braddock, Chicago, U.S.A.
	Aug. 30	Joe Louis w.pts.15 Tommy Farr (U.K.), New York, U.S.A.
1938	Feb. 23	Joe Louis w.ko.3 Nathan Mann, New York, U.S.A.
	April 1	Joe Louis w.ko.5 Harry Thomas, Chicago, U.S.A.
	June 22	Joe Louis w.ko.1 Max Schmeling (G.), New York, U.S.A.
1939	Jan. 25	Joe Louis w.rsf.1 John Henry Lewis, New York, U.S.A.
	April 17	Joe Louis w.ko.2 Jack Roper, Los Angeles, U.S.A.
	June 28	Joe Louis w.rsf.4 Tony Galento, New York, U.S.A.
	Sep. 20	Joe Louis w.ko.11 Bob Pastor, Detroit, U.S.A.
1940	Feb. 9	Joe Louis w.pts.15 Arturo Godoy (Chi.), New York, U.S.A.
	March 29	Joe Louis w.ko.2 Johnny Paycheck, New York, U.S.A.
	June 20	Joe Louis w.rsf.8 Arturo Godoy (Chi.), New York, U.S.A.
	Dec. 16	Joe Louis w.ret.6 Al McCoy (Can.), Boston, U.S.A.
1941	Jan. 1	Joe Louis w.ko.5 Red Burman, New York, U.S.A.
	Feb. 17	Joe Louis w.ko.2 Gus Dorazio, Philadelphia, U.S.A.
	March 21	Joe Louis w.ko.13 Abe Simon, Detroit, U.S.A.
	April 8	Joe Louis w.ko.9 Tony Musto, St. Louis, U.S.A.
	May 23	Joe Louis w.dis.7 Buddy Baer, Washington D.C., U.S.A.
	June 18	Joe Louis w.ko.13 Billy Conn, New York, U.S.A.
	Sep. 29	Joe Louis w.rsf.6 Lou Nova, New York, U.S.A.
1942	Jan. 19	Joe Louis w.ko.1 Buddy Baer, New York, U.S.A.
	March 27	Joe Louis w.ko.6 Abe Simon, New York, U.S.A.
1946	June 19	Joe Louis w.ko.8 Billy Conn, New York, U.S.A.
	Sept. 18	Joe Louis w.ko.1 Tami Mauriello, New York, U.S.A.
1947	Dec. 5	Joe Louis w.pts.15 Jersey Joe Walcott, New York, U.S.A.
1948	June 25	Joe Louis w.ko.11 Jersey Joe Walcott, New York, U.S.A. *Louis retired undefeated as champion.*
1949	June 22	Ezzard Charles w.pts.15 Jersey Joe Walcott, Chicago, U.S.A.
	Aug. 10	Ezzard Charles w.rsf.7 Gus Lesnevich, New York, U.S.A.
	Oct. 14	Ezzard Charles w.ko.8 Pat Valentino, San Francisco, U.S.A.
1950	Aug. 15	Ezzard Charles w.rsf.14 Freddy Beshore, Buffalo, U.S.A.
	Sep. 27	Ezzard Charles w.pts.15 Joe Louis, New York, U.S.A.
	Dec. 5	Ezzard Charles w.ko.11 Nick Barone, Cincinnati, U.S.A.
1951	Jan. 12	Ezzard Charles w.rsf.10 Lee Oma, New York, U.S.A.
	March 7	Ezzard Charles w.pts.15 Jersey Joe Walcott, Detroit, U.S.A.
	May 30	Ezzard Charles w.pts.15 Joey Maxim, Chicago, U.S.A.
	July 18	Jersey Joe Walcott w.ko.7 Ezzard Charles, Pittsburgh, U.S.A.
1952	June 5	Jersey Joe Walcott w.pts.15 Ezzard Charles, Philadelphia, U.S.A.
	Sep. 23	Rocky Marciano w.ko.13 Jersey Joe Walcott, Philadelphia, U.S.A.
1953	May 15	Rocky Marciano w.ko.1 Jersey Joe Walcott, Chicago, U.S.A.
	Sep. 24	Rocky Marciano w.rsf.11 Roland LaStarza, New York, U.S.A.
1954	June 17	Rocky Marciano w.pts.15 Ezzard Charles, New York, U.S.A.
	Sep. 17	Rocky Marciano w.ko.8 Ezzard Charles, New York, U.S.A.
1955	May 16	Rocky Marciano w.rsf.9 Don Cockell (U.K.), San Francisco, U.S.A.
	Sep. 21	Rocky Marciano w.ko.9 Archie Moore, New York, U.S.A. *Marciano retired undefeated as champion.*
1956	Nov. 30	Floyd Patterson w.ko.5 Archie Moore, Chicago, U.S.A.
1957	July 29	Floyd Patterson w.rsf.10 Tommy Jackson, New York, U.S.A.
	Aug. 22	Floyd Patterson w.ko.6 Pete Rademacher, Seattle, U.S.A.
1958	Aug. 18	Floyd Patterson w.ret.12 Roy Harris, Los Angeles, U.S.A.
1959	May 1	Floyd Patterson w.ko.11 Brian London (U.K.), Indianapolis, U.S.A.
	June 26	Ingemar Johansson (Swe) w.rsf.3 Floyd Patterson, New York, U.S.A.
1960	March 3	Floyd Patterson w.ko.6 Ingemar Johansson (Swe), Miami, U.S.A.
	June 20	Floyd Patterson w.ko.5 Ingemar Johansson (Swe), New York, U.S.A.
1961	Dec. 4	Floyd Patterson w.ko.4 Tom McNeeley, Toronto, Canada.
1962	Sep. 25	Sonny Liston w.ko.1 Floyd Patterson, Chicago, U.S.A.
1963	July 22	Sonny Liston w.ko.1 Floyd Patterson, Las Vegas, U.S.A.
1964	Feb. 25	Cassius Clay w.ret.6 Sonny Liston, Miami, U.S.A. *Clay changed his name to Muhammad Ali.* *W.B.A. withdrew recognition of Ali as champion.
1965	March 5	*Ernie Terrell w.pts.15 Eddie Machen, Chicago, U.S.A.
	May 25	Muhammad Ali w.ko.1 Sonny Liston, Lewiston, U.S.A.
	Nov. 1	*Ernie Terrell w.pts.15 George Chuvalo (Can), Toronto, Canada.
	Nov. 22	Muhammad Ali w.rsf.12 Floyd Patterson, Las Vegas, U.S.A.
1966	March 29	Muhammad Ali w.pts.15 George Chuvalo (Can.), Toronto, Canada.
	May 21	Muhammad Ali w.rsf.6 Henry Cooper (U.K.), London, U.K.
	June 28	*Ernie Terrell w.pts.15 Doug Jones, Houston, U.S.A.
	Aug. 6	Muhammad Ali. w.ko.3 Brian London (U.K.), London, U.K.
	Sep. 19	Muhammad Ali w.rsf.12 Karl Mildenberger (W.G.), Frankfurt, W. Germany.
	Nov. 14	Muhammad Ali w.rsf.3 Cleveland Williams, Houston, U.S.A.
1967	Feb. 6	Muhammad Ali w.pts.15 Ernie Terrell, Houston, U.S.A.
	March 22	Muhammad Ali w.ko.7 Zora Folley, New York, U.S.A.
	April 28	*Ali stripped of title by* *W.B.A. *and New York State Athletic Commission for ignoring U.S. army draft.*
1968	March 4	†Joe Frazier w.rsf.11 Buster Mathis, New York, U.S.A.
	April 27	*Jimmy Ellis w.pts.15 Jerry Quarry, Oakland, U.S.A.
	June 24	†Joe Frazier w.ret.2 Manual Ramos (M.), New York, U.S.A.
	Sep. 14	*Jimmy Ellis w.pts.15 Floyd Patterson, Stockholm, Sweden.
	Dec. 10	†Joe Frazier w.pts.15 Oscar Bonavena (Arg.), Philadelphia, U.S.A.
1969	April 22	†Joe Frazier w.ko.1 Dave Zyglewicz, Houston, U.S.A.
	June 23	†Joe Frazier w.rsf.7 Jerry Quarry, New York, U.S.A.
1970	Feb. 16	Joe Frazier w.ret.4 Jimmy Ellis, New York, U.S.A. (*For undisputed title*)
	Nov. 18	Joe Frazier w.ko.2 Bob Foster, Detroit, U.S.A.
1971	March 8	Joe Frazier w.pts.15 Muhammad Ali, New York, U.S.A.
1972	Jan. 15	Joe Frazier w.rsf.4 Terry Daniels, New Orleans, U.S.A.
	May 25	Joe Frazier w.rsf.4 Ron Stander, Omaha, U.S.A.
1973	Jan. 22	George Foreman w.rsf.2 Joe Frazier, Kingston, Jamaica.
	Sep. 1	George Foreman w.ko.1 Joe Roman, Tokyo, Japan.
1974	March 26	George Foreman w.rsf.2 Ken Norton, Caracas, Venezuela.
	Oct. 30	Muhammad Ali w.ko.8 George Foreman, Kinshasa, Zaire.
1975	March 24	Muhammad Ali w.rsf.15 Chuck Wepner, Cleveland, U.S.A.
	May 16	Muhammad Ali w.rsf.11 Ron Lyle, Las Vegas, U.S.A.
	July 1	Muhammad Ali w.pts.15 Joe Bugner (U.K.), Kuala Lumpur, Malaysia.
	Oct. 1	Muhammad Ali w.ret.14 Joe Frazier, Manila, Philippines.
1976	Feb. 20	Muhammad Ali w.ko.5 Jean Pierre Coopman (B.), San Juan, Puerto Rico.
	April 30	Muhammad Ali w.pts.15 Jimmy Young, Landover, U.S.A.
	May 24	Muhammad Ali w.ko.5 Richard Dunn (U.K.), Munich, W. Germany.
	Sep. 28	Muhammad Ali w.pts.15 Ken Norton, New York, U.S.A.
1977	May 16	Muhammad Ali w.pts.15 Alfredo Evangelista (Ur.), Landover, U.S.A.
	Sep. 29	Muhammad Ali w.pts.15 Earnie Shavers, New York, U.S.A.
1978	Feb. 18	Leon Spinks w.pts.15 Muhammad Ali, Las Vegas, U.S.A. †*W.B.C. stripped Spinks of title for refusing to meet Norton.*
	June 10	†Larry Holmes w.pts.15 Ken Norton, Las Vegas, U.S.A.
	Sep. 15	*Muhammad Ali w.pts.15 Leon Spinks, New Orleans, U.S.A.
	Nov. 10	†Larry Holmes w.ko.7 Alfredo Evangelista (Ur.), Las Vegas, U.S.A.
1979	March 24	†Larry Holmes w.rsf.7 Osvaldo Ocasio (P.R.), Las Vegas, U.S.A.
	June 22	†Larry Holmes w.rsf.12 Mike Weaver, New York, U.S.A.
	Sep. 28	†Larry Holmes w.rsf.11 Earnie Shavers, Las Vegas, U.S.A. *Ali announced his retirement as W.B.A. champion.*

Oct. 20   *John Tate w.pts.15 Gerrie Coetzee (S.A.), Johannesburg, South Africa.

1980 Feb. 3   †Larry Holmes w.ko.6 Lorenzo Zanon (I.), Las Vegas, U.S.A.

March 31 †Larry Holmes w.rsf.8 Leroy Jones, Las Vegas, U.S.A.

March 31 *Mike Weaver w.ko.15 John Tate, Knoxville, U.S.A.

July 7   †Larry Holmes w.rsf.7 Scott Le Doux, Minneapolis, U.S.A.

Oct. 2   †Larry Holmes w.ret.10 Muhammad Ali, Las Vegas, U.S.A.

Oct. 25   *Mike Weaver w.ko.13 Gerrie Coetzee (S.A.), Sun City, South Africa.

1981 April 11 †Larry Holmes w.pts.15 Trevor Berbick (Can.), Las Vegas, U.S.A.

June 12   †Larry Holmes w.ret.3 Leon Spinks, Detroit, U.S.A.

Oct. 3   *Mike Weaver w.pts.15 James Tillis, Rosemount, U.S.A.

Nov. 6   †Larry Holmes w.rsf.11 Renaldo Snipes, Pittsburgh, U.S.A.

1982 June 12   †Larry Holmes w.rsf.13 Gerry Cooney, Las Vegas, U.S.A.

Nov. 25   †Larry Holmes w.pts.15 Randall 'Tex' Cobb, Las Vegas, U.S.A.

Dec. 10   *Michael Dokes w.rsf.1 Mike Weaver, Las Vegas, U.S.A.

1983 March 27 †Larry Holmes w.pts.12 Lucien Rodriguez (F.), Scranton, U.S.A.

May 20   †Larry Holmes w.pts.12 Tim Witherspoon, Las Vegas, U.S.A.

May 20   *Mike Dokes drew 15 Mike Weaver, Las Vegas, U.S.A.

Sep. 10   †Larry Holmes w.rsf.5 Scott Frank, Atlantic City, U.S.A.
          Larry Holmes resigned W.B.C. title to join I.B.F.

Sep. 29   *Gerrie Coetzee (S.A.) w.ko.10 Mike Dokes, Richfield, U.S.A.

1984 March 9   †Tim Witherspoon w.pts.12 Greg Page, Las Vegas, U.S.A.

Aug. 31   †Pinklon Thomas w.pts.12 Tim Witherspoon, Las Vegas, U.S.A.

Nov. 9   ‡Larry Holmes w.rsf.12 James Smith, Las Vegas, U.S.A.

Dec. 1   *Greg Page w.ko.8 Gerrie Coetzee (S.A.) Sun City, South Africa.

1985 March 15 ‡Larry Holmes w.rsf.10 David Bey, Las Vegas, U.S.A.

April 29 *Tony Tubbs w.pts.15 Greg Page, New York, U.S.A.

May 20   ‡Larry Holmes w.pts.15 Carl Williams, Reno, U.S.A.

June 15   †Pinklon Thomas w.ko.8 Mike Weaver, Las Vegas, U.S.A.

Sep. 21   ‡Michael Spinks w.pts.15 Larry Holmes, Las Vegas, U.S.A.

1986 Jan. 17   *Tim Witherspoon w.pts.15 Tony Tubbs, Atlanta, U.S.A.

March 22 *Trevor Berbick (Can.) w.pts.12 Pinklon Thomas, Las Vegas, U.S.A.

April 19 ‡Michael Spinks w.pts.15 Larry Holmes, Las Vegas, U.S.A.

Nov. 22   †Mike Tyson w.ko.2 Trevor Berbick, Las Vegas, U.S.A.

June 9   ‡Michael Spinks w.rsf.4 Steffen Tangsted (Nor), Las Vegas, U.S.A.
          ‡Spinks forfeited I.B.F. title for refusing to meet Tony Tucker

1987 March 7   *†Mike Tyson w.pts.12 James Smith, Las Vegas, U.S.A.

May 30   ‡Tony Tucker w.rsf.10 James Douglas, Las Vegas, U.S.A.

May 30   Mike Tyson w.ko.6 Pinklon Thomas, Las Vegas, U.S.A.

Aug. 1   Mike Tyson w.pts.12 Tony Tucker, Las Vegas, U.S.A.

Oct. 16   Mike Tyson w.ko.7 Tyrell Biggs, Atlantic City, U.S.A.

1988 Jan. 22   Mike Tyson w.ko.4 Larry Holmes, Atlantic City, U.S.A.

March 20 Mike Tyson w.ko.2 Tony Tubbs, Tokyo, Japan.

June 28   Mike Tyson w.ko.1 Michael Spinks, Atlantic City, U.S.A.

World Cruiserweight Title Fights
(195 pounds: 13 stone 13 pounds)

In late 1979 the W.B.C. decided that a new weight division was required for boxers whose natural fighting weight was above the light-heavyweight limit of 175 pounds yet were too light to take on men weighing over 190 pounds (later 195 pounds) which was set as the new cruiserweight limit. The first bout at the new weight saw Mate Parlov (Yugo) draw with Marvin Camel at Las Vegas; in a return bout Camel outpointed Parlov to become the first W.B.C. champion. The W.B.A. waited until Feb. 13, 1982 and then recognized Ossie Ocasio (P.R.) as their title-holder after he had outpointed Robbie Williams (S.A.).

1979 Dec. 8   †Mate Parlov (Yugo) drew 15 Marvin Camel, Split, Yugoslavia.

1980 Mar. 31   †Marvin Camel w.pts.15 Mate Parlov (Yugo), Las Vegas, U.S.A.

1981 Nov. 25   †Carlos De Leon (P.R.) w.pts.15 Marvin Camel, New Orleans, U.S.A.

1982 Feb. 13   *Ossie Ocasio (P.R.) w.pts.15 Robbie Williams (S.A.), Johannesburg, South Africa.

Feb. 24   †Carlos De Leon (P.R.) w.rsf.7 Marvin Camel, Atlantic City, U.S.A.

June 27   †S. T. Gordon w.rsf.2 Carlos De Leon (P.R.), Cleveland, U.S.A.

Dec. 16   *Ossie Ocasio (P.R.) w.pts.15 Young Joe Louis, Chicago, U.S.A.

1983 Feb. 16   †S. T. Gordon w.rsf.2 Jesse Burnett, East Rutherford, U.S.A.

May 20   *Ossie Ocasio (P.R.) w.pts.15 Randy Stephens, Las Vegas, U.S.A.

May 21   ‡Marvin Camel w.ko.9 Rick Secorski, Billings, U.S.A.

July 17   †Carlos De Leon w.pts.12 S. T. Gordon, Las Vegas, U.S.A.

Sep. 21   †Carlos De Leon w.rsf.4 Alvaro Lopez (M.), San Jose, U.S.A.

Dec. 13   †Marvin Camel w.ko.5 Roddy McDonald, Halifax, N.S., Can.

1984 March 9   †Carlos De Leon w.pts.12 Anthony Davis, Las Vegas, U.S.A.

May 5   *Ossie Ocasio (P.R.) w.rsf.15 John Odhiambo (Ken), San Juan, Puerto Rico.

June 2   †Carlos De Leon w.pts.12 Bashiru Ali (Nig), Oakland, U.S.A.

Oct. 6   ‡Lee Roy Murphy w.rsf.14 Marvin Camel, Billings, U.S.A.

Dec. 1   *Piet Crous (S.A.) w.pts.15 Ossie Ocasio (P.R.), Sun City, S.A.

Dec. 20   ‡Lee Roy Murphy w.rsf.12 Young Joe Louis, Chicago, U.S.A.

1985 March 29 *Piet Crous (S.A.) w.pts.15 Ossie Ocasio (P.R.), Sun City, S.A.

June 6   †Alfonso Ratcliff w.pts.12 Carlos De Leon, Las Vegas, U.S.A.

July 27   *Dwight Muhammad Qawi w.ko.11 Piet Crous (S.A.), Sun City, S.A.

Sept. 21 †Bernard Benton w.pts.12 Alfonso Ratliff, Las Vegas, U.S.A.

Oct. 19   ‡Lee Roy Murphy w.ko.12 Chisanda Mutti (Zam.), Monte Carlo.

1986 March 22 †Carlos De Leon w.pts.12 Bernard Benton, Las Vegas, U.S.A.

March 23 *Dwight Muhammad Qawi w.rsf.6 Leon Spinks, Reno, U.S.A.

April 19 ‡Lee Roy Murphy w.ko.9 Dorcey Gaymon, San Remo, Italy.

July 12   *Evander Holyfield w.pts.15 Dwight Muhammad Qawi, Atlanta, U.S.A.

Aug. 10   †Carlos De Leon w.rsf.8 Michael Greer, Giardini Naxos, Italy.

Oct. 25   ‡Ricky Parky w.rsf.10 Lee Roy Murphy, Marsala, Sicily.

1987 Feb. 14   *Evander Holyfield w.rsf.7 Henry Tillman, Reno, U.S.A.

Feb. 21   †Carlos De Leon w.rsf.5 Angelo Rottali, Bergamo, Italy.

May 15   *Evander Holyfield w.rsf.3 Ricky Parkey, Las Vegas, U.S.A.

Aug. 15   *Evander Holyfield w.rsf.11 Ossie Ocasio, St. Tropez, France.

Dec. 6   *Evander Holyfield w.ko.4 Dwight Muhammad Qawi, Atlantic City, U.S.A.

1988 Jan. 22   †Carlos De Leon w.pts.12 Jose Maria Flores (Ur.), Atlantic City, U.S.A.

April 9   Evander Holyfield w.ko.8 Carlos De Leon, Las Vegas, U.S.A.

World Light-Heavyweight Title Fights
(175 pounds: 12 stone 7 pounds)

This weight division originated in America and was the brain-child of Lou Houseman, a Chicago newspaperman, who also managed boxers and promoted tournaments. One of the principal fighters in his stable was Jack Root, who found it difficult to make the middleweight limit, but was too light and on the short side to compete among the heavyweights of the day. In an article Houseman proposed that an in-between class be instituted to be known as the light-heavyweight division, the weight being restricted to 175 pounds (12 stone 7 pounds). The fistic fraternity supported this innovation and on April 22, 1903 at Detroit, Michigan, Root outpointed vetran Charles 'Kid' McCoy over ten rounds to decide the ownership of the new division. The class was not introduced in England until 1913 when it was known as the 'Cruiserweight Division', ships of this name in the Royal Navy being of lighter build than full-size battleships. In 1937, however, the British Boxing Board of Control adopted the American title when it issued its first light-heavyweight Lonsdale Belt.

1903	April 22	Jack Root w.pts.10 Charles 'Kid' McCoy, Detroit, U.S.A.
	July 4	George Gardner w.ko.12 Jack Root, Fort Erie, U.S.A.
	Nov. 25	Bob Fitzsimmons (U.K.) w.pts.20 George Gardner, San Francisco, U.S.A.
1905	Dec. 20	Philadelphia Jack O'Brien w.ko.13 Bob Fitzsimmons (U.K.), San Francisco, U.S.A.
1912	May 28	Jack Dillon w.ko.3 Hugo Kelly, Indianapolis, U.S.A.
1914	April 28	Jack Dillon w.pts.10 Al Norton, Kansas City, U.S.A.
1916	April 25	Jack Dillon w.pts.15 Battling Levinsky, Kansas City, U.S.A.
	Oct. 17	Jack Dillon w.pts.10 Tim O'Neill, New York, U.S.A.
	Oct. 24	Battling Levinsky w.pts.12 Jack Dillon, Boston, U.S.A.
1920	Oct. 12	Georges Carpentier (F) w.ko.4 Battling Levinsky, Jersey City, U.S.A.
1922	May 11	Georges Carpentier (F) w.ko.1 Ted 'Kid' Lewis (U.K.), London, England.
	Sep. 24	Battling Siki (Sen) w.ko.6 Georges Carpentier (F.), Paris, France.
1923	March 17	Mike McTigue w.pts.20 Battling Siki (Sen.), Dublin, Ireland.
	Oct. 4	Mike McTigue drew10 Young Stribling, Columbus, U.S.A.
1924	March 31	Mike McTigue ND.12 Young Stribling, Newark, U.S.A.
1925	May 30	Paul Berlanbach w.pts.15 Mike McTigue, New York.
	Sep. 11	Paul Berlanbach w.pts.15 Jimmy Slattery, New York.
	Dec. 11	Paul Berlanbach w.pts.15 Jack Delaney, New York, U.S.A.
1926	June 10	Paul Berlanbach w.pts.15 William 'Young' Stribling, New York, U.S.A.
	July 16	Jack Delaney w.pts.15 Paul Berlanbach, New York, U.S.A.
1927	Aug. 30	Jimmy Slattery w.pts.10 Maxie Rosenbloom, Hartford. U.S.A.
	Oct. 7	Tommy Loughran w.pts.15 Mike McTigue, New York.
	Dec. 12	Tommy Loughran w.pts.15 Jimmy Slattery, New York, U.S.A.
1928	Jan. 6	Tommy Loughran w.pts.15 Leo Lomski, New York, U.S.A.
	June 1	Tommy Loughran w.pts.15 Pete Latzo, Brooklyn, N.Y. U.S.A.
	July 16	Tommy Loughran w.pts.10 Pete Latzo, Wilkes-Barre, U.S.A.
1929	March 8	Tommy Loughran w.pts.10 Mickey Walker, Chicago, U.S.A.
	July 18	Tommy Loughran w.pts.15 Jimmy Braddock, New York, U.S.A.
		Loughran relinquished title to compete as a heavyweight.
1930	Feb. 10	Jimmy Slattery w.pts.15 Lous Scozza, Buffalo, U.S.A.
	June 25	Maxie Rosenbloom w.pts.15 Jimmy Slattery, Buffalo, U.S.A.
	Oct. 22	Maxie Rosenbloom w.ko.11 Abe Bain, New York, U.S.A.
1931	Aug. 5	Maxie Rosenbloom w.pts.15 Jimmy Slattery, New York, U.S.A.
1932	March 18	George Nichols w.pts.10 Dave Maier, Chicago, U.S.A.
	May 31	Lou Scozza w.pts.10 George Nichols, Buffalo, U.S.A.
	July 14	Maxie Rosenbloom w.pts.15 Lou Scozza, Buffalo, U.S.A.
		Rosenbloom gained universal recognition as world champion.
1933	Feb. 22	Maxie Rosenbloom w.pts.10 Al Stillman, St. Louis, U.S.A.
	March 1	Bob Godwin w.pts.10 Joe Knight, Miami, U.S.A.
	March 10	Maxie Rosenbloom w.pts.15 Al Heuser (G), New York, U.S.A.
	March 24	Maxie Rosenbloom w.ko.4 Bob Godwin, New York, U.S.A.
	Nov. 3	Maxie Rosenbloom w.pts.15 Mickey Walker, New York, U.S.A.
1934	Feb. 5	Maxie Rosenbloom drew 15 Joe Knight, Miami, U.S.A.
	Nov. 16	Bob Olin w.pts.15 Maxie Rosenbloom, New York, U.S.A.
1935	Sep. 17	Heinz Lazek (A) w.dis.13 Merlo Preciso (I), Vienna, Austria. *I.B.U. world title.*

1936	Oct. 31	John Henry Lewis w.pts.15 Bob Olin, St. Louis, U.S.A.
	Feb. 25	Heinz Lazek (A) w.ret.5 Rienus de Boer (Nl), Vienna, Austria.
	March 13	John Henry Lewis w.pts.15 Jock McAvoy (U.K.), New York, U.S.A.
	Aug. 3	Heinz Lazek (A) w.ko.9 Emile Olive (F), Vienna, Austria.
	Sep. 1	Gustave Roth (B) w.pts.15 Heinz Lazek (A) Vienna, Austria.
	Oct. 29	Gustave Roth (B) w.pts.15 Adolph Witt (G), Berlin, Germany.
	Nov. 9	Johny Henry Lewis w.pts.15 Len Harvey (U.K.), London, U.K.
1937	Jan. 12	Gustave Roth (B) drew 15 Antonio Rodriguez (Bra), Rio de Janeiro, Brazil.
	March 24	Gustave Roth (B); w.pts.15 Merlo Preciso (I), Brussels, Belgium.
	May 1	Gustave Roth (B) w.pts.15 John Anderson (Swe), Antwerp, Belgium.
	June 3	John Henry Lewis w.ko.8 Bob Olin, St. Louis, U.S.A.
	Dec. 1	Gustave Roth (B) drew 15 Karel Sys (B), Brussels, Belgium.
1938	Jan. 21	Gustave Roth (B) w.pts.15 Jupp Besselmann (G), Berlin, Germany.
	March 25	Adolph Heuser (G) w.ko.7 Gustave Roth (B), Berlin, Germany.
	April 25	John Henry Lewis w.ko.4 Emilio Martinez, Minneapolis, Minn. U.S.A.
	Oct. 28	John Henry Lewis w.pts.15 Al Gainer, New Haven, U.S.A.
	Nov. 28	Tiger Jack Fox w.pts.15 Al Gainer, New York, U.S.A.
1939	Feb. 3	Melio Bettina w.ko.9 Tiger Jack Fox, New York, U.S.A.
	June	*John Henry Lewis relinquished title because of failing eyesight.*
	July 10	Len Harvey (U.K.) w.pts.15 Jock McAvoy (U.K.), London, U.K.
	July 13	Billy Conn w.pts.15 Melio Bettina, New York, U.S.A.
	Sep. 25	Billy Conn w.pts.15 Melio Bettina, Pittsburgh, U.S.A.
	Nov. 17	Billy Conn w.pts.15 Gus Lesnevich, New York, U.S.A.
1940	June 5	Billy Conn w.pts.15 Gus Lesnevich, Detroit, U.S.A.
1941	Jan. 13	Anton Christoforidis (Gr) w.pts.15 Melio Bettina, Cleveland, U.S.A.
	May 22	Gus Lesnevich w.pts.15 Anton Christoforidis (Gr), New York, U.S.A.
	Aug. 26	Gus Lesnevich w.pts.15 Tami Mauriello, New York, U.S.A.
	Nov. 14	Gus Lesnevich w.pts.15 Tami Mauriello, New York, U.S.A.
1942	June 20	Freddie Mills (U.K.) w.ko.2 Len Harvey (U.K.), London, U.K.
1946	May 14	Gus Lesnevich w.rsf.10 Freddie Mills (U.K.), London, U.K.
1947	Feb. 28	Gus Lesnevich w.ko.10 Billy Fox, New York, U.S.A.
1948	March 5	Gus Lesnevich w.ko.1 Billy Fox, New York, U.S.A.
	July 26	Freddie Mills (U.K.) w.pts.15 Gus Lesnevich, London, U.K.
1950	Jan. 24	Joey Maxim w.ko.10 Freddie Mills (U.K.), London, U.K.
1951	Aug. 22	Joey Maxim w.pts.15 Bob Murphy, New York, U.S.A.
1952	June 25	Joey Maxim w.ret.14 Sugar Ray Robinson, New York, U.S.A.
	Dec. 17	Archie Moore w.pts.15 Joey Maxim, St. Louis, U.S.A.
1953	June 24	Archie Moore w.pts.15 Joey Maxim, Ogden, U.S.A.
1954	Jan. 27	Archie Moore w.pts.15 Joey Maxim, Miami, U.S.A.
	Aug. 11	Archie Moore w.ko.15 Harold Johnson, New York, U.S.A.
1955	June 22	Archie Moore w.ko.3 Carl 'Bobo' Olson (Ha), New York, U.S.A.
1956	June 5	Archie Moore w.rsf.10 Yolande Pompey (W.I.), London, U.K.
1957	Sep. 20	Archie Moore w.ko.7 Tony Anthony, Los Angeles, U.S.A.
1958	Dec. 10	Archie Moore w.ko.11 Yvon Durelle (Can), Montreal, Canada.
1959	Aug. 12	Archie Moore w.ko.3 Yvon Durelle (Can), Montreal, Canada.
1961	Feb. 7	Harold Johnson, w.ko.9 Jesse Bowdry, Miami, U.S.A.
	April 24	Harold Johnson w.ko.2 Von Clay, Philadelphia, U.S.A.
	June 10	Archie Moore w.pts.15 Guilio Rinaldi (I), New York, U.S.A.

	Aug. 20	Harold Johnson w.pts.15 Eddie Cotton, Seattle, U.S.A.
1962	May 12	Harold Johnson w.pts.15 Doug Jones, Philadelphia, U.S.A.
	June 23	Harold Johnson w.pts.15 Gustav Scholz (W.G.) Berlin, Germany.
1963	June 1	Willie Pastrano w.pts.15 Harold Johnson, Las Vegas, U.S.A.
1964	April 10	Willie Pastrano w.ko.6 Gregorio Peralta (Arg) New Orleans, U.S.A.
	Nov. 30	Willie Pastrano w.rsf.11 Terry Downes (U.K.), Manchester, U.K.
1965	March 30	Jose Torres (P.R.) w.ko.9 Willie Pastrano, New York, U.S.A.
1966	May 21	Jose Torres (P.R.) w.pts.15 Wayne Thornton, Flushing, U.S.A.
	Aug. 15	Jose Torres (P.R.) w.pts.15 Eddie Cotton (U.K.), Las Vegas, U.S.A.
	Oct. 15	Jose Torres (P.R.) w.ko.2 Chic Calderwood (U.K.), San Juan, Puerto Rico.
	Dec. 16	Dick Tiger (Nig) w.pts.15 Jose Torres (P.R.), New York, U.S.A.
1967	May 16	Dick Tiger (Nig) w.pts.15 Jose Torres (P.R.), New York, U.S.A.
	Nov. 17	Dick Tiger (Nig) w.ko.12 Roger Rouse, Las Vegas, U.S.A.
1968	May 24	Bob Foster w.ko.4 Dick Tiger (Nig), New York, U.S.A.
1969	Jan. 22	Bob Foster w.ko.1 Frank Depaula, New York, U.S.A.
	May 24	Bob Foster w.ko.4 Andy Kendall, West Springfield, U.S.A.
1970	April 4	Bob Foster (U.S.A.) w.ko.4 Roger Rouse, Missoula, U.S.A.
	June 27	Bob Foster w.ko.10 Mark Tessman, Baltimore, U.S.A.
1971	Feb. 27	*Vicente Paul Rondon (Ven) w.ko.6 Jimmy Dupree, Caracas, Venezuela.
	March 2	Bob Foster w.ko.4 Hal Carroll, Scranton, U.S.A.
	April 24	Bob Foster w.pts.15 Ray Anderson, Tampa, U.S.A.
	June 7	*Vicente Paul Rondon (Ven) w.ko.1 Piero Del Papa (1), Caracas, Venezuela.
	Aug. 21	*Vicente Paul Rondon (Ven) w.pts.15 Eddie Jones, Caracas, Venezuela.
	Oct. 26	*Vicente Paul Rondon (Ven) w.ko.13 Gomeo Brennan (Bah), Miami, U.S.A.
	Oct. 29	Bob Foster w.ko.8 Tommy Hicks, Scranton, U.S.A.
	Dec. 15	*Vicente Paul Rondon (Ven) w.ko.8 Doyle Baird, Cleveland, U.S.A.
	Dec. 16	Bob Foster w.ko.3 Brian Kelly, Oklahoma City, U.S.A.
1972	April 7	Bob Foster w.ko.2 Vicente Paul Rondon (Ven), Miami Beach, U.S.A.
	June 27	Bob Foster w.ko.4 Mike Quarry (U.K.), Las Vegas, U.S.A.
	Sep. 26	Bob Foster w.ko.14 Chris Finnegan (U.K.), London, U.K.
1973	Aug. 21	Bob Foster w.pts.15 Pierre Fouri (S.A.), Albuquerque, U.S.A.
	Dec. 1	Bob Foster w.pts.15 Pierre Fouri (S.A.), Johannesburg, South Africa.
1974	June 17	Bob Foster drew 15 Jorge Ahumada (Arg.), Albuquerque, U.S.A.
	Oct. 1	†John Conteh (G.B.) w.pts.15 Jorge Ahumada (Arg), London, U.K.
	Dec. 7	*Victor Galindez (Arg) w.ko.13 Len Hutchins, Buenos Aires, Argentina.
1975	March 11	†John Conteh (U.K.) w.rsf.5 Lonnie Bennet, London, U.K.
	April 7	*Victor Galindez (Arg) w.pts.15 Pierre Fouri (S.A.), Johannesburg, South Africa.
	June 30	*Victor Galindez (Arg) w.pts.15 Jorge Ahumada (Arg), New York, U.S.A.
	Sep. 13	*Victor Galindez (Arg) w.pts.15 Pierre Fouri (S.A.), Johannesburg, South Africa.
1976	March 28	*Victor Galindez (Arg) w.ret.3 Harald Skog (N), Oslo, Norway.
	May 22	*Victor Galindez (Arg) w.ko.15 Ritchie Kates (S.A.), Johannesburg, South Africa.
	Oct. 5	*Victor Galindez (Arg) w.pts.15 Kosie Smith (S.A.), Johannesburg, South Africa.
	Oct. 9	†John Conteh (U.K.) w.pts.15 Alvaro Lopez, Copenhagen, Denmark.
1977	March 5	†John Conteh (U.K.) w.ko.3 Len Hutchins, Liverpool, U.K.

	May 21	†Miguel Cuello (Arg) w.ko.9 Jesse Burnett, Monte Carlo, Monaco.
	June 18	*Victor Galindez (Arg) w.pts.15 Richie Kates (S.A.), Rome, Italy.
	Sep. 17	*Victor Galindez (Arg) w.pts.15 Avaro Lopez, Rome, Italy.
	Nov. 20	*Victor Galindez (Arg) w.pts.15 Eddie Gregory, Turin, Italy.
1978	Jan. 7	†Mate Parlov (Yugo) w.ko.9 Miguel Cuello (Arg), Milan, Italy.
	May 6	*Victor Galindez (Arg) w.pts.15 Alvaro Lopez, Lido Di Camaiore, Italy.
	Jun 17	†Mate Parlov (Yugo) w.pts.15 John Conteh (U.K.), Belgrade, Yugoslavia.
	Sep. 15	*Mike Rossman w.ko.13 Victor Galindez (Arg), New Orleans, U.S.A.
	Dec. 2	†Marvin Johnson w.ko.10 Mate Parlov (Yugo), Marsala, Sicily.
	Dec. 5	*Mike Rossman w.ko.6 Aldo Traversaro (I), Philadelphia, U.S.A.
1979	Apr. 14	*Victor Galindez (Arg) w.ko.10 Mike Rossman, New Orleans, U.S.A.
	Apr. 22	†Matt Franklin w.ko.8 Marvin Johnson, Indianapolis, U.S.A.
	Aug. 18	†Matt Franklin w.pts.15 John Conteh (U.K.), Atlantic City, U.S.A.
	Nov. 30	*Marvin Johnson w.ko.11 Victor Galindez (Arg), New Orleans, U.S.A.
1980	March 29	†Matthew Saad Muhammad w.rsf.4 John Conteh (U.K.), Atlantic City, U.S.A.
	March 31	*Eddie Gregory w.rsf.11 Marvin Johnson, Knoxville, U.S.A.
		Matt Franklin changed his ring name to 'Matthew Saad Muhammad'
		Eddie Gregory changed his ring name to 'Eddie Mustapha Muhammad'
	May 11	†Matthew Saad Muhammad w.rsf.5 Louis Perguad (Cameroons), Halifax, Canada.
	July 13	†Matthew Saad Muhammad w.rsf.14 Alvaro Lopez, Great George, U.S.A.
	July 20	*Eddie Mustapha Muhammad w.rsf.10 Jerry Martin, McAffe, U.S.A.
	Nov. 28	†Matthew Saad Muhammad w.ko.3 Lotte Mwale (Z), San Diego, U.S.A.
	Nov. 29	*Eddie Mustapha Muhammad w.rsf.3 Rudi Koopman (Nl), Los Angeles, U.S.A.
1981	Feb. 28	†Matthew Saad Muhammad w.rsf.11 Vonzell Johnson, Atlantic City, U.S.A.
	Apr. 25	†Matthew Saad Muhammad w.ko.9 Murray Sutherland, Atlantic City, U.S.A.
	July 18	*Michael Spinks w.pts.15 Eddie Mustapha Muhammad, Las Vegas, U.S.A.
	Sep. 26	†Matthew Saad Muhammad w.rsf.11 Jerry Martin, Atlantic City, U.S.A.
	Nov. 7	*Michael Spinks w.rsf.7 Vonzell Johnson, Atlantic City, U.S.A.
	Dec. 19	†Dwight Braxton w.rsf.10 Matthew Saad Muhammad, Atlantic City, U.S.A.
1982	Feb. 13	*Michael Spinks w.pts.15 Eddie Mustapha Muhammad, Atlantic City, U.S.A.
	March 21	†Dwight Braxton w.rsf.6 Jerry Martin, Las Vegas, U.S.A.
	Apr. 11	*Michael Spinks w.ko.8 Murray Sutherland, Atlantic City, U.S.A.
	June 12	*Michael Spinks w.rsf.8 Jerry Celestine, Atlantic City, U.S.A.
	Aug. 7	†Dwight Braxton w.rsf.6 Matthew Saad Muhammad, Philadelphia, U.S.A.
	Sep. 18	*Michael Spinks w.ko.9 Johnny Davis, Atlantic City, U.S.A.
		Dwight Braxton changed his name to 'Dwight Muhammad Qawi'.
	Nov. 20	†Dwight Muhammad Qawi w.rsf.11 Eddie Davis, Atlantic City, U.S.A.
1983	March 18	*Michael Spinks w.pts.15 Dwight Muhammad Qawi, Atlantic City, U.S.A.
	Nov. 25	*Michael Spinks w.rsf.10 Oscar Rivadeneyra, Vancouver, Canada.
1984	Feb. 25	*Michael Spinks w.pts.12 Eddie Davis, Atlantic City, U.S.A.

1985	Feb. 23	*Michael Spinks w.rsf.3 David Sears, Atlantic City, U.S.A.
	June 6	*Michael Spinks w.rsf.8 Jim Macdonald, Las Vegas, U.S.A.
		Spinks relinquished W.B.A. title
	Dec. 10	†J. B. Williamson w.pts.12 Prince Muhammad Mamah (Ghana), Los Angeles, U.S.A.
	Dec. 21	‡Slobodan Kacar (Yugo) w.pts.15 Mustafa Muhammad, Pesaro, Italy.
1986	Feb. 8	*Marvin Johnson w.rsf.7 Leslie Stewart (Tr), Indianapolis, U.S.A.
	April 30	†Dennis Andries (G.B.) w.pts.12 J. B. Williamson, London, U.K.
	Sep. 6	‡Bobby Czys w.rsf.5 Slobodan Kacar (Yugo), Las Vegas, U.S.A.
	Sep. 10	†Dennis Andries (G.B.) w.rsf.9 Tony Sibson (G.B.), London, U.K.
	Sep. 20	*Marvin Johnson w.rsf.13 Jean-Marie Emebe (F.), Indianpolis, U.S.A.
	Dec. 26	‡Bobby Czyz w.ko.1 David Sears, West Orange, U.S.A.
1987	Feb. 21	‡Bobby Czyz w.ko.2 Willie Edwards, Atlantic City, U.S.A.
	March 7	†Thomas Hearns w.rsf.10 Dennis Andries (G.B.), Detroit, U.S.A.
		Hearns relinquished W.B.C. title
	May 3	‡Bobby Czys w.rsf.6 Jim Macdonald, Atlantic City, U.S.A.
	May 23	*Leslie Stewart (Tr) w.rsf.8 Marvin Johnson, Port of Spain, Trinidad.
	Sep. 5	*Virgil Hill w.rsf.4 Leslie Stewart (Tr), Atlantic City, U.S.A.
	Oct. 29	‡Charles Williams w.ret.9 Bobby Czyz, Las Vegas, U.S.A.
	Nov. 21	*Virgil Hill w.pts.12 Rufino Angulo (F.) Paris, France.
	Nov. 27	†Danny La Londe (Can) w.rsf.2 Eddie Davis, Port of Spain, Trinidad.
1988	April 3	*Virgil Hill w.rsf.11 Jean-Marie Emebe (F.), Bismark, U.S.A.
	June 6	*Virgil Hill w.pts.12 Ramzi Hassan, Las Vegas, U.S.A.
	June 10	‡Charles Williams w.ret.11 Richard Caramanolia (F.), Annercy, France.
	June 26	†Danny La Ronde (Can) w.rsf.5 Leslie Stewart (Tr), Port of Spain, Trinidad.

World Super-Middleweight Title Fights
(168 pounds: 12 stone)

1984	March 28	‡Murray Sutherland w.pts.15 Ernie Singleton, Atlantic City, U.S.A.
	July 22	‡Chong-Pal Park (S.K.) w.rsf.11 Murray Sutherland, Seoul, S. Korea.
1985	Jan. 2	‡Chong-Pal Park (S.K.) w.ko.2 Roy Gumbs (G.B.), Seoul, S. Korea.
	June 30	‡Chong-Pal Park (S.K.) w.ko.15 Vinnie Curto, Seoul, S. Korea.
1986	April 11	‡Chong-Pal Park (S.K.) w.rsf.15 Vinnie Curto, Los Angeles, U.S.A.
	July 6	‡Chong-Pal Park (S.K.) drew 2 (tec) Lindell Holmes, Seoul, S. Korea.
	Sep. 14	‡Chong-Pal Park (S.K.) w.pts.15 Marvin Mack, Pusan, S. Korea.
1987	Jan. 25	‡Chong-Pal Park (S.K.) w.rsf.15 Doug Sam (Aus), Seoul, S. Korea.
	May 3	‡Chong-Pal Park (S.K.) w.pts.15 Lindell Holmes, Inchon, S. Korea.
	July 26	‡Chong-Pal Park (S.K.) w.ko.4 Emmanuel Otti (Aus), Kwangju, S. Korea.
	Dec. 6	*Chong-Pal Park (S.K.) w.ko.2 Jesus Gallardo (M), Seoul, S. Korea.
		Chong-Pal Park relinquished I.B.F. title to concentrate on W.B.A. title
1988	March 1	*Chong-Pal Park (S.K.) w.rsf.5 Polly Pasirlon (Ind.), Chonju, S. Korea.
	March 12	‡Graciano Rocchigiani (W.G.) w.rsf.6 Vincent Boulware, Dusseldorf, W. Germany.
	May 23	*Fulgencio Obelmejias (Ven) w.pts.12 Chong-Pal Park (S.K.), Chungju, S. Korea.
	June 3	‡Graciano Rocchigiani (W.G.) w.pts.12 Nicky Walker, West Berlin, W. Germany.

World Middleweight Title Fights
Under Marquess of Queensberry Rules
(160 pounds: 11 stone 6 pounds)

In the early days of glove fighting the middleweights were next in popularity to the heavies and the records show a world title claimant as early as 1884, eight years before there was a recognized world heavyweight titleholder. Although in England there were some notable middleweights, such as Charlie Mitchell, it was left to the Americans to establish the first universally accepted middleweight champion of the world.

At the start the recognized poundage for the middleweight class was set at 154 pounds, but in 1894 Bob Fitzsimmons raised the limit by four pounds to suit his own physical requirements. Even so the stipulated weight wavered until 1909 when the National Sporting Club in London brought matters to a head by proclaiming an 'official' weight for each of the divisions from fly to middle, the latter being set at 11 stone 6 pounds (160 pounds). Of course, the N.S.C. weights concerned only British Championships at that time, but gradually they became universally accepted and remain so to this day.

The records show that the first claimant to the world middleweight title under Marquess of Queensberry Rules was Irish-born John Kelly, who boxed under the ring name of Jack Dempsey. He was so outstandingly superior to his rivals that he was known as 'The Nonpareil'.

1884	July 30	Jack Dempsey w.ko.22 George Fulljames, New York, U.S.A.
1886	Feb. 3	Jack Dempsey w.ko.27 Jack Fogarty, New York, U.S.A.
	March 4	Jack Dempsey w.ko.13 George LaBlanche (Can), New York, U.S.A.
1887	Dec. 13	Jack Dempsey w.ko.15 Johnny Reagan, Long Island, U.S.A.
1889	Aug. 27	Jack Dempsey l.ko.32 George LaBlanche (Can), San Francisco, U.S.A. *(La Blanche used illegal pivot blow to win and Dempsey was declared not to have lost the title)*
1890	Feb. 18	Jack Dempsey w.ko.28 Billy McCarthy (Aust.), San Francisco, U.S.A.
1891	Jan. 14	Bob Fitzsimmons (U.K.) w.rsf.15 Jack Dempsey, New Orleans, U.S.A.
1894	Sep. 26	Bob Fitzsimmons (U.K.) w.ko.2 Dan Creedon (Aust.), New Orleans, U.S.A.
1896	March 2	Charles 'Kid' McCoy w.ko.15 Tommy Ryan, Long Island, U.S.A.
1897	Dec. 17	Charles 'Kid' McCoy w.ko.15 Dan Creedon (Aust), Long Island, U.S.A.
1898	Feb. 25	Tommy Ryan w.ko.18 George Green, San Francisco, U.S.A.
	Oct. 24	Tommy Ryan w.pts.20 Jack Bonner, Coney Island, U.S.A.
1899	Sep. 18	Tommy Ryan w.ko.10 Frank Craig, Coney Island, U.S.A.
1901	March 4	Tommy Ryan w.ko.17 Tommy West, Louisville, U.S.A.
1902	June 24	Tommy Ryan w.ko.3 Johnny Gorman, London, U.K.
	Sep. 15	Tommy Ryan w.ko.6 Kid Carter, Fort Erie, Canada.
1907	Sep. 2	Stanley Ketchel w.ko.32 Joe Thomas, Colma, U.S.A.
	Dec. 12	Stanley Ketchel w.pts.20 Joe Thomas, San Francisco, U.S.A.
1908	May 9	Stanley Ketchel w.ko.20 Jack 'Twin' Sullivan, Colma, U.S.A.
	June 4	Stanley Ketchel w.pts.10 Billy Papke, Milwaukee, U.S.A.
	July 31	Stanley Ketchel w.ko.3 Hugo Kelly, San Francisco, U.S.A.
	Aug. 18	Stanley Ketchel w.ko.2 Joe Thomas, San Francisco, U.S.A.
	Sep. 7	Billy Papke w.ko.12 Stanley Ketchel, Vernon, U.S.A.
	Nov. 26	Stanley Ketchel w.ko.11 Billy Papke, Colma, U.S.A.
1909	June 2	Stanley Ketchel w.ko.4 Tony Caponi, Schenectady, U.S.A.
	July 5	Stanley Ketchel w.pts.20 Billy Papke, Colma, U.S.A.
1910	May 27	Stanley Ketchel w.ko.2 Willie Lewis, New York, U.S.A.
	June 10	Stanley Ketchel w.ko.5 Jim Smith, New York, U.S.A.
1911	Feb. 11	Cycline Johnny Thompson w.pts.20 Billy Papke, Sydney, Australia.
	June 8	Billy Papke w.ko.9 Jim Sullivan (U.K.), London, U.K.
1912	Feb. 22	Frank Mantell w.pts.20 Billy Papke, Sacramento, U.S.A.
1913	March 5	Frank Klaus w.dis.15 Billy Papke, Paris, France.
	Oct. 11	George Chip w.ko.6 Frank Klaus, Pittsburgh, U.S.A.
1914	Jan. 1	‡Eddie McGoorty w.ko.1 Dave Smith (Aust.), Sydney, Australia.

	Feb. 7	‡Eddie McGoorty w.pts.20 Pat Bradley (Aust.), Sydney Australia.
	March 14	‡Jeff Smith w.pts.20 Eddie McGoorty, Sydney, Australia.
	April 6	Al McCoy w.ko.1 George Chip, Brooklyn, U.S.A.
	April 13	‡Jeff Smith w.pts.16 Pat Bradley (Aust.), Sydney, Australia.
	June 6	‡Jeff Smith w.pts.20 Jimmy Clabby, Sydney Australia.
	June 6	‡Jeff Smith w.pts.20 Jimmy Clabby, Sydney, Australia.
	Nov. 28	‡Mick King (Aust.) w.pts.20 Jeff Smith, Sydney, Australia.
	Dec. 26	‡Jeff Smith w.pts.20 Mick King, Sydney, Australia.
1915	Jan. 23	‡Jeff Smith w.dis.5 Les Darcy (Aust.), Sydney, Australia.
	Feb. 20	‡Jeff Smith w.pts.20 Mick King (Aust), Melbourne, Australia.
	May 22	‡Les Darcy (Aust) w.dis.2 Jeff Smith, Sydney, Australia.
	June 12	‡Les Darcy (Aust) w.ko.10 Mick King (Aust), Sydney, Australia.
	July 31	‡Les Darcy (Aust) wko.10 Mick King (Aust), Sydney, Australia.
	Sep. 4	‡Les Darcy (Aust) w.pts.20 Billy Murray, Sydney, Australia.
	Oct. 9	‡Les Darcy (Aust) w.ko.6 Fred Dyer (U.K.), Sydney, Australia.
	Oct. 23	‡Les Darcy (Aust) w.pts.20 Jimmy Clabby, Sydney, Australia.
1916	Jan. 15	‡Les Darcy (Aust) w.pts.20 George 'K.O.' Brown, Sydney, Australia.
	May 15	‡Les Darcy (Aust) w.ko.4 Alex Costica (R), Sydney, Australia.
	Sep. 9	‡Les Darcy (Aust) w.pts.20 Jimmy Clabby, Sydney, Australia.
	Sep. 30	‡Les Darcy (Aust.) w.ko.9 George Chip, Sydney, Australia.
		‡*Recognized only in Australia as for the world title.*
1917	Nov. 14	Mike O'Dowd w.ko.6 Al McCoy, Brooklyn, U.S.A.
1918	Feb. 25	Mike O'Dowd ND, 10 Harry Greb, Brooklyn, U.S.A.
1919	July 17	Mike O'Dowd w.ko.3 Al McCoy, St. Paul, U.S.A.
	Aug. 11	Mike O'Dowd ND, 10 Jackie Clark, Syracuse, U.S.A.
	Sep. 1	Mike O'Dowd ND, 10 Ted 'Kid' Lewis, Syracuse, U.S.A.
	Sep. 19	Mike O'Dowd ND.10 Soldier Bartfield, St. Paul, U.S.A.
	Nov. 6	Mike O'Dowd w.ko.2 Billy Kramer, Paterson, U.S.A.
	Nov. 21	Mike O'Dowd ND.10 Mike Gibbons, St. Paul, U.S.A.
1920	March 1	Mike O'Dowd w.ko.2 Jack McCarron, Philadelphia, U.S.A.
	March 31	Mike O'Dowd w.ko.5 Joe Eagan, Boston, U.S.A.
	May 6	Johnny Wilson w.pts.12 Mike O'Dowd, Boston, U.S.A.
1921	Jan. 17	Johnny Wilson ND.10 George Chip, Pittsburgh, U.S.A.
	March 17	Johnny Wilson w.pts.15 Mike O'Dowd, New York, U.S.A.
	July 27	Johnny Wilson w.dis.7 Bryan Downey, Cleveland, U.S.A.
	Sep. 5	Johnny Wilson ND.12 Bryan Downey, Jersey City, U.S.A.
1922	Aug. 14	Dave Rosenberg w.pts.15 Phil Krug, New York, U.S.A.
	Nov. 30	Mike O'Dowd w.dis.8 Dave Rosenberg, New York, U.S.A.
1923	Aug. 31	Harry Greb w.pts.15 Johnny Wilson, New York, U.S.A.
	Dec. 3	Harry Greb w.pts.10 Bryan Downey, Pittsburgh, U.S.A.
1924	Jan. 18	Harry Greb w.pts.15 Johnny Wilson, New York, U.S.A.
	March 24	Harry Greb w.ko.12 Fay Kaiser, Baltimore, U.S.A.
	June 26	Harry Greb w.pts.15 Ted Moore (U.K.), New York, U.S.A.
1925	July 2	Harry Greb w.pts.15 Mickey Walker, New York, U.S.A.
	Nov. 13	Harry Greb w.pts.15 Tony Marullo, New Orleans, U.S.A.
1926	Feb. 26	Tiger Flowers w.pts.15 Harry Greb, New York, U.S.A.
	Aug. 19	Tiger Flowers w.pts.15 Harry Greb, New York, U.S.A.
	Dec. 3	Mickey Walker w.pts.10 Tiger Flowers, Chicago, U.S.A.
1927	June 30	Mickey Walker w.ko.10 Tommy Milligan (U.K.), London, U.K.
1928	June 21	Mickey Walker w.pts.10 Ace Hudkins, Chicago, U.S.A.
1929	Oct. 29	Mickey Walker w.pts.10 Ace Hudkins, Los Angeles, U.S.A.
1931	*June 19*	*Walker relinquished title.*
1932	Jan. 25	Gorilla Jones w.ko.6 Oddone Piazza (I.) Milwaukee, U.S.A.
	April 26	Gorilla Jones w.pts.12 Young Terry, Trenton, U.S.A.
	June 11	Marcel Thil (F.) w.dis.11 Gorilla Jones, Paris, France.
	July 4	Marcel Thil (F) w.pts.15 Len Harvey (U.K.), London, U.K.
1933	Jan. 13	Ben Jeby w.ko.12 Frank Battaglia (Can), New York, U.S.A.
	Jan. 30	Gorilla Jones w.ko.7 Sammy Slaughter, Cleveland, U.S.A.
	March 17	Ben Jeby drew15 Vince Dundee, New York, U.S.A.

	July 10	Ben Jeby w.pts.15 Young Terry, Newark, U.S.A.
	Aug. 9	Lou Brouillard (Can) w.ko.7 Ben Jeby, New York, U.S.A.
	Oct. 2	Marcel Thil (F) w.pts.15 Kid Tunero (C), Paris, France.
	Oct. 30	Vince Dundee w.pts.15 Lou Brouillard (Can), Boston, U.S.A.
	Dec. 8	Vince Dundee w.pts.15 Andy Callahan, Boston, U.S.A.
1934	Feb. 26	Marcel Thil (F) w.pts.15 Ignacio Ara (Sp), Paris, France.
	May 1	Vince Dundee w.pts.15 Al Diamond, Paterson, U.S.A.
	May 3	Marcel Thil (F) w.pts.15 Gustave Roth (B), Paris, France.
	Sep. 11	Teddy Yarosz w.pts.15 Vince Dundee, Pittsburgh, U.S.A.
	Oct. 15	Marcel Thil (F) drew15 Carmelo Candel (F), Paris, France.
1935	May 4	Marcel Thil (F) w.ko.14 Vilda Jacks (Cze), Paris, France.
	June 1	Marcel Thil (F) w.pts.15 Ignacio Ara (Sp), Madrid, Spain.
	Sep. 19	Ed 'Babe' Risko w.pts.15 Teddy Yarosz, Pittsburgh, U.S.A.
1936	Jan. 20	Marcel Thil (F) w.dis.4 Lou Brouillard (Can), Paris, France.
	Feb. 10	Ed 'Babe' Risko w.pts.15 Tony Fisher, Newark, U.S.A.
	July 11	Freddie Steele w.pts.15 Ed 'Babe' Risko, Seattle, U.S.A.
1937	Jan. 1	Freddie Steele w.pts.10 Gorilla Jones, New York, U.S.A.
	Feb. 15	Marcel Thil (F) w.dis.6 Lou Brouillard (Can), Paris, France.
	Feb. 19	Freddie Steele w.pts.15 Ed 'Babe' Risko, New York, U.S.A.
	May 11	Freddie Steele w.ko.3 Frank Battaglia (Can), Seattle, U.S.A.
	Sep. 11	Freddie Steele w.ko.4 Ken Overlin, Seattle, U.S.A.
	Sep. 23	Fred Apostoli w.rsf.10 Marcel Thil (F), New York, U.S.A.
1938	Feb. 19	Freddie Steele w.ko.7 Carmen Bath, Cleveland, U.S.A.
	April 1	Fred Apostoli w.pts.15 Glen Lee, New York, U.S.A.
	July 26	Al Hostak w.ko.1 Freddie Steele, Seattle, U.S.A.
	Nov. 1	Solly Krieger w.pts.15 Al Hostak, Seattle, U.S.A.
	Nov. 18	Fred Apostoli w.ko.8 Young Corbett III, New York, U.S.A.
1939	June 27	Al Hostak w.ko.4 Solly Krieger, Seattle, U.S.A.
	Oct. 2	Ceferino Garcia (Phil) w.ko.7 Fred Apostoli, New York, U.S.A.
	Dec. 11	Al Hostak w.ko. 1 Eric Seelig (G), Cleveland, U.S.A.
	Dec. 23	Ceferino Garcia (Phil) w.ko.13 Glen Lee, Manila, Philippines.
1940	March 1	Ceferino Garcia (Phil) drew 10 Henry Armstrong, Los Angeles, U.S.A.
	May 23	Ken Overlin w.pts.15 Ceferino Garcia (Phil), New York, U.S.A.
	July 19	Tony Zale w.ko.13 Al Hostak, Seattle, U.S.A.
	Nov. 1	Ken Overlin w.pts.15 Steve Belloise, New York, U.S.A.
	Dec. 13	Ken Overlin w.pts.15 Steve Belloise, New York, U.S.A.
1941	Feb. 21	Tony Zale w.ko.14 Steve Mamakos, Chicago, U.S.A.
	May 9	Billy Soose w.pts.15 Ken Overlin, New York, U.S.A.
	Nov.	*Soose relinquished title.*
	May 28	Tony Zale w.ko.2 Al Hostak, Chicago, U.S.A.
	Nov. 28	Tony Zale w.pts.15 Georgie Abrams, New York, U.S.A.
1946	Sep. 27	Tony Zale w.ko.6 Rocky Graziano, New York, U.S.A.
1947	July 16	Rocky Graziano w.ko.6 Tony Zale, Chicago, U.S.A.
1948	June 10	Tony Zale w.ko.3 Rocky Graziano, Newark, U.S.A.
	Sep. 21	Marcel Cerdan (F) w.ko.12 Tony Zale, Jersey City, U.S.A.
1949	June 16	Jake LaMotta w.ret.10 Marcel Cerdan (F), Detroit, U.S.A.
1950	July 12	Jake LaMotta w.pts.15 Tiberio Mitri (I), New York, U.S.A.
	Sep. 13	Jake LaMotta w.ko.15 Laurent Dauthuille (F), Detroit, U.S.A.
1951	Feb. 14	Ray Robinson w.rsf.13 Jake LaMotta, Chicago, U.S.A.
	July 10	Randolph Turpin (U.K.) w.pts.15 Ray Robinson, London, U.K.
	Sep. 12	Ray Robinson w.rsf.10 Randolph Turpin (U.K.), New York, U.S.A.
1952	March 13	Ray Robinson w.pts.15 Carl 'Bobo' Olson (Ha), San Francisco, U.S.A.
	April 16	Ray Robinson w.ko.3 Rocky Graziano, Chicago, U.S.A.
	Dec. 18	*Robinson announced retirement.*
1953	Oct. 21	Carl 'Bobo' Olson (Ha) w.pts.15 Randolph Turpin (U.K.), New York, U.S.A.
1954	April 2	Carl 'Bobo' Olson (Ha) w.pts.15 Kid Gavilan (C), Chicago, U.S.A.
	Aug. 20	Carl 'Bobo' Olson (Ha) w.pts.15 Rocky Castellani, San

Francisco, U.S.A.

	Dec. 15	Carl 'Bobo' Olson (Ha) w.ko.11 Pierre Langlois (F), San Francisco, U.S.A.
1955	Dec. 9	Ray Robinson w.ko.2 Carl 'Bobo' Olson (Ha), Chicago, U.S.A.
1956	May 18	Ray Robinson w.ko.4 Carl 'Bobo' Olson (Ha), Los Angeles, U.S.A.
1957	Jan. 2	Gene Fullmer w.pts.15 Ray Robinson, New York, U.S.A.
	May 1	Ray Robinson w.ko.5 Gene Fullmer, Chicago, U.S.A.
	Sep. 23	Carmen Basilio w.pts.15 Ray Robinson, New York, U.S.A.
1958	March 25	Ray Robinson w.pts.15 Carmen Basilio, Chicago, U.S.A.
1959	Aug. 28	Gene Fullmer w.ko.14 Carmen Basilio, San Francisco, U.S.A.
	Dec. 4	Gene Fullmer w.pts.15 Spider Webb, Logan, Canada.
1960	Jan. 22	Paul Pender w.pts.15 Ray Robinson, Boston, U.S.A.
	April 20	Gene Fullmer drew 15 Joey Giardello, Boseman, U.S.A.
	June 10	Paul Pender w.pts.15 Ray Robinson, Boston, U.S.A.
	June 29	Gene Fullmer w.ko.12 Carmen Basilio, Salt Lake City, U.S.A.
	Dec. 3	Gene Fullmer drew15 Ray Robinson, Los Angeles, U.S.A.
1961	Jan. 14	Paul Pender w.rsf.7 Terry Downes (U.K.), Boston, U.S.A.
	March 4	Gene Fullmer w.pts.15 Ray Robinson, Las Vegas, U.S.A.
	April 22	Paul Pender w.pts.15 Carmen Basillo, Boston, U.S.A.
	July 11	Terry Downes (U.K.) w.ret.9 Paul Pender, London, U.K.
	Aug. 5	Gene Fullmer w.pts.15 Florentine Fernandez (C), Ogden, U.S.A.
	Dec. 9	Gene Fullmer w.ko.10 Benny 'Kid' Paret (C), Las Vegas, U.S.A.
1962	April 7	Paul Pender w.pts.15 Terry Downes (U.K.), Boston, U.S.A.
	Oct. 23	Dick Tiger (Nig.) w.pts.15 Gene Fullmer, San Francisco, U.S.A.
1963	Feb. 23	Dick Tiger (Nig) drew 15 Gene Fullmer, Las Vegas, U.S.A.
	Aug. 10	Dick Tiger (Nig) w.ko.7 Gene Fullmer, Ibadan, Nigeria.
	Dec. 7	Joey Giardello w.pts.15 Dick Tiger (Nig), New York, U.S.A.
1964	Dec. 14	Joey Giardello w.ps.15 Rubin Carter, Philadelphia, U.S.A.
1965	Oct. 21	Dick Tiger (Nig) w.pts.15 Joey Giardello, New York, U.S.A.
1966	April 25	Emile Griffith (V.I.) w.pts.15 Dick Tiger (Nig), New York, U.S.A.
	July 13	Emile Griffith (V.I.) w.pts.15 Joey Archer, New York, U.S.A.
1967	Jan. 23	Emile Griffith (V.I.) w.pts.15 Joey Archer, New York, U.S.A.
	April 17	Nino Benvenuti (I.) w.pts.15 Emile Griffith (V.I.), New York, U.S.A.
	Sep. 29	Emile Griffith (V.I.) w.pts.15 Nino Benvenuti (I.), Flushing, U.S.A.
1968	March 4	Nino Benvenuti (I.) w.pts.15 Emile Griffith (V.I.), New York, U.S.A.
	Dec. 14	Nino Benvenuti (I) w.pts.15 Don Fullmer, San Remo, Italy.
1969	Oct. 4	Nino Benvenuti (I) w.dis.7 Fraser Scott, Naples, Italy.
	Nov. 22	Nino Benvenuti (I) w.ko.11 Luis Rodriguez (C), Rome, Italy.
1970	May 23	Nino Benvenuti (I) w.ko.8 Tom Bethes, Umag, Yugoslavia.
	Nov. 7	Carlos Monzon (Arg) w.ko.12 Nino Benvenuti (I), Rome, Italy.
1971	May 8	Carlos Monzon (Arg) w.ko.3 Nino Benvenuti (I) Monte Carlo, Monaco.
	Sep. 25	Carlos Monzon (Arg) w.ko.14 Emile Griffith (V.I.), Beunos Aires, Argentina.
1972	May 4	Carlos Monzon (Arg) w.ko.5 Denny Moyer, Rome, Italy.
	June 17	Carlos Monzon (Arg) w.ko.13 Jean-Claude Bouttier (F), Paris, France.
	Aug. 19	Carlos Monzon (Arg) w.ko.5 Tom Bogs (D), Copenhagen, Denmark.
	Nov. 11	Carlos Monzon (Arg) w.pts.15 Bennie Briscoe, Buenos Aires, Argentina.
1973	June 2	Carlos Monzon (Arg) w.pts.15 Emile Griffith (V.I.), Monte Carlo, Monaco.
	Sep. 29	Carlos Monzon (Arg) w.pts.15 Jean-Claude Bouttier (F),

		Paris, France.
1974	Feb. 9	Carlos Monzon (Arg) w.ko.7 Jose Napoles (C), Paris, France.
	May 25	†Rodrigo Valdez (Col) w.ko.7 Bennie Briscoe, Monte Carlo, Monaco.
	Oct. 5	Carlos Monzon (Arg) w.ko.7 Tony Mundine (Aust), Buenos Aires, Argentina.
	Nov. 13	†Rodrigo Valdez (Col) w.ko.11 Gratien Tonna (F), Paris, France.
1975	May 31	†Rodrigo Valdez (Col) w.ko.8 Ramon Mendez (Arg), Cali, Colombia.
	June 30	Carlos Monzon (Arg) w.ko.10 Tony Licata, New York, U.S.A.
	Aug. 16	†Rodrigo Valdez (Col) w.pts.15 Rudy Robles, Cartagena, Colombia.
	Dec. 13	Carlos Monzon (Arg) w.ko.5 Gratien Tonna (F), Paris, France.
1976	March 28	†Rodrigo Valdez (Col) w.ko.4 Max Cohen (F), Paris, France.
	June 26	Carlos Monzon (Arg) w.pts.15 Rodrigo Valdez (Col), Monte Carlo, Monaco.
1977	July 30	Carlos Monzon (Arg) w.pts.15 Rodrigo Valdez (Col), Monte Carlo, Monaco.
	Aug. 29	*Monzon announced retirement.*
	Nov. 5	Rodrigo Valdez (Col) w.pts.15 Bennie Briscoe, Campione, Switzerland.
1978	April 22	Hugo Corro (Arg) w.pts.15 Rodrigo Valdez (Col), San Remo, Italy.
	Aug. 5	Hugo Corro (Arg) w.pts.5 Ronnie Harris, Buenos Aires, Argentina.
	Nov. 11	Hugo Corro (Arg) w.pts.15 Rodrigo Vaidez (Col), Buenos Aires, Argentina.
1979	June 30	Vito Antuofermo (I) w.pts.15 Hugo Corro (Arg), Monte Carlo, Monaco.
	Nov. 30	Vito Antuofermo (I) drew15 Marvin Hagler, Las Vegas, U.S.A.
1980	March 16	Alan Minter (U.K.) w.pts.15 Vito Antuofermo (I), Las Vegas, U.S.A.
	June 28	Alan Minter (U.K.) w.ko.8 Vito Antuofermo (I), London, U.K.
	Sep. 27	Marvin Hagler w.ko.3 Alan Minter (U.K.), London, U.K.
1981	Jan. 17	Marvin Hagler w.rsf.8 Fulgencio Obelmejias (Ven), Boston, U.S.A.
	June 13	Marvin Hagler w.ret.4 Vito Antuofermo (I), Boston, U.S.A.
	Oct. 3	Marvin Hagler w.rsf.11 Mustafa Hamsho, Rosemount, U.S.A.
1982	March 7	Marvin Hagler w.rsf.1 William 'Caveman' Lee, Atlantic City, U.S.A.
	Oct. 31	Marvin Hagler w.ko.5 Fulgencio Obelmejias (Ven), San Remo, Italy.
1983	Feb. 11	Marvin Hagler w.rsf.6 Tony Sibson (G.B.), Worcester, U.S.A.
	May 27	Marvin Hagler w.rsf.4 Wilford Scyplon, Providence, U.S.A.
	Nov. 10	Marvin Hagler w.pts.15 Roberto Duran, Las Vegas, U.S.A.
1984	March 30	Marvin Hagler w.ret.10 Juan Roldan (Arg), Las Vegas, U.S.A.
	Oct.19	Marvin Hagler w.ko.3 Mustafa Hamsho, New York, U.S.A.
1985	April 15	Marvin Hagler w.rsf.3 Thomas Hearns, Las Vegas, U.S.A.
1986	March 10	Marvin Hagler w.ko.11 John Mugabi (U), Las Vegas, U.S.A.
1987	April 6	Ray Leonard w.pts.12 Marvin Hagler, Las Vegas, U.S.A.
		Leonard announced retirement
	Oct. 10	‡Frank Tate w.pts.15 Michael Olajide, Las Vegas, U.S.A.
	Oct. 23	*Sumbu Kalambay (I) w.pts.15 Iran Barkley, Livorno, Italy.
	Oct. 29	†Thomas Hearns w.ko.4 Juan Roldan (Arg), Las Vegas, U.S.A.
1988	Feb. 7	‡Frank Tate w.ko.10 Tony Sibson (G.B.), Stafford, U.K.
	March 5	*Sumbu Kalambay (I) w.pts.12 Mike McCullum, Pesaro, Italy.
	June 6	†Iran Barkley w.rsf.3 Thomas Hearns, Las Vegas, U.S.A.
	June 12	*Sumbu Kalambay (I) w.pts.12 Robbie Sims, Ravenna, Italy.
	July 28	‡Michael Nunn w.rsf.9 Frank Tate, Las Vegas, U.S.A.

World Light-Middleweight Title Fights
(154 pounds: 11 stone)

Owes its origin to the amateurs who devised the class in 1951 because of the many boxers whose natural weight was between the welter and middleweight limits. First world titleholder was Denny Moyer (U.S.A.) after he outpointed Joey Giambra at Portland, Oregon, on Oct. 20, 1962. The W.B.C. was first in the field to create its own champion, awarding the distinction to Miguel de Oliveira (Brazil) after he had outpointed Jose Duran (Spain) at Monte Carlo on May 7, 1975. The W.B.A. recognized Eddie Gazo (Nicaragua) as its titleholder when he outpointed Miguel Castellini (Argentina) on March 5, 1977.

1962	Oct. 20	Denny Moyer w.pts.15 Joey Giambra, Portland, Oregon for vacant title.
1963	Feb. 19	Denny Moyer w.ps.15 Stan Harrington, Honolulu, Hawaii.
	April 29	Ralph Dupas w.pts.15 Denny Moyer, New Orleans, U.S.A.
	June 17	Ralph Dupas w.pts.15 Denny Moyer, Baltimore, U.S.A.
	Sep. 7	Sandro Mazzinghi (I) w.ko.9 Ralph Dupas, Milan, Italy.
	Dec. 2	Sandro Mazzinghi (I) w.ko.13 Ralph Dupas, Sydney, Australia.
1964	Oct. 3	Sandro Mazzinghi (I) w.rsf.12 Tony Montano (I), Genoa, Italy.
	Dec. 11	Sandro Mazzinghi (I) w.pts.15 Fortunato Manca (I), Rome, Italy.
1965	June 18	Nino Benvenuti (I) w.ko.6 Sandro Mazzinghi (I), Milan, Italy.
	Dec. 17	Nino Benvenuti (I) w.pts.15 Sandro Mazzinghi (I) Rome, Italy.
1966	June 25	Kim Ki-Soo (S.K.) w.pts.15 Nino Benvenuti (I), Seoul, S. Korea.
	Dec. 17	Kim Ki-Soo (S.K.) w.pts.15 Stan Harrington, Seoul, S. Korea.
1967	March 10	Kim Ki-Soo (S.K.) w.pts.15 Freddie Little, Seoul, S. Korea.
1968	May 26	Sandro Mazzinghi (I) w.pts.15 Kim Ki-Soo (S.K.), Milan, Italy.
	Oct. 25	Freddie Little w.rsf.9 Sandro Mazzinghi (I), Rome, Italy.
1969	March 17	Freddie Little w.pts.15 Stan Hayward, Las Vegas, U.S.A.
	Sep. 9	Freddie Little w.ko.2 Hisao Minami (J.), Osaka, Japan.
1970	March 20	Freddie Little w.pts.15 Gerhard Piaskowy (W.G.), Berlin, W. Germany.
	July 9	Carmelo Bossi (I) w.pts.15 Freddie Little, Monza, Italy.
1971	April 29	Carmelo Bossi (I) drew15 Jose Hernandez (Sp) Madrid, Spain.
	Oct. 31	Koichi Wajima (J) w.pts.15 Carmelo Bossi (I), Tokyo, Japan.
1972	May 7	Koichi Wajima (J) w.ko.1 Domenico Tiberia (I), Tokyo, Japan.
	Oct. 21	Koichi Wajima (J) w.ko.3 Matt Donovan (Tr), Tokyo, Japan.
1973	Jan. 9	Koichi Wajima (J) drew15 Miguel de Oliveira (Bra), Tokyo, Japan.
	April 19	Koichi Wajima (J) w.pts.15 Ryu Sorimachi (J), Osaka, Japan.
	Aug. 14	Koichi Wajima (J) w.rsf.13 Silvani Bertini (I), Sapporo, Japan.
1974	May 2	Koichi Wajima (J) drew15 Miguel de Oliveira (Arg), Tokyo, Japan.
	June 4	Oscar Albarado w.ko.15 Koichi Wajima (J), Tokyo, Japan.
	Aug. 10	Oscar Albarado w.rsf.8 Ryu Sorimachi (J), Tokyo, Japan.
1975	Jan. 21	Koichi Wajima (J) w.pts.15 Oscar Albarado, Tokyo, Japan.
	May 10	†Miguel de Oliveira (Bra) w.pts.15 Jose Duran (Sp), Monte Carlo, Monaco.
	June 7	*Jae Do Yuh (S.K.) w.ko.7 Koichi Wajima (J), Kitsakyushu, Japan.
	Nov. 11	*Jae Do Yuh (S.K.) w.rsf.6 Masahiro Misako, Shizuoka, Japan.
	Nov. 13	†Elisha Obed (Bah) w.rtd.10 Miguel de Oliveira (Bra), Paris, France.
1976	Feb. 17	*Koichi Wajima (J) w.ko.15 Jae Do Yuh (S.K.), Tokyo, Japan.
	Feb. 28	†Elisha Obed (Bah) w.ko.2 Tony Gardner, Nassau, Bahamas.
	April 25	†Elisha Obed (Bah) w.pts.15 Sea Robinson (Ivory Coast), Abidjan, Ivory Coast.
	May 18	*Jose Duran (Sp) w.ko.14 Koichi Wajima (J), Tokyo, Japan.
	June 18	†Eckhard Dagge (W.G.) w.rtd.10 Elisha Obed (Bah), Berlin, W. Germany.
	Sep. 18	†Eckhard Dagge (W.G.) w.pts.15 Emile Griffith, Berlin, W. Germany.
	Oct. 8	*Miguel Angel Castellini (Arg) w.pts.15 Jose Duran (Sp), Madrid, Spain.
1977	March 6	*Eddie Gazo (Nic) w.pts.15 Miguel Angel Castellini (Arg), Managua, Nicaragua.
	March 15	†Eckhard Dagge (W.G.) drew15 Maurice Hope (U.K.), Berlin, W. Germany.
	June 7	*Eddie Gazo (Nic) w.rsf.11 Koichi Wajima (J), Tokyo, Japan.
	Aug. 6	†Rocky Mattioli (I) w.ko.5 Eckhard Dagge (W.G.), Berlin, W. Germany.
	Sep. 13	*Eddie Gazo (Nic) w.pts.15 Kenji Chibata (J), Tokyo, Japan.
	Dec. 18	*Eddie Gazo (Nic) w.pts.15 Chao Koun Lim (S.K.), Inchon, S. Korea.
1978	March 11	†Rocky Mattioli (I) w.ko.7 Elisha Obed (Bah), Melbourne, Australia.
	May 14	†Rocky Mattioli (I) w.ko.5 Jose Duran (Sp), Pescara, Italy.
	Aug. 9	*Masashi Kudo (J) w.pts.15 Eddie Gazo (Nic), Akita, Japan.
	Dec. 13	*Masashi Kudo (J) w.pts.15 Ho Joo (S.K.), Osaka, Japan.
1979	March 4	†Maurice Hope (U.K.) w.rtd.8 Rocky Mattioli (I), San Remo, Italy.
	March 13	*Masashi Kudo (J) w.pts.15 Manuel Ricardo Gonzalez (Arg), Tokyo, Japan.
	June 20	*Masashi Kudo (J) w.rsf.12 Manuel Ricardo Gonzalez (Arg), Yokkaichi, Japan.
	Sep. 25	†Maurice Hope (U.K.) w.rsf.7 Mike Baker, London, U.K.
	Oct. 24	*Ayub Kalule (U) w.pts.15 Masashi Kudo (J), Akita, Japan.
	Dec. 6	*Ayub Kalule (U) w.pts.15 Steve Gregory, Copenhagen, Denmark.
1980	April 17	*Ayub Kalule (U) w.pts.15 Steve Gregory, Copenhagen, Denmark.
	June 12	*Ayub Kalule (U) w.pts.15 w.pts.15 Emiliano Villa (Col), Copenhagen, Denmark.
	July 12	†Maurice Hope (U.K.) w.rsf.11 Rocky Mattioli (I), London, U.K.
	Sep. 16	*Ayub Kalule (U) w.pts.15 Bushy Bester (S.A.) Aarhus, Denmark.
	Nov. 26	†Maurice Hope (U.K.) w.pts.15 Carlos Herrera (M), London, U.K.
1981	May 24	†Wilfred Benitez (P.R.) w.ko.12 Maurice Hope (U.K.), Las Vegas, U.S.A.
	June 25	*Sugar Ray Leonard w.rsf.9 Ayub Kalule (U), Houston, U.S.A.
	Nov. 7	*Tadeshi Mihara (J) w.pts.15 Rocky Fratto, Rochester, U.S.A.
	Nov. 14	†Wilfred Benitez (P.R.) w.pts.15 Carlos Santos, Las Vegas, U.S.A.
1982	Jan. 30	†Wilfred Benitez (P.R.) w.pts.15 Roberto Duran (Pan), Las Vegas, U.S.A.
	Feb. 2	*Davey Moore w.rsf.6 Tadashi Mihara (J), Tokyo, Japan.
	April 26	*Davey Moore w.ko.5 Charles Weir (S.A.), Johannesburg, South Africa.
	July 17	*Davey Moore w.rsf.10 Ayub Kalule (U), Atlantic City, U.S.A.
	Dec. 3	†Thomas Hearns w.pts.15 Wilfred Benitez (P.R.), Houston, U.S.A.
1983	Jan. 29	*Davey Moore w.ko.4 Gary Guiden, Atlantic City, U.S.A.
	June 16	*Roberto Duran w.rsf.8 Davey Moore, New York, U.S.A. *Duran relinquished W.B.A. title*
1984	Feb. 11	†Thomas Hearns w.pts.12 Luigi Minchillo (I), Detroit, U.S.A.
	March 11	‡Mark Medal w.rsf.5 Earl Hargrove, Atlantic City, U.S.A.
	June 15	†Thomas Hearns w.rsf.2 Roberto Duran, Las Vegas, U.S.A.
	Sept. 15	†Thomas Hearns w.rsf.3 Fred Hutchings, Saginaw, U.S.A.
	Oct. 19	*Mike McCullum (Jam) w.pts.15 Sean Mannion, New York, U.S.A.
	Nov. 2	‡Carlos Santos (P.R.) w.pts.15 Mark Medal, New York, U.S.A.

	Dec. 1	*Mike McCullum (Jam) w.ret.13 Luigi Minchillo (I), Milan, Italy.
1985	June 1	‡Carlos Santos (P.R.) w.pts.15 Louis Acaries (F), Paris, France.
	July 28	*Mike McCullum (Jam) w.rsf.8 David Braxton, Miami, U.S.A.
1986	June 4	‡Buster Drayton w.pts.15 Carlos Santos (P.R.), East Rutherford, U.S.A.
	June 23	†Thomas Hearns w.rsf.8 Mark Medal, Las Vegas, U.S.A.
	Aug. 23	*Mike McCullum (Jam) w.rsf.2 Julian Jackson (V.I.), Miami, U.S.A.
	Aug. 24	‡Buster Drayton w.rsf.10 Davey Moore, Juan-les-Pins, France.
		Hearns relinquished W.B.C. title
	Oct. 25	*Mike McCullum (Jam) w.rsf.9 Said Skouma (Alg), Paris, France.
	Dec. 5	†Duane Thomas w.ret.3 John Mugabi (U), Las Vegas, U.S.A.
1987	March 27	‡Buster Drayton w.ret.10 Said Skouma (Alg), Cannes, France.
	April 18	*Mike McCullum (Jam) w.rsf.10 Milton McCrory, Phoenix, U.S.A.
	June 27	‡Matthew Hilton (Can) w.pts.15 Buster Drayton, Montreal, Canada.
	July 12	†Lupino Aquino (M) w.pts.12 Duane Thomas, Bordeaux, France.
	July 18	*Mike McCullum (Jam) w.ko.5 Don Curry, Las Vegas, U.S.A.
		McCullum relinquished W.B.A. title
	Oct. 2	†Giafranco Rosi (I) w.pts.12 Lupino Aquino (M), Perugia, Italy.
	Oct. 16	‡Matthew Hilton (Can) w.rsf.2 Jack Callahan, Atlantic City, U.S.A.
	Nov. 21	*Julian Jackson w.rsf.3 In-Chul Baek (S.K.), Las Vegas, U.S.A.
1988	Jan. 3	†Giafranco Rosi (I) w.ko.7 Duane Thomas, Genoa, Italy.

World Welterweight Title Fights
(147 pounds: 10 stone 7 pounds)

This class has a long history, the first claimant to the world championship being Paddy Duffy from Boston who defeated William McMillan, an Englishman, in 17 rounds on Oct. 30, 1888 at Fort Foote, Vancouver. Joe Walcott, known as The Barbados Demon because of his destructive punching power, was one of the outstanding welters. He reigned for five years and was 33 before losing his crown. Following him there came such notables as Jack Britton, Ted 'Kid' Lewis, Jimmy McLarnin, Barney Ross, Henry Armstrong, Kid Gavilan and Jose Napoles. On July 18, 1976 the W.B.A. refused to acknowledge Carlos Palomino, the W.B.C. champion, and crowned Pipino Cuevas as welter king. The division was burdened with two champions until Sugar Ray Leonard (W.B.C.) stopped Thomas Hearns (W.B.A.) in 14 rounds at Las Vegas on Sept. 16, 1981 to gain the indisputed title, but split again on his retirement.

1888	Oct. 30	Paddy Duffy w.ko.17 William McMillan (U.K.), Fort Foote, U.S.A.
1892	Dec. 14	Mysterious Billy Smith w.ko.14 Danny Needham, San Francisco, U.S.A.
1893	April 17	Mysterious Billy Smith w.ko.2 Tom Williams (Aust), New York, U.S.A.
1894	July 26	Tommy Ryan w.pts.20 Mysterious Billy Smith, Minneapolis, U.S.A.
1895	Jan. 18	Tommy Ryan w.ko.3 Jack Dempsey, New York, U.S.A.
	May 27	Tommy Ryan dnc.18 Mysterious Billy Smith, New York, U.S.A.
1896	March 2	Charles 'Kid' McCoy w.ko.15 Tommy Ryan, Maspeth, U.S.A.
	Nov. 26	Tommy Ryan w.dis.9 Mysterious Billy Smith, Maspeth, U.S.A.
1897	Dec. 23	Tommy Ryan w.ko.4 Bill Payne, Syracuse, U.S.A.
1898	Feb. 24	Tommy Ryan w.ko.9 Tom Tracy, Syracuse, U.S.A.
	June 13	Tommy Ryan w.ko.14 Tommy West, New York, U.S.A.
	Aug. 25	Mysterious Billy Smith w.pts.25 Matty Matthews, New York, U.S.A.
	Oct. 7	Mysterious Billy Smith w.pts.25 Charly McKeever, New York, U.S.A.
	Dec. 6	Mysterious Billy Smith w.pts.20 Joe Walcott (Bar), New York, U.S.A.
1899	June 30	Mysterious Billy Smith drew 20 Charley McKeever, New York, U.S.A.
1900	Jan. 15	Jim 'Rube' Ferns w.dis.21 Mysterious Billy Smith, Buffalo, U.S.A.
	Oct. 16	Matt Mattews w.pts.15 Jim 'Rube' Ferns, Detroit, U.S.A.
1901	April 29	Matty Matthews w.pts.20 Tom Couhig, Louisville, U.S.A.
	May 24	Jim 'Rube' Ferns w.ko.10 Matty Matthews, Toronto, Canada.
	Sep. 23	Jim 'Rube' Ferns w.ko.9 Frank Erne, Fort Erie, U.S.A.
	Dec. 18	Joe Walcott (Bar) w.ko.5 Jim 'Rube' Ferns, Fort Erie, U.S.A.
1902	June 23	Joe Walcott (Bar) w.pts.15 Tommy West, London, England.
1904	April 30	Dixie Kid w.dis.20 Joe Walcott (Bar), San Francisco, U.S.A.
	May 12	Dixie Kid drew 20 Joe Walcott (Bar), San Francisco, U.S.A.
	Sep. 30	Joe Walcott (Bar) drew 20 Joe Gans, San Francisco, U.S.A.
1906	Oct. 16	Honey Mellody w.pts.15 Joe Walcott (Bar), Chelsea, U.S.A.
	Nov. 29	Honey Mellody w.rsf.12 Joe Walcott (Bar), Chelsea, U.S.A.
1907	April 23	Mike 'Twin' Sullivan w.pts.20 Honey Mellody, Los Angeles, U.S.A.
	Nov. 1	Mike 'Twin' Sullivan w.ret.20 Frank Field, Goldfield, U.S.A.
	Nov. 27	Mike 'Twin' Sullivan w.ko.13 Kid Farmer, Los Angeles, U.S.A.
1908	April 20	Harry Lewis w.ko.4 Honey Mellody, Boston, U.S.A.
	April 23	Mike 'Twin' Sullivan w.ret.25 Jimmy Gardner, Los Angeles, U.S.A.
	Nov. 7	Jimmy Gardner w.ret.15 Jimmy Clabby, New Orleans, U.S.A.
	Nov. 26	Jimmy Gardner drew 20 Jimmy Clabby, New Orleans, U.S.A.
1910	Feb. 19	Harry Lewis drew 25 Willie Lewis, Paris, France.
	April 23	Harry Lewis drew 25 Willie Lewis, Paris, France.
	May 4	Harry Lewis w.ko.3 Peter Brown (U.K.), Paris, France.
	June 27	Harry Lewis w.rtd.7 Harry 'Young' Joseph (U.K.), London, U.K.
	Nov. 2	Jimmy Clabby w.rsf.7 Bob Briant, Sydney, Australia.
	Dec. 26	Jimmy Clabby w.ko.1 Guy Devitt, Brisbane, Australia.
1911	Jan. 25	Harry Lewis w.ko.4 Johnny Summer, London, U.K.
1914	Jan. 1	Waldemar Holberg (D) w.pts.20, Ray Bronson, Melbourne, Australia.
	Jan. 24	Tom McCormick w.dis.6 Waldemar Holberg (D) Melbourne, Australia.
	Feb. 28	Matt Wells (U.K.) w.rsf.7 Ray Bronson, Sydney, Australia.
	March 21	Matt Wells (U.K.) w.pts.20 Tom McCormick (U.K.), Sydney, Australia.
1915	June 1	Mike Gower w.pts.12 Matt Wells (U.K.) Boston, U.S.A.
	June 22	Jack Britton w.pts.12 Mike Glover, Boston, U.S.A.
	Aug. 31	Ted 'Kid' Lewis (U.K.) w.pts.12 Jack Britton, Boston, U.S.A.
	Sep. 27	Ted 'Kid' Lewis (U.K.) w.pts.12 Jack Britton, Boston, U.S.A.
	Dec. 28	Ted 'Kid' Lewis (U.K.) ND.10 Willie Ritchie, New York, U.S.A.
1916	April 24	Jack Britton w.pts.20 Ted 'Kid' Lewis (U.K.), New Orleans, U.S.A.
	June 6	Jack Britton w.pts.12 Mike O'Dowd, Boston, U.S.A.
	Oct. 17	Jack Britton w.pts.12 Ted 'Kid' Lewis (U.K.), Boston, U.S.A.
	Nov. 14	Jack Britton drew12 Ted 'Kid' Lewis (U.K.), Boston, U.S.A.
	Nov. 21	Jack Britton w.pts.12 Charlie White, Boston, U.S.A.
1917	March 26	Jack Britton ND.10 Ted 'Kid' Lewis (U.K.), Cincinnati, U.S.A.
	May 9	Jack Britton ND.10 Ted 'Kid' Lewis (U.K.), Toronto, Canada.
	June 6	Jack Britton ND.10 Ted 'Kid' Lewis (U.K.), St. Louis, U.S.A.
	June 14	Jack Britton ND.10 Ted 'Kid' Lewis (U.K.), New York, U.S.A.
	June 25	Ted 'Kid' Lewis (U.K.) w.pts.20 Jack Britton, Dayton, U.S.A.

	July 4	Ted 'Kid' Lewis ND.15 Johnny Griffiths, Akron, U.S.A.
	Nov. 13	Ted 'Kid' Lewis w.rsf.4 Johnny McCarthy, San Francisco, U.S.A.
1918	May 17	Ted 'Kid' Lewis (U.K.) w.ret.20 Johnny Tillman, Denver, U.S.A.
	July 4	Ted 'Kid' Lewis (U.K.) ND.20 Johnny Griffiths, Akron, U.S.A.
	Sep. 23	Ted 'Kid' Lewis (N.K.) ND.8 Benny Leonard, Newark, U.S.A.
1919	March 10	Ted 'Kid' Lewis (U.K.) ND.8 Johnny Griffiths, Memphis, U.S.A.
	March 17	Jack Britton w.ko.9 Ted 'Kid' Lewis (U.K.), Canton, U.S.A.
	May 5	Jack Britton w.pts.15 Johnny Griffiths, Buffalo, U.S.A.
	May 19	Jack Britton ND.10 Joe Welling, Syracuse, U.S.A.
	Aug. 7	Jack Britton ND.12 Johnny Griffiths, Denver, U.S.A.
	Nov. 5	Jack Britton ND.12 Johnny Tillman, Detroit, U.S.A.
	Dec. 1	Jack Britton w.ko.11 Billy Ryan, Canton, U.S.A.
	Dec. 4	Jack Britton ND.10 Steve Latzo, Wilkes-Barre, U.S.A.
1920	May 31	Jack Britton w.pts.15 Johnny Griffiths, Akron, U.S.A.
	Sep. 6	Jack Britton w.pts.10 Ray Bronson, Cedar Point, U.S.A.
	Sep. 13	Jack Britton ND.10 Johnny Tillman, Cleveland, U.S.A.
	Dec. 6	Jack Britton ND.10 Pinkey Mitchell, Milwaukee, U.S.A.
1921	Feb. 7	Jack Britton w.pts.15 Ted 'Kid' Lewis (U.K.), New York, U.S.A.
	March 7	Jack Britton ND.10 Johnny Tillman, Des Moines, U.S.A.
	June 3	Jack Britton drew10 Dave Shade, Portland, U.S.A.
	June 10	Jack Britton drew10 Frank Barrieau, Portland, U.S.A.
	July 18	Jack Britton ND.12 Mickey Walker, Newark, U.S.A.
1922	Feb. 17	Jack Britton drew15 Dave Shade, New York, U.S.A.
	June 26	Jack Britton w.dis.13 Benny Leonard, New York, U.S.A.
	Nov. 1	Mickey Walker w.pts.15 Jack Britton, New York, U.S.A.
1923	March 22	Mickey Walker ND.12 Pete Latzo, Newark, U.S.A.
	Oct. 8	Mickey Walker dnc.9 Jimmy Hones, Newark, U.S.A.
1924	June 2	Mickey Walker w.pts.10 Lew Tendler, Philadelphia, U.S.A.
	Oct. 1	Mickey Walker w.ko.6 Bobby Barrett, Philadelphia, U.S.A.
1925	Sep. 21	Mickey Walker w.pts.15 Dave Shade, New York, U.S.A.
	Nov. 25	Mickey Walker ND.12 Sailor Friedman, Newark, U.S.A.
1926	May 20	Pete Latzo w.pts.10 Mickey Walker, Scranton, U.S.A.
	June 29	Pete Latzo w.ko.5 Willie Harmon, Newark, U.S.A.
	Sep. 9	Pete Latzo w.dis.4 George Levine, New York, U.S.A.
1927	Jan. 3	Joe Dundee w.pts.15 Pete Latzo, New York, U.S.A.
1928	July 7	Joe Dundee w.ko.8 Hilario Martinez (Sp), Barcelona, Spain.
	Aug. 30	Young Jack Thompson w.rsf.2 Joe Dundee, Chicago, U.S.A.
1929	March 25	Jackie Fields w.pts.10 Young Jack Thompson, Chicago, U.S.A.
	July 25	Jackie Fields w.dis.2 Joe Dundee, Detroit, U.S.A.
1930	May 9	Young Jack Thompson w.pts.15 Jackie Fields, Detroit, U.S.A.
	Sep. 5	Tommy Freeman w.pts.15 Young Jack Thompson, Cleveland, U.S.A.
1931	April 14	Young Jack Thompson w.ko.12 Tommy Freeman, Cleveland, U.S.A.
	Oct. 23	Lou Brouillard w.pts.15 Young Jack Thompson, Boston, U.S.A.
1932	Jan. 28	Jackie Fields w.pts.10 Lou Brouillard, Chicago, U.S.A.
1933	Feb. 22	Young Corbett III w.pts.10 Jackie Fields, San Francisco, U.S.A.
	May 29	Jimmy McLarnin w.ko.1 Young Corbett III, Los Angeles, U.S.A.
1934	May 28	Barney Ross w.pts.15 Jimmy McLarnin, New York, U.S.A.
	Sep. 17	Jimmy McLarnin w.pts.15 Barney Ross, New York, U.S.A.
	Dec. 10	Jimmy McLarnin w.pts.12 Bobby Pacho (M), Cleveland, U.S.A.
1935	May 28	Barney Ross w.pts.15 Jimmy McLarnin, New York, U.S.A.
1936	Nov. 27	Barney Ross w.pts.15 Izzy Jannazzo, New York, U.S.A.
1937	Sep. 23	Barney Ross w.pts.15 Ceferino Garcia (Phil), New York, U.S.A.
1938	May 31	Henry Armstrong w.pts.15 Barney Ross, New York, U.S.A.
	Nov. 25	Henry Armstrong w.pts.15 Ceferino Garcia (Phi), New

		York, U.S.A.
1939	Jan. 10	Henry Armstrong w.pts.10 Baby Arizmendi (M), Los Angeles, U.S.A.
	March 4	Henry Armstrong w.ko.4 Bobby Pacho (M), Havana, Cuba.
	March 16	Henry Armstrong w.ko.1 Lew Feldman, St. Louis, U.S.A.
	March 31	Henry Armstrong w.ko.12 Davey Day, New York, U.S.A.
	May 25	Henry Armstrong w.pts.15 Ernie Roderick (U.K.), London, U.K.
	Oct. 9	Henry Armstrong w.ko.4 Al Manfredo, Des Moines, U.S.A.
	Oct. 13	Henry Armstrong w.ko.2 Howard Scott, Minneapolis, U.S.A.
	Oct. 20	Henry Armstrong w.ko.3 Ritchie Fontaine, Seattle, U.S.A.
	Oct. 24	Henry Armstrong w.pts.10 Jimmy Garrison, Los Angeles, U.S.A.
	Oct. 30	Henry Armstrong w.ko.4 Bobby Pacho (M) Denver, U.S.A.
	Dec. 11	Henry Armstrong w.ko.7 Jimmy Garrison, Cleveland, U.S.A.
1940	Jan. 4	Henry Armstrong w.ko.5 Joe Ghnouly, St. Louis, U.S.A.
	Jan. 24	Henry Armstrong w.ko.9 Pedro Montanez (P.R.), New York, U.S.A.
	April 26	Henry Armstrong w.ko.7 Paul Junior, Boston, U.S.A.
	May 24	Henry Armstrong w.ko.5 Ralph Zanelli, Boston, U.S.A.
	June 21	Henry Armstrong w.ko.3 Paul Junior, Portland, U.S.A.
	Sep. 23	Henry Armstrong w.ko.4 Phil Furr, Washington, D.C., U.S.A.
	Oct. 4	Fritzie Zivic w.pts.15 Henry Armstrong, New York, U.S.A.
	Dec. 20	Fritzie Zivic drew10, Lew Jenkins, New York, U.S.A.
1941	Jan. 17	Fritzie Zivic w.ko.12 Henry Armstrong, New York, U.S.A.
	July 21	Freddie 'Red' Cochrane w.pts.15 Fritzie Zivic, Newark, U.S.A.
1946	Feb. 1	Marty Servo w.ko.4 Freddie 'Red' Cochrane, New York, U.S.A.
	Dec. 20	Ray Robinson w.pts.15 Tommy Bell, New York, U.S.A.
1947	June 24	Ray Robinson w.ko.8 Jimmy Doyle, Cleveland, U.S.A.
	Dec. 19	Ray Robinson w.ko.6 Chuck Taylor, Detroit, U.S.A.
1948	June 28	Ray Robinson w.pts.15 Bernard Docusen (Phi), Chicago, U.S.A.
1949	July 11	Ray Robinson w.pts.15 Kid Gavilan, Philadelphia, U.S.A.
1950	Aug. 9	Ray Robinson w.pts.15 Charley Fusari, Jersey City, U.S.A.
1951	*Feb. 15*	*Robinson relinquished welterweight title.*
	May 18	Kid Gavilan (C) w.pts.15 Johnny Bratton, New York, U.S.A.
	Aug. 29	Kid Gavilan (C) w.pts.15 Billy Graham, New York, U.S.A.
1952	Feb. 4	Kid Gavilan (C) w.pts.15 Bobby Dykes, Miami, U.S.A.
	July 7	Kid Gavilan (C) w.ko.11 Gil Turner, Philadelphia, U.S.A.
	Oct. 5	Kid Gavilan (C) w.pts.15 Billy Graham, Havana, Cuba.
1953	Feb. 11	Kid Gavilan (C) w.ko.10 Chuck Davey, Chicago, U.S.A.
	Sep. 18	Kid Gavilan (C) w.pts.15 Carmen Basilio, Syracuse, U.S.A.
	Nov. 13	Kid Gavilan (C) w.pts.15 Johnny Bratton, Chicago, U.S.A.
1954	Oct. 20	Johnny Saxton w.pts.15 Kid Gavilan (C), Philadelphia, U.S.A.
1955	April 1	Tony DeMarco w.rsf.14 Johnny Saxton, Boston, U.S.A.
	June 10	Carmen Basilio w.rsf.12 Tony DeMarco, Syracuse, U.S.A.
	Nov. 30	Carmen Basilio w.ko.12 Tony DeMarco, Boston, U.S.A.
1956	March 14	Johnny Saxton w.pts.15 Carmen Basilio, Chicago, U.S.A.
	Sep. 12	Carmen Basilio w.ko.9 Johnny Saxton, Syracuse, U.S.A.
1957	Feb. 22	Carmen Basilio w.ko.2 Johnny Saxton, Cleveland, U.S.A.
1958	June 6	Virgil Akins w.rsf.4 Vince Martinez, St. Louis, U.S.A.
	Dec. 5	Don Jordan w.pts.15 Virgil Akins, Los Angeles, U.S.A.
1959	April 24	Don Jordan w.pts.15 Vigil Akins, St. Louis, U.S.A.
	July 10	Don Jordan w.pts.15 Denny Moyer, Portland, U.S.A.
1960	May 27	Benny 'Kid' Paret (C) w.pts.15 Don Jordan, Los Angeles, U.S.A.
	Dec. 10	Benny 'Kid' Paret (C) w.pts.15 Federico Thompson, New York, U.S.A.
1961	April 1	Emile Griffith (W.I.) w.ko.13 Benny 'Kid' Paret (C), Miami, U.S.A.
	June 3	Emile Griffith (W.I.) w.ko.12 Gaspar Ortega, Los Angeles, U.S.A.

Sep. 30   Benny 'Kid' Paret (C) w.pts.15 Emile Griffith (W.I.), New York, U.S.A.

1962   March 24   Emile Griffith (W.I.) w.rsf.12 Benny 'Kid' Paret (C), New York, U.S.A.

July 13   Emile Griffith (W.I.) w.pts.15 Ralph Dupas, Las Vegas, U.S.A.

Dec. 8   Emile Griffith w.ko.9 Jorge Fernandez, Las Vegas, U.S.A.

1963   March 21   Luis Rodriguez (C) w.pts.15 Emile Griffith (W.I.), Los Angeles, U.S.A.

June 8   Emile Griffith (W.I.) w.rsf.15 Luis Rodriguez (C), New York, U.S.A.

1964   June 12   Emile Griffith (W.I.) w.pts.15 Luis Rodriguez (C), Las Vegas, U.S.A.

Sep. 22   Emile Griffith (W.I.) w.pts.15 Brian Curvis (U.K.), London, U.K.

1965   March 30   Emile Griffith (W.I.) w.pts.15 Jose Stable, New York, U.S.A.

Dec. 10   Emile Griffith (W.I.) w.pts.15 Manuel Gonzalez, New York, U.S.A.

1966   Aug. 24   *Curtis Cokes w.pts.15 Manny Gonzalez, New Orleans, U.S.A.

Nov. 28   Curtis Cokes w.pts.15 Jean Josselin (F), Dallas, U.S.A.

1967   May 19   Curtis Cokes w.rsf.10 Francois Pavilla (F), Dallas, U.S.A.

Oct. 2   Curtis Cokes w.rsf.8 Charley Shipes, Oakland, U.S.A.

1968   April 16   Curtis Cokes w.rsf.5 Willie Ludick (S.A.), Dallas, U.S.A.

Oct. 21   Curtis Cokes w.pts.15 Ramon La Cruz (Arg), New Orleans, U.S.A.

1969   April 18   Jose Napoles (M) w.rsf.13 Curtis Cokes, Inglewood, U.S.A.

June 29   Jose Napoles (M) w.ret.10 Curtis Cokes, Mexico City, U.S.A.

Oct. 17   Jose Napoles (M) w.pts.15 Emile Griffith (W.I.), Inglewood, U.S.A.

1970   Feb. 15   Jose Napoles (M) w.rsf.15 Ernie Lopez, Los Angeles, U.S.A.

Dec. 3   Billy Backus w.rsf.4 Jose Napoles (M), Syracuse, U.S.A.

1971   June 4   Jose Napoles (M) w.rsf.8 Billy Backus, Inglewood, U.S.A.

Dec. 14   Jose Napoles (M) w.pts.15 Hedgemon Lewis, Inglewood, U.S.A.

1972   March 28   Jose Napoles (M) w.ko.7 Ralph Charles (U.K.), London, U.K.

June 10   Jose Napoles (M) w.rsf.2 Adolph Pruitt, Monterrey, Mexico.

1973   Feb. 28   Jose Napoles (M) w.ko.7 Ernie Lopez, Inglewood, U.S.A.

June 21   Jose Napoles (M) w.pts.15 Roger Menetrey (F), Grenoble, France.

Sep. 22   Jose Napoles (M) w.pts.15 Clyde Gray (Can), Toronto, Canada.

1974   Aug. 3   Jose Napoles (M) w.rsf.9 Hedgemon Lewis, Mexico City, Mexico.

Dec. 14   Jose Napoles (M) w.ko.3 Horacio Saldano (Arg), Mexico City, Mexico.

1975   March 29   Jose Napoles (M) w.tec.12 Armando Muniz (M), Acapulco, Mexico.

June 28   *Angel Espada (P.R.) w.pts.15 Clyde Gray (Can), San Juan, Puerto Rico.

July 12   †Jose Napoles (M) w.pts.15 Armando Muniz (M), Mexico City, Mexico.

Oct. 11   *Angel Espada (P.R.) w.pts.15 Johnny Gant, Ponce, U.S.A.

Dec. 12   †John H. Stracey (U.K.) w.rsf.6 Jose Napoles (M), Mexico City, Mexico.

1976   March 20   †John H. Stracey (U.K.) w.rsf.10 Hedgemon Lewis, London, U.K.

April 27   *Angel Espada (P.R.) w.rsf.8 Alfonso Hayman, San Juan, Puerto Rico.

June 22   †Carlos Palomino (M) w.rsf.12 John H. Stracey (U.K.), London, U.K.

July 17   *Jose Pipino Cuevas (M) w.ko.2 Angel Espada (P.R.), Mexicali, Mexico.

Oct. 27   *Jose Pipino Cuevas (M) w.rsf.6 Shoji Tsujimoto (J), Kanazewa, Japan.

1977   Jan. 22   †Carlos Palomino (M) w.rsf.15 Armando Muniz (M), Los Angeles, U.S.A.

March 12   *Jose Pipino Cuevas (M) w.rsf.2 Miguel Campanino (Arg), Mexico City, Mexico.

June 14   †Carlos Palomino (M) w.ko.11 Dave 'Boy' Green (U.K.), London, U.K.

Aug. 6   *Jose Pipino Cuevas (M) w.ko.2 Clyde Gray (Can), Los Angeles, U.S.A.

Sep. 13   †Carlos Palomino (M) w.pts.15 Everaldo Azevedo (Bra), Los Angeles, U.S.A.

Nov. 19   *Jose Pipino Cuevas (M) w.rsf.11 Angel Espada (P.R.), San Juan, Puerto Rico.

Dec. 10   †Carlos Palomino (M) w.ko.13 Jose Palcios (M), Los Angeles, U.S.A.

1978   Feb. 11   †Carlos Palomino (M) w.ko.7 Ryu Sorimachi (J), Las Vegas, U.S.A.

March 4   *Jose Pipino Cuevas (M) w.rsf.9 Harold Weston, Los Angeles, U.S.A.

March 18   †Carlos Palomino (M) w.rsf.9 Mimoun Mohatar (Morocco), Las Vegas, U.S.A.

May 20   *Jose Pipino Cuevas (M) w.rsf.1 Billy Backus, Los Angeles, U.S.A.

May 27   †Carlos Palomino (M) w.pts.15 Armando Muniz (M), Los Angeles, U.S.A.

Sep. 9   *Jose Pipino Cuevas (M) w.rsf.2 Pete Ranzany, Sacramento, U.S.A.

1979   Jan. 14   †Wilfred Benitez (P.R.) w.pts.15 Carlos Palomino (M), San Juan, Puerto Rico.

Jan. 29   *Jose Pipino Cuevas (M) w.rsf.2 Scott Clark, Los Angeles, U.S.A.

March 25   †Wilfred Benitez (P.R.) w.pts.16 Harold Weston, San Juan, Puerto Rico.

July 30   *Jose Pipino Cuevas (M) w.pts.15 Randy Shields, Chicago, U.S.A.

Nov. 30   †Sugar Ray Leonard w.ko.15 Wilfred Benitez (P.R.), Las Vegas, U.S.A.

Dec. 8   *Jose Pipino Cuevas (M) w.rsf.10 Angel Espada (P.R.), Los Angeles, U.S.A.

1980   March 31   †Sugar Ray Leonard w.ko.4 Dave 'Boy' Green (U.K.), Landover, U.S.A.

April 6   *Harold Weston w.rsf.5 Harold Volbrecht (S.A.), Houston, U.S.A.

June 20   †Roberto Duran (Pan) w.pts.15 Sugar Ray Leonard, Montreal, Canada.

Aug. 2   *Thomas Hearns w.rsf.2. Pipino Cuevas (M), Detroit, U.S.A.

Nov. 26   †Sugar Ray Leonard w.rtd.8 Roberto Duran (Pan), New Orleans, U.S.A.

Dec. 6   *Thomas Hearns w.ko.6 Luis Primera (Ven), Detroit, U.S.A.

1981   March 28   †Sugar Ray Leonard w.rsf.10 Larry Bonds, Syracuse, U.S.A.

April 25   *Thomas Hearns w.rsf.12 Randy Shields, Phoenix, U.S.A.

June 25   *Thomas Hearns w.rsf.4 Pablo Baez (Dom), Houston, U.S.A.

Sep. 16   Sugar Ray Leonard w.rsf.14 Thomas Hearns, Las Vegas, U.S.A. *(For undisputed title.)*

1982   Feb. 15   †Sugar Ray Leonard w.rsf.3 Bruch Finch, Reno, U.S.A. *Leonard retired.*

1983   Feb. 13   *Don Curry w.pts.15 Jun-Sok Hwang (S.K.), Fort Worth, U.S.A.

Mar. 19   †Milton McCrory drew 12 Colin Jones (G.B.), Reno, U.S.A.

Aug. 12   †Milton McCrory w.pts.12 Colin Jones (G.B.), Las Vegas, U.S.A.

Sep. 3   *Don Curry, w.rsf.1 Roger Stafford, Marsala, Sicily.

1984   Jan. 14   †Milton McCrory w.rsf.6 Milton Guest, Detroit, U.S.A.

Feb. 4   *Don Curry w.pts.15 Marlon Starling, Atlantic City, U.S.A.

Apr. 15   †Milton McCrory w.rsf.6 Gilles Elbilia (F), Detroit, U.S.A.

Apr. 21   *Don Curry w.ret.7 Elio Diaz (Ven), Fort Worth, U.S.A.

Sep. 22   *Don Curry w.rsf.6 Nino La Rocca (I), Monte Carlo, Monaco.

1985   Jan. 19   ‡*Don Curry w.rsf.4 Colin Jones (G.B.), Birmingham, U.K.

Mar. 9   †Milton McCrory w.pts.12 Pedro Vidella, Paris, France.

Jul. 14   †Milton McCrory w.ko.3 Carlos Trujillo (Pan), Monte Carlo, Monaco.

Dec. 6   Don Curry w.ko.2 Milton McCrory, Las Vegas, U.S.A.

1986   Mar. 9   Don Curry w.ko.2 Eduardo Rodriguez (Pan), Fort Worth, U.S.A.

Sep. 27   Lloyd Honeyghan (G.B.) w.rsf.6 Don Curry, Atlantic City, U.S.A.

Honeyghan relinquished W.B.A. title to avoid meeting South African Harold Volbrecht (apartheid protest).

1987   Feb. 6   *Mark Breland w.ko.7 Harold Volbrecht (S.A.), Atlantic City, U.S.A.

Feb. 22	‡Lloyd Honeyghan (G.B.) w.rsf.2 Johnny Bumphus, Wembley, U.K.	
Apr. 18	†Lloyd Honeyghan (G.B.) w.pts.12 Maurice Blocker, London, U.K.	
Aug. 22	*Marlon Starling w.ko.11 Mark Breland, Columbia, U.S.A.	
Aug. 30	†Lloyd Honeghan (G.B.) w.ko.1 Gene Hatcher, Marbella, Spain.	
Oct. 28	†Jorge Vacca (M) w.pts.8 (tec) Lloyd Honeyghan (G.B.), Wembley, U.K.	
	Honeyghan was stripped of I.B.F. title after this defeat.	

1988	Feb. 5	*Marlon Starling w.pts.12 Fujio Ozake (J), Atlantic City, U.S.A.
	Mar. 29	†Lloyd Honeyghan (G.B.) w.ko.3 Jorge Vacca (M), Wembley, U.K.
	Apr. 16	*Marlon Starling drew 12 Mark Breland, Las Vegas, U.S.A.
	Apr. 23	‡Simon Brown w.rsf.14 Tyrone Trice, Berck-sur-Mer, France.
	Jul. 16	‡Simon Brown w.rsf.3 Jorge Vacca (M), Kingston, Jamaica.
	Jul. 29	†Lloyd Honeyghan (G.B.) w.ret.5 Yung-Kil Chang (S.K.), Atlantic City, U.S.A.
	Jul. 29	*Tomas Molinares (Col) w.ko.6 Marlon Starling, Atlantic City, U.S.A.

World Light-Welterweight Title Fights
(140 pounds: 10 stone)

Created in 1922 by Mike Collins, publisher of *The Boxing Blade*, a Minneapolis weekly boxing magazine. He ran a competition among his readers inviting them to choose the champion of a new weight division – the light-welterweight class, or junior-welterweight as it was known in those days. They voted for Pinkey Mitchell from Milwaukee and he held his gift title until Sept. 21, 1926 when he was outpointed over ten rounds by Mushy Callahan. When he defended his title at London's Albert Hall against Jack 'Kid' Berg in 1930, Lord Lonsdale rose from his ringside seat, waving his stick and told the announcer that there was no such class. It petered out in 1946 but was revived in 1959. On March 21, 1963 the W.B.A. acclaimed Roberto Cruz as their champion, while the W.B.C. waited until Dec. 14, 1968 when they recognized Pedro Adigue as their titleholder.

1923	July 9	Pinkey Mitchell w.pts.10 Nate Goldman, Philadelphia, U.S.A.
1926	Sep. 21	Mushy Callahan w.pts.10 Pinkey Mitchell, Vernon, U.S.A.
1930	Feb. 18	Jack 'Kid' Berg (U.K.) w.rtd.10 Mushy Callahan, London, U.K.
	April 4	Jack 'Kid' Berg (U.K.) w.pts.10 Joe Glick, New York, U.S.A.
	May 29	Jack 'Kid' Berg (U.K.) w.rsf.4 Al Delmont, Newark, U.S.A.
	June 12	Jack 'Kid' Berg (U.K.) w.rsf.10 Herman Perlick, New York, U.S.A.
	Sep. 3	Jack 'Kid' Berg (U.K.) w.pts.10 Buster Brown, Newark, U.S.A.
	Sep. 8	Jack 'Kid' Berg (U.K.) w.pts.10 Joe Glick, New York, U.S.A.
	Oct. 10	Jack 'Kid' Berg (U.K.) w.pts.10 Billy Petrolle, New York, U.S.A.
1931	Jan. 23	Jack 'Kid' Berg (U.K.) w.pts.10 Goldie Hess, Chicago, U.S.A.
	Jan. 30	Jack 'Kid' Berg (U.K.) w.pts.10 Herman Perlick, New York, U.S.A.
	April 10	Jack 'Kid' Berg (U.K.) w.pts.10 Billy Wallace, Detroit, U.S.A.
	April 23	Tony Canzoneri w.ko.3 Jack 'Kid' Berg (U.K.), Chicago, U.S.A.
	July 13	Tony Canzoneri w.pts.10 Cecil Payne, Los Angeles, U.S.A.
	Sep. 10	Tony Canzoneri w.pts.15 Jack 'Kid' Berg (U.K.), New York, U.S.A.
	Oct. 29	Tony Canzoneri w.pts.10 Phillie Griffin, Newark, U.S.A.
	Nov. 20	Tony Canzoneri w.pts.15 Kid Chocolate (C), New York, U.S.A.
1932	Jan. 18	Johnny Jadick w.pts.10 Tony Canzoneri, Philadelphia, U.S.A.
	July 18	Johnny Jadick w.pts.10 Tony Canzoneri, Philadelphia, U.S.A.
1933	Feb. 20	Battling Shaw (M) w.pts.10 Johnny Jadick, New Orleans, U.S.A.

	May 21	Tony Canzoneri w.pts.10 Battling Shaw (M), New Orleans, U.S.A.
	June 23	Barney Ross w.pts.10 Tony Canzoneri, Chicago, U.S.A.
	July 26	Barney Ross w.ko.6 Johnny Farr, Kansas City, U.S.A.
	Sep. 12	Barney Ross w.pts.15 Tony Canzoneri, New York, U.S.A.
	Nov. 17	Barney Ross w.pts.10 Sammy Fuller, Chicago, U.S.A.
1934	Feb. 7	Barney Ross w.pts.12 Pete Nebo, Kansas City, U.S.A.
	March 5	Barney Ross drew 10 Frankie Klick, San Francisco, U.S.A.
	March 27	Barney Ross w.pts.10 Bobby Pacho, Los Angeles, U.S.A.
	Dec. 10	Barney Ross w.pts.12 Bobby Pacho, Cleveland, U.S.A.
1935	Jan. 28	Barney Ross w.pts.10 Frankie Klick, Miami, U.S.A.
	April 9	Barney Ross w.pts.12 Henry Woods, Seattle, U.S.A.
	May	*Ross relinquished title.*
1946	April 29	Tippy Larkin w.pts.12 Willie Joyce, Boston, U.S.A.
	Sep. 13	Tippy Larkin w.pts.12 Willie Joyce, New York, U.S.A.
1959	June 12	Carlos Ortiz (P.R.) w.rsf.12 Kenny Lane, New York, U.S.A.
1960	Feb. 4	Carlos Ortiz (P.R.) w.ko.10 Battling Torres, Los Angeles, U.S.A.
	June 13	Carlos Ortiz (P.R.) w.pts.15 Duilio Loi (I), San Francisco, U.S.A.
	Sep. 1	Duilio Loi (I) w.pts.15 Carlos Ortiz (P.R.), Milan, Italy.
1961	May 10	Duilio Loi (I) w.pts.15 Carlos Ortiz (P.R.) Milan, Italy.
	Oct. 21	Duilio Loi (I) drew15 Eddie Perkins, Milan, Italy.
1962	Sep. 14	Eddie Perkins w.pts.15 Duilio Loi (I), Milan, Italy.
	Dec. 15	Duilio Loi (I) w.pts.15 Eddie Perkins, Milan, Italy. *Loi announced retirement.*
1963	March 21	*Roberto Cruz (Phi) w.ko.1 Battling Torres, Los Angeles, U.S.A.
	June 15	Eddie Perkins w.pts.15 Robert Cruz (Phi), Manila, Philippines.
1964	Jan. 4	Eddie Perkins w.rsf.13 Yoshinero Takahashi (J), Tokyo, Japan.
	April 18	Eddie Perkins w.pts.15 Bunny Grant (W.I.), Kingston, Jamaica.
1965	Jan. 18	Carlos Hernandez (Ven) w.pts.15 Eddie Perkins, Caracas, Venezuela.
	May 15	Carlos Hernandez (Ven) w.rsf.4 Mario Rossito (I), Maracaibo, Italy.
	July 10	Carlos Hernandez (Ven) w.ko.3 Percy Hayles (W.I.), Kingston, Jamaica.
1966	April 29	Sandro Lopopolo (I) w.pts.15 Carlos Hernandez (Ven), Rome, Italy.
	Oct. 21	Sandro Lopopolo (I) w.ret.7 Vicente Rivas (Ven), Rome, Italy.
1967	April 29	Paul Fujii (Ha) w.rtd.2 Sandro Lopopolo (I), Tokyo, Japan.
	Nov. 26	Paul Fujii (Ha) w.ko.4 Willi Quatuor (W.G.), Tokyo, Japan.
1968	Dec. 12	*Nicolino Loche (Arg) w.rtd.9 Paul Fujii, Tokyo, Japan.
	Dec. 14	†Pedro Adigue (Phi) w.pts.15 Adolph Pruitt, Manila, Philippines.
1969	May 3	Nicolino Loche (Arg) w.pts.15 Carlos Hernandez (Ven), Buenos Aires, Argentina.
	Oct. 11	*Nicolino Loche (Arg) w.pts.15 Joao Henrique (Bra), Buenos Aires, Argentina.
1970	Jan. 31	†Bruno Arcari (I) w.pts.15 Pedro Adigue (Phi), Rome, Italy.
	May 16	*Nicolino Loche (Arg) w.pts.15 Adolph Pruitt, Buenos Aires, Argentina.
	July 10	†Bruno Arcari (I) w.dis.6 Reno Roque (F), Lignano Sabbiadoro, Italy.
	Oct. 30	†Bruno Arcari (I) w.ko.3 Raimundo Dias (Bra), Genoa, Italy.
1971	March 6	†Bruno Arcari (I) w.pts.15 Joao Henrique (Bra), Rome, Italy.
	April 3	*Nicolino Loche (Arg) w.pts.15 Domingo Barrera Corpas (Sp), Buenos Aires, Argentina.
	June 26	†Bruno Arcari (I) w.rsf.9 Enrique Jana (Arg), Palermo, Italy.
	Oct. 9	†Bruno Arcari (I) w.ko.10 Domingo Barrera Corpas (Sp), Genoa, Italy.
	Dec. 11	*Nicolino Loche (Arg) w.pts.15 Antonio Cervantes (Col) Buenos Aires, Argentina.
1972	March 10	*Alfonso Frazer (Pan) w.pts.15 Nicolino Loche (Arg), Panama City, Panama.
	June 10	†Bruno Arcari (I) w.rsf.9 Joao Henrique (Bra), Palermo, Italy.

	Oct. 29	*Antonio Cervantes (Col) w.ko.10 Alfonso Frazer (Pan), Panama City, Panama.
1973	Feb. 15	*Antonio Cervantes (Col) w.pts.15 Josua Marquez (P.R.), San Juan, Puerto Rico.
	March 17	*Antonio Cervantes (Col) w.rtd.9 Nicolino Loche (Arg), Maracay, Venezuela.
	May 19	*Antonio Cervantes (Col) w.rsf.5 Alfonso Frazer (Pan), Panama City, Panama.
	Sep. 8	*Antonio Cervantes (Col) w.rsf.5 Carlos Giminez (Arg), Bogata, Colombia.
	Nov. 1	†Bruno Arcari (I) w.ko.5 Jorgen Hansen (D), Copenhagen, Denmark.
	Dec. 5	*Antonio Cervantes (Col) w.pts.15 Lion Furuyama (J), Panama City, Panama.
1974	Feb. 16	†Bruno Arcari (I) w.dis.8 Tony Ortiz (Sp), Turin, Italy.
	March 2	*Antonio Cervantes (Col) w.ko.6 Chang-Ki Lee (S.K.), Cartagena, Spain.
	July 27	*Antonio Cervantes (Col) w.ko.2 Victor Ortiz (P.R.), Cartagena, Spain.
	Aug.	*Arcari relinquished title.*
	Sep. 21	†Perico Fernandez (Sp) w.pts.15 Lion Furuyama (J), Rome, Italy.
	Oct 26	*Antonio Cervantes (Col) w.ko.8 Yasuaki Kadota (J), Tokyo, Japan.
1975	May 17	*Antonio Cervantes (Col) w.pts.15 Esteban De Jesus (P.R.), Panama City, Panama.
	July 15	†Saensak Muangsurin (T) w.rtd.8 Perico Fernandez (Sp), Bangkok, Thailand.
	Nov. 15	*Antonio Cervantes (Col) w.rtd.7 Hector Thompson (Aust), Panama City, Panama.
1976	Jan. 25	†Saensak Muangsurin (T) w.pts.15 Lion Furuyama (J), Tokyo, Japan.
	March 6	*Wilfred Benitez w.pts.15 Antonio Cervantes (Col), San Juan, Puerto Rico.
	May 31	*Wilfred Benitez w.pts.15 Emiliano Villa (Col), San Juan, Puerto Rico.
	June 30	†Miguel Velasquez (Sp) w.dis.4 Saensak Muangsurin (T), Madrid, Spain.
	Oct. 16	*Wilfred Benitez w.rsf.3 Tony Petronelli, San Juan, Puerto Rico.
	Oct. 29	†Saensak Muangsurin (T) w.rsf.2 Miguel Velasquez (Sp), Segovia, Spain.
1977	Jan 15	†Saensak Muangsurin (T) w.rsf.15 Monroe Brooks, Chiang-Mai, Thailand.
	April 2	†Saensak Muangsurin (T) w.ko.6 Guts Ishimatsu (J), Tokyo, Japan.
	June 17	†Saensak Muangsurin (T) w.pts.15 Perico Fernandez (Sp), Madrid, Spain.
	June 25	*Antonio Cervantes (Col) w.rsf.5 Carlos Gimenez, Maracaibo, Venezuela.
	Aug. 20	†Saensak Muangsurin (T) w.rsf.6 Mike Everett, Roi-Et, Thailand.
	Oct. 22	†Saensak Muangsurin (T) w.pts.15 Saoul Mamby (W.I.), Bangkok, Thailand.
	Nov. 5	*Antonio Cervantes (Col) w.pts.15 Nani Marrero (Dom), Maracay, Venezuela.
	Dec. 30	†Saensak Muangsurin (T) w.rtd.13 Jo Kimpuani (Zaire), Chantaburi, Thailand.
1978	April 8	†Saensak Muangsurin (T) w.ko.13 Francisco Moreno (Ven), Hat Yai, Thailand.
	April 29	*Antonio Cervantes (Col) w.ko.6 Tongta Kiatvayupak (T), Udon Thani, Thailand.
	Aug. 6	*Antonio Cervantes (Col) w.rsf.9 Norman Sekgapane (S.A.), Mmabatho, South Africa.
	Dec. 30	†Kim Sang-Hyan (S.K.) w.rsf.13 Saensak Muangsurin (T), Seoul, S. Korea.
1980	Feb. 23	†Saoul Mamby (W.I.) w.ko.14 Kim Sang-Hyun (S.K.), Seoul, S. Korea.
	March 29	*Antonio Cervantes (Col) w.rsf.7 Miguel Montilla (Dom), Cartagena, Spain.
	July 7	†Saoul Mamby (W.I.) w.ko.13 Esteban De Jesus, Bloomington, U.S.A.
	Aug. 2	*Aaron Pryor w.ko.4 Antonio Cervantes (Col), Cincinnati, U.S.A.
	Oct. 2	†Saoul Mamby (W.I.) w.pts.15 Maurice 'Termite' Watkins, Las Vegas, U.S.A.
	Nov. 22	*Aaron Pryor w.rsf.6 Gaeten Hart, Cincinnati, U.S.A.
1981	June 12	†Saoul Mamby (W.I.) w.pts.15 Jo Kimpuani, Detroit.

	June 27	*Aaron Pryor w.rsf.2 Lennox Blackmoore, Las Vegas.
	Aug. 29	†Saoul Mamby (W.I.) w.pts.15 Thomas Americo, Jakarta, Indonesia.
	Nov. 14	*Aaron Pryor w.rsf.7 Dujuan Johnson, Cleveland, U.S.A.
	Dec. 19	†Saoul Mamby (W.I.) w.pts.15 Obisia Nwankpa, Lagos, Nigeria.
1982	March 21	*Aaron Pryor w.rsf.12 Miguel Montilla (Dom), Atlantic City, U.S.A.
	June 26	†Leroy Haley w.pts.15 Saoul Mamby (W.I.), Cleveland, U.S.A.
	July 4	*Aaron Pryor w.rsf.6 Akio Kameda (J), Cincinnati, U.S.A.
	Oct. 20	†Leroy Haley w.pts.15 Juan Jose Giminez (I), Cleveland, U.S.A.
	Nov. 12	*Aaron Pryor w.rsf.14 Alexis Arguello (Nic), Miami, U.S.A.
1983	Feb. 13	†Leroy Haley w.pts.12 Saoul Mamby, Cleveland, U.S.A.
	April 2	*Aaron Prior w.rsf.3 Sang-Hyun Kim (S.K.) Atlantic City, U.S.A.
	May 20	†Bruce Curry w.pts.12 Leroy Haley, Las Vegas, U.S.A.
	July 7	†Bruce Curry w.ko.7 Hidekazu Akai (J), Osaka, Japan.
	Sep. 9	*Aaron Pryor w.ko.10 Alexis Arguello (Nic), Las Vegas, U.S.A.
	Oct. 19	†Bruce Curry w.pts.12 Leroy Haley, Las Vegas, U.S.A.
		Pryor announced retirement.
1984	Jan. 22	*Johnny Bumphus w.pts.15 Lorenzo Garcia (Arg), Atlantic City, U.S.A.
	Jan. 29	†Bill Costello w.rsf.10 Bruce Curry, Beaumont, U.S.A.
	June 22	‡Aaron Pryor w.pts.15 Nick Furlano, Toronto, Canada.
	July 15	†Bill Costello w.pts.12 Ronnie Shields, New York, U.S.A.
	Nov. 3	†Bill Costello w.pts.12 Saoul Mamby (W.I.), New York, U.S.A.
	Dec. 15	*Gene Hatcher w.pts.15 Ubaldo Sacco (Arg), Fort Worth, U.S.A.
1985	Feb. 16	†Bill Costello w.pts.12 Leroy Haley, New York, U.S.A.
	March 2	‡Aaron Pryor w.pts.15 Gary Hinton, Atlantic City, U.S.A.
	July 21	*Ubaldo Sacco (Arg) w.rsf.9 Gene Hatcher, Campione de Italia, Italy.
	Aug. 26	†Lonnie Smith w.rsf.8 Bill Costello, New York, U.S.A.
		Aaron Pryor stripped of I.B.F. title.
1986	March 15	*Patrizio Oliva (I) w.pts.15 Ubaldo Sacco (Arg), Monte Carlo, Monaco.
	April 26	‡Gary Hinton w.pts.15 Antonio Cruz (Dom), Lucca, Italy.
	May 5	†Rene Arredondo (M) w.ko.5 Lonnie Smith, Los Angeles, U.S.A.
	July 24	†Tsuyoshi Hamada (J) w.ko.1 Rene Arredondo (M), Tokyo, Japan.
	Sep. 6	*Patrizio Oliva (I) w.rsf.3 Brian Brunette, Naples, Italy.
	Oct. 30	‡Joe Louis Manley w.ko.10 Gary Hinton, Hartford, U.S.A
	Dec. 2	†Tsuyoshi Hamada (J) w.pts.12 Ronnie Shields, Tokyo, Japan.
1987	March 4	‡Terry Marsh (G.B.) w.rsf.10 Joe Louis Manley, Basildon, U.K.
		Marsh relinquished I.B.F. title.
	July 4	*Juan Martin Coggi (Arg) w.rsf.3 Patrizio Oliva (I), Ribera, Sicily.
	July 22	†Rene Arredondo (M) w.rsf.6 Tsuyoshi Hamada (J), Tokyo, Japan.
	Nov. 12	†Roger Mayweather w.ko.6 Rene Arredondo (Mex), Los Angeles, U.S.A.
1988	Feb. 14	‡James McGirt w.rsf.12 Frank Warren, Corpus Christi, U.S.A.
	March 24	†Roger Mayweather w.ko.3 Maurico Aceves (M), Los Angeles, U.S.A.
	May 7	*Juan Martin Coggi (Arg) Sang-Ho Lee (S.K.), Roseto, Italy.
	June 6	†Roger Mayweather w.pts.12 Harold Brazier, Las Vegas, U.S.A.
	July 31	‡James McGirt w.ko.1 Howard Davis, New York, U.S.A.
	Sep. 3	‡Meldrick Taylor w.rsf.12 James McGirt, Atlantic City, U.S.A.

World Lightweight Title Fights
(135 pounds: 9 stone 9 pounds)

This division dates back to the Prize Ring, famous bare-knuckle lightweights being Caleb Baldwin (1769–1827), Jack Randall (1794–1828), Dick Curtis (1802–1848), Barney Aaron (1836–1907), Sam Collyer (1842–1904), Owney Geoghan (1840–1885) and Abe Hicken

(1847–1910). In 1872 two Englishmen, Arthur Chambers and Billy Edwards, fought for the American title and a purse of 2000 dollars. In 1887 Jem Carney, the English champion, fought Jack McAuliffe for the world title at Revere, Mass. and was winning when the crowd invaded the ring in the 74th round and the referee declared a 'draw'. First champion with the gloves was George 'Kid' Lavigne (U.S.A.) who knocked out Dick Burge of England in 17 rounds in London on June 1, 1896. Single ownership of the class remained until 1944 when the N.B.A. and the New York body waged war and two champions appeared. In 1970 the W.B.C. and the W.B.A. carried on the duel and there have been two titleholders ever since.

1872	Oct. 6	Arthur Chambers w.dis.35 Billy Edwards, Squirrel Island, U.S.A.
1886	Feb. 27	Jack McAuliffe w.pts.17 Jack Hopper, New York, U.S.A.
1887	Nov. 16	Jack McAuliffe drew 74 Jem Carney (U.K.), Revere, U.S.A.
1894	Dec. 14	George 'Kid' Lavigne w.ko.18 Andy Bowen, New Orleans, U.S.A.
1896	June 1	George 'Kid' Lavigne w.ko.17 Dick Burge (U.K.), London, U.K.
1899	July 3	Frank Erne w.pts.20 George 'Kid' Lavigne, Buffalo, U.S.A.
1902	May 12	Joe Gans w.ko.1 Frank Erne, Fort Erie, Canada.
1908	April 1	Joe Gans w.ko.3 Spike Robson (U.K.), Philadelphia, U.S.A.
	July 4	Battling Nelson w.ko.17 Joe Gans, San Francisco, U.S.A.
1910	Feb. 22	Ad Wolgast w.ko.40 Battling Nelson, Port Richmond, U.S.A.
1911	July 4	Ad Wolgast w.ko.13 Owen Moran (U.K.), San Francisco, U.S.A.
1912	Nov. 28	Willie Ritchie w.dis.16 Ad Wolgast, Daly City, U.S.A.
1914	July 7	Freddie Welsh (U.K.) w.pts.20 Willie Ritchie, London, U.K.
1916	Sep. 4	Freddie Welsh (U.K.) w.pts.20 Charlie White, Colorado, Springs, U.S.A.
1917	May 28	Benny Leonard w.ko.9 Freddie Welsh (U.K.), New York, U.S.A.
1920	July 5	Benny Leonard w.ko.8 Charlie White, Benton Harbour, U.S.A.
1925	July 3	Jimmy Goodrich w.ko.2 Stanislaus Lloauza (Chi), Long Island, U.S.A.
	Dec. 8	Rocky Kansas w.pts.15 Jimmy Goodrich, New York, U.S.A.
1926	July 3	Sammy Mandell w.pts.10 Rocky Kansas, Chicago, U.S.A.
1930	July 17	Al Singer w.ko.1 Sammy Mandell, New York, U.S.A.
	Nov. 14	Tony Canzoneri w.ko.1 Al Singer, New York, U.S.A.
1931	April 24	Tony Canzoneri w.ko.3 Jack 'Kid' Berg (U.K.), Chicago, U.S.A.
	Sep. 6	Tony Canzoneri w.pts.15 Jack 'Kid' Berg (U.K.), New York, U.S.A.
1933	June 23	Barney Ross w.pts.10 Tony Canzoneri, Chicago, U.S.A.
1935	May 10	Tony Canzoneri w.pts.15 Lou Ambers, New York, U.S.A.
1936	Sep. 3	Lou Ambers w.pts.15 Tony Canzoneri, New York, U.S.A.
1938	Aug. 17	Henry Armstrong w.pts.15 Lou Ambers, New York, U.S.A.
1939	Aug. 22	Lou Ambers w.pts.15 Henry Armstrong, New York, U.S.A.
1940	May 10	Lew Jenkins w.rsf.3 Lou Ambers, New York, U.S.A.
1941	Dec. 19	Sammy Angott w.pts.15 Lew Jenkins, New York, U.S.A.
1942	Dec. 18	Beau Jack w.ko.3 Tippy Larkin, New York, U.S.A.
1943	May 21	Bob Montgomery w.pts.15 Beau Jack, New York, U.S.A.
	Nov. 19	Beau Jack w.pts.15 Bob Montgomery, New York, U.S.A.
1944	March 3	Bob Montgomery w.pts.15 Beau Jack, New York, U.S.A.
	March 8	Juan Zurita (M) w.pts.15 Sammy Angott, Hollywood, U.S.A.
1945	April 18	Ike Williams w.ko.2 Juan Zurita (M), Mexico City, Mexico.
1946	Sep. 4	Ike Williams w.ko.9 Ronnie James (U.K.), Cardiff, U.K.
1947	Aug. 4	Ike Williams w.ko.6 Bob Montgomery, Philadelphia, U.S.A.
1951	May 25	James Carter w.rsf.14 Ike Williams, New York, U.S.A.
1952	May 14	Lauro Salas (M) w.pts.15 James Carter, Los Angeles, U.S.A.
	Oct. 15	James Carter w.pts.15 Lauro Salas (M), Chicago, U.S.A.
1954	March 5	Paddy DeMarco w.pts.15 James Carter, New York, U.S.A.

	Nov. 17	James Carter w.rsf.15 Paddy DeMarco, San Francisco, U.S.A.
1955	June 29	Wallace 'Bud' Smith w.pts. 15 James Carter, Boston, U.S.A.
1956	Aug. 24	Joe Brown w.pts.15 Wallace 'Bud' Smith, New Orleans, U.S.A.
1959	Dec. 2	Joe Brown w.rtd.5 Dave Charnley (U.K.), Houston, U.S.A.
1961	April 18	Joe Brown w.pts.15 Dave Charnley (U.K.), London, U.K.
1962	April 21	Carlos Ortiz (P.R.) w.pts.15 Joe Brown, Las Vegas, U.S.A.
1964	April 10	Ismael Laguna (Pan) w.pts.15 Carlos Ortiz (P.R.), Panama City, Panama.
	Nov. 13	Carlos Ortiz (P.R.) w.pts.15 Ismael Laguna (Pan), San Juan, Puerto Rico.
1968	June 29	Carlos Teo Cruz (Dom) w.pts.15 Carlos Ortiz (P.R.), Santo Domingo, Dominica.
1969	Feb. 18	Mando Ramos w.rsf.11 Carlos Teo Cruz (Dom), Los Angeles, U.S.A.
1970	March 3	Ismael Laguna (Pan) w.rtd.9 Mando Ramos, Los Angeles, U.S.A.
	Sep. 26	*Ken Buchanan (U.K.) w.pts.15 Ismael Laguna (Pan), San Juan, Puerto Rico.
1971	Feb. 12	Ken Buchanan (U.K.) w.pts.15 Ruben Navarro, Los Angeles, U.S.A. *(For undisputed title.)*
	Sep. 13	Ken Buchanan (U.K.) w.pts.15 Ismael Laguna (Pan), New York, U.S.A.
	Nov. 5	†Pedro Carrasco (Sp) w.dis.11 Mando Ramos, Madrid, Spain.
1972	Feb. 18	†Mando Ramos w.pts.15 Pedro Carrasco (Sp), Los Angeles, U.S.A.
	June 26	†Roberto Duran (Pan) w.rsf.13 Ken Buchanan (U.K.), New York, U.S.A.
	June 28	†Mando Ramos w.pts.15 Pedro Carrasco (Sp), Madrid, Spain.
	Sep. 15	†Erubey Carmono (M) w.rsf.8 Mando Ramos, Los Angeles, U.S.A.
	Nov. 10	†Rodolfo Gonzalez (M) w.rtd.12 Erubey Carmona (M), Los Angeles, U.S.A.
1974	April 11	†Guts Ishimatsu (J) w.ko.8 Rodolfo Gonzalez (M), Tokyo, Japan.
1975	Feb. 21	†Guts Ishimatsu (J) w.pts.15 Ken Buchanan (U.K.), Tokyo, Japan.
1976	May 8	†Esteban De Jesus (P.R.) w.pts.15 Guts Ishimatsu (J), San Juan, Puerto Rico.
1978	Jan. 21	Roberto Duran (Pan) w.ko.12 Esteban De Jesus (P.R.), Las Vegas, U.S.A. *(For undisputed title.)*
1979	April 17	†Jim Watt (U.K.) w.rsf.12 Alfredo Pitalua, Glasgow, U.K.
	June 16	*Ernesto Espana (Ven) w.ko.13 Claude Noel (W.I.), San Juan, Puerto Rico.
	Nov. 3	†Jim Watt (U.K.) w.rsf.9 Roberto Vasquez, Glasgow, U.K.
1980	March 2	*Hilmer Kenty w.rsf.9 Ernesto Espana (Ven), Detroit, U.S.A.
	March 14	†Jim Watt (U.K.) w.rsf.4 Charlie Nash (U.K.), Glasgow, U.K.
	June 7	†Jim Watt (U.K.) w.pts.15 Howard Davis, Glasgow, U.K.
	Nov. 1	†Jim Watt (U.K.) w.rsf.12 Sean O'Grady, Glasgow, U.K.
1981	April 12	*Sean O'Grady w.pts.15 Hilmer Kenty, Atlantic City, U.S.A.
	June 20	†Alexis Arguello (Nic) w.pts.15 Jim Watt (U.K.), London, U.K.
	Sep. 12	*Claude Noel (W.I.) w.pts.15 Rodolfo Gonzalez (M), Atlantic City, U.S.A.
	Oct. 3	†Alexis Arguello (Nic) w.rsf.14 Ray Mancini, Atlantic City, U.S.A.
	Nov. 21	†Alexis Arguello (Nic) w.ko.7 Roberto Elizondo, Las Vegas, U.S.A.
	Dec. 5	*Arturo Frias w.ko.8 Claude Noel (W.I.), Las Vegas, U.S.A.
1982	May 8	*Ray Mancini w.rsf.1 Arturo Frias, Las Vegas, U.S.A.
	Feb. 13	†Alexis Arguello w.rsf.6 Bubba Busceme, Beaumont, U.S.A.
	May 22	†Alexis Arguello (Nic) w.ko.5 Andrew Ganigan, Las Vegas, U.S.A. *Arguello relinquished W.B.C. title.*
	July 24	*Ray Mancini w.rsf.6 Ernesto Espana, Warren, U.S.A.
	Nov. 13	*Ray Mancini w.rsf.14 Deuk-Koo Kim (S.K.), Las Vegas, U.S.A.

1983	May 1	†Edwin Rosario (P.R.) w.pts.12 Jose Luis Ramirez (M), San Juan, Puerto Rico.
	Sep. 15	*Ray Mancini w.ko.9 Orlando Romero (Peru), Atlantic City, U.S.A.
1984	Jan. 14	*Ray Mancini w.rsf.3 Bobby Chacon, Reno, U.S.A.
	Jan. 30	‡Charlie Brown w.pts.15 Melvin Paul, Atlantic City, U.S.A.
	March 17	†Edwin Rosario (P.R.) w.rsf.1 Roberto Elizondo, San Juan, Puerto Rico.
	April 15	‡Harry Arroyo (Arg) w.rsf.14 Charlie Brown, Atlantic City, U.S.A.
	June 1	*Livingstone Bramble w.rsf.14 Ray Mancini, Buffalo, U.S.A.
	June 23	†Edwin Rosario (P.R.) w.pts.12 Howard Davies, San Juan, Puerto Rico.
	Sep. 1	‡Harry Arroyo (Arg) w.rsf.8 Charlie Brown, Youngstown, U.S.A.
1985	Jan. 12	‡Harry Arroyo (Arg) w.rsf.11 Terrence Alli (Gu), Atlantic City, U.S.A.
	Feb. 16	*Livingstone Bramble w.pts.15 Ray Mancini, Reno, U.S.A.
	April 5	‡Jimmy Paul w.pts.15 Harry Arroyo (Arg), Atlantic City, U.S.A.
	June 30	‡Jimmy Paul w.rsf.14 Robin Blake, Las Vegas, U.S.A.
	Aug. 10	†Hector Comacho (P.R.) w.pts.12 Joe Luis Ramirez (M), New York, U.S.A.
1986	Feb. 16	*Livingstone Bramble w.rsf.13 Tyrone Crawley, Reno, U.S.A.
	June 4	‡Jimmy Paul w.pts.15 Irleis Perez (C), East Rutherford, U.S.A.
	June 13	†Hector Comacho (P.R.) w.pts. 12 Edwin Rosario (P.R.), New York, U.S.A.
	Aug. 15	‡Jimmy Paul w.pts.15 Darryl Tyson, Detroit, U.S.A. *Comacho relinquished W.B.C. title*
	Sep. 26	*Edwin Rosario (P.R.) w.ko.2 Livingstone Bramble, Miami, U.S.A.
	Dec. 5	‡Greg Haugen w.pts.15 Jimmy Paul, Las Vegas, U.S.A.
1987	June 7	‡Vinny Pazienza w.pts.15 Greg Haugen, Providence, U.S.A.
	July 19	†Jose Luis Ramirez (M) w.pts.12 Terrence Alli (Gu), St. Tropez, France.
	Aug. 11	*Edwin Rosario (P.R.) w.ko.8 Juan Nazario (P.R.) Chicago, U.S.A.
	Oct. 8	†Joe Luis Ramirez (M) w.ko.8 Cornelius Boza-Edwards (U), Paris, France.
	Nov. 21	*Julio Cezar Chavez (M) w.rsf.11 Edwin Rosario (P.R.), Las Vegas, U.S.A.
1988	Feb. 6	‡Greg Haugen w.pts.15 Vinny Pazienza, Atlantic City, U.S.A.
	April 11	‡Greg Haugen w.tec.11 Miguel Santana (P.R.) Tacoma, U.S.A.
	April 16	*Julio Cezar Chavez (M) w.rsf.6 Rudolpho Aquilar (Pan), Las Vegas, U.S.A.
	May 2	†Joe Luis Ramirez (M) w.pts.12 Pernell Whittaker, Paris, France.

World Junior-Lightweight Title Fights
Now styles Super-Featherweight class
(130 pounds: 9 stone 4 pounds)

This was the earliest of the in-between weights (apart from that of light-heavyweight). Johnny Dundee became the first champion on Nov. 18, 1921, when he won on a foul over George Chaney in five rounds at New York. Promoter Tex Rickard presented the winner with a belt valued at 2500 dollars emblematic of the new division. It died out through lack of interest in 1933 and revived in 1959. On March 16, 1960 Flash Elorde of the Philippines took over and reigned as champion until 1967. On Nov. 9, 1969 the W.B.A. recognized Hiroshi Kobayashi (Japan) as its first titleholder and on April 5, 1970, the W.B.C. set up Yoshiaki Numata (Japan) as world king. There have been two world champions ever since.

| 1921 | Nov. 18 | Johnny Dundee w.dis.5 George Chaney, New York, U.S.A. |

1923	May 30	Jack Bernstein w.pts.15 Johnny Dundee, New York, U.S.A.
	Dec. 17	Johnny Dundee w.pts.15 Jack Bernstein, New York, U.S.A.
1924	June 20	Steve 'Kid' Sullivan w.pts.15 Johnny Dundee, New York, U.S.A.
1925	Dec. 2	Tod Morgan w.ko.10 Mike Ballerino, Los Angeles, U.S.A.
1929	Dec. 19	Benny Bass w.ko.2 Tod Morgan, New York, U.S.A.
1931	July 15	Kid Chocolate w.rsf.7 Benny Bass, Philadelphia, U.S.A.
1933	Dec. 26	Frankie Klick w.ko.7 Kid Chocolate, Philadelphia, U.S.A. *Title lapsed 1934–59.*
1959	July 20	Harold Gomes w.pts.15 Paul Jorgenson, Providence, U.S.A.
1960	March 16	Flash Elorde (Phi) w.rsf.7 Harold Gomes, Manila, Philippines.
1967	June 15	Yoshiaki Numata (J) w.pts.15 Flash Elorde (Phi), Tokyo, Japan.
	Dec. 14	Hiroshi Kobayashi (J) w.ko.12 Yoshiaki Numata (J), Tokyo, Japan.
1969	Feb. 15	†Rene Barrientos (Phi) w.pts.15 Reuben Navarro (Phi), Manila, Philippines.
1970	April 5	†Yoshiaki Numata (J) w.pts.15 Rene Barrientos (Phi), Tokyo, Japan.
1971	July 29	*Alfredo Marcano (Ven) w.rsf.10 Hiroshi Kobayashi (J), Aomari, Japan.
	Oct. 10	†Ricardo Arredondo (M) w.ko.10 Yoshiaki Numata (J), Sendai, Japan.
1972	April 25	*Ben Villaflor (Phi) w.pts.15 Alfredo Marcano (Ven), Honolulu, U.S.A.
1973	March 12	*Kuniaki Shibata (J) w.pts.15 Ben Villaflor (Phi), Honolulu, U.S.A.
	Oct. 17	*Ben Villaflor (Phi) w.ko.1 Kuniaki Shibata (J), Honolulu, U.S.A.
1974	Feb. 28	†Kuniaki Shibata (J) w.pts.15 Ricardo Arredondo (M), Tokyo, Japan.
1975	July 5	†Alfredo Escalera (P.R.) w.ko.2 Kuniaki Shibata (J), Mito, Japan.
1976	Oct. 16	*Sam Serrano (P.R.) w.pts.15 Ben Villaflor (Phi), San Juan, Puerto Rico.
1978	Jan. 28	†Alexis Arguello (Nic) w.rsf.13 Alfredo Escalera (P.R.), San Juan, Puerto Rico.
1980	Aug. 2	*Yasatsune Uehara (J) w.ko.6 Sam Serrano (P.R.), Detroit, U.S.A.
	Dec. 11	†Rafael Limon (M) w.rsf.15 Idelfonso Bethelmi, Los Angeles, U.S.A.
1981	March 8	†Cornelius Boza-Edwards (U.K.) w.pts.15 Rafael Limon (M), Stockton, U.S.A.
	April 9	*Sam Serrano (P.R.) w.pts.15 Yasatsune Uehara (J), Wakayama, Japan.
	May 30	†Cornelius Boza-Edwards (U.K.) w.rtd.13 Bobby Chacon, Las Vegas, U.S.A.
	June 29	*Sam Serrano (P.R.) w.pts.15 Leonel Hernandez (Ven), Caracas, Venezuela.
	Aug. 29	†Rolando Navarrete (Phi) w.ko.5 Cornelius Boza-Edwards, Viareggio, Italy.
	Dec. 10	*Sam Serrano (P.R.) w.rsf.12 Hikaru Tomonari (J), San Juan, Puerto Rico.
1982	May 29	†Rafael Limon (M) w.ko.12 Rolando Navarrete (P.R.), Las Vegas, U.S.A.
	June 5	*Benedicto Villablanca (Chi) w.rsf.11 Sam Serrano (P.R.), Santiago, Chile. *As the champion was stopped by an eye injury, the W.B.A. ruled that Serrano was still champion.*
	Dec. 11	†Bobby Chacon w.pts.15 Rafael Limon (M), Sacramento, U.S.A.
1983	Jan. 19	*Roger Mayweather w.ko.8 Samuel Serrano (P.R.), San Juan, Puerto Rico.
	April 20	*Roger Mayweather w.ret.8 Jorge Alvarada (Pan), San Jose, U.S.A.
	May 15	†Bobby Chacon w.pts.12 Cornelius Boza-Edwards (U), Las Vegas, U.S.A. *Chacon forfeited title.*
	Aug. 8	†Hector Camacho (P.R.) w.rsf.5 Rafael Limon (M), San Juan, Puerto Rico.
	Aug. 17	*Roger Mayweather w.ko.1 Benedicto Villablanca (Chi), Las Vegas. U.S.A.

	Nov. 18	†Hector Camacho (P.R.) w.ko.5 Rafael Solis (P.R.), San Juan, Puerto Rico. *Camacho relinquished title.*
1984	Feb. 26	*Rocky Lockridge w.ko.1 Roger Mayweather, Beaumont, U.S.A.
	April 20	†Hwan-Kil Yuh (S.K.) w.pts.15 Rod Sequeran (Phi), Seoul, S. Korea.
	June 12	*Rocky Lockridge w.rsf.11 Tar-Jin Moon (S.K.), Anchorage, U.S.A.
	Sept. 13	†Julio Cesar Chavez (M) w.rsf.8 Mario Martinez (M), Los Angeles, U.S.A.
	Sep. 16	‡Hwan-Kil Yuh (S.K.) w.ko.6 Sakda Galexi (T), Seoul, S. Korea.
1985	Jan. 27	*Rocky Lockridge w.ret.6 Kamel Bou Ali (Tun), Riva-del-Garda, Italy.
	Feb. 15	‡Lester Ellis (Aust) w.pts.15 Hwan-Kil Yuh (S.K.), Melbourne, Australia.
	April 19	†Julio Cesar Chavez (M) w.ko.6 Ruben Castillo, Los Angeles, U.S.A.
	April 26	‡Lester Ellis (Aust) w.ko.13 Rod Sequeran (Phi), Melbourne, Australia.
	May 19	*Wilfredo Gomez (P.R.) w.pts.12 Rocky Lockridge, San Juan, Puerto Rico.
	July 7	†Julio Cesar Chavez (M) w.rsf.2 Roger Mayweather, Las Vegas, U.S.A.
	July 12	‡Barry Michael (Aust) w.pts.15 Lester Ellis (Aust), Melbourne, Australia.
	Sep. 21	†Julio Cesar Chavez (M) w.pts.12 Dwight Prichett, Las Vegas, U.S.A.
	Oct. 18	‡Barry Michael (Aust) w.rsf.4 Jin-Shik Choi (S.K.), Darwin, Australia.
	Dec. 19	†Julio Cesar Chavez (M) w.rsf.5 Jeff Bumpus, Los Angeles, U.S.A.
1986	May 15	†Julio Cesar Chavez (M) w.rsf.5 Faustino Barrios (Arg), Paris, France.
	May 23	‡Barry Michael (Aust) w.rsf.4 Mark Fernandez (Col), Melbourne, Australia.
	May 24	*Alfredo Wayne (Pan) w.ko.9 Wilfredo Gomez (P.R.), San Juan, Puerto Rico.
	June 13	†Julio Cesar Chavez (M) w.rsf.7 Refugio Rojas (M), New York, U.S.A.
	Aug. 3	†Julio Cesar Chavez (M) w.pts.12 Rocky Lockridge, Monte Carlo, Monaco.
	Aug. 23	‡Barry Michael (Aust) w.pts.12 Najid Daho (G.B.), Manchester, U.K.
	Sep. 27	*Brian Mitchell (S.A.) w.rsf.10 Alfredo Wayne (Pan), Sun City, South Africa.
	Dec. 12	†Julio Cesar Chavez (M) w.pts.12 Juan La Porte (P.R.), New York, U.S.A.
1987	March 27	*Brian Mitchell (S.A.) drew 15 Joe Riveron (P.R.), San Juan, Puerto Rico.
	April 18	†Julio Cesar Chavez (M) w.rsf.3 Francisco Tomas Da Cruz (Bra), Nimes, France.
	May 15	*Brian Mitchell (S.A.) w.rsf.2 Aurelio Benetez (Ven), Sun City, South Africa.
	July 31	*Brian Mitchell (S.A.) w.rsf.14 Francisco Fernandez (Pan), Panama City, Panama.
	Aug. 9	‡Rocky Lockridge w.ret.8 Barry Michael (Aust), Windsor, U.K.
	Aug. 21	†Julio Cesar Chavez (M) w.pts.12 Danilo Cabrera (Dom), Tijuana, Mexico. *Chavez relinquished W.B.C. title.*
	Oct. 3	*Brian Mitchell (S.A.) w.rsf.10 Daniel Londos (I), Gravelines, France.
	Oct. 25	‡Rocky Lockridge w.rsf.10 Johnny De La Rosa (Dom), Tucson, U.S.A.
	Dec. 19	*Brian Mitchell (S.A.) w.rsf.8 Salvatore Curcetti (I), Capo D'Orlando, Italy.
1988	Feb. 29	†Azumah Nelson (Gha) w.pts.12 Mario Martinez (M), Los Angeles, U.S.A.
	April 2	‡Rocky Lockridge w.pts.15 Harold Knight, Atlantic City, U.S.A.
	July 27	‡Tony Lopez w.pts.12 Rocky Lockridge, Sacremento, U.S.A.
	June 25	†Azumah Nelson (Gha) w.ko.9 Lupe Suarez, Atlantic City, U.S.A.

World Featherweight Title Fights
(126 pounds: 9 stone)

The first three recognized world champions in this division were neither British nor American. They came from New Zealand (Billy Murphy), Australia (Young Griffo) and Canada (George Dixon). The weight varied from 120 to 130 pounds until 1909 when it was stabilized at 126 pounds where it has remained ever since. There was a single world champion until 1932 when the N.B.A. and the N.Y.A.C. were in conflict, but things righted themselves with the Pep-Saddler saga (1942–57). Thereafter the two rival ruling bodies have got to work, the W.B.C. naming Howard Winstone as champion on Jan. 23, 1968 and the W.B.A. recognizing Raul Rojas as titleholder on March 28, 1968.

1889	March 31	Ike Weir (U.K.) drew 80 Frank Murphy (U.K.), Kouts, U.S.A.
1890	Jan. 13	Australian Billy Murphy (Aust) w.ko.14 Ike Weir (U.K.), San Francisco, U.S.A.
	Sep. 3	Young Griffo (Aust) w.pts.15 Australian Billy Murphy (Aust), Sydney, Australia.
1892	Sep. 6	George Dixon (Can) w.ko.8 Jack Skelly, New Orleans, U.S.A.
1896	Nov. 27	Frank Erne w.pts.20 George Dixon (Can), New York, U.S.A.
1897	April 7	George Dixon (Can) w.pts.25 Frank Erne, New York, U.S.A.
	Oct. 4	Solly Smith w.pts.20 George Dixon (Can), San Francisco, U.S.A.
1898	Sep. 26	Dave Sullivan w.rtd.5 Solly Smith, Coney Island, U.S.A.
	Nov. 11	George Dixon (Can) w.dis.10 Dave Sullivan, New York, U.S.A.
1899	May 29	Ben Jordan (U.K.) w.ko.9 Harry Greenfield, London, U.K.
	Oct. 10	Eddie Santry w.ko.15 Ben Jordan, New York, U.S.A.
1900	Jan. 9	Terry McGovern w.ko.8 George Dixon (Can), New York, U.S.A.
	Feb. 1	Terry McGovern w.ko.5 Eddie Santry, Chicago, U.S.A.
1901	Nov. 28	Young Corbett 11 w.ko.2 Terry McGovern, Hartford, U.S.A.
1904	Feb. 1	Abe Attell w.ko.4 Harry Forbes, St. Louis, U.S.A.
1908	Jan. 1	Abe Attell drew 20 Owen Moran (U.K.), San Francisco, U.S.A.
	Sep. 7	Abe Attell drew 23 Owen Moran (U.K.), San Francisco, U.S.A.
1909	Feb. 19	Jim Driscoll (U.K.) ND10 Abe Attell, New York, U.S.A.
1912	Feb. 22	Johnny Kilbane w.pts.20 Abe Attell, Vernon, U.S.A.
1913	Jan. 27	Jim Driscoll (U.K.) drew 20 Owen Moran (U.K.), London, U.K.
1921	May 26	Johnny Kilbane ND10 Freddy Jack, Cleveland, U.S.A.
	Aug. 17	Johnny Kilbane w.ko.7 Danny Frush, Cleveland, U.S.A.
1922	Aug. 15	Johnny Dundee w.ko.9 Danny Frush, New York, U.S.A.
1923	June 2	Eugene Criqui (F) w.ko.6 Johnny Kilbane, New York, U.S.A.
	July 26	Johnny Dundee w.ko.6 Eugene Criqui (F), New York, U.S.A.
1925	Jan. 2	Louis 'Kid' Kaplan w.rtd.9 Danny Kramer, New York, U.S.A.
1927	Sep. 19	Benny Bass w.pts.20 Red Chapman, Philadelphia, U.S.A.
	Oct. 24	Tony Canzoneri w.pts.15 Johnny Dundee, New York, U.S.A.
1928	Feb. 10	Tony Canzoneri w.pts.15 Benny Bass, New York, U.S.A.
	Sep. 28	Andre Routis (F) w.pts.15 Tony Canzoneri, New York, U.S.A.
1929	Sep. 23	Battling Battalino w.pts.15 Andre Routis (F), Hartford, U.S.A.
1932	May 26	Tommy Paul w.pts.15 Johnny Pena, Detroit, U.S.A.
	Aug. 4	Kid Chocolate w.pts.10 Eddie Shea, Chicago, U.S.A.
1933	Jan. 13	Freddie Miller w.pts.10 Tommy Paul, Chicago, U.S.A.
	May 19	Tom Watson (U.K.) w.pts.15 Kid Chocolate, New York, U.S.A.
1934	Aug. 30	Baby Arizmendi (M) w.pts.15 Mike Belloise, New York, U.S.A.
	Sep. 21	Freddie Miller w.pts.15 Nel Tarleton (U.K.), Liverpool, U.K.
1935	June 12	Freddie Miller w.pts.15 Nel Tarleton (U.K.), Liverpool, U.K.
1936	May 11	Petey Sarron w.pts.15 Freddie Miller, Washington, U.S.A.

	Sep. 3	Mike Belloise w.ko.9 Dave Crowley (U.K.), New York, U.S.A.
	Oct. 27	Henry Armstrong w.pts.10 Mike Belloise, Los Angeles, U.S.A.
1937	Oct. 29	Henry Amrstrong w.ko.6 Petey Sarron, New York, U.S.A.
1938	Oct. 17	Joey Archibald w.pts.15 Mike Belloise, New York, U.S.A.
	Dec. 29	Leo Rodak w.pts.10 Leone Efrati, Chicago, U.S.A.
1937	Oct. 29	Henry Armstrong w.ko.6 Petey Sarron, New York, U.S.A.
1938	Oct. 17	Joey Archibald w.pts.15 Mike Belloise, New York, U.S.A.
	Dec. 29	Leo Radak w.pts.10 Leone Efrati, Chicago, U.S.A.
1939	April 18	Joey Archibald w.pts.15 Leo Rodak, Providence, U.S.A.
1940	May 20	Harry Jeffra w.pts.15 Joey Archibald, Baltimore, U.S.A.
1941	July 1	Joey Archibald w.pts.15 Harry Jeffra, Washington D.C., U.S.A.
	Nov. 18	Jackie Wilson w.pts.12 Ritchie Lemos, Los Angeles, U.S.A.
1942	Nov. 20	Willie Pep w.pts.15 Chalky Wright, New York, U.S.A.
1943	Jan. 18	Jackie Callura (Can) w.pts.15 Jackie Wilson, Providence, U.S.A.
	Aug. 16	Phil Terranova w.ko.8 Jackie Callura (Can), New Orleans, U.S.A.
1944	March 10	Sal Bartola w.pts.15 Phil Terranova, Boston, U.S.A.
1946	June 7	Willie Pep w.ko.12 Sal Bartola, New York, U.S.A.
1948	Oct. 29	Sandy Saddler w.ko.4 Willie Pep, New York, U.S.A.
1949	Feb. 11	Willie Pep w.pts.15 Sandy Saddler, New York, U.S.A.
1950	Sep. 8	Sandy Saddler w.rtd.7 Willie Pep, New York, U.S.A.
1957	June 24	Hogan Bassey (Nig) w.rsf.10 Cherif Hamia (F), Paris, France.
1959	March 18	Davey Moore w.rtd.13 Hogan Bassey (Nig), Los Angeles, U.S.A.
1963	March 21	Sugar Ramos (C) w.rtd.10 Davey Moore, Los Angeles, U.S.A.
1964	May 9	Sugar Ramos (C) w.pts.15 Floyd Robertson (Ghana), Accra, Ghana.
	Sep. 26	Vicente Saldivar (M) w.rtd.11 Sugar Ramos (C), Mexico City, Mexico.
1965	Sep. 7	Vicente Saldivar (M) w.pts.15 Howard Winstone (U.K.) London, U.K.
1966	Feb. 12	Vicente Saldivar (M) w.ko.2 Floyd Robertson (Gha), Mexico City, Mexico.
1967	June 15	Vicente Saldivar (M) w.pts.15 Howard Winstone (U.K.), Cardiff, U.K.
	Oct. 14	Vicente Saldivar (M) w.rtd.12 Howard Winstone (U.K.), Mexico City, Mexico.
1968	Jan. 23	†Howard Winstone (U.K.) w.rsf.9 Mitsunori Seki (J), London, U.K.
	March 28	*Raul Rojas w.pts.15 Enrique Higgins (Col), Los Angeles, U.S.A.
	July 24	†Jose Legra (C) w.rsf.5 Howard Winstone (U.K.), Porthcawl, U.K.
	Sep. 27	*Shozo Saijyo (J) w.pts.15 Raul Rojas, Los Angeles, U.S.A.
1969	Jan. 21	†Johnny Famechon (Aust) w.pts.15 Jose Legra (C), London, U.K.
1970	May 9	†Vicente Saldivar (M) w.pts.15 Johnny Famechon (Aust), Rome, Italy.
	Dec. 11	†Kuniaki Shibata (J) w.rsf.12 Vicente Saldivar (M), Tijuana, Mexico.
1971	Sep. 2	*Antonio Gomez (Ven) w.rsf.5 Shozo Saijyo (J), Tokyo, Japan.
1972	May 9	†Clemente Sanchez (M) w.ko.3 Kuniaki Shibata (J), Tokyo.
	Aug. 19	*Ernesto Marcel (Pan) w.pts.15 Antonio Gomez (Ven), Maracay, Venezuela.
	Dec. 16	†Jose Legra (C) w.rsf.10 Clemente Sanchez (M), Monterrey, Mexico.
1973	May 5	†Eder Jofre (Bra) w.pts.15 Jose Legra (C), Brasilia, Brazil.
1974	July 9	*Ruben Olivares (M) w.ko.7 Zensuke Utagawa (J), Inglewood, U.S.A.
	Sep.9	†Bobby Chacon w.rsf.9 Alfredo Marcano (Ven), Los Angeles, U.S.A.
	Nov. 23	*Alexis Arguello (Nic) w.ko.13 Ruben Olivares (M), Inglewood, U.S.A.
1975	June 20	†Ruben Olivares (M) w.rsf.2 Bobby Chacon, Inglewood, U.S.A.
	Sep. 20	†David Kotey (Gha) w.pts.15 Ruben Olivares (M), Inglewood, U.S.A.

1976	Nov. 6	†Danny Lopez w.pts.15 David Kotey (Ghana), Accra, Ghana.
1977	Jan. 15	*Rafael Ortega (Pan) w.pts.15 Francisco Coronado (Pan), Panama City, Panama.
	Dec. 17	*Cecilio Lastra (Sp) w.pts.15 Rafael Ortega (Pan), Torrelavega, Spain.
1978	April 16	*Eusebio Pedroza (Pan) w.ko.13 Cecilio Lastra (Sp), Panama City, Panama.
	July 2	*Eusebio Pedroza (Pan) w.rsf.12 Ernesto Herrara (M), Panama City, Panama.
	Nov. 27	*Eusebio Pedroza (Pan) w.pts.15 Enrique Solis (P.R.), San Juan, Puerto Rico.
1979	Jan. 9	*Eusebio Pedroza (Pan) w.rtd.13 Royal Kobayashi (J), Tokyo, Japan.
	April 8	*Eusebio Pedroza (Pan) w.rsf.11 Hector Carrasquilla, Panama City, Panama.
	July 21	*Eusebio Pedroza (Pan) w.rsf.12 Ruben Olivares (M), Houston, U.S.A.
	Nov. 17	*Eusebio Pedroza (Pan) w.rsf.11 Johnny Aba (New Guinea), Port Moresby, New Guinea.
1980	Jan. 22	*Eusebio Pedroza (Pan) w.pts.15 Spider Nemoto (J), Tokyo, Japan.
	Feb. 2	†Salvador Sanchez (M) w.rsf.13 Danny Lopez, Phoenix, U.S.A.
	April 2	†Salvador Sanchez (M) w.pts.15 Ruben Castillo, Tucson, U.S.A.
	June 21	†Salvador Sanchez (M) w.rsf.14 Danny Lopez, Las Vegas, U.S.A.
	July 20	*Eusebio Pedroza (Pan) w.ko.9 Sa-Wang Kim (S.K.), Seoul, S. Korea.
	Sep. 13	†Salvador Sanchez (M) w.pts.15 Pat Ford, San Antonio, U.S.A.
	Oct. 4	*Eusebio Pedroza (Pan) w.pts.15 Rocky Lockridge, Great Gorge, U.S.A.
	Dec. 13	†Salvador Sanchez w.pts.15 Juan Laporte (P.R.), El Paso, U.S.A.
1981	Feb. 14	*Eusebio Pedroza (Pan) w.ko.13 Pat Ford, Panama City, Panama.
	March 22	†Salvador Sanchez (M) w.rsf.10 Roberto Castanon, Las Vegas, U.S.A.
	Aug. 1	*Eusebio Pedroza (Pan) w.ko.7 Carlos Pinango (Ven), Caracas, Venezuela.
	Dec. 5	*Eusebio Pedroza (Pan) w.ko.5 Bashew Sibaca (S.A.), Panama City, Panama.
	Dec. 12	†Salvador Sanchez (M) w.pts.15 Pat Cowdell (U.K.), Houston, U.S.A.
1982	Sep. 15	†Juan Laporte (P.R.) w.rsf.10 Mario Miran (Col), New York, U.S.A.
	Oct. 16	*Eusebio Pedroza (Pan) drew15 Bernard Taylor, Charlotte, U.S.A.
1983	Feb. 20	†Juan Laporte (P.R.) w.pts.12 Ruben Castillo, San Juan, Puerto Rico.
	April 24	*Eusebio Pedrosa (Pan) w.pts.15 Rocky Lockridge, San Remo, Italy.
	June 25	†Juan Laporte (P.R.) w.pts.12 Johnny De La Rosa (Dom), San Juan, Puerto Rico.
	Oct. 22	*Eusebio Pedroza (Pan) w.pts.15 Jose Caba (Dom), St. Vincent, Italy.
1984	March 4	‡Min-Keun Oh (S.K.) w.ko.2 Joko Arter, Seoul, S. Korea.
	March 31	†Wilfredo Gomez (P.R.) w.pts.12 Juan Laporte (P.R.), San Juan, Puerto Rico.
	May 27	*Eusebio Pedroza (Pan) w.pts.15 Angel Mayor (Ven), Maracaibo, Venezuela.
	June 10	‡Min-Keun Oh (S.K.) w.pts.15 Kelvin Lampkin, Seoul, S. Korea.
	Dec. 8	†Azumah Nelson (Gha) w.rsf.11 Wilfredo Gomez (P.R.), San Juan, Puerto Rico.
1985	Feb. 2	*Eusebio Pedroza (P.R.) w.pts.15 Jorge Lujan (Pan), Panama City, Panama.
	April 7	‡Min-Keun Oh (S.K.) w.pts.15 Irving Mitchell, Pusan, S. Korea.
	June 8	*Barry McGuigan (G.B.) w.pts.15 Eusebio Pedroza (P.R.), London, U.K.
	Sep. 6	†Azumah Nelson (Gha) w.ko.5 Juvenal Ordenes (Chi), Miami, U.S.A.
	Sep. 28	*Barry McGuigan (G.B.) w.ret.8 Bernard Taylor, Belfast, U.K.

Oct. 12	†Azumah Nelson (Gha) w.ko.1 Pat Cowdell (G.B.), Birmingham, U.K.	
Nov. 29	‡Ki-Young Chung (S.K.) w.ko.15 Min-Keun Oh (S.K.), Seoul, S. Korea.	

1986
- Feb. 15 *Barry McGuigan (G.B.) w.rsf.14 Danilo Cabrera (Dom), Dublin, Ireland.
- Feb. 16 ‡Ki-Young Chung (S.K.) w.rsf.6 Tyrone Jackson, Ulsan, S. Korea.
- Feb. 25 †Azumah Nelson (Gha) w.pts.12 Marco Villasana (M), Los Angeles, U.S.A.
- May 18 ‡Ki-Young Chung (S.K.) w.pts.15 Richard Savage, Seoul, S. Korea.
- June 22 †Azumah Nelson (Gha) w.rsf.10 Danlio Cabrera (Dom), San Juan, Puerto Rico.
- June 23 *Steve Cruz w.pts.15 Barry McGuigan (G.B.) Las Vegas (U.S.A.)
- Aug. 30 ‡Antonio Ribera (P.R.) w.rsf.10 Ki-Young Chung (S.K.), Pusan, S. Korea.

1987
- March 6 *Antonio Esappagosa (Ven) w.rsf.12 Steve Cruz, Fort Worth, U.S.A.
- March 7 †Azumah Nelson (Gha) w.ko.6 Mauro Gutierrez (M), Las Vegas, U.S.A.
- July 26 *Antonio Esppagosa (Ven) w.ko.10 Pascual Aranda (Ven), Houston, U.S.A.
- Aug. 29 †Azumah Nelson (Gha) w.pts.12 Marco Villasana (M), Los Angeles, U.S.A.
  Nelson relinquished I.B.F. title.

1988
- Jan. 23 ‡Calvin Grove w.pts.15 Myron Taylor, Atlantic City, U.S.A.
- March 7 †Jeff Fenech (Aust) w.rsf.10 Victor Callejas (P.R.), Sydney, Australia.
- Aug. 4 ‡Jorge Perez (M) w.pts.15 Calvin Grove, Mexicali, Mexico.

World Super-Bantamweight Title Fights
(122 pounds: 8 stone 10 pounds)

The W.B.C. has been generally to the fore in starting a new weight class and on April 3, 1976 it recognized Rigoberto Riasco (Panama) as champion when he stopped Waruinge Nakayama (Japan) in eight rounds at Panama City. The W.B.A. did not respond until November 26, 1977 when they nominated Soo Hwan Hong (South Korea) following his three round kayo of Hector Carrasquilla (Panama) at Panama City. There has never been a solo champion in this division.

1976
- April 3 †Rigoberto Riasco (Pan) w.rtd.8 Waruinge Nakayama (J), Panama City, Panama.
- Oct. 1 †Royal Kobayashi (J) w.rsf.8 Rigoberto Riasco (Pan), Seoul, S. Korea.
- Nov. 24 †Dong-Kyun Yum (S.K.) w.pts.15 Royal Kobayashi (J), Seoul, S. Korea.

1977
- May 21 †Wilfredo Gomez (P.R.) w.ko.12 Dong-Kyun Yum (S.K.), San Juan, Puerto Rico.
- July 11 †Wilfredo Gomez (P.R.) w.ko.5 Raul Tirado, San Juan, Puerto Rico.
- Nov. 26 *Soo Hwan Hong (S.K.) w.ko.3 Hector Carasquilla (Pan), Panama City, Panama.

1978
- Jan. 19 †Wilfredo Gomez (P.R.) w.ko.3 Royal Kobayashi (J), Kitakyushu, Japan.
- April 8 †Wilfredo Gomez (P.R.) w.rsf.7 Juan Antonio Lopez (P.R.), Bayamon, Puerto Rico.
- May 7 *Ricardo Cardona (Col) w.rsf.12 Soo Hwan Hong (S.K.), Seoul, S. Korea.
- June 2 †Wilfredo Gomez (P.R.) w.rsf.3 Sakad Porntave (T), Nakhon Ratchasima, Thailand.
- Sep. 9 †Wilfredo Gomez (P.R.) w.rsf.13 Leonardo Cruz (Dom), San Juan, Puerto Rico.
- Oct. 29 †Wilfredo Gomez (P.R.) w.rsf.5 Carlos Zarate, San Juan, Puerto Rico.

1979
- March 9 †Wilfredo Gomez (P.R.) w.rsf.9 Nestor Jimenez (Col), New York, U.S.A.
- May 21 †Wilfredo Gomez (P.R.) w.ko.2 Nelson Cruz Tamariz (Dom), New York, U.S.A.
- June 16 †Wilfredo Gomez (P.R.) w.ko.5 Julio Hernandez (Nic), San Juan, Puerto Rico.
- Sep. 28 †Wilfredo Gomez (P.R.) w.rsf.10 Carlos Mendoza, Las Vegas, U.S.A.
- Oct. 26 †Wilfredo Gomez (P.R.) w.rsf.5 Nicky Perez, New York, U.S.A.

1980
- Feb. 3 †Wilfredo Gomez (P.R.) w.rtd.6 Ruben Valdez, Las Vegas, U.S.A.
- May 4 *Leo Randolph w.rsf.15 Ricardo Cardona (Col), Seattle, U.S.A.
- Aug. 9 *Sergio Palma (Arg) w.ko.6 Leo Randolph, Spokane, U.S.A.
- Aug. 22 †Wilfredo Gomez (P.R.) w.rsf.5 Derrick Holmes, Las Vegas, U.S.A.
- Nov. 8 *Sergio Palma (Arg) w.ko.9 Ulisses Morales, Buenos Aires, Argentina.
- Dec. 13 †Wilfredo Gomez (P.R.) w.ko.3 Jose Cervantes (Col), Miami Beach, U.S.A.
- Dec. 20 *Sergio Palma (Arg) w.ko.3 Hugo Fica, Resistencia, Argentina.

1981
- April 4 *Sergio Palma (Arg) w.pts.15 Leonardo Cruz (Dom), Buenos Aires, Argentina.
- June 5 *Sergio Palma (Arg) w.ko.9 Danilo Batista, Caleta Olivia, Argentina.
- Aug. 15 *Sergio Palma (Arg) w.rsf.12 Ricardo Cardona (Col), Buenos Aires, Argentina.
- Oct. 3 *Sergio Palma (Arg) w.pts.15 Vichit Muangroi-Et, Buenos Aires, Argentina.

1982
- June 11 †Wilfredo Gomez (P.R.) w.rsf.10 Antonio Lopez (M), Las Vegas, U.S.A.
- June 12 *Leonardo Cruz (Dom) w.pts.15 Sergio Palma (Arg), Miami, U.S.A.
- March 27 †Wilfredo Gomez (P.R.) w.rsf.6 Juan Meza (M), Atlantic City, U.S.A.
- Aug. 18 †Wilfredo Gomez (P.R.) w.ret.7 Roberto Rubaldino (M), San Juan, Puerto Rico.
- Nov. 13 *Leonardo Cruz (Dom) w.ko.8 Benito Badilla Chi), San Juan, Puerto Rico.
- Dec. 3 †Wilfredo Gomez (P.R.) w.rsf.13 Lupe Pintor (M), Houston, U.S.A.
  Gomez relinquished W.B.C. title.

1983
- March 16 *Leonardo Cruz (Dom) w.pts.15 Soon Hyun Chung (S.K.), San Juan, Puerto Rico.
- June 23 †Jaime Garza w.rsf.2 Bobby Berna (Phi), Los Angeles, U.S.A.
- Aug. 26 *Leonardo Cruz (Dom) w.pts.15 Cleo Garcia (Nic), Santo Domingo, Dominican Republic
- Dec. 4 ‡Bobby Berna (Phi) w.rsf.9 Seung-In Suh (S.K.), Seoul, S. Korea.

1984
- Feb. 22 *Loris Stecca (I) w.ret.12 Leonardo Cruz (Dom), Milan, Italy.
- April 15 ‡Seung-In Suh (S.K.) w.rsf.10 Bobby Berna (Phi), Seoul, S. Korea.
- May 26 *Victor Callejas (P.R.) w.ko.8 Loris Stecca (I), Guaynato, Puerto Rico.
- May 27 †Jaime Garza w.ko.3 Felipe Irozeo (Col), Miami, U.S.A.
- July 8 ‡Seung-In Suh (S.K.) w.ko.4 Cleo Garcia, Seoul, S. Korea.
- Nov. 3 †Juan Meza w.ko.1 Jaime Garza, New York, U.S.A.

1985
- Jan. 3 ‡Ji-Won Kim (S.K.) w.ko.10 Seung-In Sun (S.K.), Seoul, S. Korea.
- Feb. 2 *Victor Callejas w.pts.15 Seung-Hoon Lee (S.K.), San Juan, Puerto Rico.
- March 30 ‡Ji-Won Kim (S.K.) w.pts.15 Dario Palacios (Col), Suwon, S. Korea.
- April 19 †Juan Meza (M) w.rsf.6 Mike Ayala, Los Angeles, U.S.A.
- June 28 ‡Ji-Won Kim (S.K.) w.ko.4 Bobby Berna (Phi), Pusan, S. Korea.
- Aug. 18 †Lupe Pintor (M) w.pts.12 Juan Meza (M), Mexico City, Mexico.
- Oct. 9 ‡Ji-Won Kim (S.K.) w.ko.1 Seung-In Suh (S.K.), Chunju, S. Korea.
- Nov. 8 *Victor Callejas (P.R.) w.ret.6 Loris Stecca (I), Rimini, Italy.
  Callejas stripped of W.B.A. title

1986
- Jan. 18 †Samart Payakaroon (T) w.ko.5 Lupe Pintor (M), Bangkok, Thailand.
- June 1 ‡Ji-Won Kim (S.K.) w.rsf.2 Rudy Casicas (Phi), Seoul, S. Korea.
  Kim announced retirement.

Dec. 10 †Samart Payakaroon (T) w.ko.12 Juan Meza (M), Bangkok, Thailand.

1987 Jan. 16 *Louie Espinoza w.rsf.4 Tommy Valoy (Dom), Phoenix, U.S.A.

Jan. 18 ‡Seung-Hoon Lee (S.K.) w.ko.9 Prayurasak Muangsurin (T), Pohang, S. Korea.

April 5 ‡Seung-Hoon Lee (S.K.) w.ko.10 Jorge Diaz (M), Seoul, S. Korea.

May 8 †Jeff Fenech (Aust) w.ko.4 Samart Parakaroon (T), Sydney, Australia.

July 10 †Jeff Fenech (Aust) w.rsf.5 Greg Richardson, Sydney, Australia.

July 15 *Louie Espinoza w.rsf.15 Manial Vilchez (Ven), Phoenix, U.S.A.

July 19 ‡Seung-Hoon Lee (S.K.) w.ko.5 Leon Collins (Phi), Pohang, S. Korea.

Aug. 15 *Louie Espinoza w.ko.9 Mike Ayala, San Antonio, U.S.A.

Oct. 16 †Jeff Fenech (Aust) w.rsf.4 Carlos Zarate (M), Sydney, Australia.
Fenech relinquished W.B.C. title.

Nov. 28 *Julio Gervacio (P.R.) w.pts.12 Louie Espinoza, San Juan, Puerto Rico.

Dec. 27 ‡Seung-Hoon Lee (S.K.) w.pts.15 Jose Sanabria (Ven), Pohang, S. Korea.

1988 *Lee relinquished I.B.F. title.*

Feb. 27 *Bernado Pinango (Ven) w.rsf.12 Julio Gervacio (Dom), San Juan Puerto Rico.

Feb. 29 †Daniel Zaragosa (M) w.rsf.10 Carlo Zarate, Los Angeles, U.S.A.

May 21 ‡Jose Sanabria (Ven) w.ko.5 Moises Fuentes (Col), Bucaramanga, Italy.

May 30 †Daniel Zaragosa (M) drew 12 Seung-Hoon Lee (S.K.), Yochon, S. Korea.

May 30 *Juan Jose Estrada (M) w.pts.12 Bernado Pinango (Pan), Tijuana, Mexico.

Aug. 21 ‡Jose Sanabria (Ven) w.pts.12 Vincenzo Belcastro (I), Capo D'Orlando, Italy.

World Bantamweight Title Fights
(118 pounds: 8 stone 6 pounds)

This is the name given to boxers of small stature weighing between the flyweight and featherweight division. It comes from the days of cock-fighting, the bantams being the most ferocious birds in a sport which is now illegal. Before the National Sporting Club first standardized the poundages into eight categories in 1909, boxers who regarded themselves as bantams could weigh anything from 102 to 122 pounds according to their best fighting weight. Fans like watching them in action because they often provide a fast and usually furious contest. The first recognized British bantamweight champion was Ben Johnson, of Hackney, London, in 1886. The first American was Tommy Kelly, 'The Harlem Spider', in 1888, who scaled only 105 pounds. He is regarded as the first world titleholder. Splits in the championship first occurred in 1927–28 when the N.B.A. recognized Bud Taylor, the N.Y.A.C. had Bushy Graham and the British claimed that Teddy Baldock was bantam king. Manuel Ortiz reigned as undisputed champion from 1942 to 1950. He was followed by Vic Toweel and Jimmy Carruthers, who retired and left a scramble for the crown, which was not resolved until Eder Jofre took the title. The W.B.C. made Rafael Herrera (Mexico) its champion on April 15, 1973 but the W.B.A. were first with Romeo Anaya (Mexico) on Jan. 20 the same year. There have been two champions ever since.

1890 Jan. 31 Tommy Kelly w.pts.10 Chappie Moran (U.K.), New York, U.S.A.

1892 Aug. 22 Billy Plimmer (U.K.) w.pts.10 Tommy Kelly, Coney Island, U.S.A.

1893 Aug. 22 Billy Plimmer (U.K.) w.ko.4 George Dixon, New York, U.S.A.

1895 May 28 Billy Plimmer (U.K.) w.ko.7 George Corfield (U.K.), London, U.K.

Nov. 25 Pedlar Palmer (U.K.) w.rsf.14 Billy Plimmer (U.K.), London, U.K.

1896 Oct. 12 Pedlar Palmer (U.K.) w.pts.20 Johnny Murphy (U.K.), London, U.K.

1897 Jan. 25 Pedlar Palmer (U.K.) w.rsf.14 Ernie Stanton (U.K.), London, U.K.

Oct. 18 Pedlar Palmer (U.K.) w.pts.20 Dave Sullivan (U.K.), London, U.K.

Dec. 6 Jimmy Barry w.ko.20 Walter Croot (U.K.), London, U.K.

1898 Dec. 12 Pedlar Palmer (U.K.) w.rsf.17 Billy Plimmer (U.K.), London, U.K.

Dec. 29 Jimmy Barry drew 20 Casper Leon, Davenport, U.S.A.

1899 April 17 Pedlar Palmer (U.K.) w.rsf.3 Billy Rotchford (U.K.), London, U.K.

Sep. 22 Terry McGovern w.ko.1 Pedlar Palmer (U.K.), New York, U.S.A.

1901 March 18 Harry Harris w.pts.20 Pedlar Palmer (U.K.), London, U.K.

April 2 Harry Forbes w.pts.15 Casper Leon, Memphis, U.S.A.

1903 Feb. 27 Harry Forbes w.pts.10 Andy Tokell (U.K.), Detroit, U.S.A.

Aug. 13 Frankie Neil w.ko.2 Harry Forbes, San Francisco, U.S.A.

1904 Oct. 17 Joe Bowker (U.K.) w.pts.20 Frankie Neil, London, U.K.

1905 March 29 Jimmy Walsh w.ko.6 Monte Attell, Philadelphia, U.S.A.

Oct. 20 Jimmy Walsh w.pts.15 Digger Stanley (U.K.), Chelsea, U.S.A.

1910 Feb. 19 Johnny Coulon (Can) w.pts.10 Jim Kendrick (U.K.), New Orleans, U.S.A.

March 6 Johnny Coulon (Can) w.ko.19 Jim Kendrick (U.K.), New Orleans, U.S.A.

1911 Feb. 26 Johnny Coulon (Can) w.pts.20 Frankie Conley, New Orleans, U.S.A.

1914 Jan. 31 Kid Williams w.ko.3 Johnny Coulon (Can), Los Angeles, U.S.A.

1917 Jan. 9 Pete Herman w.pts.20 Kid Williams, New Orleans, U.S.A.

1920 Dec. 22 Joe Lynch w.pts.15 Pete Herman, New York, U.S.A.

1921 July 25 Pete Herman w.pts.15 Joe Lynch, New York, U.S.A.

Sep. 23 Johnny Buff w.pts.15 Pete Herman, New York, U.S.A.

1922 July 10 Joe Lynch w.rtd.14 Johnny Buff, New York, U.S.A.

1924 March 21 Abe Goldstein w.pts.15 Joe Lynch, New York, U.S.A.

Dec. 19 Eddie Martin w.pts.15 Abe Goldstein, New York, U.S.A.

1925 March 30 Charlie Rosenberg w.pts.15 Eddie Martin, New York, U.S.A.

1929 June 18 Al Brown (Pan) w.pts.15 Vidal Gregorio, New York, U.S.A.

1931 Aug. 15 Al Brown (Pan) w.pts.15 Pete Sanstol (Swe), Montreal, Canada.

1933 July 3 Al Brown (Pen) w.pts.15 Johnny King (U.K.), Manchester, U.K.

1934 June 26 Sixto Escobar (P.R.) w.ko.9 Baby Casanova (M), Montreal, Canada.

1935 June 1 Baltazar Sangchilli (Sp) w.pts.15 Al Brown (Pan), Valencia, Spain.

Aug. 26 Lou Salica w.pts.15 Sixto Escobar (P.R.), New York, U.S.A.

Nov. 15 Sixto Escobar (P.R.) w.pts.15 Lou Salica, New York, U.S.A.

1936 June 29 Tony Marino w.ko.14 Baltazar Sangchilli (Sp), New York, U.S.A.

Aug. 31 Sixto Escobar (P.R.) w.rsf.13 Tony Marino, New York, U.S.A. *(For undisputed title.)*

1937 Sep. 23 Harry Jeffra w.pts.15 Sixto Escobar (P.R.), New York.

1938 Feb. 20 Sixto Escobar (P.R.) w.pts.15 Harry Jeffra, San Juan, Puerto Rico.

1940 Sep. 24 Lou Salica w.pts.15 Georgie Pace, New York, U.S.A.

1941 Jan. 13 Lou Salica w.pts.15 Tommy Forte, Philadelphia, U.S.A.

1942 Aug. 7 Manuel Ortiz w.pts.10 Tony Olivera, Oakland, U.S.A.

1947 Jan. 6 Harold Dade w.pts.15 Manuel Ortiz, San Francisco, U.S.A.

March 11 Manuel Ortiz w.pts.15 Harold Dade, Los Angeles, U.S.A.

1950 May 31 Vic Toweel (S.A.) w.pts.15 Manuel Ortiz, Johannesburg, S. Africa.

Dec. 2 Vic Toweel (S.A.) w.rtd.10 Danny O'Sullivan (U.K.), Johannesburg, S. Africa.

1952 Jan. 26 Vic Toweel (S.A.) w.pts.15 Peter Keenan (U.K.), Johannesburg, S. Africa.

Nov. 15 Jimmy Carruthers (Aust) w.ko.1 Vic Toweel (S.A.), Johannesburg, S. Africa.

1953 March 21 Jimmy Carruthers (Aust) w.ko.10 Vic Toweel (S.A.), Australia.

Nov. 13 Jimmy Carruthers (Aust) w.pts.15 Henry 'Pappy' Gault, Sydney, Australia.

1954	May 3	Jimmy Carruthers (Aust) w.pts.15 Chamrern Songkitrat (T), Bangkok, Thailand.
	Sep. 18	Robert Cohen (Alg) w.pts.15 Chamrern Songkitrat (T), Bangkok, Thailand.
1956	June 29	Mario D'Agata (I) w.rtd.6 Robert Cohen (Alg), Rome, Italy.
1957	April 1	Alphonse Halimi (Alg) w.pts.15 Marlo D'Agata (I), Paris, France.
	Nov. 26	Alphonse Halimi (Alg) w.pts.15 Raul Raton Macias (M), Los Angeles, U.S.A.
1959	July 8	Joe Becerra (M) w.ko.8 Alphonse Halimi (Alg), Los Angeles, U.S.A.
1960	Oct. 25	Alphonse Halimi (Alg) w.pts.15 Freddie Gilroy (U.K.), London, U.K.
	Nov. 18	Eder Jofre (Bra) w.ko.6 Eloy Sanchez, Los Angeles, U.S.A.
1961	May 27	Johnny Caldwell (U.K.) w.pts.15 Alphonse Halimi (Alg), London, U.K.
	Oct. 31	Johnny Caldwell (U.K.) w.pts.15 Alphonse Halimi (Alg), London, U.K.
1962	Jan. 18	Eder Jofre (Bra) w.rtd.10 Johnny Caldwell (U.K.), Sao Paulo, Brazil. *(For undisputed title.)*
1965	May 18	Masahiko Harada (J) w.pts.15 Eder Jofre (Bra), Nagoya, Japan.
	Nov. 30	Masahiko Harada (J) w.pts.15 Alan Rudkin (U.K.), Tokyo, Japan.
1968	Feb. 27	Lionel Rose (Aust) w.pts.15 Masahaki Harada (J), Tokyo, Japan.
1969	March 8	Lionel Rose (Aust) w.pts.15 Alan Rudkin (U.K.), Melbourne, Australia.
	Aug. 22	Ruben Olivares (M) w.ko.5 Lionel Rose (Aust), Inglewood, U.S.A.
	Dec. 12	Ruben Olivares (M) w.rsf.2 Alan Rudkin (U.K.), Inglewood, U.S.A.
1970	Oct. 16	Jesus Castillo (M) w.rsf.14 Ruben Olivares (M), Mexico City, Mexico.
1971	April 2	Ruben Olivares (M) w.pts.15 Jesus Castillo (M), Inglewood, U.S.A.
1972	March 19	Rafael Herrera (M) w.ko.8 Ruben Olivares (M), Mexico City, Mexico.
	July 29	Enrique Pinder (Pan) w.pts.15 Rafael Herrera (M), Panama City, Panama.
1973	Jan. 20	*Romeo Anaya (M) w.ko.3 Enrique Pinder (Pan), Panama City, Panama.
	April 14	†Rafael Herrera (M) w.rsf.12 Rodolfo Martinez (M), Monterrey, Mexico.
	Nov. 3	*Arnold Taylor (S.A.) w.ko.14 Romeo Anaya (M), Johannesburg, S. Africa.
1974	July 3	*Soo Hwan Hong (S.K.) w.pts.15 Arnold Taylor (S.A.), Durban, S. Africa.
	Dec. 7	†Rodolfo Martinez (M) w.rsf.4 Rafael Herrera, (M), Merida, Mexico.
1975	March 14	*Alfonso Zamora (M) w.ko.4 Soo Hwan Hong (S.K.), Inglewood, U.S.A.
1976	May 9	†Carlos Zarate (M) w.ko.9 Rondolfo Martinez (M), Inglewood, U.S.A.
1977	Nov. 19	*Jorge Lujan (Pan) w.ko.10 Alfonso Zamora (M), Los Angeles, U.S.A.
1979	June 3	†Lupe Pintor (M) w.pts.15 Carlos Zarate (M), Las Vegas, U.S.A.
1980	Aug. 29	*Julian Solis (P.R.) w.pts.15 Jorge Lujan (Pan), Miami, U.S.A.
	Sep. 19	†Lupe Pintor (M) w.ko.12 Johnny Owen (U.K.), Los Angeles, U.S.A.
	Nov.14	*Jeff Chandler w.rsf.14 Julian Solis (P.R.), Miami Beach, U.S.A.
	Dec. 19	†Lupe Pintor (M) w.pts.15 Alberto Davila, Las Vegas, U.S.A.
1981	Jan. 31	*Jeff Chandler w.pts.15 Jorge Lujan (Pan), Philadelphia, U.S.A.
	Feb. 22	†Lupe Pintor (M) w.pts.15 Jose Uziga, Houston, U.S.A.
	April 4	*Jeff Chandler drew15 Elijiro Murata (J), Tokyo, Japan.
	July 25	*Jeff Chandler w.ko.7 Julian Solis (P.R.), Atlantic City, U.S.A.
	July 26	†Lupe Pintor (M) w.rsf.8 Jovita Rengifo, Las Vegas, U.S.A.
	Sep. 22	†Lupe Pintor (M) w.ko.15 Hurricane Teru (J), Tokyo, Japan.

	Dec. 10	*Jeff Chandler w.rsf.13 Eijiro Murata (J), Atlantic City, U.S.A.
1982	March 27	*Jeff Chandler w.rsf.6 Johnny Carter, Philadelphia, U.S.A.
	June 3	†Lupe Pintor (M) w.rsf.11 Seung-Hoon Lee (S.K.), Los Angeles, U.S.A. *Pinter forfeited title.*
	Oct. 27	*Jeff Chandler w.rsf.9 Miguel Iriarte (Pan), Atlantic City, U.S.A.
1983	March 13	*Jeff Chandler w.pts.15 Gaby Canizales, Atlantic City, U.S.A.
	Sep. 1	†Albert Davila w.ko.12 Francisco Bejines (M), Los Angeles, U.S.A.
	Sep. 11	*Jeff Chandler w.rsf.10 Eijiro Murata (J), Tokyo, Japan.
	Dec. 17	*Jeff Chandler w.rsf.7 Oscar Muniz, Atlantic City, U.S.A.
1984	April 7	*Richard Sandoval w.rsf.15 Jeff Chandler, Atlantic City, U.S.A.
	April 16	‡Satoshi Shingarki (J) w.rsf.8 Elmer Magallano (Col), Nara City, Japan.
	May 26	†Albert Davila w.rsf.11 Enrique Sanchez (Dom), Miami, U.S.A. *Davila relinquished W.B.C. title.*
	Aug. 4	‡Satoshi Shingarki (J) w.pts.15 Joves de la Puz (Phi), Nara City, Japan.
	Sep. 22	*Richard Sandoval w.pts.15 Edgar Roman (Ven), Monte Carlo, Monaco.
	Dec. 15	*Richard Sandoval w.rsf.8 Cardenio Ulloa (Chi), Miami, U.S.A.
1985	April 26	‡Jeff Fenech (Aust) w.rsf.9 Satoshi Shingarki (J), Sydney, Australia.
	May 4	†Daniel Zaragosa (M) w.dis.7 Freddie Jackson, Aruba, D.W.I.
	Aug. 9	†Miguel Lora (Col) w.pts.12 Daniel Zaragosa (M), Miami, U.S.A.
	Aug. 23	‡Jeff Fenech (Aust) w.rsf.3 Satoshi Shingarki (J), Sydney, Australia.
	Dec. 2	‡Jeff Fenech (Aust) w.pts.15 Jerome Coffee, Sydney, Australia.
1986	Feb. 8	†Miguel Lora (Col) w.pts.12 Wilfredo Vasquez (P.R.), Miami, U.S.A.
	March 10	*Gaby Canizales w.ko.7 Richard Sandoval, Las Vegas, U.S.A.
	June 4	*Bernardo Pinango (Ven) w.pts.15 Gaby Canizales, East Rutherford, U.S.A.
	July 18	‡Jeff Fenech (Aust) w.rsf.14 Steve McGrory, Sydney, Australia. *Fenech relinquished I.B.F. title.*
	Aug. 23	†Miguel Lora (Col) w.rsf.6 Enrique Sanchez (Dom), Miami, U.S.A.
	Oct. 4	*Bernardo Pinango (Ven) w.ret.10 Ciro De Leva (I), Turin, Italy.
	Nov. 15	†Miguel Lora (Col) w.pts.12 Albert Davila, Barranquilla, Colombia.
	Nov. 22	*Bernardo Pinango (Ven) w.ko.15 Simon Skosana (S.A.), Johannesburg, S.A.
1987	Feb. 3	*Bernardo Pinango (Ven) w.pts.15 Frankie Duarte, Los Angeles, U.S.A. *Pinango relinquished W.B.A. title.*
	March 29	*Takuya Muguruma (J) w.ko.5 Anzael Moran (Pan), Moriguchi, Japan.
	May 15	‡Kelvin Seabrooks w.ko.5 Miguel Maturana (Col), Cartagena, Colombia.
	May 24	*Chan-Yung Park (S.K.) w.rsf.11 Takuya Muguruma (J), Moriguchi, Japan.
	July 4	‡Kelvin Seabrooks w.ret.9 Thierry Jacob (F), Calais, France.
	July 25	†Miguel Lora (Col) w.rsf.4 Antonio Avelar (M), Miami, U.S.A.
	Oct. 4	*Wilfredo Vasquez (P.R.), w.ret.10 Chan-Young Park (S.K.), S. Korea, Seoul.
	Nov. 18	‡Kelvin Seabrooks w.ko.4 Ernie Cataluna (Phi), San Cataldo, Sicily.
	Nov. 27	†Miguel Lora (Col) w.pts.12 Ray Minus (Bah) Miami, U.S.A.
1988	Jan. 17	*Wilfredo Vasquez (P.R.) drew 12 Takuya Muguruma (J), Osaka, Japan.
	Feb. 6	‡Kelvin Seabrooks w.rsf.2 Fernando Beltran (M), Paris, France.
	April 30	†Miguel Lora (Col) w.pts.12 Lucio Lopez (Arg), Cartagena Colombia.

May 9	*Kaokor Galaxy (T) w.pts.12 Wilfredo Vasquez (P.R.), Bangkok, Thailand.	
July 9	‡Orlando Canizales w.rsf.15 Kelvin Seabrooks, Atlantic City, U.S.A.	
Aug. 1	†Miguel Lora (Col) w.pts.12 Albert Davila, Los Angeles, U.S.A.	
Aug. 14	*Moon Sung-Kil (S.K.) w.pts.12 Kaokor Galaxy (T), Pusan, S. Korea.	

World Super-Flyweight Title Fights
(115 pounds: 8 stone 3 pounds)

The W.B.C. launched this division between flyweight and bantamweight on Feb. 2, 1980 when Rafael Orono (Venezuela) outpointed Seung-Hen Lee (South Korea) at Caracas. On Sep. 12, 1981 the W.B.A. countered with the recognition of Gustavo Ballas (Argentina) when he stopped Suk Chui Bae (South Korea) in eight rounds at Buenos Aires. There remain two champions.

1980	Feb. 2	†Rafael Orono (Ven) w.pts.15 Seung-Hen Lee (S.K.), Caracas, Venezuela.
1981	Jan. 24	†Chul-Ho Kim (S.K.) w.ko.9 Rafael Orono (Ven), San Cristobal, Venezuela.
	April 24	†Chul-Ho Kim (S.K.) w.pts.15 Jiro Watanabe (J), Seoul, S. Korea.
	July 24	†Chul-Ho Kim (S.K.) w.ko.13 Willie Jensen, Pusan, S. Korea.
	Sep. 12	*Gustavo Ballas (Arg) w.rsf.8 Suk Chui Bae (S.K.), Buenos Aires, Argentina.
	Nov. 18	†Chul-Ho Kim (S.K.) w.rsf.9 Ryotsu Maruyama (J), Pusan, S. Korea.
	Dec. 5	*Rafael Pedroza (Pan) w.pts.15 Gustavo Ballas (Arg), Panama City, Panama.
1982	Feb. 10	†Chul-Ho Kim (S.K.) w.ko.8 Koki Ishii (J), Taegu, S. Korea.
	April 8	*Jiro Watanabe (J) w.pts.15 Rafael Pedroza (Pan), Osaka, Japan.
	July 4	†Chul-Ho Kim (S.K.) drew 15 Raul Valdez (M), Daejon, South Korea.
	July 29	*Jiro Watanabe (J) w.rsf.9 Gustavo Ballas (Arg), Osaka, Japan.
	Nov. 11	*Jiro Watanabe (J) w.rsf.12 Shijo Oguma (J), Hamamatsu, Japan.
	Nov. 28	†Rafael Orono (Ven) w.rsf.6 Chul-Ho Kim (S.K.), Seoul, S. Korea.
1983	Jan. 31	†Rafael Orono (Ven) w.ko.4 Pedro Romero (Pan), Caracas, Venezuela.
	Feb. 24	*Jiro Watanabe (J) w.ko.8 Luis Ibanez (Peru), Tsuc, Japan.
	June 23	*Jiro Watanabe (J) w.pts.12 Roberto Raminez (M), Sendai, Japan.
	Oct. 6	*Jiro Watanabe (J) w.pts.11 Soon-Chun Kwon (S.K.), Osaka, Japan.
	Oct. 30	†Rafael Orono (Ven) w.ko.5 Orlando Maldonado (P.R.), Caracas, Venezuela.
	Nov. 27	†Payao Poontarat (T) w.pts.12 Rafael Orono (Ven), Bangkok, Thailand.
	Dec. 10	‡Joo-Do Chun (S.K.) w.rsf.5 Kem Kasugai (J), Osaka, Japan.
1984	Jan. 28	‡Joo-Do Chun (S.K.) w.rsf.12 Prayurasak Muangsurin (T), Seoul, S. Korea.
	March 15	*Jiro Watanabe w.rsf.15 Celso Chavez (Pan), Osaka, Japan.
	March 17	‡Joo-Do Chun (S.K.) w.ko.1 Diego de Villa (Phi), Kwangju, S. Korea.
	March 28	*Payao Poontarat (T) w.rsf.10 Gustavo Espadas (M), Bangkok, Thailand.
	May 26	‡Joo-Do Chun (S.K.) w.rsf.6 Felix Marquez (P.R.), Wonju, S. Korea.
	July 5	†Jiro Watanabe (J) w.pts.12 Payao Poontarat (T), Osaka, Japan.
	July 20	‡Joo-Do Chun (S.K.) w.ko.7 William Develos (Phi), Pusan, S. Korea.
	Nov. 21	*Kaosai Galaxy (T) w.ko.6 Eusebio Espinal (Dom), Bangkok, Thailand.
	Nov. 29	†Jiro Watanabe (J) w.rsf.11 Payao Poontarat (T), Kumamoto, Japan.
1985	Jan. 3	‡Joo-Do Chun (S.K.) w.ko.15 Kwang-Gu Park (S.K.), Ulsan, S. Korea.

March 6	*Kaosai Galaxy (T) w.ko.7 Dong-Chun Lee (S.K.), Bangkok, Thailand.	
May 3	‡Ellyas Pical (Ind) w.ko.8 Joo-Do Chun (S.K.), Jakarta, Indonesia.	
May 9	†Jiro Watanabe (J) w.pts.12 Julio Soto Solano (Dom), Tokyo, Japan.	
July 17	*Kaosai Galaxy (T) w.rsf.5 Rafael Orono (Ven), Bangkok, Thailand.	
Aug. 25	‡Ellyas Pical (Ind) w.rsf.3 Wayne Mulholland (Aust), Jakarta, Indonesia.	
Sep. 17	†Jiro Watanabe (J) w.rsf.7 Katsuo Katsuma (J), Osaka, Japan.	
Dec. 13	†Jiro Watanabe (J) w.ko.5 Yun-Sok-Wang (S.K.), Taegu, South Korea.	
Dec. 23	*Kaosai Galaxy (T) w.ko.2 Edgar Monserrat (Pan), Bangkok, Thailand.	

1986	Feb. 15	‡Carlos Cesar Polanco (Dom) w.pts.15 Ellyas Pica, (Ind), Jakarta, Indonesia.
	March 30	†Gilberto Roman (M) w.pts.12 Jiro Watanabe (J), Itami, Japan.
	May 15	†Gilberto Roman (M) w.pts.12 Edgar Monserrat (M), Paris, France.
	July 5	‡Ellyas Pical w.ko.3 Carlos Cesar Polanco (Dom), Jakarta, Indonesia.
	July 18	†Gilberto Roman (M) w.pts.12 Ruben Condori (M), Salta, Argentina.
	Aug. 30	†Gilberto Roman (M) drew 12 Santos Lacia (Arg), Cordoba, Argentina.
	Nov. 1	*Gilberto Roman (M) w.ko.5 Israel Contreras (Ven), Curacao, D.W.I.
	Dec. 3	‡Ellyas Pical (Ind) w.ko.10 Dong-Chun Lee (S.K.), Jakarta, Indonesia.
	Dec. 19	†Gilberto Roman (M) w.pts.12 Kongtorance Payakaroon (T), Bangkok, Thailand.
1987	Jan. 31	†Gilberto Roman (M) w.rsf.9 Antonio Montero (M), Montpelier, France.
	Feb. 28	*Kaosai Galaxy (T) w.ko.14 Ellyas Pical, Jakarta, Indonesia.
	March 19	†Gilberto Roman (M) w.pts.12 Frank Cedano (Phi), Mexicali, Mexico.
	May 15	‡Dae-Il Chang (S.K.) w.pts.15 Soon-Chun Kwan (S.K.), Pusan, S. Korea.
	May 16	†Santos Laciar (Arg) w.rsf.11 Gilberto Roman (M), Reims. France.
	Aug. 8	†Sugar Baby Rojas w.pts.12 Santos Lacier (Aug), Miami, U.S.A.
	Oct. 12	*Kaosai Galaxy (T) w.ko.3 Chung Byong-Kwan (S.K.), Bangkok, Thailand.
	Oct. 17	‡Ellyas Pical (Ind) w.ko.13 Chang Tae Il (S.K.), Jakarta, Indonesia.
	Oct. 24	†Sugar Baby Rojas (Col) w.rsf.4 Gustavo Ballas (Arg), Miami, U.S.A.
1988	Jan. 26	*Kaosai Galaxy (T) w.pts.12 Kongtorance Payakaroon (T), Bangkok, Thailand.
	Feb. 20	‡Ellyas Pical (Ind) w.pts.15 Raul Diaz (Col), Pontianak, Indonesia.
	April 8	†Gilberto Roman (M) w.pts.12 Sugar Baby Rojas (Col), Miami, U.S.A.
	July 9	†Gilberto Roman (M) w.rsf.5 Yochiyuki Uchida (J), Kawagoe, Japan.
	Aug. 28	‡Ellyas Pical (Ind) w.pts.15 Kichang Kim Swibye, Indonesia.
	Sep. 3	†Gilberto Roman (M) w.pts.12 Kiosturi Natanaka (J), Nagoya, Japan.

World Flyweight Title Fights
(112 pounds: 8 stone)

Before the introduction of the many intermediary classes, the flyweight division was the lowest recognized poundage for which there was an official world championship. The weight was set at 112 pounds by the N.S.C. in 1909, but prior to that anyone below the bantam limit could call himself a flyweight, which denoted someone particularly small. There were even title fights at so-called 'paperweight'. The first British flyweight champion was Sid Smith (Bermondsey, London) who also became the first world titleholder in 1913. Welshman Jimmy Wilde, who never scaled much more than 100 pounds, was a great one in this division; he reigned as world champion from 1916 to 1923. Duplicate champions were introduced by the N.Y.A.C. and the N.B.A. in 1927, then things righted themselves until 1972–73 when the W.B.C. and the W.B.A. created their own champions and this situation remains.

1916	April 24	Jimmy Wilde (U.K.) w.rtd.11 Johnny Rosner (U.K.), Liverpool, U.K.
	June 26	Jimmy Wilde (U.K.) w.rsf.11 Tancy Lee (U.K.), London, U.K..
	July 31	Jimmy Wilde (U.K.) w.ko.10 Johnny Hughes (U.K.), London, U.K.
	Dec. 18	Jimmy Wilde (U.K.) w.ko.11 Zulu Kid, London, U.K.
1917	March 12	Jimmy Wilde (U.K.) w.rtd.4 George Clark, London, U.K.
1923	June 18	Pancho Villa (Phi) w.ko.7 Jimmy Wilde (U.K.), New York, U.S.A.
1924	May 30	Pancho Villa (Phi) w.pts.15 Frankie Ash, New York.
1927	Nov. 28	Albert 'Frenchie' Belanger (Can) w.pts.10 Frankie Genaro, Toronto, Canada.
1928	Feb. 6	Frankie Genaro w.pts.10 Albert 'Frenchie' Belanger (Can), Toronto, Canada.
1929	March 2	Emile Pladner (F) w.ko.1 Frankie Genaro, Paris, France.
	April 18	Frankie Genaro w.dis.5 Emile Pladner (F), Paris, France.
1931	Oct. 27	Victor Perez (Tun) w.ko.2 Frankie Genaro, Paris, France.
1932	Oct. 31	Jackie Brown (U.K.) w.rsf.13 Victor Perez (Tun), Manchester, U.K.
1933	Sep. 11	Jackie Brown (U.K.) w.pts.15 Valentin Angelmann (F), Manchester, U.K.
	Dec. 11	Jackie Brown (U.K.) w.pts.15 Ginger Foran (U.K.), Manchester, U.K.
1934	June 18	Jackie Brown (U.K.) drew 15 Valentin Angelmann (F), Manchester, U.K.
1935	Sep. 9	Benny Lynch (U.K.) w.rtd.2 Jackie Brown (U.K.), Manchester, U.K.
1936	Sep. 16	Benny Lynch (U.K.) w.ko.8 Pat Palmer (U.K.), Glasgow, U.K.
1937	Jan. 19	Benny Lynch (U.K.) w.pts.15 Small Montana (Phi), London, U.K.
	Oct. 13	Benny Lynch (U.K.) w.ko.13 Peter Kane (U.K.) Glasgow, U.K.
1938	Sep. 22	Peter Kane (U.K.) w.pts.15 Jackie Jurich (U.K.), Liverpool, U.K.
1943	June 19	Jackie Paterson (U.K.) w.ko.1 Peter Kane (U.K.), Glasgow, U.K.
1946	July 10	Jackie Paterson (U.K.) w.pts.15 Joe Curran (U.K.), Glasgow, U.K.
1948	March 23	Rinty Monaghan (U.K.) w.ko.7 Jackie Paterson (U.K.), Belfast, U.K.
1949	April 5	Rinty Monaghan (U.K.) w.pts.15 Maurice Sandeyron (F), Belfast, U.K.
	Sep. 30	Rinty Monaghan (U.K.) drew15 Terry Allen (U.K.), Belfast, U.K.
1950	April 5	Terry Allen (U.K.) w.pts.15 Honore Pratesi (F), London, U.K.
	Aug. 1	Dado Marino (Ha) w.pts.15 Terry Allen (U.K.), Honolulu, Hawaii.
1951	Nov. 1	Dado Marino (Ha) w.pts.15 Terry Allen (U.K.), Honolulu, Hawaii.
1952	May 19	Yoshio Shirai (J) w.pts.15 Dado Marino (Ha), Tokyo, Japan.
1953	Oct. 27	Yoshio Shirai (J) w.pts.15 Terry Allen (U.K.), Tokyo, Japan.
1954	Nov. 26	Pascual Perez (Arg) w.pts.15 Yoshio Shirai (J), Tokyo, Japan.
1957	March 30	Pascual Perez (Arg) w.ko.1 Dai Dower (U.K.), Buenos Aires, Argentina.
1960	April 16	Pone Kingpetch (T) w.pts.15 Pascual Perez (Arg), Bangkok, Thailand.
1962	Oct. 10	Masahiko Harada (J) w.ko.11 Pone Kingpetch (T), Tokyo, Japan.
1963	Jan. 12	Pone Kingpetch (T) w.pts.15 Masahiko Harada (J), Bangkok, Thailand.
	Sep. 18	Hiroyuki Ebihara (J) w.ko.1 Pone Kingpetch (T), Tokyo, Japan.
1964	Jan. 23	Pone Kingpetch (T) w.pts.15 Hiroyuki Ebihara (J), Bangkok, Thailand.
1965	April 23	Salvatore Burruni (I) w.pts.15 Pone Kingpetch (T), Rome, Italy.

1966	March 1	*Horacio Accavallo (Arg) w.pts.15 Katsutoshi Takayama (J), Tokyo, Japan.
	June 14	†Walter McGowan (U.K.) w.pts.15 Salvatore Burruni (I), London, U.K.
	Dec. 30	†Chartchai Chionoi (T) w.rsf.9 Walter McGowan (U.K.), Bangkok, Thailand.
1967	Sep. 19	†Chartchai Chionoi (T) w.rsf.7 Walter McGowan (U.K.), London, U.K.
1969	Feb. 23	†Efren Torres (M) w.rsf.8 Chartchoi Chionoi (T), Mexico City, Mexico.
	March 30	*Hiroyuki Ebihara (J) w.pts.15 Jose Severino, Sapporo, Japan.
	Oct. 19	*Bernabe Villacampo (Phi) w.pts.15 Hiroyuki Ebihara (J), Osaka, Japan.
1970	March 20	†Chartchai Chionoi (J) w.pts.15 Efren Torres (M), Bangkok, Thailand.
	April 6	*Berkrerk Chartvanchai (T) w.pts.15 Bernabe Villacampo (Phi), Bangkok, Thailand.
	Oct. 21	*Masao Ohba (J) w.rsf.13 Berkrerk Chartvanchai (T), Tokyo, Japan.
	Dec. 7	†Erbito Salavarria (Phi) w.rsf.2 Chartchai Chionoi (J), Bangkok, Thailand.
1972	Sept. 29	†Venice Borkorsor (T) w.rtd.10 Betulio Gonzalez (Ven), Bangkok, Thailand.
1973	May 17	*Chartchai Chionoi (J) w.rsf.4 Fritz Chervet (Sw), Bangkok, Thailand.
	Aug. 4	†Betulio Gonzalez (Ven) w.pts.15 Miguel Canto (M), Maracaibo, Venezuela.
1974	Oct. 1	†Shoji Oguma (J) w.pts.15 Betulio Gonzalez (Ven), Tokyo, Japan.
1975	Jan. 8	†Miguel Canto (M) w.pts.15 Shoji Oguma (J), Sendai, Japan.
	Oct. 18	*Susuma Hanagata (J) w.rsf.6 Chartchai Chionoi (J), Yokohama, Japan.
1975	Jan. 8	†Miguel Canto (M) w.pts.15 Shoji Oguma (J), Sendai, Japan.
	April 1	*Erbito Salavarria (Phi) w.pts.15 Susumu Hanagata (J), Toyama, Japan.
1976	Feb. 27	*Alfonso Lopez (Pan) w.rsf.15 Erbito Salavarria (Phi), Manila, Philippines.
	Oct. 2	*Gustavo Espadas (M) w.rsf.13 Alfonso Lopez (Pan), Los Angeles, U.S.A.
1978	Aug. 13	*Betulio Gonzalez (Ven) w.pts.15 Gustavo Espadas (M), Maracay, Venezuela.
1979	March 18	†Chan-Hee Park (S.K.) w.pts.15 Miguel Canto (M), Pusan, S. Korea.
	Nov. 16	*Luis Ibarra (Pan) w.pts.15 Betulio Gonzalez (Ven), Maracay, Venezuela.
1980	Feb. 16	*Taeshik Kim (S.K.) w.ko.2 Luis Ibarra (Pan), Seoul, S. Korea.
	May 18	†Shoji Oguma (J) w.ko.9 Chan-Hee Park (S.K.), Seoul, S. Korea.
	Dec. 13	*Peter Mathebula (S.A.) w.pts.15 Taeshik Kim (S.K.), Los Angeles, U.S.A.
1981	March 28	*Santos Laciar (Arg) w.ko.7 Peter Mathebula (S.A.), Soweto, S. Africa.
	May 12	†Antonio Avelar (M) w.ko.7 Shoji Oguma (J), Mito, Japan.
	June 6	*Luis Ibarra (Pan) w.pts.15 Santos Laciar (Arg), Buenos Aires, Argentina.
	Aug. 30	†Antonio Avelar (M) w.ko.2 Taeshik Kim (S.K.), Seoul, S. Korea.
	Sep. 26	*Juan Herrera (M) w.ko.11 Luis Ibarra (Pan), Merida, Mexico.
1982	March 20	†Prudencio Cardona (Col) w.ko.1 Antonio Avelar (M), Tampico, Mexico.
	May 1	*Santos Laciar (Arg) w.rsf.12 Juan Herrar (M), Merida, Mexico.
	July 24	†Freddie Castilo (M) w.pts.15 Prudencio Cardona (Col), Merida, Mexico.
	Nov. 6	†Eleoncio Mercedes (Dom) w.pts.15 Freddie Castillo (M), Los Angeles, U.S.A.
	Aug. 14	*Santos Laciar (Arg) w.rsf.13 Betulio Gonzalez (Ven), Maracaibo, Venezuela.
	Nov. 5	*Santos Laciar (Arg) w.rsf.13 Stephen Muchoki, Copenhagen, Denmark.
1983	March 4	*Santos Laciar (Arg) w.ko.9 Ramon Neri, Cordoba, Argentina.
	March 15	†Charlie Magri (G.B.) w.rsf.7 Eleoncio Mercedes,

May 5 *Santos Laciar (Arg) w.rsf.2 Shuichi Hozumi (J), Shisuoka, Japan.

July 17 *Santos Laciar (Arg) w.ko.1 Hi-Sup Shin (S.K.), Cheju-Do, S. Korea.

Sep. 27 †Frank Cedeno (Phi) w.rsf.6 Charlie Magri (G.B.), Wembley, U.K.

Dec. 24 ‡Soon-Chun Kwon (S.K.) w.ko.5 Rene Busayong (Phi), Seoul, S. Korea.

1984

Jan. 18 †Koji Kobayashi (J) w.rsf.2 Frank Cedeno (Phi), Tokyo, Japan.

Jan. 28 *Santos Laciar (Arg) w.pts.15 Juan Herrera (M), Marsala, Italy.

Feb. 25 ‡Soon-Chun Kown (S.K.) w.rsf.12 Roger Castillo (Phi), Seoul, S. Korea.
Castillo proved to be Joaquin Caraballo – bout nulled by I.B.F.

April 19 †Gabriel Bernal (M) w.rsf.2 Koji Kobayashi (J), Tokyo, Japan.

May 19 ‡Soon-Chun Kwon (S.K.) w.pts.15 Ian Clyde (Can), Daejon, S. Korea.

June 1 †Gabriel Bernal (M) w.rsf.11 Antoine Montero (F), Nimes, France.

Sep. 7 ‡Soon-Chun Kwon (S.K.) w.rsf.12 Joaquin Caraballo (Arg), Chonju, S. Korea.

Sep. 15 *Santos Laciar (Arg) w.ko.10 Prudencio Cardona (Col), Cardoba, Argentina.

Oct. 8 †Sot Chitalada (T) w.pts.12 Gabriel Bernal (M), Bangkok, Thailand.

Dec. 8 *Santos Laciar (Arg) w.pts.15 Hilario Zapata (Pan), Buenos Aires, Argentina.

1985

Jan. 25 ‡Soon-Chun Kwon (S.K.) drew 15 Chong-Kwan Chung (S.K.) Taejon, S. Korea.

Feb. 20 †Sot Chitalada (T) w.ret.4 Charlie Magri (G.B.), London, England.

April 14 ‡Soon-Chun Kwon (S.K.), w.ko.3 Shinobu Kawashima (J), Pohang, S. Korea.

May 6 *Santos Laciar (Arg) w.pts.15 Antoine Montero (F), Grenoble, France.
Laciar relinquished W.B.A. title.

June 22 †Sot Chitalada (T) drew 12 Gabriel Bernal (M), Bangkok, Thailand.

Oct. 5 *Hilario Zapata (Pan) w.pts.15 Alonzo Gonzalez, Panama City, Panama.

Dec. 20 ‡Chong-Kwan Chung (S.K.) w.rsf.4 Soon-Chun Kwon (S.K.), Pusan, S. Korea.

1986

Jan. 31 *Hilario Zapata (Pan) w.pts.15 Javier Lucas (M), Panama City, Panama.

Feb. 22 †Sot Chitalada (T) w.pts.12 Freddie Castillo, Kuwait.

April 7 *Hilario Zapata (Pan) w.pts.15 Suichi Hozumi (J), Nirasaki, Japan.

April 27 ‡Bi-Won Chung (S.K.) w.pts.15 Chong-Kwan Chung (S.K.), Pusan, S. Korea.

July 5 *Hilario Zapata (Pan) w.pts.15 Dodie Panalosa (Phi), Manila, Philippines.

Aug. 2 ‡Hi-Sup Shin (S.K.) w.rsf.15 Bi-Won Chung (S.K.), Inchon, S. Korea.

Sep. 13 *Hilario Zapata (Pan) w.pts.15 Alberto Castro (Col), Panama City, Panama.

Nov. 22 ‡Hi-Sup Shin w.rsf.13 Henry Brent, Chunchon, S. Korea.

Dec. 6 *Hilario Zapata (Pan) w.pts.15 Claudemir Carvalho Dias (Bra), Salvador, Brazil.

Dec. 10 †Sot Chitalada (T) w.rsf.3 Gabriel Bernal (M), Bangkok, Thailand.

1987

Feb. 13 *Fidel Bassa (Col) w.pts.15 Hilario Zapata (Pan), Barranquilla, Columbia.

Feb. 22 ‡Dodie Penalosa (Phi) w.ko.5 Hi-Sup Shin (S.K.), Inchon, S. Korea.

April 25 *Fidel Bassa (Col) w.ko.13 Dave McAuley (G.B.), Belfast, U.K.

Aug. 15 *Fidel Bassa (Col) drew 15 Hilario Zapata (Pan), Panama City, Panama.

Sep. 5 †Sot Chitalada (T) w.ko.4 Rac-Ki Ahn (S.K.), Bangkok, Thailand.

Sep. 5 ‡Chang-Ho Choi (S.K.) w.ko.11 Dodie Penalosa (Phi), Manila, Philippines.

Dec. 18 *Fidel Bassa (Col) w.pts.12 Felix Marty (Dom), Cartegena, Colombia.

1988

Jan. 16 ‡Rolando Bohol (Phi) w.pts.15 Chang-Ho Choi (S.K.), Manila, Philippines.

Jan. 31 †Sot Chitalada (T) w.rsf.7 Hideaki Kamishiro (J), Osaka, Japan.

March 26 *Fidel Bassa (Col) w.pts.12 Dave McAuley, Belfast, U.K.

May 6 ‡Rolando Bohol (Phi) w.pts.15 Cho-Woon Park (S.K.), Manila, Philippines.

July 23 †Yung-Kang Kim (S.K.) w.pts.12 Sot Chitalada (T), Pohang, S. Korea.

World Light-Flyweight Title Fights
(108 pounds: 7 stone 10 pounds)

Introduced by the W.B.C. on April 4, 1975 when Franco Udello (Italy) won on a foul over Valentin Martinez (Mexico) at Milan. The W.B.A. countered by giving recognition to Jaime Rios (Panama) when he outpointed Rigoberto Marcarno at Panama City on Aug. 23 the same year. There have always been two champions to this division.

1975

April 4 †Franco Udello (I) w.dis.12 Valentin Martinez (M), Milan, Italy.

Aug. 23 *Jaime Rios (Pan) w.pts.15 Rigoberto Marcano (Pan), Panama City, Panama.

Sep. 13 †Luis Estaba (Ven) w.ko.4 Rafael Lobera, Caracas, Venezuela.

1976

July 1 *Juan Guzman (Dom) w.pts.15 Jaime Rios (Pan), Santo Domingo, Dominica.

Oct. 10 *Yoko Gushiken (J) w.ko.7 Juan Guzman (Dom), Kofu, Japan.

1978

Feb. 19 †Freddie Castillo (M) w.rsf.14 Luis Estaba (Ven), Caracas, Venezuela.

May 6 †Netrnoi Vorasingh (T) w.pts.15 Freddie Castillo (M), Bangkok, Thailand.

Sep. 30 †Kim Sung-Jun (S.K.) w.ko.3 Netrnoi Vorasingh (T), Seoul, S. Korea.

1980

Jan. 3 †Shigeo Nakajima (J) w.pts.15 Kim Sung-Jun (S.K.), Tokyo, Japan.

March 23 *Hilario Zapata (Pan) w.pts.15 Shigeo Nakajima (J), Tokyo, Japan.

1981

Jan. 31 *Pedro Flores (M) w.rtd.12 Yoko Gushiken (J), Naha, Japan.

Feb. 8 †Hilario Zapata (Pan) w.rtd.13 Joey Olivo, Panama City, Panama.

April 24 †Hilario Zapata (Pan) w.pts.15 Rudy Crawford, San Francisco, U.S.A.

July 19 *Hwan-Jim Kim (S.K.) w.rsf.13 Pedro Flores (M), Seoul, S. Korea.

Aug. 16 †Hilario Zapata (Pan) w.pts.15 German Torres (Phi), Panama City, Panama.

Nov. 6 †Hilario Zapata (Pan) w.rsf.10 Netrnoi Vorsingh (T), Nakhon Ratchasima, Thailand.

Dec. 16 *Katsuo Takashiki (J) w.pts.15 Hwan-Jim Kim (S.K.), Sendai, Japan.

1982

Feb. 6 †Amado Ursua (M) w.ko.2 Hilario Zapata (Pan), Panama City, Panama.

April 4 *Katsuo Takashiki (J) w.pts.15 Lupe Madero (M), Tokyo, Japan.

April 13 †Tadashi Tomori (J) w.pts.15 Amado Ursua (M), Tokyo, Japan.

July 7 *Katsuo Takashiki (J) w.rsf.8 Masaharu Inami (J), Tokyo, Japan.

July 20 †Hilario Zapata (Pan) w.pts.15 Tadeshi Tomori (J), Kanazawa, Japan.

Sep. 18 †Hilario Zapata (Pan) w.pts.15 Yung-Koo Chang (S.K.), Chunju, S. Korea.

Oct. 10 *Katsuo Takashiki (J) w.pts.15 Sung Nam Kim (S.K.), Tokyo, Japan.

Nov. 30 †Hilario Zapata (Pan) w.rsf.8 Tadashi Tomori (J), Tokyo, Japan.

1983

Jan. 9 *Katsuo Takashiki (J) w.pts.15 Hwan Jin Kim (S.K.), Tokyo, Japan.

March 26 †Jung-Koo Chang (S.K.) w.rsf.3 Hilario Zapata (Pan), Seoul, S. Korea.

April 10 *Katsuo Takashiki (J) drew 15 Lupe Madera (M), Tokyo, Japan.

June 11 †Jung-Koo Chang (S.K.) w.rsf.2 Masaharu Tha (J), Taegu, South Korea.

July 10 *Lupe Madera w.rsf.4 Katsuo Takashiki (J), Tokyo, Japan.
Sep. 10 †Jung-Koo Chang (S.K.) w.pts.12 German Torres (M), Taejon, S. Korea.
Oct. 23 *Lupe Madera w.pts.15 Katsuo Takashiki (J), Sapporo, Japan.
Dec. 10 ‡Dodie Penelosa (Phi) w.ko.12 Satoshi Shingaki (J), Osaka, Japan.

1984 March 31 †Jung-Koo Chang (S.K.) w.pts.12 Sot Chitalada (T), Pusan, S. Korea.
May 13 ‡Dodie Penelosa (Phi) w.rsf.9 Jae-Hong Kim (S.K.), Seoul, S. Korea.
May 28 *Francisco Quiroz (Ven) w.ko.9 Lupe Madera, Maracaibo, Venezuela.
Aug. 18 †Jung-Koo Chang (S.K.) w.rsf.9 Katsuo Takashiki (J), Poang, S. Korea.
Aug. 18 *Francisco Quiroz (Ven) w.ko.2 Victor Sierra, Panama C., Panama.
Nov. 16 ‡Dodie Penelosa (Phi) w.pts.12 Chum-Hwan Choi (S.K.), Quezon City, Philippines.
Dec. 15 †Jung-Koo Chang (S.K.) w.pts.12 Tadashi Kuramochi (J), Pusan, S. Korea.

1985 March 29 *Joey Oliva w.pts.15 Francisco Quiroz (Ven), Miami, U.S.A.
April 27 †Jung-Koo Chang (S.K.) w.pts.12 German Torres (M), Pusan, S. Korea.
July 28 *Joey Oliva w.pts.15 Mun-Jim Choi (S.K.), Seoul, S. Korea.
Aug. 3 †Jung-Koo Chang (S.K.) w.pts.12 Francisco Montiel (M), Seoul, S. Korea.
Oct. 12 ‡Dodie Penelosa (Phi) w.rsf.3 Yani Dokolamo, Jakarta, Indonesia.
Penelosa relinquished I.B.F. title.
Nov. 10 †Jung-Koo Chang (S.K.) w.pts.12 Jorge Cano (M), Seoul, S. Korea.
Dec. 8 *Yuh Myung-Woo (S.K) w.pts.15 Joey Oliva, Seoul, S. Korea.

1986 March 9 *Yuh Myung-Woo (S.K.) w.pts.15 Jose DeJesus (P.R.), Suwon, S. Korea.
April 13 †Jung-Koo Chang (S.K.) w.pts.12 German Torres (M), Kwanju, S. Korea.
June 14 *Yuh Myung-Woo (S.K.) w.ko.12 Tomosjiro Kijuna (J), Inchon, S. Korea.
Sep. 13 †Jung-Koo Chang (S.K.) w.pts.12 Francisco Montiel (M), Taejon, S. Korea.
Nov. 30 *Yuh Myung-Woo (S.K.) w.pts.15 Mario De Marco (Arg), Seoul, S. Korea.

Dec. 7 ‡Jum-Hwan Choi (S.K.) w.pts.15 Cho-Woon Park (S.K.), Pusan, S. Korea.
Dec. 14 †Jung-Koo Chang (S.K.) w.rsf.5 Hideyaki Ohashi (J), Inchon, South Korea.

1987 March 1 *Yuh Myung-Woo (S.K.) w.rsf.1 Eduardo Tunon (Pan), Seoul, S. Korea.
March 29 ‡Jum Hwan-Choi (S.K.) w.pts.15 Tacy Marcalos (Phi), Seoul, S. Korea.
April 19 †Jung-Koo Chang (S.K.) w.rsf.6 Efren Pinto (M), Seoul, S. Korea.
June 7 *Yuh Myung-Woo (S.K.) w.rsf.15 Benedicto Murillo (Pan), Pusan, S. Korea.
June 28 †Jung-Koo Chang (S.K.) w.ko.10 Augustin Garcia (Col), Inchon, S. Korea.
July 5 ‡Jum-Hwan Choi (S.K.) w.ko.4 Toshihiko Matsuda (J), Seoul, S. Korea.
July 12 ‡Jum-Hwan Choi (S.K.) w.pts.15 Cho-Woon Park (S.K.), Pusan, S. Korea.
Aug. 9 ‡Jum-Hwan Choi (S.K.) w.ko.3 Azadin Amhar, Jakarta, Indonesia.
Sep. 20 *Yuh Myung-Woo (S.K.) w.ko.8 Rodolfo Bianco (Col), Inchon, S. Korea.
Dec. 13 †Jung-Koo Chang (S.K.) w.pts.12 Isidro Perez (M), Taejon, S. Korea.

1988 Feb. 7 *Yuh Myung-Woo (S.K.) w.pts.12 Wilabardo Salazar (M), Seoul, S. Korea.
June 12 *Yuh Myung-Woo (S.K.) w.pts.12 Jose DeJesus, Seoul, S. Korea.
June 27 †Jung-Koo Chang (S.K.) w.rsf.8 Hideyuki Ohashi (J), Tokyo, Japan.

World Mini-Flyweight Title Fights
(105 pounds: 7 stone 7 pounds)

1987 Oct. 18 †Hiroki Ioka (J) w.pts.12 Mai Thomburifarm (T), Osaka, Japan.
1988 Jan. 10 *Louis Gamez w.pts.12 Bong-Jung Kim (S.K.), Pusan, South Korea.
Jan. 31 †Hiroki Ioka (J) w.rsf.12 Kyung-Yung Lee (S.K.), Osaka, Japan.
March 24 ‡Samuth Sithnakupol (T) w.rsf.11 Pretty Boy Lucas, Bangkok, Thailand.
April 29 *Louis Gamez w.rsf.3 Kenji Yokozawa (J), Tokyo, Japan.
Aug. 29 ‡Samuth Sithnakupol (T) w.pts.12 In-Ku Hwang (S.K.), Bangkok, Thailand.

Abbreviations

Match Abbreviations

d	drew
dis	disqualification
dnc	declared no contest
ko	knock-out
l	lost
ND	no decision
pts	points
ret/rtd	retired
rsf	referee stopped fight
tec	technical decision
w	won

Organizations

A.B.A.	Amateur Boxing Association
B.B.B.C.	British Boxing Board of Control
E.B.U.	European Boxing Union
I.B.F.	International Boxing Federation
I.B.U.	International Boxing Union
N.A.B.F.	North American Boxing Federation
N.S.C.	National Sporting Club
N.Y.S.A.C.	New York State Athletic Commission
U.S.B.A.	United States Boxing Association
W.B.A.	World Boxing Association
W.B.C.	World Boxing Council

Countries

A	Austria
Alg	Algeria
Arg	Argentina
Aust	Australia
B	Belgium
Bah	Bahamas
Bar	Barbados
B.G.	British Guyana
Bra	Brazil
C	Cuba
Can	Canada
Chi	Chile
Col	Colombia
Cze	Czechoslovakia
D	Denmark
Dom	Dominican Republic
D.W.I.	Dutch West Indies
E	England
E.G.	East Germany
Ei	Eire
F	France
Fin	Finland
G	Germany (pre-1945)
G.B.	Great Britain
Gha	Ghana
Gr	Greece
Gu	Guyana
Ha	Hawaii
Hun	Hungary
I	Italy
Ind	Indonesia
J	Japan
Jam	Jamaica
Lux	Luxemburg
M	Mexico
N	Norway
N.I.	Northern Ireland
Nic	Nicaragua
Nig	Nigeria
Nl	Netherlands
N.Z.	New Zealand
P	Portugal
Pan	Panama
Phi	Philippines
P.-N.G.	Papua-New Guinea
P.R.	Puerto Rico
R	Romania
S	Scotland
S.A.	South Africa
Sam	Samoa
Sen	Senegal
S.K.	South Korea
Sp	Spain
Sw	Switzerland
Swe	Sweden
T	Thailand
To	Tonga
Tr	Trinidad
Tun	Tunisia
U	Uganda
U.K.	United Kingdom
Ur	Uruguay
U.S.A.	United States of America
U.S.S.R.	Union of Soviet Socialist Republics
Ven	Venezuela
V.I.	Virgin Isles
W	Wales
W.G.	West Germany
W.I.	West Indies
Yugo	Yugoslavia
Z	Zambia
Zim	Zimbabwe

Index of Illustrations

Acknowledgements

The publishers would like to thank the following organisations and individuals for their kind permission to reproduce the illustrations in this book:

ALL-SPORT 8-9c, 14t, 15, 18b, 43, 50t, 58, 62t, 78t, 115b; David Leah 30/Andy McIntyre 90b/Graham Monro 47/Steve Powell 85t/Holly Stein front cover, back cover, 2-3, 40r, 131; COLORSPORT 33t, 62b, 99, 122r, 123, 143; MARY EVANS PICTURE LIBRARY 182, 187, 190; CHRISTOPHER M. FARINA 181t; DON MORLEY 42, 46b, 87, 103, 122l, 138, 177; OCTOPUS PICTURE LIBRARY 193; POPPERFOTO 8br, 9b, 11t, 23, 46t, 48t, 50b, 67, 72, 96, 104, 106b, 181b; SPORT AND GENERAL PICTURE LIBRARY 126, 179; SPORTING PICTURES (UK) LTD 10t, 19, 22, 23, 54t, 59, 63, 86t, 94l, 106t, 107tl, 132, 139; BOB THOMAS SPORTS PHOTOGRAPHY 94r, 119t, 134.

All other photographs are from the author's collection.